JONATHAN CAPE
PAPERBACK
JCP 12

THE THIRTY YEARS WAR

C. V. WEDGWOOD

The Thirty Years War

JONATHAN CAPE
THIRTY BEDFORD SQUARE LONDON

FIRST PUBLISHED 1938
THIS PAPERBACK EDITION FIRST PUBLISHED 1964
REPRINTED 1966, 1968, 1973

ISBN 0 224 60463 5

Condition of Sale

Printed in Great Britain by
Fletcher & Son Ltd, Norwich
and bound by
Richard Clay (The Chaucer Press) Ltd, Bungay, Suffolk

CONTENTS

MAPS AND CHARTS

FOREWORD

WRITTEN history usually reflects something of the time in which it was composed. I wrote this book in the later nineteen thirties when the depression, the Hitler régime in Germany and the Spanish War made the plight of the hungry, the displaced, the persecuted and the exiled an ever-present concern. Human distress inevitably became a major theme of the book. I do not regret this emphasis. The suffering caused by the Thirty Years War was beyond all reckoning, and I believe it to be an important part of the educational purpose of history to indicate the repercussions of policy on the lives of the people. But it must also be remembered that the Thirty Years War and its supposed consequences have become a popular myth in German history. Every calamity — economic, moral and social — is apt to be ascribed to the effects of this conflict. Such exaggerated views are misleading. The long-term effects of the war differed in different parts of the country and all generalizations are suspect. It is, however, clear that the economic decline of Germany long ante-dated the war, while the political disintegration of the Empire was a cause rather than a result of it. Three questions are discussed in the first and last chapters of this book, and I hope readers will measure what is said there against the accounts in other chapters of immediate destruction and suffering.

In the present edition I have corrected some errors of fact, but I have resisted the temptation to substitute the more cautious judgments of my later years for the confident pronouncements on character and motive which I made in my more fiercely idealistic youth. Although I would not today be so stern in my assessments of individuals, I should not wish to alter the general theme of the book. The dismal course of this war still seems to me to be an object lesson on the dangers and disasters which can arise when men of narrow hearts and little minds are in high places.

London, 1963.   C. V. W.

7

CENTRAL EUROPE
IN 1618

Frontiers of the Empire...........
Other frontiers................

Scale of Miles

100   50   0   100

DEN

SEA

NORTH

KIEL
RENDSBURG
SEGEBERG
GLUCKSTADT
HAMBUR
LUNEBURG   R.

UNITED PROVINCES

AMSTERDAM

THE HAGUE

BREMEN
VERDEN

R. Aller

R. Ems

R. Weser

HANOVER
OSNABRÜCK   MINDEN   HILDESHEIM   WOLF
MUNSTER   HAMELN   LUTTER
CORVEY   NORDHEIM
STADTLOHN   PADERBORN   GÖTTINGEN
WESEL   ARNSBERG   DUDERSTAD

BREDA
BERGEN OP ZOOM

VENLOO
ROERMONDE

WEI
ERFURT

CALAIS   DUNKIRK
BRUSSELS
Spanish   MAASTRICHT
LENS   FLEURUS
CAMBRAI   AVESNES
CORBIE   ROCROY
COMPIÈGNE
SENLIS
PARIS

ANTWERP

JÜLICH
COLOGNE

Hesse

R. Meuse

Netherlands

R. Rhine

AACHEN

EHRENBREITSTEIN

BACHARACH   HÖCHST   HANAU   SCHWEINFUR
MAINZ   FRANKFURT   PASCHAFFENBURG
KREUZNACH   O.M.   WURZBURG
TREVES   OPPENHEIM   DARMSTADT
LUXEMBOURG   WORMS   Main   MERGENTHEIM
THIONVILLE   FRANKENTHAL   MANNHEIM   HERBSTHEN   FÜRTH
Palatinate   HEIDELBERG   OROTHEN
VERDUN   GERMERSHEIM   SPEIER   WIMPFEN
METZ   LANDAU   PHILIPPS-   HEILBRONN
MOYENVIC   BURG   NORDLINGEN
NANCY   HAGENAU   STUTTGART   O-A
OZABERN   DONAUWORTH
STRASBOURG   Wurtemberg   ZUS
BENFELD   WITTENWEIER   TUBINGEN
SCHLETTSTADT   ULM   B
BREISACH   ROTTWEIL
SENNHEIM   FREIBURG   TUTTLINGEN
HOHENTWIEL
BELFORT   ÜBERLINGEN   KEMP
RHEINFELDEN   LINDAU
BASEL   BREGENZ

BESANÇON

BERNE   CHUR

Lorraine   R. Moselle   R. Rhine   R. Neckar

FRANCE

R. Seine

TOUL

To
R.L.W. and I.V.W.

GERMANY AND EUROPE
1618

How many stand around waiting to share thy[1] garments? Are they not already promised to many, who await only the hour of thy destruction? How long dost thou think to continue in prosperity? Verily, for as long as Spinola wills it.

PAMPHLET, 1620

[1] Germany

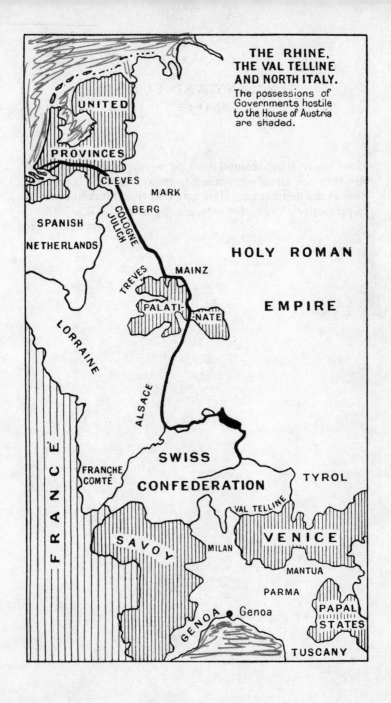

THE RHINE,
THE VAL TELLINE
AND NORTH ITALY.

The possessions of
Governments hostile
to the House of Austria
are shaded.

UNITED

PROVINCES

CLEVES

MARK

COLOGNE JULICH

BERG

SPANISH

NETHERLANDS

HOLY ROMAN

MAINZ

TREVES

PALATI- ENATE

EMPIRE

LORRAINE

ALSACE

FRANCE

FRANCHE COMTÉ

SWISS

CONFEDERATION

TYROL

VAL TELLINE

SAVOY

MILAN

VENICE

MANTUA

PARMA

PAPAL STATES

GENOA • Genoa

TUSCANY

GERMANY AND EUROPE

I

THE year 1618 was like many others in those uneasy decades of armed neutrality which occur from time to time in the history of Europe. Political disturbances exploded intermittently in an atmosphere thick with the apprehension of conflict. Diplomatists hesitated, weighing the gravity of each new crisis, politicians predicted, merchants complained of unsteady markets and wavering exchanges, while the forty million peasants, on whom the cumbrous structure of civilization rested, dug their fields and bound their sheaves and cared nothing for the remote activities of their rulers.

In London the Spanish ambassador demanded the life of Sir Walter Raleigh while the people, crowding about the palace, shouted imprecations at a King too weak to save him. In The Hague the rivalry of two religious factions broke again and again into open riot, and the widow of William the Silent was hissed in the streets. Between France and Spain relations were strained to the uttermost, each government claiming control of the Val Telline, the key pass between Italy and Austria. In Paris they feared immediate rupture and European war;[1] in Madrid they doubted whether the recent marriage of the Infanta Anne to the young King of France would withstand the strain. At seventeen Louis XIII treated his wife's advances with an icy indifference,[2] so that the dissolution of an unconsummated marriage might at any moment remove the last guarantee of friendship between the ruling dynasties of France and Spain. In vain the Austrian cousins of the Spanish King intervened from Vienna with the tentative offer of a young Archduke for a French princess;[3] the regency government in

[1] *La Nunziatura di Francia del Cardinale Guido Bentivoglio. Lettere a Scipione Borghese* . . . ed. L. de Steffani. Florence, 1863-70, II, p. 409.
[2] *Nunziatura di Bentivoglio*, II, pp. 394, 520; N. BAROZZI E G. BERCHET, *Relazioni dagli Ambasciatori Veneti, Francia.* Venice, 1856-78, II, p. 101.
[3] Ibid., p. 99.

Paris, disregarding the suggestion, opened negotiations for a marriage with the eldest son of the Duke of Savoy, the avowed enemy both of the Austrian and the Spanish rulers.

The discovery of a Spanish plot to overthrow the republican government of Venice and a rising of the Protestants in the Val Telline threatened to submerge Italy in war. In northern Europe the ambitious King of Sweden secured Esthonia and Livonia from the Tsar of Russia, and projected a firm alliance with the Dutch[1] which, had it succeeded, would have established their joint control over the northern waters of Europe. In Prague an unpopular Catholic government was overthrown by a well-timed Protestant rising.

The political world was in a state of nervous exasperation acute enough to invest any one of these incidents with an exaggerated importance. The probability of war was a commonplace among the well-informed who doubted only the immediate cause and scope of the conflict; the material and moral antagonisms which divided political life were clear.

May 23rd, 1618, was the date of the revolt in Prague; it is the date traditionally assigned to the outbreak of the Thirty Years War. But it was not clear until seventeen months later, even to the leading men in the countries most deeply concerned, that this revolt rather than any other incident in that stormy time had lighted the fire. During the intervening months the affairs of Bohemia became slowly identified with the problems of the European situation. That situation itself brought forth the war.

II

The partial elimination of certain administrative and physical disabilities in the last hundred years has so far altered conditions that it is not easy to appreciate seventeenth-century politics without understanding their mechanism. The routine of government was ill-organized; politicians worked with inadequate help; honesty, efficiency and loyalty were comparatively rare, and the average statesman seems to have

[1] *Nunziatura di Bentivoglio*, II, pp. 435, 498.

worked on the assumption that a perpetual leakage of funds and information was inevitable.

The diplomatic tempo of Europe was that of the horse traffic on which all communications rested, and political necessity was subjected to the meaningless interventions of nature: contrary winds or heavy snows played their part in averting or precipitating international crises. Vital decisions had to be postponed or in some desperate case thrust upon an underling without time to consult a higher authority.

The faulty transmission of news excluded public opinion from any dominant part in politics. The peasantry for the most part lived in ignorance of the events happening about them, suffered their effects mutely and broke into revolt only when conditions became intolerable. Among townsfolk a better diffusion of knowledge made possible the rudimentary expression of public opinion, but only the relatively wealthy and well-educated consistently assimilated or made use of political information. The great majority of the people remained powerless, ignorant and indifferent. The public acts and private character of individual statesmen thus assumed disproportionate significance, and dynastic ambitions governed the diplomatic relations of Europe.

The insecurity and discomfort of life encouraged irresponsibility in the ruler. Wars brought with them no immediate upheaval since they were fought largely by professional armies, and the civilian population — except in the actual area of fighting — remained undisturbed at least until the need for money caused an exceptional levy on private wealth. Even in the actual district of the conflict the impact of war was at first less overwhelming than in the nicely balanced civilization of to-day. Bloodshed, rape, robbery, torture and famine were less revolting to a people whose ordinary life was encompassed by them in milder forms. Robbery with violence was common enough in peace-time, torture was inflicted at most criminal trials, horrible and prolonged executions were performed before great audiences; plague and famine effected their repeated and indiscriminate devastations.

The outlook even of the educated was harsh. Underneath a veneer of courtesy, manners were primitive; drunkenness and cruelty were common in all classes, judges were more often severe than just, civil authority more often brutal than effective, and charity came limping far behind the needs of the people. Discomfort was too natural to provoke comment; winter's cold and summer's heat found European man lamentably unprepared, his houses too damp and draughty for the one, too airless for the other. Prince and beggar were alike inured to the stink of decaying offal in the streets, of foul drainage about the houses, to the sight of carrion birds picking over public refuse dumps or rotting bodies swinging on the gibbets. On the road from Dresden to Prague a traveller counted 'above seven score gallowses and wheels, where thieves were hanged, some fresh and some half rotten, and the carcases of murderers broken limb after limb on the wheels'.[1]

The pressure of war on such a society had to be intensified and prolonged before any popular outcry was evoked, and by then the matter was usually beyond control.

France, England, Spain, Germany — already in the seventeenth century the historian is faced by these conglomerate abstracts. The self-conscious nation existed even if its connection with the individuals who composed it was hard to define; all peoples had their border problems, their minorities, their divisions. In certain professions there was a fluidity which is startling to the modern mind: no one thought it strange that a French soldier should command an army against the French, and loyalty to a cause, to a religion, even to a master, was commonly more highly esteemed than loyalty to a country. In spite of this, nationality was gaining a modified political significance. 'There is a necessity all men should love their country;' wrote Ben Jonson, 'he that professeth the contrary, may be delighted with his words, but his heart is there.'

But for the most part national feelings could be exploited by the sovereign with whose rule they were connected, and the dynasty was, with few exceptions, more important in European diplomacy than the nation. Royal marriages were the rivets of international policy and the personal will of the sovereign or

---

[1] *Taylor his Travels: from the Citty of London in England to the Citty of Prague in Bohemia ... with many relations worthy of note.* London, 1620.

the interests of his family its motive forces. For all practical purposes France and Spain are misleading terms for the dynasties of Bourbon and Hapsburg.

Meanwhile the basis of society was altering so that the ruler was faced with new problems. In the majority of western European countries, government was aristocratic and had been evolved in a society where land and power were one. This form outlived the actual replacement of land by money as an effective force, so that political authority remained in the hands of those who had not the wealth to execute their will, and the merchant classes, who had the means but not the authority, were in perpetual opposition.

The rise of a class independent of the land had been balanced by a corresponding decline of the peasantry. In the feudal system, based on the mutual obligations of master and tenant, the serf had a recognized if inferior position. The vocal discontent of the peasant dates from the collapse of feudalism, from the period when the landed and governing classes converted the labour of their serfs into money and exploited the conditions of their tenure to make their farms profitable.

The feudal system had presupposed a world in which everyone was connected with the land and the responsibility for his bodily welfare rested with the landlord. As that supposition came to bear less relation to the facts, new duties devolved on Church and State. Slow transport, bad communications and lack of money prevented the central government from creating the necessary mechanism to support these growing burdens, so that the State repeatedly delegated its power to already existing bodies — to the Justice of the Peace in England, to the parish priest or the local landowner in Sweden, to the headman of the village or the burgomaster of the town in France, to the nobility in Poland, Denmark and Germany. Thus no government could rely on the execution of its measures unless it had the support of these indispensable assistants. This was what gave the Polish, German, Danish nobility and the English gentry a power over the central government unjustified by their actual wealth and redressed the balance between the landed and the merchant classes.

But there was no adequate connection between the legislative and executive powers, nor any clear conception of the uses of public money. Because taxation had been evolved for the most part to replace the old service in arms, demands for money were inextricably confused in the popular mind with the emergency of war. The idea of taxation for public services had hardly yet been born. Parliaments, Estates, Stände and Cortes, all those partly representative bodies which had grown up in past centuries, considered that a crisis alone justified the demand for money and persistently refused to help the government to bear its daily responsibilities. Out of this misunderstanding more than one evil arose. Rulers recklessly anticipated their revenue, sold Crown lands, mortgaged their royal privileges, and thus progressively weakened the central government.

This confusion explains the bitterness and suspicion towards their rulers common to the middle classes in the early seventeenth century, a bitterness manifested in permanent obstruction and occasional revolt. Periods of transition are always periods of mismanagement; thus the predominant demand of the time was for efficiency. Acutely conscious of the prevailing insecurity, that small section of the populace which exercised its influence was in general prepared to accept any government which could guarantee peace and order.

The underlying cause of the demand for a voice in politics was thus not so much the principle of liberty as the desire for efficient government. Theories of right and wrong, of divine ordination or the innate equality of men, formed the rallying cries, the symbols for which men died with profound sincerity, a king of England by the axe no less than an Austrian peasant on the wheel. But success or failure in the end depended on the efficiency of the administrative machine. Few men are so disinterested as to prefer to live in discomfort under a government which they hold to be right rather than in comfort under one which they hold to be wrong. Representative government in Bohemia failed because it was signally worse managed than the despotism it replaced, and the Stewarts fell not because Divine Right was unsound but because their government was incompetent.

III

The generation which preceded the Thirty Years War may not have been more virtuous than its predecessors, but it was certainly more devout. The reaction from the materialism of the Renaissance which had begun towards the middle of the previous century had now reached its widest limits; the spiritual revival had penetrated to the very roots of society and religion was a reality among those to whom politics were meaningless and public events unknown.

Theological controversy became the habitual reading of all classes, sermons directed their politics and moral tracts beguiled their leisure. Among the Catholics the cult of the Saints reached proportions unheard of for centuries and assumed a dominant part in the experience of the educated as well as of the masses; miracles once again made the life of everyday bright with hope. The changes of the material world, the breakdown of old tradition and the insufficiency of dying conventions drove men and women to the spiritual and the inexplicable. Those whom the wide arms of the Churches could not receive took refuge in the occult: Rosicrucianism had crept from Germany to France, Illuminism was gaining hold in Spain. Fear of witchcraft grew among the educated and devil-worship spread among the populace. Black magic was practised from the desolate north of Scotland to the Mediterranean islands, holding the fierce Celts, the oppressed peasants of Russia, Poland, Bohemia in vengeful terror, no less than sensible merchants of Germany and stolid yeomen of Kent.

Superstitious beliefs were fostered by a pamphlet literature in which every strange happening was immediately recorded and magnified. Gruesome fears lingered even among the educated. A distinguished scholar in Württemberg ascribed the death of his brother either to 'robbers or ghosts'.[1] A Prince of Anhalt, an intelligent and sober young man, recorded the seeing of phantoms in his diary[2] without a flicker of surprise or

[1] J. V. ANDREAE, *Vita*, Berlin, 1849, IV, p. 120.
[2] HERMANN WÄSCHKE, *Eindrücke vom Kurfürstentag zu Regensburg*, 1630. *Deutsche Geschichtsblätter*, XVI, iii and iv, p. 67.

incredulity. The Electoral family of Brandenburg believed firmly in the 'White Lady' who appeared to warn them of approaching death and who on one occasion had dealt such a box on the ear to an officious page who had incommoded her that he died soon after.[1] The Duke of Bavaria had his wife exorcized to lift the curse of sterility which he believed had been placed upon her.[2]

A pseudo-scientific interest in astrology was the fashion. Kepler himself, half humorously, half indignantly, averred that the astronomer could only support himself by ministering to the follies of astronomy's 'silly little daughter', astrology.[3] He himself was one of that small group of acute thinkers whom the unrest of the times drove to explore not the heights of faith but the structure and possibilities of the material world. In the latter half of the sixteenth century schools of anatomy had been established at Padua, Basel, Montpelier and Würzburg. At Rome in 1603, at Rostock in 1619, attempts were made to form societies for the study of natural history.[4] At Copenhagen and in all the schools of Denmark a young and enlightened King was encouraging the teaching of physics, mathematics and the natural sciences. The discovery of the circulation of the blood by William Harvey was within a few years to revolutionize the practice of medicine, even as the study of the material world had been revolutionized by Galileo's assertion that the world revolved round the sun.

Before Galileo's discovery the antithesis between faith and science had been partly admitted. Luther had cried out against the 'harlot reason'. Philosophy, science and the processes of reasoned thought were felt to be safe only so long as they were guided by revealed religion. Truth sprang from direct and divine revelation; scientific facts, for which man had no better evidence than that of his own faculties, might be merely the calculated deception of the devil. The natural conservatism of the human mind helped the Churches in their opposition to the new outlook. Men wanted certainties, not more causes for

[1] STRECKFUSS, 500 Jahre Berliner Geschichte. Berlin, 1900, pp. 206-7.
[2] RIEZLER, Geschichte Bayerns. Gotha, 1903, VI, p. 129.
[3] JANSSEN, VI, p. 500.
[4] PAULSSEN, Geschichte des gelehrten Unterrichts. Dritte Auflage, ed. R. Lehmann. Leipzig, 1919, I, p. 471.

doubt, and since the discoveries of science perplexed them with strange theories about the earth on which they walked and the bodies they inhabited, they turned with all the more zeal to the firm assurances of religion.

Never had the Churches seemed stronger than in the opening decades of the seventeenth century. Yet a single generation was to witness their deposition from political dominance. The collapse was implicit in the situation of 1618. The fundamental issue was between revealed and rationalized belief, but the sense of danger was not strong enough to bring the Churches together. The lesser issue between Catholic and Protestant obscured the greater, and the Churches had already set the scene for their own destruction.

Superficially there seemed to be two religions in Europe, the Catholic and the Protestant, but in fact the latter was so clearly divided against itself that there were three hostile parties. The Reformation had had two outstanding leaders, Luther and Calvin, and was divided by their teaching, or more exactly by the political consequences of their teaching, into two successive and far from complementary movements. An emotional rather than an intellectual man, Luther had easily fallen a victim to the ambitions of the governing classes: secular rulers had welcomed his teaching because it freed them from the interference of a foreign Pope, and the young movement, too weak to stand on its own feet, had become the servant of the State. Its spiritual force was not destroyed but was at least partly stifled by its material power, and the new Church flourished in the wealth and respectability of its members, grew because kings protected it and merchants approved. This is not to condemn Lutheranism, for men follow their own interests for the highest as well as for the lowest causes, and neither princes nor peoples accepted Lutheranism in the blandly cynical spirit which a later analysis of their motives seems to reveal. They believed, doubtless, because they wanted to believe, but the stress in their own minds was on belief, not on desire. And some at least of them died for their faith.

Moreover, the initial defiance of the Pope did not altogether lose its significance because it was so immediately adapted by the secular powers to serve their age-old quarrel with spiritual authority. If the reformed Church gave little encouragement to rebels once it was entrenched behind the State, it had at least shattered the unity of Catholic Christendom and made way for the exercise of a freer judgment.

Nevertheless, Luther's well-meant interference in spiritual matters solved the problem of religion for a section of society only; popular unrest was aggravated, not allayed, by the advent of a new faith which, thanks to its immediate exploitation by the governing powers, showed no spiritual superiority over the Catholic Church. The re-birth of both Catholic and Protestant Europe was not the work of Luther but the simultaneous achievement of two men working from two opposing sides. In 1536 Calvin published his *Institutio Christianae Vitae*; two years before, Ignatius Loyola had founded the Society of Jesus.

Luther, impulsive and emotional, saw religion as the mainstay and comfort of humanity, felt for his fellow-men and spoke because he could no longer remain silent. Calvin, more logical and intellectual, saw religion as a revelation of God's reason, an essemblage of inescapable deductions from the inspired writings, a thing good in itself, without regard to the material needs of human kind. The fundamental doctrines of Calvinism are those of Grace and Predestination; the ultimate fate of each soul, whether for Heaven or Hell, is fore-ordained by an all-knowing God, and a man is born either with or without Grace.

This harsh teaching, so lacking in apparent comfort, had one quality which raised it above Luther's. It was not merely a new theology, it was a new political theory. By the institution of Elders, Calvin entrusted the moral well-being of the community and the control of the ministers of God to laymen. This new theocracy, which set God above all, but the community above the priest, combined the authoritarian and the representative principles with the theory of the responsibility of the individual towards the community. As the organization and the doctrine spread, the monarchic governments of Europe found themselves challenged each in turn by a religion which supplied in itself a rival political formation.

The Catholic Church of the Renaissance had reached a pitch of cultural civilization in which the ruder ethics of its founders were altogether out of place and the priesthood of Rome had forgotten that the barbarians beyond the Alps demanded both more and less of their Pope than that he should stand first among European princes as a patron of the arts. The only answer which could now be made to the redoubled onslaught from without was by reform within and in this the Catholic Church proved its unexhausted vitality.

The first step towards inner reform was taken in Rome when in 1524 the order of Theatines came into being. This pioneer order was not monastic, although its members took the triple vow of chastity, poverty and obedience; its members were secular priests, leading a life partly of contemplation and study, partly of preaching and work among the people. Membership was confined to sons of noble families and its founders intended to make it the training place for a priesthood with renewed spiritual power. The appeal was too limited and the seminary became not a school for clergy but a forcing house for the future leaders of the Church; hence the Counter-Reformation drew not its parish priests but its Bishops, its Cardinals, its Popes.

Only with the foundation of the Society of Jesus in 1534 did the Counter-Reformation truly begin. It was in a sense the last of the military orders and the greatest; in its ultimate development a hierarchy of highly trained men bound by an oath of unquestioning obedience to their superiors and controlled by the General, its organization was essentially that of an army. When the Catholic Church arose at length from the Council of Trent armed for conflict, it had a fighting force in the Jesuits who were prepared to carry the faith by any means and at any personal cost into any land of the globe. Under their influence the Inquisition, native in Spain, had been re-established at Rome as the effective instrument for the discovery and extirpation of heresy.

Calvinism gained ground in Germany, Poland, Bohemia, Austria, Hungary, France — but it had not the essential strength to maintain what it had won. A new religion, it could not strike deep down to the roots of tradition as the teaching of the Jesuits did. Moreover the Jesuits were a picked force, chosen for their vocation. The Calvinists, as their religion spread, became a heterogeneous mass of scattered communities without a central government. Besides which, although they were the most active and efficient of the new heresies, they could not fulfil the part of defenders and missionaries of the Protestant faith as the Jesuits did for the Church of Rome. They formed the militant left wing of the Protestants as the Jesuits formed the militant right wing of the Catholics, but with this difference, that the Jesuits championed a comparatively united cause, but the Calvinists hated their fellow-Protestants, the Lutherans in particular, almost more than the Papists themselves.

The only serious opposition which the Jesuits encountered within their own Church was that of the Capucins, and even this opposition took the form of rivalry rather than open enmity. A reformed branch of the Franciscans, the Capucins had been founded some years before the Society of Jesus but had failed to make so definite a mark on the course of the Counter-Reformation. In the opening years of the seventeenth century they were, however, not far behind the Jesuits in their missionary zeal and far in advance of them in their understanding of political intrigue. They specialized in diplomacy and had constituted themselves the unofficial go-betweens of the leading Catholic monarchies, an office in which the Jesuits, always more interested in the actual propagation of the faith and the education of the young, did not attempt to replace them. Had the two orders worked together they had between them all the resources necessary to unite Catholic Christendom against the heretic. But as the years passed their rivalry developed into antagonism and widened instead of closing the estrangement between the Catholic governments of Europe. It is significant that the Jesuits were most influential in Spain and Austria, the Capucins in France.

In this way there was a fissure in the Catholic Church, not so apparent but actually as serious, as that between the two leading Protestant Churches. When it came to a conflict between Rome and the heretic there was bound to be on both sides a division of interests which would gravely modify the alignment of the parties.

Meanwhile hatred between the opposing religions gained in bitterness. Those who practised by some precariously held privilege a religion other than that of the country where they lived were in perpetual danger. In parts of Poland the Protestant pastors carried their lives in their hands; in Bohemia, Austria, Bavaria, Catholic priests went armed.[1] Travellers were not always safe; in the canton of Lucerne and in the Black Forest Protestant merchants had been seized and burnt.[2]

In the first years of the Reformation the weakness of Catholic rulers had forced many of them to make concessions to their Protestant subjects, so that, officially at least, there were more Protestant communities in Catholic countries than there were Catholics in Protestant ones. Apart from Italy and Spain, almost all Catholic states tolerated some sort of a Protestant community in their midst. This fact undoubtedly increased the sense of injustice and danger among the Catholic party, just as the slightest infringement of Protestant privilege sent a tremor of indignation through the officially Protestant governments.

The possibility of a clash was constantly present. On the face of it Catholicism, as the older and the more united faith, should have emerged victorious from the conflict. Barely a century had passed since the Reformation, and the Catholic Church cherished the far from illusory hope of re-uniting Christendom. The attempt failed. No single cause can explain that failure, yet one stands out above all others. The fortune of the Church became fatally interwoven with that of the House of Austria, and the territorial jealousy evoked by that dynasty reacted upon the Catholic Church by dividing those who should have been her defenders.

I V

In 1618 the Hapsburg dynasty was the greatest power in Europe. 'Austriae est imperatura orbi universo' ran their proud

[1] RANKE, *Sämmtliche Werke.* Leipzig, 1872-85, XXXVIII. *Die Römische Päpste,* II, p. 261.
[2] WELLER, *Annalen der poetischen National-Literatur der Deutschen.* Freiburg-i-B., 1862-64, p. 267; KHEVENHÜLLER, *Annales Ferdinandei.* Leipzig, 1721, XII, p. 1281.

device, nor within the narrow limits of the world as conceived by the average European was the boast unfounded. They owned Austria and Tyrol, Styria, Carinthia, Carniola, all Hungary that was not in the hands of the Turk, Silesia, Moravia, Lusatia, and Bohemia; farther west Burgundy, the Low Countries and parts of Alsace; in Italy the duchy of Milan, the fiefs of Finale and Piombino, the kingdom of Naples which covered the whole southern half of the peninsula with Sicily and Sardinia. They were Kings in Spain and Portugal and reigned in the New World over Chile, Peru, Brazil and Mexico. A policy of marriage rather than conquest, they boasted, had made them great, but when heiresses were not to be had they strengthened the solidarity of the dynasty by marriages among themselves; it happened that one prince would be brother-in-law and son-in-law and cousin to another, thrice bound to him in love and duty. [1]

The spectacle of so much concentrated power alone might have roused the envy of neighbouring princes, but in the half-century preceding 1618 the dynasty had given warrant for the enmity of its rivals by identifying its policy with two ideas. Its princes stood forth without compromise for absolutism and the Catholic Church and had so relentlessly pursued these convictions that the outside world no longer distinguished between the men and their actions.

The head of the family was the King of Spain, the representative of the elder line; their policy was therefore identified with the militant right wing of Catholicism, that of Saint Ignatius and the Jesuits. Besides which the subjection of particular interests to that of the Spanish King flung into relief one of the oldest feuds in Europe. The rulers of France and Spain had been rivals for the last three centuries: now that the King of Spain was head of a dynasty which controlled most of Italy, the Upper Rhine and the Low Countries, France was threatened on all the landward frontiers. For the last quarter of the sixteenth century the King of Spain had piled fuel on the fire by persistent interference in the internal politics of his neighbour in order to gain control of the Crown itself. He failed and there

[1] Thus Philip IV of Spain to the Emperor Ferdinand III and the Elector Maximilian of Bavaria to the Emperor Ferdinand II.

emerged triumphant from the conflict the founder of a new French dynasty, the Bourbon, Henry of Navarre. His murder in 1610, at the moment when he had been ready to continue the contest, left his country to a regency too feeble to carry out his projects. Peace was made with Spain and the boy-king married to a Spanish princess. The temporary and deceptive friendship veiled but did not alter the latent enmity of Bourbon and Hapsburg. It remained the most important underlying factor in the European situation.

The immediate problem was the Dutch revolt. The so-called United Provinces, the Protestant northern Netherlands, had rebelled successfully against Philip II; after forty years of fighting they signed a truce with his successor in 1609 by which they gained independence and immunity from attack for twelve years. But the provinces were too valuable to be lightly relinquished, and the Spanish government had granted the long armistice not as a prelude to peace but to give itself leisure to prepare the final reduction of the rebels. The end of the truce in 1621 would precipitate a European crisis — the opportunity for all Protestant rulers to defend a free republic from extinction, or the occasion for the Hapsburg dynasty and the Catholic Church to make a triumphant advance.

The concealed enmity of Bourbon and Hapsburg, the imminent attack of the King of Spain on the Dutch — these dominated the actions of European statesmen in 1618.

Spain was a favourite enigma among politicians who talked incessantly of her weakness and took every precaution against her strength. 'Daily doth the weakness of the government . . . discover itself more and more unto me. The wisest and most judicious of the nation itself, are contented both to acknowledge and lament it . . . Such is the extremity of their idleness and loose regard of their most important affairs . . . as it could not but lay open to the whole world, the nakedness and miseries of their estates,' wisely proclaimed an Englishman as early as 1605, while both Dutch and Italian travellers confirmed his views.[1] Yet the King of England assiduously wooed a Spanish

---

[1] SAWYER, *Memorials and Affairs of State in the reigns of Elizabeth and King James I, collected from the original papers of Sir Ralph Winwood.* London, 1725, II, p. 95; CANOVAS DEL CASTILLO, *Bosquejo Historico*, Madrid, 1911, p. 221.

alliance for years to come. The Spaniards were a race of priest-ridden decadents, declared German pamphleteers, yet in the same breath they told of gigantic armies and secret fortresses on the Rhine that were a strange comment on the decadence of those who raised them.[1]

The truth was midway between the two. The economic decline of Spain had begun and was gaining in speed while the population, particularly in Castile, dwindled with terrifying rapidity. The economic policy of the government was equally unconstructive both in industry and agriculture, and financial policy there was none. So great had been the demands on the royal revenues for the past three generations that many of the taxes were now paid directly to the creditors of the Crown without passing through the royal treasury. In 1607 the government had repudiated its debts for the fourth time in fifty years without gaining more than the briefest respite. The exemption of the clergy from the financial burdens of the community increased the pressure on the middle classes and the peasants and further hampered the possibility of recovery. In spite of all this, a great state in its decline may yet be more powerful than a small state not yet arrived at greatness. England was more prosperous than Spain but she was not a quarter as powerful, and even France could not in a crisis have drawn on such resources as were still at the disposition of this once great and now sickening monarchy. The enfeebled government rested on four strong supports — the silver mines of the New World, the recruiting grounds of northern Italy, the loyalty of the southern Netherlands and the genius of a Genoese soldier, Ambrogio Spinola.[2] The government still had an army, reputedly the best in Europe, could still pay it since the bullion of Peru was reserved for little else,[3] had a base in Flanders whence to re-conquer the Dutch, and a general who could do it. Should the prosperous northern provinces be regained economic recovery would be possible for the whole of the Spanish Empire.

[1] *Spannische Sturmglock und Teutsches Warngloecklein*, 1616, p. 2.

[2] R. EHRENBERG, *Das Zietalter der Fugger. Geldkapital und Kreditverkehr im 16. Jahrhundert.* Jena, 1896, II, pp. 199-200, 259; ALTAMIRA Y CREVEA, *Historia de España*, Barcelona, 1900, III, p. 447 f. E. J. HAMILTON, p. 74 f.

[3] *Relazioni dagli Ambasciatori, Spagna*, I, p. 566.

The southern provinces of the Netherlands, the base for the coming attack, had emerged from the war with the Dutch in 1609 impoverished and dependent on Spain for financial support. They presented, nevertheless, the appearance of prosperity. Given as the dowry of the Infanta Isabella, daughter of Philip II, when she married her cousin the Archduke Albert, they were technically independent at least until the death of her husband, when, as the marriage had been childless, they would revert to the Spanish Crown. Naturally, therefore, in spite of their conscientious employment of native officials and encouragement of national self-respect, the aged Archduke and his wife guided their policy to suit their inevitable heir — the King of Spain.[1]

Active, generous, benevolent and just, they had long devoted themselves to the service of their people. A profound religious revival gave vigour and unity to national life, an intelligently extravagant Court made Brussels the artistic centre of Europe, while the well-disciplined and punctually paid army caused a temporary but beneficial economic activity throughout the country. Gracious and impressive, the Archduchess Isabella had sought and won the love of her people;[2] her popularity made for the popularity of the government while the immediate activity and independence of the provinces concealed the fact that they had no future.

An arbitrarily drawn frontier, corresponding merely to the best defensive line which the Dutch had been able to maintain, divided the southern provinces from the northern. This frontier was itself the symbol of undecided conflict, for it corresponded to no line of religious or linguistic cleavage; Dutch was spoken south of it in Flanders and Brabant and there were Catholics north of it in Holland, Zeeland and Utrecht, as there were Protestants to the south.[3] The armistice had solved no problem of race or faith and by removing the pressure of attack it had all but destroyed the precarious unity of the rebels.

The Spanish Netherlands, whatever their inner weakness, were at least united under a strong and popular government.

---

[1] *Opere del Cardinal Bentivoglio.* Venezia, 1644, pp. 63-4.
[2] Ibid., p. 57.
[3] GEYL, *Geschiedenis van de Nederlandsche Stam,* II, p. 9; H. G. R. READE *Sidelights on the Thirty Years War,* I, p. 133.

But each of the seven United Provinces claimed independent privileges in despite of the general good. The people feared that minority of secret Catholics which was menacingly large in at least three of the provinces, and the Protestants themselves were divided into two irreconcilable factions. The only element of unity was provided by Maurice, Prince of Orange, the son of William the Silent, who commanded the army and was stadholder of five out of the seven provinces. He was not without enemies; a growing party suspected him of dynastic ambition and feared that their country had escaped the tyranny of the Hapsburg to become subject to that of the House of Orange. The two religious factions which divided his Protestant people corresponded more or less to the supporters and the opposers of Prince Maurice. Sooner or later there was bound to be a clash.

The internal danger was increased by external threats. The phenomenal development of Dutch trade had provoked the enmity of the English, once her firm allies, not to mention the Danes and Swedes. Dependence on commerce, and the devotion of a great part of the agricultural land to dairy-farming made the provinces dependent on Poland and Denmark for corn, on Norway for wood. And in the cities successful private enterprise had piled up the national wealth in a few hands so that there was great poverty and great discontent among the populace.

England, the most important of the three northern powers, was in 1618 at cross-purposes with herself and therefore the less likely to play any significant part in Europe. The governing class were too Protestant and too much opposed to the absolutist principle to favour a Spanish alliance while their economic fears prevented them from helping the Dutch.

The other two northern powers, Sweden and Denmark with its subordinate Norway, were less likely to remain quiescent. Both countries were Lutheran. In both the centralizing authority of the Crown was checked by an ambitious nobility and both were under the government of highly gifted kings who intended by the encouragement of the merchant and professional classes to subdue the aristocracy. Of these two monarchs the youthful Gustavus Adolphus of Sweden was

likely to be the more successful: his father had already partly
reduced the nobility, and after defeating the Tsar of Russia he
had secured for his traders an important stretch of the southern
coast of the Baltic. On the other hand, Christian of Denmark
was master of the Sound where he exacted a toll from every
passing ship; the proceeds were used to strengthen the power
of the Crown. As overlord of Holstein he had an important
foothold in northern Germany.

There was one other northern power, or rather the shadow of
one — the Hanseatic League. This once important confederation of trading ports was now sinking into decadence while
those of its members who still flourished were emancipating
themselves from its control.

Denmark, Sweden, the Hanseatic League — all were alike
jealous of each other and of the Dutch. They might form
ephemeral alliances within the group but a joint defensive
league against the Hapsburg was out of the question.

There was one other state on the Baltic, linked both to north
and central Europe. This was Poland, with an eastern frontier
on Russia and Turkey, a southern on the Hapsburg dominions
in Silesia and Hungary. The King, Sigismund, was bound to
the dynasties of both north and south. Son of a Swedish king,
he was by hereditary right King of Sweden but had lost that
country through his religion. He was a devout Catholic and a
pupil of the Jesuits, so that both his faith and his policy — he
had fought doggedly against the demands of the Polish Diet —
inclined him towards an alliance with the Hapsburg. Twice
he had chosen himself a wife from that family.

With the northern kingdoms thus divided, with Sigismund of
Poland to check the action of any one of them, with the Dutch
at odds among themselves and suspicious of their ruler, the
King of Spain had every prospect of subduing the provinces
once the truce had expired. Should this take place France
would be shut in between the re-united dominions of the Hapsburg on the north-east, the east and the south. Her government
had therefore more interest than any other in Europe to prevent
the reduction of the Dutch.

By 1618 France had recovered from the devastations of the
religious wars and had a rich export trade in wine and corn to

England, Germany, Italy and Spain; the southern ports competed with Venice and Genoa in the Levantine trade and the country was becoming the European mart for sugar, silks and spices. As the royal revenues on import and export duties rose the power of the Crown increased. On the other hand, the trading and farming population grew less tractable with prosperity and the landed nobility were critical and restive. Meanwhile the large and privileged Protestant minority resented the Catholicism of the royal government and encouraged the interference of foreign powers. To this ever-present internal danger was added the further external danger, that Spanish and Austrian agents tampered perpetually with the rulers of the border states of Savoy and Lorraine, both vantage points whence an attack could be made on France.

The French government had one important potential ally. As head of Catholic Christendom the Pope should have rejoiced at the Crusading policy of the Hapsburg dynasty, but as an Italian prince he feared the growth of their power both in the peninsula and throughout Europe. It was therefore natural that he should favour their rivals. The jealousy of the two leading Catholic powers cut clean across the religious alignment of Europe and the highest mission of the Pope should have been to reconcile their quarrel and unite the Catholic world within itself. He lacked both the spiritual authority and the political means; the Vatican moved steadily away from the Hapsburg and towards the Bourbon.

Intermittently, too, the French government commanded the alliance of the Duke of Savoy and the republic of Venice. Both were important. The Duke of Savoy commanded the Alpine passes from France into Italy and was for this reason assiduously wooed by both Hapsburg and Bourbon. His inclination bound him to the latter whenever his timidity did not force him to yield to the former. On the other hand, the territories of the republic of Venice bordered the Val Telline for thirty miles; this valley was the essential pivot of the whole Hapsburg Empire. It was the passage through which convoys of men and money from northern Italy reached the upper waters of the Rhine and Inn, thence to descend either to Austria or the Netherlands. The structure of the Hapsburg Empire was cemented by Spanish money and supported by Spanish troops. Block the Val Telline and the house would fall. Small wonder therefore that the republic of Venice could assert herself with effect against the dynasty; small wonder that the Archduke of Styria and the King of Spain both sought means to overthrow her before she could overthrow them.

The Spaniards aimed to control the Val Telline single-handed but could not afford to offend the Swiss Confederation, one of whose cantons, the Grisons or Grey Leagues, bounded the valley on the northern side. They contented themselves therefore with forming a party in the Grisons, an example instantly followed by the French. The weakest point in the Hapsburg defences was this one valley, and its possession was to play a part in the politics of the next twenty years out of all proportion to any intrinsic merit which it boasted.

From Spain to Poland, from France to the eastern confines of Swedish Finland and the ice-bound ports of the Baltic, the arch of European politics rested on the keystone of Germany. That immense conglomerate of interdependent states which went by the name of the Holy Roman Empire of the German Nation formed both the geographical and the political centre of Europe. In the contest between Hapsburg and Bourbon, between the King of Spain and the Dutch, between Catholics and Protestants, the part that Germany played would be decisive. Every government had realized this and each had tried to establish an interest in that much-divided country.

The Spanish King wanted the Rhine so that his troops and money could be easily transported from north Italy to the Netherlands. The King of France, and the Dutch no less, wanted allies on the Rhine to stop this. The Kings of Sweden and Denmark each sought allies against the other on the Baltic coast, against the King of Poland or against the Dutch. The Pope attempted to form a Catholic party in Germany opposed to the Hapsburg Emperor, the Duke of Savoy intrigued to be elected to the imperial throne.

From Rome, Milan, Warsaw, Madrid, Brussels and The Hague, Paris, London, Stockholm, Copenhagen, Turin, Venice, Bern, Zurich and Chur, attention was focused on the Empire. The larger issue was that between the dynasties of Hapsburg and Bourbon: the conflict immediately expected was that between the King of Spain and the Dutch republicans. But it was a revolt in Prague and the action of a prince on the Rhine which precipitated the war. The geography and politics of Germany alone give the key to the problem.

v

Germany's disaster was in the first place one of geography, in the second place one of tradition. From remote times she had been a highway rather than an enclosure, the marching ground of tribes and armies, and when at last the tides of movement ceased, the traders of Europe continued the ancient custom.

Germany was a network of roads knotted together at the intersections by the great clearing-houses at Frankfort on the Main, Frankfort on the Oder, Leipzig, Nuremberg, Augsburg. West Indian sugar reached Europe from the refineries of Hamburg, Russian furs from Leipzig, salt fish from Lübeck, oriental silks and spices from Venice through Augsburg, copper, salt, iron, sandstone, corn were carried down the Elbe and Oder, Spanish and English wool woven in Germany competed with Spanish and English cloth in the European market, and the wood that built the Armada was shipped from Danzig. The continual passage of merchants, the going and coming of strangers had more powerfully affected German development than any other single cause. Commerce was her existence, and her cities were more thickly spread than those of any country in Europe. German civilization centred in the small town, but the activities of her traders, the concourse of foreigners to the fairs at Leipzig and Frankfort, drew the interests of the Germans outwards and away from their own country.

The political traditions of Germany emphasized the development which had originated in a geographical chance. The revival of the Roman Empire by Charlemagne was not wholly fantastic, since he held lands on both sides of the Rhine and the Alps, but when the title passed in time to a line of Saxon kings holding relatively little land in France and Italy the term

32

'Roman Empire' exerted a distorting influence. Classical and medieval ideas, theories and facts in conflict, gave birth about the fifteenth century to the almost apologetic modification of the term 'Holy Roman Empire' by the additional phrase 'of the German Nation'. It was already too late; classical tradition and lust for power attracted the German rulers to campaigns of conquest in Italy, and the German nation was from the outset fatally submerged in the Holy Roman Empire.

Pursuing the shadow of a universal power the German rulers forfeited the chance of a national one. German feudalism, instead of becoming absorbed in the centralized state, disintegrated utterly. Custom and the weakness of the central government increased the self-reliance of each small unit at the expense of the whole until one Emperor declared with blasphemous humour that he was indeed a 'King of Kings'.[1] Foreign rulers held fiefs within the Empire — the King of Denmark was Duke of Holstein, and the great and scattered estates which made up that whole section of the Empire known as the Burgundian Circle were virtually independent under the King of Spain. Direct vassals of the Emperor, such as the Elector of Brandenburg, held lands outside the Empire and independent of imperial authority. The system had long ceased to conform to any known definition of the state.

The long succession of the Hapsburg to the imperial throne had gravely intensified the danger. Powerful in their hereditary lands they intimidated, but did not control, the lesser princes, who in return opposed all efforts at centralization because they came from a dynasty already too strong. The connection between the Spanish and imperial families was the final disaster, for the Emperor appealed to the King of Spain for help against those who defied his authority, and the princes retaliated by appealing to the enemies of Spain, above all to the King of France. Little by little the German princes laid their country open as a battlefield for foreign rivals.

Meanwhile internal divisions grew more complicated. As late as the turn of the century — in Hesse-Cassel as late as 1628 — primogeniture was not an established principle in the

---

[1] *Obras del Ilustrissimo excellentissimo y venerable siervo de Dios Don Juan de Palefox y Mendoza.* Madrid, 1762, x; *Dialogo politico del estado de Alemania*, p.63.

Empire, and princes divided their lands between their sons, giving to each independent or almost independent rights.[1] In a single province as many as half a dozen smaller states might arise, each independent, each having for centre some little township, sometimes no more than a village with a royal hunting lodge, which was its prince's capital and palace. These segments each bore the name of the parent state together with that of its own nucleus town, thus complicating imperial geography with terms like Hesse-Cassel, Hesse-Darmstadt, Baden-Baden, Baden-Durlach; apart from the Electoral or Rhenish Palatinate there were the related principalities of Zweibrücken, Neuburg, Zimmern and Sulzbach, and in the little state of Anhalt, itself scarcely larger than Essex, there were in 1618 the four principalities of Zerbst, Dessau, Bernburg and Cöthen.

Scattered among these princely lands were the free cities, smaller and larger divisions of land independent of anyone save the Emperor. Some, like Nuremberg and Ulm, owned whole provinces; others, like Nordhausen or Wetzlar, no more than the tidy orchards and gardens about their walls. There were even free imperial villages. Again, among all this confusion of boundaries were the Church lands, abbeys and prince-bishoprics with independent rights, varying from the compact province of Münster to the scattered estates of Freising separated from each other by stretches of more than a hundred miles.

These were only the more important members of this federation of individual governments; the free knights and counts who could declare themselves, like Götz von Berlichingen, 'dependent only on God, the Emperor and himself', were innumerable. There were perhaps two hundred whose wealth and lands gave them some claim to consideration, and nearly two thousand whose economic position was the equivalent of that of an English country gentleman. Thus a population of twenty-one millions depended for its government on more than two thousand separate authorities. The lesser nobility,

[1] ROMMEL, *Geschichte von Hessen*. Marburg, Cassel, 1820-43, II, p. 14; DOMKE, *Die Viril-Stimmen im Reichsfürstenrat von 1495-1654. Untersuchungen zur deutschen Staats- und Rechtsgeschichte*, No. xi. Breslau, 1882, pp. 111 ff.; J. S. PÜTTER, *Historical Development of the Political Constitution of the German Empire*, London, 1790, I, p. 14.
[2] ELSAS, p. 78.

the knights and free tenants of the Emperor formed confederations among themselves where they were thickest on the ground, or came to an understanding with the chief administrator of the surrounding province where they were few. Yet even making allowances for such arrangements there were over three hundred potentially conflicting authorities in Germany.

The mechanism of imperial government could not control the situation. Theoretically the Emperor could call a Reichstag or Diet of all the independent rulers, lay his schemes before them and seek their consent to make them law. No general laws or taxes were valid unless they had been passed at such a meeting. Unhappily the Diet never met without fruitless wrangling over precedence and the right to vote. Among the various princes between whom a single province had been divided it was often doubtful how many could vote in the Diet; the four divisions of Brunswick having dwindled to two, each prince exercised a double vote, but when Anhalt split into four, its representatives had to share one vote between them.[1] Again, had there been some dispute over the division of land the rivals would inevitably claim equal rights, cause ill-feeling within the assembly and bloodshed outside it.

By origin the Diet had been an advisory body and the right of individual voting was confined to the higher princes and prelates alone. Thus a relatively small number of princes could gain a majority vote and ride roughshod over their fellows and inferiors. Certain princes had therefore recently asserted a right not to be bound by any decision to which they had not personally consented. Their action made the Diet as a legislative body for the whole Empire wholly useless. If the Emperor wished to govern Germany in anything but name he must evolve some other means of legislating. He fell back on government by proclamation, enforced where possible by the prestige of the dynasty. It was hardly fair, although it was usual, to charge the Emperor with tyranny for thus governing without the Diet: governing with it had become impossible.

The Emperor might free himself of the Diet. He could not evade the control of the Electoral College. Although the result

[1] DOMKE, p. 23; PÜTTER, pp. 14-15.

was usually a foregone conclusion, the ceremony of an election was always scrupulously performed on the death of an Emperor. Thus the seven Electors were the true controllers of the Empire, since no Emperor could be chosen without them; the Diet could not meet without their consent; they could be convened by their president without the knowledge of the Emperor, and their decrees were binding with or without imperial confirmation. One further peculiarity of the Electoral College removed it entirely from Hapsburg control: there were seven Electors but only six of them had the right to sit at ordinary meetings. The King of Bohemia, who was in fact not a prince of the Empire but a neighbouring and independent monarch, might vote at an imperial election, but was allowed on no other occasion to meddle in the affairs of the Empire. This kingship had belonged for many years to the Hapsburg dynasty; thus while their candidate could always be certain of one favourable voice at an election, he could not after he became Emperor exert any further control over the deliberations of the College. As the Emperor was bound to consult them before he called a Diet, imposed a new tax or altered an old one, disposed of escheated land, made an imperial alliance or declared war, he was left without any right of independent action.

Fiscal and military organization were as little in imperial control as legislation. For these purposes the Empire had been divided into ten circles, each with its local Diet and elected president. Should a circle be attacked the president could appeal to the two neighbouring circles to assist him, and if the three together were still unable to defend themselves a further two might be called in. If this did not ease the situation the five circles might then ask the Elector of Mainz to call the leading members of the Diet to Frankfort, a form of meeting without the imperial consent which was called a Deputation-stag. If this meeting agreed that the attacked district needed further help, they in turn appealed to the Emperor for a general Diet. By this amazing procedure it was possible for one half of the Empire to be fully engaged in civil or external war before anyone was bound so much as to inform the Emperor.

The division into circles in fact weakened the central power without solving any problem of organization. Endless confusions arose from the anomalous relations between the circle and its individual members, endless quarrels over their relative responsibility for defence, currency, the peace and management of the district. Moreover, the president of each circle, while in theory an official of the Empire, was in fact always the most powerful of the local princes, and his policy would thus depend on his personal opinions. He might carry out imperial edicts but nobody could force him against his will. The presidency merely added another power to those already enjoyed by a ruling prince.

The administration of justice alone left some scope for imperial intervention, although even here it was limited. A body called the Reichskammergericht dealt with all appeals from local justice except in those cases, and they were many, where the prince had the right of ultimate justice himself. If justice, was however, refused or delayed even by a privileged ruler, the Reichskammergericht could take the cause out of his hands, but this right could only be exercised if the prince were weak and the central authority had strong local support. The other cases brought before the Reichskammergericht were disputes between direct vassals of the Emperor and breaches of peace by arms. In this last case the Emperor had also the right to levy imperial troops against the rebels.

The Reichskammergericht consisted of twenty-four members and a president. The Hapsburg family, as Emperors, Arch-dukes of Austria and Dukes of Burgundy, controlled six nominations, the remaining eighteen being in the hands of the princes and presidents of circles. A commission consisting of one of the electors, two princes, a free count, a ruling prelate, the representative of a free city, and plenipotentiaries of the Elector of Mainz and the Emperor met yearly to consider the findings of this Court and embody them in the written law of Germany. In 1608 the election of a Protestant president caused the Catholic members to refuse to allow his jurisdiction; since that date all proceedings had been discontinued pending the solution of an insoluble problem.

The suspension made way for the increase of imperial power. There had always existed one other Court through which, in cases affecting the succession or possession of a ruling prince, the Emperor could take the cause out of the hands of the Reichskammergericht. This was the Reichshofrat, a body composed entirely of imperial councillors, which dealt with problems of succession and privileges, and judged crimes committed by the direct vassals of the Emperor; only in cases of actual revolt or breach of the imperial peace when the safety of the whole Empire was endangered, the Reichskammergericht had the right to deal with the culprit. The collapse of the Reichskammergericht thus automatically increased the power of the Reichshofrat.

The imperial constitution defied codification. At every election therefore an oath was administered to the Emperor in which the privileges of his subjects were tediously recapitulated. He had to undertake to rule only with the consent of the Diet, to appoint no foreigners to imperial offices, to declare no war and to outlaw none of his subjects by pronouncing the imperial ban against him without the general agreement. This oath or Capitulation varied slightly at every fresh election, and precedent could be found for breaking many if not all of its provisions. Imperial power rested ultimately not on the constitution but on force.

The imperial army was raised by demanding contingents from the separate states and paying for them with money voted in the Diet. The subsidies were confusingly styled 'Roman months' — an amount of a hundred and twenty-eight thousand gulden or the sum which the army was supposed to cost for a month. But in the clash of arms which invariably formed the last act of a dispute about imperial authority the Emperor would probably be unable to raise an army at all except through his own private resources. The resources of the Hapsburg dynasty being greater than those of any of their predecessors they had maintained their position comparatively well.

Empty as was the imperial title in 1618, the dynasty had not abandoned the hope of restoring to it the reality of power. With a people as traditional as the Germans a lurking respect for the person of the Emperor was always to be found even among the most rabid exponents of the 'German Liberties' — a feeling which an intelligent Emperor could often exploit.

'The German Liberties' was a phrase which had become

popular in the sixteenth century. It stood in theory for the constitutional rights of the individual rulers of the Empire, in fact for anything which the caprice or interest of the princes dictated, a bald truth which does not derogate from the personal sincerity with which most of them believed in their own motives. In the smaller group of authoritarians which centred about the Emperor the corresponding rallying cry was 'Justice'; the emphasis was on government here, on independence there. Ultimately there must come a breaking-point.

Had the division between the Emperor and his subordinates been clear the disaster might have been less grave. It was Germany's fate that no division should be clear. The free cities feared the princes more even than the princes feared the Emperor, and although they subscribed to the theory of the 'German Liberties' they were sceptical of the sincerity of the princes in the same cause. Suspicious of the landed aristocracy, from whom they had wrested their freedom in the past, they would rather let things be than exert themselves to win anything that they would have to share with the suspected class. The Catholic rulers of the Church, on the other hand, supported the Catholic Emperor on whom they relied to protect them against hostile and often heretic princes. A highly developed class-consciousness divided landowners, burghers, churchmen and peasants so that the commonweal was sacrificed to sectional interests. The evolution of military organizations by each of these groups added a further menace to a situation already dangerous.

Even so the political divisions of these sections were not rigid. Some of the free cities regarded their neighbours with embittered commercial jealousy — Lindau and Bregenz each refused to receive ships that had touched at the other, Lübeck resented the prosperity of Hamburg. A weak prince might be intimidated by a strong neighbour and seek protection with the Emperor, or a succession dispute might divide a royal house against itself, as the dynasties that ruled in Saxony, Hesse and Baden were divided. Private fears and petty interests split the party of the German Liberties into innumerable warring fragments.

Of all these independent princes, prelates, counts, knights and gentlemen, only about a dozen had enough reputation to be reckoned with in European politics; around these outstanding figures the ant-heap politics of the Empire grouped themselves. They were diplomatically in an ambiguous position, being minor pawns in the European game but giants at home; their politics reflected both the pettiness and the grandeur of their position, veering from dignified diplomacy to backstairs intrigue, from ostentation to parsimony as their interest dictated.

First in dignity came the seven Electors. Their president was the Elector of Mainz who, with the Electors of Cologne and Treves, took precedence over all the princes in Germany. These three represented the interests of religion, or rather of the Catholic Church in the government of the Empire, and their prestige rested on tradition rather than power. The remaining four Electors were temporal princes — the King of Bohemia, the rulers of the Palatinate, of Saxony and of Brandenburg.

The sovereignty of Bohemia, as also that of Hungary, had for nearly a century been vested in a member of the House of Hapsburg. Outside the imperial family the Elector of the Palatinate, briefly the Elector Palatine, was the first secular prince in Germany. The title had been hereditary for many generations in the south German family of Wittelsbach, which had once held the imperial Crown. The Elector Palatine had his capital at Heidelberg on the Neckar and owned the greater part of the rich wine-growing district between the Mosel, the Saar and the Rhine, an irregular triangle riddled by the lands of the Bishops of Speier, Worms, Mainz and Treves. This was called the Rhenish or Lower Palatinate; but the Elector owned also the Upper Palatinate, a comparatively poor agricultural district between the Danube and the Bohemian Forest. Other princes might be richer, but the Elector Palatine held two of the key positions in Germany, vantage points on the Rhine and on the Danube whence he could threaten the communications between the scattered Hapsburg possessions.

The sixth Elector, Saxony, had his capital at Dresden whence he governed the fertile plains of the Elbe and Mulde. It was a rich well-populated province with Leipzig, the mart of eastern Europe, to feed its wealth. Leipzig was not a free city but the cherished possession of the Elector. A disinherited elder line of the same family held a string of minor Saxonies — Gotha, Weimar, Altenburg — lying westwards from the parent state.

The seventh Elector, Brandenburg, had the largest but the poorest possessions, the sandy north-eastern plain of Germany without the trading seaboard. The Elbe and the Oder watered his land but the mouth of the one was at the free city of Hamburg and of the other in the separate dukedom of Pomerania. For capital his thinly populated agricultural land had only the little wood-built town of Berlin with less than ten thousand inhabitants. Not until 1618 did the Elector inherit Prussia with its fine city of Königsberg, and this remote land beyond the Vistula was not part of the Empire but a fief of the Polish Crown.

Beside the Electors there were several other princes of leading rank. The Duke of Bavaria, the governor of five hundred square miles and nearly a million subjects, maintained a position of unrivalled importance. A distant cousin of the Elector Palatine, he was head of the younger branch of the Wittelsbach dynasty and his lands formed the bulwark between Austria and the central German princes. The duchy of Bavaria was chiefly agricultural and there were few towns; Munich itself, in spite of its new ducal palace, cathedral and imposing gates, was more like an overgrown mountain village than a capital city.

The Duke of Württemberg with his capital at Stuttgart, the Margraves of Baden and the Landgraves of Hesse were also princes of some eminence. The Duke of Lorraine, who controlled one of the gateways to France, was more important in the diplomacy of Europe than in the politics of the Empire. The Dukes of Brunswick, princes of the Guelph dynasty, and further east the Dukes of Mecklenburg and Pomerania, dominated the politics of the northern part of the Empire.

VI

If it was hard to form two parties on the question of imperial reform when so many currents ran against the main stream of princely interest, religious division made it finally impossible.

A common faith had alone given unity to the disintegrating Empire. When Protestantism rent the confederate principalities asunder, when the more adventurous princes seized upon it as an additional weapon against the Emperor, the theories of five hundred years went up in smoke. At the religious settlement of Augsburg in 1555 the principle of *cujus regio ejus religio* was formulated, by which every prince was permitted to enforce either the Catholic or the Lutheran faith in his lands so that subjects who could not conform must emigrate. This extraordinary compromise saved the theory of religious unity for each state while destroying it for the Empire.

So far the divisions between princes and Emperor might have been made the clearer by the religious difference, for the Hapsburg family held by the Catholic faith and were not popular with their Protestant subjects, while the seizure of many bishoprics by the Lutherans in north Germany increased the territorial power of the princes. But Calvinism, appearing within a decade of the settlement, destroyed all chance of a clean issue. 'The Calvinist dragon', declared a Lutheran writer, 'is pregnant with all the horrors of Mohammedanism.'[1] The frantic fervour with which certain of the German rulers adopted and propagated the new cult gave some justification for the statement. The Elector Palatine in particular demonstrated his disbelief in transubstantiation in the crudest manner. Loudly jeering, he tore the Host in pieces, 'What a fine God you are! You think you are stronger than I? We shall see!'[2] In his austerely whitewashed conventicles a tin basin served for a font and each communicant was provided with his own wooden mug.[3] The Landgrave of Hesse-Cassel took the additional precaution of having the toughest possible bread provided for the sacrament so that his people should have no doubt whatever of the material nature of what they were eating.[4]

The Lutherans were doubly shocked. Although they no longer revered the symbols of the ancient faith, they had preserved them respectfully as the outward signs of their worship and they had a natural esteem for the settlement which had guaranteed them their liberty. They feared that the Calvinists would discredit the whole Protestant movement and they were panic-stricken when, in direct contravention to the settlement of Augsburg, the Calvinists began to proselytize with

[1] JANSSEN, IV, p. 360.   [2] Ibid., p. 204.   [3] Ibid., p. 201.   [4] Ibid., V, p. 533.

ruthless thoroughness. The principle of *cujus regio ejus religio* was subject to one reasonable modification. No ruling prelate, abbot, bishop or archbishop, might retain his lands if he should at any time be converted to the Protestant religion. This important rule, the Ecclesiastical Reservation, was as little respected by the Calvinists as the settlement of Augsburg itself, the terms of which had made no provision for any Protestant belief other than the Lutheran.

The Lutherans now began to fear the subversion of that very settlement by right of which they existed. The disregard of imperial edicts by a party who declared that all who were not with them were against them, threatened the Lutherans no less than the Catholics, and among the princes of both these religions there were stumbling gestures towards friendship. Between the uncompromising Catholics on the one side and the Calvinists on the other, a centre party was emerging.

There was one element common to the Catholic, Lutheran and Calvinist religions; each was used by the prince as a means of enforcing his authority. This was well enough for the Hapsburg who held in all their dealings unerringly to the absolutist principle; but for princes who were clamouring for liberties it was a blatant contradiction. They were demanding from the Emperor what they refused to their own people. The libertarian movements, the convulsive outbursts of mercantile or peasant insurrection, terrified those unhappy rulers who were perched between rebellion beneath and oppression above. Two battles were being fought, one between princes and Emperor, another between princes and peoples, and the princes bore the brunt in both, facing both ways, carrying the torch of liberty in one hand and the tyrant's sword in the other.

Unconsciously the natural alliance between those who demanded liberty of conscience and those who demanded political freedom was broken asunder. The religious policy of the reformed princes perverted the natural issue and obscured without destroying the antagonism between the Catholic authoritarian states and their Protestant opponents. The Catholic powers gained. Their position remained clear while that of the Protestants, Calvinists and Lutherans alike, was self-contradictory.

The individual caprice or conscience of rulers played havoc with the welfare of their subjects. Saxony, Brandenburg and the Palatinate jerked from Lutheranism to Calvinism and back, blazing a trail of dispossession, exile and violence. In the Palatinate a Calvinist regent dragged the child successor of a Lutheran prince, screaming and struggling, to the conventicle.[1] In Baden, the ruler dying while his wife was yet with child, the regent imprisoned the widow and carried off the infant prince at birth to educate him in his own faith.[2] In Brandenburg the Elector declared that he would rather burn his only University than allow one Calvinist doctrine to appear in it.[3] Nevertheless his successor became a Calvinist and introduced a pastor at Berlin, whereat the Lutheran mob broke into the newcomer's house and plundered it so effectively that he had to preach on the following Good Friday in a bright green undergarment, which was all that the rioters had left him.[4]

The energy of the educated was perverted into the writing of scurrilous books, which were joyfully received by an undiscriminating public. The Calvinists exhorted all true believers to violence and took special delight in the more bloodthirsty psalms. But the Catholics and Lutherans were not innocent and force was everywhere the proof of true faith. The Lutherans set upon the Calvinists in the streets of Berlin; Catholic priests in Bavaria carried firearms in self-defence; in Dresden the mob stopped the funeral of an Italian Catholic and tore the corpse in pieces; a Protestant pastor and a Catholic priest came to blows in the streets of Frankfort on the Main, and Calvinist services in Styria were frequently interrupted by Jesuits disguised among the congregation who would tweak the prayer book from the hands of the worshipper and deftly substitute a breviary.[5]

Such things did not happen every day nor everywhere. There were years of comparative quiet; there were undisturbed districts; there was marrying and giving in marriage between the three religions; there was friendship and peaceful discussion. But there was no security. The individual might be generous or indifferent, the local priest or pastor a man whom all parties

[1] JANSSEN, V, pp. 61-2. [2] Ibid., v, p. 426. [3] Ibid., v, p. 538.
[4] STRECKFUSS, pp. 200 ff.
[5] Ibid., p. 195; JANSSEN, IV, pp. 44, 116; v, p. 105; ADALBERT HORAWITZ, *Die Jesuiten in Steiermark. Historische Zeitschrift*, XXVII, p. 134.

could and did respect, but everywhere, open or concealed, there was inflammable material, and the central authority was too powerless or too partial to guard against an outbreak of fire.

VII

With an administration chronically diseased and a disintegrating moral background, the intellectual reputation of Germany and her social amenities had declined. Here and there a great man towered above his contemporaries: the Saxon musician Heinrich Schütz, the Silesian poet Martin Opitz, the Augsburg architect Elias Holl, and Johann Valentin Andreae, the theologian of Württemberg. But these men stand out by their very rarity; they are alone. Although there were movements, particularly among the ruling class, to improve education and encourage German culture, the results were small. The intellectual and social life of Germany was overshadowed no less than the political by the rivalry of France and Spain; at the imperial Court manners, arts and dress were based on Spanish models, at the Courts of Stuttgart and Heidelberg on French. Dresden and Berlin scorned foreign intervention and paid for it by intellectual eclipse. Music, dancing and poetry came from Italy, pictures from the Low Countries, romances and fashions from France, plays and even players from England. Appealing eloquently for the recognition of the German language as a literary medium, Martin Opitz wrote in Latin, so that he might be sure of a hearing. A princess of Hesse turned elegant verses in Italian, the Elector Palatine wrote his love-letters in French, and his wife, who was English, never found it necessary to learn German.

Germany was in fact celebrated throughout Europe at this period for nothing so much as eating and drinking. 'Oxen', said the French, 'stop drinking when they are no longer thirsty. Germans only begin then.' Travellers from Spain and Italy were alike amazed at the immense appetites and lack of conversational talent in a country where the rich of all classes sat eating and drinking for hours to the deafening accompaniment of a brass band.[1] The Germans did not deny the accusation. 'We Germans', ran a national proverb, 'pour money away through our stomachs'.[2] 'Valete et inebriamini' a jovial prince was in the habit of closing his letters to his friends.[3] The Landgrave of Hesse founded a Temperance society but its first president died of drink;[4] Lewis of Württemberg, surnamed the Pious, drank two challengers into stupor, and being himself still sober enough to give orders, had them sent home in a cart in company with a pig.[5] The vice ran through all classes of society; young gentlemen in Berlin, reeling home in their cups, would break into the houses of peaceful burghers and hunt them into the street. At the weddings of peasants in Hesse more would be spent on food and drink than could be saved in a year, and the bridal party arrived at the Church more often drunk than sober.[6] In Bavaria and less successfully in Pomerania the government legislated again and again to prevent these outbursts.[7]

This was not a reputation of which the intelligent German could be proud, yet there was a tendency among the simpler sort of patriots to glorify the national enjoyment of meat and wine. They had the authority of Tacitus that their ancestors had behaved in much the same way. That peculiar form of racial nationalism which later reached its highest development in Germany had already begun in the sixteenth century. Arminius, optimistically Germanized into Hermann, was already on the way to being a national hero, and one scholar at least had tried to prove the unblemished descent of the entire German race from a fourth son of Noah born after the flood.[8] The word 'Teutsch' was used as the equivalent of all that was upright and brave, and every ruler appealing for popular support arrogated to himself a particular share of German

[1] PALAFOX, Diario del Viaje a Alemania, p. 91; Dialogo politico, p. 67.

[2] HANDSCHIN, Die Kuche des 16. Jahrhunderts nach Johann Fischart. Journal of English and German Philology, v, p. 65.

[3] Philip Hainhofers Reisetagebuch im Jahr 1617. Baltische Studien, 11, p. 173.

[4] JANSSEN, VIII, pp. 173-4.

[5] THOLUCK, Die Vorgeschichte der Rationalismus. Halle, 1853, 1861, 11, i, pp. 212-13.

[6] GOTHEIN, Die Oberrheinischen Lande vor und nach dem dreissigjährigen Kriege. Zeitschrift für die Geschichte des Oberrheins. Neue Folge, 1, p. 40.

[7] RIEZLER, Geschichte, VI, pp. 64f.; Hainhofers Reisetagebuch, p. 29.

[8] KARL SCHULTZE-JAHDE, Der dreissigjährige Krieg und deutsche Dichtung. Historische Zeitschrift, CXLIII, pp. 266-7.

blood and German virtues. The self-consciousness of the German nation remained unimpaired, perhaps the best guarantee for the continued existence of a state whose cultural and political vitality were on the wane.

There was a deeper cause for the sterility of intellectual life than the absorption of energy into the religious conflict. The conditions which had produced Germany's greatness were ceasing to exist. Her culture had rested on the towns: but the towns were declining. The uncertainty of transport in a politically disturbed country and the decline of Italian commerce had disastrously affected German trade. Besides which, her currency was wholly unreliable; there was no effective central authority to control the issues from the countless local mints; princes, towns and prelates made what profit they chose. The Saxon dynasty controlled forty-five mints, the Dukes of Brunswick forty; there were eighteen in Silesia, sixty-seven in the Lower Rhenish Circle. [1]

Meanwhile German credit declined and dangerous speculation led to the collapse of one great banking house after another. The firm of Manlich of Augsburg failed as early as 1573, that of Haug a year later; the larger business of the Welsers collapsed in 1614 and the world-famed family of Fugger itself could not work out the storm but went into liquidation shortly after with a total loss of more than eight million gulden. [2]

Swedish, Dutch and Danish competition was all this while choking the Hanseatic League, and in all Germany only at Hamburg, and at Frankfort on the Main were there signs of stable and progressive prosperity.

The decline of agriculture was even graver than that of the cities. After the Peasants War mutual fear between the peasant and the landowner had altogether replaced the old sense of mutual obligation. Landowners grasped every opportunity to increase their power, and serfdom was either stationary or increasing. [3] The secularization of Church land in north

[1] FRIEDENSBURG, *Munzkunde und Geldgeschichte der Einzelstaaten*. Münich and Berlin, 1926, p. 118; W. A. SHAW, *Monetary Movements of 1600-21 in Holland and Germany. Transactions of the Royal Historical Society*, Second Series, IX, pp. 199-200; MAYR, p. 11.

[2] EHRENBERG, *Das Zeitalter der Fugger*, I, pp. 184-6, 210, 225, 234.

[3] BRUCHMULLER, *Die Folgen der Reformation und des dreissigjährigen Krieges*. Crossen, 1897, p. 17.

Germany was another cause for discontent, since the peasants, even though they had now long been Protestant, did not feel the attachment to a lay master that they had felt towards the bishops and abbots of old.[1] The morality of the small free landowner, the 'knight' class, had undoubtedly declined; in general he was a lazy, irresponsible and exacting lord. The passion of the aristocracy for hunting caused destructive and dangerous game to be carefully preserved, and the peasant was forced to give his services free at the hunting parties of his master in the course of which whole stretches of cultivation might be laid waste.[2]

Poverty, political unrest, religious divisions, conflicting interests and individual jealousies — these were tinder for a war. Fire was not lacking.

In 1608 a riot between Catholics and Protestants at Donau-wörth, a free city on the Danube, kept the Empire for some months on the edge of disaster. The Reichshofrat, with imperial approval, divested Donauwörth of its rights and restored its church, wrongfully appropriated by the Protestants, to the Catholics. A storm of indignation from Protestant Germany met this decree and had any leader been forthcoming war must have ensued. But the dispute grew cold among the bickerings of parties, for the cities would not side with the princes nor the Lutherans with the Calvinists.

In 1609 an insurrection in Bohemia forced the Emperor to guarantee religious freedom in that country, but beyond weakening imperial prestige the incident had no immediate results.

In 1610 the death of the Duke of Cleves-Jülich without heirs brought the third and worst crisis. His lands, the provinces of Jülich, Cleves, Mark, Berg and Ravensberg, formed a scattered group on the Rhine from the Dutch frontier to Cologne and were an essential military base either for the Hapsburg or their opponents. Two claimants, both Protestants, presented themselves, and the Emperor immediately occupied the district with his own troops pending a decision. In order to prevent a serious clash between the rivals the Emperor could hardly have

[1] BRUCHMULLER, *Die Folgen der Reformation und des dreissigjährigen Krieges.* p. 20.
[2] JANSSEN, VIII, pp. 135-50.

done less, but the Protestant princes interpreted his actions as an attempt to lay hold of the lands for his own dynasty, and Henry IV of France surmised that the King of Spain, anxious to secure this valuable district for his operations against the Dutch, had prompted the Emperor. Henry did not hesitate; acting in alliance with a group of German allies he made ready to invade, and only the chance of his murder averted European war. The leader gone, the controversy dragged from negotiation to negotiation until one of the claimants tried to solve the problem by becoming a Catholic. His rival, the Elector of Brandenburg, in the hope of gaining the support of the extreme Protestant party, became a Calvinist, but the step involved him in so many private difficulties that he was forced in the end to acquiesce in a temporary settlement which gave Jülich and Berg to his rival and left him only Cleves, Mark and Ravensberg.

As the Empire was flung from crisis to crisis, each time righting itself with more difficulty, individual rulers sought their own safety. Strong defences seemed essential, and a traveller in 1610 was amazed at the threatening show of arms in even the smallest cities.[1] An English tourist, who had been rapidly and roughly ejected from the precincts of a ducal palace, indignantly averred that 'these inferior Princes' houses are guarded with hungry halberdiers and reverent musty bill-men with a brace or two of hot shots so that their palaces are more like prisons than the free and noble courts of commanding potentates'.[2] Arms were supplemented by alliances until the bristling network of hostility was such that the ablest statesman living could not have told where the break would ultimately come and what groups would stand on either side. Solomon himself, said the Emperor's chief adviser, could not have solved the problem of Germany;[3] inside and outside the Empire every diplomatist held his own views and acted on them, waiting for the inevitable explosion.

---

[1] *Relazioni Veneziane. Venetiaansche berichten over de Vereenigde Nederlanden van 1600-1795, verzameld en uitgegeven door Dr. P. J. Blok. Rijks geschiedkundige publicatiën*, No. 7, p. 63.

[2] *Taylor his Travels.*

[3] Konstantin Höfler, *Böhmische Studien. Archiv für Oesterreichische Geschichte*, XII, Vienna, 1854, p. 388.

49

As the second decade of the century drew to its close and the Empire continued to drift hazardously between the reefs, the conviction became general in Europe that the end of the Dutch truce in 1621 would be the signal for war in Germany.

Ambrogio Spinola, the Genoese general of the Spanish army, was cautiously completing his plan of attack. If he could bring the manpower of the north Italian plains into action in Flanders and ensure his communications from the Milanese to Brabant he had won his war. Dutch power and money were not inexhaustible. If, by way of Genoa and the Val Telline, Spinola could depend on the supply of bullion from Spain while the population of north Italy furnished his cannon fodder, he could exhaust the enemy. From Milan to Brabant his way was through the Val Telline, along the north shore of Constance, thence through Alsace and northwards down the left bank of the Rhine through the Catholic bishopric of Strasbourg. The lower Rhine was held by friendly powers, the bishops of Cologne and Treves and the new Duke of Jülich and Berg. But between the well-disposed lands of Strasbourg and Treves were fifty miles of the Palatinate, held by a Calvinist prince. So long as this prince was the ally of the Dutch the land route by the Rhine was dangerous and Spanish troops and money would have to be brought round by sea, interminably delaying Spinola's plans. The subjection of this stretch of land was therefore essential.

His design, long suspected by the opposing party, made the Rhenish Palatinate the keystone of European policy and thrust the young man who ruled it into the front of diplomatic intrigue. The Elector Palatine did not stand entirely alone. The panic among the German cities caused by the attack on Donauwörth, the still greater panic among the Protestant princes caused by the imperial occupation of Cleves, had made it possible for his advisers to persuade some at least of the princes and cities to sink their animosity and enter into an alliance known as the 'Union'. Theoretically Protestant, the Union was predominantly Calvinist. The nucleus of an opposition to the Hapsburg in Germany, it was not negligible and had gained the moral support of the Venetians and the financial support of the Dutch. Furthermore, the King of England had given his only daughter to the Elector Palatine to wife.

The conventions of royal marriages in the early seventeenth century were well enough marked for the English wedding to cause a stir. Princess Elizabeth, the only surviving daughter of James I, was among the most exalted brides in Europe and had been considered both for the heir of France and the heir of Spain, not to mention the King of Sweden. German Electors seldom entered the lists against such rivals and up to the last moment the bridegroom's party feared that their diplomacy might break down. A prejudice in favour of a Protestant marriage, the emphatic interference of the Prince of Wales, and the immediate popularity of the pleasant young suitor both with the King, his ministers, the bride and the London mob, all played their part in preparing a triumph for Palatine diplomacy. The triumph was barren; the contracting parties had been at cross-purposes. European statesmen saw the Elector as the pivot of the Hapsburg problem, the necessary ally of the Dutch and the Protestant governments, a pawn of immense importance but only a pawn in their game. Yet, inside the Empire he was the leader of the Protestant party and the chosen defender of the German Liberties. The Elector and his ministers were Germans; to their way of thinking the chief problem was the humiliation of the Emperor, the establishment of princely rights and unquestioned religious freedom in Germany. The animosity of Bourbon and Hapsburg, the imminent Dutch war, were to them merely cards to be ingeniously played in order to gain them the support of foreign powers.

For the Elector and his friends the storm-centre of Europe was neither Madrid, Paris, Brussels, nor The Hague, but Prague. The reason was simple: the reigning Emperor Matthias was old and childless, so that the occasion for breaking the Hapsburg succession to the imperial throne would be opportune at the next election, and a Protestant majority in the Electoral College would have an excellent chance of effecting it. There were three Catholic Electors, all bishops; there were three Protestant Electors, Saxony, Brandenburg and the Elector Palatine. And then there was the seventh Elector, the King of Bohemia, for many elections past always a Catholic and always a Hapsburg. But the Bohemian Crown was elective, not hereditary, and the Bohemians were many of them Protestants. If some bold German prince could engineer a revolt in Bohemia, wrest the Crown and with it the right of voting at the imperial election from the Hapsburg family, then the Protestant party would outnumber the Catholic in the Electoral College by four to three and the imperial dynasty would be doomed.

Hints of this kind had been dropped at the time of the Elector Palatine's wedding.[1] The Bohemian project was therefore known to all those who signed the alliance, but while the Elector's advisers assumed that the English king would help them to put it into action, the King had equally assumed that these remote German follies would never enter into the actual politics of Europe.

These were the two problems: European diplomacy forming a wide circle about Madrid, Paris, Brussels, and The Hague; German diplomacy groping round the control of imperial power and the Bohemian Crown. Connecting the two and essential to both was the Elector Palatine. Seldom in the history of Europe have such immense consequences hung upon the character of one man.

The Elector Frederick V was in the twenty-second year of his age and the ninth of his reign in 1618. Slender and well made, he added to pleasing features and fine eyes a singular charm of expression.[2] Apart from an intermittent moodiness he was a gracious host and a good companion, high-spirited and easily pleased. Gentle, trustful, equally incapable of anger, hatred or resolution, he strove conscientiously to fulfil his responsibilities although the pleasures of hunting, playing tennis, swimming and even lying in bed were very tempting to him.[3] Ironic fate had given him no vices, and all the virtues most useless to a ruling prince. He was strong neither in body nor in spirit,

---

[1] GINDELY, *Geschichte des dreissigjährigen Krieges*, Prague, 1869.

[2] SAWYER, *Memorials*, III, p. 404.

[3] SPANHEIM, *Mémoires sur la vie et la mort de Loyse Juliane, Electrice Palatine*. Leyden, 1645, p. 315.

and the gentle education which had been planned to stimulate his timorous nature[1] and to fit him for the arduous championship of a cause had softened out of existence what little character he had.

His mother, a daughter of William the Silent, had with admirable fortitude remained unswervingly devoted to her diseased and drunken husband, but she had removed her son from the range of his father's uncontrolled humours by sending him to be educated by her sister at Sedan in the court of her sister's husband, the Duke of Bouillon. This nobleman was the acknowledged leader of the Calvinist party in France.

A backward boy of fourteen, Frederick had been brought back to Heidelberg at his father's death and his education had been completed under the care of his own and his father's chancellor, Christian of Anhalt. Sensitive and affectionate, the young prince allowed himself to be moulded into the pattern his elders chose, believed unquestioningly in the mission they had planned for him, subjected his judgment utterly to theirs and turned as by second nature to Bouillon, to his chaplain or to Anhalt for advice.

None of these men had the qualities necessary to meet a European crisis; Bouillon was the turbulent nobleman of an earlier age, brave, chivalrous, ambitious but without any profound insight. The chaplain, Schultz, was like most of his kind, an academic bigot, intoxicated with the power he had obtained over his conscience-ridden master.

Christian of Anhalt, the most important of the three, was a prince in his own right, but he had abandoned the little state of Anhalt-Bernburg to deputies in order to find a better outlet for his talents in the Palatinate. He was an immensely confident, managing little man with a mop of startlingly red hair.[2] In arms, in administration and in diplomacy he showed a superficial excellence. How brilliant for instance had been his management of the English marriage! But he had not paused to consider that a day of reckoning would come when the English King realized that he had been inveigled into a German

[1] FRIEDRICH SCHMIDT, *Geschichte der Erziehung der pfälzischen Wittelsbacher*. *Monumenta Germaniae Paedagogica*. Berlin, 1899, XIX, pp. xlv f., 61 f.
[2] WÄSCHKE, XVI, v, p. 124.

war. Anhalt's diplomacy, with England, with the United Provinces, with the German princes and later with the Duke of Savoy, was based on a simple principle: he always promised everything. He calculated that when the German crisis came his allies would fulfil their side of the bargain before they called on him to fulfil his. He calculated wrong: when the moment came not one of his far-sought alliances bore the strain.

His masterstroke outside Germany was the English marriage, inside Germany it was the Protestant Union. Acting on the panic caused by the judgment at Donauwörth, he had brought that confederation into being and kept it alive ever since. But Christian of Anhalt was not a man who inspired confidence, and the princes and cities of the Union already suspected that he exploited the Protestant Cause and the German Liberties for the aggrandizement of the Elector Palatine. The Elector himself was so obviously in the hands of his minister that he could do nothing to alleviate these growing doubts. It was Frederick's misfortune to be wholly inoffensive and wholly inadequate, so that his allies drifted with him to the approaching abyss without gaining confidence to support him or finding the occasion to break with him.

The one excuse for Anhalt's transparent dishonesty was that he invariably deceived himself; no one could have been more aggressively certain that he was master of the situation. Added to his confidence he had other qualities calculated to enslave the respect of his master. He was a model of all the private virtues, the most devoted of husbands and beloved of fathers, while his household might have served as a pattern for all the princes of Germany. It is easy to understand why the Elector so far violated all the conventions of his time as to address his minister as 'Mon père', and subscribe himself 'your very humble and very obedient son to do you service'.[1]

There was one other influence to be reckoned with in the household of the Elector Palatine, his wife Elizabeth. This princess combined buoyant health and high spirits with

---

[1] LUNDORP, Frankfort, 1688, III, p. 603; see also J. K. KREBS, *Christian von Anhalt und die Kurpfälzische Politik am Beginn des dreissigjährigen Krieges.* Leipzig, 1872, pp. 1-60 *passim*.

character, intelligence and beauty. Her loveliness was that of colour and animation, and her begrimed and faded portraits can do no more than indicate a forgotten glory. The splendour of auburn hair, the subtlety of flushed cheek and swift gesture, the expressive changes of the shrewd, observant eyes and witty mouth, mirrors of that 'wild humour' which scandalized and bewitched her contemporaries — these are lost for ever. Her letters give us fragmentary flashes of the brave, frivolous soul, fragments too of the harder substance beneath, a courage matched by resolution in which obstinacy and pride played their part.

A contract which had been arranged for the most prosaic reasons had quickened into a marriage of love. Elizabeth despised her husband's language and never learnt it, quarrelled with his family and made chaos of his household affairs, but with the Elector himself she lived in a perpetual honeymoon, bestowing on him a pet-name from the fashionable love-story of the day,[1] sending him little gifts and indulging in the most delightful disputes and reconciliations. But it was not the moment for an idyll and the Elector Palatine was not the man.

The Protestant party in Europe and the supporters of the German Liberties looked towards Frederick and his elegant Court at Heidelberg. Those who believed in the political and religious mission of the Hapsburg dynasty looked towards Graz in Styria where the Archduke Ferdinand, cousin of the reigning Emperor, kept his duller Court. Since the death of Philip II there had been a dearth of effective ability within the family. His successor as head of the line, Philip III of Spain, was an undistinguished and insignificant man. His daughter, the gifted Infanta Isabella, now ruling in the Netherlands with her husband the Archduke Albert, was debarred by her sex and childlessness from playing a leading part in dynastic politics. Her cousin, the old Emperor Matthias, had only one ambition — to postpone the crisis until he should be safely in his grave. He too was childless and the family had selected his cousin Ferdinand of Styria to succeed him. The support of

[1] He signed his letters 'Céladon', the name of the lovesick shepherd in d'Urfée's 'Astrée'.

Philip III for this candidature had been bought by a significant concession: on his election to the imperial throne Ferdinand agreed to make over the Hapsburg fiefs in Alsace to his Spanish cousins. This was tantamount to a promise to give the King of Spain every possible help in the transport of troops for the Dutch war. Spinola had been consulted as to the terms of the treaty long before it was actually signed.[1] Once again the internal problems of Germany were linked to those of Europe.

A godson of Philip II,[2] Ferdinand had early conceived the idea of completing the work begun by his godfather. His duty to the Church had been impressed upon him in childhood, for he had been educated at the Jesuit College of Ingolstadt. Later he had made a pilgrimage to Rome and Loreto, where it was widely but falsely believed that he had made a vow to eradicate heresy from Germany.[3] Ferdinand had no need of such vows. His was an unquestioning mind, and the mission to which he had been educated was as natural to him as the breath he drew.

No sooner did he attain his majority than he enforced Catholicism in Styria with more conviction than caution. The Protestants formed so large a minority that his father had never dared to attack them; Ferdinand took the risk — taking risks was to be the hall-mark of his career. Once he declared that he would sooner lose everything than tolerate the heretic, but he was shrewd enough to see that his own authority depended very much on the growth of the Catholic faith. It was generally, and not unjustifiably, believed in his family that all opposition to the secular government came from the Protestants.[4]

Ferdinand's policy combined cunning with boldness; he undermined the Protestants by civil disabilities, seduced the younger generation by education and propaganda, and gradually tightened the screw until the Protestants realized too late that they had no longer the means to resist. The triumph of this policy in Styria was a warning to Germany. The religious

[1] LONCHAY ET CUVELIER, I, p. 492.
[2] KHEVENHÜLLER, *Jahrbücher*. Leipzig, 1778 I, p. 4.
[3] HURTER, *Geschichte Kaiser Ferdinands II und seiner Eltern*. Schaffhausen, 1850-61, III, pp. 436, 589; IV, p. 593.
[4] Ibid., III, p. 410.

settlement of 1555 rested on custom only; by a remarkable oversight it had never been ratified. What if there should come an Emperor who chose to disregard it?

In 1618 the Archduke Ferdinand was forty years old, a cheerful, friendly, red-faced little man with a reassuring smile for everyone. Frank good nature beamed from his freckled countenance and short-sighted, prominent, light blue eyes. Red-haired, stout and bustling, he presented a wholly unimpressive figure, and the familiarity of his manners encouraged his courtiers and his servants to take advantage. Friends and enemies agreed that an easier tempered man was not to be met with. His rule in Styria was conscientious and benevolent; he had started public schemes for the care of the sick and destitute and the provision of free legal defence for the poor in the law courts. His charity was boundless; he had a memory for the faces of his humblest subjects and a kindly curiosity into their private troubles. His two overwhelming passions were the Church and the chase; he was punctilious in his devotions and he hunted three or four times a week. His relations with his children and his wife were extraordinarily happy. Only the practice of certain morbid austerities throws an unexpected light on his otherwise ordinary private life.[1]

General and private opinion flattered the archduke's virtues but not his ability. Kindly contemptuous, the greater number of his contemporaries wrote him off as a good-natured simpleton wholly under the control of his chief minister Ulrich von Eggenberg. Yet Ferdinand's apparent lack of personal initiative may have been a pose; as a young man he had been taught by the Jesuits to cast the onus of political decision on to others in order to spare his own conscience.[2] He does not appear to have taken political advice from his confessors, and his subjection to the Church did not prevent him from laying violent hands on a Cardinal and defying the Pope in pursuit of what he himself felt to be right. Repeatedly in the course of his life he twisted disaster into advantage, wrenched unexpected safety out of overwhelming danger, snatched victory

[1] *Relationen Venetianischen Botschafter*, ed. FIEDLER, *Fontes Rerum Austriacarum*, II, XXVI, Vienna, 1866, p. 102.

[2] CARAFA. *Relatione dello stato dell' imperio. Archiv für oesterreichische Geschichte*, XXIII, Vienna, 1859, p. 265.

from defeat. His contemporaries, unimpressed, commented on his astonishing luck.[1] If it was luck, it was certainly astonishing.

Baffled by the apparent contradiction between Ferdinand's well-known kindliness and his ruthless policy, they evolved the explanation that he was, politically speaking, merely a puppet, and they did not grasp the fact that, for a puppet, he showed phenomenal resource and consistency. The only evidence in support of this common view was the relationship between Ferdinand and Eggenberg. He was certainly devoted to the minister whose suave manners, unruffled temper and clear judgment made a strong appeal to him. When Eggenberg was ill Ferdinand would be for ever trotting off to his bedroom with matters of state to discuss.[2] This is proof that Ferdinand did not act without Eggenberg's approbation. It is not proof that Eggenberg initiated Ferdinand's policy. When, much later, another minister gradually took Eggenberg's place, Ferdinand's policy did not alter. That Ferdinand trusted him above all men and depended much on him for advice, there is no doubt; but there was here no such subjection of one will to another as there was between the Elector Frederick and Christian of Anhalt.

Personal good-nature and political ruthlessness are not mutually exclusive qualities and if Ferdinand's ability was not, of a kind to show itself either in conversation or in writing, that is still no proof that he had none. In fact men hoped for or feared the coming of Ferdinand because they believed him to be the instrument of his dynasty and the Jesuits, because they believed him to be bound by sacred vows to the extirpation of heresy, because they believed he had no will but that of the immense forces of militant Catholicism behind him. They would have been wiser to fear him because he was one of the boldest and most single-minded politicians that the Hapsburg dynasty ever produced.

IX

Ferdinand of Styria was the candidate for the imperial throne. Frederick, Elector Palatine, was the leader of the party

[1] FIEDLER, p. 114. [2] CARAFA, p. 296.

of the German Liberties. Neither of these men stood for the solidarity of the German nation. Between the extremes there were two men whose interests were exclusively German, whose policy held a middle course, and whose inclination to one side or the other would be decisive. The Elector John George of Saxony and the Duke Maximilian of Bavaria — these two were the basis of that possible centre party which might yet save the German nation intact from the wreck of the Holy Roman Empire.

John George, Elector of Saxony, was a little over thirty; a blond, broad, square-faced man with a florid complexion. His outlook on life was conservative and patriotic; he wore his beard in the native fashion, clipped off his hair and understood not a word of French.[1] His clothes were rich, simple and sensible[2] as befitted a prince who was also a good Christian and the father of a family, his table generously supplied with local fruit, game and beer. Three times a week he attended a sermon with all his court and partook of the sacrament in the Lutheran fashion.[3] According to his lights John George bore out his principles, leading an unimpeachable private life in an oppressively domestic atmosphere.[4] Although hunting was a mania with him he was not without culture, took an intelligent interest in jewellery and goldsmiths' work and above all in music.[5] Under his patronage Heinrich Schütz performed his miracle of welding German and Italian influences into music that foreshadowed a later age.

In spite of these claims to culture John George had preserved the good old German custom of carousing in a manner that shocked men under French or Spanish influence, Frederick of the Palatinate and Ferdinand of Styria. John George, who scorned foreign delicacies, had been known to sit at table gorging homely foods and swilling native beer for seven hours on end, his sole approach at conversation to box his dwarf's ears, or pour the dregs of a tankard over a servant's head as a signal for more.[6] He was not a confirmed drunkard; his brain

---

[1] BARTHOLD, *Geschichte der Fruchtbringenden Gesellschaft.* Berlin, 1848, p. 54
[2] *Hainhofers Reisetagebuch*, pp. 239-40.
[3] KERN, *Deutsche Hofordnungen*, II, p. 67.
[4] *Hainhofers Reisetagebuch*, p. 188.
[5] Ibid., p. 211 f. [6] THOLUCK, II, i, p. 213.

when he was sober was perfectly clear, and he drank through
habit and good fellowship rather than weakness. But he drank
too much and too often. Later on it became the fashion to say
whenever he made an inept political decision that he had been
far gone at the time, and the dispatches of one ambassador
at least are punctuated with such remarks as, 'He began to
be somewhat heated with wine', and 'He seemed to me to be
very drunk'.[1] It made diplomacy difficult.

But it did not alter the situation, for John George, drunk
or sober, was equally enigmatical. Nobody knew which
side he would support. There was no harm perhaps in keeping
the two parties guessing if John George himself knew which
side he favoured; unhappily he was as much in the dark as his
suitors. He wanted above all peace, commercial prosperity,
and the integrity of Germany; unlike Frederick or Ferdinand
he had no mission and did not wish to risk present comfort
for doubtful future good. Seeing that the Holy Roman Empire
of the German Nation was in danger of collapsing, he knew no
remedy save that of shoring it up again. Between the two parties
that were wrenching the structure apart, between German
liberties and Hapsburg absolutism, he stood for the solidarity
of ancient things. First and last he was a constitutionalist.

Of the three leaders he was probably the most intelligent, but
he had neither Ferdinand's self-confidence nor Frederick's
confidence in others; he was one of those who, seeing both sides
to every question, have not the courage to choose. When he
did act his motives were wise, honest and constructive, but he
always acted too late.

Two people exercised great though not decisive influence
on him, his wife and his Court preacher. The Electress
Magdalena Sybilla was a woman of character, virtuous, kind,
conventional and managing. Her insight was limited; she
believed that Lutheranism was right, that the lower orders
should know their place and that a public fast was a seemly way
of meeting a political crisis. She controlled the Electoral
children and the Electoral household admirably and was
partly responsible for the close sympathy engendered between

[1] VOIGT, *Des Grafen von Dohna Hofleben. Historisches Taschenbuch. Dritte
Folge*, IV, pp. 135, 137.

her husband and his people, being one of the first princesses to recognize the importance of a middle-class standard of respectability in building up the prestige of a royal family.[1]

The Court chaplain, Doctor Hoë, was an excitable Viennese of a noble house, whose education among Catholics had given him some understanding of their outlook;[2] the Calvinists, he said, had forty times four more errors in their creed.[3] On the other hand, he was a sincere Protestant and like his master a constitutionalist. As venomous a writer as he was an eloquent speaker, he had an unslaked passion for print, first displayed in his sixteenth year,[4] and was known as a controversialist all over Germany. The Calvinists, making a play on the pronunciation of his name, called him the high-priest[5] — Hohepriester. Intellectually vain and socially exclusive, the learned Doctor was an easy target for ridicule. 'I cannot thank God enough', he had been heard to say, 'for the great and noble gifts that His holy omnipotence has bestowed on me.'[6]

Posterity has not been kind to John George and his advisers. As the defenders of a nebulous constitution and a divided people they had a thankless task, and as events showed they performed it badly, but the Elector must at least have credit for some qualities unusual enough in the years to come. He was always honest, he always said what he meant, he worked sincerely for peace and for the commonweal of Germany, and if now and again he put Saxony first and grasped more than he should for himself, the fault was of his time and at least he never asked the foreigner to help him. History knows him as the man who betrayed the Protestants in 1620, the Emperor in 1631, the Swedes in 1635. In fact he was almost the only man who preserved a consistent policy among the veering schemes of enemies and allies. Had he been different he might have found a *via media* for his country that would have saved her from disaster. It is one of the major tragedies of German history that John George was not a great man.

---

[1] BARTHOLD, *Geschichte der Fruchtbringenden Gesellschaft*, p. 55.
[2] H. KNAPP, *Matthias Hoë von Hoenegg*. Halle, 1902, p. 77.
[3] HURTER, *Ferdinand II*, VIII, p. 77.
[4] LUDWIG SCHWABE, *Kursächsische Kirchenpolitik im dreissigjaehrigen Kriege. Neues Archiv für Sächsische Geschichte*, XI, p. 300.
[5] KNAPP, p. 12.
[6] SCHWABE, pp. 302-4.

Maximilian of Bavaria although not an Elector had of all the princes in Germany the greatest reputation abroad. A distant cousin of the Elector Palatine, he too belonged to the family of Wittelsbach whose prestige in some parts of Germany stood higher than that of the less ancient Hapsburg. In the opinion of his contemporaries he was the ablest prince in Germany; a man of infinite resource, patience and calculation, he had ruled Bavaria for over twenty years, since the abdication of his father, and was now at forty-five one of the most successful and the least prepossessing rulers in Europe. By economy and supervision he had built up so great a reserve of treasure in his coffers that he not only controlled the Bavarian Estates when he deigned to let them meet, but when he entered into an alliance with another potentate he was accustomed to pay the lion's share and dictate the joint policy.

Coldly benevolent, accurately just and rigidly moral, Maximilian did not spare himself in the arduous task of government. He had built hospitals and organized public relief, encouraged education and the arts and given to his people the sense of security which comes of stable and solvent government. But he decreed the death penalty for adulterers; he traded some of his criminals yearly to the galleys and he had assisted at the interrogation of witches by torture. He had a standing army and had organized conscription throughout his country. He even interfered in the most private concerns of his subjects: no one, not even a nobleman, might possess a carriage until he was fifty-five years old, so that the breed of riding horses and the skill of his people as cavalrymen might not be impaired, and within three years he passed seven restrictions on dress, so that the clothes of his subjects might not only be more seemly but more practical in warfare. There was no corner but he would be ferreting out crime in it. Scandalized at the immorality of the peasantry, he prohibited their dancing and insisted that men and women labourers should not sleep in the same shelters, nor does it appear to have crossed his mind that the poor have few pleasures and are not always responsible for the conditions under which they live.[1] His

[1] RIEZLER, *Geschichte*, VI, p. 61 f.; *Geschichte der Hexenprozesse in Bayern*, Stuttgart, 1896, pp. 194-5.

meanness was a by-word in Europe;[1] he had cut down the allowance of his old father because he considered it to be excessive for one who was no longer a ruling prince, and although he paid his servants regularly he paid them very little and ruled his household by respect and fear.

Unattractive in his political life, Maximilian was equally unattractive in his personal characteristics. Fate had unkindly bestowed upon him a singularly unimpressive presence; he was lanky, lean and small with mouse-coloured hair and a pasty complexion, his speech and features much affected by adenoids. His manners were polished and his conversation fluent and well-informed, but the shrill pitch of his voice startled those who were not prepared for it. In honour of his wife, a princess of Lorraine, he affected the French fashion, whose elegant elaborations can hardly have concealed the shortcomings of nature.[2]

Abler and more politically effective than John George, Maximilian had not that dogged honesty which was the saving grace of the Elector of Saxony. Cautious to a fault, he would never commit himself and thereby raised delusive hopes in all who courted him. Like John George he was sincere in striving for the common good of Germany, but unlike John George he had a clear sense of policy and an accurate judgment. His excuse was the less when, like John George, he allowed his individual advantages to take precedence. In this respect both the Elector of Saxony and the Duke of Bavaria failed their country, but Maximilian always with the more shameless egoism. Never was man more anxious that others should sacrifice their gains for the general good; never did man stand more jealously, more fatally by his own.

Doubly allied by marriage to the Archduke Ferdinand[3], Maximilian had begun his reign as an ardent supporter of the Counter-Reformation, and in all Germany his lands were said to be the cleanest of heresy.[4] In 1608 he had been chosen to carry out the judgment passed on Donauwörth. His immediate

---

[1] PALAFOX, *Dialogo Politico*, p. 65.
[2] CARAFA, p. 336 f.
[3] Maximilian's aunt was Ferdinand's mother, his sister was Ferdinand's first wife.
[4] CARAFA, p. 338.

acceptance of this task was calculated to place him irrevocably on the side of imperial authority. So unpopular did he become with the defenders of the German Liberties that he founded the Catholic League almost out of self-defence as an answer to Christian of Anhalt's Protestant Union.

Later, as he grew more apprehensive of the interference of the Spanish Crown in Germany, he altered his policy. He first attempted to drive all Hapsburg princes out of the Catholic League. Then he dissolved it altogether and founded a new League consisting only of princes subservient to his influence. Writing to the Elector Palatine, he represented this body as a purely political association for the maintenance of the constitution[1] and suggested its fusion with the Protestant Union in an undenominational bond. The suggestion was not at the time as ridiculous as the subsequent history of the two bodies was to make it appear, and there is no reason to suppose that he was not in earnest.

Both Catholics and Protestants had breathed of a scheme to put Maximilian forward as a rival candidate to Ferdinand at the next election. His reputation would be equal to the honour and he had no dangerous foreign commitments. Outside Bavaria he had shown no particular enmity towards the Protestants and he had been extremely friendly to the Elector Palatine. This would give him the support of the three Protestant Electors; of the three Rhenish bishops, Cologne was his own brother, Mainz could be intimidated by the Elector Palatine, and Treves was under the control of the French Court.[2] Thus all save the King of Bohemia would be favourable. But in June 1617 Ferdinand of Styria himself had been elected King of Bohemia. If somebody could wrest the Crown from him ... But the conjecture was neither here nor there since Maximilian himself had so far taken no decision to stand. He had the ability to choose, but his caution was stronger than his judgment; he lacked the unhesitating yet careful boldness which knows when and for what cause to take a risk.

[1] RIEZLER, Geschichte, v, p. 116.
[2] La Nunziatura di Bentivoglio, III, p. 406. Some attempt was made to gain the support of the French government for this scheme. See TAPIÉ, Politique étrangère de la France au début de la Guerre de Trent Ans, p. 252.

There were few other princes in Germany who counted for anything. The Elector John Sigismund of Brandenburg, a Calvinist ruling over a people who were for the most part Lutheran, was an insignificant old man harassed by palace intrigue. Besides, he had just acquired Prussia as a fief of the Polish Crown and dared not move an inch against the Hapsburg dynasty lest they should loose their watch-dog, the King of Poland, to worry him. In general he drifted drearily in the wake of Saxony.

Of the three spiritual electors, John Schweikard of Mainz was an intelligent, conscientious and peaceful man but with small influence outside the Electoral College. Treves was a nonentity, so much so that one may read the great mass of the literature of the period without so much as finding his name, yet it was an outstanding name in history, for it was Metternich: enough that this scion of the family added nothing to its reputation. Cologne too was insignificant save as Bavaria's brother.

At Vienna the Emperor Matthias tottered towards the grave. Dreadful things would happen when he was gone, he gloomily predicted. But he had not even the barren contentment of dying in time. In common with Europe he miscalculated the crisis by three years. The signal for war was given not by the end of the Dutch truce in April 1621, but in May 1618, by revolt in Bohemia.

A KING FOR BOHEMIA
1617-1619

MOREOVER we considered that if we came to reject this rightful calling, the effusion of much blood and the wasting of many lands must have been laid to our account. . . .

DECLARATION OF FREDERICK V.

A KING FOR BOHEMIA

I

THE kingdom of Bohemia was only a small province, but the kingship carried with it sovereign rights in the duchies of Silesia and Lusatia and the margravate of Moravia. The four provinces had separate capitals at Prague, Breslau, Bautzen and Brünn, held separate Estates, made and kept separate laws. German and Polish were spoken in Silesia, German and Wendish in Lusatia, German and Czech in Bohemia, Slovak in Moravia.

It was doubtful whether all or any of the four were within the boundaries of the Holy Roman Empire.

Bohemia, the richest province, dominated the other three. Here the movements towards religious independence, national integrity and political liberty which were stirring in the rest of Europe had attained an early maturity. The Czechs were divided from the Germans by language, and from the Slavs by religion and character; self-reliant and resourceful, they had early gained a reputation for commercial acumen, and their folklore glorified the virtues of labour. They had learnt Christianity from Byzantine missionaries, but had modified their form of worship to suit themselves; when they were later merged in the Catholic Church they maintained their native speech in the services and adopted for their patron not one of the famous saints of Christendom but their own King Wenceslas, whose sanctity rested on scarcely better authority than popular affection.

Inevitably they were among the first to defy the authority of Rome, giving Europe at the same time two great teachers, John Hus and Jerome of Prague, who were burnt for heresy at Constance in 1417. The reformers were condemned, but the Czechs set their national honour on their teaching, and finding a leader in Zizka and a fortress on the wide hill of Tabor, reconquered their country. A generation later George of Podiebrad, the first non-Catholic King in Europe, established the religion of Hus throughout Bohemia and set up on the front of every church a sculptured chalice, the symbol of reform. The distinguishing mark of Utraquism, the new religion, was that the laity might receive the Communion in both kinds; otherwise it differed only in detail from Catholicism. Fifty years later the German Reformation burst upon Europe and spread Lutheranism followed by Calvinism into Bohemia.

About this time Bohemia fell into the hands of the Hapsburg dynasty with whom it remained. The kingdom was an important prize, being in fact so rich both in agriculture and commerce that the yield of its taxes covered more than half the total cost of the administration of the Empire.[1] 'Everything that belonged to the use and commodity of man was and is there ... nature seemed to make the country her storehouse or granary' an admiring traveller commented.[2] It is difficult to understand why the Czechs submitted for so long to Hapsburg kings who used their wealth for foreign purposes; this was the more extraordinary because the monarchy was not hereditary but elective.

The truth was that Bohemia in the later sixteenth century was in the most dismal confusion. While Utraquists, Lutherans and Calvinists fought among themselves for privileges, the Hapsburg kings re-established Catholicism as the official religion, granting the other three toleration only. Meanwhile a decline had begun; the old values based on land died hard in Bohemia, where there were no less than fourteen hundred noble families dividing a small country between them and each asserting social distinctions which had to be wastefully maintained.[3] The greater number of these families were Lutheran, but fear of the fanatical Calvinist minority made them cling for safety to the Hapsburg government, Catholic though it was. In addition, the nobility were on equally bad terms with the burghers and the peasants.[4]

These internal divisions gave the Hapsburg throne a negative security. Nevertheless, an occasional crisis brought the

[1] GINDELY, *Geschichte*, I, p. 156.
[2] *Taylor his Travels*.
[3] GINDELY, *Geschichte*, I, pp. 137 ff.
[4] Ibid., I, pp. 138 ff.

Bohemians together: in 1609, when the Emperor Rudolf had attempted to withdraw toleration from the Protestants, even the Catholic nobility cried out against an infringement of privilege. A threat of general revolt forced the Emperor to grant the so-called Letter of Majesty by which Protestant worship was guaranteed and a body known as the Defensors set up to safeguard it.

The Emperor Rudolf made Prague his imperial capital. Here he passed the darkening later years of his reign among the astrolabes and celestial diagrams of his laboratories, filling the stables with horses he never rode, the imperial apartments with works of art he no longer cared to enjoy, closeting himself for hours with his astrologers and astronomers, while edicts and dispatches accumulated the dust of weeks, unsigned upon his desk. The Lutheran nobility in Bohemia finally enforced his deposition and elevated his brother Matthias to the throne.

'The Bohemians', wrote an anonymous politician, 'intend everything for the destruction of the Catholic Church and nothing for the greater glory of Matthias',[1] and indeed the Lutheran party had intended to bind the new ruler by ties of gratitude, but the Catholic tradition of the Hapsburg dynasty was too strong for them. It was not long before Matthias infringed the spirit if not the actual provisions of the Letter of Majesty; meanwhile he moved his residence to Vienna, thus adding economic distress to heighten the indignation of his subjects. Both nobility and townsfolk felt themselves betrayed, and resentfully suspected that their country was being degraded into a mere province of Austria.[2] In revenge the Estates at Prague passed laws forbidding any man to settle in the country or acquire rights of citizenship unless he could speak Czech.[3]

The Estates of Bohemia consisted of three divisions, nobles, burghers and peasants, of which only the first had the right to vote, while the others acted as advisory bodies. Land was

[1] HURTER, *Ferdinand* II, VI, p. 694.
[2] J. SVOBODA, *Die Kirchenschliessung zu Klostergrab und Braunau und die Anfänge des dreissigjährigen Krieges. Zeitschrift für Katholische Theologie*, x. Innsbruck, 1886, p. 404. GINDELY, *Geschichte*, I, pp. 133-4.
[3] Ibid., pp. 117-19.

the sole basis of nobility and its loss entailed the forfeiture of all right to sit or vote; conversely, the man who acquired land acquired also the privileges of the landowner. Thus the Bohemian estates consisted of fourteen hundred landed proprietors, for the most part scarcely more than gentlemen-farmers, acting on the advice of committees of peasants and burghers. These latter, on whom the government depended for the collection and provision of taxes, could exert a decisive pressure on the actions of the voting nobility; in particular the forty-two free royal cities were important enough in the national economy of Bohemia to make their goodwill worth courting. [1]

The landowners were divided into two classes, the lords and the knights, the lords exercising two votes each. The knights, on the other hand, outnumbered the lords by about three to one. The total lack of the representative principle has blinded many observers to the elements of democratic government in the Bohemian Estates; England, with a larger population, had a Parliament of less than half the number, counting Lords and Commons, and although there was some rudimentary idea of territorial representation there was no attempt, as in Bohemia, to account for the varying interests of different classes. There was nothing rotten in the constitution of Bohemia.

The danger lay in her too active political and religious life, in the conflicting aspirations of religions and classes. Some wanted to assert national independence, some to gain religious liberty, some to establish the Estates in actual control of the central government. All three could have been combined but the burghers feared that the nobility, the country's natural leaders in time of war, might turn armed rebellion to their personal advantage; the free peasants, living a life too close to the level of subsistence to risk present security for future improvement, feared alike greedy townsfolk and oppressive landowners. Lutherans, Utraquists, Calvinists, Catholics, each feared the intolerance of the others. National independence could in fact only be gained by deposing the one dynasty which, unpopular as it was, yet guaranteed a balance between the parties.

But this uncomfortable neutrality was drawing fast to an end,

[1] GINDELY, *Geschichte*, I, pp. 140-1.

for Matthias was childless and his successor both in the Empire and in Bohemia was likely to be that Archduke Ferdinand of Styria whose political and religious views were already notorious. No one doubted that he would treat Protestantism and popular government in Bohemia with the same thoroughness he had used in Styria.

It remained to be seen whether, as in the crisis of 1609, the Bohemians would be able to stand together. The three guiding principles of nationalism, toleration, democracy alike drew them away from Ferdinand, an Austrian, a Catholic, and a despot — but drew them in three different directions. If religious liberty was to be their banner, then they must join their cause to that of the German Protestants, already preparing to unite against Ferdinand; if popular government, then nobles and burghers must make common cause to thrust constitutional reform on their future king; if nationalism, then the Bohemians must fly to open revolt, and sacrifice all to the immediate necessities of war. The three points of view were each held by an approximately equal number of people throughout the country but none was distinct enough to produce the alignment of a party. All outlines were blurred by private interests and local quarrels, with the dead weight of conservative timidity dragging behind.

The right man might have found some common rallying cry, but while on the one side the Archduke Ferdinand stood ready to contest Bohemian liberty in three fields, there was no one in Bohemia who could combine those elements by political skill which were combined in Ferdinand by the chances of race, birth and conviction. By seniority and rank the leader of the Protestant nobility was a nobleman of ancient family, Andreas Schlick. In religion a Lutheran, Count Schlick was an honourable, peace-loving gentleman who had spent a useful life defending the privileges of his countrymen by constitutional means. Intelligent, brave, conscientious, Schlick was no leader; he had too philosophic an outlook, too much sense of humour, and perhaps also too much to lose. With a tradition of honourable citizenship behind him, he saw the future in terms of security for his sons.

This weakness of Schlick left the initiative to a less important and less intelligent man. Heinrich Matthias, Count Thurn, was of that type which is often thrown into a position of leadership in times of unrest. A German-speaking nobleman with lands outside Bohemia as well as a small estate that gave him a seat in the Estates, he knew little Czech and had been educated in Italy; at first a Catholic, he had become a Lutheran and was now verging towards Calvinism.[1] A soldier by profession, he was quick in decision, resolute and unscrupulous in action, endowed with all too much of that quality in which Schlick was lacking — self-confidence. He fancied himself both as a diplomat, a political leader and a general. Unhappily he possessed few of the qualities on which he prided himself: his diplomacy was mere intrigue, his political acumen a blundering guess-work, his soldiering largely bluster. He was brave and, according to his own peculiar standard, honourable, but he had neither tact, patience, judgment nor insight; moreover he was covetous, overbearing and boastful, so that although he had many supporters he had few friends.

The choice of a ruler for Bohemia should have concerned no one but the Bohemians. The unhappy fact that their King was also an Elector of the Holy Roman Empire, and had been for nearly a century an Elector in the Hapsburg interest, made it an event of European importance; but the Bohemians were interested in the government of their country, the rest of Europe simply in the disposal of one vote at an imperial election.

The Emperor Matthias had been elected to the Bohemian throne, on the deposition of his brother Rudolf, by a strong Protestant party within the country. He had disappointed that party and by disappointing it had made the election of yet another Hapsburg to succeed him extremely questionable. Knowing this he had postponed the election until the eleventh hour, even arranging for his wife to simulate pregnancy as an excuse for leaving the succession open. There was a time limit, however, to such a pretence and by 1617, with Matthias every day more old and feeble, further delay was impossible.

The situation was not hopeful for the Hapsburg dynasty. Some of the family felt that the Archduke Ferdinand was the

[1] GINDELY, *Geschichte*, i, pp. 90-2.

last man who could safely be put forward. To say the least of it, he was hardly a ruler who would inspire confidence in a predominantly Protestant country on edge with anxiety for its privileges. The Spaniards argued, justifiably, that to let Ferdinand stand was to court a defeat which might be disastrous for the dynasty. But what other candidate was there? The remaining Austrian archdukes were all too old to offer any permanent safety. The sons of the King of Spain, the eldest of them in his early 'teens, would be no less suspect to the Protestant Bohemians and, as foreigners educated in Madrid, were even less likely to be popular than the Archduke Ferdinand who at least spoke German and had visited Prague. The suggestion that one of the Spanish princes should stand was therefore hardly serious and, in June 1617, the government at Madrid agreed to drop the project if in return the Archduke Ferdinand would renounce his rights on the Hapsburg fiefs in Alsace in favour of the Spanish crown. This was that celebrated secret agreement by which the united support of the dynasty was gained for Ferdinand on the understanding that he, as King of Bohemia and later as Emperor, should make a way across Germany for Spanish troops.[1]

The election of the Archduke Ferdinand thus provided an occasion for the Bohemian Protestants and for the enemies of the Hapsburgs in Europe to put forward a rival candidate. The necessity was apparent, the candidate was lacking. Christian of Anhalt had coveted the Bohemian throne for the last five years for his young master, the Elector Palatine, but all his efforts had not sufficed to build up a party strong enough to support Frederick's candidature. The Elector was a Calvinist, was still without experience and without reputation among European princes; naturally enough the Protestant party in Bohemia, which was mainly Lutheran, was not attracted by the prospect of having him for a king. The only other possible candidate was the neighbouring prince, John George of Saxony. A Lutheran, a mature and tolerant ruler, he would have been more acceptable, but as he persistently disregarded all overtures it was impossible to put his name forward.

[1] See *supra*, p. 56.

The kingship would thus fall to Ferdinand in default of better candidates unless the Protestant party refused altogether to elect or attempted to impose terms which the new king could not accept. Possibly Thurn would have blocked the election in this way had it fallen to him to do so. But Thurn, as a mere knight in the Estates, had no vote at the election. At this critical moment the guidance of the Protestant party fell to Count Schlick, and Schlick, like the Emperor Matthias, believed in postponement. Rather than precipitate a dangerous crisis he let the opportunity pass, and when Ferdinand's election was put to the vote on June 17th, 1617, he gave his voice without demur in his favour, whilst the bewildered but docile Protestant nobility followed him to a man.[1]

On the next day the Estates, all but two members, Jaroslav Martinitz and William Slavata, both fanatical Catholics, demanded that the King-elect should guarantee the Letter of Majesty. Slavata urged Ferdinand to refuse, arguing that the extraordinary conduct of Schlick could not be typical of Protestant opinion in general; he felt that the moment had come to deliver a final and crushing blow. The Emperor Matthias and his pacific adviser Cardinal Khlesl thought differently; both of them genuinely wanted Ferdinand to guarantee the Letter of Majesty. Even if he meant to attack the Protestants later, it was not necessary to proclaim his intentions from the housetops. Ferdinand himself hesitated: he did not for one moment contemplate standing by the Letter of Majesty, but he was uncertain whether the time was favourable for making his position clear. He was troubled in his conscience at the thought of making even a formal concession to heretics. At the same time he had the measure of Thurn and the extremists and fully realized that he had only to hold his hand until this party perpetrated some act of direct hostility towards the government and gave him the excuse he needed for rescinding Protestant privileges. Some consultation with his confessor convinced him that political necessity did in fact justify a deviation from absolute sincerity and on the following day he formally guaranteed the Letter of Majesty.[2]

There is no justification for Ferdinand's disingenuous

[1] GINDELY, *Geschichte*, I, pp. 167 ff.   [2] HURTER, *Ferdinand II*, VII, p. 243.

conduct save the consideration that a definite refusal to guarantee the Letter of Majesty must inevitably have produced a general revolt. As things stood there was still the possibility that Thurn would act aggressively and ill-advisedly, that the Protestant party would become hopelessly divided and that Ferdinand, playing off one group against another, would manage to destroy religious freedom without actual bloodshed.

It is probable that neither Matthias nor Khlesl fully understood what was happening. Nevertheless, in the autumn following the election two edicts were issued. Neither of them was contrary to the constitution although both showed that Ferdinand was already influencing the government. The first gave the King's judges the right to be present at all local and national meetings, the second brought the press of Prague under royal censorship. Matthias, on leaving the city shortly after, appointed five deputy-governors among whom were Slavata and Martinitz, but neither Thurn nor Schlick.[1]

Into this atmosphere, surcharged with suspicion, two causes came to be decided. At Klostergrab, a village belonging to the Archbishop of Prague, the Protestants were building a church, asserting that they were freemen of a royal borough and not vassals of the Archbishop. The demand for liberty of conscience was thus dangerously fused with a claim to civic rights. The same fusion occurred at the little town of Braunau where the Protestants were not only building a church but stealing wood from the neighbouring conventual estates to do so. In both cases they claimed that they were building churches on royal land and that the Letter of Majesty expressly guaranteed them such a right. The government replied that, although Protestants were allowed to build on royal land, the Letter of Majesty did not prevent the King from alienating such land; that he had in fact made a gift of this estate subsequently to the Church and that the rights of the Protestants had accordingly lapsed. Protest and answer alike showed the same fusion of ideas; this was not merely a case of Protestant against Catholic, but of the subject against the sovereign. Had the King in fact any right to alienate land without the subject's consent? The Protestant Bohemians thought not, and thought

[1] GINDELY, *Geschichte*, I, pp. 242-5.

it the more emphatically that Matthias in the course of the last five years had in this way restored a hundred and thirty-two parishes to the jurisdiction of the Archbishop of Prague alone.[1]

When he left for Vienna, Matthias had given orders that any further objections from the people of Klostergrab and Braunau were to be withstood if necessary by force. The Catholic deputy-governors immediately took advantage of these instructions to imprison some of the more recalcitrant burghers of Braunau. As by a magnetic force the disunited particles of the Bohemian opposition rushed together: Protestants were indignant at an outrage on their privileges, townsfolk insulted by an attack on the rights of free burghers, and the nobility leaped at the occasion for curtailing the territorial power of the Church.

Thurn called a meeting of Protestant officials and deputies from all over Bohemia and appealed for the release of the prisoners. When this demonstration proved useless, he urged the Defensors of the Letter of Majesty to call a yet larger assembly of Protestants. This second meeting was fixed for May 1618; it was now March. In the intervening time both parties set themselves to work up the feelings of the people and of the townsfolk of Prague in particular. In spite of Catholic propaganda the Protestant meeting assembled on May 21st, a formidable gathering of noblemen, gentry and burghers from all over the province. The imperial governors in vain commanded them to dissolve. Only then did Slavata and Martinitz grasp the danger in which they stood, and on the evening of the 22nd a secretary of state escaped in disguise towards Vienna to implore immediate help.[2]

It was too late. That very night Thurn called on the leading nobility to form a plan of action. Overruling the protests of Schlick he demanded death for Slavata and Martinitz and the establishment of a Protestant emergency government. The city was already alive with excitement and when on the following morning the Protestant deputies were seen making their way towards the royal castle of the Hradschin an immense

---

[1] See the exhaustive article by Svoboda in the *Zeitschrift für Katholische Theologie*, x, p. 385 f., for a careful examination of these questions.
[2] GINDELY, *Geschichte*, I, p. 275.

crowd followed in their wake. Through the portals surmounted by the outspread eagle of the Hapsburg they surged into the courtyard; up the staircase the deputies led the way, through the audience hall and into the small room where the governors sat. Trapped between the council table and the wall, the crowd before and the blank stones behind, Slavata and Martinitz stood at bay. Neither doubted that his last hour had come.

A hundred hands dragged them towards the high window, flung back the casement and hoisted them upwards. Martinitz went first. 'Jesu Maria! Help!' he screamed and crashed over the sill. Slavata fought longer, calling on the Blessed Virgin and clawing at the window frame under a rain of blows until someone knocked him senseless and the bleeding hands relaxed. Their shivering secretary clung to Schlick for protection; out of sheer intoxication the crowd hoisted him up and sent him to join his masters.

One of the rebels leant over the ledge, jeering: 'We will see if your Mary can help you!' A second later, between exasperation and amazement, 'By God, his Mary has helped,' he exclaimed, for Martinitz was already stirring. Suddenly a ladder protruded from a neighbouring window; Martinitz and the secretary made for it under a hail of misdirected missiles. Some of Slavata's servants, braving the mob, went down to his help and carried him after the others, unconscious but alive.[1]

The extraordinary chance which had saved three lives was a holy miracle or a comic accident according to the religion of the beholder, but it had no political significance. Martinitz fled that night in disguise and Slavata continued, ill and a prisoner, in the house whither he had been carried. That evening his wife knelt before the Countess Thurn entreating some guarantee for her husband's life, a request which the

[1] P. Skály ze Zhoře Historie Česka, ed. K. TEEFTRUNK. Prague, 1865; Monumenta Historiae Bohemica, II, pp. 132-3; Paměti Nejvyššího Kancléře Království českeho Vilema Hraběte Slavata, ed. JIRICEK. Prague, 1866; Monumenta Historiae Bohemica, I, p. 81. Slavata subsequently embellished the story with a circumstantial account of the number of times he had bounced and told it in this form twelve years later to the younger Christian of Anhalt. A story current in Spain shortly after adds the apocryphal detail that the secretary was so little hurt that he sprang lightly to his feet and apologized for having inconsiderately fallen on top of his masters. (PALAFOX, Dialogo Politico, p. 59.)

lady granted with the pessimistic stipulation that the Countess
Slavata should do her a like service after the next Bohemian
revolution.[1]

Murder or no murder, the *coup d'état* was complete, and since
Thurn had overruled many of his supporters in demanding
death it was as well for the conscience of his allies that a pile
of mouldering filth in the courtyard of the Hradschin had made
soft falling for the governors.

No time was lost in setting the mechanism of the State once
more in order. All officials who agreed to recognize the new
power were confirmed in their positions, nor was there at first
any attempt to displace Catholics. A provisional government
of thirteen Directors was appointed by the Protestant assembly
which then voted the raising of an army of sixteen thousand
men at the country's expense, Thurn to be in command.
For the better enlightenment of Europe they issued an Apologia
setting forth the causes of the revolt.[2] Having thus provided
for the continuance of civil government and against the
possibility of war, the meeting dissolved within five days of
the revolt and within ten of its original opening.

II

In speed, efficiency and moderation the revolt might serve
as a model, but under a smooth surface the new state concealed
disastrous elements. The pressure which had forced the various
parties to combine could not last and, as the immediate
crisis lessened, the united front resolved into its component
parts. Was it a revolt purely for religious liberty, or for national
freedom, or for the rights of the subject against the sovereign?
The truth was that nobody knew, and each party was prepared
to sacrifice the interests of the other to further its own.

Besides, the country had not even been fully united in revolt.
The extreme Catholics, of whom Slavata and Martinitz were
typical representatives, were indeed a minority, but they were
not negligible. The original intention of the new government

[1] *Annales*, IX, p. 32.
[2] LÜNIG, *Teutsches Reichsarchiv.*, Leipzig, 1710, VI, ii, p. 133 f.

to give equal rights to all their compatriots proved utterly un-
practical, for Catholic nobility everywhere, Catholic burghers,
even Catholic townships — Budweis, Krummau, Pilsen — were
storm-centres of resistance.[1]

Had Thurn made himself the leader of the State, had he
choked the protests of his allies and concentrated his forces on
the struggle for independence, the revolt might at least have
ensured the national future of Bohemia. But constitutional
tradition was too strong, and Thurn either could not or would
not overrule it. He commanded the army but it was subject
to the thirteen Directors; they in turn were subject to the
Estates who alone could vote supplies. Thurn, as a knight,
had a seat and a vote in the Estates, but he refused to be made
a Director. He seems to have thought that while Bohemia's
safety depended on her ability to defend herself in arms the
power of the Directorate over the army would be theoretical
only. He was wrong. Throughout the thirty months of
Bohemia's struggle he remained dependent on the grudging
subsidies of quarrelsome Estates and a disunited Directorate.[2]

The internal truce with the Catholics broke down at once.
On June 9th the Jesuits were expelled the country[3] and before
midsummer Thurn had attacked and subdued Krummau.
Acting on the advice of his pacific adviser, Khlesl, the Emperor
Matthias at first sent offers of amnesty and peaceful discussion.[4]
The rebels defiantly refused to consider them, shocking the
Catholic opinion of Europe and confirming their enemies in
the belief that religion was a mere cover for national and
political motives.[5] Slowly the revolt assumed significance
in the problems of Europe; in Brussels and Madrid the prestige
of the dynasty was felt to be at stake; money and troops were
hastily dispatched to help the Archduke Ferdinand defend
his throne,[6] while the Papal Nuncio in Paris received commands from the Vatican to impress the King of France with
the danger to the Bohemian Catholics.[7]

[1] *Epitome Historica Rerum Bohemicarum, authore Bohuslao Balbino e Societate
Jesu.* Prague, 1677, pp. 626-9.
[2] STANKA, *Boehmische Confederationsakten,* pp. 74 ff.
[3] LÜNIG, VI, ii, p. 141 f.
[4] Ibid., p. 144 f.   [5] BENTIVOGLIO, *Opere,* p. 650.
[6] *Letters and Documents,* I, p. 12; LONCHAY ET CUVELIER, I, p. 524 f.
[7] *La Nunziatura di Bentivoglio,* II, pp. 500, 518.

The Archduke Ferdinand who, as the King-elect of the rebellious country, stood to lose the most, asked for nothing better than the immediate inception of a Crusade while the enthusiasm of the Catholic world was yet warm. Only the waning life of Matthias and the persistent desire of Cardinal Khlesl for compromise stood in his way. On July 20th, 1618, Ferdinand seized Khlesl and sent him prisoner to a fortress in Tyrol. The Emperor's indignant outcry was in vain; Ferdinand apologized courteously but would not release the Cardinal; Matthias was forced to bow before his cousin's inspired obstinacy and to trust the guidance of his policy in future to hands which had already seized it for themselves.

Less than a month after Khlesl's fall the first imperial army crossed the Bohemian border. The army and the general came from Flanders, the money from Spain; in answer the rebels would inevitably appeal to the enemies of Spain and Flanders. Thurn, bringing his vaunted talents as a diplomatist to reinforce his prowess as a general, had in fact already done so. But the appeal to France was coldly rejected by a king who had not yet grasped the dynastic significance of the revolt and was too devout a son of the Church to support Protestant rebels.[1]

On the other hand, the Elector Palatine, Frederick, or at least his chancellor Christian of Anhalt, hastened to meet Thurn's overtures half-way. Before the end of June Frederick had an agent in Prague, and met the indignant protest of the Emperor with the cool explanation that he only wished to persuade the rebels towards compromise. His ambassador chose a curious means to this end, in urging the Bohemians to increase and improve their army and in suggesting that Anhalt himself should take command.[2]

These were not words without deeds, for at the same time couriers had gone from Heidelberg to the Duke of Savoy's capital at Turin to negotiate with him for the loan of the large mercenary army at present in his employ. The Duke, an old enemy of the Hapsburg family, grasped joyfully at the occasion of injuring them, and terms were rapidly signed by which he

[1] *La Nunziatura di Bentivoglio*, II, p. 528.
[2] KREBS, *Christian von Anhalt*, pp. 94 ff.; LUNDORP, III, pp. 606.

agreed with the Elector Palatine to share the expenses of transporting and maintaining an army for the Bohemians.[1] The joint offer of the two princes reached Prague not a moment too soon. One imperial army was already over the border and a second was preparing to follow. Thurn's rapidly recruited troops were without the experience to stand against the Flemish professionals, even had their numbers been adequate. When the Duke of Savoy and the Elector Palatine offered to provide a highly trained army which was already only a few days' march away under the command of Ernst von Mansfeld, a general of European reputation, hesitation was impossible.

On August 28th, 1618, the second imperial army left Vienna and two days later the Bohemians accepted the offer of help.[2] On September 9th the two invading armies joined and would infallibly have marched on Prague but for the rumoured approach of Mansfeld. Harassed by skirmishing attacks from Thurn, the invaders fell back towards Budweis, while Mansfeld crossed the border with twenty thousand men and laid siege to Pilsen, the richest and most important stronghold of the Catholic loyalists. All over Bohemia enthusiasm for the Protestant cause flamed up once again. On November 21st, after fifteen hours of desperate fighting, Pilsen fell[3] and with the deepening winter Thurn and Schlick at the head of the native army shut in the Flemish troops in Budweis and laid waste the Austrian border.

Bohemia had been saved, and for the moment no one counted the cost. But she had been freed from Austrian domination only to be sold to the Elector Palatine and the Duke of Savoy; jealous lest their country should be exploited by the Hapsburg dynasty, the rebels exposed her to exploitation by the enemies of the Hapsburg, and the individual problem of Bohemia was gradually sucked in towards the centre of the European whirlpool.

While the Austrian frontiers went up in flames, the Elector Palatine called a meeting of the Protestant Union at Rothenburg. If Frederick or Christian of Anhalt had expected to be

[1] KREBS, *Christian von Anhalt*, pp. 596, 603.   [2] GINDELY, *Geschichte*, I, p. 387.
[3] LUNDORP, I, p. 502 f.

congratulated on their actions, they were gravely disillusioned, for the princes of the Union took discretion to be the better part of valour and indignantly repudiated all that had been done. They did not wish to pay Mansfeld or to enter into any understanding with the rebels; they absolutely refused to raise a joint army at Frederick's suggestion, and they established their impartiality by publishing a memorial exhorting both the Emperor and his subjects to compromise. [1]

Probably no one was more astonished by the behaviour of the Union than its youthful President. There is evidence that the Elector Frederick was, of all the princes assembled at Rothenburg, the most in ignorance as to his own policy. Christian of Anhalt had been working only to one end: he wanted to create a party in Bohemia which would elect Frederick for King. He had hoped to arrange this before the election of Ferdinand and, having signally failed, [2] had leapt upon the renewed opportunity which the rebellion offered him. It did not need very much political acumen on the part of the princes of the Union to penetrate Anhalt's schemes. Resenting the policy in itself, they resented still more his assumption that he could throw dust in their eyes with fine words about the defence of Protestantism.

Among those assembled at Rothenburg, Frederick was one of the few who believed in Anhalt's professions. From the outset he wanted peace in Bohemia. The letters on this subject which he had written to the Emperor, to the King of England and to the Duke of Bavaria, [3] disingenuous as they may seem, were in fact the outcome of a real innocence. Frederick was twenty-one, technically of age, but he had not the character or the desire to replace Anhalt, whom he trusted in all things. Nevertheless, he took his duties seriously and when the revolt in Bohemia had been made clear to him in all its aspects he had timorously evolved a policy. His suggestion was that the Union should raise an army and persuade the Elector of Saxony to join them in a protest to the Emperor Matthias. He hoped in this way to show that the Protestants of Germany

[1] LUNDORP, I, p. 508 f.
[2] KLOPP, Tilly im dreissigjährigen Kriege. Stuttgart, 1861. I, pp. 215-6.
[3] Letters and Documents, I, p. 9; LUNDORP, I, pp. 503 ff.

were united and were, in the last resort, prepared to use force. Once this was evident to the Emperor, Frederick assumed that there would be no actual necessity to appeal to arms. Protestantism in Bohemia would be guaranteed and a significant warning would have been issued against any future attempt at coercion in Germany itself.

Frederick's plan was the fruit of youth and optimism, and Anhalt could probably have persuaded him that, in view of Saxony's rabid hostility towards the Calvinists, it was quite impracticable. But it was one thing to persuade Frederick that his peace plan would not work and quite another to suggest that an intrigue to gain the Bohemian Crown for himself was the only alternative. Anhalt found it simpler to use Frederick's trivial project as the cover for his private intrigues. Exploiting his master's confidence, he could give instructions to ambassadors that certainly never reached Frederick's ears and keep the well-intentioned but incurious prince totally ignorant of the things which were being done in his name. [1]

After the meeting of the Union at Rothenburg concealment was no longer so easy. Even Frederick must have felt that there was some substance behind the suspicions of his fellow princes, and about November 1618 Anhalt judged it wise to reveal his schemes to one who was to be the principal actor in them. [2] A strong man might still have been able to redeem the situation, however gravely endangered, but Frederick was not strong, and his trust in Anhalt, although shaken, was not destroyed. The Bohemians had meanwhile responded to the persistent hinting of the Palatine ambassadors, and Thurn privately asked them whether they would guarantee their master's acceptance of the Crown should it be offered to him. [3] At the same time Anhalt approached the Prince of Orange to support the plan and bought the favour of the Duke of Savoy by promising to further his candidature for the imperial throne. [4] All this while Frederick, the impotent figure-head of the whole scheme, drifted in a state of bewildered melancholy towards the abyss whither his chancellor was blithely steering.

---

[1] WEIGEL, *Franken, Kurpfalz und der Böhmische Aufstand*, I, pp. 192 ff. and pp. 145 ff.
[2] Ibid., I, pp. 144-5.   [3] GINDELY, *Geschichte*, I, p. 445.   [4] LUNDROP, III, p 608.

Busily pushing the pieces on the chessboard into alignment for European war, Anhalt was assisted by an ally whose motives were more questionable than his own. Ernst von Mansfeld, general of the army which had been pitchforked to the help of Bohemia, was the bastard son of a nobleman, Peter von Mansfeld, one time governor of Luxembourg. While his father had brought him up at his Court, he had early and brutally checked the boy's pretensions to consider himself a true scion of his family, leaving him with a personal sensitiveness on this point which he never outgrew.[1] Birth and education made him an adventurer. The whole world was his oyster and the sword the best tool to open it.

The military practice of his time was an invitation to him. With the development of artillery and more especially of the musket, the feudal levy, consisting of unskilled peasants, had become almost useless. Professional soldiers alone could acquire the necessary precision in tactics. Infantry was now composed of pikemen and musketeers, the musketeers chiefly for attack, the pikemen to cover them in defensive action; with the continuous improvement in the efficiency of the musket the importance of pikemen was dwindling in proportion, but in the first quarter of the century the numbers of each in the average infantry regiment were roughly equal. For the effective handling of both weapons long practice was essential. The cavalry who formed about a third part of the normal army and were still by far the most important section, at least in attack, were also armed some with lances, some with pistols; here fire-arms were replacing the lance faster than among the infantry. In pitched battles, which formed the crux of warfare, ill-trained cavalry were worse than useless, well-trained cavalry all-important, since on the execution of certain complicated movements might depend the success or failure of the whole army.[2] So far no state had evolved a system of conscription capable of keeping a national army fully trained. When it came to war a wise government at once enlisted the service of a professional general.

[1] STIEVE, *Ernst von Mansfeld. Sitzungsberichte der philosophisch-philologisch und historischen Classe der Königlich bayerisch Akademie der Wissenschaften.* 1890, p. 521.
[2] DELBRÜCK, pp. 171 ff.

These professionals usually kept about them a small staff of officers expert in rapid recruiting and training. The armies thus raised without regard to race or religion were the outcasts of society or the surplus population of over-crowded districts. Switzerland and north Italy, for instance, where the land could never support the healthy and prolific race that it bred, produced better recruits than the German States, where the population question was less acute. The soldiers once enlisted were faithful only to their banners. The oath which they took was not to any personal leader or State but to the flag, and if the flag were captured in battle the soldiers were at liberty to follow it.[1] Even loyalty to the flag was not always apparent, and it was usual for prisoners of war to enlist in the army of the victors whether their banner had been taken or not. Besides this, a soldier served only under contract; should he choose at the expiration of his time to try another army he was free to do so. Officers and men shifted from service to service without the least compunction and discussed the merits of each round the camp fires in the evening. The Emperor paid well, but it was considered 'a hard service, to lie out wet and dry'; the King of Poland paid even better but would not undertake to feed the army in winter; the Governess of the Netherlands made the wages sound tempting to those who did not know that she calculated a month at six to eight weeks; 'the best service is accounted the States[2] because constant, and if they lose any joint or be made unserviceable they are during their life to have the same pay that they had when they were disabled'.[3]

Generals were accustomed to see their armies dwindle to half their size by desertion during the winter months or when the quarters were more than usually uncomfortable. Theoretically death was the penalty for desertion, but since a number of the men came back in the spring encouraged by the prospect of fresh plunder, wise officers did not discourage them by a rigid inquiry into their absence.

Mansfeld's professional reputation rested on his organizing

[1] KLOPP, III, i, p. 228.
[2] The United Provinces.
[3] *The Diary of Thomas Crosfield*, ed. F. S. BOAS for the Royal Society of Literature. London, 1935, p. 67.

ability. He was not a very gifted tactician, but he had a genius for putting the money of his employers to the best advantage in recruiting and quartering the troops. He could raise an army in record time and maintain it at very reasonable cost — to the employers at least. To the peasantry on whom he quartered his men the cost may well have seemed less reasonable.

Since it was more expensive to raise a new army than to keep on an old one, the mercenary general began to search out new employment for his men as soon as a war came to an end. The Bohemian revolt had been manna in the wilderness to Mansfeld, who had found himself in 1618 faced with the prospect of disbanding his men. Fundamentally he was a less dangerous adventurer than others who were to follow him in the disastrous years to come, because he was not a very ambitious man. All that he wanted was to secure for himself a recognized position in society and a little free principality to which he could retire in old age. He would not be over-scrupulous in the means he used to gain this end, for although he had virtues they were those of the soldier only. The courage, endurance and self-discipline for which he was famous were balanced by no social virtues and he was as devoid of common honesty as he was of cowardice. The Elector Palatine's money, the Duke of Savoy's ambition, the Bohemian revolt, the very war which was to engulf all Germany, were but so many incidents in the path of his desire. He saw nothing among the mountainous ranges of European politics but the footholds by which he would climb to his personal goal.

In the winter following his reduction of Pilsen, Mansfeld left his men in their quarters and set out to see for himself how the land lay. Having visited Heidelberg he went on to Turin where he found the Duke of Savoy in a more than usually exuberant mood. In February 1619, he had secured the sister of the King of France as a wife for his son and heir. Mistaking this for an indication that the French government was at last preparing an attack on Spain, the Duke proposed to make himself Emperor and King of Bohemia; he would then present the Elector Palatine with Hungary and Alsace.[1] Mansfeld was more concerned for the immediate payment of

[1] LUNDORP, III, pp. 619, 632 f.

his army than for the partition of Europe, and it needed the smooth diplomacy of Anhalt, who arrived from Heidelberg in March, to bring them to an agreement. Mansfeld was sent back to Bohemia with the guarantee of further support, and the Duke of Savoy was satisfied after eight weeks more diplomacy by a treaty of alliance conceived in Anhalt's usual vein. Charles Emmanuel should certainly have the Empire and probably Bohemia too if he would support the Elector Palatine in the meanwhile.[1]

Some of the Duke of Savoy's enthusiasm seems to have infected Anhalt, for he was blind to the weakness of his cause. He hardly noticed the intractability of the Union and did not pause to consider the King of England. When an ambassador was sent to obtain James's assistance, the King had made it clear both in the King's English, which was Scots, and in three lines of Virgil that he would have nothing to do with Bohemia.

'O praestans animi juvenis, quantum ipse feroci
Virtute exsuperas, tanto me impensius aequum est
Prospicere, atque omnes volventem expendere casus.'

recited James, ingeniously misquoting the *Aeneid*.[2]

While Anhalt fondly imagined that he was building up an international alliance, the Archduke Ferdinand was striving to regain the wavering support of his own dynasty. The King of Spain and the governors of the Netherlands had helped him gladly so long as they believed that Bohemia could be easily quelled. The intervention of Mansfeld had altered that. In the spring of 1618 the rebels were not only strong in Bohemia, but the loyalty of Moravia, Hungary, Lusatia and Austria was weakening.[3] Silesia had already joined in the revolt. It was rumoured in Germany that Maximilian of Bavaria had at last decided to contest the imperial election, and at Brussels Ferdinand's disillusioned cousins debated whether it would not be wiser to sacrifice him altogether, since he could only be upheld at great and perhaps fruitless expense. Was there, from

[1] LUNDORP, III, pp. 632 ff.
[2] VOIGT, pp. 127-8.
[3] LUNDORP, I, pp. 559-72, *passim*.

the dynastic point of view, any object in re-establishing a man whose weakness would be a menace to their prestige and whose chances of the imperial crown were dwindling?

All this time Maximilian of Bavaria and John George of Saxony were working with immense industry and apparent good faith for a solution of the Bohemian problem before Matthias died. Should an imperial election occur while the revolt lasted, some desperate effort of the Elector Palatine's party to gain control of the Bohemian vote was to be feared. Both John George and Maximilian implored the rebels to submit their cause to arbitration by the princes.[1] John George, by persistent entreaty, at length persuaded them to send deputies to a general Conference at Eger in April 1619. His labour was in vain, for before the conference met the last feeble bond of German union snapped.

At nine o'clock on the morning of March 20th, 1619, the Emperor Matthias died.

III

In the face of this new situation the extremist party in Bohemia at once gained the upper hand. The projected conference at Eger was tacitly abandoned and strenuous efforts were made to increase the army,[2] fill the empty treasury and drag the provinces of Moravia and Lusatia into revolt. The lands of all loyal Catholics, some of whom had already fled, were seized by the victorious party.[3] At Braunau the Abbot barely escaped with his life.[4] The process was the more thorough because Thurn was now in deadly fear of a rupture within the country itself. Along the Moravian and Austrian borders villages and farms lay waste, and the peasants were everywhere loud in their outcry against a government which had taken their savings, wasted their lands and enlisted their sons. Thurn's native army, raised by compulsion, unprofessional and badly officered, was sick, hungry, mutinous and unpaid. The townsfolk, rich and poor, had been pressed to subscribe to loans, and

[1] LUNDORP, I, pp. 496-7, 503-8, 535-7, 575-6.
[2] Ibid., I, p. 643 f. [3] GINDELY, *Geschichte*, I, p. 476. [4] SVOBODA, pp. 414.

the wanton debasement of the coinage had injured their trade. Prague was crowded with hungry and fever-stricken fugitives.[1]

On March 27th, Ferdinand offered oblivion, indemnity and the confirmation of their privileges if the rebels would but submit themselves to his mercy.[2] Distressed as they were, the Estates could not bring themselves to trust him. Their refusal was followed in a few weeks by the open revolt of Moravia in panic for her liberties. A landslide in the Hapsburg dominions had begun. The Protestants of Upper and Lower Austria were loudly criticizing Ferdinand; Carinthia, Carniola, even Styria, were alleged to be on the verge of insurrection.[3]

In Europe the situation was even darker for Ferdinand. The weathercock French government had withdrawn its earlier offer of support.[4] In Brussels they had abandoned Ferdinand and were talking of putting forward the Archduke Albert for the imperial throne.[5] He was old, but at least he had more control of the states he ruled than that 'silly Jesuited soul'[6] as they now contemptuously called him, who, with all his dominions in revolt, was proposing to stand for the Empire.

Thurn meanwhile, at the head of an army encouraged by the spring weather and the hope of revolt in Austria, had cleared Moravia of all Ferdinand's allies and marched on Vienna. There Ferdinand had assembled the Estates of Lower Austria. He was met by a demand for the expulsion of the Jesuits, for a Protestant Church in Vienna, for autonomy within Austria and the immediate cessation of war on the Bohemians.[7] The Estates were in session when Thurn himself appeared outside the walls.

Ferdinand's lack of imagination and unquestioning faith served him well. Through the long summer when seven weeks of blistering rainless heat[8] added physical discomfort to the tension of the atmosphere, he had maintained his customary cheerfulness. Even when the random firing of the Bohemians

[1] GINDELY, Geschichte, I, p. 472; Letters and Documents, I, p. 198.
[2] LÜNIG, VI, ii, pp. 947 ff.
[3] Letters and Documents, I, p. 88; see also LUNDORP, I, p. 610 f.
[4] La Nunziatura di Bentivoglio, III, p. 379.
[5] Loc. cit.; LONCHAY ET CUVELIER, I, p. 537 f.
[6] Letters and Documents, I, p. 107.
[7] GINDELY, Geschichte, II, p. 74 f.
[8] LAMMERT, Geschichte der Seuchen, Hungersund Kriegsnot, Wiesbaden, 1890, p. 49.

made his own study unsafe he retained his calm, nor did the rumour that Hungary too was in revolt unduly depress him.[1] When his confessor came to speak some words of comfort to him he found him prostrate before his crucifix. Rising, he declared with confidence rather than resignation that he had been seeking counsel where alone he knew it to be found, and that he was now prepared to die, if need be, in the only righteous cause. Had the Saviour spoken to him from the cross, as the Viennese afterwards averred, Ferdinand could not have been more serenely confident.[2]

Almost immediately he met an angry deputation from the Estates with unruffled obstinacy and good-temper. Knowing that Thurn was outside the gates, that the people of Vienna might themselves rebel and let the Bohemians in, that it would need but little for the angry protests of his subjects to find vent in personal violence, Ferdinand nevertheless refused to accede to their demands.[3] Suddenly the clamour of the deputies was interrupted by the clatter of horses' hooves in the courtyard outside. One at least of Ferdinand's allies had remained loyal to him, his younger brother Leopold of Tyrol who had dispatched four hundred cavalry to his immediate help. It was this troop which evaded Thurn's casual guard and now burst into the courtyard of the palace. They had no intention of seizing the representatives or terrorizing the city; their numbers were too few for any such rash undertaking, but the mere sight of their colours was enough for the deputies of the Estates, who fled in confusion, leaving Ferdinand master of the situation.[4] He had not trusted in vain.

Fortune had veered. Four days later on June 10th, 1619, Mansfeld, marching on Budweis with the larger part of his army, was cut off by the imperial forces near the little village of Sablat. He fought for seven hours, sending desperate scouts for the Bohemian reinforcements which he believed to be close at hand, and only at nightfall withdrew, leaving fifteen hundred

[1] HURTER, *Ferdinand II*, VII, p. 553.   [2] *Annales*, XII, pp. 2386-7.
[3] The story that one of the deputies addressed him as 'Nandel' – the colloquial abbreviation of Ferdinand – and took hold of him by his doublet buttons rests on doubtful authority. SCHMERTOSCH, *Vertriebene und bedrängte Protestanten in Leipzig. Neues Archiv für Sachsische Geschichte*, XVI, p. 271.
[4] GINDELY, *Geschichte*, II, pp. 76-80; KLOPP, I, pp. 353-4.

dead and prisoners and most of his baggage in the hands of the enemy.[1] Used to the fortunes of war, he made ready at once for a new march on Budweis, but the citizens of Prague were in panic and the morale both of the native army and of the mercenaries was so badly shaken that the Estates had no choice but to recall Thurn from Austria. The two generals were thus together thrown back upon the defensive in a city now rotten with fear and discontent.

In this dark hour the Elector Palatine still proved the best friend of the rebels. On the very day of Sablat he had written to the Elector of Saxony urging the postponement of the imperial election at least until the Bohemian question was settled;[2] he had a scheme, not officially divulged, for filling Frankfort with Protestant troops and forcibly preventing Ferdinand's arrival until the election was over.[3] There were only three drawbacks to this plan: the first that no candidate could be found to oppose Ferdinand, for the Duke of Savoy was ridiculous and Maximilian of Bavaria had refused; the second that John George of Saxony would not postpone the election; the third that of all men in Germany Frederick was the least fitted to carry out a plan which needed audacity and determination.

The battle of Sablat, the first Catholic victory, had repercussions outside Bohemia. The Crusade sprang once more into life; and followers flocked to Ferdinand with as much zeal as previously they had fled from him. In France, after some weeks of doubt, the young King's religious convictions triumphed over his political judgment and he agreed to further Ferdinand's election to the imperial throne by exerting the necessary pressure on the Elector of Treves.[4] In Germany the Catholic League under the presidency of Maximilian of Bavaria declared itself in favour of Ferdinand in the Bohemian quarrel.[5]

Towards the end of July the Electors or their representatives arrived in Frankfort for the Election. Here the atmosphere was heavy with rumour, and Ferdinand's cavalcade of servants — he had avoided a half-hearted ambush arranged by the

[1] *Theatrum Europaeum*, Francfort, 1635, I, i, p. 153.   [2] LUNDORP, I, pp. 657 ff.
[3] GINDELY, *Geschichte*, II, pp. 148-9.
[4] *Relazioni dagli Ambasciatori Francia*, II, p. 134; *La Ninziatura di Bentivoglio*, pp. 405-6.
[5] LÜNIG, VII, iv, pp. 286-7.

Elector Palatine — was set upon by the citizens, who declared that he intended to overawe the Electors. The diplomatic Elector of Cologne quieted the uproar by inviting Ferdinand to a hunting expedition in the neighbouring country until the day of the election.[1]

Meanwhile on July 31st, 1619, Lusatia, Silesia, and Moravia signed the terms of a joint confederation with Bohemia in the name of their national integrity and the Protestant faith.[2] Writing to his wife from a sunny seat 'at the top of the little tower' at Amberg, the Elector Frederick gave way to irresponsible jubilation. 'They have agreed to many conditions', he wrote, 'that will hardly please Ferdinand.'[3] His doubts lulled to rest by Anhalt, he felt once again confident and safe.

Hard upon the news of this confederation, Ferdinand received yet worse tidings. On the outskirts of his lands another enemy was in arms. The small principality of Transylvania along the north-eastern border of Hungary acted as the bulwark between the Hapsburg dominions and the Turks; its princes, theoretically vassals of the Hungarian Crown, were virtually independent, since they were too valuable as allies to be treated unceremoniously as subjects. Gabriel Bethlen, or as he is familiarly known, Bethlen Gabor, had been Prince of Transylvania since 1613; his path to the throne had been devious, beset with intrigue and stained, his enemies said, with murder. His method of keeping it was crudely effective, for he staved off internal unrest almost annually by leading his excitable subjects into battle. A brilliant soldier and a wily diplomat, he rang the changes of wars and alliances with the Turks, the Poles and the Emperor in turn. As he was not only a Calvinist but in his curious way a very devout one, the distress of the Bohemian Protestants gave him all the excuse he needed for his summer campaign in 1619. Thus while Ferdinand was on his way to Frankfort, the swarthy little Tartar with his loyal followers came marching over the border into Hungary. Half Protestant, Hungary rose at once; rebels sprang up on all sides to throw off the yoke of the absent Ferdinand. It was but

---

[1] *Annales*, IX, p. 414.   [2] See STANKA, 74 f.
[3] ARETIN, *Beitrage zur Geschichte und Literatur*, VII, *Sammling noch eunedrückter Briefe des Churfursten Friedrich V von der Pfalz*, Munich, 1806, p. 148.

a few weeks before Thurn entered into communication with this new friend, and on August 20th, 1619, they signed an offensive and defensive alliance.

Only a day before, the confederate states of Bohemia, Lusatia, Silesia and Moravia had declared that the election of Ferdinand was invalid and that he had ceased to be their king.[1] The Elector Frederick was one of the first to receive the news. He had not gone in person to Frankfort but had stayed, suspiciously enough, in the Upper Palatinate not far from the Bohemian border. The happy confidence of three weeks before had evaporated, and he now wrote querulously to his wife that the rebels had deposed Ferdinand and he for his part did not know what course to decide on.[2] It was a little late for the Elector to be in doubt; Anhalt was not.

On August 26th the Bohemians at last met to choose their new king. Of the five candidates named, only two, the Electors of Saxony and of the Palatinate, received serious consideration. Count Schlick, striving to guide his compatriots to the less dangerous alternative, urged them to choose John George of Saxony. The Elector had shown little sympathy with the revolt, but his prestige and his wisdom were not to be despised; in a dangerous situation, he might be able to come to an understanding with Ferdinand. The choice of Frederick must mean war to the death, and it might be Bohemia's death, not Ferdinand's. Schlick's moderation was once more swept aside; with Bethlen Gabor in the field and Ferdinand pleasantly remote at Frankfort, the extremists were again in the saddle. Frederick was chosen king by a hundred and forty-six votes to seven.[3]

Two days later, amid a host of lugubrious prognostications, the imperial election took place at Frankfort. The news from Bohemia had not yet reached the Main, but bees had swarmed in front of the Rathaus, which the people reckoned an evil omen,[4] and when Ferdinand took his place among the Electors as King of Bohemia a deputation of the rebels protested and had to be silenced before the meeting could proceed.[5] He wore

---

[1] Lünig, vi, i, p. 167 f.; Lundorp, i, p. 675 f.
[2] Aretin, *Beitrage*, vii, p. 148.
[3] Gindely, *Geschichte*, pp. 227-8.
[4] *Letters and Documents*, i, p. 199.
[5] d'Elvert, *Beiträge zur Geschichte des dreissigjährigen Krieges in Mähren*, Brünn, 1867, i, p. 45; Lundorp, i, pp. 657 ff.

a new and hastily contrived diadem, for the time-honoured crown of Bohemia was in the hands of the insurgents.

The three Catholic Electors unhesitatingly gave their votes for Ferdinand, the representative of the Elector of Saxony did likewise. He had no alternative, for his master had dispatched him to Frankfort with the discouraging words, 'I know no good will come of it, I know Ferdinand', but had not indicated whom else he should support. The Elector, it was said, had been drunk at the time; but the same judgment might well have been given with complete sobriety. The representative of the Elector of Brandenburg copied the others. There followed a tedious dissertation from the deputy of the Elector Palatine, whose instructions were on no account to vote for Ferdinand. After suggesting seven other candidates all equally absurd, he registered a vote for the Duke of Bavaria.[1] The Archbishop of Mainz tactfully pointed out that the Duke of Bavaria had agreed to forgo all his votes in favour of Ferdinand. The Palatine deputy had no choice but to withdraw his vote and register it again for Ferdinand.

The bulky capitulation of constitutional rights which each new Emperor had to guarantee was next handed to Ferdinand, who flicked over the pages with disconcerting rapidity and stood up to take the oath with as little gravity as if he had been stepping out to a dance.[2] Outside, a great crowd had gathered to hail the new Emperor when he appeared according to custom on the balcony, but just before he came out to them a rumour started on the edge of the crowd — news from Prague. It passed, gathering momentum, from lip to lip across the excited throng. Ferdinand had been deposed in Bohemia.[3] And while their voices rose in a hubbub of excitement, the great windows above them were thrown open and before them on the balcony stood the man himself, Ferdinand, deposed King of Bohemia, but irrevocably chosen and sworn, Holy Roman Emperor of the German Nation.

[1] *Letters and Documents*, II, p. 31.
[2] MOSER, *Patriotisches Archiv*, Frankfort, 1781, VII, p. 45.
[3] HURTER, *Ferdinand II*, VIII, p. 50.

IV

The news of the Bohemian and imperial elections reached the Elector Frederick hard upon each other, bringing him face to face with a problem he had not foreseen. His vote had been given to Ferdinand at Frankfort, and almost in the same moment he was asked to assume a crown which had been forcibly taken from Ferdinand. Like his rival he met the situation by prayer, but unlike his rival his prayers remained unanswered, ending only in despondency and tears.[1]

Pleading for time, Frederick withdrew to Heidelberg to consult his councillors and the princes of the Union. At his Court nearly all voices were loud against the offer, even his mother, a daughter of William the Silent, besought him not to go to Bohemia. His council drew up a list of fourteen reasons for refusal against six for acceptance.[2] His chaplain, on the other hand, saw the hand of God in the Bohemian choice and vehemently urged Frederick to agree.[3] The young Electress Elizabeth valiantly assumed a neutral attitude in public, but popular report attributed a different policy to her, and legend put into her mouth the proud statement that she would rather eat sauerkraut with a king than roast meat with an Elector. Whatever her open conduct, she expressed herself frankly in favour of her husband's acceptance in her letters,[4] and it is difficult to believe that the Bohemian Crown was a subject altogether barred in the electoral bedchamber. Her contempt for Ferdinand was boundless. 'He hath but one eye, and that not very good,' she wrote light-heartedly; 'I am afraid he will be lousy for he hath not money to buy himself clothes.'[5]

On September 12th the Union met at Rothenburg, where the deputies, with few exceptions, advised Frederick not to meddle with Bohemia. Anhalt's other allies were equally intractable. The Duke of Savoy, indignant that neither the imperial nor the Bohemian Crown had been secured for him, threatened to

---

[1] GINDELY, *Geschichte*, II, p. 230.
[2] MOSER, *Patriotisches Archiv*, VII, p. 109.
[3] HAEBERLIN, *Neueste Teutsche Reichsgeschichte*. Halle, 1774-1804, XXIV, pp. 376-7.
[4] *Letters and Documents*, II, p. 2.   [5] Ibid., p. 1.

withdraw all help, and the Venetians declined to invest their money in so crazy a venture.[1] The Prince of Orange, it was true, urged Frederick forward, but the recent internal revolution in the Provinces which had ended in the temporary extinction of the anti-Orange party and made Maurice virtually dictator, was not yet complete and the government was still weak. The King of England had not ceased to deplore the policy of his son-in-law ever since the revolt began. From Hungary the irrepressible Bethlen Gabor sent cordial messages of encouragement, but only a rash man would trust so variable an ally.

Ultimately the decision would be taken on moral and not on political grounds. The education of seventeenth-century princes inured them to this practice, and Frederick was no exception when he submitted the fate of Bohemia to the judgment of his conscience. He was uncertain both as to the morality of supporting rebels even in a good cause,[2] and as to the sacred nature of his duty to the Emperor. On the one hand, there was his loyalty as a German prince; on the other, the expectations that his policy had so rashly created among the Bohemians. If he abandoned Ferdinand, he could always plead that his quarrel was not with the Emperor as such but with the deposed king of a province outside the bounds of imperial control. If he abandoned Bohemia he would have betrayed a people who had trusted in him. On the one hand, he would be guilty of a common political subterfuge, on the other of a moral treachery. On September 28th, 1619, he secretly informed the rebels that he would accept the Crown. Whatever the suspicions of the world there is little doubt that Frederick expressed the sum of his intentions when he wrote to his uncle, the Duke of Bouillon, 'It is a divine calling which I must not disobey ... my only end is to serve God and His Church.'[3]

Frederick had forgotten one prince in his calculations. Since the outbreak of the revolt his kinsman, Maximilian of Bavaria, had been working for a peaceful settlement; Frederick's acceptance of the Crown destroyed that tenuous hope. It destroyed

---

[1] *Letters and Documents*, I, p. 110.   [2] GINDELY, *Geschichte*, I, p. 447.
[3] *Ambassade extraordinaire de Messieurs les Duc d'Angenlême, Comte de Béthune ... en l'année MDCXX*, ed. H. DE BÉTHUNE. Paris, 1667, p. 95.

also Maximilian's other scheme for the coalition of the Catholic and Protestant princes, of the League and the Union, [1] for the defence of the German constitution. It was natural that Maximilian should be indignant with Frederick, but indignation alone did not drive him into the camp of the enemy. As a Catholic, he did not wish to see a Protestant king in Bohemia; as a German prince, he did not wish to see Frederick defeated by troops sent from Spain and Flanders. He found but one way out of this quandary — to espouse the cause of Ferdinand and restore him to his rightful kingdom by the arms of the Catholic League. In this way the Church would be saved in Bohemia, and Ferdinand would be bound by gratitude to the Catholic princes of Germany.

The argument would have been sound had it ended there. Personal and dynastic ambition, strengthened perhaps by some obscure jealousy of his handsome cousin whose wife was young and fruitful, induced this ageing and childless man to go yet farther. As the leader of the Catholic League and the master of one of the best professional armies in Europe, he could afford to sell his alliance dearly. On October 8th, 1619, he signed an agreement with Ferdinand by which he was to have absolute control of all operations in Bohemia and was to hold in pledge against the repayment of his expenses all such lands as he conquered. [2] Furthermore, and in this single point personal ambition triumphed over political discretion, by a secret article, Maximilian, on the defeat of Frederick, was to have his Electoral title.

The fatal alliance was all but signed when Frederick rode out of Heidelberg amid the lamentations of his people. 'He is taking the Palatinate with him into Bohemia,' said his mother as she watched him go. But he was taking more than the Palatinate into Bohemia. The truce between Spain and the United Provinces was coming to an end, and here was the man on whom the Dutch depended to guard the Rhine leaving his post to chase a phantom in Bohemia, setting out to dethrone a Hapsburg, blandly defying the lightning of Spain. Here was the leading Protestant ruler in the Empire pledging the cause of constitutional liberties and religious freedom to the support of a

---

[1] See *supra*, p. 64.
[2] LÜNIG, v, i, pp. 691 ff.

national rising in Bohemia. Here was a German prince assuming the leadership of a Slavonic rebellion. When Frederick rode out of Heidelberg in the drizzling mists of an October day[1] he was taking more than the Palatinate into Bohemia, he was taking the fate of Germany and the peace of Europe.

[1] JOHN HARRISON, *A Short Relation of the Departure of the Most High and Mighty Prince Frederick.* Dort, 1619.

SPANISH TOCSIN, GERMAN ALARUM
1619-1621

Qu'ILS se battent en Bohême tant qu'ils voudront, nous serons bons voisins en ces quartiers icy.

THE ELECTOR OF TREVES

SPANISH TOCSIN, GERMAN ALARUM

I

WERE it ever possible in history to single out one action as decisive for the developments which followed it, the acceptance of the Crown of Bohemia by the Elector Frederick was such an act. By that acceptance he drew together the guiding threads of European diplomacy and combined the interests of Protestant Germany with those of the European enemies of the Hapsburg dynasty. As Elector Palatine he was already the bulwark between the Dutch resistance and the Spanish advance: as King of Bohemia he would be the safeguard of princely liberties against imperial infringement. Could he maintain both positions, his lands would form a barrier against Hapsburg aggression from the Rhine to the Oder. France, the United Provinces, Denmark, Sweden, England, the German princes should have recognized the decisive moment and acted. According to the scheduled schemes of Anhalt the time had come.

Anhalt was no fool; neither was his colleague of Ansbach when he declared that: 'We have in our hands the means to overturn the world'; neither was the Venetian agent in Vienna who predicted that all Germany would fly to arms, nor the leaders of the Bohemian revolt who confidently awaited the action of the European princes, nor the imperial councillors who feared the intervention of France, nor the Duke of Bouillon who wrote to demand it.[1] But all made one error; they calculated without the human element. Seldom in the history of Europe has the insignificance of one man had so profound an effect upon his period. Frederick was no leader; indeed he was a man of so blank a personality as to defy all attempts to make him one. In vain to say that the occasion mattered more than the man. In the long run the enemies of the Hapsburg must

[1] LUNDORP, III, p. 616; HÖFLER, p. 391; BÉTHUNE, p. 97 f.

be drawn into Frederick's quarrel or perish, but afraid to trust so mild a leader they hesitated until Frederick had fallen, until Bohemia and the Palatinate were lost, and then spent a generation in trying to fill the breach which had been made.

The personal tragedy of Frederick was the more bitter because for the first weeks after his decision the signs were deceptively favourable. While his youthful cavalcade made its way to the Bohemian frontier, Ferdinand had retired from Frankfort to Graz among the Styrian hills where his eldest son, smitten with an incurable disease, lay wasting slowly. On all sides disquieting rumours, stilled momentarily by the imperial election, broke out afresh. It was said that there were traitors even among the imperial council.[1] In Styria there was discontent, the Protestants of Austria and Hungary had entered into alliance with the Bohemians;[2] Bethlen Gabor, joining his forces with theirs, had taken Pressburg and driven Ferdinand's unpaid, undisciplined troops back over the Danube. Defence proved impossible on the long line of frontier, and before the autumn was over he was marching unhindered for Vienna, laying the country waste about him. God alone, reported the Venetian agent, could now save the House of Austria.[3]

Beyond his own borders events were no less distressing to Ferdinand. The United Provinces, Denmark,[4] Sweden and the Venetian republic, recognized Frederick as king. The Duke of Bouillon promised help, and from Davos, high up in the mountains of the Grisons, the Swiss sent word that they would hold the Val Telline against all Spanish reinforcements. Even Ferdinand's brother-in-law and close ally, the King of Poland, was prevented by the protests of the Diet from making a diversion in Silesia.[5]

Meanwhile Vienna, overcrowded with fugitives and wounded, with plague raging and famine imminent, awaited the coming of Bethlen Gabor. From the bedside of his dying son, Ferdinand hastened to the capital, believing that his presence alone might

---

[1] HÖFLER, p. 393.
[2] LÜNIG, VI, ii, p. 150 f.
[3] HÖFLER, p. 391.
[4] BRUCHMANN, *Archivalia inedita zur Geschichte des Winterkönigs.* Breslau, 1909, p. 10.
[5] HÖFLER, p. 394; LUNDORP, I, p. 850.

hearten the citizens. Drought, followed by torrential rain and thunderstorms, had damaged the harvest, and the heat of the late summer had brought out the plague in the valleys of Austria.[1] All across the duchy, Ferdinand met straggling bands of fugitives — Catholic peasants fleeing from Bohemia, Hungary, Upper Austria, monks and nuns driven from their plundered convents, who knelt at the muddy roadside, lifting thin hands and anxious faces to him. When he entered his capital Bethlen Gabor was already at the gates, while the country for miles to the eastward was the prey of his foraging hordes.[2]

While Ferdinand strove to encourage Vienna, Frederick had been enthusiastically welcomed at Prague. The frankness with which he had guaranteed the Bohemian constitution before he crossed the frontier,[3] the bustling competence of Anhalt, the hope of powerful allies, the beauty of the young queen and the flattering fact that although she was far advanced in pregnancy she had risked the arduous journey in order to bear her child among her husband's new subjects — all these things contributed to form a favourable first impression. Besides, Prague, notoriously gay, welcomed an occasion for festivity even though the country towards the borders was already desolate, and fugitives were camped in the streets and open places of the city.[4]

Soon the new king would learn that there was no money for arms or men; in the meantime there was money to hang the whole city in blue and silver, to furnish out a guard of honour in the dress of Zizka's time, to set up fountains running red and white wine, and to throw largess of silver coins stamped with the device, 'God and the Estates gave me the Crown'. The joyous entry of the King and Queen, their separate and splendid coronations, the hysterical gaiety of the city delighted at the return of a Court, were enough at first to deceive Frederick. His spirits reached such heights that when, in the small hours of December 18th, his wife gave birth to a son, he was with difficulty restrained from arousing the whole town with joy bells.[5]

---

[1] LAMMERT, p. 50.   [2] *Annales*, IX, p. 414; GINDELY, *Geschichte*, II, p. 286.
[3] LÜNIG, VI, ii, p. 179.   [4] LUNDORP, I, pp. 717, 722.
[5] Ibid., I, pp. 724 ff., 926; D'ELVERT, I, p. 62 f.

Ferdinand's ill fortune kept pace with his rival's triumph. While in Prague preparations were made for the christening of Rupert, Duke of Lusatia, as Frederick entitled his new-born child, in Graz on Christmas Eve Ferdinand's eldest son had died.

The omens played Frederick false, for weeks lengthened into months and still the united rising of the Protestant powers did not take place.

The Princes of the Union after long deliberation agreed to recognize Frederick's sovereignty, but made no further effort to help him. The German cities in the first flush of Protestant enthusiasm offered a gift of money,[1] but nothing more was ever heard of it. Emerging for one moment into the light of history the Elector of Treves remarked, 'Let them fight as much as they like in Bohemia; we others, we will remain good friends in these parts',[2] and relapsed into optimistic inactivity. As far as the princes on the Rhine were concerned, his prophecy was accurate.

It was different in Saxony. In spite of his discouragement of the rebels, John George had been sure that if they elected a new king they would choose him; he had not fully realized the strength of the Palatine party in Prague. Had the crown been offered to him he would not have accepted it, but he would have taken the opportunity to establish himself as the protector of the Protestants in Bohemia and to dictate a settlement to Ferdinand. Now this hope was gone and instead he was faced with a potential increase in the power of the Elector Palatine.

Only the most selfless politician in John George's place could have regarded the establishment of a fellow-elector in Bohemia with equanimity. If Frederick succeeded he would be the most powerful prince in Germany, with two electoral votes in his hands and control of the upper waters of the Elbe and Oder and the middle waters of the Rhine. Added to this, Frederick had a sister married into the Hohenzollern family, a dynasty whose expansion John George regarded with the utmost suspicion. Before the Bohemian election he had seen himself as the arbiter of the Empire; after it, he was merely a prince whose heritage was in danger of isolation between the growing power of Brandenburg in the north and of the new King of Bohemia in

[1] LUNDORP, I p. 727.　　[2] BÉTHUNE, p. 143.

the south.[1] John George's anxiety was fanned into active hatred by his Court preacher, the irascible Höe who denounced the Bohemian government for having betrayed the Lutheran faith to the Calvinistic Antichrist. He went farther; he espoused without more ado the cause of the dispossessed Ferdinand. 'God', he cried, 'shall smite the cheeks of your imperial majesty's insolent enemies, scatter their teeth, turn them backwards, and bring them to shame.'[2]

Dismayed but not yet at the end of his resources, Anhalt threw out one more bait to tempt the Elector of Saxony. He advised Frederick to invite all the Protestant German rulers to a conference at Nuremberg, hoping that in the interests of peace even the least favourable princes would appear. Had Anhalt planned a demonstration of Frederick's weakness he could have thought of none better. Hardly a ruler in Germany, save the members of the Union, sent representatives; above all John George of Saxony remained unmoved. Those who did assemble half-heartedly agreed to guarantee Frederick's lands on the Rhine while he was away, but would not be moved to any decision in the matter of Bohemia. The agent whom Ferdinand had sent to sound the intentions of the meeting was able to return to Vienna with wholly reassuring news.[3]

The Nuremberg assembly laid bare Frederick's weakness and the disunion of the Protestant princes. Four months later, in March 1620, a meeting called by Ferdinand at Mühlhausen demonstrated the strength and union of the opposing party. Frederick had asserted on taking the Bohemian Crown that he wrested it not from the Emperor, but only from an Austrian Archduke.[4] This argument rested on the assumption that Bohemia was outside the bounds of the Empire: Frederick was not breaking the imperial peace, but merely indulging in an external war, so that Ferdinand could not extend his authority as Emperor to oppose him.

This specious argument was shattered by the meeting at Mühlhausen. Here were gathered the representatives of Maximilian of Bavaria and the Catholic League as well as the delegate

---

[1] J. G. DROYSEN, *Geschichte der Preussischen Politik*. Berlin, 1885-86, THEIL III, pp. 23-4.
[2] SCHWABE, pp. 306, 315; KNAPP, p. 15.
[3] GINDELY, *Geschichte*, II, p. 301 f.   [4] LUNDORP, III, p. 678.

of the Elector John George. Here Ferdinand bought the united support of Lutherans and Catholics by offering a guarantee not to interfere with the religion of the secularized bishoprics in the Upper Saxon Circle. In response they pronounced Bohemia to be an integral part of the Empire. Frederick had therefore broken the imperial peace and laid himself open to the direst penalties of the law. On April 30th an imperial mandate was issued summoning him to withdraw from Bohemia before June 1st; his disregard of this ultimatum was the real declaration of war. From June 1st, 1620, the hand of every loyal German must be lifted against him as the deliberate destroyer of public peace; henceforward the Emperor might bring up all the forces he could command as Emperor, as Archduke of Austria and as the rightful King of Bohemia, to the destruction of the usurper.[1]

II

Frederick's position was weak in Germany; it was weaker still in Europe. The King of England celebrated his son-in-law's accession by officially denying to every sovereign in Europe that he had countenanced or even known of the project.[2] The enthusiasm of the Londoners who attempted to stage an illumination in the new king's honour,[3] and of the ardent Protestants throughout the country who at once began to collect money for his cause,[4] did nothing to move James from his initial obstinacy. 'His Majesty hath a purpose to join with the French King in doing all good offices for the weal of Christendom to pacify the present broils that are on foot in Germany', his ambassador explained, to the exasperation of Frederick's advisers.[5] The defection of so near an ally discouraged Frederick's other friends: his cause, they whispered, must be bad indeed if not even his nearest kin would support it.[6]

---

[1] LUNDORP, II, p. 12 f.; LÜNIG, VI, i, p. 321 f.
[2] GARDINER, *History of England*, London, 1883, III, p. 24.
[3] *Letters and Documents*, II, p. 23.
[4] *Calendar of State Papers. Domestic Series* 1619-23. London, 1858, p.132 and elsewhere.
[5] *Letters and Documents*, II, p. 189; LUNDORP, I, p. 860.
[6] G. GROEN VAN PRINSTERER, *Archives de la Maison d'Orange-Nassau.* Leyden, Hague, Utrecht, 1835 sq., II, ii, p. 572.

The King of Denmark admonished the Elector of Saxony to assist Frederick[1] but was too deeply engaged in a commercial dispute with Hamburg to spare time, money or men for personal intervention. The King of Sweden, with Frederick's warm encouragement, descended on Brandenburg and carried off the eldest princess for his wife, but the marriage was not a prelude to armed intervention on the Protestant side in Germany. Intent on his wars with the King of Poland, Gustavus was more anxious to gain Frederick's help than to offer any himself.

The Venetians grudgingly agreed to prevent as far as possible the shipping of troops from Spain to Germany,[2] but were otherwise too much afraid of intrigues in Italy and too little interested in a revolt which no longer promised to be good business. The Duke of Savoy, justly indignant because Anhalt had secured for him neither the imperial nor the Bohemian crown as he had promised,[3] withdrew his subsidies from Mansfeld's army and allowed passage across his dominions to a contingent of Spanish troops bound for Germany. Troubles in Transylvania had forced Bethlen Gabor to raise the siege of Vienna. After settling his own difficulties, he sold his alliance dearly to Frederick, demanding a perpetual stream of titles, subsidies and rewards to keep him even superficially loyal. Had the Bohemian government realized that he was still negotiating with Ferdinand, they would have thought his alliance even dearer at the price.[4] Worst of all a sudden rising in the Grisons threw open the Val Telline to Spain.

There remained the most important of all Anhalt's allies, the United Provinces. Here at least were friends who could not afford to abandon Frederick; if he were defeated and his lands on the Rhine endangered, they would be the first to suffer. It might be presumed therefore that they would defend the Palatinate for him. This was the part for which Anhalt had cast them, and again he had miscalculated. Anxious to undermine the power of the Hapsburg, the Dutch had encouraged

---

[1] LUNDORP, II, p. 19.
[2] H. V. ZWIEDINECK-SÜDENHORST, *Die Politik der Republik Venedigs*. Stuttgart, 1882-85, I, pp. 101-3.
[3] *Letters and Documents*, II, p. 31.
[4] GINDELY, *Geschichte*, II, p. 283 f.; III, p. 156.

the revolt from the outset,[1] but they had not considered the probability of Frederick's abandoning his post on the Rhine, still less had they foreseen the defection of the Union. They now found that they alone were expected to defend the Rhine should the Spaniards choose to invade the Palatinate. And they were not prepared to accept the responsibility. The final clash between the two religious parties which divided the country had coincided with a conflict between the central aristocratic authority of Prince Maurice and the demands of the States of Holland. Internal revolution had made Prince Maurice military dictator. But the dictatorship was not yet firm, and Maurice needed all the time that remained before the expiry of the truce with Spain to consolidate his power. He could not risk precipitating war by any rash movement on the Rhine. Perhaps he would have acted had he been supported by the King of England and the Protestant Union; he dared not, even to save the Rhineland, act alone. As it was, the United Provinces voted a subsidy of fifty thousand florins a month to Frederick[2] and sent a small contingent to strengthen the Bohemian army. This was hardly the help for which Anhalt had been waiting. As for the Rhine, Maurice placed a few troops on the right bank, facing the episcopal lands of the Bishop of Cologne.[3] By no stretch of imagination could this be interpreted as an act of hostility towards Spain; Maurice had saved what remained of the truce. Whether this tiny gesture would also save the Palatinate was more doubtful.

III

There were still two rulers in Europe whose decision to act or to acquiesce would be decisive: the Kings of France and Spain. Anhalt had regarded Philip's intervention for Ferdinand as a foregone conclusion; that being so, he regarded the intervention of Louis for Frederick as equally certain. Again he had reckoned without the personal element.

[1] LUNDORP, I, pp. 545-6.
[2] HÖFLER, p. 400.
[3] GINDELY, *Die Berichte über die Schlacht auf dem Weissenberge bei Prag.*
Archiv für Oesterreichische Geschichte, LVI. Vienna, 1878, pp. 23-4.

Frederick relied on his uncle, the Duke of Bouillon, to enlist the support of the French government. As a Protestant, as a quondam rebel against royal authority, as a persistent and unscrupulous intriguer, Bouillon was ill qualified to gain the trust of the young King,[1] a devout Catholic, jealous for the prestige of the monarchy, and bred in an atmosphere of suspicion. The ruling favourite, the handsome and vacuous Duke of Luynes, clung to power only by flattering the opinions of his master.

Bouillon talked too much. When in the early spring of 1619, before the deposition of Ferdinand, the King of France had created a new order of knighthood, he had burst out irrepressibly that Louis might make knights in France, but that he, Bouillon, was making kings in Germany.[2] This admission of intrigues, better concealed, suggested that Bouillon's was the master-hand behind the Bohemian incident. This was not the case, but so long as Bouillon boastingly implied it he was unlikely to persuade Louis to support Frederick. The idea of a French nobleman manipulating a puppet king was of all things most calculated to alienate the young monarch.

Poised unsteadily between an intriguing Court and a discontented people, the royal ministers felt that the safety of the government depended on suppressing the demands of the King's Protestant subjects. Louis himself was a devout Catholic; on hearing of the Bohemian election he declared at once that, for the sake of the Church, this new kingship was not to be tolerated and when Frederick sent ambassadors to Paris he accorded them only the precedence of Electoral envoys.

Besides, Frederick's wife stood next but one in succession to the English throne. The possible death of the unmarried and delicate Prince of Wales would mean that in a few years the new King of Bohemia would be as good as King of England. So large an extension of power was not at all to be encouraged in a neighbouring prince.[3]

On the other hand, should the Emperor or the King of Spain

---

[1] RICHELIEU, *Mémoires*, ed. *Societé de l'histoire de France*, Paris, 1907, II, pp. 400-1.

[2] BENTIVOGLIO, *Opere*, p. 668.

[3] PONCHARTRAIN, *Mémoires*. Petitot, II, xvii, Paris, 1822, p. 297; *Nunziatura di Bentivoglio*, I, pp. 110-11, III, p. 504, IV, pp. 9, 153.

make Frederick's revolt into an excuse to seize the Rhenish Palatinate, France would feel the ill-effects only less than the United Provinces. A middle course seemed best, and with this in view an embassy left Paris for Germany in the early summer of 1620.

At Ulm the French ambassadors found the princes of the Protestant Union with their small army, sulky and undecided what action to take; on the opposite side of the river Maximilian of Bavaria was gathering the larger and better trained forces of the Catholic League, ready to march on Bohemia in accordance with his promise to Ferdinand. It was touch and go whether the armies should try the issue; none of the princes wished to be involved in Frederick's war, but all feared that Maximilian would attack them or perhaps attempt to march through their lands. The French at once put forward a suggestion: if the Union would guarantee the lands of all Catholic princes from attack, would not the League give an equivalent guarantee to respect the neutrality of Protestant states? Maximilian of Bavaria warmly supported the plan, and the princes of the Union, who asked for nothing better than safety and freedom from responsibility, were easily persuaded to come to terms. On July 3rd the Treaty of Ulm was signed.[1]

French diplomacy was based on two assumptions: the first and correct assumption that Frederick would not be able to hold Bohemia; the second that the Union, freed from the menace of the League, would defend the Rhine from Spanish attack. The Treaty of Ulm was intended to neutralize the peril to which Frederick's rashness had exposed the party of the German Liberties; he was to suffer alone for his folly, and the Hapsburg victory with its consequences was to be confined to Bohemia. The policy would have been sound had the members of the Union behaved as the French government expected, but instead they made the Treaty an excuse for total inaction, and the ministers of France realized too late that their diplomacy had removed the last check on Frederick's enemies, without securing the Rhine.[2]

[1] RICHELIEU, *Mémoires*, III, p. 112 f.; LÜNIG, V, i, p. 285; BÉTHUNE, pp. 144 f., 163 f.
[2] See TAPIÉ, *Politique Etrangère de la France au commencement de la Guerre de Trente Ans*, pp. 510 f., 624 f.

Almost at the same moment as the conclusion of the Treaty, the governors of the Spanish Netherlands informed the King of France that Spinola was preparing to march on the Palatinate. There were doubts in Madrid and Brussels as to how Louis would take this news; he took it as a good Catholic and showed no displeasure.[1] His advisers were trusting that the Union would avert the danger; only later did they hear that their emissaries, on leaving Ulm for Vienna, had found the imperial Court rotten with Spanish bribery, the Emperor wholly in the hands of the Spanish ambassador, and their own projects for moderation and compromise in Bohemia barely treated with civility.[2] It was too late then to initiate a new policy, for both the Queen-mother's intrigues and the Huguenot rising had come to a head, and the French government, having casually destroyed the last barrier against the Hapsburg advance, slid out of European politics for the next three years.

Meanwhile the Hapsburg dynasty had united little by little in support of the deposed Ferdinand. Suspicious, apprehensive, doubtful of Ferdinand's ability to hold Bohemia even if it were reconquered for him, and fearing the growing poverty and discontent of his country, Philip III of Spain at first hesitated. He wished to husband his strength for the renewal of the Dutch war.[3] In the Netherlands, nearer to the scene of action, the Archduke Albert and his advisers saw more clearly. For them, Frederick's seizure of the Crown put a new face on Ferdinand's cause: an excuse for invading the Palatinate and occupying that one dangerous Protestant outpost on the Rhine might never occur again. The lethargy of Philip III could not be allowed to stand between Spinola and his far-reaching strategy.[4]

Ambrogio Spinola, a Genoese nobleman and a natural soldier, had made his reputation fighting against Prince Maurice in the opening years of the century. Political cartoonists represented him as a gigantic spider weaving a web to entangle Protestant Europe.[5] In fact, he thought of little else

---

[1] *Nunziatura di Bentivoglio*, IV, pp. 295, 308.
[2] BÉTHUNE, pp. 225-31.
[3] GINDELY, *Geschichte*, II, p. 406.
[4] See LONCHAY ET CUVELIER, I, pp. 546 f., 558 ff.
[5] E. A. BELLER, *Caricatures of the Winter King of Bohemia*, 1928, *passim*.

but the coming war with the Dutch, slept little, ate sparingly without noticing what was set before him, worked for eighteen hours a day and spent the greater part of his private fortune on the improvement of the army.[1] For eleven years, since the truce with the Dutch, he had been building up the plan for their final defeat; Europe was to him but the outworks of his own problem, and that problem the control of the Rhine. At the first rumour of unrest in Germany, he tried to gain a voice in the military plans of the League. As soon as Frederick's election was known, he began to collect and mass troops from Spain and from Spanish Italy, in the Milanese, the Netherlands and Alsace.[2] Three years before, in 1617, Ferdinand had bought Spanish support for his candidature to the imperial throne by the offer of part of Alsace; now, in his anxiety for military help, he offered more. Spinola acted in the knowledge that, if he conquered Frederick's lands on the Rhine, a share of them would fall to Spain, and with that the Protestant barrier between the source of his military power and his objective would be obliterated.

Frederick had forfeited his lands by wilfully breaking the imperial peace, and the Emperor could dispose of them to his friends. On paper it sounded fair enough, and if in fact it was directly contrary to the oath that Ferdinand had sworn when he assumed the imperial Crown — the oath not to dispose of German lands without permission of the Diet[3] — this legal aspect of the matter could always be considered after the actual seizure had taken place. The decision to invade the Palatinate was taken in Brussels before the end of 1619,[4] the treaty between Ferdinand and the Spanish government was signed in February 1620, and the order which at length gave Spinola leave to march was dated at Madrid on June 23rd;[5] before it reached him the French had negotiated their treaty at Ulm, the Union had withdrawn their army and the Rhineland lay open to all comers.

---

[1] LONCHAY ET CUVELIER, pp. 510, 564.
[2] Ibid., I, p. 547; HÖFLER, p. 399; *Fortescue Papers*, p. 91.
[3] Ferdinand's capitulation oath is given in LÜNIG, III, p. 57 f.
[4] LONCHAY ET CUVELIER, I, p. 550.
[5] LUNDORP, II, p. 171.

IV

For the last ten years pamphleteers had been warning the people of the Spanish menace; for more than ten years the independent rulers of Germany had dreaded the increase of imperial power and an attack on their liberties. Anhalt had reckoned on these fears to bring the majority of the princes to Frederick's side. Were they then so blind when the moment came that they could not guess, even if they did not know, what Spinola, Ferdinand and the King of Spain intended?

The princes were not blind. At the imperial court everyone knew that Ferdinand's two chief advisers, Eggenberg and Harrach, were under Spanish control,[1] and it was common knowledge too that no decision was taken without consulting Oñate, the Spanish ambassador.[2] No ruler of importance can possibly have been so ill-informed as to ignore the fact that Spinola was gathering troops, or so simple as to think that he was doing it for a pastime.

The princes of the Union were frankly afraid to act; their only anxiety was to establish their innocence of participation in Frederick's revolt. But the Electors of Saxony and Brandenburg and the Duke of Bavaria, these three, Lutheran, Calvinist and Catholic, had all alike declared themselves at one time or another firm defenders of the constitution. Did none of them now perceive that the constitution was in danger?

The Elector of Brandenburg could plead an excuse. George William, the eldest and Calvinist son, had succeeded his Calvinist father at Christmas 1619. The Lutheran Electress-mother determined to dethrone him in favour of her second Lutheran son and enlisted the help of John George of Saxony. The young Elector, with half his subjects ready to revolt against him, appealed for help to the neighbouring King of Poland. His mother immediately arranged for her eldest daughter to marry, without her brother's consent, the King of Sweden, mortal enemy of the King of Poland. Cut off from Poland, George William offered to help the Bohemians in the hope that they in return would help him. At once the Elector

[1] FIEDLER, p. 117.   [2] BÉTHUNE, p. 227.

of Saxony threatened to invade Brandenburg and raise the whole Lutheran population against him. There remained only one alternative for George William; to throw himself sycophantically on the mercy of John George and to order his policy as he was told.[1]

There was less obvious excuse for the behaviour of the Elector of Saxony. Whatever his jealousy of Frederick and resentment that he had not himself been chosen King, as a Protestant and as a constitutional ruler he was expected to support the new monarchy against Catholic tyranny. If he valued the German Liberties he could not stand inactive while Frederick was crushed by troops from Spain and Flanders.

John George of Saxony was no selfless statesman; the desire for personal gain put an ugly face on many of his actions, but he was genuine in his respect for the German Liberties. He saw that Frederick by his provocative usurpation of Bohemia had seriously, perhaps fatally, compromised the Protestant and constitutionalist party. His object was therefore to redeem Frederick's blunder. He achieved this, or tried to achieve this, by abandoning Frederick. At the Mülhhausen meeting he had shown that he disapproved of the seizure of the crown. Shortly after, he signed a treaty with Ferdinand, by which in return for his armed intervention he exacted a guarantee of the Lutheran faith in Bohemia and the recognition of all secularized Church land in the Lower and Upper Saxon Circles. The justification for this extraordinary move, which Frederick's friends regarded as the most callous treachery, was that John George had seen the Spanish danger and adopted the best means of defence — that of making Spanish help unnecessary. Ferdinand restored by German Protestant arms as a constitutional monarch in Bohemia, Ferdinand owing his prestige as Emperor to the loyalty of a German prince, would be a thousand times safer than Ferdinand re-established by the help of Spanish troops and his own dynasty.

This was not only the subsequent justification, it was probably the actual cause of John George's action. Unhappily his dynastic ambitions were stronger than his political instinct. The guarantee of Lutheranism in Bohemia, the confirmation

[1] DROYSEN, *Preussische Politik*; THEIL III, pp. 30 ff.

of the secularized lands in North Germany, these were so many pillars of John George's constitutionalist, Protestant policy; but unfortunately he also asked for the cession of Lusatia to Saxony. This selfish stipulation weakened a position otherwise unassailable.

Maximilian of Bavaria, the Catholic counterpart of John George, had in his treaty with Ferdinand of the previous October followed the same line of thought. He too had sought to make the Emperor dependent for his restoration on German and not on Spanish arms, and he too had tripped over his dynastic ambition by stipulating for the Electorate of Frederick as his reward.

Although both John George and Maximilian were influenced by the same ideas, dynastic ambition prevented their alliance. When Maximilian heard of John George's treaty, he became so jealous that he could only be satisfied by a guarantee that he himself should have the supreme direction of the war in Bohemia while John George confined his attack to Silesia and Lusatia.[1]

Intensely alive to immediate advantage, these partial patriots nullified their common policy. Neither of them realized that by bargaining with Ferdinand for lands and titles they were giving him a dangerous mandate for cutting up and re-distributing the Empire in any way that he chose. Neither of them realized that Ferdinand did not forgo Spanish help when he sought theirs; nor did he give them any undertaking with regard to Frederick's lands on the Rhine.[2]

v

The tragedy of Frederick moved swiftly to a close. Some Catholic prophets had hoped that he would prove but a Winter King, and although he had now the spring and summer to his credit each month brought some new forewarning of disaster. Early in the year he visited the chief parts of his new realm, and at Brünn, at Bautzen, at Breslau, he was enthusias-tically received. At Olmütz, however, the authorities filled the

---

[1] HURTER, VIII, *Ferdinand II*, p. 673.
[2] GINDELY, *Geschichte*, II, p. 442.

hall for his reception with peasantry and soldiers lest the
absence of the Catholic gentry should be perceived. Frederick
remained unaware that half his subjects in that town hated
him because his party had desecrated their churches.[1] He was
innocently busy planning future hunting parties for his Queen;
in the cold season he had been persuaded to leave her in Prague.
'Il m'ennuie fort de coucher seul'[2] he lamented in his letters.

Little by little he realized his danger. On the night of his
coming to Brünn, a contingent of Polish troops crossed the
frontier in answer to an appeal from Ferdinand, and the distant
glare of flaming villages reddened the horizon. He did not
speak of it in his letters to Elizabeth, admitting only that he
was very tired — 'l'esprit rompu'.[3]

There was cause enough to break a stouter spirit. His
friends failed him on every side, and the enthusiasm of his
subjects evaporated with his hopes. They had elected him
not for love of his person but for the help he could bring them[4],
and he had brought them none. At first his private means had
sufficed to increase the Bohemian army by seven thousand
men,[5] but by March 1620 he was appealing for a loan as far
afield as London, by midsummer he was pledging his jewellery
and persecuting the Jews and Catholics for ready money.[6]
Conditions among his troops grew desperate; demoralized by
camp-fever, penniless, hungry and insecure, they plundered the
country bare. Anhalt's spasmodic execution of culprits availed
nothing, and here and there the peasantry, taking the law
into their own hands, broke into revolt.[7] Efforts to organize
conscription broke down: the province of Silesia managed to
furnish only four hundred cavalry and those very bad, and at
Olmütz in Moravia the conscripted peasants, finding no officers
ready to take charge of them, dispersed within a few days
to their homes.[8]

---

[1] LUNDORP, I, p. 986; D'ELVERT, I, p. 113.
[2] ARETIN, Beyträge, VII, pp. 155, 158.
[3] Ibid., II, vi, pp. 74-5; VII, p. 153.   [4] LUNDORP, I, pp. 859-60, 987.
[5] MOSER, Patriotisches Archiv, VII, p. 65.
[6] LÜNIG, VI, ii, pp. 172, 175; Calendar of State Papers. Domestic Series, 1619-1623, p. 131.
[7] Annales, IX, p. 1002.
[8] B. DUDIK, Chronik der Stadt Olmütz über die Jahre 1619, 1620. Schriften der historischen-statistischen Section der mährisch-schlesischen Gesellschaft zur Beförderung des Ackerbaues, I, p. 44.

Short of horses, short of artillery, short of money, Ernst von Mansfeld still occupied Pilsen in Frederick's name. In the summer he journeyed to Prague in search of pay for his men. He was followed at a little distance by a regiment which he had disbanded for lack of funds: led by their indignant officers they broke into Prague and surrounded his lodging so that he had to cut his way out, sword in hand, and call up the royal life-guard to protect him.[1] Nor were these disbanded men alone in creating disturbance, for the officers of the conscript army seized every excuse to abandon their dwindling forces and swagger about the streets and taverns of the capital.[2]

The city, indeed, provoked comparison with Sodom and Gomorrah, making merry under skies heavy with disaster. There were balls and banquets at the houses of the nobility, sleighing parties in the winter and bathing parties in the summer, while the King himself drove about the town in a bright red cloak with a yellow feather stuck jauntily in his hat. When the warm weather came he bathed stark naked in the Moldau before the Queen and all her ladies, so that the burghers of Prague strained disapproving eyes to catch every detail of the immodest spectacle.[3] Visitors flocked to stare at the gay young King and Queen who gave 'free and bountiful entertainment to strangers in abundance' and allowed the curious to gape at the state rooms in the Hradschin and even to dandle the latest royal infant. One of them deftly removed his woollen shoes for a souvenir.[4]

Seldom can such innocent and well-intentioned rulers have made themselves more readily disliked. Frederick's one hope was to gain the devotion of his new subjects; but he provoked the contempt of his ministers and the hatred of the populace. Shy of his advisers, bewildered by the language and the peculiarities of the constitution he had pledged himself to defend, Frederick displayed even less than his usual intelligence. At the Protestant assembly of Nuremberg he answered an

---

[1] *The Appollogie of Ernestus, Earle of Mansfielde,* 1622, pp. 34-5.

[2] LOYSE JULIANE, *Mémoires,* p. 164.

[3] LUNDORP, I, pp. 925-6; RIEZLER, *Kriegstagebücher aus dem ligistischen Hauptquartier,* 1620. *Abhandlungen der Königlichen Akademie der Wissenschaften Historische Classe, XXIII.* Munich, 1906, p. 187.

[4] *Taylor his Travels.*

ambassador, repeating by heart the reply to a totally different question.[1] In Bohemia he scandalized his courtiers and advisers by receiving them always bare-headed, by turning to Anhalt for the answer to every question, by allowing his hand to be kissed far too often, by giving precedence to the Queen in public and letting her appear in dresses which no respectable Bohemian husband would have permitted to his wife.[2]

He annoyed the leading statesmen and above all the nobility of Bohemia by suggesting that serfdom should be abolished, by attempting to impose a new oath of allegiance and by urging the Estates to elect his five-year-old son as his successor.[3] He annoyed the people by blundering efforts to check the immorality of Prague[4], and worst of all by desecrating their churches. The great church of the Jesuits and the cathedral were ruthlessly stripped of images, while Frederick's chaplain sent his two maidservants to carry the relics away for firewood. The Queen, it was rumoured, had even wanted to break open the tomb of Saint Wenceslas, and she had certainly insisted with misplaced modesty that the 'naked bather' in the middle of the Charles Bridge be torn down. She was not obeyed, for the citizens came out armed to prevent the desecration of the crucified Saviour above the Moldau.[5]

Misguided as Frederick and his wife were, their subjects did little to help them. The Bohemians, Frederick's advisers asserted, thought of nothing but 'gratifying their brothers and friends' in the administration both of the army and the State. Some of them were even said to have told the King, when he called a meeting at seven in the morning, that it was against their privileges to rise so early.[6] The State was honeycombed with disaffection, for the old animosities of nobility, burghers and peasantry were sharpened by the distresses of the country, and treason was suspected at the very Court of the King.[7]

[1] GINDELY, *Geschichte*, II, p. 308.
[2] HURTER, *Ferdinand II*, VIII, p. 126; LUNDORP, I, pp. 926, 861.
[3] HURTER, loc. cit.; HÖFLER, p. 400; H. PALM, *Acta Publica. Verhandlungen und Correspondenzen der schlesischen Fürsten und Stände.* Jahrgang, 1620. Breslau, 1872, p. 132 f.
[4] HURTER, loc. cit.
[5] LUNDORP, I, pp. 923 ff.; *Kriegstagebücher*, p. 205.
[6] LUNDORP, II, p. 221.
[7] *Berichte über dem Weissenberge*, p. 130.

So matters stood when on July 23rd, 1620, Maximilian of Bavaria crossed the Austrian frontier with the army of the Catholic League, twenty-five thousand men[1] under his general, Count Tilly. The troops, mercenaries of many tongues, marched to the encouragement of Jesuit preachers, the twelve largest cannon were each called after an apostle, and their general's especial patroness was the Virgin Mary. As a young man, Tilly had wished to enter the Society of Jesus, but later, deciding to fight God's battles in another field, had maintained throughout his life in camps so strict a morality and so unfailing a devotion to his Patroness that he was popularly known as the 'monk in armour'.[2]

Maximilian intended first to make certain of Austria where many of the Protestant gentry were in arms. Before Tilly's forces the peasantry fled, carrying with them what they could and Maximilian advanced in the blustering storms of a cold summer across a deserted country and over roads strewn with the carcasses of cattle and swine wantonly slaughtered by his men.[3] At Linz on August 4th he enforced the submission of the Austrian Estates, who were unable to organize resistance to so large an army without help from Bohemia.

At the same time, Spinola with nearly twenty-five thousand men[4] set out from Flanders, amidst scenes of such devout enthusiasm that many compared the campaign to a new Crusade.[5] As the head of the column advanced towards the Rhine, the Prince of Orange, afraid to break the truce and powerless to intercept the army, appealed in despair to the King of England.[6] At this eleventh hour, James permitted a regiment of two thousand volunteers under Sir Horace Vere to put out from Gravesend for the Low Countries.[7] At the same time, he wrote to the government at Brussels demanding to know the destination of their army, and on August 3rd he received the disingenuous reply that they did not know.[8]

[1] Morel Fatio, *L'Espagne au XVI at au XVII siècle*, Heilbronn, 1878, p. 348.
[2] *Kriegstagebücher*, p. 117; Klopp, I, p. 545.
[3] *Kriegstagebücher*, pp. 114, 147.
[4] Morel-Fatio, p. 340; Lonchay et Cuvelier, I, p. 553.
[5] Lonchay et Cuvelier, p. 552.   [6] Prinsterer, II, ii, pp. 571, 572.
[7] A. Wilson, *The History of Great Britain*. London, 1653, p. 136.
[8] Lundorp, II, p. 127.

Spinola, crossing the Rhine at Coblenz, turned his face towards
Bohemia, and the anxious powers of western Europe breathed
again. It was a brilliant feint, designed to keep his enemies out
of action, for, wheeling in his tracks in the third week of August,
he headed again for the Rhine. 'It is now too late to doubt
whether Spinola's large army is destined against the Palatinate,
it is already at our door', lamented the Electress-mother from
Heidelberg.[1] On August 19th, Spinola occupied Mainz. In
vain the distracted Prince of Orange besought the Electress-
mother to defend the threatened country. In vain he appealed
to the princes of the Union. Alone, the two thousand English
volunteers forced their way up the Rhine, evading Spinola's
outposts and established themselves at the key fortresses of
Frankenthal and Mannheim.[2] On September 5th, Spinola
crossed the Rhine, on the 10th he took Kreuznach, and four
days later Oppenheim.[3] Far away in Bohemia Frederick's
heart bled for his people, but he could do nothing save appeal
once more to the King of England and console himself with
pious thoughts. 'I commend all to God', he wrote to Elizabeth.
'He gave it me, he has taken it away, he can give it me again,
blessed be his name.'[4]

At Linz, meanwhile, Tilly had joined with what remained
of the imperialist army, and on September 26th had crossed the
Bohemian border. He was first in the field by a narrow margin;
on October 5th, the Elector of Saxony swept down from the
north, and the town of Bautzen, the capital of Lusatia, surrendered almost without a blow.[5] At the same time, Maximilian
was summoning Pilsen to surrender, and Mansfeld had opened
negotiations. On a peremptory order from Frederick to hold
the town, Mansfeld sulkily obeyed, but he could no longer be
relied on to harass the rear of the enemy: serving an insolvent
master, he was not so foolish as to make himself unpopular
with Maximilian, a wealthy prince and a potential employer.[6]

With Pilsen quiescent in his rear, Maximilian turned towards
Prague, and in mid-October came up with Frederick's mis-

[1] M. A. E. GREEN, p. 153.
[2] WILSON, p. 139.   [3] MOREL-FATIO, pp. 360 ff.
[4] ARETIN, *Beyträge*, VII, p. 163.   [5] *Theatrum Europaeum*, I, p. 373.
[6] See REUSS, *Ernst von Mansfeld im böhmischen Kriege*. Brunswick, 1865,
pp. 86 ff.

cellaneous forces at Rokitzan, two days' march from the capital. The King himself was in the camp, trying vainly to check the furious rivalry of Thurn and Anhalt. Here, a few days later, Mansfeld appeared in person to announce that his contract had run out, and since the King had not the means to renew it he would take leave to consider himself free of his obligations.[1]

Frederick still trusted in Bethlen Gabor, who had once more overrun Hungary. But the troops which he sent to reinforce the Bohemians were a hindrance rather than a help, for their unbridled licence robbed the King of his last vestige of popularity among the wretched peasants, and on foraging expeditions they not only attacked their allies, but even fought with each other.[2] They slaughtered their prisoners, and so ill-used one of Maximilian's colonels who had been returning wounded to Austria that, Frederick himself intervening too late, he died within a few days.[3]

Meanwhile the surrounding country was desolate. Empty villages, burnt-out farms, and the carcasses of starved cattle marked the passing of the armies. The winter had come on early after the storms of autumn, and in both camps the bitter cold and fevers engendered by the damp and the lack of food decimated the armies.

On November 4th, the Bohemian army celebrated the anniversary of the King's coronation with hollow rejoicings; the soldiers had threatened a general mutiny unless pay should be forthcoming at latest by the end of October, and only the presence of the enemy prevented them from carrying out their threat.[4] Anhalt and Thurn were agreed only on one point, that something must be done and quickly. The King too was anxious to make sure of Prague where he had left his wife, once again within a few weeks of her confinement.

Doubts of the same kind, though not so acute, disturbed the councils of Maximilian and the imperialist general Bucquoy. Here, too, neither of them knew which was to have the higher authority, Maximilian claiming it by right of his agreement

[1] See REUSS, *Ernst von Mansfeld*, p. 89.
[2] ARETIN, *Beyträge*, III, i, pp. 88, 99, 100.
[3] *Kriegstagebücher*, pp. 128-9, 176.
[4] ARETIN, *Beyträge*, III, p. 112; *Berichte über dem Weissenberge*, p. 142.

with Ferdinand, and Bucquoy being loath to surrender to the new-comer the control of operations which he had so long maintained unassisted. Ferdinand, to avoid the resentment of either party, had officially stated that the only commander-in-chief of his army was and should always be Our Lady Herself, to whose care he committed his fortunes.[1] This decision did not settle the immediate problems of Maximilian and Bucquoy. Their troops were exhausted, hungry and plague-stricken; it would be folly, Bucquoy argued, to advance through the autumnal fogs, over country stripped of fodder and partly occupied by the enemy.[2] Maximilian, on the other hand, put all his faith in an immediate assault on Prague: once the capital was taken, he argued, the revolt would be at an end. He was no soldier but his political instinct was right.

On the night of November 5th the Bohemians stealthily withdrew to defend the capital, and as soon as the innumerable and cumbrous baggage wagons of Maximilian could be set in order, the imperialist and Bavarian troops followed. For thirty-six hours the two armies marched almost parallel, the Bohemians on the high road, their enemies on the wooded hills, neither seeing the other clearly through the damp November mists. On the evening of the 7th, Anhalt halted within a few miles of Prague, and the King, after he had ridden along the lines exhorting his troops not to desert his own or the Bohemian cause, hastened into the city to implore the Estates for money to pay the army. He had not gone long before Anhalt struck camp and moved under cover of darkness to the top of the White Hill, a broad eminence scarred with chalk pits, divided by a small stream from the advancing enemy and overlooking the undefended city. It was one o'clock before Anhalt reached the summit. He had told the King that there was no likelihood of a battle and, since he let his men sleep where they halted without giving any orders for the morning, he apparently did not expect one.

Meanwhile Bethlen Gabor's undisciplined troops were plundering the countryside, so that here and there a light from a burning farmhouse lit up a segment of the hilly, wooded country. In one of these flashes the Catholic sentries saw the

[1] *Annales*, XII, p. 2405.   [2] *Kriegstagebücher*, p. 171.

Bohemian army straggling forward towards the White Hill. At once the word was given and at midnight Maximilian and Bucquoy were in pursuit.

The misty day had scarcely broken on November 8th when a band of Bethlen Gabor's troops galloped into the Bohemian camp. Some of Tilly's men, reconnoitring in the dawn, had dislodged them from an outpost, and before Anhalt had altogether grasped their proximity, the enemy crossed the stream and, moving warily in the shelter of the steep incline which protected them from Anhalt's guns, took their stand about a quarter of a mile from the Bohemian lines.

It was still misty, and Anhalt calculated that they would not attack until it grew clearer, for the rising ground was against them and they could have no certain knowledge of the numbers or positions of the Bohemian army. Between seven and eight o'clock he hastily drew up his troops across the brow of the hill, covering a front nearly a mile long. Later, when he was explaining away his defeat, he estimated his numbers at fifteen thousand, and the enemy at forty thousand. His estimate of his own forces was probably fairly exact, but he doubled the number of his enemies.

On the extreme right of Anhalt's line lay a pleasure garden called the 'Star', before the walls of which some hasty breast-works were thrown up; to the extreme left the hill sloped steeply away over sodden ploughland. Anhalt placed the cavalry on the wings, the foot and cannon in the centre, but so great was his fear of mutiny that he divided up several regiments, and here and there set contingents of German professional cavalry among the conscripted Bohemian foot soldiers. The bulk of the Germans were, however, on the left, the Bohemians on the right, and the King's own banner, yellow velvet with a green cross and the words 'Diverti nescio', was in the centre. Bethlen Gabor's unruly Hungarians, who had at last come to rest below the 'Star', were ordered to move across the hill to a similar position on the left, whence they could attack the flank of the enemy.

The Catholic forces were disposed across the lower slope of the hill: Maximilian's troops under Tilly on the left facing the Bohemians, Bucquoy's on the right over against the Germans, and the foot in two separate detachments in the centre, backed by small reserves of cavalry. Bucquoy, who had been seriously wounded a few days before and was unable to take command, was unwilling to risk an engagement, seeing that the Bohemians had the advantage of the ground. He wanted to bring them down from the heights by outflanking the hill and threatening Prague. Maximilian, on the other hand, was determined to stake everything on a battle, and urged Tilly to charge the Bohemians at the 'Star', in order to test their resistance. They stood their ground and Tilly fell back, but Maximilian remained unconvinced. The mist was by now clearing and a council of war was hastily called. Maximilian still pressed for action and Bucquoy's unwilling lieutenants at length yielded. The leaders then heard the 'Salve Regina', gave the holy name of 'Sancta Maria' as the word for the day, and made ready for the attack.

This long delay convinced Anhalt that the enemy, holding the worst position, would draw off without fighting. He was taken completely unawares when Tilly, supported by a steady bombardment from the artillery in the centre, suddenly charged up the hill. At first the Bohemians stood to their posts, and on the right wing, where Anhalt's valiant son was in command, all but forced Tilly to give way. Meanwhile the imperialists on the right seconded Tilly's charge, and the infantry in the centre, gaining the plateau at the top of the hill under cover of the guns, engaged the Bohemian centre. Ill-armed and mutinous, the centre soon gave ground, two standards were taken, the lines broke and the officers tried in vain to drive their men back to their posts at the sword's point.

. At this moment Bucquoy struggled from his sick bed, called for his horse and, wounded as he was, led the imperialist reserves to the support of the main body. On the Bohemian right wing young Anhalt, twice wounded, went down among a circle of enemies, while his soldiers took panic, and fled breaking the ranks behind them. On the extreme left the Hungarians, thrown into disorder by Tilly's first charge, were even now streaming across the Moldau in full flight. Unsupported, the troops on the Bohemian left broke in hopeless panic, scattering towards Prague, and Anhalt, hoarse with his efforts to rally his men — Alexander, Caesar, or Charlemagne, he explained later, could have done no more — rode after them. The King's great banner, a hundred standards and all the cannon were taken, and on the brow of the hill only the Moravian life-guard stood to their places about the walls of the 'Star', not a man surrendering.

In Prague the King and Queen sat at dinner with the two English ambassadors. Both were in good spirits and Frederick asserted confidently that there would be no fighting; the enemy were too weak and would soon draw off. He had been told so, and he was in the habit of believing what he was told. After dinner, nevertheless, he thought he would ride out to see his gallant soldiers. As he passed the city gate he met the first fugitives from the battle, and while he vainly inquired the cause of their panic Anhalt himself came up, incoherent and dishevelled. This was the first that the King knew of the battle which he had lost.[1]

Anhalt, so fluent once in council, had but one solution to offer — the King must fly at once. Frederick made a last effort to redeem his shattered fortune; ignoring Anhalt's council of despair, he moved his wife and children rapidly across the Moldau — so rapidly that the youngest prince was all but forgotten and the Queen's frivolous books were left lying about in her rooms to scandalize the piety of the conquerors.[2] Fortunately someone had the wit to lay hands on some of the Crown jewels; they were to be the chief source of the King's diminishing income for many years to come. In the new town across the river Frederick called a council to discuss the situation. Neither the King nor the Queen, 'our blessed undaunted lady' the English ambassador called her, showed any sign of fear, and if they decided to leave their capital, it was not they who abandoned their subjects but their subjects who abandoned them.

Confusion reigned in Prague, and the people closed the gates inexorably against the flying troops.[3] Since they would not

<hr>

[1] The best accounts are in *Berichte über dem Weissenberge* and *Kriegstage-bücher*. KREBS, *Die Schlacht am Weissenberge bei Prag*, Breslau, 1879, is a careful reconstruction of events.

[2] *Annales*, ix, p. 1116; KREBS, *Schlacht*, p. 126; SCOTT London, 1899, *Rupert, Prince Palatine*, p. 5.

[3] *Berichte über dem Weissenberge*, p. 133.

receive their defenders there was no hope of saving the town; indeed the burghers gave vent to their hatred of the foreign King who had despised their churches and disregarded their conventions. On the night after the battle Frederick's nearest followers feared for his life, and all alike besought him to escape before the citizens delivered him to the victorious enemy as the price of their own immunity.[1] If anything was still to be done for the Bohemian cause, it could only be by joining Mansfeld, or by making a stand in Silesia. Early in the morning Frederick set out for Breslau, accompanied only by Elizabeth and some few councillors; it was not a moment too soon, for the mob had already decided to sacrifice him, and his departure was all but prevented.[2]

Almost without a shot fired, the town had unconditionally surrendered, and Maximilian of Bavaria wrote that night to his wife from the palace where for the last year Frederick had kept his Court. The news reached Munich on November 13th,[3] on the 23rd cannon thundered the rejoicings of Vienna.[4] Churches echoed with psalms of thanksgiving and from the high pulpits under the image of Christ crucified the voices of the clergy cried for vengeance.

At Breslau Frederick sought to retrieve his fortune; he called the Estates of Silesia to help him[5] and appealed to the Union.[6] He had still Mansfeld's troops at Pilsen if he could raise money to re-engage them; Bethlen Gabor and his army were expected from Hungary. But money was not to be had. Mansfeld made no movement and Bethlen Gabor collected his plunder and marched for safety and Transylvania.

Frederick snatched despairingly at straws; he tried first to make terms with the invading Elector of Saxony, and next to organize resistance in Moravia, but on December 20th news came that Moravia too had yielded. Frederick dared not wait to fall with his wife and children into the hands of his encircling enemies; dismissing the few loyalists who remained with him, he slipped away towards Brandenburg between the nearing

[1] *Berichte über dem Weissenberge,* p. 136.
[2] Ibid., pp. 136, 158.   [3] HÖFLER, p. 404.
[4] BÉTHUNE, p. 347.
[5] PALM, 1620, p. 227 f.
[6] *Berichte über dem Weissenberge,* p. 56.

fronts of the Saxon and Bavarian armies, leaving the Silesians to throw themselves on the mercy of the conquerors.[1]

Subjects and friends alike deserted the fugitive. Thurn's eldest son had joined the victors on the morrow of the battle with three thousand men,[2] and Anhalt fled to Sweden from whence he wrote requesting the Emperor's pardon on the grounds that he had been led astray by his master.[3] Catholic and Protestant pamphleteers did not spare the defeated. A post boy was represented seeking high and low over Germany for 'a young man with a wife and children who was a King last winter', and he was familiarly referred to as 'faithless Fritz' or the King of Hearts, the most worthless King of the pack, a title which the chivalrous later adapted for his wife and endowed with a prettier meaning.[4]

Meanwhile in Prague, on the afternoon following the battle the Duke of Bavaria had received in Ferdinand's name the submission of the Bohemian Directorate. At a little distance his confessor watched with an overflowing heart the spectacle of heresy defeated; he could not hear the broken words of the Bohemians, nor the Duke's low-spoken answer, but he saw that 'the words of His Excellency whatever they were drew tears from the Directors'.[5]

There was no mercy for the conquered. For a week after the battle the gates of the city were closed and the troops given licence to take what they would. Theoretically the rebels only were to suffer, but the soldiery could not conduct a political catechism on every doorstep in Prague, nor did they see why they should. Walloon, French and German, Pole, Cossack and Irish,[6] the mercenaries cared nothing for the niceties of policies, and it was not every day nor every year that a capital city and one of the richest in Europe was laid open to them.

Eight wagon-loads of King Frederick's household stuffs were found blocking the Hradschin gates, on which the soldiers

---

[1] ARETIN, *Beyträge*, VII, p. 173; D'ELVERT, III, p. 89; PALM, 1620, p. 265 f.; LUNDORP, II, p. 381.

[2] *Berichte über dem Weissenberge*, p. 42.

[3] LUNDORP, II, p. 481.

[4] OPEL and COHN, *Der dreissigjährige Krieg*, Halle, 1862, p. 122; BELLER, *Caricatures, passim*.

[5] *Kriegstagebücher*, p. 105.

[6] ARETIN, *Beyträge*, III, i, p. 56.

fell with undiscriminating greed, scattering silks and jewellery, firearms and swords upon the ground. Among it all a Walloon picked up a finely wrought pendant of St. George on a pale blue ribbon; he took it to the Duke of Bavaria and got a thousand talers for his pains. It was the insignia of the Garter belonging to the defeated King. Henceforward he appeared in the crude caricatures of his enemies with his garterless stockings hanging about his ankles.[1]

The sack was not yet over when Maximilian, taking the finest horses in Frederick's stable as his share of the booty, left again for Munich.[2] Early on the morning of Saint Catherine's Day he rode into his capital where his subjects crowded the streets to welcome him. At the doors of the great church he dismounted, received the blessing of the Bishop of Freising and went in to give thanks to God while the choir joyfully sang: 'Saul hath slain his thousands, and David his ten thousands.'[3] Maximilian had much to be thankful for; he was the only prince in Germany who could afford the war which had just been waged, and for his services the Emperor already owed him three million gulden, against which he now held Upper Austria in pledge.

In Vienna Ferdinand rode bare-headed to give thanks to the Blessed Virgin, and commanded a crown of pure silver costing ten thousand florins to be made, that he might himself offer it at her shrine at Mariazell in his own Styria. Another, even more splendid, he sent to the Church of Santa Maria della Scala at Rome.[4] With such shining gifts he might express a gratitude acceptable to Heaven; Spain and Bavaria would not be so easily satisfied.

VI

Bohemian resistance had collapsed at the battle of the White Hill, and no Protestant power came forward to save the defeated. The war was over: Frederick had but to ask pardon, the Spaniards to withdraw from the Palatinate, Mansfeld to dis-

[1] *Kriegstagebücher*, p. 72.   [2] KREBS, *Schlacht*, p. 130.
[3] *Kriegstagebücher*, p. 138 f.   [4] HAEBERLIN, XXV, p. 67.

solve his army and Ferdinand to pay his debts — four simple postulates that could not be fulfilled.

While the world thus fell about them, Frederick and his wife resolutely closed their eyes to the catastrophe. The Queen had been rushed to safety in Brandenburg, where she had given birth to a son whom she christened Maurice as a sufficiently broad hint to the Prince of Orange, and wrote with irrepressible gaiety to her friends telling them how they would laugh to hear of the '*beau voyage*' she had so suddenly made from Prague.[1] Frederick, meanwhile, was spending a cheerful visit with the Duke of Saxe-Lauenburg, where he invested something over three hundred florins on pearls for his three-year-old daughter.[2]

His irresponsible behaviour arose from no lack of conscience, rather the reverse. Weak and bewildered so long as he had power, the loss of it brought out the fundamental coherence of his character. He could not cease to believe in his cause because he had been defeated; lacking the reckless courage, the gift of leadership which might have saved Bohemia, he lacked also the facile selfishness which might have saved his own possessions. Defeat simplified for him all complicated differences between right and wrong; henceforward there was only one right, to assert the justice of his lost cause regardless of persuasion or treachery. 'Neither greed nor ambition brought us to Bohemia,' he proclaimed in a letter to Thurn, 'neither poverty nor distress shall make us rebel against our dear God nor do anything against honour and conscience.'[3] From the White Hill to the hour of his death he was to follow the rulings of that conscience with superb faith and deplorable consequences.

Ferdinand demanded a formal submission and apology; Frederick replied, with inspired simplicity, that a man who was in the right could not apologize; if, however, the Emperor would guarantee the constitution of Bohemia, pay off the conscripted army and indemnify him for his expenses, he would consider abdicating.[4] This was more than a personal defiance; it was a challenge to the German princes. At Mühl-

[1] *Archaeologia*, XXIX, p. 161.   [2] ARETIN, *Beyträge*, VII, pp. 174-5.
[3] LUNDORP, p. 243.   [4] Ibid., II, p. 444.

hausen they had declared his seizure of the Crown illegal: by denying the validity of that judgment, Frederick tacitly indicated that he believed they had been forced or bribed by the Emperor. To the end of his life he still declared that he had not broken the imperial peace, that he had rebelled not against the Emperor but against an Archduke of Austria. This was the corner-stone of his policy: he was the rightful King of Bohemia, unlawfully attacked both there and in his German lands.

If Frederick would not submit, Spinola's troops would stay in the Palatinate. Two of the four postulates were unfulfilled and two doors to peace closed. There remained the questions of Mansfeld's army and Ferdinand's debts.

Ernst von Mansfeld, with his unemployed army, lay encamped at Pilsen, under the imperial ban and with a price of three hundred thousand talers on his head. For the immediate future his actions were governed by two considerations, the necessity of getting food for his men and the problem of making himself so valuable to one side, or so dangerous to the other, that he would either find new service or be bought out of the war. Meanwhile he replenished the gaps in his ranks by recruiting, with or without permission, over all south Germany.

He had not only an army to feed but a State to govern. The usual reckoning of a woman and a boy for each soldier was a narrow estimate; in Tilly's army they counted five servants to each lieutenant and up to eighteen for a colonel. As the men grew rich in booty they hired drudges to carry it. The gunners were hired mechanics who, with their mastergunner, grooms for their huge horse teams, wives and servants, formed a compact unit, separate from, yet essential to, the army.[1] Peasant girls dragged from plundered farms, children kidnapped for ransom and forgotten, hawkers, tricksters, quacks and vagabonds swelled the ranks. In Bucquoy's army six or seven children were born in a week[2] and Mansfeld's women were doubtless as prolific.

The mercenary leader had a responsibility to all these, which he must fulfil or let loose a disorder as dangerous to him as to

[1] Camon, *Condé et Turenne*, Paris, 1933, p. 3.
[2] *Kriegstagebücher*, pp. 156-7.

the country in which he quartered. 'Neither they nor their horses can live by air,' wrote Mansfeld. 'All that they have, whether it be arms or apparel, weareth, wasteth and breaketh. If they must buy more they must have money, and if men have it not to give them, they will take it where they find it, not as in part of that which is due unto them, but without weighing or telling it. This gate being once opened unto them they enter into the large fields of liberty: . . . they spare no person of what quality so ever he be, respect no place how holy so ever, neither Churches, Altars, Tombs, Sepulchres nor the dead bodies that lie in them.'[1] Such was the state which Mansfeld ruled, such the anarchy which followed if his rule broke down.

Mansfeld spent the winter confusing the politics of Europe by offering his troops to Savoy, Venice and the United Provinces. With the early spring he hastened to Heilbronn to urge the princes of the Union there assembled to sign a contract for his services. It was in vain; retracing his steps to the Bohemian border, he was met by the garrison of Pilsen which had evacuated the town during his absence for the sum of a hundred and fifty thousand gulden[2]. The money was not to be despised, and the troops were more useful to him than the possession of the place; Mansfeld accepted the situation.

Soon after he found out that the Dutch would be willing to subsidize his old master Frederick, and making a virtue of necessity he signed a further contract with the defeated prince. He was staking his own and his army's fortune on a gamble, but he had a double chance of winning. Either he could re-establish Frederick by force of arms in his own lands, or — and this was likelier — he could make himself so dangerous to the Catholic commanders that they would pay him off on his own terms. A landless man with a price on his head, Mansfeld wanted a free pardon, a generous grant of money and a modest but independent principality: he would get those by continuing the war in the heart of Germany. The third gate to peace was closed.

Lastly there was the problem of Maximilian's payment. He was already occupying Upper Austria until Ferdinand could redeem it by reimbursing his war expenses, and at the

[1] MANSFELD'S *Appollogie*, p. 23. [2] GINDELY, *Geschichte*, IV, p. 32.

New Year of 1621 that day seemed far distant. Ferdinand's private resources had never been large, and Bohemia, the richest province of all the Hapsburg dominions, the source from which so many of the imperial charges had been met, was after two years of war a ruined country.

More serious was Ferdinand's promise to give Frederick's Electoral title to the victor. Frederick could not be deprived of his title without the consent of his fellow-princes, and when at Mühlhausen in the previous year Ferdinand had attempted to sound them on this question he had found them obdurate; apart from Maximilian of Bavaria, none of the princes who had wished to drive Frederick out of Bohemia had also wished to deprive him of his lands and titles in Germany. They had made this clear by opposing Ferdinand's suggestion that Frederick should be put to the ban of the Empire.[1] Ferdinand, therefore, could not satisfy Maximilian without offending the majority of his powerful subjects, and could not punish Frederick without opposing the decisions reached at Mühlhausen.

To depose Frederick was to force the issue with the princes, and wisely Ferdinand decided to approach it slowly, first placing Frederick under the ban, and when he had watched the effect of this, transferring the Electorate to Maximilian. With whatever specious pretences he might surround these two acts, they had to be performed by his authority and prestige alone, to be in fact a trial of strength between the Emperor and the constitution.

Maximilian of Bavaria was, in the eyes of his contemporaries, a very much cleverer man than Ferdinand, over whom his wealth and army gave him the whip hand. But Ferdinand, who never in the course of his career freed his policy from the control of wealthier allies, had a gift for twisting the ambitions of his paymasters to suit his own. Pitied by many for being bound to Maximilian by an agreement which inevitably continued the war, he was in fact using the agreement as an excuse, and Maximilian's ambition as a cover for his own. Ferdinand was preparing to lay a new foundation for imperial power by redistributing the land itself. Maximilian gave him the opportunity.

HURTER, *Ferdinand II.*, VIII, pp. 211-12.

On January 29th, 1621, the ban was pronounced against
Frederick.[1] Eight days later the princes and cities of the
Protestant Union assembled at Heilbronn. If Frederick had
broken the constitution by seizing the Bohemian crown,
Ferdinand had violated it further by issuing the ban. He had
by this action wilfully broken the oath which he had sworn at
Frankfort, when he was crowned and thereby linked the cause
of the German Liberties irrevocably once again with that of the
broken King of Bohemia.

The moment had come for the Union to stand out in defence
of the constitution, the moment at which they could be certain
of the support of the Elector of Saxony and even of some
Catholic constitutional princes. The first fruit of the meeting
was a vigorous protest to Vienna.[2] Now came the trial of
strength which Ferdinand had anticipated. In answer to their
protest he refused to withdraw the ban and commanded them
in the name of imperial peace to disband the few troops which
they still had in arms. At the same time a detachment of
Spinola's troops on the Rhine made a significant movement.
It was a brilliant bluff, for the truce with the United Provinces
had only a few weeks to run, and the Brussels government had
ordered Spinola to make an armistice with the Union on any
terms and return at once to the Netherlands.[3] With admirable
coolness he made the menacing gesture which he knew he
could not carry to its conclusion, and he was successful.
The cities of the Union, knowing nothing of Spinola's obligations, gave way, unwilling to be overrun by Spanish armies
for the sake of a constitutional quibble. Bereft of their support
the princes collapsed. On April 1st the delegates of the Union
agreed with Spinola to disband their army if he would guarantee
their rights as neutrals.[4] The Mainz Accord, as the treaty was
called, was the last public document signed by the Protestant
Union, and on May 14th the delegates broke up, never to
reassemble. The evidence of immediate danger had been
stronger than the fear of disaster to come; without a blow the
defenders of the constitution had abandoned their leader and

[1] LUNDORP, II, p. 307 f.; LÜNIG, VI, i, p. 88 f.
[2] LUNDORP, II, p. 377.
[3] LONCHAY ET CUVELIER, I, p. 584.
[4] LUNDORP, II, p. 382.

their principles, and made way for foreigners and adventurers to fight the cause of German liberty on German soil.

The Protestant princes had thought to end the war by sacrificing Frederick; the Catholics to prevent foreign inter-ference by themselves supporting Ferdinand. They had alike forgotten that although no one cared for Frederick or Bohemia, there were all too many princes in Europe who feared the House of Austria or coveted the valley of the Rhine. With the collapse of Bohemia the centre of conflict had shifted two hundred miles to the west. Prague fell into the background and all eyes were turned to the Emperor's Spanish allies in the Palatinate. In an emphatic protest to Vienna, the King of Denmark laid an unerring finger on the spot: not Frederick's broken forces, he said, but Spanish troops were the source of unrest in Europe.[1]

But what had the King of Denmark to do with it? Judging by his actions, a great deal, for he had received Frederick at Segeberg in Holstein on his flight from Bohemia and had urged the authorities of the Lower Saxon Circle, in which Holstein was situated, to defend his cause. When this had failed, he had himself come forward with an offer to mediate at Vienna between Frederick and the Emperor.[2] And all because the King of Denmark feared that the destruction of the Protestant opposition in Bohemia would increase Hapsburg power on the head-waters of the Elbe and encourage them to push their dominion northward to the Baltic.

The King of Denmark was the first but not the most important prince to move. The governments of the United Provinces, of France, of England, all alike realized with dismay that under the smoke clouds of the Bohemian war they had allowed the Spaniards to occupy the Palatinate. The phantom danger against which they had made plots and treaties for the past ten years had become real, and they had looked away. Too late the English government had sent thirty thousand pounds to the princes of the Union;[3] the handful of troops which had gone to the Palatinate under Sir Horace Vere were already cut off at Mannheim and Frankenthal, while at Heidelberg a

[1] LUNDORP, II, p. 400. [2] Ibid., II, p. 391 f.
[3] *Calendar of State Papers. Domestic Series*, 1619-1623, p. 198.

136

mixed garrison of Germans and Dutch still held the city. A temporary obstruction to the Spanish army these garrisons might be, but no permanent barrier. At Vienna the French ambassador was exposed to the acrimonious reproaches of the English, as the author of the fatal Treaty of Ulm.[1] Meanwhile, since the Catholic rising of the previous year, the passes of the Val Telline were open to Spain, so that armies and funds could be plentifully replenished from North Italy.

The United Provinces stood in graver and more immediate danger than France, England or Denmark. For some anxious weeks the Prince of Orange contemplated signing an unfavourable peace with the Brussels government but, certain of their military advantage, they would not offer terms which he could accept. There was an alternative: while defending their own frontiers as best they might, the Dutch could subsidize Frederick and his allies to regain the Rhine. An alliance was hastily signed with the King of Denmark, and letters sent to Mansfeld promising him rewards if he should be loyal to the Protestant cause.[2] On April 9th, 1621, the truce with Spain expired; five days later the King and Queen of Bohemia were received in The Hague with all the honours due to reigning sovereigns, and on April 27th Frederick set his hand to a treaty by which he accepted the subsidies of the Dutch to reconquer his lands on the Rhine. The second act of the German tragedy had begun.

---

[1] BÉTHUNE, p. 346.   [2] GINDELY, *Geschichte*, IV, p. 23.

THE EMPEROR FERDINAND AND THE ELECTOR MAXIMILIAN
1621—1625

L'Allemagne perdue, la France ne peut subsister — Richelieu

THE EMPEROR FERDINAND AND THE ELECTOR MAXIMILIAN

I

THE centre of interest had shifted from the Moldau to the Rhine, and in Bohemia Ferdinand was laying the foundation of despotic power unhampered by foreign intervention. All four provinces had submitted, Silesia and Lusatia gaining generous terms from the Elector of Saxony,[1] Moravia and Bohemia yielding unconditionally to the Duke of Bavaria. Maximilian made a perfunctory promise to intercede for the lives and property of the rebels. So little did he care for his word that he explicitly requested Ferdinand to disregard it. Later he dispatched to Vienna a Capuchin friar, of whom it was reported that he spoke of the vengeance which God demanded on the Bohemians with the vehemence of a prophet breathing divine revelation.[2]

'Thou shalt break them with a rod of iron; thou shalt dash them to pieces like a potter's vessel', had been the verse chosen by one of Vienna's preachers on the news of the Bohemian surrender, and Ferdinand himself could not have chosen a better text. On Maximilian's withdrawal he had appointed Karl von Liechtenstein governor in Prague. Liechtenstein was an undistinguished politician, timid, cautious, mildly dishonest and fairly shrewd; the Bohemians might have gained more from his intelligence and mercy, had he not been in all things merely the mouthpiece of the Emperor. Less than five weeks after the fall of Prague the Jesuits had returned, the exiled Catholic officials had been reinstated, the people disarmed, the press brought under control, the coinage of the usurper called in and the rebels prohibited from leaving the country.[3]

---

[1] LUNDORP, II, p. 381.
[2] GINDELY, *Geschichte*, III, p. 377; IV, p. 49.
[3] D'ELVERT, II, p. 1 f.

Ferdinand was determined to reform but not to depopulate his reconquered lands; both in Moravia and Bohemia stringent measures were taken to prevent the emigration of Protestants.[1]

On the night of February 29th, 1621, thirty of the leading rebels were arrested in Prague.[2] Thurn had fled with the King and was safe beyond the border, but the unhappy Schlick, hoping always for moderation and amnesty, had lingered in Silesia; he was seized in Friedland by Saxon soldiers and delivered up to join his compatriots in the dungeons of Prague.[3]

Ferdinand's judgment on his unhappy country was pronounced soon after. Elective monarchy was abolished, and the Crown became henceforward hereditary in the Hapsburg dynasty. The Letter of Majesty, the charter of religious liberty, had been taken in the sack of Prague and sent to Vienna, where it was said Ferdinand had personally cut it in pieces. Rumour exaggerated, for the removal of the imperial seal served to make it valueless, and in this degraded condition the paper long survived its purpose. The Calvinist and Utraquist heresies were alike to be rooted out, and only in consideration of the promise made to the Elector of Saxony was the Lutheran Church still to be tolerated.[4] Ferdinand's policy was three-sided. He desired the political and economic destruction of all who had been concerned in the revolt, the extinction of national privileges and the extermination of the Protestants. Liechtenstein's anxious protests for mercy or at least for caution fell on deaf ears. The punishment of Bohemia was to inaugurate a new policy, by which the Hapsburg lands were to be moulded into one state united in religion and controlled from Vienna, the essential foundation for the rebuilding of Catholic Europe.

The first necessity was to impress Ferdinand's power on his defeated subjects in letters of blood. The arrested leaders were tried by a special commission from which there was no appeal, and more than forty of them were sentenced to imprisonment and death. Foremost among them was Andreas Schlick, whose fortitude in these last hours gave strength to the most wretched

---

[1] D'ELVERT, II, p. 7.   [2] Ibid., p. 31 f.
[3] Ibid., pp. 41, 45, 55, 58-9.
[4] Ibid., pp. 47-8; LUNDORP, II, p. 555.

of his fellow-prisoners. This was the last and perhaps the noblest service that he performed for those who had so persistently disregarded his counsels. Whichever side had won, the generosity and moderation for which he had pleaded would have been alike impossible; life had long lost its sweetness for him.

In the last week of May 1621, the sentences reached Vienna for Ferdinand's signature.[1] He felt that it was his duty and knew that it was in his interest to strike hard, but when it came to condemning so many men to death, even his imagination was touched, and starting up from the council table he fled from the room, mopping the sweat from his forehead.[2] In the morning, after consulting his confessor, he was calm again, signed upwards of twenty death sentences without more ado and sent orders for immediate execution.[3]

They died in Prague on June 21st, 1621, in the great square before the Rathaus, while seven hundred Saxon horsemen patrolled the city. But there was no demonstration as Liechtenstein had feared,[4] no attempt at rescue. They died for the most part silently, one only crying out, 'Tell your Emperor I stand now before his unjust judgment; warn him of the judgment of God', before the drums of the soldiery drowned his words. Twelve heads were spitted on the Charles Bridge and the right hand of Count Schlick, grisly reminders through ten long years of the revolt which had failed.[5]

Prague acquiesced, its riches vanished, its trade stopped up, its people sick with fear, its leaders gone. Beyond Prague, beyond Bohemia, the Protestant news-letters screamed their indignation; men spoke of Alva and the Council of Blood[6] which fifty years before had roused the Netherlands to throw off the tyrant. But the Dutch had had a champion beyond their borders who had come back at a nation's call. For Bohemia no deliverer came. The best of her manhood had died on the White Hill and in the market-place, by the sword

[1] D'ELVERT, II, pp. 54, 56.   [2] FIEDLER, p. 109.
[3] D'ELVERT, II, p. 67 f.; HURTER, *Ferdinand II*, VIII, p. 596.
[4] D'ELVERT, II, p. 76.
[5] *Annales*, IX, p. 1310; LUNDORP, II, p. 428.
[6] REIFFERSCHEID, *Quellen zur Geschichte des Geistigen Lebens*. Heilbronn, 1899, p. 114.

and the axe. Beyond her borders there was only a fugitive king and a band of exiles, within them only the victorious party, the cowards, the indifferent, the widows and the children of the slain.

II

Absolute power was Ferdinand's ambition: absolute power in his own dominions and throughout the Empire; he saw the future of the Hapsburg dynasty from this angle. The King of Spain, on the other hand, saw the safety and greatness of his family in the reconquest of the Netherlands and the renewed prosperity of Spain. While both ultimately desired the good of the dynasty above all, inevitably each was unwilling to sacrifice his policy to that of the other. The two policies came into conflict in the spring and summer of 1621.

The deaths of the Archduke Albert and of Philip III had substantially altered the relations of Spain with the Netherlands. The independence of the provinces ended with the life of the Archduke; superficially it seemed at first that the Spanish Crown would not take advantage of this, for the widowed Isabella continued to govern and Ambrogio Spinola remained the dominant power in the state.[1] But gradually the new rulers of Spain infringed the independence of those who were now legally no more than appointed deputies; these new rulers were a boy still in his 'teens and his favourite, Olivarez.

The new King, Philip IV, was slightly more intelligent and considerably less conscientious than his father; interested in music, painting and the arts, with a taste for display, for masques, dances and the drama, a devotee of hunting and bull-fighting, and promising already to become an uncontrolled libertine, he was unimaginative in politics and bigoted in religion rather by education than by a natural bent.[2] Power passed entirely into the hands of Olivarez, a man whose immense energy and imagination made up for the lacka-daisical indifference of his master. At his prompting, almost

[1] HENNEQUIN DE VILLERMONT, *L'Infante Isabelle*, Paris, 1912, I, p. 162 f.; RODRIGUEZ-VILLA, *Ambrosio Spinola*, Madrid, 1904, I, p. 731.
[2] *Relazioni dagli Ambasciatori, Spagna*, I, p. 600 f.

every minister of the late King was removed from office, and a new government came into being under the absolute control of the favourite.[1] Gaspar de Guzman, Count of Olivarez, was a man in the middle thirties; he had established his position with the King largely by means of a vivid personality, for he was not apparently the type of friend most acceptable to Philip. In person he was a stout, florid, robust man, with an easy flow of conversation, who disliked sport and was bored by frivolous amusements. He was devoured by a passion for power, and he commanded rather than advised the King. He had the good of the monarchy at heart but his faith in his own judgment was unalterable and he went through life guiding the fate of his country exclusively by the light of his own brilliant but unstable mind.[2]

In 1621 his chief concern was to find the surest means of controlling the Palatinate. He had a plan for restoring Frederick under Spanish protection. This scheme fulfilled a double purpose. England could always make herself dangerous in the Narrow Seas by hindering the ships which passed between Spain and Flanders, and the restoration of a chastened Frederick under Spanish influence was designed at least partly to pacify English public opinion. No scheme could have been more unwelcome to Ferdinand, who had determined to transfer the Electorate to Maximilian and also to pay off his debts by bestowing on him a large portion of the displaced Elector's land.

Happily for Ferdinand, Frederick's troops under Mansfeld and Sir Horace Vere were forced by hunger to resume the offensive, thus temporarily blocking the Spanish scheme. Better still, their movement provided a bait to tempt the Duke of Bavaria into compromising himself yet further. Torn between ambition and anxiety for the German constitution, Maximilian had half-realized the peril of his position, and when the execution of the ban against Frederick was entrusted to him,[3] with the suggestion that he should invade the Upper Palatinate, he had at first refused. In public he had even assumed a lofty

[1] RICHELIEU, Mémoires, III, p. 203.
[2] Relazioni dagli Ambasciatori, Spagna, I, p. 65.
[3] LUNDORP, II, p. 376; LÜNIG, VI, i, p. 339 f.

detachment with regard to the ban itself. Alas that Maximilian, in appearance so subtle and so shrewd, had not the firmness to maintain this posture. When Mansfeld's troops suddenly began to use the Upper Palatinate as a base for a new attack on Bohemia, Ferdinand had only to suggest that he would himself attack them, to bring Maximilian hurrying into the field lest he should lose his share of the spoils.[1]

On September 23rd, 1620, Maximilian stormed and took the town of Cham on Frederick's side of the German-Bohemian frontier. Mansfeld, strong in his army but hard pressed for funds, seized his opportunity; after brief negotiations he signed, in return for a large sum of money, an undertaking to fight no more for Frederick. No sooner was this done than he turned his face westwards and, with the most callous disregard for his promise, marched to join Frederick's English allies in the Rhenish Palatinate. On October 25th, fifteen days after the signing of the treaty with Maximilian, the glad sight of his vanguard burst on the eyes of Vere's hard-pressed garrison at Frankenthal.

This breach of trust gave Maximilian the justification for which he had been waiting, to attack Frederick's lands on the Rhine. Even less than Ferdinand did he wish to see the Spaniards established there in sole command, and quick as thought he dispatched his general Tilly in pursuit of Mansfeld. It would be something to have his own troops on the Rhine next to those of Spain, but if Maximilian hoped that Tilly could rush the Spaniards into action on his behalf he was mistaken. Spinola was in the Netherlands organizing a frontal attack on the Dutch; neither the governments at Brussels nor Madrid wished to waste money fighting for a strip of country they could get more safely by treaty, and their general on the Rhine, Cordoba, obeyed their orders. Tilly, unable to attack Mansfeld alone, had to retire disappointed to winter quarters in the Upper Palatinate while Cordoba remained inactive, Vere entrenched his minute forces on both banks of the Rhine, and Mansfeld crossed over into Alsace in search of food and shelter for his army.

Bohemia, the Rhenish Palatinate, the Upper Palatinate,

[1] GINDELY, *Geschichte*, IV, pp. 182 ff.

the Rhine bishoprics, Alsace—gradually the war was spreading. 'God help those where Mansfeld comes!' was a cry by this time well known in Germany.[1] His troops had carried plague across the heart of Franconia, leaving the virulent infection to smoulder in towns and villages;[2] he brought typhus into Alsace,[3] and of the twenty thousand refugees who fled before him to the safety of Strasbourg one-fifth died in the ensuing months.[4] The winter came early with heavy snows, and Mansfeld's troops wasted the country for food, burning and breaking what they could not carry off. From the walls of Strasbourg a man might count sixteen fires at once flaming through the night, and none dared leave the city for fear of straggling plunderers. Those peasants that could drove their cattle and swine before them into the city, but many left their beasts to die of hunger or to be driven off by the soldiery.[5] In the Catholic bishoprics the soldiers fell upon the churches, tearing down all that they could carry off, wrenching the Christs from the crosses and gibbeting them like thieves on trees along the roadways. As far south as Ensisheim and Breisach spread the marauders, and it was credibly reported that for fifteen miles round the citadel of Hagenau they had set fire to every house they passed.

A year had gone by since the battle of the White Hill, and peace was still far off. Olivarez at Madrid and the Archduchess at Brussels made a united front with the King of England in favour of Frederick's restoration to the Palatinate, but Ferdinand was warmly if unintentionally assisted in his efforts to prevent it by Frederick himself. Confident in the new forces which he was building up with Dutch help, bound by his treaty with the Provinces to go back to his lands as a conqueror at the head of Dutch-paid armies, he had no intention of creeping home under Spanish protection. He was as willing to fight as Ferdinand. The Anglo-Spanish plan foundered on the opposition of both the principals. And peace receded.

Theoretically there was still no civil war between factions

---

[1] HURTER, *Ferdinand II*, IX, p. 77. [2] LAMMERT, p. 55 f. [3] Ibid., p. 56.
[4] Ibid., p. 57.
[5] WALTHER, *Strassburger Chronik*, pp. 14-15.
[6] *Annales*, XI, p. 1701; *Acta Mansfeldica*, p. 118 f.; REUSS, *Alsace au dix-septième Siecle*, Paris, 1898, p. 61.

within Germany, but a war directed against a single breaker of the peace. Whether Ferdinand altogether wished that it should remain so is doubtful: he was annoyed by the deadlock created by the Spaniards on the Rhine, but rather because he wished to settle with Maximilian than because he feared the international complications which might arise out of it. In his earliest youth he had chosen the warlike device 'Legitime certantibus corona', and the idea of fighting justly for the rights of the imperial crown cannot therefore have been displeasing to him. Optimistic as he was, he had never thought to increase his power as Emperor without conflict, and he regarded the prospect of continued war with conventional distress only. He had not the imagination which grasps the meaning of famine, fire and sword in their effect on individuals, and he resembled the greater number of his contemporaries in thinking it more dreadful that the Protestant soldiery should spike out the eyes of an image of the Virgin than that they should hunt the peasants into their burning houses. Ferdinand was as unwilling to accept plans for mediation and peace as Frederick or Mansfeld, but politically and morally his position was stronger because he could put the onus of responsibility for further war on to them. Confident that his own and not the Spanish view was safer for the dynasty, confident that the Dutch or Frederick himself would soon make the Anglo-Spanish scheme impossible, confident that some nervous ineptitude on the part of the Protestant princes would shortly provide him with yet another excuse to attack their power in Germany, the situation was unrolling itself for him with singular felicity. There is a gift in knowing when to move and when to be still, when to interpose a guiding finger and when to let the world drift. This was Ferdinand's gift. In the winter of 1621 he had only to wait.

III

Had Frederick and Elizabeth acquiesced in the Anglo-Spanish plan and gone back to Heidelberg on terms, there would have been no Thirty Years War.

Neither of these young people — their united ages were still under fifty — showed the least inclination to do any such thing. Frederick had convictions if he had not strength of character, and Elizabeth had courage enough for two.

Incompetent, over-trustful, perpetually defeated and perpetually gathering their spent forces for a new attack, betrayed by one ally only to look for another, obstinate, wrong-headed and sincere, the King and Queen drew the interests of Protestant Europe towards Germany, and for nine disastrous years kept their cause alive until the genius of Richelieu and Gustavus Adolphus came to destroy for ever the Empire of the Hapsburg and the dominion of Spain.

In the dual combination Frederick was the figure-head, Elizabeth the spirit. His lands, his titles, real or assumed, his rights — these were the pieces in the game; Elizabeth's wit and ability shifted them about on the board. 'The grey mare', wrote her brother the Prince of Wales, 'is the best horse.'[1] It was Elizabeth who wrote voluminously to all the unofficial powers, her father's favourite and the leading courtiers of France, Elizabeth who tactfully christened her new-born daughter Louisa Hollandina and asked the Dutch States to be godfathers, Elizabeth who dazzled ambassadors and substituted the currency of her favours for the money which her husband had not got.

Their first important ally was the youthful Prince Christian of Brunswick, who offered his services to recruit and lead a new army for which the Dutch were to pay. A younger brother of the Duke of Brunswick-Wolfenbüttel, Christian had been created at eighteen 'Administrator' of the secularized bishopric of Halberstadt; he possessed little qualification for this office save an unreasonable dislike of the Catholics. 'I must confess', he wrote once to his mother, 'that I have a taste for war, that I have it because I was born so, and shall have it indeed to my end.'[2] Handsome, lively and vigorous, Christian was his mother's favourite son and had been spoilt from childhood. Irresponsible and opinionated, he affected soldierly manners and a blasphemous turn of speech, from which

---

[1] M. A. E. Green, p. 250 n.
[2] Opel, *Elisabeth Stuart, Königin von Böhmen, Kurfürstin von der Pfalz. Historische Zeitschrift*, XXIII, p. 320.

superficial tricks of adolescence he gained the reputation for reckless cruelty and vice which has clung to him for over two centuries. When he was excited and a little drunk he certainly shouted down his elders, characterized the Archduchess Isabella as an *alte Vettel*,[1] and characterized the German princes and the King of England with obscene brevity as *cojones*.[2] The best known of his atrocities, namely that he forced the nuns of a plundered convent to wait, naked, on him and his officers,[3] was invented by a journalist in Cologne. In fact, he showed consideration to his prisoners and courtesy to his enemies.[4]

Suspicious of the Hapsburg dynasty and hostile to the Catholic Church, Christian invested his commonplace political views with an aura of romance by declaring himself passionately, although chivalrously, in love with the beautiful Queen of Bohemia.[5] When she dropped her glove he pounced upon it with a flourish and to her laughing request for its return cried, 'Madam, I will give it you in the Palatinate'.[6] Thereafter he wore it in his hat with the motto 'Pour Dieu et pour elle', a device which he also carried on his banners.

Christian was the material of which great leaders are made, had he had the patience to learn. With almost no money and very few officers, he raised an army of more than ten thousand men in the autumn of 1621. This feat, however ill-armed and ill-disciplined his troops, proves at least his dauntless energy and should earn a better name for the man who accomplished it than that of mere freebooter.[7] The 'mad Halberstädter' his contemporaries called him, but his madness smacked of inspiration.

Another ally had appeared at the same time in George Frederick, Margrave of Baden Durlach. He was a devout Calvinist and a good German, who was impelled to act by the menace of the Spaniards on the Rhine. George Frederick was

---

[1] Old hag, dirty old witch.
[2] WERTHEIM, *Der tolle Halberstädter*, I, pp. 223-4.
[3] Ibid., p. 230.   [4] Ibid., p. 217 f.; KLOPP, II, p. 151.
[5] OPEL, p. 306; WERTHEIM, I, p. 200 f.; Wertheim's re-assessment of Christian's character and merits may be a little exaggerated, but his appreciation of his military skill is founded on no less an authority than Delbrueck, and his defence of his moral character seems highly justified and is certainly long overdue.
[6] BLOK, *Relazioni Veneziane*, p. 223.   [7] WERTHEIM I, p. 232.

a popular ruler and despite his sixty years as energetic and high-spirited as a young man; these characteristics enabled him to raise an army of eleven thousand men, largely from among his own subjects. Thus by the spring of 1622 Frederick's cause fluttered three gallant little flags in defiance of the Emperor — Mansfeld in Alsace, Christian of Brunswick in Westphalia, George Frederick in Baden.

The junction of these three forces on the Rhine would give Frederick an army of about forty thousand men, enough with dexterous leadership to handle Tilly and the Spaniards. At present the armies were far apart, Christian's in Westphalia, the other two in the upper valley of the Rhine. Between them lay over a hundred miles of country and the rivers Main and Neckar, so that there was time for Tilly and the Spaniards to intercept them, and time, too, for the Archduchess Isabella, frightened at this recrudescence of Protestant arms,[1] to send her agents to suborn Mansfeld.

Frederick himself, meanwhile, left The Hague secretly in disguise and on April 22nd, 1622, joined Mansfeld at Germersheim in his own Palatinate, to the delight of his subjects and the stupefaction of the general.[2] Mansfeld, indeed, who had not expected him so soon, was engaged as usual in bargaining for the price of his withdrawal with the agents of the enemy.[3] The arrival of his employer decided him to postpone the discussion and, crossing with the greater part of his forces on to the right bank of the Rhine, he intercepted the junction of Tilly with the Spanish general, Cordoba, and thrust him back with some loss on April 27th at the little village of Mingolsheim. Nevertheless, Tilly proved the better strategist, for while Mansfeld waited for the Margrave of Baden to come up with his army, he circumvented him unhindered and joined with Cordoba early in May.

The problem now before Frederick's allies was how to outmarch the enemy's joint forces and meet Christian of Brunswick, who was advancing slowly and with immense booty from the north. Mansfeld and the Margrave of Baden together

[1] RODRIGUEZ-VILLA, *Correspondencia de la Infanta, Isabella Clara Eugenia con el Duque de Lerma*. Madrid, 1906, p. 241.
[2] AITZEMA, *Saken van Staet en Oorlogh*. The Hague, 1657, I, p. 116.
[3] *Annales*, IX, p. 1705.

hardly had enough troops to risk engaging Tilly and the
Spaniards, but above all they needed the help of Christian's
treasure to keep their armies paid. The young prince had
occupied the past months in extracting immense sums of
money and precious metals, by blood-curdling threats, from the
wealthy bishoprics of Münster and Paderborn. He had issued
startling letters, suggestively burnt at the four corners, and
bearing the words 'Fire! Fire! Blood! Blood!' to every
sizeable village he passed. This method seldom failed to extract
a ransom in hard cash from the people. He had also
systematically stripped Catholic churches of their gold and
silver ornaments, minting some of them into money with the
impertinent superscription, 'God's friend and the priests' foe'.[1]
The letters and the money had sufficed to give him a reputation
for blasphemous barbarity which was already broadcast over
Germany by the pamphlet press. Curiously enough, his proven
conduct was of the mildest: at Paderborn the cathedral
chapter could find no fault with his manners, and he was at
pains to restore the bones of their saints uninjured, provided
that he might melt down the reliquaries.[2]

The first barrier between Christian and Frederick's troops on
the Rhine was the line of the Neckar. Unwisely, Mansfeld
and the Margrave of Baden decided to cross it apart, hoping
thus to divide Tilly and Cordoba. The plan failed; on May 6th
the Margrave, trying to make the crossing at Wimpfen, found
himself cut off by Tilly and Cordoba in person with the
greater part of their troops. Although he was outnumbered his
case was not hopeless, his loyal and zealous soldiers were pitted
against an army seriously weakened by lack of provisions[3] and
under a divided command. Relying on his cannon, the Margrave took up his position on a low hill dominating the flat
country and entrenched his artillery with conscientious
thoroughness. He had planned to break the advancing Spanish
and Bavarian troops by a cavalry charge supported by a heavy
cannonade. At first his plan seemed to work, Cordoba's front
line broke before his horsemen and the terrific bombardment

[1] WESKAMP, *Das Heer der Liga*, Munich, 1891, pp. 50, 86.
[2] KLOPP, II, p. 151.
[3] DU CORNET, *Histoire Générale des Guerres de Savoie, de Bohême, du Palatinat et des Pays Bas*. Bruxelles, 1868, p. 30.

of his well-placed batteries. Two of the Spanish cannon were seized and the whole of the Spanish wing began to waver, when suddenly, so suddenly that afterwards it was attributed to a miracle, the Margrave's cannon ceased their murderous fire and his troops fell back in disorder. A white-robed woman, half-seen in the smoky air, floated above the heads of Cordoba's men, and one of them, dumb from birth, cried out 'Victory, victory!' and urged his wavering comrades back to fight. Thus the legend: the white-robed woman was a cloud of smoke from George Frederick's arsenal blown sky-high by a random shot. Seizing the chance, Tilly and Cordoba simultaneously closed in on the hill and forced the Badeners, after a long and murderous resistance, to relinquish their guns and fly.[1]

Rumour had it that at nightfall, alone and dropping on his spent horse, George Frederick was battering on the gates of Heilbronn, calling to the astonished watchman, 'Give me a drink, friend, I am only the old Margrave'. It was a fact that on the day after the battle, May 7th, 1622, he rode into Stuttgart with a few wretched companions, a broken man.[2]

Yet from the military point of view very little had happened. Within the next few days more than two-thirds of the army were again collected; Christian of Brunswick would be able to make good the loss in artillery and ammunition from his funds when he came up. The destruction among Cordoba's troops was nearly as serious, and Tilly's men were in need of rest, refreshment and better fodder for their horses. The passage of the Neckar could still be made while Tilly and Cordoba repaired their losses, was indeed made by Mansfeld who now struck boldly northwards across the neutral lands of the Landgrave of Hesse-Darmstadt. But the old Margrave, bowed down by the horror through which he had passed, the memory of the shambles to which he had brought his own loyal and trusting subjects, had no heart for further campaigning; as an ally he had ceased to be significant, and his reassembled army melted again for lack of organization.[3]

The chief necessity for Frederick was that Mansfeld and

---

[1] Carafa, p. 371; du Cornet, p. 32; *Westenrieders Beyträge*, Munich, 1792, IV, pp. 110-11.
[2] Dieffenbach, *Das Grossherzogtum Hessen*, Darmstadt, 1877, p. 159.
[3] Wertheim, II, p. 412 f.

Christian should meet. The Neckar valley lay behind, and Mansfeld and Tilly both raced for the Main, the one to assist Christian's crossing, the other to prevent it. Mansfeld's quickest way lay across the lands of the Landgrave of Hesse-Darmstadt. This unoffending prince was a good imperialist, but he was unarmed, and when Frederick and Mansfeld appeared outside his small capital he was forced to shelter their army and give the leaders hospitality. In vain he himself attempted to evade responsibility by secret flight: brought back ignominiously, muddy and footsore from a long nocturnal walk, he was peremptorily required to hand over Rüsselsheim, a small fortress on the Main. With obstinacy that was almost heroic the Landgrave refused, and Mansfeld continued his march to the Main, indignant at the useless detour and carrying off the prince and his young son as hostages.[1]

This brief resistance saved the situation for Tilly and Cordoba. They reached the Main before Mansfeld and found Christian newly arrived at the bridge-head of Höchst, a mile or two west of Frankfort.

Christian's army consisted of about twelve to fifteen thousand men, very moderately armed and with an artillery of three cannon, of which two were unfit to be used. He was therefore in no position to offer battle to his enemies. But he knew that Mansfeld was not far off and that he needed above all reinforcements and money. The problem for Christian was to cross the Main with as many men as he could and all his booty; and this, in the face of the united Spanish and Bavarian forces, Christian did. He lost two thousand men, he lost much of his baggage, he lost his famous three cannon, but he crossed the Main and joined Mansfeld with nearly all his cavalry intact and his treasury triumphantly saved.[2]

It was typical of the hide-bound military theory of the time that Christian's exploit, because it had been foolhardy and extravagant of lives, should be decried throughout Europe as a crushing defeat. It was natural, no doubt, that Tilly and Cordoba should claim the victory, although they had signally

[1] LUDWIG SCHÄDEL, *Der Gründer der Ludoviciana in der Haft des Winter-königs. Mitteilungen des oberhessischen Geschichtsvereins. Neue Folge.* XIV, p. 54.
[2] WERTHEIM, II, p. 512 f.; DU CORNET, p. 51.

failed in their only important object. It was less natural and very galling for Christian that when he joined Mansfeld and Frederick in the highest spirits, visibly denying the rumour that he had been killed,[1] the professional soldier should have nothing but hard words for what he had done.[2]

The united armies can hardly have numbered less than twenty-five thousand men, and if Tilly and Cordoba had more, their troops were by this time dispirited by continuous marches and the impact of two hard-fought engagements. Mansfeld may have been jealous of the youthful princeling who took precedence of him at meals and seems to have had a habit of dominating the conversation; certainly he had been intermittently ill throughout the spring and summer[3] and was tired and bad-tempered. His men were so short of money that Christian's booty failed to satisfy them, and the question of fodder in the occupied country was becoming for them, no less than for Tilly's troops, acute.[4]

Mansfeld's only valuable possession was his army, and he did not wish to risk it in a joint action with the reckless Christian; he had neither the prince's belief in the Protestant Cause nor his carelessness of the common soldiers' lives. Unsupported, Christian could do nothing, and Mansfeld within a few days of the battle of Höchst insisted on retreating with the united armies over the Rhine to Landau, leaving the enemy in unhampered occupation of the right bank.

They were an ill-assorted and quarrelsome company which trailed southwards towards Alsace, Frederick explaining at intervals to the Landgrave that he was not technically at war with the Emperor,[5] Mansfeld arguing about what should have been done at Höchst, Christian declaring noisily to shocked listeners that he had peopled the bishopric of Paderborn with 'young Dukes of Brunswick' who would all grow up to keep the priests in order.[6]

Three weeks of Mansfeld's company on a retreat was

[1] ARETIN, *Beyträge*, VII, p. 185.
[2] KLOPP, II, pp. 194-5. Again, I follow Wertheim's reading of this incident. If he loads the balance a little too heavily in Christian's favour, he has at least collected a great deal of material to support his opinion.
[3] SCHÄDEL, pp. 54-5.   [4] WERTHEIM, II, p. 516 f.
[5] HURTER, *Ferdinand II.*, IX, p. 121.
[6] KLOPP, II, pp. 194-5; WERTHEIM, I, p. 227.

enough for Frederick. Making across Alsace, the troops set
fire to one town and thirty villages; what shreds of reputation
were left to Frederick were torn away by this conduct. In
Strasbourg, where ten thousand fugitives had fled for shelter
with all their cattle, famine was feared both for man and
beast. Small wonder that a high-flown manifesto on the
defence of the German Liberties was received with the utmost
scepticism. The country was by this time so far wasted, the
villages so deserted, that Mansfeld could not feed his army and
must perforce march into Lorraine.[1] 'There ought to be some
difference made between friend and enemy', lamented
Frederick, 'but these people ruin both alike ... I think these
are men who are possessed of the devil and who take a pleasure
in setting fire to everything. I should be very glad to leave
them.'[2] Mansfeld was equally tired of Frederick's service, and
on July 13th, 1622, he secured the revocation of his and
Christian's commission.[3] This done, Frederick, without armies
or possessions, almost without servants, retired to his uncle
the Duke of Bouillon at Sedan, there in the intervals of bathing
and tennis to search for new allies.[4]

Mansfeld was looking for employment, Christian for some
new way to serve the Protestant Cause. For the time being
they decided to act together. Rumour of distress in the United
Provinces decided them to make northwards. Since the
expiration of the truce everything had gone amiss for the
Dutch; Spanish troops had overrun the neighbouring German
province of Jülich, and with all his efforts Maurice could barely
guarantee the safety of the frontiers. Offensive war was out
of the question, and in the summer of 1622 Spinola crossed the
border and laid siege to the key fortress of Bergen op Zoom.

Hardly waiting for a definite invitation, Mansfeld and
Christian set off by the straightest way to the threatened city,
trailing a belt of fire, famine and disease across the neutral
bishoprics of Metz and Verdun and into the Spanish Netherlands. Their march was utterly unexpected, and in vain

---

[1] REUSS, *Alsace*, pp. 61, 65; KLOPP, II, p. 200 f.
[2] GARDINER, *History of England*, IV, pp. 323, 339.
[3] LUNDORP, II, p. 636.
[4] ARETIN, *Beyträge*, VII, p. 188; RITTER, *Untersuchungen über die pfälzischen
Politik. Historische Zeitschrift*, LXXIV, pp. 410 ff.

Cordoba, racing northward with a handful of troops, attempted to block their way at Fleurus. Here on August 29th Christian carved a way through the Spanish lines for himself and Mansfeld by five desperate charges, the fifth at last shattering the opposing troops and leaving the roads clear to what remained of the victorious army. He had been wounded in the right arm and had to have it amputated a few days later, an occasion which he used for a spectacular display of physical courage. The operation was performed to a fanfare of trumpets and he commemorated the occasion by striking a medal with the superscription 'Altera restat'.[1] On October 4th, meanwhile, he had arrived with Mansfeld just in time to raise the siege of Bergen op Zoom.

While Mansfeld and Christian were cutting heroic figures in the Netherlands, Tilly and Cordoba completed the subjection of the Palatinate. After a siege of eleven weeks the garrison of Heidelberg, hopeless of relief, marched out with the honours of war on September 19th, 1622; the townsfolk, whose indignation at hardship had found vent in ceaseless bickering with their defenders, received less courteous treatment, and Tilly allowed his soldiery the customary reward of plunder.[2] 'Voilà mon pauvre Heidelberg pris,' wailed Frederick from Sedan, and wrote desperately to the Kings of England and Denmark for help. None was forthcoming, and on November 5th Sir Horace Vere abandoned Mannheim on the same terms. Of all Frederick's rich and beautiful country there was nothing left to him but the little fortress of Frankenthal, where a single English garrison still flew the forlorn banner of the Protestant Cause.

That winter in The Hague he and his wife were busy with new schemes. Bethlen Gabor and the Turks, the King of Denmark, the Electors of Saxony and Brandenburg, all these were to unite to encircle and destroy the Hapsburg.[3] It was in vain, for money and confidence were lacking. 'The

[1] DU CORNET, pp. 69-70; J. A. WORP, *Briefwisseling van Constantin Huygens.* Hague, 1911, I, p. 125; *Theatrum Europaeum*, I, pp. 66-8.

[2] LUNDORP, II, pp. 630, 743-53; *Die Schicksale Heidelbergs im dreissigjährigen Kriege. Archiv fur die Geschichte der Stadt Heidelberg* II. Heidelberg, 1869, p. 29 f.

[3] See RITTER, *Untersuchungen über die pfälzischen Politik. Historische Zeitschrift*, LXXIV, pp. 407-41.

Palatinate', said the wits, 'was likely to have a numerous army shortly on foot, for the King of Denmark would furnish them with a thousand pickled herrings, the Hollanders with ten thousand butter boxes, and England with one hundred thousand ambassadors.'[1]

Frederick's defences were gone, and Ferdinand realized that he need wait no longer. The time had come to fulfil his promise to Maximilian.

IV

There was a constitutional provision that the Emperor could not call a Diet on his own authority. It was not a Diet, therefore, but only a general Electoral meeting or Deputationstag, called rather unwillingly by the Elector of Mainz, which Ferdinand opened at Regensburg on January 10th, 1623.[2] The Electors of Mainz, Treves, and Cologne, of Saxony and Brandenburg, the Dukes of Brunswick-Wolfenbüttel, Pomerania and Bavaria, the Landgrave of Hesse-Darmstadt, the bishops of Salzburg and Würzburg either came in person or sent representatives, but the meeting was neither full nor enthusiastic.

Ferdinand had spent the intervening months canvassing the leading princes in preparation for the transference of the Electorate from Frederick to Maximilian. Apart from the Elector of Cologne, Maximilian's own brother, almost every important prince in Germany was opposed to it. The Electors of Mainz and Treves objected on constitutional grounds; the Electors of Saxony and Brandenburg had additional religious motives, fearing equally the increase of Ferdinand's imperial power and the extension of his religious policy. In the course of the last year he had broken his word to John George of Saxony by forbidding the practice of the Lutheran faith in Bohemia,[3] so that the protection which the Elector had thought to give to the oppressed Protestants had failed utterly. His protests to Ferdinand, alike on behalf of the Bohemian

[1] R. COKE, *State of England*, p. 109.
[2] Two long accounts of the meetings are given in great detail in GOETZ, *Briefe und Akten*, Leipzig, 1907, II, i, pp. 10-22 and pp. 26-46.
[3] LUNDORP, II, p. 630.

Lutherans and in favour of more constitutional treatment of
Frederick, met with the coolest response.[1] He was beginning
to see that he had intervened to save the Emperor from an
unconstitutional attack, only to lay Germany open to an
onslaught more dangerous and more unconstitutional than
anything of which Frederick had dreamed. Conscious of his
weakness, he wavered from side to side, and Ferdinand realized
that, while he could not count on John George's further support,
he would not have to reckon with his enmity.

The Elector of Brandenburg was in an equally uncomfortable
and powerless position. His wife was Frederick's elder sister,
and she had persuaded him to give a refuge to her mother and
youngest brother, while the latter prince had married a princess
of Brandenburg, thus increasing the bond of obligation between
the two families. No less had the Bohemian persecutions
turned the Elector of Brandenburg against the Emperor, but
he was neither intelligent nor determined, his lands were
troubled by the existence of a large Lutheran party personally
opposed to his own Calvinism, and he had dynastic reasons
for seeking to preserve peace. Besides, the King of Poland,
Ferdinand's brother-in-law, had once again made an opportune
intervention by ceding the much-disputed province of Prussia
to Brandenburg as a fief of the Polish Crown.[2] The Elector
could hardly accept the bribe without committing himself to
support the Hapsburg dynasty. Indeed, had he wished to
oppose it, he had no army worth the name, nor were his Estates
prepared to advance him money to raise one. His cue was to
follow in the wake of Saxony and above all to make no rash
decision.

While the two Protestant Electors played for safety,
Ferdinand could carry through his unconstitutional act. No
effective power in Germany would prevent him.

It was different in Europe. The Spaniards did not want
the Electorate transferred to Maximilian. The Archduchess
Isabella, with the approval of Madrid, had evolved the perfect
scheme: Frederick should be made to abdicate in favour of his
eldest son, a child of seven, who should then be dispatched to

[1] *Annales*, IX, pp. 1653, 1799; LUNDORP, II, pp. 605, 631, 649-52.
[2] DROYSEN, *Preussische Politik*, II, p. 638.

Vienna, educated with the Emperor's family, and ultimately married to one of his daughters. This plan, which among other things saved the imperial constitution intact, for an abdication under pressure was allowable where a deposition would be illegal, was sponsored by Philip IV and James I, and even taken up by John George of Saxony. That Frederick refused to abdicate, refused to relinquish his son, and continued to demand an indemnity for the sufferings of the Protestant Bohemians, disturbed no one.[1]

But Maximilian had not been idle in the defence of his own interests. The reconquest of the Palatinate had given him the opportunity to prove that he, no less than Ferdinand, was the champion of the Church. Every effort had been made to reconvert the people. As soon as Tilly's troops were well established, missionaries had descended upon the hungry and plague-stricken populace, and orders had been promulgated forbidding emigration; the Protestant churches of Heidelberg itself had been closed, the University dissolved and the superb library packed into boxes and trundled in wagon loads over the Alps to Rome, Maximilian's thankoffering to the Vatican.[2]

Such bribery was, however, not necessary to enlist the Pope's help. The plan of the Archduchess would have caused an increase in Hapsburg power which as an Italian prince he could not afford to allow. With the King of England supporting it, with the King of France apparently not strong enough to resist, Spain would in all probability reconquer the Dutch Netherlands and regain thereby all its lost prosperity. If the Hapsburg were not to master the world, Maximilian must be advanced as a counterweight within the Empire to the power of Austria, in Europe to that of Spain.

All this time Ferdinand appeared to be cast about like a rudderless boat on the stormy currents of conflicting intrigue. On the one side the Pope pressed him to make a written promise of the Electorate to Maximilian,[3] on the other the King of Spain urged the English plan upon him, while the constitutionalist Elector of Mainz warned him of the dangerous

[1] *Annales*, x, pp. 86, 117-18; GOETZ, *Briefe und Akten*, II, i, pp. 4, 22-3.
[2] GOETZ, *Briefe und Akten*, II, i, p. 568; *Schucksale Heidelbergs*, p. 188; CARAFA, *Germania Sacra Restaurata*, Cologne, 1637, I, p. 340 f.
[3] GINDELY, *Geschichte*, IV, p. 383.

enmity of Saxony, should he fulfil Maximilian's desire.[1] Certainly in Europe the Emperor, who had apparently so few personal resources and no command of his own destiny, was an object of faintly contemptuous pity, and the result of the Regensburg negotiation was generally assumed to depend on the relative pressure exerted by Spain and Bavaria. It was to Ferdinand's advantage that it should be so, for just as he seems to have had no doubt whatever as to his intentions, so also it was best for him to figure throughout as the victim of circumstance. If he enforced the cession of the Electorate to Maximilian his imperial power would be strengthened; if he failed, he could plead his innocence of all responsibility and be no worse off than before.

In the meantime he was prepared to make a temporary sacrifice of Spanish interests for the furtherance of his own more subtle plans. A Hapsburg on the father's side, on the mother's Ferdinand was a German, and the illusion of nationality was strong with him. Ultimately he would, like all his forebears, serve the interests of his dynasty, but he would serve them in a German, an Imperial, not a Spanish sense, and he saw salvation not through the reconquest of the Dutch Netherlands but through the reform of the Empire. Once imperial power had become a reality again, no nation in Europe, no reigning dynasty, would be able to stand against the Hapsburg. He was prepared to shelve the immediate demands of Spain, not indeed to please Bavaria, but to serve the larger ends of the dynasty.

The princes who met at Regensburg in January 1623 were few of them favourable to Ferdinand's proposition. In order to avoid a difficult decision, the Electors of Saxony and Brandenburg had not sent plenipotentiary ambassadors; therefore no decision would be legally binding on them. But what hairsplittings were these constitutional quibbles, when the only armed force in Germany belonged to the Duke of Bavaria and was at the Emperor's disposal! What Ferdinand did would be effective whether it were legal or not, and the princes would have to recognize the accomplished fact.

The Regensburg meeting lasted for six weeks, every kind of

[1] GOETZ, *Briefe und Akten*, II, I, p. 20.

argument being adduced both by the princes and by the Spanish
ambassador to prevent the transference of the Electorate. The
claims of Frederick's innocent children, four healthy sons,
were urged in vain against those of Maximilian; no less, the
rights of Frederick's younger brother and of the Prince of
Neuburg, a Catholic and a nearer relation of the rebellious
prince than was Maximilian of Bavaria. But Maximilian and
Ferdinand stood to their decision, Maximilian earning the
opprobrium and Ferdinand the pity of the assembly.

The Duke was playing into the Emperor's hands. His
personal ambitions blinded him to the breach he was making
in the German Liberties. His old father, who had been
nearly thirty years in retirement, thrust himself forward for
one last moment to warn his son to consider his actions. But
Maximilian, himself grown grey in government, would not stop
to listen to a voice from the past century.[1]

Ferdinand made only one concession to the doubts of the
princes. The Electorate was bestowed for life only, and there
would be the possibility of restoring it to Frederick's children
on Maximilian's death; the Duke was already old and his wife
past the age of child-bearing.[2] On February 23rd, 1623,
Frederick was deposed, and two days later Maximilian was
invested with his titles.[3] The hall was dismally deserted at his
investiture, for neither the representatives of Saxony and
Brandenburg nor the Spanish ambassador had come. The
Elector of Mainz performed the ceremony with an embarrassed
air, frequently stopping to scratch his head as if for inspiration,
and Maximilian's speech of gratitude lacked polish and confidence;[4] at that last moment, too late to retract, perhaps even
he began to wonder whither his dynastic ambition had led him.
He had gained a personal advantage at the expense of those very
Liberties by which he, no less than all the princes of Germany,
maintained his power. He might stand to-morrow in the
place in which Frederick stood to-day, for he had put a weapon
into the Emperor's hands that Ferdinand would not fear to use.
The time was fast approaching when he would regret that he

[1] LUNDORP, II, p. 501.   [2] Ibid., p. 657 seq.
[3] LÜNIG, III, ii, p. 64 f.; v, i, p. 693 f.; LUNDORP, II, pp. 673, 676.
[4] GOETZ, Briefe und Akten, II, i, pp. 44-5.

had sacrificed the constitution of Germany to the ambition of Bavaria and made way for the unimpeded rule of violence. He, who of all men had been most jealous lest imperial power should increase, had lent his hand to the destruction of the constitution which he had championed.

V

The elevation of Maximilian evoked a storm of protest for which Ferdinand had not been unprepared. The Spanish ambassador offered no congratulations, the Archduchess Isabella openly expressed her disapproval and regret.[1] The Electors of Saxony and Brandenburg jointly refused to recognize their new colleague, and the Regensburg meeting came to an untimely end because the Protestant delegates would not take their seats with the so-called 'Elector' of Bavaria.[2]

Ferdinand now knew the limit of his power. It stretched as far and no farther than his armed force could carry it, and for that armed force he still depended on the Catholic League and Maximilian of Bavaria. The Protestant delegates at Regensburg had expressed their disapproval by refusing any further grants of money for the war; they might be too weak to resist, but they were not quite so simple as to subsidize an attack on their Liberties. The transference of the Electorate had completed the work of the ban by forcing the constitutionalist party into sympathy, if not alliance, with the dispossessed Frederick.

On the other hand, the cleavage between Catholic and Protestant princes had been dangerously widened at Regensburg, where the delegates of the Catholic League had naturally supported Maximilian, their president and paymaster, and some of the more indiscreet had foolishly boasted that the Church would soon reconquer all Germany. As a result, the Electors of Saxony and Brandenburg held a protest meeting, at which there was talk on Saxony's part of forming a new Protestant Union, and on Brandenburg's of an appeal to force.

---

[1] *Annales*, x, p. 71; GOETZ, *Briefe und Akten*, II, i, pp. 76, 101.
[2] LUNDORP, II, p. 733; GINDELY, *Geschichte*, IV, p. 515.

The chief result of these gestures was merely to cement more firmly than before the alliance between Ferdinand and the League.[1]

The delegates of the League, under the auspices of Maximilian, had been holding their own annual meeting at Regensburg in the intervals of imperial business. Exploiting his new triumph, Maximilian overrode the doubts of the more timorous members and persuaded the gathering to vote for the continued maintenance of Tilly's army.[2] He saw well enough that after the unmasking of Catholic and dynastic ambition which had taken place, it would be essential to check by a show of arms all possibility of Protestant and constitutionalist attack. The resources of his allies and of Bavaria itself were already strained, and for the last months Tilly had had difficulty in keeping his troops satisfied;[3] nevertheless, the new Elector's arguments were unanswerable, and the members of the League prepared to raise yet more money from their already overtaxed subjects.

The second essential for Maximilian was to strengthen his hold over Ferdinand, which was not difficult to accomplish when the Emperor needed armed force and the League alone could provide it. By the end of March 1623 the original alliance had been renewed; Ferdinand, it was estimated, already owed the Elector of Bavaria between sixteen and eighteen million florins for his original services, a debt which showed every sign of increasing and none of being paid. To redeem this immense sum he now contracted to give Maximilian control of the revenues of Upper Austria and the complete possession of the Upper Palatinate at least for the time being.[4] Although a final transference of these tracts of land was not made, no one who understood the rudiments of Hapsburg policy could doubt that Ferdinand meant in course of time to buy back Upper Austria by the total cession of the Palatinate. He was feeling his way towards the re-distribution of the Empire and once again he was concealing his policy under cover of his obligations to Maximilian.

---

[1] LUNDORP, II, p. 733 f.; GINDELY, *Geschichte*, IV, pp. 501 ff.
[2] GOETZ, *Briefe und Akten*, II, i, pp. 48-64.
[3] Ibid., II, i, *passim*. [4] Ibid., II, i, pp. 137-44.

Ferdinand had successfully defied the limitations on imperial power which had crippled his predecessors since Charles V, but the victory would be wasted unless he could carry it to its logical conclusion. So long as he remained indebted to any party in the state, Catholic or Protestant, his despotism would be an illusion and there would come a point at which it would no longer be safe to exploit the ambitions or the convictions of one prince for the destruction of another, a point at which the power of Bavaria might become dangerous to the Hapsburg dynasty itself. After all, Maximilian had once been mentioned as a possible candidate for the imperial throne.

A clever statesman in Ferdinand's position would have played off one party against the other, John George of Saxony against Maximilian of Bavaria. A religious fanatic would have sold himself body and soul to the Catholic League and re-conquered Germany for the Church, at whatever cost to imperial prestige. Ferdinand, by the peculiarities of his birth and out-look, could do neither. He was ardently, intensely Catholic, and therefore to speak of his 'exploitation' of the Catholic League is to do an injustice to his convictions for, in so far as the League served the Church, Ferdinand's heart was with it; but when the League began to endanger his dynasty a new force came into play. His political and religious convictions were inextricably mingled; he genuinely believed that the Hapsburg dynasty alone could restore Germany to the Church, and that, if the League endangered the stability of his dynasty, it endangered the welfare of Catholic Europe. This profound conviction alone justifies his actions and explains the apparent insincerity of his conduct. He had won half his battle with the help of the Catholic League; he had now to find some new weapon with which to bring the League itself under control. It is probable that Ferdinand, being a simple man, and more given to exercise than thought, hardly conceived of the problem in explicit terms, but henceforward two motives dominated his policy: he must strengthen the Hapsburg power in the dynastic lands themselves, and find means whenever possible to evade all further obligations to Maximilian of Bavaria. This he set out to achieve in the time conscientiously allotted to state affairs between prayers and hunting.

He had to help him in his task two men of exceptional ability, his friend and chief minister, Eggenberg, and the Jesuit father, Lamormaini,[1] who together exerted the only permanent influences on his pliable but slippery judgment. Eggenberg had been his leading councillor for several years, but Lamormaini only became Ferdinand's confessor in 1624. He came from Luxemburg, of well-to-do peasant stock, a lean, tall man with an ugly limp, the deformity which had driven him as a boy into the shelter of the seminary. His manners were austere, his habits simple, his convictions fanatical. Ferdinand had never cherished any illusion as to the political sanctity of the ministers of the Church. Although he showed a meticulous respect to the merest village priest, he had thought nothing of arresting and forcibly detaining a Cardinal[2] and, as a young man, he had removed the confessor of one of his brothers because he did not approve of the way in which he used his influence. Nevertheless, a clever man could establish such relations with him as would make the confessional a potent if never a guiding instrument of policy. Lamormaini suited Ferdinand admirably: he took a genuine and sympathetic interest in his family and his hunting, avoided all appearance of political dominance and gave his advice when it was asked with that logic, accuracy and clearness which Ferdinand had learnt to expect of the Jesuits.

On April 5th, 1623, Ferdinand left Regensburg for Prague,[3] there to initiate his policy for the strengthening and stabilizing of Hapsburg power. In his suite travelled the Papal Nuncio, Cardinal Carafa, one of the ablest members of that family from which the greatest of the Counter-Reformation Popes had sprung. He was the man to whom Ferdinand looked to restore Bohemia to the Church.

Five years had passed since Ferdinand last travelled to Bohemia, and the country through which he went showed cruel signs of change. From Regensburg to the frontier his road lay across the Upper Palatinate, where the troops of Tilly had made

---

[1] This appears to be the most accurate form of the name which is supposed to be a corruption of La Moire Mannie in the Ardennes, the place of origin of the family. *Correspondenz Kaisers Ferdinand II herausgegeben von* Dr. B. DUDIK, *Archiv für Oesterreichische Geschichte*, LIV. p. 228.

[2] Cardinal Khlesl. See *supra*. p. 82.   [3] GINDELY, *Geschichte*, IV, p. 523.

horrible devastation. The peasantry of the country seem to have had a real devotion to their dispossessed Elector[1] and had often refused food and shelter to the Catholic soldiery, thus bringing down on themselves the unbridled fury of the invaders.[2] Maximilian, to prevent further trouble, had had the whole province forcibly disarmed;[3] meanwhile the natural protectors of the peasantry, the local gentry, less loyal than their people, had made haste to come to terms with the new government, leaving their peasants to suffer undefended. Shortage of pay had undermined the discipline of Tilly's army as early as the summer of 1621. They had avenged their poverty, with the licence of a conquering army, on the wretched villages of the Palatinate. In the towns they had even broken into and plundered the hospitals and pest-houses, thus spreading disease through their own ranks and carrying it across the province.[4] Crossing the Bohemian border, Ferdinand came upon the track of Mansfeld's depredations, nor were other parts of his lands less affected. The province of Moravia, which for the past two years had been safeguarded by Cossack troops against the possible invasion of Bethlen Gabor, was a waste in which plague, hunger and flight had reduced the population by more than three quarters.[5]

Ferdinand had not come to organize relief, and the measures which he adopted were not calculated to pour balm on the sores of Bohemia. In the preceding autumn he had issued an edict that every participant in the recent revolt was to forfeit part or all of his lands,[6] and he now came to see the effect of his orders. Six hundred and fifty-eight families in Bohemia, fifty towns, and land amounting to one half of the whole province, came within the scope of the decision, while in Moravia over three hundred landowners were affected, the greatest culprits losing the whole of their estates, the lesser as little as a fifth. Neither Ferdinand nor his councillors were blind to the advantage of keeping the spoils in the hands of the Crown, but the immediate need for money to meet the expenses of

---

[1] As late as 1638 Maximilian feared that the passage of one of Frederick's sons, as a prisoner of war, through the Upper Palatinate might cause trouble.
[2] HOEGL, *Die Bekehrung der Oberpfalz.* Regensburg, 1903, pp. 52-3.
[3] Ibid., pp. 85 ff.   [4] Ibid., p. 52.
[5] D'ELVERT, III, p. 114; IV, p. 118.   [6] Ibid., II, p. 151 f.

the State was too great to allow of argument. They had to sell.

But there was too much land on the market and too few possible buyers. The prospects were further darkened by a financial crisis throughout the Empire. The uncontrolled monetary system of Germany had completely broken down; the gulden, the more or less standardized coin of south Germany, had begun as early as 1619 to fluctuate in relation to the taler of the north. In the course of three years the taler reached a value of four gulden in Austria, eight at Strasbourg, ten in Ansbach and Hildesheim, twelve in Saxony and Silesia, and soared to fifteen at Nuremberg. At Ulm the municipality fixed it forcibly at eight, at Vienna the gulden sank to less than an eighth of its normal value and at Prague the taler began to disappear altogether from circulation. In Saxony the government was losing half the normal yield on the taxes through bad money.[1]

In Prague the gravity of the situation was increased by the necessities of the government. Frederick had begun the trouble by slightly debasing the currency during his year of rule; Ferdinand's nominee, Liechtenstein, continued the process, reduced the amount of silver in the coinage by more than seventy-five per cent and attempted to fill the imperial coffers — and his own — with the profit which he made on the mint.[2] In January 1622 Ferdinand, in hope of further gain, made a contract with a group of speculators for the establishment of a privately controlled mint in Prague. The currency was drastically debased while prices were forcibly stabilized; the plan failed utterly, for the people became suspicious and hoarded what good money they had, while in spite of the provision of the government, food alone rose to twelve times its normal price. External trade stopped altogether and for the ordinary exchanges of everyday life the people took to barter. To add to the damage done by this crazy scheme, the chief object of the contractors was rather their own enrichment than the payment of Ferdinand's debts.

At this moment Ferdinand was besieged with demands to

---

[1] D'ELVERT, III, p. 119; II, p. 33; R. WUTTKE, *Zur Kipper und Wipperzeit in Kursachsen. Neues Archiv für Sächsische Geschichte*, XVI, p. 155; WALTHER, p. 15.
[2] GINDELY, *Geschichte*, IV, pp. 326-9.

buy the confiscated lands. The loyal nobility and many wealthy merchants offered him what had once been fair prices in the Prague money, prices which he could not now refuse to take without repudiating his own currency. It was one thing to sell the lands and another to make use of the money; Ferdinand had accepted his own coin, but his soldiers threw it back in their officers' faces, because the local peasantry would not take it in exchange for the necessities of life. Throughout Bohemia trade came almost to a standstill, the peasants would not supply the towns with food, the army was mutinous, the civil population starving and certain contractors, of whom Liechtenstein was not the least, were among the richest men in Europe. At Christmas 1623, Ferdinand devaluated the money and broke the contract. By that time the greater part of the confiscated land had been sold for an average price of less than a third its normal value.[1] His first move towards financial security had been catastrophic, for not only had he lost the advantage of the confiscation, but he had completed the economic ruin of Bohemia. Wealth, which had been widely distributed among an industrious peasantry and an active urban population, had become, through political persecution and the disastrous effects of the inflation, concentrated in a few unscrupulous hands. As a source of imperial revenue Bohemia had become useless.

Politically Ferdinand had achieved one slight advantage: private fortunes had been engulfed and the ruthless confiscation of land had ruined or partly ruined almost all the municipalities;[2] whatever immediate poverty might face his government, he had at least destroyed the restless and critical merchant classes and removed the bulwark between the ruler and the people. One of the most progressive and commercialized countries in Europe had slipped back two centuries in little more than two years and the field was free for despotism.

Politically, too, the redistribution of land was successful. The leading Protestant aristocracy were replaced by men whose Catholicism was unimpeachable and whose right to the

---

[1] GINDELY, Geschichte, IV, p. 338; D'ELVERT, III, pp. 117, 128.
[2] GINDELY, Geschichte der Gegenreformation in Böhmen. Nach dem Tode des Verfassers herausgegeben von T. Tupetz. Leipzig, 1894, Chapter VIII, passim.

land depended on their support of the government which had given it to them. Liechtenstein himself had bought ten estates, Eggenberg eight. But there was one man who above all others had made himself known as a ready buyer. Albrecht von Waldstein, or as he was more euphoniously called, Wallenstein, the military governor of Prague, had accumulated no less than sixty-six estates,[1] the most important being the province of Friedland and the town of Gitschin.

Wallenstein was forty years old in 1623; the son of a small Protestant landowner, he had been left an orphan early and educated as a Lutheran at the celebrated school of Altdorf until the authorities requested his removal, not without cause, since he had once taken part in a murderous brawl, and once nearly killed one of his servants.[2] Travel in Italy and conversion to the Catholic religion sobered his over-excitable spirits, and he settled down in his early twenties to make himself a career. At the imperial Court he attached himself to Ferdinand's party, when he was still only Archduke of Styria. Next he married a wealthy widow who shortly after died leaving him a rich man. The foundations of his public and private fortune thus laid, he had but to husband and increase his resources while watching his opportunities. In his financial affairs he showed a judgment and discretion which grew with his wealth, and although he was not a sympathetic landowner he was an exceptionally good one. He developed his estates to their uttermost limit, establishing industries where possible in the towns, inspecting and controlling agriculture, building store-houses for superfluous crops, exporting produce for sale, and at the same time increasing the efficiency of his people by organizing education, poor relief, medical services and provision for times of famine.[3] His capital at Gitschin was not unworthy of the state he was creating; he himself built his own palace and Church and lent money to the burghers at a moderate rate to reconstruct their houses according to his plans.[4]

[1] D'ELVERT, II, pp. 257, 258, 261.

[2] SIEGL, Wallenstein auf der 'hohen Schule', zu Altdorf. Mitteilungen des Vereins für Geschichte der Deutschen in Böhmen, XLIX, pp. 127-52.

[3] ERNSTBERGER, Wallenstein als Volkswirt in Herzogtum Friedland. Reichenberg, 1929, pp. 96-9, 46; see also HUNZIKER, Wallenstein als Landesherr, insbesondere als Herzog von Mecklenburg. Zurich, 1875.

[4] ERNSTBERGER, p. 88.

Count Wallenstein's tastes were sumptuous but sombre, and his entourage was impressive rather from the exactness with which he had everything arranged, the order and regularity of his household, than by any ostentatious expense. He was not a popular man; tall, thin, forbidding, his face in the unexpressive portraits which have survived is not prepossessing. No great master painted him[1] and the limners who attempted his saturnine features agree only in a few particulars. The irregular features, the high cheek-bones and prominent nose, the heavy jowl, the thick, out-jutting underlip — these are present more or less in all pictures. Later portraits exploited the dramatic possibilities of that strangely unsympathetic face, for when Wallenstein became great there was no detail of his conduct or appearance that did not become common property — his ungovernable temper, his disregard of human life, his unsteady nerves, his immutable chastity, his faith in astrology. As time went on, he himself cultivated the spectacular, dressed in a bizarre mixture of all European fashions and relieved his habitually dark attire with a sash or plume of unexpected and violent red. In his pale, dry face the equally vivid colour of his lips may perhaps not have been nature's work alone.[2] But stripped of the character he later created, what was Wallenstein in 1623 but an unscrupulous and able careerist? Neither the unsteady nerves nor the blind rages to which he was subject, neither his unusual chastity nor his comparatively usual belief in astrology, are attributes of singular greatness or of peculiar mystery.

Born, like Elizabeth of England, under a conjunction of Saturn and Jupiter, Wallenstein's stars gave him a peculiar mixture of weakness and strength, vice and virtue. His was, so his horoscope informed him, a restless, exacting mind, impatient of old methods and for ever striving for the new and the untried, secretive, melancholy, suspicious, contemptuous of his fellow-

[1] Van Dyck never set eyes on Wallenstein. The portrait in the Bavarian State Collections which is often reproduced is a fancy picture drawn as one of a series of well-known soldiers. The fine portrait in the Liechtenstein Collection in Vaduz may or may not be intended to represent Wallenstein; but even if the identification of the subject is accurate – and this seems more than doubtful – it cannot have been painted from the life.

[2] PRIORATO, *Historia della Vita di Alberto Valstein, Duca di Fritland*. Lyons, 1643, p. 64.

men and their conventions. He would be avaricious, deceitful, greedy for power, loving no one and by no one beloved, changeable in his humours, quarrelsome, friendless and cruel. So far the analysis of Johan Kepler from the position of the stars over Hermanice at four in the afternoon on September 14th, 1583, when Wallenstein was born.[1] The estimate was searching and true enough.

Wallenstein had been in command of the local levies of Moravia when the rebellion broke out in 1618. Finding that his troops were deserting to the rebels he had, with his usual presence of mind, escaped to safety, taking with him the military treasury of the province, thus bringing much-needed financial help to Ferdinand and depriving the Moravian rebel army of its pay.[2] In the following year he had advanced forty thousand gulden to the Emperor from his own estates and offered to raise a thousand men in Flanders, in 1620 he had lent four times as much again, in 1621 nearly two hundred thousand gulden, and in 1623, the year in which he bought the greater number of his new estates, half a million. And these were real gulden, not the debased currency of Prague. Wallenstein was not the man to throw away his money, and every loan put the Emperor deeper into his debt, a debt for which when the time came he would exact every farthing of interest, in favour if not in money. Ferdinand's obligations to Maximilian of Bavaria were based at least on a diplomatic treaty; these private obligations were based on nothing but a business agreement, and Wallenstein had a harder head for a deal than Ferdinand.

Already Wallenstein had a reputation for insolence and pretensions beyond his station. A Czech by birth, speaking the language fluently and allied to many of the leading families, dispossessed and otherwise, Wallenstein was influential if not popular in many sections of society. He now controlled a quarter of the land in Bohemia, was overlord of more than three hundred vassals and held in his hand more power than any of the rebel parties who had once dethroned Ferdinand. The rigid efficiency of his management together with his strict adherence to the Catholic faith were coming to be the dominant

[1] HELBIG, *Der Kaiser Ferdinand und der Herzog zu Friedland, während des Winters* 1633-34. Dresden, 1852, pp. 62-71.
[2] RANKE, *Sämmtliche Werke*, XXIII. *Geschichte Wallensteins*, p. 12.

influences in the consolidation of the country.[1] Ferdinand had to conciliate him or take the risk of further trouble in Bohemia.

Meanwhile, before the end of 1623 Wallenstein had contracted a second marriage, with Isabella von Harrach, a lady who regarded him with the nearest approximation to love which we may suppose it was ever his fate to inspire,[2] and whom he treated as he had his previous wife, with faultless courtesy and respect. The importance of the marriage was not, however, in the personal contentment which it gave to either party, but in the fact that Isabella von Harrach was the daughter of one of Ferdinand's closest advisers. In the same year Wallenstein was created Count of Friedland.[3]

This elevation was an integral part of Ferdinand's policy. In order to curb the demands of the too numerous petty nobility, of his lands, he seized upon every opportunity to replace them by a small aristocracy dependent entirely on himself. The individual power of his nominees might be greater than that of the innumerable gentry whom they superseded, but their influence as a class was conditioned by their dependence on the Crown, and it would be many years before they gained the understanding and support of their local peasantry; their estates were too far scattered, their presence too often required at Prague or Vienna. They were a governing aristocracy bound only to the Crown, not the leaders of a feudal hierarchy. Ferdinand further accentuated this separation of the nobility from the people by introducing foreigners into the conquered land, Austrians, Italians, Germans. So many of the original nobility had been tainted with rebellion that the persecution had stripped the country bare of its natural leaders and made way for the strangers. Italian and French were heard in the streets of Prague, German supplanted Czech as the official language, and on the battered ruins of the medieval Slavonic city grew up the stately palaces, the spacious courtyards, the cool loggias, the opulent baroque churches, which told of Spanish, Italian and Jesuit influence.

---

[1] STIEVE, *Wallenstein bis zur Ubernahme des ersten Generalats. Historische Vierteljahrschrift*, 1899, p. 228.

[2] See her letters in FOERSTER, *Wallenstein als Feldherr und Landesfürst.* Potsdam, 1834, pp. 320 ff.

[3] LÜNIG, XXIII, pp. 1454-7.

As he changed the course and almost the whole nature of Czech culture, damned up its natural stream and forced it into foreign channels, so Ferdinand also changed the religion of his people. Seldom was persecution more effective or reform more far-reaching, for if the Emperor and his advisers had the courage[1] and the cruelty of their convictions, they had also the wisdom to plant again where they destroyed and to salve the scars they inflicted with balm from the same source.

Religion in Bohemia, even the Catholic religion, was closely connected with national feeling. The Utraquist King, George of Podiebrad, and the Utraquist leader, Zizka, were the two heroes of popular imagination, and among the Catholics the favourite saint was the heroic Duke Wenceslas, the 'good King Wenceslas' of the carol, a prince who had been canonized not by the Vatican but by the common devotion of his people. Times out of mind religious services had been held in Czech, even among the most scrupulous adherents to the old faith. The bringing of Bohemia into line with the rest of Catholic Europe entailed therefore the eradication of age-old tradition and a direct attack on Czech nationality itself. Had Ferdinand been a less devout man than in fact he was, he must have seen the importance of carrying through this reform. As it was he had his personal convictions to support him, and doubtless imagined that he was doing as well for the souls of his subjects as he was for the stability of his own government.

This double conviction gave him the strength of mind to sweep aside the protests of the more cautious Liechtenstein and give whole-hearted approval to the ruthless thoroughness of Cardinal Carafa. Liechtenstein would have spared all but the Calvinists, because he feared the intervention of John George of Saxony; Carafa, on the other hand, would not permit so superficial a deviation from orthodoxy as the saying of Mass in Czech, even if the safety of the Bohemian Crown itself depended on it.[2] And politically Ferdinand did well to support this extreme view; the cautious politicians of the Empire shook

---

[1] See Ferdinand's indifference to the possibility of Saxon intervention. GOETZ, *Briefe und Akten*, II, ii, pp. 67-70.

[2] D'ELVERT, II, p. 98; CARAFA, p. 151.

their heads and warned him he would drive the Elector of Saxony to arms.[1] Ferdinand knew his Saxony; the Court of Dresden deluged him with written protests, adjured him to remember his past promises, called down the wrath of heaven on his head, overwhelmed him with recriminations, and stirred not a finger to stop him.[2]

A policy of torture and violence had lost the northern Netherlands for ever to the Catholic Church. The same mistake was not made in Bohemia; but civil and economic persecution fastened upon the Protestants like a vice from which the only means of escape was the denial of their faith. The University of Prague was given to the Jesuits in 1623, and education throughout the country placed wholly in the hands of the Church, so that the younger generation imbibed naturally the lessons which their parents were learning in a harder school.[3]

Prague itself presented few difficulties. The Archbishop made conversion the price of pardon for participation in the revolt, and this, acting upon the natural indifference of a religiously divided and cosmopolitan city, brought the greater number of citizens into the Catholic fold within little more than a year.[4] The outlying towns proved more difficult, and towards them sterner measures were used. Taxes and extraordinary levies were demanded from the Protestants, and the billeting of imperialist troops was found to be a particularly effective form of coercion unless, as sometimes happened, the inhabitants got wind of their coming, burned their houses and fled to the woods with all that they could carry.[5] Otherwise the exactions and disorders of the troops would wear down the resistance of the people in a few months. Tabor, the stronghold of Zizka, was entirely reconverted before Easter 1623; Komotau, after bearing heavy contributions for three years, broke down at a threat of occupation; at Kuttenberg the miners, a hardy and obstinate people, bore a contribution three times as large as the normal taxes for the whole of the rest of Bohemia, and suffered for three years under the quartering of troops until the greater number

---

[1] GOETZ, *Briefe und Akten*, II, i, pp. 67 ff.
[2] LUNDORP, II, pp. 631, 633.
[3] GINDELY, *Geschichte der Gegenreformation*, p. 246.
[4] Ibid., p. 245.   [5] Ibid., p. 255; HURTER, *Ferdinand II*, x, p. 163.

of the population drifted away and the mines fell into disuse through lack of workers.[1] The Catholic nobility assisted in the conversion of their villagers; the tyrannical Count Kolowrat, it was said, drove his peasants to church with blows;[2] at Gitschin, Wallenstein founded a Jesuit school to which he compelled his serfs to send their children. He built a church copied from Santiago de Compostela, and followed this up by suggesting that the duchy of Friedland be converted into a bishopric.[3] The idea was set aside by the imperial court, where Wallenstein was thought to be powerful enough without having a pocket bishopric in his control.

No measures which could serve to discourage the national as well as the heretical spirit of the Bohemians were neglected. On John Hus's Day, hitherto a national holiday, the churches were closed; the statue of George of Podiebrad in the Prague market-place was destroyed, and the sculptured chalice, the Bohemian symbol of reform, was erased from the façades of innumerable churches.[4] Ferdinand also procured the canonization of John of Nepomuk, a Czech priest who had been murdered by Wenceslas IV for refusing to reveal the secrets of the confessional. The move was ingenious, for the new Saint's life-story cast a slur on the forerunners of the Hapsburg on the Bohemian throne, and among the younger generation the popularity of Nepomuk soon outstripped that of the remote Saint Wenceslas.

The chief hindrance to the conversion of Bohemia was the lack of priests for so immense a task. The Jesuits poured their crusaders into the country but could never fill the breach made by the removal of Calvinist, Lutheran and Utraquist pastors; in many cases easygoing Protestant ministers agreed to become Catholic in order to keep their cure, and it was years before the irregularities arising out of this practice could be put down. The pastors were commanded to send away their wives; many made no effort to obey this order, while others merely called their wives 'housekeepers' and continued to live with them, to the great scandal of the neighbourhood. In one case a

[1] GINDELY, *Geschichte der Gegenreformation*, pp. 221 ff.
[2] HURTER, *Ferdinand II*, x, p. 162.
[3] ERNSTBERGER, p. 88; RANKE, *Geschichte Wallensteins*, p. 17.
[4] CARAFA, pp. 251-2.

Utraquist vicar persistently said he was a Catholic when interrogated, but continued to preach the tenets of the Utraquist heresy and to administer the sacrament in both kinds.[1] Carafa could fulminate in vain against such conduct; time alone and the growth of a native priesthood would ultimately cure the evil.[2] In remote districts Protestantism persisted openly for at least another generation and died hard or sometimes not at all, living on as a secret tradition among the people.[3]

The conversion of Bohemia completed its political subjection and stilled for ever the factious religious quarrels which had disturbed the country for a century past; but the forcible restoration of Church lands completed its economic ruin. The second and the third Estates of the Bohemian parliament, the small gentry and the merchants, declined. Ferdinand, after restoring the clergy to the place in the Estates which they had forfeited at the Reformation, was able to continue the appearance of representative government, in the certainty that it would mean government by his own Church and his own higher aristocracy.[4]

In Moravia, where Cardinal Dietrichstein had enlisted the help of both Jesuits and Capuchins, the conversion was equally rapid and successful. The peasantry clung less firmly to their religion than in Bohemia, and after the Protestant nobility had been sufficiently penalized and the Anabaptists expelled from the country, the Church met with little further oppposition.[5]

Silesia and Austria received slightly better treatment than Moravia and Bohemia. Silesia had been promised religious freedom by the Elector of Saxony when he reconquered it for Ferdinand, and here at least Ferdinand kept his word. Nevertheless, he insisted on the unconditional restoration of all Church land and flooded the country with Jesuit missionaries. At the same time he gradually suppressed the liberties of the Silesian

[1] GINDELY, *Geschichte der Gegenreformation*, pp. 195 ff.

[2] See also CARAFA, *Germania Sacra Restaurata*, pp. 283 ff.

[3] KRÖSS, *Zur Geschichte der Katholischen Generalreformation in Böhmen unter Ferdinand III. Zeitschrift für Katholische Theologie*, 1916, p. 772.

[4] GINDELY, *Geschichte der Gegenreformation*, p. 475 f.; CARAFA, *Germania Sacra Restaurata*, I, p. 162.

[5] *Bericht über die Diöcese Olmütz durch den Kardinal Franz von Dietrichstein, von* B. DUDIK. *Archiv für Oesterreichische Geschichte*, XLII, p. 223; WOLNY, *Die Wiedertaüfer in Mähren. Archiv für Oesterreichische Geschichte*, v, pp. 124-5; D'ELVERT, I, pp. 147, 229, 282.

Estates; he limited the right of argument and protest so drastic-ally that one delegate at length bitterly remarked that he could have spared himself the trouble of coming to Breslau, for it was cheaper to say 'yes' at home.

In Austria Protestant pastors and schoolmasters were exiled and the exercise of the Reformed religion was only permitted to certain privileged nobility. As late as 1628 Carafa complained that the pastors were still practising their 'abominations' in private houses under cover of these guarantees,[1] and there was no doubt that Ferdinand would have been glad of any excuse to withdraw them.

Hungary alone escaped with religious liberty and political privileges intact. With so dangerous a protector as Bethlen Gabor across the border, the Hungarians could be certain of preferential treatment. The barrier land between Europe and the Turk, Hungary was too precious to be roughly used, and kept its solitary flag of liberty firmly planted on the outer edge of the Hapsburg Empire.

At the same time Ferdinand altered the traditional con-stitution of the Hapsburg dominions, replacing the old idea of a family confederation by a system of primogeniture in his own house. The Archdukes of a previous generation had died without issue, leaving Ferdinand and his brother Leopold as the sole representatives of the Austrian branch. Ferdinand, but for Leopold's protests, would have united the whole southern block of land from Tyrol to Hungary under a single head, making one monarchy. The younger Archduke, with a fore-sight which was not altogether prompted by personal jealousy, dissuaded him from an act which could only irritate the German princes. Ferdinand compromised. His brother and his brother's heirs were to have the county of Tyrol, while Austria, Hungary, Styria, Carinthia, Carniola, Bohemia, Moravia and Silesia were to pass as a whole to his own eldest son and continue so in the direct line. To accentuate the solidarity of this block of land, he reorganized the imperial administration, centralized the postal system and even made some impression on the hitherto confused and divided finances of the hereditary lands.

---

[1] LUNDORP, III, p. 770 f.; CARAFA, *Germania Sacra Restaurata*, I, pp. 225, 288.

Gradually, too, he began to divide the state business of these provinces from that of the Empire.[1] His intention was that this Austrian centre should be a nucleus for the revivified German Empire. The progress of events altered the effect of his plan. He was to be the creator of the Austrian, not the restorer of the Holy Roman Empire.

This creation is Ferdinand's greatest, perhaps his only, claim to the gratitude or condemnation of posterity; on the whole, where he has had recognition for his act, he has received little thanks for it. To the German nationalist he is the man who confirmed that fissure between Austria and the north which they once so bitterly lamented. They forget that Ferdinand never meant that it should be so, and it was the unwillingness and separatism of the Protestant north which caused his dream of a united Empire to fail. To the Czech, Hungarian and southern Slav nationalists his name can only be that of a tyrant and oppressor, and they forget that, whatever the unrelenting despotism of his government, he gave unity and order where there had been none before.

It is not easy, it is probably impossible, to judge the religious issue, from which all others depended, with an unbiassed mind. It was a period of natural and bitter prejudice, and inevitably a period, for Bohemia at least, of intense unrest, misery, heart-sickening exile, poverty, change and recrimination. It was not a period from which any sane and balanced evidence could be left to after ages. The exiles who reached the shelter of Protestant lands salved their sick hearts with reports of outrages which, founded on fact, were swollen by the vengeful wretchedness of the defeated. The imperial soldiery were oppressive and brutal; life and property, women and children were not sacred to them. The harsh mandates of the government and a gratifying sense of their own righteousness gave them a licence which they used to the uttermost. There is a fundamental truth in the horrors which crowd the pages of the *Historia Persecutionum* compiled by the exiles, overdrawn as are the details, crude as are the colours. Yet the new government and the new religion were neither of them unpopular when the 'storm had passed. The people

[1] See BIDERMANN, *Geschichte des Oesterreichischen Gesammtstaatsidee.* Innsbruck, 1867, I, pp. 27-36.

defended the one and upheld the other a bare generation later against the onrush of the 'liberating' Swedes.

Ferdinand must be judged neither by the means he used — for of these there is no untainted evidence — nor by the end he achieved, for it was different from the one he sought. As the creator of the Austrian Empire, his reputation rests on an unstable thing which failed to withstand the explosive forces of liberal nationalism in the nineteenth century and illiberal nationalism in the twentieth. As the last Emperor who made a sustained effort to unite central Europe, he deserves more recognition from later ages than he has gained. The tragedy was that he not only failed to complete his work, but left behind him something which by its very incompleteness fatally retarded the national development of Germany.

VI

That Ferdinand's project of reorganization stretched beyond the frontiers of the Hapsburg states was made clear by the reckless redistribution of land which he initiated at the same time within the Empire. The Margrave of Baden-Durlach was forcibly dispossessed of part of his lands. John George was confirmed in his tenure of Lusatia, a colossal bribe which must stifle his constitutional objections for some time to come. The loyal Landgrave of Hesse-Darmstadt was rewarded with part of the lands of his less loyal cousin Maurice of Hesse-Cassel. He was also given a piece of the Rhenish Palatinate, probably as a counter-weight to Maximilian of Bavaria, who was gaining more prestige than Ferdinand wished him to have by converting that country.[1] Maximilian's monopoly was further infringed when Ferdinand gave the Bishop of Speier licence to seize any lands on the Rhine which he regarded as having originally belonged to his diocese.

This was the first clear indication that Ferdinand intended to restore the Church to the position which it had held at the Peace of Augsburg.

In the secularized bishoprics of Halberstadt and Osnabrück there was uncomfortable speculation, for Christian of Brunswick,

[1] GOETZ, *Briefe und Akten*, II, i, p. 568; *Schicksale Heidelbergs*, pp. 182-4.

the administrator of Halberstadt, had been in open arms against the Emperor, and the administrator of Osnabrück died in April 1623. The death of one, the possible deposition of the other, left each of these sees open to a Catholic appointment. Ferdinand intended his second son, the fair-haired little Archduke Leopold, for the Church; his installation in the see of Halberstadt or Osnabrück would carry the Counter-Reformation and the Hapsburg dynasty a long step farther towards the control of all Germany.

Ferdinand, however, was not the only father with sons destined for the Church. The Elector of Saxony was interested in Halberstadt, Maximilian of Bavaria in Osnabrück, where he would have liked to establish one of his family. [1] But Osnabrück was coveted no less ardently by the King of Denmark for his younger son Frederick, an ambition far more dangerous to the Hapsburg than the vague schemes of Bavaria or Saxony. Even if the bishopric could not be seized for the dynasty, it must not be allowed to fall into the control of so active and powerful a Protestant prince as Denmark, himself an ally of the United Provinces and uncle to Elizabeth of Bohemia.

To combat these new Hapsburg claims, the Elector of Brandenburg vainly urged John George to found a new Protestant Union. A lesser prince, William of Saxe-Weimar, had founded a party grandly known as the 'Alliance of Patriots of all Classes', whose object was to secure a renewed guarantee for the Protestant lands within the Empire and to restore Frederick to the Palatinate. As it had almost no resources this alliance was unlikely to be effective. Throughout the year 1623 the defenders of the German Liberties and the Protestant Cause continued to have their headquarters at Frederick of Bohemia's overcrowded house in The Hague.

This year the exile's negotiations covered Europe from the Bosphorus to the White Sea, and a plan was made for the total destruction of the Hapsburg dynasty, in which Turks, Russians, Danes, Swedes, Venetians, English and French were each to play their part. There were to be simultaneous risings in Hungary, Bohemia, Moravia, Silesia and Austria. The Sultan was to be bribed by the offer of Hungary and Bohemia as fiefs

[1] GOETZ, *Briefe und Akten*, II, i, pp. 124-5.

if he would establish a Protestant king there. The Tsar was to harry Poland while the united forces of the Danes, Swedes, English and Dutch were to invade North Germany, where Anhalt, secretly returned to Frederick's service, was to raise native troops with money found in Holland. Mansfeld and Christian of Brunswick were to attack the northern bishoprics and thence carry the war south into Bavaria. For his reward Mansfeld was to have the Rhenish fief of Hagenau and a part of Hungary. Saxony and Brandenburg were to be bought by the promise of Cleves-Jülich to divide between them. The French were to seize the Val Telline with the help of the Venetians and the Duke of Savoy.[1]

Unhappily for the projectors of Frederick's policy, the King of England, wishing to negotiate a marriage between the Spanish Infanta and the Prince of Wales, guaranteed his good faith by withdrawing the English garrison from Frederick's last stronghold in Germany, the fortress of Frankenthal. At the same time he urged Frederick to lay down arms and permit his eldest son to be betrothed either to a daughter of the Emperor or to a niece of Maximilian.[2] The Kings of Sweden and Denmark would not agree to fight side by side, the government of France was a prey to internal disturbances, the Prince of Orange was fully occupied defending his own borders and could not even afford to continue paying subsidies for the winning back of the Rhine. All that came of the great scheme was an attack on Hungary by Bethlen Gabor and the advance of Christian of Brunswick into the Lower Saxon Circle.

The Lower Saxon Circle was that division of the Empire, lying for the most part between the Weser and the Elbe, in which was situated the bishopric of Halberstadt, already earmarked by Ferdinand for his son Leopold. This district was marked out by Frederick's councillors as the base for their attack on the Emperor. When, inevitably, some of their letters fell into Ferdinand's hands, he joyfully seized the opportunity of carrying the war northwards and urged Maximilian to send his forces at once to the threatened area.

---

[1] LUNDORP, II, pp. 728-9.
[2] RUSDORF, *Mémoires et négociations secrètes*, Leipzig, 1789, I, *passim;* GOETZ, II, i, *passim.*

The quaking rulers of the Lower Saxon Circle thus shortly found themselves between Christian of Brunswick, exhorting them to rise in defence of the German Liberties, on the one hand, and Tilly at the head of the Bavarian and League army demanding a guarantee of their neutrality, on the other.[1] Neutral the princes and people were and wished to remain, but they had no choice: Christian forcibly established himself as 'protector' of the lands of his elder brother, the Duke of Brunswick-Wolfenbüttel, marched unhindered across the country and sent for Mansfeld to join him. Tilly demanded the expulsion of Christian, a request which the Estates of the Circle would most willingly have obeyed had they had the means to do so.

For a brief while they considered raising an army in their own defence but the plan was hardly feasible. In the end they chose what seemed to be the lesser of two evils and threw themselves on the mercy of Tilly and the Emperor. His was the larger army and the more likely to win in the long run. On July 13th, 1623, Tilly crossed their border and three days later sent an ultimatum to Christian, excluding him from all hope of imperial pardon unless he withdrew immediately. Rejecting the offer with several expressive oaths, the prince sent again to Mansfeld suggesting a joint attack on Tilly, and to the Prince of Orange offering to enter his service in the Netherlands. He then proclaimed his abdication of the bishopric of Halberstadt in favour of a son of the King of Denmark.[2] After which he had the drums beaten to call in his straggling hordes, packed up the loot and set off, fifteen thousand strong, for the Netherlands, leaving the country bare to Tilly's advance, and the Cathedral Chapter of Halberstadt a prey to Dane or Emperor.

The retreat of the 'mad Halberstädter', as he was now generally called, was by no means that of a defeated man. He still intended to join with Mansfeld for a conclusive trial of arms against Tilly. In his over-confidence he miscalculated the actions of Mansfeld, who had found secure quarters in the bishopric of Münster and was not sufficiently impressed by Christian's military judgment to exchange his present safety for a fruitless and expensive campaign.

[1] LUNDORP, II, pp. 758-9.   [2] LÜNIG, V, iv, p. 108.

Christian crossed the Weser at Bodenwerder on July 27th, 1623, Tilly in pursuit a few miles farther south at Corvey on the 30th, but the prince lost his advantage by loitering on the border of the bishopric of Münster for three days, waiting for Mansfeld who never came, before striking out once more, this time in full flight, with Tilly half a day's march behind, for the Dutch border. He crossed the Ems with Tilly close behind him at Greven, and in the early morning of August 6th, 1623, his rearguard fought off a sudden charge from the van of Tilly's army. Less than ten miles from the Dutch border and safety, Christian was compelled to turn and give battle to the pursuing forces which, under better control and less burdened with plunder, gained on him with every moment. Outside the little village of Stadtlohn he seized the advantage of a small hill overlooking the road and protected from flank attack on two sides by a bog, and here wheeled round to face the enemy, having barely time to marshal his troops in the traditional order and throw up emplacements for his guns before his pursuers were upon him. It was about midday on August 6th, a Sunday and the feast of the Transfiguration. Tilly, who took the holy season as a good omen for his pious cause, was astonished and horrified to see on Christian's banners the device, 'All for God and for Her'. There could surely be no victory for people so blasphemous as to put the name of 'a sack of mortal corruption' — so inelegantly did he refer to the beautiful Queen of Bohemia — on one banner with that of their Creator.

For reasons that were physical rather than spiritual, Tilly had an easy victory. Christian had the advantage of the ground, but Tilly had the greater numbers and used his forces with more discretion, first only employing his vanguard and gradually reinforcing it as the rest of his army and the artillery came up. Under the persistent and increasingly heavy attacks the cavalry on the wings of Christian's army began to give way; there was too little room for skirmishing on the hill-side, and seventeenth-century horse were notoriously bad at defensive tactics. The flight of the cavalry made the resistance of the foot useless against overwhelming odds, and Christian's troops deserted the hill-top in disorderly flight, only to find themselves cut off by the bog behind them. Most of the cavalry got through, but the infantry, the wagons and the artillery stuck fast. Of the whole army six thousand were killed and four thousand taken, among them fifty of Christian's leading officers and his ally, that Duke William of Saxe-Weimar whose 'Alliance of Patriots of all Classes' was to have saved the German Liberties from Ferdinand. More important was the seizure of sixteen cannon and most of the ammunition; in the flight one of the powder wagons had exploded, adding a further disorder to the terror-stricken rabble. Christian crossed the Dutch border late that night with a bare two thousand men and neither artillery nor supplies.[1]

The defeat was so decisive that even the mad Halberstädter's spirits were damped. He gave way to sullen rage and was with difficulty prevented from shooting one of his colonels, whom he chose as the scapegoat for his misfortune. The actions of his victor contrasted all too strikingly with his own, for Tilly in his report of the battle gave the glory to Heaven and to his subordinates.[2]

The shattering defeat of Stadtlohn brought Frederick's castles toppling down from the clouds. The year's endeavours had ended once more, as they so often ended for him, in tragical disaster; instead of a reconquered Bohemia and a restored Palatinate, he had only an additional mouth to feed at his poverty-stricken table in The Hague, for Christian had lost so much of his fortune in the flight that he could no longer afford a household of his own.[3]

Three weeks after Stadtlohn, Frederick yielded to the persuasions of the English King, temporarily abandoned his diplomatic schemes and signed an armistice with the Emperor.[4]

VII

The armistice had been made with a total disregard for Mansfeld. All this while he had maintained his army as best he could in East Friesland, to the impotent annoyance of the Dutch

---

[1] LUNDORP, II, pp. 768 ff.; GINDELY, *Beiträge zur Geschichte des dreissigjährigen Krieges. Archiv für Oesterreichische Geschichte*, LXXXIX, p. 22.

[2] AITZEMA, I, p. 231; HURTER, *Ferdinand II*, ix, p. 295; LUNDORF, II, 769.

[3] OPEL, *Elisabeth Stuart*, p. 323.   [4] RUSDORF, I, p. 117.

government. 'The Kings of France, England and Denmark gave him nothing, the King of Bohemia had nothing'[1] — Mansfeld's only means of existence was by plunder, and his men had stripped the province bare and committed damage reckoned at about ten million talers. In the neighbourhood of his quarters nearly four-fifths of the inhabitants had fled to evade paying tribute to the army, a crime which Mansfeld punished by tearing down their deserted homes, so that five out of every six houses were alleged to be in ruins. Law and order had ceased to exist, the civil population defended itself as it could, the men by ambushing and slaughtering the soldiers, the women, in some cases, by destroying themselves. The troops, in circumstances which daily grew more hopeless, had sunk to less than half their original numbers.[2] To crown these accumulating evils, Tilly's army now appeared on the border, fresh from the victory of Stadtlohn and evidently prepared to make short work of their enemies.

During the early part of the year Mansfeld had lived in hope that the French government would hire him to invade the Val Telline.[3] This scheme never came to fruition and meanwhile he was still in arms, without that principality for which he had hoped, without pay, under the ban of the Empire and with his chances of pardon daily dwindling. Tilly's advance prompted him to action. Staking all on the reputation which, despite the disasters of his last years, still clung to his name, he abandoned his army to its fate, left East Friesland and set out alone to canvass the political powers of northern Europe. On April 24th, 1624, he arrived in London, where the Protestant populace acclaimed him as the champion of their Princess, and the Prince of Wales lodged him in the very rooms which had been destined for his Spanish bride.[4]

So experienced a mercenary as Mansfeld did not act without good knowledge of European diplomacy. He knew that there were two powers, France and, in a lesser degree, England, whose decision to act, belated though it was, might yet be decisive for the Protestant Cause. By the spring of 1624 a

[1] AITZEMA, I, p. 131.   [2] GINDELY, *Beiträge*, pp. 28-9.
[3] REIFFERSCHEID, p. 153.
[4] *Calendar of State Papers. Domestic Series*, 1623-1625, p. 223; GINDELY, *Beiträge*, p. 120.

change had come over the diplomacy of these two hitherto timorous governments; of this change he hastened to take advantage.

King James's plan for the Spanish marriage of his son and the imperial marriage of his grandson, Frederick's eldest child, had fallen to the ground. At the very time when Frederick, worn out with the arguments of his father-in-law and crushed by the defeat of Stadtlohn, had agreed to countenance the scheme, James's policy had broken down. His son and his favourite Buckingham, indignant at their reception in Spain whither they had gone to hasten the negotiations, returned to England and declared themselves unwilling to participate further in the unholy alliance. The London mob had been demanding war with Spain for months past, and the prince and Buckingham were for taking the tide of popular feeling at the flood. The two governments drifted rapidly towards the final breach. In December 1623, James was already toying with the idea of an alliance with the King of Denmark and Bethlen Gabor on behalf of his son-in-law. In January 1624, he was about to approach the United Provinces, and when Mansfeld came to London the King gave him permission to recruit twelve thousand men at England's expense.[1]

A change of policy made itself felt at the same time in France, where a minister had newly arisen who had something more to recommend him to the King than the excellent knowledge of falconry which had distinguished Luynes. Armand Jean du Plessis, Bishop of Luçon and Cardinal de Richelieu, was slowly acquiring that control over the King's actions which only death was to dissolve. The son of a noble but not a wealthy family of Poitou, he had been intended first for a soldier, but a change in the family plans had caused him to be hastily ordained, that he might succeed to the little bishopric of Luçon, long the perquisite of the family. Richelieu's ambitions had never been confined to the narrow boundaries of his see, although he fulfilled his episcopal duties, as he did everything in his intricate career, with scrupulous thoroughness. Attaching himself at first to the party of the Queen-mother, he had gained his first ministerial appointment

[1] RUSDORF, I, p. 287.

in 1616; since then he had contrived to maintain, except for a short interlude, his foothold on the slippery ground of advancement. He had not risen without abandoning his old friends and protectors, without arousing many bitter enemies — the Queen-mother the bitterest of all — but in the larger field of politics his ambitions were impersonal and he had used intrigue as the means to a greater end. He had the organizer's careful ability, the percipience of the statesman and that unrestrained ambition to serve his country regardless of domestic happiness which is often the accompaniment of political genius. The national egoism of the ardent patriot mingled in him with a belief in monarchy as the essential form of government for France. France, he said, had two diseases — heresy and liberty. Sooner or later he and his King would cure them both. She had one imminent and dangerous enemy: the house of Hapsburg, whose power and influence encompassed her on the landward frontiers, on the Pyrenees, on the Alps, on the Rhine, in Flanders. His ambition was to see a united France freed from this perpetual menace, assuming her natural part as the protectress of European peace. But meanwhile he must unify and defend this exposed country of industrious and unarmed peasants, shut in between the Hapsburg lands and the sea. The guiding motive of Richelieu's policy was not aggression but defence.[1]

The Cardinal was barely forty in 1624, a thin, dark man with a commanding presence and cultured manners. His interests did not end with politics: he had time to be a connoisseur in jewels, antiques, works of art and music; the theatre was above all his passion and he held himself inferior to none as a critic. He even fancied himself as a poet. 'In what do you think I take the greatest pleasure?' he once asked a friend who tactfully answered, 'In creating the happiness of France.' 'Not at all,' countered Richelieu, 'in writing verses.'[2] Doubtless he practised an innocent self-deception, for when his fortune momentarily forsook him he had not taken kindly to the prospect of turning verses at Luçon for the rest of his life.

[1] W. MOMMSEN, Richelieu als Staatsmann. Historische Zeitschrift, CXXVII, p. 230 f.

[2] G. HANOTAUX et LE DUC DE LA FORCE, Histoire de Richelieu. Revue des Deux Mondes. Juillet 1934, p. 97.

Nevertheless, the pretence in itself indicated the peculiar nature of his generous and civilized genius. However much he gave himself up to the service of the State, however much he appeared to make the monarchy his God, and subject all to that overwhelming deity, he had too clear a sense of proportion to assume that man was made for the State, not the State for man. He was a despot, but never a totalitarian.

Too wise to rely wholly on his own judgment, Richelieu learnt early to assume a quiet confidence that he was far from feeling. Few men have faced more exacting problems with less help for so long a period. The only confidant in whom he entirely trusted was his confessor, François le Clerc du Tremblay, known in religion as Father Joseph, and popularly throughout France as 'l'Eminence grise'. This ardent Capuchin monk, who had devoted his whole life to the propagation of the faith, saw in Richelieu the possible leader of a united Catholic power that would not subordinate the interests of religion to those of a dynasty. Being a Capuchin and not a Jesuit, Father Joseph shared the papal suspicion of the motives of the Hapsburg Crusade. Under his influence the religious element, one might almost say the Crusading element, in Richelieu's policy was never altogether submerged in the political.

The Cardinal had been forced to remain in the background during the ineffective ministry of Luynes and his incompetent successor, Sillery, whose fall in January 1624 made the way at last clear. Meanwhile Louis XIII had grown from an oppressed neurotic adolescent, ready to fall under the control of the first affectionate and flattering friend, into a secretive, moody, intelligent, critical young man with an acute judgment and a will of his own. His reign, and Richelieu's, was beginning.

With the alteration in the politics of France and England the deadlock was at an end. All once again began to move towards an assault on the Hapsburg position. No sooner had the Spanish marriage fallen through than Richelieu suggested Madame Henriette, sister of the French King, as a bride for the Prince of Wales, at the same time covering this Protestant alliance from criticism at home by demanding guarantees of protection for Catholics in England.[1] The changed policy of

---

[1] RICHELIEU, *Mémoires*, IV, pp. 46-7.

the French government had immediate repercussions, not only in England but farther north. The King of Sweden turned his attention suddenly towards Germany, recklessly lengthened an existing truce with the Poles in order to have his hands free, and offered to sink his differences of opinion with the King of Denmark.[1] Christian of Denmark seemed amenable; his eyes also were fixed on Germany, where he hoped to secure the bishoprics of Halberstadt and Osnabrück for his son and had, in preparation, already offered his 'protection' to the Estates of the Lower Saxon Circle. The offer had been welcomed by the wretched princes, powerless as they were against the advancing Catholic army, but when they innocently appealed to the Emperor to confirm the King of Denmark's son as Bishop of Halberstadt, he responded indirectly but effectively by ordering Tilly to make his winter quarters in the Circle. Faced by so clear an indication that his son should only retain Halberstadt over Ferdinand's, or at least Tilly's, dead body, Christian of Denmark enthusiastically accepted an offer of French subsidies and prepared to enter the lists for the German Liberties, the Protestant Cause, and his son's bishopric.

Richelieu did not intend to confine the war to north Germany. The House of Hapsburg was his enemy, but he feared Spain rather than Austria, and his object was to hold Austria in check in Germany while the main onslaught was upon Spain on the Rhine and in North Italy. Savoy and Venice had been approached even before he came to power, and he continued in that friendship. Above all, the United Provinces must enter the coalition. The exiled Frederick and Elizabeth, allied by marriage to almost all the Protestant rulers of Europe, became the central link of the chain which was to draw England, Denmark, Sweden and the Provinces into one grand alliance with Savoy, Venice and France. Bethlen Gabor himself was to play his part in attacking Hungary, so that the Hapsburg power should be attacked at once on flank and front and rear. Richelieu had given substance at last to those airy schemes which Frederick and his ministers had evolved vainly year by year.

The issue was still far from simple. 'I mean to make use of

[1] RYDBERG OCH HALLENDORF. *Sverges Traktater*, Stockholm, 1877, v, i, pp. 317 f.; 321 f.

all religions to compass my ends', the King of England had said,[1] but if it seemed as easy as that to James I, it was not so easy for Richelieu. He was embracing the Protestant Cause in Europe in order to break the Hapsburg dynasty, but whatever cynical indifference to religion reigned among the nobility and in diplomatic circles, the Cardinal had to reckon with the still profoundly devout French bourgeoisie, and he could not do anything too extravagantly unorthodox, for fear of shaking the stability of the monarchy. Happily for Richelieu, an election in Rome, completed on the very day of the defeat at Stadtlohn, had placed Cardinal Barbarini in the chair of St. Peter. Urban VIII, as he was now known throughout Christendom, was a comparatively young and vigorous man. A keen politician, he had for many years acted as legate in France, had held Louis XIII himself at the font and admitted on this account to a peculiar affection for him. Urban VIII was to reign twenty-one years, a time almost exactly coeval with the ministry of Richelieu. Without him the Cardinal's policy would have been, if not impossible, at least very much more difficult of realization, for Urban VIII, although he sincerely desired the peace of Christendom, regarded the Hapsburg dynasty as a perpetual menace. He wanted peace in Europe, but if that could not be, he would stretch out the hand of blessing over those who curbed Hapsburg aggression, so that the Catholics of France could sleep contented while their taxes were poured out in subsidies to Dutch and German heretics.

The excuse, and it was a good one, was that the inextricable combination of temporal and spiritual interests which characterized Hapsburg policy was harmful to the Church. In spite of the conversion of Bohemia, in spite of the rout of Calvinism in Germany, there was much to be said for the view held by Richelieu and the Pope. It was a view equally and fanatically held by the Capuchins. If both the Hapsburg Crusade and the Papal and French opposition arose from non-religious roots, both could be justified with equal fervour on purely spiritual grounds. The tragedy for the Catholic Church was that neither party could win a complete victory over the other.

With European dangers closing in upon him, Ferdinand

[1] *Calendar of State Papers. Domestic Series*, 1623-1625, p. 195.

must make redoubled efforts to establish his position in Germany. The weak Spanish monarchy, on whose account alone he was to be attacked, did not help him. Philip IV, the head of the dynasty and the master of the Peruvian mines, was still wholly under the control of the erratic Olivarez. The favourite, after persistently sacrificing Ferdinand to his own plan for an English alliance, had lamentably failed to complete that alliance itself. Lastly, in Flanders the Archduchess Isabella, starved of financial support by the incompetent government at Madrid, was concentrating all her forces on the comparatively weak defences of the Dutch; her only salvation lay in the reconquest of the rebellious United Provinces and she had no help to spare for Ferdinand.

The position throughout 1624 was pregnant with danger for Austria. In the early summer it was believed that Bohemia and Moravia, too hard-pressed by confiscations and penalties, were about to revolt[1] — the alarm was false but none the less dismaying while it lasted. In the summer a French agent visited the Elector of Brandenburg, and at Vienna doubts were entertained as to his loyalty, doubts which appeared to be confirmed when his sister was given in marriage to Bethlen Gabor.

The Elector of Saxony was wavering. In dudgeon since the elevation of Maximilian, he would not for many months be pacified, and when he was at length reconciled to the new Elector, it was in circumstances not calculated to reassure Ferdinand. The President of the Electoral College, the Elector of Mainz, asked John George to meet him at Schleusingen in July 1624, where in the intervals of hunting and carousing the wily bishop showed him a newly printed selection of documents relating to the Bohemian affair, which had been discovered in the castle of Heidelberg. Better propaganda for Maximilian against Frederick could not have been found, for here lay revealed to all the world the secret machinations behind the Bohemian revolt. John George was shocked to the depths of his honest soul. Mainz pressed home the advantage, showed the anxious prince how the King of Spain stood behind the Emperor, the Prince of Orange and perhaps the

[1] GOETZ, *Briefe und Akten*, II, i, p. 549.

King of France behind Frederick, and that the only hope for German integrity lay in friendly union between the Electors of Bavaria and Saxony, honest native princes, opposed to foreign factions. Over-persuaded, John George recognized Maximilian's Electorate, not to please Ferdinand, but to further the formation of the constitutional opposition to him.[1]

Had the moment come for that nebulous centre party to take form at last, for the German princes to assert themselves against Hapsburg and Bourbon? The Electors of Saxony and Mainz fought in vain against the current which was dragging their fellows towards French and Dutch alliances. George William of Brandenburg, seduced by French and Swedish councils, refused to recognize Maximilian's Electorate and signed a provisional treaty with the United Provinces. Maximilian of Bavaria himself, on whose army both the Electors of Saxony and Mainz counted to give reality to their constitutional party, had for the last eighteen months steered a doubtful course. He hated and suspected the Spanish monarchy and had proved it openly by denying to the agents of the Archduchess Isabella any influence in, or even access to, those lands on the Rhine occupied by his own troops under Tilly.[2] Moreover, after the battle of Stadtlohn he had forbidden Tilly to pursue the defeated army into the United Provinces.[3] Under Capuchin influence, he had next attempted a *rapprochement* with France; one of the monks, who acted as his unofficial ambassadors, cherished the hope of uniting Europe for a crusade,[4] and a scheme was breathed for the formation of an international Catholic League consisting of France, Venice, Savoy and Bavaria.[5] Maximilian's plan to secure the friendship of France foundered on the Palatinate question: the King of England was arranging a French marriage for his son to further the restitution of his son-in-law on the Rhine, and Richelieu could not stretch out his right hand to the kin of the dispossessed and his left hand to the usurper simultaneously. In vain Maximilian attempted to settle the difference by suggesting

<hr />

[1] GOETZ, *Briefe und Akten*, II, i, pp. 557-67; GINDELY, *Beiträge*, p. 57.
[2] GOETZ, *Briefe und Akten*, II, i, p. 115.
[3] Ibid., II, i, p. 283.
[4] GOETZ, *Pater Hyacinth. Historische Zeitschrift*, CIX, p. 117.
[5] GOETZ, *Briefe und Akten*, II, i, pp. 67, 104, 108.

the marriage of his niece to Frederick's eldest son;[1] the scheme
found little favour and Richelieu rejected his alliance for that
of the English King.

Panic gripped Maximilian; he had information that England,
Denmark, Savoy and Venice were arming; that England,
Denmark and Sweden were tampering with the princes of
north Germany. If this meant danger for the Hapsburg power,
it meant danger too for his ill-gotten titles; his only safety
lay in combating the new champions who had sprung up for
the defeated Frederick, even if in so doing he had to assist the
Hapsburg. In the spring of 1624 he called a meeting of the
Catholic League at Augsburg and persuaded his fellow-
members to strengthen Tilly's army against possible danger.[2]
The move stirred both Olivarez and Richelieu to descend upon
Maximilian; Richelieu, too late in the day, offered friendship.[3]
Olivarez flattered him with praise of the League as Christen-
dom's one bulwark and offered to stand his friend in the
Rhenish Palatinate. Maximilian seemed to waver towards
the Spanish alliance, perhaps for safety, perhaps to frighten the
French. Going back on his constitutionalism yet again, he
openly declared that he would 'live and die for the House of
Austria'.[4]

Vainly the constitutional party fought against the gathering
storm; Saxony and Mainz suggested that a Diet should be
called, or at least an Electoral meeting, to discuss and if
possible to settle the problems of the Empire before Danish,
French and English soldiery flooded in.[5] Without the support
of Maximilian, without his prestige and his money, little could
be done. Intentionally or no, Ferdinand had robbed the constitutional party of its strongest defender when he gave
Maximilian the Electorate of Frederick.

Except for Bavaria, the circle of Richelieu's alliances closed
in about the common enemy. On June 10th, 1624, at
Compiègne, the governments of France and the United

---

[1] RUSDORF, I, pp. 156 ff.
[2] GOETZ, *Briefe und Akten*, II, i, pp. 452-510.
[3] Ibid., II, i, pp. 516 f., 528 f.; FAGNIEZ, *Fancan et Richelieu. Revue Historique*,
CVII, p. 61 f.; WIENS, *Fancan und die fransösische Politik*, 1624-1627. Heidelberg, 1908, pp. 18, 27.
[4] GOETZ, *Briefe und Akten*, II, ii, pp. 19, 23-4, 28, 39, 40.
[5] Ibid., II, i, pp. 620, 635, 642, 651.

Provinces signed a treaty of friendship: the fundamental rival and the chief antagonist of the Hapsburg dynasty were in alliance at last. Five days later England entered the bond; on July 9th the Kings of Sweden and Denmark came to terms; on the 11th France, Savoy and Venice agreed on joint intervention in the Val Telline; on October 23rd the Elector of Brandenburg allied himself with the United Provinces; on November 10th Henrietta of France was betrothed to the Prince of Wales.

Meanwhile the Protestants of the Grisons had risen and defeated Ferdinand's brother, the Archduke Leopold, with heavy loss; before Christmas they seized Tirano and blocked the Val Telline. With the melting snows of spring, 1625, the Duke of Savoy, with French and native troops, descended from his barren dukedom, fell upon Asti and encircled Genoa from the precipitous heights his mountaineers could guard so well.

The vital line was cut. With the Val Telline blocked, with hostile English ships watching the narrow seas, the King of Spain could send bullion to Flanders and Austria neither by sea nor land. It seemed that the contest whose causes lay outside Germany had ended outside Germany, and that Ferdinand who had fastened the prestige of his dynasty on that of the Empire had been wrong. Spinola had seized the Rhine in vain, and the diplomacy of Richelieu had undone the victories of Tilly from the White Hill to Stadtlohn.

But the war had begun in Germany, and in Germany it was to end. Seven years of fighting across a country whose politics were as intricate as those of the Empire left a situation which even Richelieu could not control. There was matter for too much dispute among the north German Bishoprics alone. The situation slipped suddenly out of his hands, and the victories in Italy fixed a milestone but set no limit to the war.

TOWARDS THE BALTIC
1625 — 1628

Legitime certantibus corona — Device of Ferdinand II

CHAPTER V

TOWARDS THE BALTIC

I

THE Val Telline was occupied and the divided members of the Hapsburg Empire in Flanders and Austria were thrown on their own resources, with Mansfeld's army disembarking on the Dutch coast, and the Kings of northern Europe planning a descent on the Baltic shore. The moment had come for the wisdom of Ferdinand's imperial policy to be proven; since bullion could not come from Spain, the Emperor was cast on the loyalty of his own subjects.

In the winter of 1624-25 Albrecht von Wallenstein had been in Vienna, suggesting to the Spanish ambassador that he should recruit an army in their interest for service in Italy.[1] At the catastrophic turn of events in that country, he changed his mind, and on the fall of the Val Telline he repeated the offer to the Emperor himself. He would raise fifty thousand men at his own expense, securing quarters and provisions for them by mere force of arms[2] and demanding their pay alone from the imperial coffers.

Ferdinand dared not refuse. His acceptance would place a dangerous power in the hands of Count Wallenstein, but in his present peril he had no alternative. Maximilian was his only other ally, and while Ferdinand was probably glad to halve his obligations by allowing someone else to put an army in the field, Maximilian himself, in panic at the gathering storm, had urged him to raise troops independently if he could.[3] In the spring of 1625 the Elector of Bavaria saw safety only in arms and was too much afraid for his own possessions to care whose arms they were.

[1] GINDELY, *Waldstein während seines ersten Generalats im Lichte der gleichzeitigen Quellen.* Prague-Vienna, 1886, I, pp. 46 ff.; ZWIEDINECK-SUDENHORST, II, p. 223.
[2] HURTER, *Zur Geschichte Wallenstein*, Schaffhausen, 1855, p. 27.
[3] GOETZ, *Briefe und Akten*, II, ii, pp. 39-40.

Wallenstein's only serious opponent was his rival, the governor of Bohemia, Karl von Liechtenstein, who attempted in vain to wreck the scheme by preferring forty-two charges of financial dishonesty against him.[1] Ferdinand could not pause to consider them. In February 1625 Liechtenstein himself was recalled, and in April Wallenstein was summoned to Vienna.[2] Nevertheless, Ferdinand acted warily, reduced the number of the proffered army from fifty thousand, which would make Wallenstein dangerous, to twenty thousand, which would be enough to meet the immediate crisis, and confined the functions of the general for the time being to the Hapsburg lands alone. If need be, he would use Wallenstein elsewhere later on, but in the meantime he confirmed to Maximilian of Bavaria the dominating control of the operations of war.[3]

While Ferdinand thus used the loyalty of one of his own creatures to help him in Austria, Spinola redoubled his efforts in the Low Countries, trying to bring the Dutch War to a conclusion before the seizure of the Val Telline could tell on his men and his supplies. Hitherto his progress, though slow, had been continuous, and it seemed that his long-planned scheme for wearing down his opponents was all but realized. Bergen-op-Zoom had been preserved from the Spaniards only by the chance intervention of Mansfeld and Christian of Brunswick in 1622; the Rhine was lost, the neighbouring province of Jülich was overrun by Spanish troops, and two savage winters had nipped for the time being the prosperity of the Dutch farmers. The phenomenal frosts of January and February 1624 had been followed by the bursting of dykes and destructive floods which sent crowds of homeless peasants flocking into the towns; bitter winds raced over the country, tearing the thatch off the roofs, while Spinola's disciplined troops, recking nothing of the weather, broke the frontier defences, and the Dutch army, underfed, underpaid, wet and cold, mutinied at Breda; it looked for a moment as though there was nothing left for the Provinces to do but ask for terms.[4] The Dutch rallied in time to stem the invasion, but matters had not greatly altered by the

---

[1] STIEVE, *Wallenstein bis zur Ubernahme des ersten Generalats*, pp. 229-30.

[2] D'ELVERT, III, p. 135; GOETZ, *Briefe und Akten*, II, ii, p. 148.

[3] GINDELY, *Waldstein*, p. 54.

[4] AITZEMA, p. 269.

spring of 1625, when Spinola formed the siege of Breda, the key fortress on the frontier of Brabant which guarded the roads to Utrecht and Amsterdam.

At this time Maurice of Orange died in The Hague. On his deathbed he sent for his younger half-brother, Frederick Henry, the prince who would undoubtedly succeed him in the stadholderate of five provinces and the command of the army. To the Dutch in general this youngest son of William the Silent was still unknown; believed to have sympathies with the defeated party, he had lived in retirement since the *coup d'état* of 1619, anxious above all to avoid forming a party in the State against the elder brother to whom he was devoted. He was over forty; by the standards of his times he was therefore old to assume the reins of government, and he was still un-married.

Maurice's mind during his last illness hovered between his anxiety for the Dutch people and for his own dynasty; he commanded his brother to save Breda and to find a wife. As far as the latter duty went, Frederick Henry was willing enough; it seemed that he had for some time loved a buxom young maid-of-honour of the Queen of Bohemia. Dowerless but for her peerless beauty — so the courtly Venetian ambassador put it [1] — Amalia von Solms was nevertheless welcome to the dying Maurice as the instrument through whom the dynasty should be continued. She was the daughter of a noble German house devoted to the interests of the dispossessed Frederick, and she would bind her husband closely to that Rhenish alliance which was likely to be the only means of breaking Spanish power on the Rhine. The wedding was privately solemnized in The Hague early in April; a few days later Maurice died, and the bridegroom left the capital at the head of an army bound for Breda. [2]

Spinola's outworks proved too strong for the Dutch relieving force to break through. Frederick Henry hoped in vain that Mansfeld would bring up his English troops to the rescue, but James I wished them to be employed rather in north Germany, [3] and they themselves, or such as were left of them after a winter spent without pay and almost without the

[1] Blok, *Relazioni Veneziane.*
[2] See Moser, *Patriotisches Archiv,* XI, pp. 175-206.
[3] Rusdorf, I, p. 485.

necessities of life, took the law into their own hands and deserted wholesale to the Spaniards.[1] Defeated at last by hunger, the garrison of Breda sued for terms, and on June 5th, 1625, marched out with the honours of war after a defence of more than six months. Spinola himself, deeply moved, embraced the Dutch commander before the whole army.[2]

The Hapsburg dynasty could now set off the help of Wallenstein against the help which their enemies might receive from France, the fall of Breda against the seizure of the Val Telline. There remained that dangerous northern coalition, and here too the dynasty had a plan. The possible alliance of Sweden, Denmark, England and the United Provinces left one jealous northern power in the cold, the Hanseatic League. In February 1625 Olivarez dropped hints to the Austrian ambassador in Madrid,[3] and in April the Spanish ambassador at Vienna approached the Emperor with a scheme, by which the Hanseatic League were to be tempted into an alliance with the Hapsburg dynasty by the offer of a fleet to protect them against their rivals, and special trading preferences in the Spanish Indies — so many bribes to make Lübeck, Stralsund, Hamburg, Bremen into naval bases on the Baltic.[4]

Should the towns be unwilling, it was thought that a demonstration of imperial force would persuade them to accept the offer, and in June Wallenstein's military commission was enlarged to cover the whole of the Empire.[5] He had already been as good as his word and stood ready on the Bohemian border with a well-equipped army, with which in the late summer he crossed into Germany and made northwards to join with Tilly. He had recently been elevated to the rank of a count palatine of the Empire, a patent which gave him the right to ennoble others at his discretion. During the summer he tacitly arrogated to himself the title of Duke of Friedland.[6]

With a new imperial army in the field and Breda lost, the situation was becoming untenable for the French in the Val Telline; Richelieu's government had not the resources necessary

[1] AITZEMA, I, p. 405.   [2] Ibid., I, pp. 408, 416.
[3] MESSOW, Die Hansestädte und die Habsbürger Ostseepolitik, p. 11.
[4] GINDELY, Die maritimen Pläne der Habsbürger, Vienna, 1891, pp. 2-3.
[5] HALLWICH, Fünf Bücher zur Geschichte Wallensteins, Leipzig, 1910, III, p. 12.
[6] HURTER, Zur Geschichte Wallensteins, pp. 20-1.

to occupy the valley indefinitely and was still uncertain at home. Palace intrigue or local rebellion might at any moment throw him off his balance, and meanwhile in the north the great arc of his projected alliances was beginning to crack.

The King of Denmark and the King of Sweden burnt with equal ardour to intervene in Germany; both of them deluged Paris and London with their plans of campaign,[1] but each assumed that the other would act under his orders. France, on the whole, favoured the King of Sweden; the English government vacillated, was enthusiastic for the Swedish plan and then, as suddenly, was attracted by the Danish, and tactlessly asked Gustavus Adolphus to sign an alliance giving Christian IV full controlling powers.[2] The rage with which Gustavus heard this demand was not unjustified: he did not trust Christian of Denmark and he feared that, unless he had absolute military control, his armies and money would be exploited for the advantage of others.[3] Virtually he held a pistol to the heads of the English and French governments: he had made a truce with his old enemy the King of Poland, which would end in a few weeks — either he must be given the chief control of operations, or he would resume his war in Poland and leave Germany to take care of itself. The English and French governments remained unmoved, and on June 11th, 1625, Gustavus Adolphus turned his back on the German war and launched a further attack on Sigismund of Poland.[4]

Of all the impressive group of projected allies, only one, the King of Denmark, appeared in the field for the Protestant Cause of Germany in the summer of 1625.

II

Christian IV was not negligible. His misfortune was to reign at the same time as Gustavus of Sweden, so that popular report, dazzled by so brilliant a rival, has given him too small a

[1] RUSDORF, I p. 439 f.; MOSER, *Patriotisches Archiv*, V, p. 107.
[2] RUSDORF, I, pp. 464, 496, 545-9, II, p. 29.
[3] Ibid., I, p. 554 f.; see also MOSER, *Patriotisches Archiv*, V, pp. 159 *seq.*, *passim*.
[4] MOSER, *Patriotisches Archiv*, VI, p. 21.

place in European history. At the time of his intervention in Germany he was forty-eight years old and had been on the throne for thirty-seven years. He was a straight, broad-shouldered man, rather florid in complexion, his light brown hair by this time rather grey; his life of hard exercise interspersed with hard drinking had left him only the heartier. Monogamy had never suited his exuberant nature, and the number of his bastards grew in time to be a Danish problem and a European joke. In spite of his energetic tastes, he was an intellectual man and made use of his gifts; he had even conducted a learned correspondence in Latin with that prince of pedants, James I of England.[1] A good linguist, he was also a good talker. He had encouraged the arts and sciences in his northern capital as few had done before him, and his palaces at Kronborg and Copenhagen reflected in their opulent decorations, their lavish gold ornaments and plump plaster cherubs realistically tinted pink, something of their master's warm and vigorous personality. 'One could hardly believe that he had been born in so cold a climate', an Italian had once commented.[2]

As a king, Christian had shown outstanding ability, determination and courage, promoting the interests of his people both at home and abroad by combating the exorbitant claims of the nobility and encouraging overseas trade. If he did not altogether succeed, it was because he had to fight the rooted power of a selfish and irresponsible aristocracy at home, and abroad the transcendent genius of Gustavus Adolphus. Throughout Christian's life too much always turned on the King himself: his intellectual powers and his character were always strained to their uttermost, for he had no deputies to lift the burden from him. His charm of manner, his masterful personality, his reckless courage, rough, astringent humour and moody temper had to be constantly at the service of his political acumen, and it was small wonder if the man was sometimes too tired to uphold the King unaided. In comparing his failure with the success of his rival the King of Sweden, it must not be forgotten that Gustavus was as fortunate in his

---

[1] BENTIVOGLIO, *Opere*, p. 90.
[2] Loc. cit.

servants as in his own gifts. Christian, from his majority to the day of his death, fought his battles alone.

Half a German, Christian spoke and wrote the language as well as his own, and he had influence and interests in Germany. He was Duke of Holstein, his son had just been elected to the vacant bishopric of Verden, and Christian claimed both Osnabrück and Halberstadt in his name; with these territories under his influence, and more particularly with the incontrovertible possession of Holstein to back him, Christian intended to put pressure on wavering neutrals. Unhappily, both he and his allies miscalculated the confusions of German politics. The Electors of Saxony and Brandenburg, no less than Christian or the Emperor, had sons to provide for, and they too had nourished hopes of the bishoprics of Osnabrück and Halberstadt. Bitterly resenting the idea that a Hapsburg prince should snatch these prizes from their own children, they were equally unwilling to assist the King of Denmark to do the same. Both princes declared their continued loyalty to the Emperor.

Meanwhile the unhappy rulers of the Lower Saxon Circle continued in their quandary. They were still unwilling to abandon their neutrality, but were powerless to maintain it when Tilly's troops were encamped within their southern border, and the King of Denmark was gathering his forces to the north. Christian proved the more successful intimidator and in May 1625 the bewildered Estates first elected him President of the Circle and then took an unwilling decision to arm.[1] This, in fact, meant only that Christian was free to recruit within their borders.

No declaration of war had hitherto passed between the King and the Emperor, so that Tilly met these activities by sending a note to Christian to ask his intention. The reply was a conciliatory letter explaining that as President of the Lower Saxon Circle he found it necessary to make arrangements for its defence.[2] There followed, all that autumn and winter, an interchange of exquisitely courteous letters between Ferdinand and the assembled Estates of the Circle, in which he attempted to win them generally and singly from their allegiance to the King

[1] LUNDORP, III, p. 807.
[2] Ibid., III, pp. 812, 813.

of Denmark. Clinging to the shreds of neutrality, they wavered
pitiably; at first they considered Ferdinand's specious offer of a
religious guarantee for the north German bishoprics, and then
called off the deal when he tried to except Magdeburg. They
were rapidly falling into that double distress which in time
overtook all the neutral states of Germany, that of being at
war with both parties.[1]

Meanwhile in the field nothing significant happened.
Christian, advancing down the Weser, was checked at Hameln
by a dangerous accident. Riding round his lines one evening,
he was thrown from his horse eighty feet off the ramparts
and only by a miracle survived. He was rumoured dead,[2]
which gave Tilly courage to advance, but better information
and shortage of food drove him back again.[3] Even the coming
of Wallenstein with nearly thirty thousand men[4] increased
rather than lessened Tilly's difficulties, for there were now two
armies to feed, on land which had already been eaten bare by
one alone.[5]

A cold spring had deepened into a bitter summer; snow fell
in June and the drenched crops rotted in the ground. Plague
swept over Europe, checking political and economic life; in
Austria and Styria, in Mecklenburg and Prussia, in Würzburg
and on either side of the Rhine, from Württemberg to Aachen,
it raged through the summer; sixteen thousand died in Prague.[6]
By October eight thousand of Tilly's eighteen thousand men
were sick and the rest ill-clad; all were without safe or decent
quarters for the winter.[7]

Wallenstein was more fortunate. The imperial name had
more terrors than that of the League, and Tilly was amazed to
see cities which had refused entry to his troops open their gates
to Wallenstein.[8] The imperial general seized as by right the
best quarters, settling down in the bishoprics of Magdeburg
and Halberstadt,[9] while Tilly, his men mutinous, hungry and

[1] LUNDORP, III, pp. 824 ff.
[2] GOETZ, *Briefe und Akten*, II, ii, p. 324.
[3] Ibid., pp. 355, 377.   [4] GINDELY, *Waldstein*, I, p. 63.
[5] GOETZ, *Briefe und Akten*, II, ii, pp. 377-8.
[6] LAMMERT, p. 67 f.; *Theatrum Europaeum*, I, p. 999; D'ELVERT, II, p. 193 f.;
III, p. 138 f.; GOETZ, *Briefe und Akten*, II, ii, p. 308.
[7] GOETZ, *Briefe und Akten*, II, ii, p. 408.   [8] Ibid., p. 438.
[9] Ibid., p. 441.

deserting, had to do as best he could in the smaller and less prosperous diocese of Hildesheim.[1] The legitimate search for food degenerated into a scramble for plunder and women, in which the perverted cruelty of mankind, unloosed from the social controls of peace, found horrible expression. In vain townships and villages asked for guarantees of safety on the grounds of their loyalty; the general gave, but could not enforce them.

Wantonly destructive, the soldiery set fire to villages and slaughtered such cattle as they did not drive off. In their lust for plunder they dug up the graveyards for concealed treasure, combed the woods in which the homeless peasants had taken refuge, and shot down those they found, in order to steal their ragged bundles of savings and household goods. They wrecked the churches, and when a pastor, braver than the rest, denied them entrance, they cut off his hands and feet and left him bleeding on the altar, a mangled sacrifice to his Protestant God. Nor did they spare those of their own faith; at the convent of Amelungsborn they ripped up the vestments and shattered the organ, carried off the chalices and ransacked even the graves of the nuns.[2]

Wallenstein's men were on the whole less destructive than Tilly's. His quartering and provisioning was far better organized, and although his exactions in money fell more heavily than those of Tilly on the leading burghers of the towns he occupied, he saw to it that his men were contented, and thereby lessened the chances of wanton plundering.[3] Out of the monstrous contributions which he levied on the occupied country, he kept his troops punctually paid, and accumulated a reserve to replace and improve the artillery.[4] Against all emergencies, he had in his own granaries in Bohemia the means to keep the army fed should all else fail.[5]

Throughout the desolate summer and autumn of 1625, the Danish King strove to tighten the ring of his alliances. In

[1] GOETZ, *Briefe und Akten*, II, ii, p. 407.
[2] HURTER, *Ferdinand II*, VIII, pp. 658-60.
[3] RANKE, *Geschichte Wallensteins*, p. 29.
[4] RITTER, *Das Kontributionssystem Wallensteins. Historische Zeitschrift*, XC, pp. 211-20, 239-46.
[5] V. LOEWE, *Die Organisation und Verwaltung der wallensteinischen Heere*. Leipzig, 1895.

December he signed a treaty with England and the United Provinces,[1] hoping that these two wealthy States would feed his troops with money. Short-lived expectations, for money belonged to individuals not to the government; the Dutch Estates voted him less than he expected, the English Parliament nothing. They had given money to Mansfeld in 1624, to Christian of Brunswick in 1625, and they felt that it was enough to send a small troop of pressed men under Colonel Morgan to help the King of Denmark.[2]

Final catastrophe came when the support of France was withdrawn. Richelieu was the Atlas upholding this tottering world of allies; in the spring of 1626 a Huguenot revolt broke out in France and he was forced to recall his troops from the Val Telline to meet the graver danger at home. To salvage the wreck, the Prince of Orange fitted out a small fleet to sail against the Huguenot fortress of La Rochelle, but the Dutch sailors refused to man the boats against fellow-Protestants and by this mistimed zeal contributed to the collapse of the Protestant Cause in Germany. By the Peace of Monzon on March 26th, 1626, Richelieu withdrew from the Val Telline, and the passes were once more open to Spain. The blood flowed again in the veins of the Hapsburg Empire.

There remained for the defence of the Protestant Cause and the German Liberties Christian of Denmark, Christian of Brunswick and Ernst von Mansfeld. The King of Denmark had the largest army and was the natural director of the war, but Mansfeld, with forces which he had once again swelled by new recruiting, regarded himself as the leader who, *par excellence*, understood the situation; Christian of Brunswick, on the other hand, with an army which he recruited from the peasants as he passed and armed primitively with heavy iron-bound sticks,[3] was willing to act under the King of Denmark but not on any account under Mansfeld.[4] Three separate operations were therefore indicated, since a concerted attack would lead only to bickering; and besides, a divided onslaught

---

[1] AITZEMA, I, p. 482; LUNDORP, III, p. 802.
[2] RUSDORF, II, pp. 58, 189.
[3] WESKAMP, *Das Heer der Liga*, p. 357.
[4] C. F. BRICKA og J. A. FRIDERICIA, *Kong Christian den Fjerdes egenhaendige Breve.* Copenhagen, 1878-91, I, pp. 461-2.

was more likely to separate the combined armies of the enemy. Mansfeld was to invade the bishopric of Magdeburg, Wallenstein's headquarters, thus drawing his fire, circumvent him if possible, and make for Silesia where Bethlen Gabor had promised to join him. Christian of Brunswick was to evade Tilly's outposts and make for Hesse, where he was to raise the Landgrave Maurice for the Protestants and fall on Tilly's rear, while Christian of Denmark, advancing down the Weser, took him full in front.

Christian of Brunswick's attack failed utterly. Worn out at twenty-eight, broken in reputation and fortune, ravaged by disease, he urged his tattered forces across the Hessian border, only to find that the Landgrave, without an army, without resources, already sentenced to the loss of his estates and terrified lest the imperial judgment should be put into force, would have nothing to do with the projects of the King of Denmark. Utterly dejected, Christian fell back on Wolfenbüttel where on June 16th, 1626, he died, his vitals, so the Catholics reported, gnawed by a gigantic worm: the death of Herod.

Mansfeld was hardly more successful. Advised of his movements, Wallenstein himself marched with a large detachment of his army to Dessau on the Elbe, where he knew the Protestant army must cross, and where on April 25th, 1626, Mansfeld appeared with twelve thousand men. For both generals much depended on the issue of that day; Mansfeld, the veteran of his trade, whose ill-luck was becoming proverbial in Europe, relied on a brilliant passage of the Elbe to revive his withering reputation. Wallenstein, still a beginner in the art of mercenary leadership, had all his reputation yet to make. In the previous year he had been slow to march northward and had arrived too late in the field to show his mettle; since then they had been saying in Vienna that he was an empty boaster, an expensive luxury not worth the Emperor's favour, useless as a soldier, dangerous as a subject. A faction wished to depose him from the head of the troops he had raised and give the command to an experienced Italian professional, Collalto. In the very ranks of his army there were officers who took down his chance words and sent them to Vienna with their own interpretations, so at least the Lorrainer, Colonel Aldringer.[1] The action at the Dessau bridge was to Wallenstein something more than the defence of the Elbe; it was the defence of his own reputation.[2]

Mansfeld made the fatal mistake of under-estimating his enemy. When he stormed the bridge-head at Dessau, he had not realized that he had to do with a man whose thoroughness made up for his lack of experience. With the best artillery that had yet been seen in the war, with his troops concealed to minimize their apparent strength, Wallenstein made the Dessau bridge a death-trap, and Mansfeld who trusted in the experience of his soldiers and the massed weight of his charges fell back that night, leaving one-third of his army dead under Wallenstein's guns.

'God gave me the good fortune to smite Mansfeld on the head', wrote Wallenstein to the Emperor.[3] A few days later he accused and upbraided Aldringer for his meddling letters to Vienna, flinging the parting taunt 'ink-swiller'[4] at his discomfited subordinate; it was a jibe which struck home to the self-made man who had been a secretary before he held a commission:[5] a light word thrown out in the heat of anger, but a word which Aldringer would remember when Wallenstein had forgotten.

Divided from Christian of Denmark, on the wrong bank of the Elbe, Mansfeld turned north-eastward into neutral but defenceless Brandenburg, sent out his officers to make good his losses by recruiting and waited for news from Bethlen Gabor. Angry, dejected, ill, but obstinate in his purpose, he planned to strike down the line of the Oder into Silesia when his strength should be sufficiently recruited.

The triumphs in the north had not only saved Wallenstein's reputation. They had brought up for consideration in Brussels a plan which had long been maturing. This was no less than a scheme to establish a naval base for the Spanish fleet on the Baltic and thus reduce the Dutch by an attack on both sides

---

[1] TADRA, *Briefe Albrechts von Waldstein an Karl von Harrach*, 1625-1627. *Fontes Rerum Austriacarum*, II, xli, p. 356; HALLWICH, *Gestalten aus Wallensteins Lager*, Leipzig, 1885, II, 118 f., 144 f.
[2] HALLWICH, *Fünf Bücher*, I, p. 375.　　[3] Ibid., III, p. 42.
[4] 'Tintenfresser'; lit. 'ink eater'.
[5] HALLWICH, *Gestalten aus Wallenstein's Lager*, pp. 144, 163, 164.

at once. On July 1st a Flemish envoy met the two generals at Duderstadt and offered them the financial and military help of Spain if they would occupy Lübeck. Tilly and Wallenstein both shrugged their shoulders. The enterprise, they said, would not be worth the risk. This was certainly true as things then stood in north Germany, and the envoy travelled back with nothing achieved.[1] But Wallenstein did not forget the interview. The fruits of the Duderstadt meeting ripened slowly.

In the meantime there were disturbing reports of Mansfeld's movements: before the end of July he had collected enough recruits to cross the Silesian border and was making gradually southwards to join with Bethlen Gabor. Early in August Wallenstein, leaving Tilly alone to deal with Christian of Denmark, set off in pursuit. The decisive separation of the forces gave the Danish King the opportunity for which he had waited all the summer in vain. Leaving his base in the Duchy of Brunswick, he marched south towards Thuringia, intending to strike between the divided armies of his enemies for the heart of unarmed south Germany.

Informed of his advance, Tilly sent scouts after Wallenstein, and Christian soon learnt that Tilly, strengthened by the return of eight thousand of Wallenstein's men, was marching against him. Christian swung round and raced back to his base in Brunswick. On August 24th, 25th and 26th the rear of his army held the road against the swiftly advancing enemy, beating them off each time with trifling losses. By the 27th, however, he saw that he could not hope to cover the remaining twenty miles to Wolfenbüttel without disaster and, taking up a position across the road just outside the small fortified village of Lutter, he prepared to challenge the advancing army. Woods and a slight inequality of the ground afforded him a little advantage. He placed his twenty cannon where they could sweep the road, and disposed the greater number of his musketeers singly among the trees and hedges through which the enemy were bound to advance. He had a few hundred more cavalry, but his infantry were outnumbered and fled before Tilly's determined charge. The cavalry did better, and the King himself, a reckless rather than a gifted commander, three times rallied

[1] ARETIN, *Bayerns auswärtige Verhältnisse*, Passau, 1839, *Urkunden*, pp.224-40.

his broken lines for a renewed resistance before the seizure of the cannon turned the day hopelessly against him. Some of the cavalry attempted to make a stand at the Castle of Lutter but, deserted by the main body of the army with which Christian himself had fled, they surrendered that evening. The numbers of the taken were reckoned at two thousand five hundred, the numbers of the dead at six thousand on the Danish side. Even allowing for the faulty statistics and habitual exaggerations of the time, Christian had lost more than half his army. All his cannon were gone and he was lucky to have escaped with life and liberty, for in his headlong courage he had been surrounded by the enemy, his horse had been shot under him, and he had with difficulty been saved by the self-sacrifice of one of his officers. [1]

It was useless to attempt to hold the district round Wolfenbüttel. Already the neighbouring rulers were flinging themselves with every profession of loyalty into the arms of Tilly[2], and of all his fair-weather allies Christian had none left save his own son and the two dukes of Mecklenburg. He had no choice but to retreat northwards to the coast and fix his winter quarters at Stade in the flat plain to the south-west of the estuary of the Elbe.

Christian of Brunswick was dead. Christian of Denmark was shattered at Lutter. Mansfeld's army in Silesia was useless, for the general himself had quarrelled with his second-in-command and made united action impossible. Bethlen Gabor, grown suddenly very old and weary, entered into negotiations for a final peace with the Emperor. Deserted by his ally and at odds with his own people, Mansfeld left his quarters in Silesia with only a few followers, and through the deepening autumn of 1626 made south-westwards to the Dalmatian coast. What his destination was on that last journey, or what his projects, no one knew. Some said he went to get the help of Venice, others of the Turks. Undoubtedly, scattered Turkish troops joined his army, though for little purpose beyond plunder. Mystery and legend surround his last days, but somewhere on the way to the Dalmatian coast among the hills above Serajevo, he

[1] LUNDORP, III, p. 876 f.; BRICKA og FRIDERICIA, II, pp. 31-2; see also H. VOGES, *Die Schlacht bei Lutter am Barenberge.* Leipzig, 1922.
[2] LUNDORP, III, pp. 977 f., 991-2.

died, leaving his leaderless companions to starvation or captivity.[1] It was rumoured untruthfully that the Turks had poisoned him, rumoured too, perhaps with more truth, that when his body and soul were in their last struggle he called for two of his men and, leaning a heavy arm on the shoulder of each, dragged himself to his feet so that he should die at least as befitted a soldier and the son of a noble house[2] — a defiant and futile gesture to end that defiant and futile life.

III

The years 1625-26 had seen the rise and fall of a European movement against the Hapsburg dynasty. They had also seen the rise and fall of a more significant and tragic movement within the hereditary lands. The peasants of Upper Austria, sacrificed to pay the imperial debts, had been for five years under the rule of Maximilian of Bavaria, the most exacting of masters. Under his auspices the far-reaching religious edicts of the Emperor were rigorously enforced. All Protestant ministers and schoolmasters were expelled under penalties which did not stop short of death, no child might be educated abroad, no one might visit Protestant churches over the border. All officials of the government were to be Catholic; church-going and fasting were compulsory, all shops and markets were closed during the time of services, all goods which had at any time belonged to the Church were to be restored, and all Protestant books to be given up. Even the old nobility who claimed, and were supposed to receive, preferential treatment, were allowed no more than the empty privilege of calling themselves Protestant, without permission either to practise their religion or to instruct their children in it.[3]

The moral and economic depression of the peasantry, the result of the war, was aggravated by an upheaval in the administration of the district and the disappearance of those mild influences that local pastors and schoolmasters had exerted over the barren, laborious lives of the people. The

---

[1] POYNTZ, p. 50.   [2] HAEBERLIN, XXV, p. 471; POYNTZ, p. 50.
[3] LUNDORP, III, p. 767 f.

Catholic church could not replace the pastors quickly enough or, if it did, then local suspicion and prejudice against a faith too intimately connected with a sense of political oppression prevented the new-comer from filling the place of his predecessor. Moreover, the systematic weakening of the Protestant nobility removed the class which had stood as a bulwark between the people and the government, and left the peasant defenceless.[1]

Herbersdorf, Maximilian's governor of Upper Austria, was neither ruthless enough to stamp out all opposition nor liberal enough to disarm it; a foreigner, in the eyes of the Austrian peasant, and the instrument of an unpopular regime, he evoked an almost insane hatred.[2] In the spring of 1625 he quelled an abortive rising and in the following October published a yet more stringent edict against the Protestants. Through the winter the peasants suffered inactively, but with the spring of 1626 they could bear no more. On May 17th there was a fight at Haibach between some of the imperial soldiers, sent to enforce the edicts, and the natives.[3] Before Herbersdorf had realized what was happening, the peasants were streaming across the province, sixteen thousand strong, towards Linz, the capital and seat of government. They carried black banners bearing a death's head and the words 'It must be', because, as they grimly knew, the revolt would probably mean death for its leaders, whether they won or lost.[4]

> 'Our lives, our faith, hang on our sword,
> Endue us with thy courage, Lord,'

they chanted, with an almost mystical enthusiasm, and they headed the manifestos that they issued to the countryside with the words 'At our Christian camp'.[5]

[1] GINDELY, *Die Gegenreformation und der Aufstand in Oberoesterreich im Jahre 1626. Sitzungsberichte der philosophisch-historische Klasse der Kaiserliche Academie der Wissenschaften. cxviii. Vienna*, 1889, p. 7 f.

[2] See the song in STIEVE, *Der oberösterreichische Bauernaufstand*, Munich, 1891, I, p. 90:

> 'Von Bayerns Joch und Tyrannei,
> Und seine grossen Schinderei
> Mach uns, o lieber Herr Gott, frei!'

[3] GINDELY, *Die Gegenreformation und der Aufstand*, p. 21.

[4] HARTMANN, *Historische Volkslieder*, Munich, 1907, I, p 177.

[5] LUNDORP, III, p. 927; CZERNY, *Bilder aus der Zeit der Bauernunruhen in Oberösterreich*. Linz, 1876, p. 61 f.

A small farmer, Stephan Fadinger, had established himself as leader and under his direction they raided the neighbouring garrisons and strong places for artillery, until they had thirty cannon, and demanded one grown man from every house in each village through which they passed, until their numbers reached seventy thousand. Defeated at Wels, the governor fell back on Linz itself, where on June 24th the peasants shut him in; fortunately for Herbersdorf, he had a reliable garrison, for Stephan Fadinger sent in a manifesto demanding his immediate personal surrender on pain of the total destruction of the town.[1]

Both Ferdinand and Maximilian sent troops, and the death of Fadinger, killed by a chance shot, brought the revolt to a temporary standstill, but the imperialist soldiery avenged themselves on the peasants with such barbarity that revolt flamed up from its smouldering ashes again in August,[2] and once more Linz was threatened. The peasants with frantic zeal blocked the fairway of the Danube with iron chains, to prevent help from the river side, and although the city itself was relieved by superior forces on August 30th, the rebels again defeated the imperial troops at a second battle fought at Wels on October 10th.

At length, on November 8th, 1626, new reinforcements crossed the frontier under Gottfried Heinrich, Count Pappenheim, the son-in-law of Herbersdorf, a soldier trained in Spanish service. The peasants had the advantage of numbers, they knew their country, they had artillery, and they had the friendship of the people among whom and for whom they fought, but they had to face the picked troops of Bavaria under a commander of more than ordinary skill. The issue was never really in doubt. Pappenheim outmanœuvred them, forced them back westwards from Wels, charged and scattered them at Wolfsegg in the open hilly country on the fringe of the district from which the greater number of the rebels came. The army of the peasants dwindled by desertion; Pappenheim's cavalry outmarched them and came between them and their homes, forcing them southwards up the Traun into the steep defiles of the Höllengebirge. Surrounded and crushingly

---

[1] Lundorp, iii, pp. 925-7; Hurter, *Ferdinand II*, x, p. 92.
[2] Stieve, *Bauernaufstand*, i, p. 228.

defeated at Gmunden, the remnants scattered towards the open country, were pursued and finally defeated in two more murderous fights at Vocklabrück and Wolfsegg.[1]

Count Pappenheim presented a gilded statue of Saint George to the village Church of Gmunden, as a thank-offering for his inevitable victory[2] and at Linz in the following spring twenty of the leaders died by the judgment of their rulers. They had prophesied rightly when they blazoned the death's head on their banners: whoever lost or gained by the war, whatever religion throve or prince grew rich, they paid and suffered for all.

IV

The old year went out stormily on the northern coasts and the new year came in wet, cold and gloomy,[3] the New Year of 1627, heralding the tenth year of the war. Outside Germany, the Val Telline was open to Spain, and the Huguenot revolt continued to spread. The favourite who governed England, Buckingham, made nonsense of the diplomacy of the past two years by declaring war on France and sailing to help the rebels at La Rochelle, while Richelieu, to save the monarchy, swung full circle on his alliances and sued for the friendship of Spain.

Within Germany, Tilly's forces held the bishopric of Hildesheim, Wallenstein's were in Magdeburg and Halberstadt, in Brandenburg and parts of Bohemia. The Rhineland was occupied by Spanish and Bavarian troops; Austria, Bohemia, Hungary supported detachments of the imperial army. Mansfeld's mercenaries were in Silesia and Moravia, and Christian's soldiers on the western plain of the Elbe. Over the whole of western Germany the harvests had failed,[4] and there was famine in Franconia and the Rhine valley.[5] Plague had been very bad at Strasbourg, in Brandenburg round

[1] Stieve, *Bauernaufstand*, I, pp. 298-303; Lundorp, III, p. 952.
[2] Czerny, *Ein Tourist in Oesterreich*, Linz, 1874, p. 17.
[3] Jacob Franc, 1626-27, p. 81.
[4] Walther, p. 20.
[5] Duhr, *Geschichte der Jesuiten in den Ländern deutscher Zunge*. Freiburg, 1907, II, ii, p. 130.

Stendal and Kottbus,[1] in Silesia, at Sagan, at Goldberg, in Nassau, in the Saar; in the province of Württemberg hunger and the pestilence had accounted for twenty-eight thousand.[2] Disease could not be checked with the armies passing; typhus, scurvy, smallpox, syphilis, marched under the banners and bred in the countryside. Diseased horses and cattle trailed along among the baggage wagons, spreading contagion in the farms through which they passed.

Violence and insecurity were the accompaniment of life. '13th May, 1626. Catherine, my old servant, shot', entered a pastor of Brandenburg in his diary without further comment.[3] Savage reprisals followed the least attempt at resistance. At Weiss Kirchen in Moravia the people paid dearly for refusing shelter to Mansfeld's men for, as an English mercenary recorded, 'we entered killing man, woman and child: the execution continued the space of two hours, the pillaging two days'.[4]

From the north-east bitter complaints assailed the Emperor. A deputation from Silesia arrived at Vienna in February, honest burghers who did not take their task too heavily and found time to visit the sights and get drunk in the intervals of their more serious business.[5] Silesia had indeed suffered so much less than either Moravia or Bohemia that her people still had the energy to make their distresses known. On the way to Vienna their emissaries found evidence of conditions far worse than those of which they came to complain. At Glatz the suburbs had been altogether destroyed; beyond Mittelwalde on the Bohemian border the peasants had left the fields untilled, weary of sowing harvests to be wantonly destroyed or stolen from them.[6]

Conditions were worse in Brandenburg, where Wallenstein had established his troops at Crossen on the Oder, as well as at Stendal and Gardelegen in the basin of the Elbe, whence he would be able to prevent the junction of the Danes with the

[1] GEBAUER, *Kurbrandenburg in der Krisis des Jahres* 1627. Halle, 1896, p. 9.
[2] LAMMERT, p. 80 f.
[3] *Tägliche Aufzeichnungen des Pfarrherrn Garcaeus*, Brandenburg, 1894, p. 75.
[4] POYNTZ, p. 48.
[5] KREBS, *Zacharias Allerts Tagebuch aus dem Jahre* 1627. *Jahresbericht der schlesischen Gesellschaft für Väterländische Kultur*, LXIV, p. 24 f.
[6] *Allerts Tagebuch*, pp. 22-6.

remains of Mansfeld's army in northern Silesia.[1] Here his quartermasters demanded not only food and drink for the soldiers but clothes and shoes; the obligation of the province was assessed at sixty-six thousand gulden, and when the local authorities failed to raise it they were seized by the soldiers and held as hostages against payment. Unlike Tilly's veterans, Wallenstein's men were young, the sons of poverty-stricken peasant families, ruffians still in their teens, inexperienced, unmanageable and demoralized by spreading sickness; at Gardelegen they were burying their dead daily, twenty together, in open pits.[2] 'Is there then no God in Heaven that will take our part?' wailed the Brandenburgers to their Elector who had prudently fled to Prussia. 'Are we then such utterly forsaken sheep? . . . Must we look on while our houses and dwellings are burnt before our eyes?'[3]

The answer was self-evident, for George William's piteous embassy to Vienna brought no relief. Ferdinand received the ambassador personally and impressed him with his courtesy — it was noticeable that he lifted his hat every time the name of the Elector was mentioned — but the upshot of the interview was merely that certain 'inconveniences' could not be avoided in war-time, and the ambassador must apply to Eggenberg for further help. Eggenberg's reception was no less courteous although illness confined him to bed at the time. Having no hat, he saluted the ambassador by graciously removing his night cap, and repeated in more detail the observations made by his master. Elsewhere the ambassador learnt that Wallenstein's conduct in Moravia was worse than in Brandenburg, and it stood to reason, his informant added, that if the Emperor could not protect his own lands he could hardly protect those of others.[4]

The insistence of the ambassador at last forced the imperial government to draw up a memorandum pointing out to Wallenstein that he was quartering in Brandenburg without the Emperor's leave. At the last minute the sentence was

---

[1] OPEL, *Das Kurfürstentum Brandenburg in den ersten Monaten des Jahres,* 1627. *Historische Zeitschrift,* LI, p. 194.
[2] GEBAUER, *Kurbrandenburg in der Krisis,* p. 9.
[3] OPEL, *Das Kurfürstentum Brandenburg,* p. 194.
[4] Ibid., op. cit., pp. 199-202.

altered to without the Emperor's knowledge', confirming the ambassador's nascent suspicion that the government itself was afraid of its general.[1]

The Elector of Brandenburg now took the task into his own hands and wrote two personal letters to Wallenstein, without eliciting the least response. He learnt later that he had given mortal offence by addressing the general merely as his 'well-beloved friend' instead of 'well-beloved lord and friend' as did the more tactful Elector of Saxony.[2] The experience of a rash deputation from Halle had shown that Wallenstein was not to be trifled with: he had imprisoned its members in chains and declared that he would shoot any further complainants out of hand.[3]

Germany was not yet a ruined country, but unless some limit was set to the spreading war, she soon would be. With Christian of Denmark defeated and France at peace with Spain, it seemed that the hostilities must end, and in the winter it was confidently prophesied that Wallenstein's army would be partly disbanded and he himself dismissed.[4] Of all the German princes only the Dukes of Mecklenburg, the Protestant administrator of Magdeburg and the exiled Frederick remained unreconciled to imperial power. All the rest were either indifferent or in arms for the Emperor. The occupied country was almost without exception neutral country; the town of Magdeburg and its district had, for instance, emphatically disassociated itself from the rebellion of its ruler.[5] There was nothing to prevent peace. Yet in the New Year of 1627 Wallenstein, who had recruited his army to nearly a hundred and forty thousand fighting men,[6] was sending his officers out with their commissions as far afield as the Rhineland, and had brought down upon Ferdinand the complaints of all the ecclesiastical Electors.[7]

The emissary from Brandenburg had imagined that the Emperor was afraid of his general, but there was a more profound reason for Ferdinand's behaviour. Wallenstein had digested the Spanish Baltic plan and was prepared to execute it.

[1] OPEL, *Das Kurfürstentum Brandenburg*, p. 202.
[2] Ibid., pp. 203, 205.
[3] KLOPP, op. cit., II, p. 707.   [4] GINDELY, *Beiträge*, p. 155 f.
[5] LUNDORP, III, pp. 1021-2.   [6] GINDELY, *Beiträge*, pp. 223-4.
[7] HALLWICH, *Fünf Bücher*, pp. 140-1.

Hence his preliminary occupation of the Mark of Brandenburg, and his intention to carry the war forward into Mecklenburg on one side and Holstein on the other in the coming spring. He seems, however, to have been already working on his own authority, for he had made himself unpopular with the court by occupying part of the imperial lands for winter quarters, and the Spaniards had lost confidence in him since the previous summer. Already at the time of the Battle of Dessau the Emperor owed Wallenstein half a million gulden[1] for the expenses of the army, and as the months passed the debt grew; no great political acumen was needed to see that the general was gaining a dangerous hold over the government. The Spanish party were right in their view that the Baltic plan would be most conveniently carried through by Wallenstein's army without Wallenstein himself.

They were right, but Wallenstein already had too strong a hold to be dislodged. On the first rumour of complaint to Vienna, he threatened to resign incontinently, an action which would have left the imperial government with the dangerous task of taking over his army without money to pay it. A little later he met Eggenberg at Brück on the Leitha to discuss his future policy.

What took place at that meeting will for ever remain doubtful; the evidence is tainted and no biographer of Wallenstein is able to approach it in an impartial spirit. The interpretation of his career is too closely involved in that occasion. The most balanced of German historians[2] considers that in fact Wallenstein merely discussed details of organization, and that the report which depicted him outlining the Baltic plan and foreshadowing the spreading power of the Hapsburg was a forgery for the especial deception of Maximilian of Bavaria. This much, however, is true: that there was a Baltic plan; that shortly after the meeting at Brück the whole yield of the taxes in Bohemia was ear-marked for the use of Wallenstein's army, and that he himself was invested with full sovereign rights within his own large estates;[3] that Maximilian of Bavaria

---

[1] HALLWICH, *Fünf Bücher*, III, p. 327.
[2] MORITZ RITTER, *Zur Geschichte Wallensteins. Deutsche Zeitschrift für Geschichtswissenschaft*, IV, pp. 24-38.
[3] Ibid., p. 31; STIEVE, *Wallenstein bis zur Ubernahme des Generalats*, p. 228.

heard of the Baltic plan and of Wallenstein's part in it in some probably exaggerated form.[1]

Ferdinand was in some sort intoxicated by the victory of Lutter and the collapse of the Danish King. He was justified, if he was not right, in thinking Christian the most powerful of the northern monarchs. If he could be so easily shattered, neither the King of Sweden nor England seemed dangerous, and within Germany itself no other prince had power to stand alone against imperial arms.[2] Thus the victory of Lutter did not dispose Ferdinand to peace; on the contrary it disposed him very much to war. With Wallenstein's army he could establish his authority in the northern bishoprics and gain control of the Baltic Sea.

Now, if ever, was the moment for Maximilian to return to his honourable German policy and make a stand for peace before Ferdinand's power overtopped all bounds. He called the Catholic League to Würzburg in January 1627, and here, for the sake of peace and the stability of princely rights, threatened to withdraw support from Ferdinand unless the power of Wallenstein was curtailed. The members of the League feared the consequences of Ferdinand's aggression more than they desired the re-establishment of the Catholic Church throughout Germany. They demanded peace and inevitably they suggested Louis XIII as a mediator — a Catholic king who had shown friendship to Maximilian. The suggestion of peace died with the naming of the mediator, for the government in Vienna suspected Richelieu's motives, and the Protestant party, such as it was, had not yet forgiven him his betrayal. Maximilian had signally failed either to establish an armistice or to curb Wallenstein.

In the spring of 1627 the general opened his campaign by a further shameless violation of princely rights. George William of Brandenburg was the most harmless ruler in Germany except on the rare occasions when he was rushed into a decision against his will. His policy was of a naked, dynastic simplicity; his only desire was that he should continue to be an Elector

[1] HALLWICH, *Fünf Bücher*, I, p. 677; RITTER, *Zur Geschichte Wallensteins*, pp. 15-40.
[2] G. DROYSEN, *Gustaf Adolf*, Leipzig, 1869, I, pp. 286-7; J. G. DROYSEN, *Geschichte der Preussischen Politik*, III, I, p. 13.

for all his days and that his son should succeed him.[1] Before judging this principle too harshly, it is fair to remember that George William had ascended the throne in the teeth of intense resistance, and that his court was an asylum for his wife's relations — she was the sister of Frederick of Bohemia. But a mere chance of geography robbed George William of the fruits of his inoffensive neutrality. His lands lay between the wreck of Mansfeld's army in Silesia and the King of Denmark's headquarters. Either of these armies might march across to join the other, and Wallenstein would certainly think nothing of invading Brandenburg to prevent it. Worse still, the King of Sweden was using Prussia as a base in his Polish war, whether George William liked it or no, and had bullied him into ceding the convenient port of Pillau.[2] It was rumoured in 1627 that Gustavus Adolphus might consider coming to help the defeated Christian. If he did, he too would march across Brandenburg, and so would the imperial army which tried to stop him.

Hoping in vain to save himself, George William had even agreed to recognize Maximilian as an Elector,[3] in the mistaken hope that the League would prevent Wallenstein from attacking him. All in vain; in vain too his protests to Vienna. When his ambassador forced a way into Wallenstein's presence to entreat the removal of the forces stationed at Crossen, the general, who was in bed, unceremoniously buried his head under the pillows and would not listen.[4]

Before the summer of 1627 Wallenstein's troops under the best of his lieutenants, Hans Georg von Arnim, himself a Protestant and a native of Brandenburg, had advanced into the Elector's country. The unhappy George William attempted in vain to raise a small force to protect his lands, but when a band of sixty soldiers, the utmost that could be collected, attempted to occupy Berlin, they were driven out by the indignant people who tore up the cobble stones and pelted them out of the town because, being Lutherans, they were insanely convinced that this was some attempt of the Elector to enforce Calvinism at the sword's point. In the rest of the

[1] DROYSEN, *Preussische Politik*, III, i, pp. 52-3.
[2] GINDELY, *Die maritimen Pläne der Habsbürger*, p. 4 f.
[3] *Annales*, X, p. 1227; LUNDORP, III, pp. 941-80.
[4] OPEL, *Das Kurfürstentum Brandenburg*, p. 204.

province George William's subjects preferred submission to the unequal contest: at Neu-Brandenburg resistance was punished by the plundering of the town, so that at Havelberg the people, forewarned, violently expelled the garrison and threw open the gates at the approach of Arnim's troops.[1] George William had no choice but to follow their example, submit with as good a grace as possible and proclaim throughout the land that the invaders were to be received as friends.[2] About this time his unsuccessful ambassador was on his way back from Vienna, bearing a letter from Ferdinand assuring the Elector of his unalterable regard;[3] it is to be hoped that this was balm to George William.

With Brandenburg thus occupied, it was easy for Wallenstein to settle the scattered forces of the Protestants. The King of Denmark had passed the winter trying vainly to enlist fresh help. The English government, his only hope now Richelieu had failed, sent him neither ships nor subsidies.[4] Frederick of Bohemia had nothing to send, for the Dutch paid his pension grudgingly, the English not at all, and his house was besieged by unpaid tradesmen. He owed £140 for milk alone and could not lay his hand on a penny.[5] Knowing that the King of Denmark was as good as defeated,[6] he was turning again towards the King of Sweden.[7] The Dukes of Mecklenburg, Christian's remaining allies, had done likewise, and the subsidies they owed to his army came in slowly or not at all.[8] The Duke of Brunswick-Wolfenbüttel had long since made peace with the Emperor and was trying to drive Christian's troops out of the few districts they still occupied in his land.[9] Short of food and money for his men, short of horses for his cavalry, Christian tried in vain to keep order among the defeated and demoralized troops.[10]

[1] OPEL, Das Kurfürstentum Brandenburg, pp. 215-17.
[2] LUNDORP, III, pp. 985-6.
[3] OPEL, Das Kurfürstentum Brandenburg, p. 205 f.
[4] RUSDORF, I, pp. 604, 611; MOSER, Patriotisches Archiv, VI, p. 106.
[5] MOSER, Patriotisches Archiv, VI, p. 109; M. A. E. GREEN, Elizabeth Queen of Bohemia, revised by S. C. Lomas. London, 1909, p. 258.
[6] MOSER, Neues Patriotisches Archiv, I, p. 77.
[7] LUNDORP, III, pp. 952-60; RUSDORF, II, passim.
[8] GEBAUER, Kurbrandenburg in der Krisis, p. 2; BRICKA og FRIDERICIA, II, pp. 94-5; LUNDORP, III, p. 461.
[9] LUNDORP, III, pp. 977-9.   [10] Ibid., pp. 976-8.

On August 4th, 1627, the remnants of Mansfeld's army surrendered or fled at Bernstein, and their leader, the Dane Mitzlaff, escaped with a few bedraggled regiments to join the Swedes in Poland. In September Wallenstein and Tilly joined in the march down the Elbe, in October Tilly reduced the remaining garrisons in Germany while Wallenstein pursued Christian over the frontiers of Holstein; the last of his cavalry surrendered in the far north at Halborg, and Wallenstein's army made ready to winter in the unspoiled villages of Jutland.

V

While Wallenstein conquered in the north, Ferdinand continued his work of consolidation in the south. This same year saw the promulgation of a new constitution for Bohemia in a form which it retained for over two hundred years. Bohemia was still autonomous in theory but the Crown was hereditary, the King appointed his own officials and the Estates lost all coercive power.[1] This was followed in the summer by an edict requiring all those who still persisted in the Protestant religion to choose immediately between conversion and exile. The final purge sent twenty-seven thousand more of Ferdinand's subjects out of the country.[2]

In the summer of 1627 Ferdinand had once again taken his favourite pilgrimage to Mariazell, in order to thank his Patroness for the happy completion of half a century of life,[3] and he decided to end the year by a visit to Bohemia. He had never been personally unpopular in Prague and he wisely sought to soften his increasing despotism by giving the townsfolk an excuse for rejoicing and putting money into the pockets of the shop-keepers.

A lavish coronation had won Frederick and Elizabeth what little popularity they had ever enjoyed: Ferdinand could not be crowned again, but he decided instead to crown the Empress Eleanora, a handsome woman still under thirty, who would make a dignified centrepiece to his political stagecraft. Her

[1] See DENIS, La Bohème depuis la Montagne Blanche, Paris, 1903, pp. 107-19; D'ELVERT, II, pp. 204 f. , 266 f.

[2] D'ELVERT, II, pp. 206 ff.

[3] GINDELY, Geschichte der Gegenreformation, p. 514.

coronation, which took place with unexampled splendour, was attended by cheering crowds so thick that she had difficulty in making her way through them, and was followed by fireworks, plays, banquets and dances, while the fountains, as in Frederick's time, ran red and white wine. Afterwards at a lance-running contest the Emperor's eldest son, the nineteen-year-old Archduke Ferdinand, carried off the prize,[1] a feat which won him the immediate adulation of the populace and proved highly convenient to his father's plans. The prince had been privileged to sit on his father's council since the previous year, and his quiet discretion, so different from his father's garrulous confidence, fitted him well for the office that the ageing Emperor now put upon him. The Archduke Ferdinand was to have the disagreeable task of being the first hereditary King of Bohemia under the new constitution.

His coronation, which took place in the same week as that of the Empress his step-mother, was signalized by the same attention to popular taste, so that the bitter sense of wrong was drowned in the temporary prosperity of the overfilled town, where the innkeepers were making their fortunes and everyone who wished could get drunk for nothing. Prague had long had the sinister reputation of being the most vicious town in Europe; the virtuous Ferdinand relied on the baser tastes of his subjects to drown their more noble aspirations. Of the Bohemian revolt nothing now remained but a bankrupt court at The Hague and a hundred and fifty thousand exiles.[2]

At Brandeis, about a month after the double coronation, Ferdinand met Wallenstein. As things now stood, there was no power in Germany which could make head against them, and Wallenstein informed the Emperor that he could conduct the war for six years more on the resources of the conquered countries without troubling the government for a penny.[3] He intended to establish Ferdinand's power over all the Empire, by occupying Jutland, Holstein, Pomerania, Mecklenburg, parts of Brandenburg, Franconia, Swabia and Alsace.[4] In the north, his position was unassailable; Spanish money had

[1] PISTORIUS, *Historische Beschreibungen*, 1627-28, p. 47.
[2] BRETHOLZ, *Geschichte Böhemns und Mährens*, Reichenberg, 1921, III, p. 16.
[3] GINDELY, *Die maritimen Pläne der Habsbürger*, p. 17.
[4] CHLUMECKY, *Wallensteins Briefe an Collalto*, Brünn, 1856, p. 55.

breathed new life into the Polish monarchy,[1] so that the King of Sweden had his hands fully occupied and could not come to the rescue of the chastened King of Denmark. At the same time the bewildered Elector of Brandenburg had actually been bullied into sending help, not to his brother-in-law of Sweden but to the Poles: he could not afford to defend himself, but he was forced to dispatch all the men and arms he could raise to fulfil his duty as a vassal to Sigismund of Poland.[2] In these circumstances the Hapsburg plans for launching a fleet on the Baltic and founding a new trading company in conjunction with the Hanseatic towns were all but realized. In the spring, Wallenstein was already arranging to build twenty-four warships for the Baltic, provided Spain sent a like number.[3]

Ferdinand had dispossessed Frederick in order to secure the Rhine; now, to make doubly certain of the Baltic coast, he again seized the property of a rebel and bestowed it on an ally. On March 11th, 1628, he signed a patent conferring the duchies of Mecklenburg, with all the titles and privileges pertaining to them, on Albrecht von Wallenstein.[4]

Europe reeled. It had shocked statesmen enough when the Duke of Bavaria had been raised to an Electorate, but he was at least a leading prince, and the transfer had been conducted with the actual, if grudging, approval of the spiritual electors. Wallenstein was by birth no more than a nobleman of Bohemia, a subject of that Crown. And was he now to take his place as an independent prince beside the rulers of Württemberg and Hesse? If the Emperor's word were enough to depose a reigning prince and set up a creature of his own, the whole of Germany would shortly be a province of Austria.

Within the Hapsburg dynasty the movement would have been greeted with more enthusiasm had Ferdinand's cousins been convinced that he was in fact the master of the situation. The Spaniards shared with the German princes and with Wallenstein himself the belief that the Emperor was a mere pawn in the general's hand. 'The Duke is so powerful,' wrote the Spanish ambassador, 'that one must almost be grateful to him for contenting himself with a land like Mecklenburg . . . The

---

[1] GINDELY, *Die maritimen Pläne der Habsbürger*, pp. 11-12.
[2] Ibid., p. 11.   [3] Ibid., p. 17.
[4] LUNDORP, III, p. 1012.

Emperor in his goodness, in spite of all warnings, has given
the Duke such power that one cannot fail to be anxious.'[1]
It is clear from this report that Ferdinand had yet again
refused to listen to Spanish advice, and perhaps not entirely
out of such weakness as the writer imagined. Ferdinand's
generosity was dictated by motives of policy more complicated
than the ambassador had wit to grasp.

Nailing the constitutional colours to the mast, John George
protested against the elevation of Wallenstein with dignified
futility.[2] The Dukes of Mecklenburg, in exile, set up a wail for
help and threw themselves on the mercy of the King of Sweden.
But the act was bitterest of all to Maximilian of Bavaria, who
had first instructed Ferdinand in the practice of disregarding
the constitution. He was now nearly sixty, an age at which the
seventeenth-century ruler began to think of abdication and
rest, but with all his ambition and dynastic greed, he could
nevertheless recognize his duty, and it was not for himself but for
the Liberties of the German princes that he now collected his
wasted forces for a new resistance.

All through the winter and early spring a meeting of the
German Electors had been in session at Mühlhausen. At first it
revealed only the deepening fissures of the Empire.[3] The
ecclesiastical princes wanted the victories of Wallenstein used
to advance the Church in north Germany, and were not
impressed by Maximilian's warning that Wallenstein was
becoming a serious menace;[4] he had weakened his position
shortly before the assembly met by accepting the right bank of
the Rhine and the Upper Palatinate in hereditary possession
from Ferdinand.[5] But the elevation of Wallenstein in March
proved Maximilian's prognostications right and frightened his
fellow Electors into forgetting his personal ambition and their
jealousy. On the eve of dissolution the meeting at last found
unity.

The alliance of Ferdinand and Wallenstein had one weak
point. The Emperor was fundamentally conventional. He
prided himself that he had never broken his word, and could
justify all his unconstitutional acts on specious grounds.

[1] GINDELY, *Waldstein*, I, p. 368.   [2] LUNDORP, III, p. 1009.
[3] Ibid., p. 996.   [4] Ibid., p. 998 f.   [5] LÜNIG, v, i, pp. 695-700.

Finding it very easy to believe what he wanted to believe, he deceived himself into thinking that he had kept the letter of every oath he had ever sworn unless circumstances had made it impossible. He revered the forms of the Empire and for the past year had been wooing the Electors to make his eldest son 'King of the Romans', a formality tantamount to a guarantee of his succession to the imperial throne. Apparently it did not occur to Ferdinand that if he made full use of the power Wallenstein was pouring into his hands he could dispense altogether with forms. Even should the Elector of Bavaria stand against him,[1] young Ferdinand would be Emperor, because he would be the strongest prince in Germany. Destroying the constitution with one hand, Ferdinand clung to it with the other, and he wanted now, above everything, to secure his dynasty on the throne in the traditional fashion.

Seventeen days after the elevation of Wallenstein to the dukedom of Mecklenburg, the Elector of Mainz indicted a manifesto to Ferdinand in the name of all his fellows, emphatically stating that while the imperial armies continued under Wallenstein's command, he would not guarantee the the election of the prince.[2] It was not difficult to guess who had prompted the Elector of Mainz. Across the victorious advance of Ferdinand and his general, Maximilian of Bavaria interposed the barrier of his disapproval, saying: thus far and no farther.

[1] This was the contingency Ferdinand the elder is alleged to have feared: see RUSDORF, II, p. 367.
[2] LUNDORP, III, pp. 1012-17.

DEADLOCK
1628 — 1630

God send that there may be an end at last; God send that there may be peace again.   God in Heaven send us peace.

Diary of HARTICH SIERK (a peasant), 1628

DEADLOCK

I

EVERYTHING depended on the judgment of the Emperor Ferdinand. He had before him a choice: either he could yield to Maximilian and the Catholic princes, and gain the succession of his son to a throne neither stronger nor weaker for ten years of war, or he could place himself unreservedly in the hands of Wallenstein, risk the open hostility of an ever wider circle of princes, and rely on force of arms to build him a sovereignty such as no Emperor had enjoyed for centuries.

Wallenstein stood for the military autocracy of the Emperor, but he also stood for an Empire of Central Europe unconnected with Spain. As a practical man he objected to an alliance which was geographically impossible, and in his apparent acceptance of the Spanish Baltic plan he never intended to go beyond the point at which it was useful to his own ambition. The centre of the Spanish conflict was the plain of the Netherlands, but Wallenstein's interests lay in Bohemia; just as the Rhine valley formed the spinal column of the Hapsburg Empire, so the valley of the Elbe was the connecting passage between the Hapsburg lands and the northern seas, the central nerve of the state that Wallenstein projected.

Albrecht von Wallenstein was a visionary; the most practical of men in the management of financial affairs, the most unimaginative in his dealings with human beings, his politics soared to fantastic heights, into that borderland between genius and insanity. It is impossible to study his career or his writings without realizing that something more than the self-interest of each particular moment guided his actions, impossible equally to grasp what that something was. The historian asks the nature of his patriotism in vain — was he a Czech at heart, or a German? — for Wallenstein's dreams defied a national circumscription. His ambition was always imperial, although at the end he abandoned the thought of Ferdinand as the figure-head; he was not interested in the rights of individuals, of races, of religions; to his thinking, north-eastern Germany and Bohemia could form one block with the southern domains of the Hapsburgs and become a powerful state dominating the Turks on one side and Western Europe on the other.

Basing his power on the nucleus of his own lands, he had extended his influence by purchase over the greater part of Bohemia, so that the reorganization of his estates alone was a consolidating force in Ferdinand's regenerated kingdom. From this Slavonic base, Wallenstein, with sublime indifference to national distinctions, now stretched out his hand to pluck Mecklenburg. It was rumoured that if he could goad the Elector to open war he would pluck Brandenburg as well. [1]

Whether this Central European Empire was the Empire which Ferdinand wished to govern remains doubtful; Wallenstein, with that over-confidence in himself which was to be his downfall, forgot the dynastic prejudice which dominated Ferdinand's policy. The Emperor disliked all foreign customs; he could not, or would not, speak Spanish; [2] he had never visited Spain, he had no personal knowledge either of his nephew, [3] the present King, or of the Archduchess Isabella. But he had never for one moment forgotten the ultimate advantage of the dynasty. Stronger than any personal feelings, the pressure of tradition held the family together. Poor himself, the Emperor needed the financial help of others, and since he must mortgage his policy to one paymaster or another, he would get what he could from Wallenstein but in the last resort call in the King of Spain to buy him free. Deep under the alliance of Ferdinand and his general ran this hidden fissure.

Ferdinand was prepared to call on the resources of Spain when he wished to be rid of Wallenstein. He was also prepared to sacrifice Wallenstein to gain the support of the German princes for his son. But not in March 1628. The ultimatum

---

[1] GAEDEKE, *Zur Politik Wallensteins und Kursachsens in den Jahren* 1630-1634. *Neues Archiv für Sächsische Geschichte*, x, p. 35.

[2] CARAFA, p. 264.

[3] The mother of Philip IV was the Archduchess Margaret of Styria, Ferdinand's younger sister.

from the Electors at Mühlhausen showed Ferdinand clearly one thing: that he could buy the election of his son as King of the Romans by the sacrifice of Wallenstein. Reverse the threat of the Electors, and what else did it mean? Ferdinand cannot at once have embraced the scheme of throwing his general to the wolves; dismissing Wallenstein would be difficult and dangerous now that he was among the most powerful men in Germany. Ferdinand was always more than a little afraid of the act itself. [1] Nevertheless, it is clear from the passage of events during the next two years that he calculated for no less. But he was determined to exploit his general's power to its uttermost before renouncing him.

The princes, meanwhile, concentrated on overthrowing Wallenstein before his army should rob them both of their rights and the means to protect them. Again, for the undoing of Germany, two parties and not one stood in opposition to the Emperor and to each other. One party, consisting of Maximilian and the Catholic princes, demanded the stabilization of Germany in the condition prevailing after the Battle of Lutter and before the elevation of Wallenstein to the dukedom of Mecklenburg. Opposed to this party was the Protestant consti-tutionalist group headed by John George of Saxony, who, with the Elector of Brandenburg, demanded the restitution of Frederick to the Palatinate. Their position was more logical than that of the League princes, who were fiercely indignant about the transference of Mecklenburg, but ignored, for obvious reasons, the transference of the Palatinate.

Had these groups coalesced as the Elector of Mainz had hoped four years earlier, [2] there would have been some chance of forcing the will of the princes on the Emperor and ending the war by settlement. But the generous, intelligent John Schweikard of Mainz had died, and his successor was kept from decisive action by fear of Wallenstein's troops. The two parties remained divided. The group led by John George held to his firm principles, sought no help abroad and was totally without effect on imperial policy; the group led by Maximilian exploited the enmity of the Bourbon for the Hapsburg, and with foreign

---

[1] Dukid, *Correspondenz Kaiser Ferdinands II*, p. 273.
[2] See *supra*, Chapter II, pp. 192-3.

support reached up again to grasp the helm of government. Steering the ship clear of the Spanish quicksand, they wrecked her on the French reef.

II

For Wallenstein the centre of Europe was the slavonic block at the sources of the Elbe and Oder; for Ferdinand it was the group of German-speaking states on the upper Danube; for the Kings of France and Spain it remained the Rhine, the Low Countries and the north Italian passes. In the Rhine and its tributary valleys two minor incidents had wakened again the feud of Bourbon and Hapsburg. At Verdun, occupied by a French garrison since 1552 in accordance with an ancient treaty, the bishop, whose sympathies were with the Hapsburg, had excommunicated the French soldiers for attempting to build a fortress. In answer Richelieu burnt the excommunication and tried to seize the bishop. The bishop, in turn, appealed to Wallenstein to send troops, while Ferdinand urged the Spaniards to arm in Luxemburg. There the incident ended; it served to show which way the wind was blowing. Not long after, the French government quarrelled with the new Duke of Lorraine, Charles III, over the suzerainty of Bar. The Duke immediately appealed to the Emperor and for the time being the quarrel lapsed.

In fact Richelieu did not want war.[1] France, he said, suffered from four evils: 'the unbridled ambition of Spain, the excessive licence of the nobility, the lack of soldiers and the absence of any reserve of savings for the prosecution of war'. Clearly the abolition of the first evil depended on the previous settlement of the other three. In 1628 they were not yet settled. The French army consisted of recalcitrant local lévies — the Bretons asserted that only wars with England concerned them — which were under the control of the nobility. War automatically increased the power of the aristocracy, and by a dangerous feudal survival the King himself was not absolute master of his own army, the ultimate control lying with the Constable of France.[2]

---

[1] See RICHELIEU, *Mémoires*, VIII, pp. 114 ff.
[2] HANOTAUX ET DE LA FORCE. *Revue des Deux Mondes*, March, 1935, p. 62.

Besides this underlying trouble, the Huguenot rebels were still making head against the government, and a long siege had not yet reduced their great stronghold at La Rochelle.

In the Low Countries, meanwhile, a gradual change had come over the face of affairs. Frederick Henry had failed to relieve Breda, but his intelligent and vigorous government neutralized the effects of its capture. The strain of war was beginning to affect the unstable finances of the Spanish Netherlands; the army was less regularly paid, the expenditure of the Court had diminished and the ephemeral prosperity of the state melted away. The emigration of the artisan population grew annually more serious and legislation was of no effect.[1] In the long run the temporary blocking of the Val Telline had told on the army, and the persistent harrying of Spanish ships by Dutch in the narrow seas checked the stream of subsidies from Madrid. It had been the Spanish custom to lie in English waters off the Downs until a good moment came to make the harbour of Dunkirk without Dutch interference;[2] but from 1624 the English were at war with Spain and gave no shelter to her vessels. In 1626 Frederick Henry took Oldenzaal with immense store of arms and ammunition, thereby making good the defence of his eastern frontier.

But it was in north Italy that the serious crisis came. The Duke of Mantua died, leaving as his nearest heir Charles, Duke of Nevers, a subject of the French Crown. While nobody cared particularly who owned Mantua, the Spanish Hapsburg were determined that the small related county of Montferrat, with its fortress of Casale on the borders of the Milanese, should not pass into the hands of a Frenchman. Richelieu was equally determined not to lose this happy occasion of obtaining foothold in northern Italy. On the flimsy pretext that the Duke of Nevers had not asked the imperial permission, Ferdinand unloosed the Mantuan war on April 1st, 1628, by declaring Montferrat and Mantua sequestered. Charles of Nevers retaliated by urging the French government to free Italy from the Spanish yoke.[3] Immediately, the Spaniards occupied Mont-

[1] BRANTS, *Albert et Isabelle*, Louvain, 1910, p. 180.
[2] H. G. R. READE, *Sidelights on the Thirty Years War*, I, p. 75.
[3] QUAZZA, *Guerra di Mantova*, I, p. 130; LÜNIG, op. cit., x, ii, pp. 694-6; RICHELIEU, *Mémoires*, VIII, p. 184.

ferrat, all except Casale, for the reduction of which Spinola himself was shortly afterwards recalled.

While the crisis between Hapsburg and Bourbon drew near, the heads of the Austrian and Spanish lines made a significant movement towards closer union. The Emperor's eldest son was marriageable and the bride chosen for him was the Infanta Maria of Spain, his first cousin, who had four years before been wooed in vain by the Prince of Wales. The graceful Infanta, with her German blue eyes and pink complexion, had always been considered something of a beauty in Spain; reports of the Archduke, on the other hand, were unnecessarily gloomy, and his bride formed the apprehensive impression that he was ugly and stupid. Knowing her duty, she did not complain and, having prepared herself to meet a deformed and short-witted husband, contrived to fall in love at first sight out of mere relief at finding the Archduke normally shaped and normally gifted.[1] In the meantime nobody consulted the inclinations of the bride and bridegroom. Long before they met the marriage contract was irrevocably signed.[2]

III

The Baltic plan went steadily on towards completion. Ferdinand offered alliances to Lübeck and Hamburg,[3] and when his overtures were received without enthusiasm Wallenstein introduced a second line of argument by sending an army against Stralsund. The show of violence fluttered the Hanseatic League but still had not the desired effect for, instead of accepting imperial friendship, the deputies of the Hanse merely offered Wallenstein eighty thousand talers to withdraw.[4] He proved incorruptible and on July 6th, 1628, arrived in person before Stralsund.

The city lies on the coast of Pomerania, opposite the island of Rügen which forms a natural shelter for its harbour. The indentation of the sandy coast at that point is such that Stralsund itself is all but an island. Three days before Wallenstein's

[1] *Annales*, xi, p. 1504; FIELDER, p. 190.
[2] ABREU Y BERTODANO, *Collection de los Tratados*, Madrid, 1740, IV, p. 89 f.
[3] LUNDORP, III, pp. 1006-7, 1083.
[4] GINDELY, *Die maritimen Pläne*, pp. 28-9.

coming, the municipality signed a treaty with the King of Sweden by which he was to protect them for thirty years, while they in turn provided a base and landing place for him in Germany.[1] Strong in this defence, the burgomaster and councillors of Stralsund rejected Wallenstein's offers. 'The town shall yield though it were bound with chains to Heaven', the general is alleged to have challenged them in mounting anger.[2] From the distance of Prague he had set great store on the reduction of this key port on the Baltic,[3] but when he had twice attacked in vain he recognized that it was impregnable. He was still without a fleet, while the King of Sweden's ships were off the coast and the King of Denmark, with a new army, was waiting to disembark. On July 28th he himself withdrew and a week later the army broke camp before the walls.

The check was more effective morally than physically. In fact neither Ferdinand nor Wallenstein was worse off than before, but this first successful resistance was seized on by the pamphleteers of the opposing party as a presage of Hapsburg defeat. 'Eagles', the polemists facetiously asserted, 'cannot swim'.[4]

The King of Denmark's unquenchable optimism gave Wallenstein the chance he needed to redeem his reputation. Christian had landed to the south-east of Stralsund on the sandy dunes of Pomerania, swooped upon the town of Wolgast and made ready to invade Mecklenburg. He was safe in his sandhills, Wallenstein admitted, but report asserted that the King was drinking heavily and would soon do something foolhardy. 'If he ventures out', boasted Wallenstein, 'he is ours for sure.'[5] He was right. On September 2nd, 1628, he intercepted the Danish forces just outside Wolgast and slaughtered all that did not surrender or fly. Christian himself took refuge with his ships, fled to Denmark and sued for peace.

Wallenstein's success brought down fresh complaints on Ferdinand. At a conservative estimate, the general had a hundred and twenty-five thousand troops under arms and was

---

[1] *Sverges Traktater*, v, 1, pp. 242-5.
[2] MONRO, 1, p. 67, gives one version of this story.
[3] CHLUMECKY, p. 75; FOERSTER, *Wallenstein*, 1, pp. 342 ff.
[4] DROYSEN, *Gustaf Adolf*, 1, pp. 346-7.
[5] CHLUMECKY, p. 78.

still recruiting[1] — three times the number of men that Tilly had once declared to be the utmost any general could want against an enemy in normal conditions.[2] And after the final defeat of Christian there was not even an enemy.

But the complaints which most perturbed the Emperor came from his own allies. 'We shall repent in the end of the excessive power given to Friedland', wrote Ferdinand's brother, Leopold of Tyrol.[3] The Elector of Saxony, on whose lands Wallenstein had, without any permission, quartered a detachment of his swelling armies, burst out in bitter lamentation both to Ferdinand and to Maximilian of Bavaria.[4] Most persistent in his complaints was Maximilian himself[5] who, for the last two years, had received plentiful intimation of Wallenstein's enormities. His general, Tilly, had suffered and protested ever since the winter of 1626. Wallenstein persistently forced him to quarter his troops in the most inconvenient and barren places, so that they deserted in great numbers and were re-enlisted by Wallenstein's officers. Worse than this systematic weakening of the actual man-power of Tilly's army was the undermining of the morale of his officers who, seeing that the rival general paid better and provided a more pleasant life, waited impatiently for the close of their contracts to leave the Bavarian service for the imperial. Pappenheim himself had considered transferring his allegiance.[6]

Ferdinand could not afford to disregard these complaints. He sent to ask Wallenstein's withdrawal from the siege of Stralsund,[7] and protested several times about the nature and extent of the quartering, although it was commonly believed in Vienna that the general paid no attention.[8] Wallenstein obeyed, it was said, when he wished to obey. He had the discretion to perceive that it would be unwise to alienate all the Catholic princes of Germany, and for this reason he evacuated

[1] KIEWNING, *Nuntiatur des Pallottos*, Rome, 1895, I, p. 81.
[2] RIEZLER, *Geschichte Bayerns*, VI, p. 170.
[3] DUDIK, *Correspondenz*, p. 316.
[4] *Annales*, IX, p. 93; LUNDORP, III, pp. 1009, 1042.
[5] LUNDORP, III, p. 1023.
[6] ARETIN, *Wallenstein*, Regensburg, 1846, I, p. 20; GINDELY, *Wallenstein während seines ersten Generalats*, I, p. 87.
[7] LUNDORP, III, pp. 1018-19; also HALLWICH, *Fünf Bücher*, III, pp. 355-6.
[8] KIEWNING, I, p. 82.

Swabia and Franconia, where many Catholic bishoprics were situated, to pour his troops the more ruthlessly into Saxony and Brandenburg. In north Germany from Krempe in Holstein to the borders of Prussia only Mecklenburg escaped his armies. Mecklenburg was his own estate and he carefully respected the imperial patent which exempted all that he owned from war contributions.

IV

In Vienna, meanwhile, Ferdinand pursued the less spectacular part of his policy. He was not a clever man but he had a certain unconscious ability for appropriating the ideas of clever men and converting them to his own uses. Just such a transformation he was now engaged upon. During the past year the Catholic princes, and particularly Maximilian, had pressed energetically upon his notice the excellent opportunity he now had of restoring the lands seized from the Church in the three-quarters of a century which had elapsed since the settlement of Augsburg.[1] This enthusiasm had not at first been reciprocated by the Emperor, who feared both the upheaval that the change might cause and the danger that Maximilian would make it an occasion for increasing his own power. He wanted Osnabrück for a cousin, and his brother had already engrossed the bishoprics of Münster, Liège, Hildesheim and Paderborn with that of Cologne.[2]

With the increasing strength of Wallenstein Ferdinand's attitude gradually altered. An Edict of Restitution properly carried out could be advantageous to the sovereign power of his dynasty. In the latter part of the year 1628 the idea assumed the first place in Ferdinand's internal policy, and now the Catholic princes hung back,[3] for Maximilian had as much reason to contest an Edict of Restitution which gave lands and power to the Hapsburg as he had previously had reason to advocate one that would increase his own. Besides, there had been talk at different moments in his long career of making him the

---

[1] LUNDORP, III, pp. 998-1000; RITTER, *Der Ursprung des Restitutionsediktes. Historische Zeitschrift*, LXXVI, pp. 94-5.
[2] CARAFA, p. 374.
[3] See LUNDORP, III, pp. 1054-7.

champion of the Church in place of Ferdinand — it had been partly his motive in founding the Catholic League and was being urged upon him now by the Pope himself — so that his rival's sudden appropriation of the plan for restitution, at the best possible moment for himself and the worst for Maximilian, was acutely embarrassing. Ferdinand stole the thunder that the Bavarian ruler had been so carefully preparing.

It would be unfair to Ferdinand to suppose that the processes of his mind were so deliberate or so cynical as they appear on analysis of the bare facts. He was genuinely devout, and if his education had made it impossible for him to distinguish between the needs of his Church and of his dynasty, the fault is one which is inherent in all political education. What political party, what political leader in the recorded history of the world could plead innocent? He had always wanted the restitution of the usurped lands of the Church: but when it was first suggested to him the occasion had not seemed propitious and now, in the course of the year 1628, it had become so.

Ferdinand was supported in his plan by his confessor, Father Lamormaini; he was a Jesuit, and circumstances had inclined the Jesuits to regard the house of Hapsburg as the special instrument of Heaven in re-establishing the Catholic Church. It will for ever remain an undecided point whether the Jesuits were correct in their calculations and the Pope wrong. Ferdinand, Wallenstein and the united Catholic Church would surely have swept the Reformation out of Germany; but with the Church disunited by an irrelevant political issue, Cardinal Richelieu, Maximilian and Father Joseph could, with the blessing of Rome, be undoing in Munich and Paris all that Ferdinand and Father Lamormaini were doing in Vienna.

Ferdinand had formulated a general and a particular plan, the first embracing all Germany, the second affecting the bishopric of Magdeburg only. The first and larger plan was to effect the return of all Church lands wrongfully usurped since 1555. Since no Diet could possibly be expected to vote for this, the scheme was to be executed on the strength of an imperial edict. This would serve the double purpose of expelling the Protestants and putting the Emperor's power of government by proclamation to a decisive test.

The change that Ferdinand intended to force upon his subjects was little less than revolutionary. It entailed the alteration of boundaries over all north and central Germany; princes who had grown rich on secularized property would sink at one blow to the level of minor nobility. The Duke of Wolfenbüttel alone held the lands of thirteen convents and a great part of what had once been the bishopric of Hildesheim, while the situation in Hesse, Württemberg and Baden was nearly as grave, and the Electors of Saxony and Brandenburg were not safe. Ferdinand had indeed guaranteed the lands of Saxony as the price of John George's initial alliance, but now that he could safely dispense with that alliance, there was no further security for his word; he had not kept his promise to maintain freedom for the Lutherans in Bohemia.

More perilous still was the position of the free cities. Augsburg, the greatest Lutheran city in Germany, was in the heart of a Catholic bishopric and had been Catholic in 1555; the conversion of the small German town had been the work of the latter part of the sixteenth century, and what was to happen at Dortmund, with all its churches now Protestant and only thirty Catholics in it?[1] — at Rothenburg, at Nördlingen, at Kempten, at Heilbronn? The return to the situation of 1555 would mean the destruction of property rights that had the sanction of three generations, the expulsion of noblemen from their estates and burghers from their towns; if the principle of *cujus regio ejus religio* was to be enforced in the lands restored to the Church, there would be a disturbance in the actual population which could not but lead to widespread distress and the stopping of all such commercial activity as had so far survived the war.

Moreover, Ferdinand was making no allowance for the size of the Catholic party in Germany in relation to the amount of new land it would have to digest. Even in Bohemia he had had difficulty in finding Catholic overlords fast enough for the estates, and Catholic priests fast enough for the people. He did not himself realize the enormity of the change that he wished to effect in Germany, if he imagined that the Jesuits and the Hapsburg dynasty alone would be able to engross the restored lands of the Church.

[1] RITTER, *Ursprung des Restitutionsediktes*, p. 85.

This was the general aspect of the question. The particular case of Magdeburg revealed Ferdinand's intentions at their simplest. This bishopric covered a large stretch of country on the Elbe between the small principality of Anhalt to the south and the Electorate of Brandenburg to the north. Since the Elbe was the chief highway between the Hapsburg dominions and the North Sea, the land was of the utmost strategic importance. The old Wendish name of the great episcopal town, Magataburg, had been slurred into the popular German form which meant the virgin city, and the accidental corruption had acquired in the last century a romantic significance from the prolonged resistance of the burghers to the attack of Charles V. Over their chief gate was the wooden statue of a young girl with a virgin's wreath in her hand and the device, 'Who will take it?' Although her burghers were for the most part Lutheran, Magdeburg had been technically a Catholic bishopric at the time of the Augsburg settlement. In 1628 she still tolerated just within her walls a small and harmless monastery, and among her thirty thousand inhabitants there were a few hundred Catholics. The cathedral and all the churches had been long since seized and the bishopric had passed into the hands of a Protestant administrator.

Christian William, a prince of the house of Brandenburg, who had been administrator when the Danish King invaded, had rashly entered into open alliance with him. Forced to abandon his bishopric at the approach of Wallenstein, he had since then fled for help to the King of Sweden, while his forsaken subordinates, anxious only for peace, had elected a son of the neutral Elector of Saxony in his place.[1] It was too late, for already the Emperor had declared the bishopric sequestrated in favour of his son Leopold. This was an enterprise, said Ferdinand, on which 'the salvation and happiness of many thousand souls depended, nay the rest and well-being of our house, as well as of the whole realm, the Holy Catholic Church and true religion'.[2] But if the Emperor had his way, the salvation and happiness of many thousand souls would also

[1] LUNDORP, IV, pp. 1021-2.
[2] WITTICH, *Magdeburg als Katholisches Marienburg. Historische Zeitschrift*, LXV, p. 416.

depend on the spiritual guidance of a twelve-year-old boy who was appalled at the prospect of becoming a priest.[1]

With Wallenstein ready to seize Magdeburg for the young Archduke,[2] and his troops holding all north Germany in check, Ferdinand sent a draft of the proposed Edict of Restitution to Maximilian of Bavaria and John George of Saxony. It was a challenge to the constitutionalists, Catholic and Protestant alike, but it was a safe challenge. John George could not object without risking a quarrel with Ferdinand that he was too weak to sustain alone, Maximilian could not object without compromising that position of Catholic leader which he was so carefully building up. Gradually Ferdinand was forcing his concealed enemies to abandon either their enmity or their concealment.

Grasping unhesitatingly at the same defence, the two electors demanded a Diet to discuss the matter.[3] Ferdinand declared that the wounds of the Church could not wait for a Diet to heal them, and on March 6th, 1629, he promulgated his Edict of Restitution to a defenceless Germany.

It was a searching document. In the first place it denied legitimate existence to the Calvinists. In the second place it denied the right of a Protestant to buy Church land, for Church land was inalienable and could not legally be sold. Thus even those who had honestly acquired the quondam spoils of the Church were to suffer. In the third place, and this was the most important of all, it denied the validity of any previous legal judgments in respect of Church land, thus asserting the private right of the Emperor to alter laws and legal decisions according to his will. The commissioners were instructed furthermore that if any complained that the Edict had not the sanction of a Diet, they should expound to them the doctrine of imperial absolutism.[4]

Ferdinand took little notice of the instant outcry from the administrative circles of Swabia and Franconia, where a very large proportion of land would have to change hands as a result of the Edict; he paid only polite attention to the lengthy

[1] FIEDLER, p. 194.
[2] CHLUMECKY, p. 94.
[3] LUNDORP, III, pp. 1045-7.
[4] Ibid., IV, pp. 1-2; LÜNIG, pp. 71-80.

and highly constitutional protest of the Elector of Saxony, answering it in a letter scarcely less long and quite as complicated.[1] He was, however, anxious to pacify Maximilian and took the occasion to offer him the sees of Verden and Minden for his family as soon as the Archduke Leopold had been appointed to Magdeburg, Halberstadt and Bremen. But Maximilian could not be so easily calmed when the property rights of all the princes in Germany were endangered and the Emperor was frankly enforcing his will at the sword's point — Wallenstein's sword.

Soldiers were pouring into the bishopric of Halberstadt, and the Duke of Wolfenbüttel, who already owed more than the market value of all his lands in war contributions, was to be forcibly divested of about a third of his territory, wrongfully appropriated from the Church; in Württemberg fourteen convents had already been seized by the troops.

Ferdinand was ingenious in using Wallenstein's army for the enforcement of the Edict, since he could plead the advancement of the Church as an excuse for maintaining the general's power. Surely the League would not wish to hinder the cause of true religion by attacking its mightiest supporter? But true religion or no, the members of the Catholic League had their own princely rights nearer at heart, and in December 1629 they demanded drastic reductions in the army. The fact that they did not definitely ask for the general's dismissal must be attributed to one of those temporary changes of front which were a disturbing feature of Maximilian's policy;[2] he appears at this moment to have wanted the army reduced but the general kept. In fact, he got neither, for Ferdinand issued a disingenuous order by which Wallenstein was forbidden to form new regiments, but given a free hand to enlarge his old ones, and his recruiting went forward unchecked.[3]

All this while Ferdinand built his power stone by stone, not on his own strength but on the weakness of his people. Rather than submit to the Edict of Restitution, stormed the Protestant pamphleteers, 'the Germans would cast away all laws and

---

[1] LUNDORP, IV, pp. 3-8.
[2] See RIEZLER, *Geschichte*, V, p. 357.
[3] HURTER, *Ferdinand II*, X, p. 265.

customs and let their country become a wilderness once more.'[1]
The angry broadsheet, the popular song, the formal protest —
these they issued in hundreds, but of active resistance there was
none.

The city of Augsburg had, since the celebrated Confession of
Augsburg, a special significance which made it almost sacred
to Lutherans.[2] An attack on this town might reasonably be
expected to awaken a new spirit of resistance in the Empire.
Although the so-called Catholic bishopric of Augsburg had
never ceased to exist, the town itself, unlike Magdeburg and
Halberstadt, was a free city of the Empire, independent of the
bishop. By reason of this divided control, the citizens exercized
the religion they had chosen, while the bishop retired to a
residence outside the boundaries of the free territory and continued to administer his episcopal lands.

When Wallenstein enforced the Edict of Restitution at
Magdeburg he was partly at least within the letter of existing
laws. There was no specific constitutional fault in the Edict
itself, only the weight of tradition against it. Magdeburg
was an episcopal town, not a free city. The question of Augsburg
was on an altogether different plane, for the right of a free city
had never yet been contested with impunity. Ferdinand had
only to look back twenty years and remember what had
happened when even the petty little Donauwörth had been
deprived of its rights by an imperial judgment. But Ferdinand
had never yet hesitated because a task was dangerous. The
challenging and subduing of Augsburg was worth the supposed
risk: it would put the power of the free cities to the test and it
would prove the effectual force, if any, of the Protestant
opposition.

On August 8th, 1629, after certain preliminary discussions
with the municipality, the exercise of the Protestant religion
was altogether forbidden and its ministers were exiled from the
city.[3] Augsburg collapsed without a sword drawn or a shot
fired. Eight thousand citizens went into exile, among them an
old man, Elias Holl, who had been master-mason for thirty

[1] RANKE, *Die römische Päpste*, p. 363.
[2] HURTER, *Ferdinand II*, IV, p. 97.
[3] LUNDORP, IV, pp. 25-7, 35-6.

years and had but recently completed the town hall which was the burghers' greatest pride.[1] It stands to this day, massive and grey, a monument to the extinguished hopes of a great commercial city.

Great was the indignation of the Protestants, but no man raised a finger save only John George of Saxony who wrote his habitual letter of dignified protest.[2] The reason was clear: there was neither courage nor hope left in Germany.

V

Within the Empire, Ferdinand had never been stronger; he had a power unequalled since the days of Charles V, a power which might, with time and skill, be the foundation of a re-vivified, re-united German state in which princely rights would be limited and Hapsburg absolutism with the Catholic Church reign supreme.

Outside the Empire, the storm gathered against him. It gathered in Mantua and the Low Countries, it was to break in the north from Sweden, and the cause behind it was the enmity between France and Spain. Ferdinand paid dearly for the faults of his Spanish cousins; he might have achieved a renewed power alone, he could not drag the carcass of Spain with him. Financially the master of imperial policy, Philip IV was politically worse than a dead-weight, he was dangerous. He introduced complications into Ferdinand's straight course which ruined him: he drew off the military strength of Germany to Italy, he forced the man who was rebuilding the Empire as a Catholic federation to quarrel with the Pope, he made him risk the solidarity of his new creation by driving him into war with the Dutch. Last of all, the fear of Spanish aggression prompted Richelieu to arrange a truce between the Kings of Poland and Sweden, thereby unleashing a Protestant champion against the rising Catholic Empire to destroy it for ever.

First came the Mantuan war. When Ferdinand, on a hint from Spain, sequestered the duchy, the Pope was at once in

[1] *Hauschronik der Familie Holl*, Munich, 1910, p. 87.
[2] LUNDORP, IV, p. 31 f.

terror of further Hapsburg intervention in Italy. In vain Ferdinand, supported by his confessor Father Lamormaini,[1] hung back to avoid this crisis; the Spanish King rated him soundly for not acting more emphatically against the French Duke of Mantua,[2] and Ferdinand was compelled to send imperial troops to Italy. The indignant Pope wavered only for a little; at the desire of the nuncio in Vienna he made one mild effort to buy Ferdinand off by sending him a relic,[3] but when this did not check the Mantuan campaign he turned almost brutally against him. He would not canonize either Wenceslas of Bohemia or Stephen of Hungary at his request; he refused to give him the right to appoint bishops to the reclaimed sees — a refusal which Ferdinand disregarded; he insisted that monastic lands should be given back to the orders from whom they had been taken and not to the Jesuits.[4] An excitable, talkative little man, Urban VIII soon let the whole of Rome know which way the wind blew. He could not speak above a whisper, he announced, because of Spanish spies in the Vatican, and he slept so ill at nights for worry over Mantua that he had all the birds in his gardens killed lest they should disturb him with untimely chirruping.[5]

Insignificant in itself, the Mantuan crisis was the turning point in the Thirty Years War, for it precipitated the final division of the Catholic Church against itself, alienated the Pope from the Hapsburg dynasty and made morally possible the calling in of Protestant allies by Catholic powers to redress the balance.

The year 1629, the twelfth year of the war, was more eventful in theory than in fact. Not in the field but in the chancelleries of Europe things moved towards a new formation. The Spanish monarchy asserted itself over the Empire and turned Ferdinand's hitherto successful policy into a difficult and dangerous channel. Spanish interests in Mantua thrust Ferdinand into opposition against the Pope; Spanish interests in the Low Countries forced him to risk his new-found imperial power on a Dutch war and to risk it in vain. While Ferdinand had been successful in

---

[1] KIEWNING, i, pp. 130, 141, 242.
[2] Ibid., i, p. 141.   [3] Ibid., i, pp. 158-9.
[4] RANKE, Die römische Päpste, p. 358.
[5] Relazioni dagli Ambasciatori, Roma, i, pp. 319, 339, 360.

Germany his Spanish cousins had been unsuccessful in Flanders, and they turned now not so much to ask as to exact help from him.

In the Netherlands, Frederick Henry, a commander as thorough as he was unspectacular and by now the idol of his people, carried all before him. On August 19th, 1629, he took Wesel, a fortress on the German border whence he could guard the passage of the Rhine, and hardly a month later the great town of Hertogenbosch on the frontier of Brabant. In Flanders, defeat after defeat demoralized the army and the civilian population and undermined the once popular rule of the Archduchess among her Flemish subjects.[1] Meanwhile Dutch ships infested the Narrow Seas and prevented the transport of bullion to the Flemish ports. In 1628 the Dutch admiral, Piet Hein, captured the entire treasure fleet off Cuba with spoils in bullion and goods valued at eleven and a half million Dutch florins — the shareholders of the Dutch West India Company received a fifty-per-cent dividend in 1629 from money that had been meant for the Spanish army in Flanders.

Ill-feeling spread among the unpaid Spanish soldiers, flaming at last into mutiny. Sheets of paper with the superscription, 'Money! Money! Money! We will not fight without money!' were thrown into the officers' quarters at Breda; at Herstal the men despoiled the neighbouring woods for faggots and supported themselves by selling these to the burghers; at Liège they were with difficulty prevented from plundering the town; at Sanfliet desertion thinned three full companies to less than sixty men. The discipline of the far-famed Spanish infantry was breaking down, and small wonder, for the troops went hungry and ill-clad, and in the winter two sentries at Liège had been found dead at their posts, frozen in their threadbare rags. The Archduchess staved off disaster by first pawning her jewellery and later raising exceptional levies from the people; the arrangement was unpopular and could not last.[2] In this extremity Ferdinand alone could help. The Spanish government called upon him to stigmatize the Dutch as breakers of

---

[1] LONCHAY ET CUVELIER, II, pp. 471, 482.
[2] *Annales*, XI, pp. 831-2; 400-1. See also RODRIGUEZ VILLA, *Spinola*, p. 461 f.; HENNEQUIN DE VILLERMOND, II, p. 259; LONCHAY ET CUVELIER, II, p. 471.

the imperial peace by their operations across the frontier at Wesel, and thus to force the German princes to take action against them.

This exertion of Spanish pressure on Ferdinand had two results. The first was that he had to divide his attention in Germany between persuading the princes to elect his son and forcing them to make war on the Dutch; the other that he had to sacrifice Wallenstein earlier than he intended. Frankly, Wallenstein's interest in the Baltic plan and the restitution of Church lands lasted only so long as he could use them to advance his own scheme for a German-Slav Empire, centred about the Elbe, commanding the northern seaboard and dominating the lands to east and west. He wanted Brandenburg silenced, Saxony quiescent, Poland and Transylvania as tributary allies, Denmark and Sweden humbled. In so far as he had any views on the subsequent policy of this reformed Empire, he wanted it to attack the Turk. Born in eastern Europe, fighting his first campaign in a Turkish war, Wallenstein conceived of the Turk as the great hereditary enemy.[1]

The first essential was a quiescent north Germany, and while the general undoubtedly believed that his troops could silence opposition, the economist and the politician in him revolted against the enforcement of the Edict of Restitution. By his campaigns against the King of Denmark, Wallenstein had reduced the northern provinces to political submission; why provoke the Protestant powers of Europe or rouse any remnants of resistance in the north by interfering unnecessarily with religion? After the battle of Lutter he was said to have inadvisedly burst out with a statement that he would redeem no more abbeys for the Church until she had better men to send to them.[2] Since the promulgation of the Edict of Restitution Wallenstein had provoked ever sharper criticism from Vienna by the way in which he occupied the lands in question without facilitating the task of the priests and monks who were sent to take charge.[3]

He had shown a curious lack both of political and of human understanding in exploiting the schemes of the Spanish government; for, while they might in time have forgiven him had he

---

[1] See CHLUMECKY, 1628-9, *passim*.
[2] PRIORATO, *Valstein*, pp. 27-8.
[3] See RANKE, *Wallenstein*, p. 166 f.

refused to handle their Baltic plan, they could never forgive him for both appropriating the plan and excluding them from its execution. At a comparatively early period he had advised the Emperor to refuse Spain's help and leave the building and management of the Baltic fleet entirely to him,[1] a line of conduct which had ended in the failure of both parties to raise ships and the successful defiance by Stralsund.

Wallenstein had miscalculated; he had never reckoned on serious opposition from the Baltic ports, and in 1629 he found himself in a position of unexpected danger. The resistance of Stralsund and her alliance with the King of Sweden had seriously affected the King of Poland; now that Gustavus Adolphus had got Pillau from Brandenburg and Stralsund, he could wage war on Poland with such dangerous effect that Sigismund III would be bound to give up the struggle.[2] The Polish watchdog being thus chained up, nothing would prevent the King of Sweden from invading Germany. The Hanse towns, which would not receive Wallenstein, would many of them joyfully receive Gustavus Adolphus, and he could thus make himself master of the Baltic and stretch out a hand to the oppressed Protestants of Germany.

All through 1629 this danger came nearer. In February the King of Sweden arranged a meeting with the King of Denmark; Christian, a defeated man suing for peace,[3] might at last be willing to accept the position of subordinate ally to the King of Sweden. But Gustavus Adolphus had left it just too late. A year before, Christian IV had some tenuous hope of redeeming his good name; after the defeat of Wolgast he had none.

In vain Gustavus plied him with tales of Wallenstein's hypothetical fleet and urged him to meet the danger half-way. The King of Denmark shrugged his shoulders; the German princes would not help, he said, and his poor, exhausted country, half overrun by the enemy, could raise not another penny. Gustavus waxed enthusiastic; Sweden had been fighting continuously for thirty years, he boasted, and would go on if he said so. As for himself, he had a bullet in his shoulder and would carry three if

---

[1] GINDELY, *Die maritimen Pläne*, p. 15.   [2] Ibid., p. 30.
[3] Christian issued credentials for the negotiation of peace on December 7th, 1628, Ferdinand on the 19th. HALLWICH, *Fünf Bücher*, III, pp. 423, 426.

it were the will of God, and with that he invited the King of Denmark to feel the scar. Christian remained unmoved. A dissertation on the duties of Protestants to their religion, on which the King of Sweden embarked some time later, at length stirred the older and defeated man to a cogent protest. 'What business has Your Majesty in Germany?' he suddenly threw in his face. Gustavus, for the fraction of a second, was at a loss. 'Is that worth asking?' he shouted indignantly, and then, launching again into his discourse, inveighed against the enemies who wronged the Protestant Churches. Quivering with emotion, he bore down on the King of Denmark, shaking his fist almost under his nose. 'Your Majesty may be sure', he cried, 'that be he who he will that does this to us, emperor or king, prince or republic or — nay, or a thousand devils — we will so take each other by the ears that our hair shall fly out in handfuls.' His histrionics were lost on Christian of Denmark; the only possible retort was that he regretted that the King of Sweden had not felt so strongly five years before. With astonishing restraint Christian did not make it.[1]

The chief effect of the meeting was that Wallenstein sent reinforcements to Sigismund of Poland, so that he might engage the Swedes for as much longer as he could,[2] and hastened to soften his terms of peace for the King of Denmark. They were still hard enough: Christian was to give up the north German bishoprics and accept the imperial sovereignty over Holstein, Stormarn and Ditmarschen, but whatever his opinion of the treaty, and it was not favourable,[3] he had little choice but to accept it. 'If he has not lost his wits he will grasp at it with both hands', said Wallenstein dryly.[4] In June 1629 peace was concluded at Lübeck.

The Peace of Lübeck did not end the danger in the north, for in the early part of the year the Elector of Brandenburg, driven at last to desperation by Wallenstein's exactions, had made overtures towards the United Provinces,[5] and later joined

---

[1] *Riksrådet G. G. Oxenstiernas Berättelse om Mötel mellan Gustaf Adolf och Kristian IV. Historiske Handlingar*, VIII, iv, pp. 4-16; *Oxenstjerna Brefvexling*, II, i, pp. 463-4; II, iii, pp. 173-4; FRIDERICIA, II, p. 179.

[2] CHLUMECKY, pp. 131-3.

[3] FRIDERICIA, II, pp. 195-6, 237 f.

[4] CHLUMECKY, p. 132.

[5] LUNDORP, IV, pp. 1092-3.

in a suspicious correspondence with the King of Sweden.[1] Worse still, agents of France and England arranged a truce between Gustavus and Sigismund of Poland[2] and before the end of the year a French ambassador visited the Swedish King at Upsala, to find him already discussing with his council the project of invading Germany.[3]

In these circumstances only one solution presented itself to Wallenstein — to increase his army so that a landing in north Germany would be impossible. Only in this way could the Baltic plan be brought to completion.[4] This determination of Wallenstein precipitated his quarrel with the Spanish monarchy. Early in 1629 Richelieu had invaded Italy, occupied Susa, relieved Casale and signed a treaty with Savoy, Venice and the Pope.[5] Olivarez struck him in the back by assisting the Huguenots,[6] but Richelieu by skilful diplomacy brought this inner peril to an end at the Peace of Alais. The attack on Italy was postponed, not prevented; the Hapsburg had gained breathing space only. To the disgust of the belligerent Olivarez, Spinola advised settlement by treaty and not by war; he was overruled.[7] Henceforward the ungrateful government at Madrid sought only to undermine the veteran general.[8] In his place they demanded that Wallenstein's army should be sent them from Germany. What was the use of that great force on the Baltic, now that the naval project had failed and the only remaining enemy was the petty King of Sweden? So argued Olivarez, and Ferdinand, even if he were better informed, had no choice but to obey.

In May 1630 he asked Wallenstein for thirty thousand men to be sent to Italy, not under the general's personal command but under the Italian mercenary, Collalto, in whose favour the Spanish party in Vienna had long sought to oust him. Wallen-

---

[1] LUNDORP, IV, p. 19.
[2] *Sverges Traktater*, V, i, pp. 347-56; RICHELIEU, *Mémoires*, ed. Petitot, II, XXV, p. 133 f.
[3] *Handlingar hörande till Konung Gustaf Adolfs historia. Handlingar rörande Skandinaviens Historia*, II, pp. 79 ff.; RICHELIEU, *Mémoires*, II, XXV, pp. 150 ff.
[4] See GINDELY, *Die maritimen Pläne*, pp. 53-4.
[5] ABREU Y BERTODANO, IV, pp. 105 f., 113 f.
[6] Ibid., p. 127 f.
[7] RODRIGUEZ VILLA, *Correspondencia de la Infanta*, p. xxxi; *Spinola*, p. 590 f.
[8] RODRIGUEZ VILLA, *Spinola*, pp. 590 ff.

DEADLOCK

stein replied categorically that he could not spare a soldier.[1]
The crisis between Ferdinand and the man to whom he owed
his greatness had come.

Early in that same month the King of Sweden's councillors
had let their master persuade them that Sweden's very life
depended on an immediate invasion of Germany.[2] Thus on
May 29th, having commended his only child, the Princess
Christina, to the protection of his council, he set sail from
Stockholm.[3] He was 'the rising sun' to Richelieu,[4] the 'Protestant Messiah' to Maximilian of Bavaria,[5] but to Ferdinand
of Hapsburg he was nothing but the insignificant usurper[6] of a
frozen country on the arctic edge of civilization. Since the
King of Denmark had been so easily overcome, surely he could
snap his fingers at the 'Schwedische canaglia'.[7] This was
Wallenstein's term, but his theoretical contempt, unlike Ferdinand's, was not reflected in practice. He thought it wiser to
prevent the Swedes from landing than to have to expel them
subsequently, and had he been allowed to keep the north coast
satisfactorily guarded, no landing would have been possible.
Ferdinand would not agree, Wallenstein was overruled and
thirty thousand men marched south for Italy.

Wallenstein's power was threatened. 'I wage more war with
a few ministers than with all the enemy', he declared;[8] and it
was true. The imperial councillors had all turned against him.
His occupation of the hereditary lands was draining the meagre
resources of the Crown; and his exactions elsewhere were making
Ferdinand unpopular. 'No one knows', wailed the Elector of
Brandenburg in a letter to Vienna, 'how long I shall remain
Elector and master in my own land'; he complained that he
had not only to support the troops quartered on his country
but to pay contributions for others and, he added bitterly, 'the
actual cause of this war is unknown to me'.[9] He did well to

[1] HALLWICH, *Briefe und Akten zur Geschichte Wallensteins*, Vienna, 1912,
I, p. 33; see also KIEWNING, I, pp. 147-8; II, pp. 26, 377, 462.
[2] *Svenska Riksradets Protokoll*, II, p. 2.
[3] ARCHENHOLTZ, *Historische Merkwürdigkeiten*, Liepzig, 1751, II, p. 29.
[4] RICHELIEU, *Mémoires*, ed. Petitot, II, xxv, p. 119.
[5] HURTER, *Ferdinand II*, x, p. 231.
[6] Ferdinand, of course, regarded Sigismund III of Poland as Sweden's
rightful King.
[7] FOERSTER, *Wallenstein*, I, p. 387.   [8] CHLUMECKY, p. 218.
[9] HALLWICH, *Briefe und Akten*, I, pp. 12-19.

mention this, for since the Peace of Lübeck there was, theoretically, no war.

Far more serious was the menacing attitude of the exasperated Maximilian. He had openly admitted to the French envoy in Munich that he intended to force the Emperor to disarm. For some time a rumour had been current that he would now, at this eleventh hour, make that effort to break the Hapsburg succession to the imperial throne which he had failed to make in 1619. He would himself contest the election of the Emperor's son by standing for the title of King of the Romans. The French agent had whispered it to the English agent in the previous year as they hung about the draughty encampment of the King of Sweden in Prussia. 'I pray God this be not a French nightingale that sings sweetly but is all voice', the Englishman wrote home.[1] When a little later the League, under Maximilian's influence, voted money to keep Tilly's army ready against emergencies,[2] notwithstanding the Peace of Lübeck, it seemed indeed that Maximilian had learnt a lesson from the technique of Wallenstein and that the nightingale would not be all voice.

In March 1630 the Elector of Mainz issued a summons to his colleagues to attend an Electoral meeting at Regensburg[3] in the summer, and thither towards the end of May Ferdinand set out. For his own part he wanted to buy the election of his son by the sacrifice of Wallenstein, a movement for which the time was now well ripe. But for the sake of his Spanish cousins he had to add another demand, namely that the Electors should agree to send troops against the Dutch. Wallenstein's dismissal might conceivably buy one or the other concession from the weakened princes, but could it possibly buy both? The government of Spain was forcing Ferdinand to risk the success of his own policy by merging it with theirs. It had done worse; it had conjured up the power of France to play an active part in Germany. Moving darkly on the edge of imperial politics, Richelieu had first delivered the King of Sweden from the Polish danger, had then committed himself to an alliance with the Dutch, and now made ready to send representatives to the Electoral meeting

---

[1] ROE, *Negotiations*, p. 43.
[2] LUNDORP, III, pp. 1084-8.
[3] Ibid., IV, p. 45.

itself, who, under cover of negotiating for the French Duke of
Mantua, would tamper with the Electors of the Holy Roman
Empire.

Possibly, even probably, Ferdinand alone would have been
a match for the divided princes, but Ferdinand harassed by his
Spanish cousins could never be a match for the German princes
and Richelieu together. The meeting at Regensburg in 1630
was a prelude to the conflict between Bourbon and Hapsburg,
not an epilogue to the German war, and Ferdinand neither
wholly abandoned nor wholly completed his policy; it was
tacitly superseded.

VI

In the summer of 1630 there was no war in Germany. With
the withdrawal of the King of Denmark, the last armed resistance of the Protestants ended. It should have been the mission
of the assembled Electors to give sanction to that peace by
settling the still outstanding problems and demobilizing the
army. It was high time.

In ten years of war more than half the Empire had borne the
actual occupation or passage of troops, the immediate disaster
leaving a train of evils behind — disease among the cattle,
famine for man and beast, the ineradicable germs of plague.
Four bad harvests in succession between 1625 and 1628 added
their burden to the tale of German misery. Plague took terrific
toll of the hungry people and wiped out whole encampments
of wretched refugees. Poverty and starvation robbed a naturally
industrious people both of hope and of shame, so that it was no
longer a disgrace to beg. Once-respected burghers were not
ashamed to knock for alms at their neighbours' houses,[1] and
charity was exhausted not for lack of sympathy but for lack of
means. Exiled pastors wandered about the country looking for
those not who *would* but who *could* take them in, and looking in
vain. In the Upper Palatinate the Catholic priests, to make
room for whom they had been expelled, implored the government to relieve their now starving predecessors.[2]

[1] ANDREAE, III, p. 109.
[2] HOGL, *Die Gegenreformation in Waldsassen*, Regensburg, 1905, p. 78.

In Tyrol in 1628 they ground bean-stalks for bread, in Nassau in 1630 acorns and roots.[1] Even in Bavaria starved bodies lay unburied on the roads.[2] The harvest of 1627 on the banks of the Havel had promised well, but retreating Danes and pursuing imperialists destroyed it.[3] 'I hear nothing but lamentations nor see variety but of dead bodies', wrote Sir Thomas Roe from 'miserable Elbing' on the gulf of Danzig in 1629. 'In eighty English miles not a house to sleep safe in; no inhabitants save a few poor women and children vertendo stercorarium to find a corn of wheat.'[4]

No matter what the destitution of the people, the soldiers continued their exactions and plied their nefarious sports. The sword to till the land, and plunder for their harvest, such was the burden of their outspoken songs,[5] and they practised what they sang. At Kolberg alone they burnt five churches with all the barns and storehouses belonging to them, and this as often for the fun of the bonfire as for any other purpose; they would let off their pistols for sport into the haystacks, and once they deliberately set fire to a quarter of the town and came back when the houses were in ashes to plunder the people who were camping in the church with all that was left of their goods.[6] At nearly every occupied town the pleasant suburbs where the burghers tended their fruit and vegetable gardens were burnt to make room for fortifications.[7]

On the back of an exorbitant list of demands the burgomaster of Schweidnitz scribbled a prayer:[8] it seemed the only possible comment. Tilly's officers had had the church spires torn down and melted for the lead when money could not be found, and along the Elbe they had improvized new tolls to satisfy their demands.[9] Even if a town could supply all that was needed, there was no guarantee that the money or pro-

---

[1] LAMMERT, pp. 97, 109.
[2] Ibid., p. 119.
[3] GEBAUER, *Kurbrandenburg in der Krisis des Jahres 1627*, pp. 127-9.
[4] ROE, *Negotiations*, pp. 36-8.
[5] ZIEGLER, *Deutsche Soldatenlieder*, Leipzig, 1884, p. 18.
[6] COSMUS VON SIMMERN, *Bericht über die von ihm erlebten Geschichtsereignisse. Baltische Studien*, XL, pp. 28, 47-8.
[7] Ibid., p. 34.
[8] J. KREBS, *Die Drangsale der Stadt Schweidnitz. Zeitschrift des Vereins für Geschichte und Altertum Schlesien*, XIV, p. 36.
[9] HURTER, *Zur Geschichte Wallensteins*, p. 47.

visions would be used to satisfy the soldiers and prevent further disturbance; one commander was commonly reported to have melted down the plate he had confiscated to make himself a dinner service,[1] and Wallenstein fulminated against officers who kept their companies below strength in order to appropriate the pay given them for the men.[2]

In Thuringia a party of Wallenstein's men, who had dined too well in one of those eating places in the cellars of the town-hall which seem then as now to have provided the best food and drink in Germany, discovered that they could have fine sport firing at the feet of the passers-by through the low-set windows of the cellar.[3]

In the Mark of Brandenburg they carried off respectable burghers as hostages, dragged them for miles along the rough roads bound to their horses' tails and tied them like dogs under tables and benches for the night.[4] The virulent hatred between soldiers and civilians, rising almost to a frenzy, increased the horrors of war. Civil war between the peasants and the troops raged in Ditmarschen with daily killings, burnings, raiding of camps and answering attacks on villages.[5] In his nightmare novel, Grimmelshausen speaks of soldiers thrusting the peasants' thumbs into their pistols, thus improvizing a hideously effective thumbscrew; of the cord twisted round the head until the eyes began to start; of roasting and smoking over fires and in ovens; of pouring liquid filth into the mouths of the victims, which was later known as the Swedish drink. It was sport to shoot the prisoners tied in long rows one behind the other, and lay wagers on the number that one charge of shot would penetrate.[6]

Germany had but one chance of recovery and that was by the conclusion of the war. Yet hardly a prince or ruling poten-

[1] SIMMERN, p. 37.
[2] LUNDORP, III, p. 996.
[3] EINERT, *Ein Thüringer Landpfarrer, Arnstadt*, 1893, pp. 2-3.
[4] GINDELY, *Waldstein während seines ersten Generalats*, I, p. 348 f.
[5] *Die Bauernchronik des Hartich Sierk*. Flensburg, 1925, pp. 173-5.
[6] GRIMMELSHAUSEN, *Simplicissimus*, I, IV, XIV. The novelist, although he had experienced some of the incidents described in his book, naturally allowed himself a certain licence in the compilation of his story. One critic has pointed out the suspicious likeness between one of his scenes and a picture by Callot showing the same subject – the plundering of a farm-house. Both of these are set-pieces in which every form of atrocity is shown happening at the same moment. In the text I have been careful to mention only such things as are plentifully supported by other evidence.

tate in 1630 so much as considered the quickest way of settlement. John George of Saxony penned a protest of compelling eloquence to Ferdinand, in which he drew the conditions of the country almost in tears of blood,[1] but he revealed the extent to which the sufferings of the populace had touched his blunted sensibilities by refusing to come to Regensburg. He asserted that Ferdinand was trying to intimidate him, and persuaded the Elector of Brandenburg to join with him in a protest meeting at Annaburg.[2] He acted, no doubt, from the highest political motives, but there was small prospect of peace for Germany when two of the Electors refused even to join in a general discussion.

Maximilian was little better. In one respect he was worse, for, in his determination to break Wallenstein, he arrived at Regensburg armed with the secret support of the Pope and Richelieu.[3] Believing that Spanish intervention was at the root of the German disaster, Maximilian displayed a fatal, if a common, lack of perception when he sought to rid the Empire of one foreign influence by calling in yet another.

Had Maximilian refused to help or be helped by the French agents at Regensburg, had the Electors of Saxony and Brandenburg accepted the defeat of Protestantism instead of making an eleventh hour stand, there would have been peace in Germany. The King of Sweden must have withdrawn and the war between Bourbon and Hapsburg would have been fought out in Flanders and Italy. Surrender in 1630 would have saved Germany from eighteen more years of war, and although the settlement would have been very different from that ultimately enforced by the governments of France and Sweden in 1648, it would not have been appreciably worse. Surrender in 1630 would have meant the abandonment of the German Liberties; these Liberties were the privileges of ruling princes, or at most of municipalities, and had nothing to do with the rights of peoples. Popular liberty was unknown, before, during and after the war. Ferdinand's victory would have meant the centralization of the Empire under Austrian control, the establishment of one

---

[1] LUNDORP, IV, p. 40.
[2] GEBAUER, *Die Restitutionsedikt in Kurbrandenburg*, pp. 72-88.
[3] RICHELIEU, *Mémoires*, ed. Petitot, II, xxv, p. 115; *Relazioni dagli Ambasciatori, Roma*, I, pp. 296, 337.

despotism rather than several in the German-speaking world. It would have meant a heavy defeat for Protestantism but not its extinction. The Catholic Church was already proving itself too weak to carry out the gigantic task which Ferdinand had given it, and the spiritual redemption of secularized lands lagged far behind the political seizure. Admirable as was the constancy of many Protestants, great as was the number of exiles who drifted north to Saxony and Brandenburg and Holland, among the younger generation on both sides indifference was growing. Ferdinand's organization was already proving unequal to the execution of the Edict of Restitution, and even had he achieved all that was implied by that document, Protestantism would not have been extinguished. There remained Saxony and Brandenburg and the undisputed fragments of Württemberg, Hesse, Baden and Brunswick.

It would be absurd to pretend that the victory of Ferdinand in 1630 would have been an unmixed blessing. Great was the suffering that the Edict of Restitution had already caused, and great would have been the distress which its further execution would have engendered, but it is at least permissible to ask whether eighteen more years of war were not infinitely worse. There are strong arguments in favour of those who preferred to continue the war: surrender would have been a fatal encouragement to the Hapsburg dynasty both in Germany and in Europe; Ferdinand might be encouraged to further aggression and he would almost undoubtedly assist the King of Spain against the Dutch. The power of the Hapsburg would overshadow all Europe. Yet in point of fact the continuation of the struggle led only to the no less threatening dominance of the Bourbon. By the settlement of 1648 the German Liberties were preserved intact by thoughtful foreign allies who saw in them a guarantee of German weakness. Eighteen years of conflict produced a settlement which was no better from the internal point of view, and infinitely worse from the external point of view, than any which could have been made in 1630. The German Liberties were certainly very dearly bought.

They may not have seemed so expensive to the princes, for it was not they who paid the price. Famine in Brunswick-Wolfenbüttel caused the Duke to notice that his table was less plentifully supplied than usual, and three bad wine harvests on the Lower Danube once prevented Ferdinand from sending his annual gift of tokay to John George of Saxony — such minute draughts blew in through palace windows from the hurricane without.[1] Mortgaged lands, empty exchequers, noisy creditors, the discomforts of wounds and imprisonment, the loss of children in battle, these are all griefs which man can bear with comparative equanimity. The bitter mental sufferings which followed from mistaken policies, loss of prestige, the stings of conscience and the blame of public opinion gave the German rulers cause to regret the war but seldom acted as an incentive to peace. No German ruler perished homeless in the winter's cold, nor was found dead with grass in his mouth, nor saw his wife and daughters ravished; few, significantly few, caught the pest.[2] Secure in the formalities of their lives, in the food and drink at their tables, they could afford to think in terms of politics and not of human suffering.

VII

The Regensburg Electoral meeting of 1630 is only important in imperial history because its governing considerations were remote from Germany. The old problem of the Dutch war, the old enmity of Bourbon and Hapsburg, controlled the discussion on both sides.

Now that Ferdinand was master in Germany, the Spanish government demanded that he should summon the princes to help them subdue the Dutch. They were not discouraged at Madrid by the failure of all the efforts they had hitherto made to induce in the German rulers a more favourable attitude towards this programme. Bribes in the shape of pensions were regularly paid to the Electors of Cologne and Treves, to the Duke of Neuburg, to certain officers in the army and ministers at the Court of Vienna, even to servants in Wallenstein's household — all without result.[3] The Elector of Cologne made a few protests against Dutch military operations actually within his own

---

[1] HURTER, *Zur Geschichte Wallensteins*, pp. 247-8.
[2] Perhaps only the luckless Frederick of Bohemia; a case of poetic justice?
[3] H. GÜNTER, *Die Habsburger Liga*, Berlin, 1908, pp. 213-23.

lands, but even when their proximity caused Tilly some military anxiety, Maximilian forbade any attack on them.[1] Once indeed the Electors had requested the Archduchess Isabella to withdraw all restrictions on Dutch trade, seeing that the Provinces, whatever their relations with Spain, were technically members of the Empire and ought to share its privileges.[2]

Ferdinand needed all his optimism to think that he could induce the princes to declare war on the Dutch. Yet his obligation to Spain forced him to set this point almost first among his demands when he opened the meeting at Regensburg early in July 1630. Justifying his own armaments by a reference to the Mantuan war, he pointed out that the Dutch had infringed the integrity of the Empire, and urged the Electors to take measures against them. Led by Maximilian, they answered that they could discuss nothing until Ferdinand reduced his army and found a new commander-in-chief. As for Dutch hostility, they had noticed none; on the other hand the Spaniards were making unpardonable use of German soil for their military operations.[3]

This was attack and counter-attack leading to deadlock. Ferdinand's answer was conciliatory in manner but not in matter. He pointed out that he had personally always insisted on discipline in his army, and promised that he would find a new commander-in-chief.[4] The answer was ill-received, partly because of its vagueness, but more because of the rumour that Ferdinand intended his own son for the new commander, a change which would be in some respects a change for the worse. On July 29th, the Electors responded with a second and more emphatic series of complaints.[5]

Ferdinand had gone hunting while the Electors discussed their grievances, and did not get back until the evening of July 31st. In the intervening time two French agents had arrived, one of them being Father Joseph himself. The news of these arrivals, or a more mature consideration of the Electoral complaints, or both, destroyed Ferdinand's good cheer, and when he rode in on the evening of the 31st he passed silently to his

[1] LUNDORP, III, p. 1103; IV, pp. 111-16.
[2] GINDELY, *Die maritimen Pläne der Habsburger*, p. 21.
[3] LUNDORP, IV, pp. 53-4.   [4] Ibid., p. 59 f.
[5] Ibid., p. 61 f.

apartments and sat until three in the morning of August 1st closeted with his nearest councillors.[1]

The events of the next days justified anxiety. Both Father Joseph and the Papal nuncio strengthened the princes in their determination neither to sanction a war against the Dutch, nor to elect the young Archduke as King of the Romans. Father Joseph saw to it so thoroughly that no aspect of Spanish intervention in Germany was lost on the Electors,[2] that Brulart, the second of the French agents, was able to assert complacently soon after that these princes were all 'good Frenchmen'.[3] John George of Saxony, meanwhile, made his position clear by sending in a schedule of six leading stipulations which he considered essential preliminaries to any discussion of peace. The chief of these were the religious settlement of the Empire as it had been in 1618, the withdrawal of the Edict of Restitution and the drastic reduction of war contributions.[4]

On August 7th, at Regensburg, Ferdinand once again attempted to reduce the Catholic Electors by argument. He denied that he had ever acted as anything but a defender of the constitution against aggression, and inserted unobtrusively in his speech the suggestion that the duchy of Cleves-Jülich, the succession of which was still doubtful, should be sequestered.[5] This was a further sidelong attempt to help the Spanish in the Dutch war by giving them strong foothold on the Lower Rhine. To sweeten their consideration of these propositions, Ferdinand entertained the princes on the following day with an exhibition of riding at the ring, in which his eldest son again carried off the prize.[6] Fortunately for the Emperor's stage-management, young Ferdinand had a keen eye and a good seat on a horse, but if his father thought that these qualities would soften the hearts of the assembled Electors, he thought wrong. Their answer to his new propositions was cold to the point of hostility. They

[1] HERMANN WÄSCHKE, *Tagebuch Christians II von Anhalt. Deutsche Geschichtsblätter*, XVI, v, p. 122.
[2] RICHELIEU, *Mémoires*, ed. Petitot, II, xxvi, p. 285.
[3] HERMANN WÄSCHKE, *Tagebuch Christians II von Anhalt, Deutsche Geschichtsblätter*, XVI, v, p. 132.
[4] LUNDORP, IV, p. 73.
[5] Ibid., pp. 65-72.
[6] HERMANN WÄSCHKE, *Tagebuch Christians II von Anhalt. Deutsche Geschichtsblätter*, XVI, v, p. 129 f.

dragged the slyly inserted reference to Cleves-Jülich into the daylight, recognized its full implications and flatly refused to countenance any sequestration.[1]

Ferdinand had two trumps in his hand, Wallenstein and the Edict of Restitution. The abandonment of the general might pacify the Catholic Electors, the abandonment of the Edict would pacify Saxony and Brandenburg and possibly force them, belatedly, to attend the meeting. He decided to play the first of these cards at once, and on August 17th called his councillors together to discuss the best means for dismissing the general. Wallenstein was only a few miles off at Memmingen with a large following, and the Emperor himself admitted that he could not answer for the way in which he might take a demand for his resignation.[2] Surprisingly, however, a preliminary messenger brought the news that Wallenstein would withdraw if the Emperor personally desired it. On August 24th an imperial embassy arrived at Memmingen;[3] Wallenstein received its members with sombre dignity and sent them back to Regensburg with his formal resignation. He had shown them an astral diagram on which it was shown that the fate of Ferdinand was controlled at certain crises by Maximilian. Within certain limits Wallenstein let the decrees of Heaven govern his actions, but submitting in public he nourished in private the well-laid plans of his revenge.[4]

His dismissal robbed the French agents of Bavarian support. With Wallenstein gone, Maximilian saw his way to regaining his military dominance over Ferdinand and was no longer interested in foreign allies. At the same time Ferdinand's troops had taken Mantua and forced the French duke to fly. Defeated in Italy and deprived of Maximilian's support in Germany, the French were in a weak position, and Ferdinand pushed his advantage home. He offered to confirm Charles of Nevers as Duke of Mantua, provided Casale and Pinerolo were guaranteed to Spain, and that the French government undertook to enter into no alliance with those at war within the Empire. It was a direct thrust at the Franco-Dutch alliance, a barrier against

[1] LUNDORP, IV, pp. 72-3.
[2] DUDIK, Correspondenz, p. 273.
[3] HALLWICH, Briefe und Akten, pp. 54-5, 75 f.
[4] Annales, XI, p. 1133; PEKAŘ, Wallenstein.

Richelieu's projected Swedish treaty. In France the King was ill and the desperate requests of the ambassadors for further instructions remained unanswered. Father Joseph and Brulart had to decide for themselves. On October 13th, 1630, they agreed provisionally to all Ferdinand's demands, and the Treaty of Regensburg was signed.

The news was received with dismay in France. Richelieu, his features drawn with anxiety and anger, declared to the Venetian ambassador that he intended to abandon politics and enter a monastery.[1] Casale and Pinerolo lost, the alliances with the Dutch and Swedes renounced, the friendship of the German princes waning — this was the outcome of Father Joseph's diplomacy. Meanwhile Ferdinand, suffused with the benevolence of the victor to the vanquished, was saying farewell to the ambassadors with expressions of exceptional regard for Richelieu and the King of France.[2]

Ferdinand had squeezed all that he could out of Wallenstein's dismissal. His other move, the withdrawal of the Edict of Restitution, might yield even greater advantages. Eggenberg besought him to make it.[3] The King of Sweden was invading; every day brought fresh rumours of his advance — he had fifty thousand men — he had taken Gustrow — he had taken Weimar — Regensburg was alive with misinformation and fear.[4] This was no moment to quarrel with the Protestant Electors. Abandon the Edict of Restitution, and the protest meeting of Saxony and Brandenburg must come to an end, since they had themselves issued a manifesto declaring that the Edict alone prevented peace in the Empire.[5] The Catholic Electors were prepared to discuss the matter with them. Surely Ferdinand for the sake of his dynasty would yield.

But Eggenberg came up against uncompromising obstinacy. Ferdinand had played half his hand admirably; he refused to play the second half. The abandonment of Wallenstein and of the Edict were for him on incomparably different planes. The one was concerned merely with politics, the other was an

[1] *Relazioni dagli Ambasciatori, Francia*, II, p. 272.
[2] RICHELIEU, *Mémoires*, ed. Petitot, II, xxvi, p. 377.
[3] Ibid., VI, p. 360.
[4] WÄSCHKE, XVI, v, pp. 104, 110, 116.
[5] LUNDORP.

article of faith. That underlying fanaticism, which had so far carried him safely through all the risks of his career, played him false here.

Before the end of August it was said in Regensburg that he would never yield,[1] and all through the Electoral meeting imperial troops in Württemberg continued their brutal redemption of monastic lands. His triumph therefore at Regensburg was over Richelieu alone, not over the princes, and the meeting broke up in November with almost every problem it had come to settle still unsolved.

On the agreement of the Dutch to withdraw any troops they had in Cleves and Jülich, Ferdinand was forced to promise the evacuation of all other troops, thus abandoning the idea of sequestration and shelving the vexed question of Dutch neutrality.[2] The imperial army was to be placed under the command of Maximilian and Tilly, leaving the Emperor in his position of five years previously, before the intervention of Wallenstein. The Edict of Restitution was to be fully discussed at a general meeting of the princes.[3] No King of the Romans was elected, no war in the Spanish interest declared.

Against the single diplomatic victory over France, Ferdinand had to balance these two heavy defeats. Nor did he receive any sympathy from that very government to whose interests he had so fatally sacrificed his own. At Madrid they were indignant at the Cleves-Jülich settlement and had not the intelligence to appreciate what had been done for them in the Mantuan affair.

Within the Empire Ferdinand's policy had broken down. The pressure of Spain's demands had been too heavy on the still unstable structure. Instead of uniting Germany, the Regensburg meeting had divided it, leaving Maximilian and the League to dominate Ferdinand's policy once again, and the two Protestant Electors to dissociate themselves by a new minority protest from the actions of their colleagues.[4] Into this growing rift the invading King of Sweden was

[1] Wäschke, p. 131.
[2] Lundorp, iv, pp. 116-25.
[3] Ibid., pp. 103-14.
[4] See Heyne, *Der Kurfuerstentag zu Regensburg von* 1630. Berlin, 1866, pp. 190-1.

even now driving a wedge which split the Empire like a rotten plank.

Ferdinand had failed, Maximilian had failed, John George had hardly tried, to create a native body strong enough to deal with native problems. The Regensburg meeting marks the end of what alone has some right to be called the German period of the war, and the beginning of the foreign period. The King of Sweden had landed in Pomerania, and the German people bowed once again under the scourge of a war they had not started and could not stop. The conference which should have brought relief after twelve years of disaster, heralded only the eighteen that were to come.

THE KING OF SWEDEN
1630—1632

I hope more of the King of Sweden's own person than of all his country . . . he is all and worth all.

THOMAS ROE

I make account of Your Majesty as of an angel of God.

JOHN DURIE

THE KING OF SWEDEN

I

THERE was conflict between France and Spain; Germany was the fighting ground. This alone had come out of the jangled discords at Regensburg; Hapsburg or Bourbon must dominate this little section of the world. Ferdinand and his vision of united Empire, Maximilian and the German Catholic party, John George and the Lutheran constitutionalists, Wallenstein and his army, these were the weapons with which the dynasties fought out their rivalry.

The war was covert still, for neither Richelieu nor Olivarez could afford open hostility. The French monarchy still rode insecurely on the waves of barely stilled revolt; the Spanish treasury was drained by the Dutch and Italian wars, and each rival sought to ruin the other by indirect attack. The true welfare of Germany, Richelieu had stated, lay in her government by Germans to the exclusion of Spaniards;[1] Regensburg had shown him that the Germans, at least as represented by their quarrelling rulers, were incapable of carrying out that policy. He had no choice, therefore, for the safety of France but to exclude the Spaniards by means of foreign allies.

The Dutch were useful against Spain in the Low Countries, but they had no strength to spare for Germany. The English alliance had broken lamentably in his hand. The King of Denmark had retired defeated. By a process of trial and exclusion Richelieu's interest had fastened at last upon the King of Sweden. The German Protestants looked towards Gustavus as towards the dawn, Richelieu had declared, and he made haste to secure for France the warmth of the rising sun. The preliminaries of a Franco-Swedish treaty had been outlined in December 1629,[2] and although Gustavus Adolphus had so

[1] AVENEL, *Lettres de Richelieu*, Paris, 1853, III, p. 878.
[2] MOSER, *Patriotisches Archiv*, VI, pp. 133 f.

far not confirmed these, French agents hovered on the outskirts of his march, and the ultimate alliance depended only on the detailed settlement of terms. Richelieu had lost no time in repudiating the guarantee, which his agents had given at Regensburg, that he would give no help to the Emperor's enemies.

While Richelieu negotiated with the King of Sweden, substituting vicarious attack for open war, Olivarez sought to strengthen Spain so that open war would become too dangerous. He concentrated not on Germany, but on the Netherlands, and tried to forge the way to Spain's recovery by the suppression of Dutch competition, the rehabilitation of Antwerp's trade and the reconquest of the colonies.

II

On July 4th, 1630, the King of Sweden landed at Usedom. Stepping from the ship down the narrow gangway, he stumbled and slightly injured his knee,[1] an incident which contemporary historians, with a fine sense of the dramatic, instantly converted into a deliberate act; the Protestant hero, as soon as his foot touched the land, had fallen upon his knees to ask the blessing of God on his just cause.[2] The legend embodies at least a poetic truth, for whatever the forces behind the King of Sweden, his personal belief in his mission never faltered.

At the time of his landing, Gustavus Adolphus was thirty-six years old. Tall, but broad in proportion so that his height seemed less, fair, florid, his pointed beard and short hair were of a tawny colouring, so that Italian soldiers of fortune called him '*il re d'oro*', and his more usual soubriquet, 'the Lion of the North', gained an additional meaning. Coarsely made and immensely strong, he was slow and rather clumsy in movement, but he could swing a spade or pick-axe with any sapper in his army. In contrast his skin, where it was not tanned by the weather, was as white as a girl's. He held himself erect, a

---

[1] G. DROYSEN, *Gustaf Adolf*, II, p. 151; *Gustaf Adolfs Landungsgebet. Mitteilungen des Instituts für Oesterreichische Geschichtsforschung*, XXII, pp. 269-87.
[2] CHEMNITZ, *De Bello Suecico*, Stettin, 1648, I, p. 55.

King in his every gesture, no matter to what task he lent himself.
As the years went by, he stooped a little forward from the neck,
contracting his short-sighted light blue eyes.[1] The King's appetites were hearty and his dress simple; he wore for preference
the buff coat and beaver hat of a soldier, relieved only by a
scarlet sash or cloak. He could look as well in the ballroom as
in the camp, but he did not on that account evade the toils
of campaigning: he would sweat and starve, freeze and thirst
with his men, and had stayed fifteen hours at a stretch in the
saddle. Blood and filth mattered nothing to him — the kingly
boots had waded ankle-deep in both.

Yet no greater mistake could be made than to imagine that
Gustavus was simple because he was soldierly. Ambassadors,
who were shocked by his too easy manners and the tactless
directness with which he expressed his opinions, overcame their
initial repugnance when they discovered the concentrated
thought and practical knowledge behind his rapid judgments.
Courtiers who took advantage of his friendliness raised a storm
that they could rarely allay; servants who lingered to ask
unnecessary questions were sharply sent about their business,
and ambassadors whose credentials were not correctly inscribed
with his titles could find no admission until the mistake was
set right.[2]

Educated from his earliest childhood to the task of kingship,
he had played in his father's study during the transaction of
state affairs almost before he could stand upright. At six years
old he had accompanied the army on campaign, at ten sat at
the council table and given voice to his opinions, and in his
teens received ambassadors unaided. He had a smattering of
ten languages, an interest in learning, perhaps a little perfunctory, and a passion for practical philosophy; he carried a
volume of Grotius with him everywhere.[3]

Not excepting either Richelieu, or that prince so much
advertised among his contemporaries, Maximilian of Bavaria,
Gustavus was the most successful administrator in Europe. In
the nineteen years of his active reign, for he had been king in
word and deed since his seventeenth year, he had stabilized the

---

[1] HAEBERLIN, XXVI, pp. 28-9.   [2] ROE, *Negotiations*, p. 56.
[3] *Oxenstiernas skrifter och brefvexling, Stockholm*, 1888, I, i, pp. 247-8.

finances of Sweden, centralized the administration of justice, organized relief, hospitals, postal services, education, evolved an elaborate and successful conscription scheme for his army and tackled the problem of an idle and ambitious nobility by forming the Riddarhus, an assembly of nobles who were responsible to the Crown for the government of Sweden. He was in no sense a democratic king; his theory of politics was aristocratic, but while his guiding hand controlled the aristocracy, one and a half million people in Sweden and Finland[1] enjoyed the smoothest rule in Europe. Moreover, he had encouraged commerce and developed the natural resources of his country, her mineral wealth especially. Sweden had the materials to manufacture her own armaments and she had used them; there had hardly been a full year of peace since the accession of the King.[2] In these circumstances, it was hardly remarkable that the Swedish Estates in 1629 had unanimously voted the subsidies for a three years' war in Germany.

Gustavus had applied to war that same ardent and adventurous intelligence which he applied to the affairs of peace. An admirer of Maurice of Orange, he had developed the tactics of that prince so as to get the utmost mobility and efficiency from his troops. He had brought over Dutch professionals to instruct his men in the use of artillery and in siege warfare, and had himself experimented in the manufacture of a light and mobile form of cannon. His so-called 'leathern' guns were, however, only partly successful and he relied in general on quick-firing four-pounders, light enough for one horse or three men to move.[3]

Like all great leaders, Gustavus believed in himself as well as in his cause. Repeatedly in the moment of crisis he declared his unshaken conviction that God was with him. By education he was a Lutheran, but his toleration of the Calvinists more than once aroused doubts among his subjects and allies.[4] He

---

[1] See DROYSEN, *Gustaf Adolf*, II, p. 71.

[2] *Brefvexling*, I, i, pp. 351-459; the standard works on Gustavus Adolphus are: AHNLUND, *Gustav Adolf den Store*. Stockholm, 1932; G. WITTROCK, *Gustav Adolf*, 1932; JOHANNES PAUL, *Gustav Adolph*. Leipzig, 3 vols., 1927-32; and the authoritative two volumes by Michael Roberts, *Gustavus Adolphus, a History of Sweden*, 1611-32, 2 vols., London, 1953, 1958.

[3] See DROYSEN, *Gustaf Adolf*, I, pp. 59-60, 77.

[4] G. WESTIN, *Negotiations about Church Unity*. Uppsala, 1932, p. 208.

was nevertheless convinced of the peculiar rightness of his own broad Protestantism, and could not easily conceive how any man could be persuaded by force to change his religion. Yet he was tolerant at least in this respect, that as he scorned those who were converted by compulsion, he scorned himself to use it. He was willing to allow the defeated, of whatever faith, to continue in their errors.

Gustavus was a brilliant administrator, a skilful soldier, fearless, resolute, impetuous; but these characteristics alone do not explain his power over his contemporaries. The cause lay rather in his own mind, in that terrific confidence in himself which hypnotized not only his followers but those who had never seen him. An Italian in Gustavus's army, a soldier of fortune with neither nation nor faith to make him love the Swedish King, was paid to shoot him. More than once he levelled his pistol for the act, yet though the opportunity were never so favourable he could not fire; for as he looked his heart would turn to lead and his hand refuse the act.[1] Did fate indeed endow the King with supernatural armour, or did his own gigantic confidence, imparting itself to others, give him his virtue? 'He thinks the ship cannot sink that carries him';[2] that was the King's secret, that his revelation, the inspired egoism of the great leader.

His dearest friend was his grey, taciturn, scholarly chancellor, Axel Oxenstierna, from whom alone he would accept advice and reproof. Gustavus had the impulsive passions of genius, Oxenstierna the cooler brain of the man of affairs; he was the expert who could translate his master's dizzy conceptions into the same language of fact. 'If we were all as cold as you,' the King rated him, 'we should freeze.' 'If we were all as hot as Your Majesty,' replied Oxenstierna, 'we should burn.'[3]

The chancellor needed something more than his actual twelve years' seniority to give him his unique power over the King; his qualities were in some respects equal and in others supplementary to those of his master: he had the same immense energy, the same rapidity of judgment and flexibility of mind, the same or even greater powers of memory and gifts of organiz-

---

[1] *Annales*, XI, p. 1326. [2] ROE, *Negotiations*, p. 74.
[3] MOSER, *Patriotisches Archiv*, v, p. 8.

ation. Both men enjoyed the same robust health, a characteristic important enough in a time of perpetual danger and unskilful doctoring: Oxenstierna in particular boasted of his ability to sleep soundly at nights in the midst of anxiety and danger. Twice only, he averred, did the political situation keep him awake; both occasions were during the German war.[1]

If Oxenstierna gives less the impression of a dominating personality than his master it is because his genius was less aggressive; he was a natural diplomat, courteous yet reserved, opportunist yet fundamentally honest, impossible to outwit yet difficult to dislike. He spoke German and French, particularly the latter, with astonishing fluency, and never missed those delicate ambiguities on which the French diplomatists occasionally relied. Brilliant as was his diplomacy, effective as he made his government in Europe both before and after the King's death, he never found full outlet for his humane talents. He appears in his personal outlook and interests a far more civilized and generous man than the King himself: selfless, devoted, kindly in his personal relations, capable of profound affection, intensely interested in the improvement of Swedish culture and the welfare of the subject — such was the man whose chief part in European history was to engineer the continuance of war in Germany for sixteen years. That he performed, both before and after, much constructive work in Swedish administration is not to be denied, yet what he did for peace serves only to stress the loss to Sweden and Europe through the absorption of such men as he in the organization of slaughter. And in the end, whatever immediate glory the ruler and generals of Sweden gained, whatever impetus was given to Swedish trade, the bad even in Sweden outweighed the good, for the central authority was weakened by the ambitions of the soldiers, the people exhausted by the demands of the war, and the territorial gain untenable. Oxenstierna served his government and his King with all his powers, but both they and the times exacted the wrong service.

Never had Germany seen an army such as that which landed with Gustavus. There were twenty-eight warships and as many

[1] ARCHENHOLTZ, *Historische Merkwürdigkeiten*. Leipzig, Amsterdam, 1751, 1752, II, p. 46.

transports lying off the Pomeranian coast, sixteen troops of horse and ninety-two companies of foot with a strong detachment of artillery, thirteen thousand men in all.[1] This was a small army, but the King was already recruiting in Germany and he did not intend to win the war by numbers alone. Unlike the polyglot herds of mercenaries, his army had a collective knowledge of its purpose. The cavalry and the artillery were for the most part his own subjects, strong in the sense of national unity; from the tall, muscular men of southern Sweden with their pale hair and light eyes, to the squat, swarthy Laplanders on their shaggy ponies, whom the Germans imagined to be only half human,[2] and the lean, colourless Finns, children of a wintry land — all alike were subjects of the King and all alike his fellow-soldiers. He was their sovereign, their general, almost their god.

The infantry was different, having but a nucleus of Swedes, the rest mostly Scots and Germans with other soldiers of fortune recruited during the course of his wars. Gustavus did not despise the usual custom of enrolling prisoners in his army, but with this difference, that his principles were not those of other generals: he exacted loyalty not only to the banner but to the ideals for which he fought and for which he was himself prepared to die. He enlisted men of all religions, but Lutheranism was the official creed of his troops. Prayers were held twice daily and each man was provided with a pocket hymn-book of songs suitable for battle.

Discipline was faultless in theory and comparatively effective in practice. There was a standing order that no attack be made on hospitals, churches, schools or the civilians connected with them. One quarter of the breaches of discipline mentioned in his military code were punishable by death; in the King's absence his colonels were empowered to pronounce sentence out of hand.[3]

Even such severity might have been ineffective without the

[1] LORENTZEN, *Die Schwedische Armee im dreissigjährigen Kriege und ihre Abdankung.* Leipzig, 1894, p. 9.

[2] DITFURTH, *Die historisch-politischen Volkslieder des dreissigjährigen Krieges.* Heidelberg, 1882, p. 177 f.

[3] *Annales*, XI, p. 1757; *Brefvexling*, I, vi, p. 584 f.; II, i, p. 619; I, v, pp. 10, 16, 46, 316; GEBAUER, *Ein Schwedischer Militärprozess. Historische Zeitschrift*, XCVIII, p. 547 f.

personality of the King. The chief cause of disorder in all armies was the lack of prompt and regular pay, and this neither Gustavus nor Axel Oxenstierna could prevent. Sweden was a poor country and could not be pressed too hard; the chancellor, who controlled the finances, attempted to pay for the war out of the tolls and customs raised at Riga and the lesser ports of the Polish seaboard,[1] but they were insufficient and the arrangements for distribution broke down very frequently. Gustavus paid his men in another currency. He cared unceasingly for their welfare, and if money was scarce they had at least proper food and clothing. Each man was equipped with a fur cloak, gloves, woollen stockings, and boots made of waterproof Russian leather.[2] Chiefly, as Sir Thomas Roe observed, the King 'hath the singular grace to content his followers without money, because he is "commiles" with every man, and gives besides excellent words and good usage as much as he hath'.[3] In extreme cases, and only in extreme cases, he allowed his army a limited licence to raise the necessities of life by plunder.

There was a reverse side to the King's admirable discipline. When for political or strategic reasons he wished to ruin a country, his men, released from the customary restraint, made up with interest for the opportunities they had been forced to miss.

Gustavus added a sense of publicity to his other qualities. His agent, Adler Salvius, had been stirring up north Germany with talk of the German Liberties and abuse of the imperial government for a month or more before the King sailed, and on the eve of his embarkation had issued a manifesto in five languages to the people and rulers of Europe, justifying the King's espousal of the Protestant Cause.[4] As soon as he landed he issued a second manifesto, declaring that the intervention of Ferdinand in Poland had provoked him to take up arms for the oppressed. He had tried in vain to argue peaceably with the Emperor, but both at Lübeck and at Stralsund his ambassadors had been turned away, and at last perceiving that the German Electors

---

[1] SONDEN, *Axel Oxenstierna och hans Broder*, Stockholm, 1903, p. 18; WITT-ROCK, p. 251.
[2] DROYSEN, *Gustaf Adolf*, II, p. 76.   [3] ROE, *Negotiations*, p. 57.
[4] BOETHIUS, *Gustaf II. Adolfs instruktion för Salvius den 30 juni 1630. Historisk Tidskrift*, 1913, p. 120.

would not protect their own Church, he had taken up arms to do it himself.[1]

On July 20th, he entered Stettin, the capital of Pomerania, insisted on seeing the unwarlike old Duke and forced him to become his ally and provide money. The unhappy man agreed but wrote immediately after to Ferdinand apologizing abjectly and pleading *force majeure*.[2] Should the promised monies not be paid, Gustavus proposed to hold Pomerania in pledge; thus within three weeks of landing he had already staked out Sweden's claim to a valuable strip of the Baltic coast.

He had foothold, or the possibility of foothold, in other parts of Germany. The exiled Dukes of Mecklenburg were his allies; he had declared himself ready to restore Frederick of Bohemia to the Palatinate,[3] and before the end of 1630 he had secured the alliance of the Landgrave of Hesse-Cassel. More important than any of these, was the friendship of Christian William, the deposed Protestant administrator of Magdeburg. Magdeburg, the key fortress of the Elbe and one of the wealthiest cities of Germany, was the strategic base coveted by both Gustavus and Tilly. It had, moreover, sullenly resisted the crusading zeal of the Emperor, so that if Gustavus could hold it he would at once justify himself as a Protestant champion.

With the help of Swedish arms and men, Christian William re-entered the city on August 6th, 1630, and declared that he would defend his bishopric, with God's help and the King of Sweden's, against all comers. In Germany, Protestant news-sheets published the statement in joyous verse, but at Magdeburg itself relief was tempered by fear, for while the majority of the burghers loved their religion they feared the consequences of revolt. When Christian William was reinstated in his episcopal chair, a flight of ravens wheeled screeching over the town, and in the angry sunsets of succeeding nights strange armies fought among the clouds, while under the lurid reflections of the sky the Elbe ran blood-red.[4] Europe applauded the splendid defiance, but at Magdeburg the people sulked, quarrelled and obstructed their defenders.

[1] LUNDORP, IV, pp. 73-7; LÜNIG, VI, i, pp. 359-65.
[2] LUNDORP, IV, p. 80.   [3] ROE, *Negotiations*, pp. 60-1.
[4] *Zacharias Bandhauers Deutsches Tagebuch der Zerstörung Magdeburgs*, ed. P. P. Klimesch. *Archiv für Oesterreichische Geschichte*, XVI. Vienna, 1856, p. 279.

Gustavus wintered in Pomerania and the Mark of Branden-burg, but lack of supplies forced him early to take the field.[1] On January 23rd, 1631, he was at Bärwalde on his way to Frank-fort on the Oder, the next object of his campaign. Here he received the agents of Richelieu and signed the long-projected treaty of alliance.

The Treaty of Bärwalde was for liberty of trade and the mutual protection of France and Sweden. After this prelimi-nary flourish came the more serious clauses. Gustavus was to keep on foot an army of thirty thousand foot and six thousand horse in Germany, at the expense or part-expense of France, while Richelieu undertook on every 15th of May and November to pay the equivalent of twenty thousand imperial talers into the Swedish treasury. In return for this support, Gustavus was to guarantee freedom of worship for Catholics throughout Germany, to leave the lands of Maximilian of Bavaria, France's friend, unmolested, and to make no separate peace at least until the lapse of the treaty in five years' time.[2]

Gustavus showed himself as good a diplomatist as he was administrator and soldier. He forced up Richelieu's offer from fifteen to twenty thousand talers, and insisted that the sly Cardinal be openly compromised by the publication of this treaty with a Protestant power.[3] He knew well enough that if the treaty remained technically secret, men would whisper that he was ashamed to be the pawn of France. As a party to a secret treaty, he would seem a mere puppet, as a party to an open treaty, he was an equal ally.

Was it a distinction without a difference? In his struggle against the Hapsburg, Richelieu intended to make good use of the surplus energies of such inspired champions as the King of Sweden. The people of north Germany were already flocking to his banners, their ministers praying for him, their sons hastening to join his ranks. The Protestant Cause was alive again. But Richelieu and his secretaries, in the stuffy ante-rooms of the Louvre, imagined they knew better. The exploita-tion of courage and spiritual ardour has been the opportunity

[1] *Brefvexling*, II, ix, p. 846.   [2] *Sverges Traktater*, v, i, pp. 438-42.
[3] L. WEIBULL, *Gustave-Adolphe et Richelieu. Revue Historique*, CLXXIV, pp. 219-25.

of the practical politician since the world began, and at Bärwalde the King of Sweden was — they thought — limed and
taken.

They were mistaken. The King's faith was genuine, his
desire to help oppressed Protestants genuine, but he was neither
simple soldier nor fanatic. 'He is a brave prince,' Sir Thomas
Roe meditated, 'but wise to save himself, and maketh good
private use of an opinion and reputation that he is fit to restore
the public.'[1] He stood, the English diplomat considered, even
now upon the banks of the Rubicon, but 'he will not pass over
unless his friends build the bridge.'[2] Richelieu would hardly
have described his policy as building a bridge for the King of
Sweden; rather the King of Sweden was to build a bridge for
him. But the Cardinal and his agents had overreached themselves, and the King of Sweden had signed the Treaty of
Bärwalde with his eyes open. With the help of French money
he would shortly make himself independent of French policy:
exploitation is a game that two can play.

III

The Treaty of Bärwalde was open to any German ruler who
wished to join in throwing off the oppression of the Emperor.
This was a direct invitation to the Protestants to take up arms
against Ferdinand. Eleven years before, when Bohemia was in
revolt, they had had a like opportunity to band themselves
against the Emperor. They had lost it. Now in 1630 it was
given them again. As in 1619, John George of Saxony stood
out for the stability of the constitution against those who sought
to overthrow it. He who had once held the balance between
Ferdinand and Frederick, now held it between Ferdinand and
Gustavus. In 1619 he had had to choose between Protestantism
and Catholicism, the one openly, the other surreptitiously
attacking the German constitution. But now, in 1630, there
was virtually no constitution to defend, and the choice between
Catholic and Protestant had lost its meaning. Hapsburg
aggression had driven the Papacy and Catholic France, the one

[1] Roe, *Negotiations*, p. 39. [2] Ibid., p. 69.

into sympathy, the other into alliance with the Protestants, and Europe no longer presented even the approximate outline of a religious cleavage. The political aspect of the conflict had destroyed the spiritual.

The statesman, no less than the fanatic, will always simplify a complex situation in order to see his way more clearly. Thus for Gustavus and Ferdinand, for the great man as for the small man, the issues were much the same as they had been in 1619. To their thinking, religion still dominated the conflict. For John George everything had altered. He saw on one side Ferdinand with his unconstitutional demands, and on the other Gustavus with his menacing foreign power, and crushed between the two, the forgotten interests of Germany as an Empire and as a nation.

The choice between Ferdinand and Gustavus was easier for John George than had been that between Frederick and Ferdinand — for Frederick had at least been a German. Gustavus was a foreigner, an invader, a trespasser on the soil, and in the politics, of the Holy Roman Empire. John George could decide clearly and immediately against Gustavus. But to decide was one thing, to act another.

To understand what happened in Germany in the next two years, it is necessary to see one thing clearly. The real enemy of Gustavus was not Ferdinand, but John George of Saxony, whatever his open policy. Ferdinand was the simplest, the most frank, the most considerate of enemies; he stood fair and square without pretence, extending the whole front of his religious and dynastic policy before the onslaught of the Swedish King. There were no concealments here. But he was fighting for a cause that, with the desertion of the Pope, had ceased to have any reality. He was nothing but the target for Gustavus's attack. And Gustavus himself, sincere as was his religion, was fighting for the material aggrandizement of Sweden and the Baltic seaboard. His enemies were not the Catholics but all who stood for the solidarity of Germany. Of these the leader was John George.

There were three elements in the situation. There was the conflict between Catholic and Protestant, the open issue between Ferdinand and Gustavus, which, for all its unreality still seemed to the average European the ultimate and only question. There was the political rivalry between Hapsburg and Bourbon which dominated the official policy of Paris, Madrid and Vienna. Buried under these there was the direct issue between the native German and the Swedish invader.

This is a discussion of facts, not of motives. There can be no doubt of Gustavus's sincerity. He had, like most great leaders, an unlimited capacity for self-deception. In his own eyes the Protestant champion, in Richelieu's eyes a convenient instrument against the House of Austria, he was in sober fact the protagonist of Swedish expansion on German soil. Sweden stood to gain, Protestantism stood to gain, but the German people stood to lose. John George alone saw the danger through the emotional smoke and the diplomatic mirage which blinded Europe, and guided his policy by his conviction.

An unexpected ally came to his aid in the winter of 1630. George William, the handsome, well-intentioned Elector of Brandenburg, had spent the eleven years of his reign in a state of gloomy bewilderment. Under the influence of his chief minister, the Catholic Schwarzenberg, this Calvinist ruler of a Lutheran state had played for neutrality. It was not an easy thing to do, for he had married a sister of Frederick of Bohemia, and harboured in Berlin his mother-in-law who ceaselessly urged him to perform some valiant action for her dispossessed son. Inconveniently, too, Gustavus Adolphus had, at an early period, carried off and married his sister, thus plunging him into an aggressively Protestant alliance. In spite of all, George William clung doggedly to his imperial loyalty, urging the defeatist excuse that he thought it would be safest for the dynasty. Unhappily, he reaped no benefit for what the English agent not unnaturally described as 'too cold and stupid a neutrality';[1] Wallenstein used his lands for campaigning against the Dane, Gustavus Adolphus made them a base against the Pole, and the wretched Elector, driven to desperation, was forced to realize that Wallenstein, if not the Emperor himself, actually wanted him to declare war so that there would be an excuse for depriving him of his Electorate.[2]

[1] ROE, *Negotiations*, pp. 39-40.
[2] GAEDEKE, *Zur Politik Wallensteins und Kursachsens. Neues Archiv für Sächsische Geschichte*, x, pp. 36-7.

In 1630 the worm turned at last. At their meetings at Annaburg in April and December of that year, John George persuaded George William to disregard Schwarzenberg's advice, first to refuse to go to Regensburg and secondly to call a Protestant Convention at Leipzig to discuss Ferdinand's policy.[1]

Here John George in his opening speech declared that the purpose of the assembly was to establish trust between the two parties for the peace of Germany;[2] undoubtedly, he hoped that the sight of Brandenburg and Saxony united against him would induce Ferdinand to compromise with them, lest they should join the King of Sweden. Even he knew by this time that it was no good speaking gentle half-hints to Ferdinand, and he had opened his diplomatic campaign by advertising the news that he was arming for the defence of his lands and the rights of the German Protestants. On March 28th, the Leipzig meeting issued a manifesto which had the nature of an ultimatum. They cited the Edict of Restitution as the root cause of continued disturbance in the Empire, in the next place the imperial and League army; they lamented the decay of princely rights, the disregard of the constitution, and the straits to which the war had reduced the country. If Ferdinand would not immediately join with them for the remedying of these evils, they could not be responsible for the consequences. The manifesto was, in fact, a qualified declaration of war. It was signed by the Elector of Saxony and his cousins the princes of the lesser Saxon principalities, by the Elector of Brandenburg, by the representatives of Anhalt, Baden, Hesse, Brunswick-Lüneburg, Württemberg, Mecklenburg, and innumerable independent nobility, not to mention the Protestant Abbess of Quedlinburg, the towns of Nuremberg, Lübeck, Strasbourg, Frankfort-on-the-Main, Mühlhausen, Nordhausen, and the lesser independent cities of Swabia.[3]

Incontrovertibly, John George had done the best thing to save Germany. He had stood forth with his colleague of Brandenburg as the defender of Protestantism and the constitution, and

---

[1] See GEBAUER, *Kurbrandenburg und der Restitutionsedikt von 1629.* Halle, 1899, pp. 72-89, 132-7.
[2] LUNDORP, IV, pp. 133-4.   [3] Ibid., pp. 142-3.

he had the great majority of Protestant opinion behind him. Calvinists and Lutherans were standing side by side at last. Even the Dukes of Mecklenburg and the Landgrave of Hesse, allied as they were with the King of Sweden, had shown by signing the Leipzig manifesto that they were not unwilling to settle without foreign intervention. That left only Magdeburg, the Duke of Pomerania and Frederick of Bohemia as the unqualified allies of Gustavus. John George's position was a strong one and he used it.

If he could frighten the Emperor into a compromise settlement, he would have defeated the King of Sweden without a blow. For Gustavus, everything depended on his reception in Germany. If the army that John George was now straining every resource to raise, the army for which he had secured Wallenstein's best commander, Hans Georg von Arnim, a Brandenburger and a Protestant, if this army were to assert the neutrality of Germany in the face of the King's advance, to challenge him in the recruiting grounds of the northern plain and drain away to its own ranks the man power that he relied on for his, then Gustavus had best sail back to Sweden and think matters over. John George's army was not yet very large nor very well-trained, but no one, least of all an experienced soldier like the King of Sweden, would be so foolish as to discount any army under the command of Hans Georg von Arnim.

Arnim was about forty years old, a soldier by taste and not by necessity. He had been largely responsible for the victorious Silesian campaign of 1627, in which Wallenstein's reputation had been made. A deeply religious man and the loyal subject of the Elector of Brandenburg, Arnim had taken service with the imperialists for much the same reasons that John George had joined Ferdinand in 1620. He did not at first regard the war as a religious war, but rather as a war against rebels and disturbers of the imperial peace. But the Edict of Restitution forced him, as it forced John George, to change his mind.

Protestant Germany, therefore, had leaders at last in John George and George William, a programme in the Leipzig manifesto, and a soldier who understood how to make good a threat. The Electors of Saxony and Brandenburg were offering the support of united and armed Protestant Germany to Ferdinand if he would yield over the Edict of Restitution. Should he refuse, they could not be answerable for the consequences, for the intervention of Gustavus made further neutrality impossible; Ferdinand could not expect the Protestants to let themselves be crushed between his own advance and that of the Swedish King. If they were not against the King of Sweden, they would have to be with him.

It is just, but only just, conceivable that Ferdinand realized this. More probably, he failed to understand the power and prestige of Gustavus and took the Leipzig manifesto for the habitual impotent demonstration with which John George had been saving his face since the beginning of the war.[1] But whether he realized the danger before him or not, he could only have given one answer. He was not a politician but the leader of a Crusade, and he could as easily deny Christ as abandon the Edict of Restitution.

On April 4th, 1631, John George dispatched the manifesto to the Emperor, accompanied by a personal appeal.[2] Before he could answer, the Swedish danger had drawn a decisive step nearer. Marching up the Oder, the King drove back the imperialist troops — Wallenstein's army, but without Wallenstein — into the strong city of Frankfort. The Swedes carried it by assault on April 13th, replenishing their own dwindling stores from the sack of the town and scattering, killing or capturing the remnant of eight regiments.[3]

Four days later, Ferdinand returned an inconclusive answer to the Leipzig protest. He had presumably as yet no news of the fall of Frankfort-on-the-Oder, for a little later he moderated his tactics and sent an ambassador to Saxony with a message of conciliation — but he would not withdraw the Edict of Restitution. And on May 14th he changed again from conciliation to command, and issued an order forbidding all his loyal subjects to assist in any way the recruiting operations of the Protestant princes.[4] He had burnt his own and the Elector of Saxony's boats.

[1] See HURTER, *Friedensbestrebungen Kaiser Ferdinands II.* Vienna, 1860, pp. 9-10.
[2] LUNDORP, IV, pp. 143-4.
[3] *Arkiv till upplysning om Svenska Krigens,* I, p. 413; MONRO, II, p. 34.
[4] LUNDORP, IV, pp. 148-58.

Meanwhile the King of Sweden made good his position in north Germany. His troops had overrun Pomerania, seizing Greifswald and Demmin, so that he now held the hinterland of the Baltic coast from Stralsund to Stettin, and the line of the Oder for eighty miles from its mouth. He had encircled the whole province of Brandenburg on its northern and eastern frontiers. The Dukes of Mecklenburg were preparing to reconquer their land with Swedish arms from the sea, Magdeburg was his ally already, he had but to make sure of Brandenburg, and the whole north-eastern block of the Empire was his, with the lower waters of the Elbe and Oder, the highways into the heart of Ferdinand's country.

The Elector of Brandenburg was surely the unluckiest man in Germany, for the spring of 1631 found him again the chosen victim of both Emperor and invader. Both saw that they must put an immediate stop to his activities on behalf of the constitutionalist party, the Emperor to frighten the King of Sweden by occupying Brandenburg, the King to rob John George of his best supporter and force each of the constitutionalist champions, singly, to accept his alliance.

Gustavus was in the better position, for unexpected disaster had befallen Tilly in the winter. It had come upon him through the man he had superseded. Wallenstein knew from the stars that he would be recalled, but he was not so simple as to leave the matter entirely to the stars, and he had taken certain measures to prove himself indispensable. Quartered in Mecklenburg and the Oder valley, Tilly's troops relied on supplies from the well-stocked granaries of Friedland and Sagan as well as from Mecklenburg itself. But these were all Wallenstein's lands, and while he had fed the army admirably when it was his, he saw no reason to feed it now that it was another's. He refused all provisions from Friedland except such as were paid for in money, which meant virtually that he refused provisions altogether; he gave as little as possible from Sagan, and profited by the shortage to let the prices of his corn rise; even in Mecklenburg he privately instructed his officials to make the quartering of the troops as difficult as possible.[1] The hungry

[1] ERNSTBERGER, *Wallenstein als Volkswirt*, pp. 34-5; ERNSTBERGER, *Wallensteins Heeressabotage und die Breitenfelder Schlacht. Historische Zeitschrift*, CLXII, pp. 46-9, 51-3; PEKAŘ, I, pp. 75 f.; II, pp. 32-6.

soldiers deserted to join Arnim's newly-recruited troops, the horses died and the army which had been Wallenstein's creation melted before the eyes of his successor. 'All the days of my life', wrote Tilly, 'I have never seen an army so lacking in everything at one and the same time from the most important to the least; no draft horses, no officers, no cannon in a condition to be used, no powder, no ammunition, no picks or shovels, no money and no food.'[1] In vain he appealed for help; Wallenstein would not and Ferdinand could not give it.

In this desperate state, Tilly yielded to his lieutenant Pappenheim's insistence and set his hopes on the reduction of Magdeburg. Strategically the most important point on the Elbe, he believed it also to be well stocked with provisions. He made one sharp attempt to strike between Gustavus on the Oder and his base on the Baltic seaboard, carried Neubrandenburg with horrible slaughter,[2] but fell back because his men had not the stamina to go farther, and in April 1631 joined Pappenheim at the siege of Magdeburg with the greater number of his forces.

At Magdeburg itself the situation was complicated by the unwillingness of the citizens to be made martyrs. Some of the municipality displayed a more heroic spirit and gave what help they could to Dietrich von Falkenberg, the Hessian soldier whom Gustavus had dispatched to organize the defence. But the people in general made perpetual difficulties and supplied the necessary stores so unwillingly that Falkenberg's hungry cavalry mutinied and were with difficulty brought to order.[3] 'There is little wisdom here', he wrote to the King, 'we live from day to day.' The King's attempt to draw Tilly off by his attack on Frankfort-on-the-Oder[4] failed. By May 1631 the besiegers were on the alert within speaking distance of the defenders on the walls, and the leading burghers of Magdeburg were clamouring for surrender by treaty lest the city should fall by assault and be put to sack.[5]

---

[1] HALLWICH, *Briefe und Akten*, I, pp. 204-5, 210-12, 214-15, 232, 251, 255, 288-90.

[2] *Brefvexling*, II, viii, pp. 34, 37; HALLWICH, *Briefe und Akten*, I, p. 308.

[3] WITTICH, *Dietrich von Falkenberg*. Magdeburg, 1892, pp. 73-4.

[4] R. USINGER, *Die Zerstörung Magdeburgs. Historische Zeitschrift*, XIII, p. 388; *Brefvexling*, II, viii, p. 39.

[5] WITTICH, *Falkenberg*, p. 159; DROYSEN, *Gustaf Adolf*, I, pp. 313-14.

Protestant Europe looked to the King of Sweden. Broad-sheets poured from the press, exhorting Magdeburg to stand firm, abjuring the maiden city to deny access to the elderly wooer who pressed her so hard.[1] Nothing lay between the rescuer and his objective but a hundred and fifty miles of ill-defended country and the decisions of the Leipzig Conference. Between Magdeburg and her saviour the Electors of Branden-burg and Saxony interposed the enigma of their policy. Gustavus had appealed to them, when they were in session at Leipzig, to enter into alliance with him and march to the rescue of Magdeburg, an offer which they had received with icy indifference.[2] Once before, the King of Sweden had burst out furiously against the German rulers. 'They know not whether they would be Lutheran or Popish, imperialist or German, slave or free', he had raged.[3] But he did them wrong, for they knew one thing very certainly, that they did not want the interference of the King of Sweden. Without the alliance of the two Protestant Electors, Gustavus dared not move: the peasants of Brandenburg had fled before his advance; the local authorities, knowing their Elector's policy, had not been friendly, and Gustavus's troops, on short rations both for men and horses, were gravely weakened.[4] Without help from Arnim it would be difficult to relieve Magdeburg, and far from helping him, the two Electors seemed inclined to hinder. It was conceivable that, should he advance across Brandenburg, the army sup-ported by the Leipzig Convention would fall on his rear and try to force him out of Germany.

At the end of April, Gustavus informed Falkenberg that he must hold out another two months;[5] early in May he struck at the Elector of Brandenburg, seized his fortress of Spandau and frightened him into a provisional treaty of alliance.[6] The first step, the separation of the Protestant allies, was accom-plished. John George, without the assurance of whose friend-ship Gustavus dared not make towards the Elbe, remained alone. But before he could be forced to terms, all Europe echoed to the catastrophe of Magdeburg.

---

[1] DITFURTH, *Volkslieder*, pp. 143 ff.; *Bandhauers Tagebuch*, p. 267.
[2] DROYSEN, *Gustaf Adolf*, II, p. 295.   [3] Ibid., p. 296.
[4] *Brefvexling*, II, viii, p. 45; II, i, p. 695.
[5] DROYSEN, *Gustaf Adolf*, II, p. 289.   [6] *Sverges Traktater*, V, i, pp. 449-54.

Rumour gave the King of Sweden credit for moving faster than he did, and fear of his arrival drove the besiegers to desperate efforts.[1] In the exhausted condition of the Catholic army, failure to take Magdeburg would mean certain destruction; if the troops turned eastwards they would meet Gustavus, southwards Arnim, northwards Wallenstein's inhospitable Mecklenburg where they could not live.

For two days from May 17th, 1631, the city was stormed in vain, until the burghers implored Falkenberg to make terms, fearing the plunder which must follow a fighting conquest. The commander stood firm, convinced, it would seem, in the strength of his defences. On the 20th, between six and seven on a windy morning, the storm began again, for Pappenheim, fearing Tilly's hesitancy, had led his men to the assault without orders.[2] The defenders were taken at a disadvantage, and after a frantic resistance in which Falkenberg himself was killed, the attackers forced an entrance on two sides, and Magdeburg had fallen.

Drunk with victory, the troops defied all efforts to control them. Pappenheim himself only by force rescued the wounded Administrator, Christian William, from the rough hands of his plundering captors,[3] and the aged Tilly, riding among the tumult, was seen unhandily nursing a baby which he had plucked, living, from the arms of its dead mother. Seeing the prior of a local monastery, the general shouted to him to herd the women and children into the cathedral, the one sanctuary which he could guard against his troops. The dauntless old monk, defenceless in his white habit, did what he could and managed to lead about six hundred to safety.[4]

Pappenheim had fired one of the gates during the assault, and a strong wind blew the acrid fumes of gunpowder across the town, but towards midday flames suddenly shot up at almost the same moment in twenty different places. There was no time for Tilly and Pappenheim to ask whence came the fire; staring in consternation, they rallied their drunken, disorderly, ex-

---

[1] W. LAHNE, *Magdeburgs Zerstörung in der zeitgenossischen Publizistik*. Magdeburg, 1931, p. 33; USINGER, pp. 391-3.
[2] KLOPP, III, ii, pp. 167-8; FOERSTER, *Wallenstein*, II, p. 94.
[3] F. SPANHEIM, *Le Soldat Suedois*. Geneva, 1633, p. 39.
[4] *Bandhauers Tagebuch*, pp. 276 ff.

hausted men to fight it. The wind was too strong, and in a few minutes the city was a furnace, the wooden houses crashing to their foundations in columns of smoke and flame. The cry was now to save the army, and the imperialist officers struggled in vain to drive their men into the open. Rapidly whole quarters were cut off by walls of smoke, so that those who lingered for booty or lost their way, or lay in drunken stupor in the cellars, alike perished.

Far into the night the city burnt, and smouldered for three days after, a waste of blackened timber round the lofty gothic cathedral. How it happened no one then knew or has ever learnt. One thing, however, was clear to Tilly and Pappenheim, as they looked at the sulphurous ruin and watched the dreary train of wagons that for fourteen days carried the charred bodies to the river — Magdeburg could no longer feed and shelter either friend or foe.

Because of that, some have thought, not without justification, that Dietrich von Falkenberg planned the fire, leaving its execution in the hands of some few trusted citizens and soldiers, the fanatics of his party, thus to destroy Tilly's prey and possibly Tilly's army in the moment of victory. It is not impossible; at the time it was widely rumoured, and the fallen city was called the Protestant Lucretia because she had destroyed herself rather than outlive her shame.[1] To the fanatic mind, and such was Falkenberg's, a holocaust of twenty-four thousand men and women might seem a reasonable sacrifice to the Protestant Cause and the King of Sweden. Proof of the crime is lacking, for the blackened pyre left no evidence; in the sack of a great city accidental fires may easily break out, the high wind and the wooden houses doing all the rest. One thing only is certain, that neither Tilly nor Pappenheim would have deliberately destroyed the city on whose wealth they had planned to feed and pay their army.[2]

The greater part of the food in the town was burnt, but when the soldiers came back to plunder among the ruins they found here and there cellars with wine casks which had escaped

[1] WITTICH, *Magdeburg, Gustav Adolf und Tilly*. Berlin, 1874, I, p. 15.
[2] See STIEVE, *Abhandlungen*. Leipzig, 1900, pp. 181-94; also WITTICH, *Dietrich von Falkenberg*, and *Magdeburg, Gustav Adolf und Tilly*. The problem of responsibility has been variously but never conclusively solved.

the flames, and for two days the army reeled about blind drunk, uncontrolled and uncontrollable.

On May 22nd Tilly began to set his world in order. The refugees were brought out of the cathedral, given food, and lodged in the cloisters of the monastery, where they lay for three weeks, huddled together under blankets, few of them having any other covering. In the monks' vineyard a little camp was organized for the lost children, but of eighty gathered there fifteen only survived.[1] Famine hung over civilians and soldiers alike, while scavenging dogs fought over the dead and scratched up the buried. To prevent an outbreak of plague, Tilly had the bodies thrown into the Elbe. For miles along the banks below the city the current washed the swollen corpses among the reeds, where birds of prey gathered screeching above them.[2]

Of the thirty thousand inhabitants of Magdeburg about five thousand had survived, and these for the most part women. The soldiers had secured them first, carrying them off to the camp before returning to plunder the city. When the sack was over, Tilly attempted to regulate the situation. He sent priests among the soldiers to persuade them where possible to marry their victims, failing that to give them up for a reasonable sum. The surviving men of Magdeburg were allowed to buy back their women and ransom themselves, but those who could not afford the luxury had to march with the troops as the servants of their captors.[3]

If he could do little for his army, Tilly could at least do something for his Church, and five days after the fall of the city he arranged the solemn rededication of the cathedral. The men were called in to their colours, the leading officers with some picked soldiers marched into the cathedral with their banners flying, heard Mass and listened to a Te Deum. The cannon were brought into position on one of the larger fragments of the city wall, whence a salute was fired to announce the return of the cathedral to its true faith. Afterwards the general proclaimed that the black wreck at his feet was no longer Magdeburg but Marienburg, a city dedicated to his Patroness.[4]

[1] *Bandhauers Tagebuch*, p. 278.   Ibid., p. 282.
[3] Ibid., p. 287; WITTICH, *Magdeburg als Katholisches Marienburg. Historische Zeitschrift*, LXV, p. 433.
[4] Ibid., *Magdeburg als Marienburg*, p. 444.

The wooden statue of the maiden that had crowned the gate for so long had been found after the fire, charred and broken, in a ditch.[1] She had been wooed and won at last, and for years to come men remembered the 'marriage of Magdeburg'.

The news came upon Europe with a shock of horror. At Vienna the thanksgivings were hushed, and in Protestant countries no words could describe the outburst of disgust and indignation. The appalling accident which robbed the conquest of its military significance was trumpeted to the world as the deliberate act of its conquerors, and Tilly's name was to pass into history for ever coupled with Magdeburg. Years later, imperialist soldiers crying for quarter would be met with the answer 'Magdeburg quarter' as they were shot down.

'Our danger has no end, for the Protestant Estates will without doubt be only strengthened in their hatred by this',[2] Tilly wrote to Maximilian. He was right. Throughout Europe Magdeburg was the signal for Protestant action; on May 31st the United Provinces entered into an agreement with the King of Sweden, by which they undertook to add their subsidies to those of the French,[3] and directly after made ready to invade Flanders.

More immediately disastrous was the treaty signed in mid-June between George William of Brandenburg and Gustavus Adolphus. The Elector of Brandenburg had agreed to yield Spandau in April but attempted subsequently to evade the obligation. Gustavus acted quickly. On June 15th he declared that George William's further refusal to carry out his obligations would be treated as a declaration of war, and six days later he appeared outside Berlin and trained his cannon on the Electoral palace. The timorous prince broke down utterly, sent out his wife and mother-in-law to soften the invader, following himself some hours later with the sycophantic suggestion that they should settle the little misunderstanding over a friendly drink. Gustavus, now master of the situation, was nothing loth; gaily he pledged the Elector in four bumpers, and on the next day, June 22nd, 1631, enforced a treaty which placed the resources of Brandenburg and the fortresses of Spandau and Küstrin at

---

[1] *Bandhauers Tagebuch*, pp. 280-1.   [2] USINGER, p. 399.
[3] LUNDORP, IV, pp. 214-15.

his disposal for the duration of the war.[1] For the rest of the day and most of the ensuing night George William solaced his wounded pride by riotous eating and drinking with the Swedish King.[2]

Meanwhile Tilly's position was becoming untenable. Added to his military difficulties, he was in a political quandary. Although he was commander-in-chief of all the imperialist forces, he had not on that account ceased to be the general of the Catholic League and thereby under the authority of Maximilian. All the spring, this prince had pursued his old policy of forming a Catholic constitutionalist party regardless alike of the Emperor and the King of Sweden. He calculated that he needed only the alliance within Germany of a sufficient number of princes, John George if possible, and the moral support of Richelieu. In accordance with this theory he had on May 8th, 1631, signed a secret treaty with the French government for eight years, by which they recognized his Electorate and bound themselves to assist him in case of attack. Maximilian in return undertook to give no assistance to their enemies.[3]

The confusion caused by this secret treaty can scarcely be conceived. Richelieu recognized Maximilian's claim to a title which his other ally, Gustavus Adolphus, intended to restore to its rightful holder. Moreover, he bound the French government to defend Maximilian in case of attack. Did Richelieu not realize that, even if Gustavus were fighting the Emperor, the Emperor's army was paid largely by Maximilian's resources and commanded by his general? Was Richelieu so simple as to imagine that Gustavus either could or would respect the purely technical neutrality of Bavaria, whatever his promises? The diplomacy of Maximilian and the Cardinal rested still on the fatuous assumption that the King of Sweden was their malleable instrument, that he could be used to frighten the Emperor, kept neatly within bounds in Germany, paid off and sent back to Sweden.

The man who suffered most by this uncomprehending

---

[1] *Sverges Traktater*, v, i, pp. 457-63.

[2] See DROYSEN, *Gustaf Adolf*, II, pp. 303, 351-3; REINHOLD VON KOSER, *Gustav Adolfs letzter Besuch in Berlin. Festschrift zum 50 jährigen Jubiläum des Vereins für die Geschichte Berlins.* Berlin, 1917, pp. 3-10; MONRO, II, p. 43.

[3] LÜNIG, VIII, pp. 78-9.

diplomacy was the faithful Tilly. As commander-in-chief of the imperialist forces it was his plain duty to hold back the King of Sweden. But as the general of Maximilian of Bavaria it was the last thing he could do, for it had been made clear to him, as soon as the treaty was signed, that he was to avoid all open contact with Gustavus, his master's friend's friend.[1] Failing this, Tilly might advance boldly into Saxony, using the terror which his name, as the reputed butcher of Magdeburg, now inspired to intimidate John George. But Maximilian was determined on no account to provoke the hostility of John George; he gauged the situation well enough to know that an attack from Tilly would drive the Elector into the arms of Sweden and destroy his own hopes of a new princely party.

Once again the possibility of alliance between the two constitutionalists flickered up and was snuffed out. The armies of Tilly and Arnim acting together might have saved Germany, but a mild interchange of letters between John George and the Catholic Electors bore no fruit.[2] There is an immediacy in the conduct of war that cannot wait for the delays of ministers; the decisive fact in the summer of 1631 was that Tilly's men were hungry.

Four days after the fall of Magdeburg, Tilly vainly implored Wallenstein to provide food for his men.[3] As the summer advanced every hopeful outlet was cut off. The Swedes beat him back in the north, taking Havelberg on July 22nd and overrunning Mecklenburg. Tilly had hoped that in this extremity Wallenstein would put his lands and resources at his disposal rather than lose his duchy to the enemy. But Wallenstein preferred to lose his duchy; he knew what he wanted.[4]

Desperate for food and quarters but still true to Maximilian's policy, Tilly turned away from the Saxon border and marched south-westwards for Hesse; the Landgrave incontinently signed a treaty of alliance with the King of Sweden and called on Gustavus for immediate help.[5] Not daring to risk a pursuit, Tilly faced about once more and now, cut off on all sides in the

---

[1] GARDINER, *History of England*, VII, p. 188.
[2] LUNDORP, IV, pp. 175-8.
[3] HALLWICH, *Briefe und Akten*, I, pp. 389-90.
[4] PEKAŘ, p. 75.
[5] *Sverges Traktater*, V, i, pp. 476 ff.

wasted plain of Magdeburg, he had no choice but to march for Saxony.

It was John George's turn to stand between two fires. On the one hand was the King of Sweden, more than ever anxious for his alliance since the destruction of Magdeburg had robbed him of his projected base on the Elbe; on the other hand was Tilly with his hungry troops, ravenous for the fleshpots of Saxony. One way or another, the pacific policy of John George was doomed, but he had acted more cautiously and could make better terms than his colleague of Brandenburg. When Tilly sent word that he was to disband his army or be declared contumacious to imperial authority, he evaded an immediate answer,[1] having the determination left to play off one enemy against another. He did not intend any open breach with the Emperor until he had sold himself dearly to the King of Sweden. Until the last minute he made it appear to Gustavus that he might yet jump in the other direction.

On August 31st, about fourteen thousand fresh troops, hastily gathered from the south and west, joined Tilly, bringing his numbers up to thirty-six thousand,[2] and four days later he crossed the Saxon border. Wild with renewed strength, Tilly's troops flung themselves into the conquest of Saxony with a zeal they had not shown for months, and the rich town of Merseburg fell at their first attack. By the 6th they were already on the road to Leipzig, laying the province waste about them, their march slowed down by the weight of their booty.

In the crisis the two soldiers, Gustavus and Arnim, swept the negotiations out of John George's hands.[3] Neither dared move without the other, for each misjudged Tilly's strength. The terms of the alliance were hastily agreed and signed on September 11th, 1631, the Elector promising to join Gustavus with all his troops as soon as he should cross the Elbe, to give him quarters and food in his lands, to hold the Elbe for him and perform all necessary actions for the defence of the key positions on the river in conjunction with him. He also agreed to make no separate peace and to give the chief, though not the uncon-

---

[1] LUNDORP, pp. 199-204.
[2] HALLWICH, *Briefe und Akten*, p. 473.
[3] WITTICH, *Zur Würdigung Hans Georgs von Arnim. Neues Archiv für Sächsische Geschichte*, XXII, p. 31.

trolled, command of the two armies to the Swedish king *so long as the emergency continued.* Here was his loophole, for there was no criterion laid down by which the emergency could be measured, and John George was in fact free to withdraw from the alliance when he thought good. In return the King promised to keep good discipline in his army, to restrict the operations of war in Saxony as far as possible and to clear the Electorate of enemies before he proceeded to any further action.[1]

There was all the difference in the world between this treaty and the alliance concluded with Brandenburg; George William was bound helplessly to the invader's policy, John George asserted his own dominance. The treaty might on the surface appear to give the King of Sweden all he wanted, but, in his anxiety for immediate help, he had agreed to that nebulous time limit on his ally's obligations — a time limit to be judged and set by John George alone. From the moment of signing the treaty until his death, Gustavus was never certain of this ally; he had to act always so as to be sure of his continued goodwill. John George had neither created a German constitutional party nor defended the integrity of the Empire, but he had at least secured for himself, a native prince, a controlling vote in the decisions of the invader.

I V

Three days later, on September 14th, 1631, Tilly stormed and took the fortress of Pleissenburg which guards Leipzig; on the following day he entered the city, his soldiers gathering an immense booty. Twenty-five miles to the north, the forces of the King of Sweden and the Elector of Saxony met at Düben and turned their faces southwards. It could mean nothing but annihilation for Tilly. Retreat was out of the question, even had he been able to drag his unwilling troops without a mutiny from the earthly paradise into which so many of them had come after months of wretchedness.[2] The nearest friendly country

---

[1] *Sverges Traktater*, v, i, pp. 513-16.
[2] See FOERSTER, *Wallenstein*, II, p. 120.

was Württemberg, but he would have to cross a hostile Thuringia, with the King of Sweden close on his heels, before he reached it. If he attempted to strike in the opposite direction, traverse the still undefended southern part of Saxony and fall back on Bohemia, he would find no welcome from Wallenstein, the un-crowned ruler of Bohemia, and would encourage the advance of the Swedish King into the very heart of the imperial lands. Retreat was therefore impossible; Tilly's best hope was to barricade himself in Leipzig and play for time until General Aldringer should come up with the reinforcements which the Emperor was desperately raising.[1]

Gustavus, on the other hand, stood to gain by hazarding a battle. A startling victory would confirm the recent friendship of John George, who was clamorous for the rescue of his cherished Leipzig; besides, the joint Saxon and Swedish army outnumbered Tilly's by ten thousand men.[2]

The veteran Catholic general was a conscientious but had never been a great soldier, and with age his natural caution had increased beyond all proportion. Unhappily, he had Pappenheim for his second-in-command, and while this skilful cavalry leader lacked the patience and grasp of detail necessary for the chief command, he lacked also the temperament for a subordinate post. He regarded Tilly as incompetent, if not actually senile. At Magdeburg he had given the order for attack without his chief's assent and had carried the city; encouraged no doubt by this recollection, he did the same at Leipzig. On September 16th he left the camp with a recon-noitring party, and late that night sent back word that he had sighted the enemy, could not return without grave danger and must be supported where he stood. Never yet defeated, the arrogant nobleman doubtless already saw himself slaughtering these barbarian Swedes and raw Saxons as easily as he had slaughtered the peasants at Gmunden. Utterly without fear, the marks on his body bore witness to his repeated defiance of death; moreover there was a legend in his family that a scion of their house should kill an invading king and save the father-land. Never a realist, Pappenheim throughout his military

[1] FOERSTER, *Wallenstein*, II, p. 109.
[2] DROYSEN, *Gustaf Adolf*, II, p. 401.

296

career attempted the impossible and often achieved it by the very madness of his courage. But Leipzig was an ill-chosen moment for such a venture, and Tilly, clutching his head in anguish when he heard the news, loudly lamented: 'This fellow will rob me of my honour and reputation, and the Emperor of his lands and people.'[1] Pappenheim had engineered a battle and Tilly had no choice but to follow him.

About nine o'clock on Wednesday, September 18th, the Protestant forces, cautiously advancing, came on the imperialists outside the village of Breitenfeld four miles to the north of Leipzig. The day was hot and a gusty wind made choking whirlwinds of the powdery dust which lies three or four inches deep on that dry ground; both sun and wind were against the King of Sweden. So also was the slight, but almost imperceptible, incline of the ground.

Tilly's army was drawn up in the traditional formation, the infantry in the centre, the cavalry massed on the wings, Tilly commanding in the centre and Pappenheim on the left. As soon as the enemy came in sight, the imperialists opened fire and continued to bombard Gustavus's lines, although with singularly small effect, while he marshalled his men for action. On the left wing was the Saxon cavalry with the Elector himself, very spick and span with well-polished arms and handsome uniforms, the officers, young noblemen of Saxony, in gay scarves and cloaks; 'a cheerful and beautiful company to see', said the Swedish King. Next came the Saxon detachment of infantry, and then part of the Swedish infantry in the centre, and on the right wing the rest of the infantry with Gustavus's cavalry. Here Tilly's veterans saw a strange formation rapidly come into shape: instead of massing his horsemen in columns riding almost knee to knee, the King formed his cavalry in small squares, each square having room to skirmish, and each man space to move on all sides. Between these groups were smaller detachments of musketeers, so that in place of the uniform appearance to which they were accustomed, Tilly's officers perceived a loosely extended chess-board in which squares of infantry and cavalry alternated. Hardly had they had time to note this peculiarity than they became aware of another and an even more disturbing

[1] FOERSTER, *Wallenstein*, II, p. 104.

characteristic. Gustavus had trained his musketeers to stand in files of five, one behind the other, the front man kneeling so that the first two could fire simultaneously; they then walked to the back of the file, and the process was repeated by the next two, the men making ready to fire as they came up to the front. By dint of unceasing practice, Gustavus had brought this drill to such brisk perfection that his firing was not only three times as fast as Tilly's, but far more than three times as effective. No matter which way the attack came, the chess-board forma-

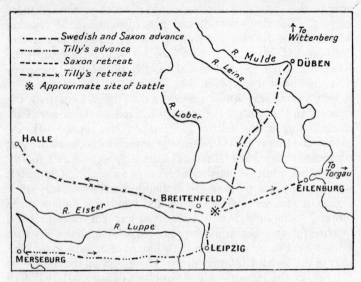

tion made it possible for both cavalry and musketeers to change their direction with the slightest possible delay. For seven hours on end, through clouds of blinding dust, Tilly was to hear the regular, unceasing chatter of the Swedish musketry.[1]

It was nearly half-past two before either side moved, and the sun was shining almost full into the faces of the Swedes. Pappenheim moved first; sweeping outwards, he made a wide circle beyond the immediate range of Gustavus's deadly firing, and crashed in behind the main body of the Swedish cavalry on to the reserves. Had Gustavus's troops been drawn up in the

[1] DELBRUECK, pp. 232 f; DROYSEN, *Gustaf Adolf*, II, p. 404.

habitual formation, this charge of Pappenheim's must have been fatal, but the Swedish cavalry immediately faced about so that the enemy was trapped at right angles between the reserves and the main body. Baffled, Pappenheim withdrew as best he could; seeing the embarrassment of their left wing and judging that it would be best to attack the Saxons when the Swedes were fully engaged, both Tilly in the centre and Fuerstenberg, his commander on the right, took the opportunity to charge for the Saxon guns, which were massed between the Saxon horse on the left wing of the opposing army and the Saxon foot in the centre.

John George's untried forces had faced the redoubtable foe boldly for the last two hours, but now a sudden redoubled energy among the enemy musketeers played havoc with their front line, and when the great mass of the opposing column moved forward with deafening uproar, more than half concealed in dust, the Saxon front line was already wavering. The Croatian cavalry led the charge, their red cloaks streaming in the wind, their sabres flashing, while such outlandish cries issued from their mouths that the Saxons imagined nothing less than that these were the devil's minions hot from hell. John George himself, brave enough in the hunting field, had never imagined such fury as was now bearing down upon him. The gunners fled first, and the cannon were seized; sweating and straining in the stifling dust, the imperialists dragged them round to face the Saxon cavalry and opened fire. Until that moment Arnim might yet have rallied his wavering troops, but the new disaster overpowered them. John George himself spurred his horse out of the battle without more ado, and never drew rein until he reached Eilenburg, fifteen miles away. Of his cavalry, two whole regiments, being Saxon subjects and more inclined to follow their ruler's example than to obey their newly appointed general, defied Arnim's efforts, threw away their arms and ran or rode for safety. They were wiser or less well mounted than the Elector, for they had not gone a mile before they realized there was no pursuit and, snatching an immediate advantage from their disaster, fell upon the Swedish baggage wagons in the rear and carried off all that they could lay hands on.

The Saxon cavalry being thus broken, and most of the infantry gone, the imperialist cavalry on both wings reformed and charged the Swedes. For all the good that the Saxon arms had done, the King might never have signed his treaty with John George; the whole brunt of the imperialist attack must now be borne by the Swedes alone, and the once incredible victory of the imperialists seemed now assured. Two things saved the King of Sweden — his own genius and the caprice of the wind. The Swedish squares stood like a rock against which Tilly's cavalry broke in vain, and up each of the innumerable alleys between the narrow groups of horsemen, on whichever side the imperialists attacked, came that unrelenting stream of deadly fire. The King and his officers, without armour, in their buff coats and plumed hats, showed themselves fearlessly wherever the danger was greatest, the King himself seeming to be everywhere at once, so that when the day was over he, of all men, had the most confused recollection of the fight. Blinded with dust, the sweat streaming from his face, he galloped up and down the lines, exhorting his men until his throat gave out, bawling hoarsely for a drink of water, and spurring off again before any one had time to hand him a flask.

Meanwhile the westering sun no longer shone into the eyes of the Swedes. The wind had veered and the powdery dust, the curse of that hard-fought day, blew in hot gusts into the faces of the exhausted imperialists. It was the occasion for which Gustavus had waited. After the first attack, his reserves of cavalry had taken no further active part in the fight and were now the freshest troops in the field. They were in two detachments, comprising about a thousand men whom the King now called forward: he intended himself to charge with the main body of the army, making a swerving movement to divide the imperialist cavalry from the infantry, while the reserves followed and engaged the cavalry alone. The manœuvre succeeded; infantry and cavalry were cut off one from another, the Saxon guns recaptured and turned on the broken enemy. Already Tilly's men had had more than enough, and now they were thinking of their booty stored in Leipzig. They began to break and fly, the Swedes pursuing them with great slaughter. Tilly himself, wounded in the neck and chest, his right arm shattered, left the field with only a few companions, too ill to know which way he rode or what was happening to his men. Pappenheim was left alone to save the army. The dust clouds, once his worst enemies, were now his only friends; under cover of fog and twilight he beat off the pursuers, and with about four regiments made good his retreat on Leipzig. He himself fought in the hottest of the rearguard action all the way; once, it was said, he cut himself free of fourteen Swedish soldiers. But he could not hold Leipzig, and on the following morning he withdrew his bedraggled troops towards Halle. More than twenty cannon — all the artillery — were gone, with nearly a hundred standards. Of the army, twelve thousand lay on the parched field of Breitenfeld and the long road to Leipzig, seven thousand were prisoners in the Swedish camp that night and soldiers in the Swedish army by the morning.

And whither now? In his weary mind, hot with the fiery images of pain, the drooping Tilly must have asked himself this question as he took shelter at an inn late that night on the road to Halle. But Pappenheim, burning with anger, indignant and contemptuous, snatched the first opportunity to write to Wallenstein: 'It is hard for me to bear the burden of this disaster alone', he said. 'I see no other way to set the work on foot again but that your Excellency will once more take charge of this war to serve God and the faith, to help the Emperor and the Fatherland.'[1]

The first charge was made at half-past two in the afternoon, but the 'blue darkness' had come up cool above the dust clouds before Gustavus was satisfied that the day was his. There was little rest that night round his camp-fires, and in the small hours he could not sleep for the deafening clatter that his men were making with the sacred bells they had looted from the priests in the defeated army. 'How merry our brothers are', the King laughed.[2]

It was thirteen years since the war had begun, and the Protestant fortunes had turned at last. From the day of Breitenfeld

---

[1] FOERSTER, *Wallenstein*, II, p. 108.
[2] The account of the battle is assembled from the various contemporary accounts given in *Archiv für Sächsische Geschichte*, VII, pp. 342 ff.; in *Arkiv till upplysning Svenska Krigens*, pp. 492-5; in *Brefvexling*, II, i, pp. 739-42; in FOERSTER'S *Wallenstein*, pp. 119 ff.; MONRO, *His Expedition*, II, pp. 63-7; and few indications in the *Relation* of Sydnam Poyntz. See also *Sveriges Krig 1611-1632*, IV, pp. 477-523.

no man feared again the conquest of the Fatherland by the Hapsburg dynasty or the Catholic Church, and for more than a hundred years they kept September 17th as a day of thanksgiving at Dresden.[1] What the German princes could not do for themselves the King of Sweden had done for them, and the battle which freed their country from the Austrian gave it to the Swede.

Certain events have a moral effect irrespective of their physical importance. The battle of Breitenfeld is one of these. It seemed to the Protestants of Europe both then and later that Gustavus on that day liberated Europe from the fear of Catholic-Hapsburg tyranny which had haunted her since the time of Philip II. But in fact the animosity of the Pope and Richelieu undermined the religious policy of the House of Austria before Gustavus himself set foot on German soil. And on the field of Breitenfeld he had struck not at the root but only at a branch of the Hapsburg tree. A bare week before, off the coast of Zeeland, a Spanish fleet bearing an army ready to land had been destroyed by the Dutch. This event, overshadowed in the popular report by the battle at Leipzig, struck a harder blow at the House of Austria. Its future depended above all on the recovery of Spain, and every defeat in the Netherlands made that recovery less possible.

The battle of Breitenfeld was a heavy blow to Ferdinand, but it did not break him. The most perilous time for the Protestants had not yet come. It was not the weeks which preceded the Swedish victory at Breitenfeld, but those which followed the Swedish defeat three years later at Nördlingen.

Yet this cannot affect the position of Breitenfeld in the history of Europe. Almost at once it became a symbol. The giant personality of the King, and his belief in himself, endowed his every action with miraculous significance, most of all this great battle, the first Protestant victory. And therefore it must take its place in the simplified tradition which is customarily called history, not because of what it achieved but because of what men thought it had achieved. It was as though the King of Sweden had written the incontrovertible truth about the

---

[1] G. MÜLLER, *Dresden im dreissigjährigen Kriege*. *Neues Archiv für Sächsische Geschichte*, XXXVI, p. 255.

situation in letters that every man could read. The Hapsburg dynasty was defeated; the last crusade had failed.

Two hundred years later, in the liberal nineteenth century, a monument was erected on the field, bearing one significant phrase: 'Freedom of belief for all the world'. The monument still stands, set back from a quiet country road in the shade of a line of trees. Three centuries have smoothed every scar from that placid landscape, even as the philosophy of the New Germany has submerged the spiritual landmark. 'Freedom of belief for all the world' — forgotten yearning of an age forgotten among men who have no choice but to believe what they are told.[1]

V

The remains of the imperial army separated in order to stem the tide of invasion, Tilly fell back southwards to Nördlingen in the Upper Palatinate, Pappenheim to the Weser to check the advance of the King's subsidiary army along the northern coast. The League treasury was lost in the retreat and only the inadequate imperial funds were left to pay the army.

All Europe confidently expected that Gustavus would march on Vienna. John George urged him on; they had agreed before the battle that, in the event of victory, the Elector should keep watch on central Germany while the King invaded Bohemia. After the battle Gustavus reversed the plan: his reasons were simple and sound. He did not trust John George. It would be a fine thing if he should find, on his arrival in Vienna, that his ally had come to an understanding with his enemies, and that he must either make a bad peace or fight his way back to the coast. But if he forced the Elector to invade the Hapsburg lands himself, he would be less able to make his peace with the offended Emperor, and, even if he did, Gustavus would still control central and northern Germany with the roads back to the coast. These reasons were strong but there was another. Wallenstein had offered to surrender Prague;[2] Gustavus, while

[1] Written in 1936.
[2] See GAEDEKE, *Wallensteins Verhandlungen mit den Schweden*, Frankfort, 1885, pp. 108-9; IRMER, *Die Verhandlungen Schwedens und seinen Verbündeten mit Wallenstein*, Leipzig, 1888, I, p. 87.

he encouraged this cool treachery, knew that Wallenstein would act in the last resort only as best suited his own advantage. He might hand over Prague, or he might merely use the King's advance to hold a pistol at the head of the imperial government, resume his old command and, with the help of his immense resources, entrap the advancing army.

The latent enmity of Gustavus and John George clashed in a brief struggle. The Elector wanted to use the King merely as an instrument to bring Ferdinand to reason; the King wanted to be the dominant power in Germany. His national egoism and his desire for the north German waterways mingled with his devotion to the Protestant Cause. Justifiably he could not believe in the ability of John George, or of any German prince, to defend that Cause, and justifiably therefore, as it seemed to him and many of his contemporaries, he set himself up as the arbiter of Germany.

The Elector was in no position to protest against the new arrangement, for the flight of his troops at Breitenfeld had robbed him temporarily of the power to deal with Gustavus on equal terms. The circumstances were ignominious and, being himself partly to blame for what had happened, he did not improve matters by parading his indignation and threatening to hang every one of the fugitives. He would have to begin by hanging himself, an English volunteer impertinently declared;[1] the laugh was certainly against John George.

There was nothing for it but to yield, and in the early days of October 1631 the Saxon troops under Arnim crossed the Silesian border to redeem their shattered reputation in the imperial lands. On the 25th they were over the Bohemian frontier, on November 10th Wallenstein withdrew from his trust at Prague, and on the 15th Arnim occupied the town in the name of the Elector, while from a hundred hiding places the silenced Protestants crept out to welcome him.[2]

Meanwhile the King of Sweden marched westwards into the heart of Germany, blazing his trail down the Pfaffengasse, the 'Priests' alley', the hitherto unspoiled lands of the great Catholic

[1] POYNTZ, p. 58.
[2] See FOERSTER, *Wallenstein*, II, p. 168 f.; GAEDEKE, *Die Eroberung Nordböhmens. Neues Archiv für Sächsische Geschichte*, IX, pp. 243 ff.

bishoprics. On October 2nd he entered Erfurt. On the 14th he was at Würzburg, which he carried by assault on the fourth day. Here, for the first time, the vindictive cry 'Magdeburg quarter' resounded through the streets as the Swedish soldiers cut down the garrison, but the civilians, both citizens and fugitives from the surrounding country, were spared, and order was restored more rapidly and effectively than it had been at Frankfort-on-the-Oder. Nevertheless, great was the booty collected, and the King exacted a ransom of eighty thousand talers.[1]

At Frankfort-on-the-Main, the Catholic Princes had assembled for that futile discussion of the Edict of Restitution to which the Protestant Electors had refused to come; in the small hours of October 14th the Bishop of Würzburg woke the town with the lamentable news that he was a fugitive before the invader, and the deputies scattered in ignominious flight.[2] On November 11th Gustavus occupied Hanau, on the 22nd Aschaffenburg, on the 27th he entered Frankfort-on-the-Main, the constitutional centre of the Holy Roman Empire. Hither he called his Chancellor, Axel Oxenstierna, to direct the administration of his conquests.

He was now approaching that country which had been occupied by Spanish garrisons for over ten years, but he feared the King of Spain as little as or less than the Emperor. At Höchst he was joined by the Landgrave William of Hesse-Cassel with reinforcements, with whom he crossed the Rhine and marched for Heidelberg. But the season being advanced and the land well garrisoned, he turned back, leaving his ally, the young Duke Bernard of Saxe-Weimar, to win his spurs by seizing Mannheim. He himself five days before Christmas occupied Mainz; the Elector fled, the Spanish garrison surrendered before overwhelming odds.

Everywhere on his victorious march he had been received with jubilation by the Protestants, with gratitude by all, as the fame of his discipline spread. At Schweinfurt they spread rushes before him in the streets and hung banners from their windows, and 'they adored him wheresoever he came like a

[1] DROYSEN, *Gustaf Adolf*, II, p. 437; MONRO, II, p. 81.
[2] GEBAUER, *Die Restitutionsedikt in Brandenburg*, p. 201.

God come from Heaven'.[1] One after another, now with ease, now with difficulty, he plucked the German rulers from allegiance to the Emperor. By Christmas he had the Dukes William and Bernard of Saxe-Weimar serving in his army, the Landgrave of Hesse-Cassel and the Duke of Brunswick-Lüneburg as his allies in arms, the Landgrave of Hesse-Darmstadt, the regent of Württemberg, the Margraves of Ansbach and Bayreuth, the free city of Nuremberg and the Franconian Circle all under his protection.[2] The alliance of the Dukes of Mecklenburg he had always had, and in The Hague Frederick of Bohemia was preparing to join him.

He had seven armies and nearly eighty thousand men within the Empire. On the Rhine, he had fifteen thousand under his personal command, in Franconia under Marshal Horn eight thousand, in Hesse eight thousand, in Mecklenburg four thousand, in the Lower Saxon Circle thirteen thousand, near Magdeburg twelve thousand, in Saxe-Weimar four thousand, and the rest in garrisons over the country. He intended to raise another hundred and twenty thousand men in the course of the winter, of which a bare nine thousand were to come from Sweden.[3] His conquests made both recruiting and feeding so huge an army comparatively easy.

The King's name was spoken from end to end of Germany with joy and fear; he was prayed for in a thousand churches, known to great and small by a hundred names, the Golden King, the Lion of the North, biblically as Elias, as Gideon, as the Lion from Midnight.[4] In the winter, his Queen was expected and in her honour he had the initial letters of her name Marie Eleanore Regina traced in the brickwork of the fortifications he was building at Mainz. She joined him at Hanau on January 22nd, 1632; a tall, handsome, slender woman, who, before the whole assembly, putting her arms round the neck of the conqueror, greeted him with, 'Now you are my prisoner'.[5]

---

[1] POYNTZ, pp. 56, 62.

[2] *Sverges Traktater*, v, i, pp. 1631-2 *passim*.

[3] DROYSEN, op. cit., II, pp. 464-7; *Arkiv till upplysning Svenska Krigens*, I, pp. 546-8.

[4] DITFURTH, pp. 180, 241.

[5] *The Swedish Intelligencer*, second part, p. 68.

At Vienna in the drizzling rain, a procession of penitents besought their God to turn his wrath away; among them went the
Emperor, on foot in the mud, the water trickling down his
neck.[1] His prayers were not heard. His appeals to Rome
brought only the cold answer that the Pope did not consider
the war to be one of religion.[2] Letters to Madrid served only
to confirm the truth that the reserves of Spain were, for the
moment at least, exhausted. An embassy to Warsaw received
the same unhelpful reply.[3]

Thrown on his own resources, Ferdinand had no choice but
to look once again towards Wallenstein. The general's friends
had been agitating for his recall since the preceding spring,[4]
but at first the Emperor hesitated, torn between his inclination
and his necessity. His own son, the younger Ferdinand, pleaded
to be made commander-in-chief,[5] but even the fond father had
to realize that his appointment would not solve the financial
problem. The army could only be fed, clothed and paid again
by the man whose resources had fed, clothed and paid it before.
Three times, between November and December 1631, the
Emperor wrote imploring Wallenstein to come back; the last
time he penned the letter throughout in his own hand.[6] On
December 10th, he sent an embassy, not so much to suggest
terms as to find out what terms the general himself would
offer.[7] Not until the last day of the old year did Wallenstein
yield to persuasion, and then he merely guaranteed to raise a
new army by the following March, but agreed neither to pay
nor to lead it beyond that date.

The situation of the Spaniards on the Rhine was even more
perilous than that of Ferdinand at Vienna. Not only were
Mainz and Mannheim lost and the troops in the remaining
garrisons unpaid, mutinous and hungry, for the land from which
their support naturally came was overrun by the advancing
Protestants, but the Swiss at Gustavus's suggestion had closed

[1] *Annales*, XII, p. 2399. [2] SPANHEIM, pp. 122-3.
[3] CHEMNITZ, I, p. 297. [4] HALLWICH, *Briefe und Akten*, I, p. 306.
[5] Ibid., pp. 648-9. [6] FOERSTER, *Wallenstein*, II, pp. 186-92.
[7] HALLWICH, *Briefe und Akten*, I, pp. 657 ff.

the passes,[1] the Dutch had offered him subsidies for the coming year,[2] and on the left bank of the Rhine the French, without any declaration of war, had moved threateningly forward.

The excuse had been given by Charles of Lorraine. Closely attached to the interests of the Hapsburg, this reckless and unscrupulous young man watched for advantages against the Bourbon. In 1631 an abortive intrigue of the Queen-mother against Richelieu ended in the full confirmation of the Cardinal's power and the flight of the dowager Queen to Brussels, while her younger son, Gaston of Orleans, fled to Lorraine. The meaning of this flight was clear; the malcontents threw themselves on the mercy of the Hapsburg and their allies, against their own dynasty. Charles of Lorraine, encouraged alike from Brussels and Vienna, joyfully espoused their cause. On the first news of Breitenfeld, even Maximilian of Bavaria, panic-stricken, added his urgent plea.[3] But the Duke was an optimistic rather than a reliable ally. On January 3rd, 1632, he defied Richelieu and sowed the seeds of perpetual conflict by marrying his sister Margaret to the apparently infatuated Gaston; but fear, with the fat Duke of Orleans, was a stronger passion than love, and at the advance of a French army towards Nancy, he abandoned his young wife on their wedding night and fled to Brussels. On January 6th the Duke of Lorraine, unequal to the invasion, ceded the strong places on his frontier at the ignominious Peace of Vic. His rash intervention merely served as an excuse for trapping the Spanish garrisons on the Rhine between the armies of Gustavus and Richelieu.

Worse still, the Electors of Treves and Cologne, the two remaining Catholic princes on the Rhine, thought to save their skins by placing themselves unreservedly under the protection of France. The Elector of Cologne went even further, and refused passage to troops which were bound for the strengthening of the Spanish Netherlands.[4]

The Hapsburg position was thus in less than eighteen months completely undermined. So far from reconquering the northern provinces of the Netherlands, the government at Brussels

[1] PAUL, III, pp. 84-6.   [2] *Sverges Traktater*, v, i, pp. 601-3.
[3] HALLWICH, *Briefe und Akten*, I, p. 501.
[4] *Brefvexling*, II, viii, p. 69.

feared for its own safety, robbed alike of naval defence and financial support. Seldom had the Spaniards been more unpopular in Flanders, among populace and nobility alike. The cry 'Long live the Prince of Orange!' had been heard in the streets of Brussels,[1] and the danger of internal conspiracy was added to that of external attack.

In the face of so many perils — the joint attack in the Empire and the Low Countries, and the gathering of the French, Dutch and northern Protestant interests into so dangerous a coalition — the two branches of the Hapsburg dynasty once again made a formal treaty of offence and defence.[2] Meanwhile, the criticism of a certain section of Catholic society drove the Pope to give a little grudging support. 'Is His Holiness by chance a Catholic?' ran a significant pasquinade, with the suggestive answer, 'Hush, hush! He is most Christian.'[3] Under persuasion, Urban VIII at length made a small grant on Church lands in Spain, to be employed to support the German Catholics.[4]

Yet although disaster had swept down upon the Hapsburg dynasty, there was little jubilation at Paris. Indeed, Richelieu was far from satisfied with his Swedish ally; French policy in Germany for the last hundred years had been based on the establishment of France as the 'protector of the German Liberties', on gaining and using the alliance of the princes to curb the power of the Emperor. But the King of Sweden had shown as little respect for French policy as for Saxon, and had established himself incontrovertibly as the arbiter of German destinies.

The situation was grave for Richelieu. His policy was anti-Hapsburg but it was Catholic, and much depended for him on the maintenance of a good understanding between Maximilian's League and the French Court. Gustavus first distressingly compromised the Cardinal by proclaiming the alliance of Bärwalde to all the world, and secondly by plunging straight across the bishoprics of central Germany, not altering their form

[1] GEYL, p. 127.
[2] ABREU Y BERTODANO, IV, p. 342 f.
[3] The allusion is, of course, to the titles of the Kings of Spain and France, 'His Catholic Majesty' and 'Most Christian King'.
[4] ABREU Y BERTODANO, IV, p. 330 f.

of worship, it is true, but driving out their bishops and slicing the lands up as gifts for his marshals with cheerful unconcern. It was hardly surprising that Maximilian and the League turned on Richelieu to ask what his intentions had been when he subsidized the King of Sweden.

Richelieu hastily sent one ambassador to pacify Maximilian[1] and another to call the King of Sweden to order. The task of the first was hard, that of the second impossible. The Cardinal's brother-in-law, Brézé, had instructions to secure neutrality for the League. In return the League was to ally itself with France and to yield the key fortresses on the Rhine as guarantees of good faith.[2] The instructions of Brézé reveal how far Richelieu still under-estimated Gustavus. As arbiter of Germany, the King knew that he must keep control of the Rhine, and had no intention of yielding up his conquest. When Brézé in despair hinted that he could have north Germany for his own if he would only guarantee the Rhine to France, the King exploded with rage and stormily told the ambassador that, speaking for his own part, he was the protector and not the betrayer of Germany. A second ambassador, Hercule de Charnacé, who had negotiated the earlier treaty with the King, was hurried to Frankfort to calm the infuriated ally,[3] but weeks of enervating argument resulted only in his gaining a partial guarantee of neutrality for the Elector of Treves,[4] while Brézé was pacified with the gift of a gold hatband worth sixteen thousand talers as a parting gift.[5]

The bewildered annoyance of Richelieu was shared by the German princes. Although he had been approached by the Emperor and the Spanish ambassador,[6] although Wallenstein had opened a second line of negotiations with Arnim,[7] John George dared not make peace now that Gustavus was so powerful in Germany. In vain he urged the King to make a settlement while the occasion was favourable; his ally met these demands with a galling mixture of anger, contempt and suspicion. He believed that Arnim and Wallenstein were

[1] FAGNIEZ, Le Père Joseph et Richelieu, Paris, 1894, II, pp. 494-500.
[2] AVENEL, IV, pp. 251-4.   [3] Ibid., IV, pp. 257-9.
[4] LUNDORP, IV, pp. 275-8.   [5] Brefvexling, II, i, p. 760.
[6] HALLWICH, Briefe und Akten, I, p. 527 f.
[7] IRMER, Die Verhandlungen Schwedens, I, pp. 107-8.

treating secretly, or that his old rival the King of Denmark had tampered with John George, and he flung off the repeated entreaties of the Saxon ambassador at length with the apocalyptic words that he 'had begun this work with God, and with God he would finish it.'[1]

Adler Salvius, the King's most persuasive agent, had been busy soothing the Elector of Brandenburg ever since the march across central Germany began, and temporarily flattered him into acquiescence by the suggestion that the only daughter and heiress of Gustavus should marry his eldest son.[2] But when early in 1632 the Elector's ambassadors at Frankfort mentioned peace to the Swedish King, he informed them that he could not possibly consider it in the interests of Protestant Germany. Protestant Germany, at least as represented by its quavering rulers, thought, not without justification, that further conquest would only embitter the Catholic party and rouse fresh enemies; better take a stand on what they had than risk the position to gain more. But Gustavus was thinking in terms of imperial conquest; he had drastically reorganized the conquered lands, was encouraging trading schemes and commercial enterprises, planning to unite the Calvinist and Lutheran Churches,[3] projecting in fact the destruction of the old chaotic Empire and the creation of another. Taking the long view, he may have been justified in fighting for a better conclusion; taking the nearer view and looking more closely at the spreading distress of the country, one sympathizes with the princes.

What part Gustavus planned for himself in the new Empire is doubtful. Officially he spoke of himself merely as the defender of the Protestants; unofficially he had certainly let slip to the Duke of Mecklenburg a phrase beginning: 'If I become Emperor . . .'[4] There was nothing intolerable in the idea: the Empire was not theoretically a national German state, but an

---

[1] G. DROYSEN, *Die Verhandlungen über den Universalfrieden im Winter* 1631-32. *Archiv für Sächsische Geschichte. Neue Folge*, VI, pp. 223-6.

[2] R. SCHULZE, *Die Projekt der Vermählung Friedrich Wilhelms von Brandenburg mit Christina von Schweden.* Halle, 1898, pp. 2-3 f

[3] WESTIN, *Negotiations about Church Unity*, pp. 135-6; GEBAUER, *Die Restitutionsedikt in Kurbrandenburg*, pp. 235-6.

[4] KRETZSCHMAR, *Gustav Adolfs Pläne und Ziele in Deutschland und die Herzöge von Braunschweig und Lüneburg.* Hannover, 1904, p. 176 n. 1.

international state of which the vicissitudes of fortune had left only the German-speaking fragment. French and even English kings, Italians, Spaniards and the King of Denmark had considered standing at past elections. The Swedish King, with his Baltic interests, his Protestant religion and his fluent German speech, was a no less suitable Emperor than Ferdinand with his Spanish obligations, his Italian interests and his Catholic religion. In the north he was a more suitable candidate. Besides which he had an only daughter, and his wife was unlikely to have other children; if this daughter were married according to plan to the heir of Brandenburg, there would be a progressive Germanization of the Swedish dynasty and of Sweden itself, until it became merged in the more advanced and thickly populated states of Germany.

In spite of this, the idea of substituting Gustavus for Ferdinand appealed not at all to the leading German princes. From the purely selfish view-point they did not wish to be saddled with a ruler who with his own army and a career of conquest behind him was even more potentially despotic than Ferdinand. The rift between the north and south of the German-speaking world having not yet become inevitable, it was obvious to any German statesman of ordinary acumen that the elevation of Gustavus to the imperial throne would lead only to a schism, and the domination of a Protestant ruler would force the Catholic princes into firmer alliance among themselves and with Ferdinand. Whatever the merits of Gustavus's plan, in practice it rested on the goodwill of the German rulers, which, with few exceptions, he never had. Speaking of them he himself had said, 'I fear stupidity and treachery more than force'.[1] By appearing to aim at Empire and by redistributing German land among his marshals,[2] he did not increase his popularity.

In February Frederick of Bohemia made his appearance at Frankfort and was received by the King with exaggerated respect. To the indignation of the constitutional party, Gustavus gave him the precedence not of an Elector but of a

[1] *Arkiv till upplysning Svenska Krigens*, 1, p. 521.
[2] F. BOTHE, *Gustav Adolfs und seines Kanzlers Wirtschaftspolitische Absichten*. Frankfurt, 1910, p. 179; IRMER, *Die Verhandlungen Schwedens*, 1, p. 111.

reigning monarch, and insisted on the perpetual use of all his titles without omission.[1] This was fair treatment indeed, but even the dispossessed prince shortly began to suspect his ally's intentions. He confessed to the Brandenburg ambassador that he saw no further cause for war except that 'the King of Sweden was hard to content',[2] and when later he found that Gustavus intended to restore him to the Palatinate as a vassal of the Swedish Crown, he gathered the rags of his self-respect about him and emphatically refused.[3] A welcome ally, the King was an unwelcome master. From Frederick of Bohemia to Gustavus of Sweden, this attitude was doubtless in practice absurd; in theory it was the only possible course for a loyal German prince.

The son-in-law of John George, the Landgrave of Hesse-Darmstadt, suffered most. He had acted during the summer as a go-between for the Emperor and his father-in-law, and when in the autumn he had been forced to ally himself with Gustavus, he continued to use all his petty influence to guide the conqueror towards peace.[4] The King suspected him of being in imperial pay, and when the prince complained of the bad discipline of the soldiers quartered at Rüsselsheim, asked him scornfully if he was thinking of selling it to the Emperor. Indeed he referred to him mockingly in public as 'peace-maker in ordinary to the Holy Roman Empire'.[5]

The atmosphere at Frankfort was not improved by an after-dinner conversation on February 25th, 1632. Gustavus had undertaken to fight for the Germans out of pure generosity, he pointed out. 'Let [the Emperor] not inquire after me', he said, 'and I shall not inquire after him', and then to the Landgrave of Hesse-Darmstadt, 'Your Highness can tell him so, for I know you are a good imperialist'. The Landgrave opened his mouth to protest but the King cut him short: 'He who gets thirty thousand talers reward must be a good imperialist', he stated scornfully. White with anger, the prince relapsed

[1] SPANHEIM, p. 226.
[2] AITZEMA, I, pp. 1260-1.
[3] MOSER, Patriotisches Archiv, VI, pp. 176-84.
[4] HURTER, Friedensbestrebungen Ferdinands, II, p. 14 f.; IRMER, Die Verhandlungen Schwedens, pp. 8-68 passim; DROYSEN, Die Verhandlungen über den Universalfrieden, pp. 144-5.
[5] IRMER, Die Verhandlungen Schwedens, I, p. 109; SPANHEIM, p. 211.

into silence,[1] while Gustavus continued to enlarge on the necessity of further war to a bewildered and irritated audience.

VII

On March 2nd, 1632, the King again took the field; leaving Bernard of Saxe-Weimar to guard the Rhine, he marched to join Marshal Horn at Schweinfurt, and thence to Nuremberg for a general rendezvous of his forces. Here he was received with jubilation by the citizens and overwhelmed with gifts from the municipality;[2] after assembling forty thousand men he made ready to march south. His objective was Augsburg and, inevitably, Bavaria.

Torn between his trust in Richelieu and his fear of Gustavus, Maximilian had played into the King's hands. The French agent had persuaded him to assert his neutrality, but Maximilian's terrors were so great that he had never made any attempt to dissociate himself from Tilly's army, and in March he had written to Ferdinand imploring him to recall Wallenstein.[3] Terror lest he should lose his lands drove him both to forgo all he had once gained by the dismissal of the general and to renounce his neutrality. On April 1st he joined Tilly and his army at Ingolstadt, giving Gustavus all the justification he wanted for his march into Bavaria.

Reinforced by five thousand new troops which Wallenstein after long refusal had grudgingly agreed to send him, Tilly fell back eastwards, meaning to hold the line of the river Lech. On April 7th Gustavus crossed the Danube at Donauwörth and marched eastwards, laying the land waste about him so that no second army could find sustenance. His troops even rooted up the young corn to feed their horses and left the spring fields desolate.[4] All this time Wallenstein lay on the Bohemian border with an army of twenty thousand men,[5] which he had

<hr>

[1] MOSER, *Patriotisches Archiv*, IV, pp. 466-73.
[2] MONRO, II, p. 111.
[3] HALLWICH, *Briefe und Akten*, II, p. 277.
[4] LAMMERT, pp. 120, 124.
[5] DROYSEN, *Gustaf Adolf*, II, p. 553.

raised but would not lead. For weeks the government at Vienna besought him to move, the Emperor and the Emperor's son, the proud young Archduke Ferdinand, imploring him only to name his terms and bring his army to save them.[1] When the King of Sweden crossed the Danube, he had still taken no decision. On April 14th Gustavus reached the Lech, on the far side of which Tilly was encamped upon rising wooded ground. Reconnoitring, he saw sentries on the opposite bank who, not recognizing him, hailed him with the friendly insolence of their kind. 'Where's your King?' they called. 'Nearer than you think,' shouted Gustavus and cantered off.[2] In the night he constructed a bridge of boats, and in the morning sent three hundred picked Finnish troops across the river under Tilly's ceaseless fire, to throw up earthworks for his batteries. In the shelter of these the rest of the army crossed, Tilly not daring to risk his position by a charge. Once over, the King stormed the hill; his tactics were good and his luck better, for Tilly, shot in the leg at the outset, was carried to the rear and his second, Aldringer, fell only a few minutes later unconscious, with a fractured skull. Failing these, Maximilian saved what was left of the army by immediate retreat. The baggage and the artillery for the most part remained on the field, and the army itself would not have got so clean away had not the winds turned imperialist and blocked the roads with fallen trees in the stormy night that followed.[3]

Two hundred and fifty miles away at Göllersdorf in Austria, Wallenstein had at last come to terms with the Emperor. What those terms were will probably never be known. No untainted evidence exists. But this much is clear, that rumour credited Wallenstein with having stipulated not only for absolute control in the army, but for absolute control of all peace negotiations and the right to conclude treaties when and where he would, for the exclusion of the Emperor's son from any part in the command, and of Spain from any influence upon it, while he, Wallenstein, was to receive as his reward a part of the Hapsburg lands and the title of Elector — Bohemia and the

[1] FOERSTER, *Wallenstein*, II, pp. 196 f., 202 f.
[2] DROYSEN, *Gustaf Adolf*, II, p. 537.
[3] CHEMNITZ, I, p. 310; see also *Brefvexling*, II, viii, p. 55; POYNTZ, p. 65; *Swedish Intelligencer* II, p. 142.

Electorate of Brandenburg or the Palatinate. This was mostly rumour with a little leakage of inside information.[1]

Baldly, whatever the terms of his recall, Wallenstein came back with a practical power which was unquestioned; he had proved beyond doubt that he alone could support and pay the army, and in the intervening time he had brought all his previous arrangements to such perfection that he could turn on or turn off the supplies at will. His estate of Friedland in particular, and the sphere of his influence in general, had become one vast magazine for supplying food, clothing and stores. Munition factories had sprung up, mills were grinding night and day, bakers baking hundreds of thousands of loaves, brewers brewing, weavers weaving, while his officials everywhere were collecting and bringing in the taxes for him to pay away in wages for his army. Friedland was covered over by a network of clearing houses and roads down which supplies were transported to the troops, or carried to huge store-houses for any sudden emergency.[2] Wallenstein, first perhaps among European rulers, had conceived of a state organized exclusively for war.

His return still did not mean an immediate check to the King of Sweden, for Bohemia had first to be cleared of the Saxons. Wallenstein took his time; holding the absolute control of the situation on the Catholic side, he saw — as he had always seen — that he could undermine the King's position best by suborning John George. Consequently, instead of attacking the Saxons he made it possible for them to withdraw unmolested over the border to the accompaniment of polite suggestions of alliance.[3] This did not separate John George from the King but it accomplished half Wallenstein's intention, for Gustavus had counted on the Saxon army to hold Bohemia, and its withdrawal filled him with doubts of his ally's loyalty, which before the end of the year lured him to his death.

For the moment the King's triumphal progress went on.

---

[1] GINDELY in the *Historische Zeitschrift*, XCVII, and in *Waldsteins Vertrag mit dem Kaiser, Abhandlungen der Classe für Philosophie, Geschichte und Philologie der Königlich böhmische Gesellschaft der Wissenschaften*, VII, iii, 1890; RITTER, *Der Untergang Wallensteins. Historische Zeitschrift*, LXXXVIII; GLUIBICH, *Gli ultimi successi di Alberte di Waldstein narrati dagli Ambasciatori Veneti. Archiv für Oesterreichische Geschichte*. Vienna, 1863, XXVIII, pp. 361-2.
[2] ERNSTBERGER, *Wallenstein als Volkswirt*, pp. 20-2, 38-9, 47.
[3] GAEDEKE, *Wallenstein und Arnim*, pp. 11-13.

On April 24th he entered Augsburg among the plaudits of the Protestant citizens and addressed the people in the warmest terms from the balcony of the Fuggers' house in the wine market; he demanded, however, an oath of loyalty from the leading citizens and a monthly subsidy of thirty thousand talers.[1] That evening he gave a banquet and ball at which, throwing off the dignity of the King, he engaged, according to a local legend, in a pleasingly human scramble for a kiss with a pretty and coy Augsburgerin.[2]

Five days later he arrived outside the strongly fortified city of Ingolstadt where, among the small but loyal garrison, the wounded Tilly lay dying. On his sick-bed, hearing the news of Wallenstein's appointment, he had the strength of body and character left to write a letter of good wishes to the man who, having ruined him, now stepped in over his dying body to rescue the imperial cause.[3] His mind rested much on God and the Holy Patroness to whom he had dedicated his arid and blameless life, but he forgot neither his men nor his duties, drew up a will leaving sixty thousand talers to the veteran regiments of the League army, and died, it was said, with the word 'Regensburg' on his lips.[4] The defence of that key-point on the Danube had in his last moments driven all thoughts of Heaven or Hell from the failing mind of the old soldier.

Outside, in the Swedish camp, Gustavus displayed himself with his usual recklessness and had his horse killed under him. He was unimpressed: earlier, when he had been entreated to take more care for his person, he had cogently asked what was the use of a King in a box?[5] His self-confidence was equally apparent in an interview with the French agent from Munich who sought, once again, to secure a guarantee of neutrality for Maximilian. The Frenchman began badly by explaining that the Elector knew nothing of the clash of arms between Tilly and the Swedish King. In that case, Gustavus replied, why had Tilly not been arrested and hanged? The Frenchman, attempting to redeem a tactical error, suggested suavely that

[1] *Chronik des Jakob Wagner*, Augsburg, 1902, pp. 10-12.

[2] KLOPP, III, ii, p. 646 n.

[3] DUDIK, *Waldsteins Correspondenz. Archiv für Oesterreichische Geschichte*. Vienna, 1866, XXXVI, p. 222.

[4] SPANHEIM, p. 272.   [5] *Swedish Intelligencer*, II, p. 161; SPANHEIM, p. 211.

there was much to be said for the Elector. Gustavus answered that he believed there was much to be said for lice by those who cared for them. This was too much for the French agent, whose indignant protest was, however, cut short by a volume of threats. Maximilian should have his neutrality if he laid down arms at once without further question, stormed the King; otherwise Bavaria should be burnt from end to end, so that the Elector could distinguish his enemies from his friends. Truculent in his turn, the Frenchman reminded Gustavus of Richelieu's promise to help Maximilian should he be attacked. What if forty thousand men were sent from France? Trembling with rage, the King declared that he would fight them all. God was with him. To this unanswerable asseveration the French agent had no rejoinder, and the interview came to an end.[1]

On May 3rd the King marched on; he had not the time to spare for a long siege and decided to risk leaving Ingolstadt unreduced. While Marshal Horn pursued the remnants of Tilly's battered troops towards Regensburg, wasting as he went,[2] the King made for Bavaria, intending by this movement to draw Wallenstein out of Bohemia. Maximilian, now in personal command of his wrecked army, faced a cruel alternative. Either he could throw his army into Munich and save his capital, thereby abandoning Regensburg, which was not his own town, and allowing Horn to cut the line of communication between him and Wallenstein, or he could sacrifice his own Bavaria, stay where he was and maintain the line unbroken. There is no doubt which was wiser for the imperial cause, but the temptation must have been sharp, for Maximilian had given forty years of his life to the welfare of Bavaria. Nevertheless, with one of those flashes of self-abnegation which here and there illumine his career of dynastic egoism, he chose to let the army hold Regensburg. He himself descended on Munich, garrisoned it with two thousand picked cavalry, collected his more important papers and treasury and fled to Salzburg.[3]

[1] HALLWICH, Briefe und Akten, II, p. 404 f.; ARCHENHOLTZ, Mémoires concernant Christine, Reine de Suède, II, App. pp. 21-4.
[2] Brefvexling, II, viii, p. 56.
[3] Ibid., loc. cit.; FOERSTER, Wallenstein, II, p. 225 f.

He was not a moment too soon. By mid-May the King of Sweden was at the gates; the troops, realizing that resistance was useless, retreated over the Isar, blowing up the bridges, and the citizens and clergy bought immunity from the conqueror with the gigantic sum of a quarter of a million talers.[1]

After the passage of the Lech they had said it would take the King three weeks to reach Vienna.[2] But that had been in April, and at the end of May he was still in Bavaria. John George was holding him back. Frankly, the information from Bohemia was puzzling, contradictory and suspicious. Count Thurn, the veteran rebel, in command of the small Swedish contingent that had accompanied the Saxons, had been insinuating against Arnim's loyalty all the year.[3] Arnim had made no effort to prevent Wallenstein's recruiting, he had openly said that he would cease to fight if peace were not made by May,[4] and last of all he had retreated without a shot fired, back into Silesia. On May 25th Wallenstein reoccupied Prague, and with Wallenstein in Prague and Arnim apparently unwilling to fall on his rear, Gustavus could not march on Vienna. It would put him in just the position he had avoided in the previous year; some separate treaty between John George and Ferdinand might leave him stranded in Austria. The King hesitated; in spite of Thurn's malice, Gustavus had a better opinion of Arnim than of John George and tried to solve the problem by suborning the general to abandon the Electoral service for his own.[5] Arnim would not be bribed; on June 7th he withdrew the last of his troops from Bohemia, and Gustavus sent an envoy post haste to Dresden to inquire what John George was about.[6]

In the circumstances the King had to make certain of his political position in Germany. On June 20th he again entered Nuremberg and began to organize himself a party. There, in a busy forty-eight hours, he revealed his plan for Germany. The

---

[1] *Brefvexling*, loc. cit.; DROYSEN, *Gustaf Adolf*, II, p. 557.

[2] W. MICHAEL, *Wallensteins Vertrag mit dem Kaiser im Jahre* 1632. *Historische Zeitschrift*, LXXXVIII, p. 387.

[3] HILDEBRAND, *Wallenstein und die Schweden*. Frankfort, 1885, p. 10.

[4] *Letter from George Fleetwood giving an account of the battle of Lützen. Camden Miscellany*, I. London, 1847, p. 5.

[5] *Brefvexling*, II, i, pp. 766, 798 f.

[6] IRMER, *Die Verhandlungen Schwedens*, I, p. 211.

terms of the only treaty he would make with the Emperor comprised the toleration of the Protestant religion everywhere, the restoration of all Protestant lands, the north coast from the Vistula to the Elbe for Sweden, a seizure of land which was to be made good to the Elector of Brandenburg by the gift of Silesia. Chiefly, the Protestant princes were to form a united Corpus Evangelicorum, with a strong standing army under an elected president, which should have full and equal recognition within the Empire and at the Diet.

The city of Nuremburg declared itself at once ready to join the Corpus, but for the moment the King had to shelve politics again, for Wallenstein had at last crossed the Bohemian frontier and was marching to join Maximilian. The King attempted to separate them, but Wallenstein evaded him and at Schwabach on July 11th came up in person with Maximilian. Dismounting from their horses, the allies courteously embraced one another, neither the resentment of the one nor the mortification of the other betraying itself.[1] Momentarily, it seemed that the past was forgotten and both would work in unison to redeem the fallen fortunes of the Church and the imperial dynasty.

The King retreated again to Fürth on the outskirts of Nuremberg. Wallenstein followed and built himself a strong encampment on a long ridge overlooking the little river Rednitz and threatening Gustavus's position. On July 27th he had information that the King, outnumbered, and too weak to risk moving from his camp, had sent for almost the whole of his scattered armies from south and western Germany. There was, Wallenstein calculated, no fodder for horse or man, and the King would have to fight or starve. If he starved, that was an end of his army; if he fought, that too, in the relative positions of the troops, would be death.[2] Meanwhile Wallenstein was feeding his men from his own supplies; the communications were not faultless, and the troops, particularly in Maximilian's army, were dying fast. But there was this difference between Wallenstein and Gustavus: Wallenstein could afford to lose one army and raise another, Gustavus could not. Maximilian could not afford it either; he said as

[1] *Annales*, XII, p. 24. [2] HALLWICH, *Briefe und Akten*, II, pp. 644-5.

much, but fruitlessly.[1] Wallenstein had never been sensitive to the wants of the League army.

On August 16th the King's reinforcements came up, and at last, on September 3rd and 4th, he attacked the enemy position. All in vain, for on the uneven ground, thick with scrub, he could not bring his cavalry into action and he had to withdraw with a loss heavy in men, but heavier in reputation.[2] Bad discipline among his troops, particularly those recruited in Germany, was robbing him of his previous popularity, and even his personal intervention was unsuccessful. Stolen cattle had been traced to some German officers, and the King burst out in almost tearful rage. 'God be my witness, you yourselves are the destroyers, wasters and spoilers of your fatherland', he stormed, 'my heart sickens when I look upon one of you . . .'[3] It was rumoured that his allies were slipping from him. 'His power is not in his own subjects but in strangers; not in his money but in theirs; not in their goodwill but in mere necessity as things now stand between him and them; therefore if the necessity be not so urgent as it is . . . the money and the power and the assistance which it yieldeth unto him will fall from him'; so predicted a Scottish divine, shrewdly watching the passage of events. 'He is not well settled yet in Germany', he wrote, 'he is far from home.'[4]

In September at Nuremberg the King attempted to right this last evil. He offered peace terms to Wallenstein, in which the main points of his scheme for establishing a strong Protestant party were clearly outlined; he demanded that all land ever occupied by Protestants should remain Protestant, that the Edict of Restitution should be unconditionally withdrawn and toleration be granted in every State of the Empire including the imperial lands, that the dispossessed should be reinstated, that Wallenstein should take Franconia in place of Mecklenburg, that Maximilian be given Upper Austria in exchange for the Palatinate, that he himself should have Pomerania, and the Elector of Brandenburg be given Magdeburg and Halberstadt

[1] HURTER, *Wallensteins vier letzte Lebensjahre.* Vienna, 1862, pp. 155-6; HALLWICH, *Briefe und Akten,* III, p. 95.
[2] *Swedish Intelligencer,* III, pp. 38 ff.
[3] *Chronik Jakol Wagners,* pp. 20-1; see also *The Swedish Intelligencer,* III, p. 24.
[4] WESTIN, p. 208.

in its place.[1] These terms showed clearly the scope of the King's plans. The Church and the Hapsburg dynasty were to be ruthlessly sacrificed, and an Empire, in which the constitutional secular princes predominated, was to be in fact controlled by the Corpus Evangelicorum and its president, the King of Sweden. The marriage of his only daughter Christina to the heir of Brandenburg would create a dynastic territorial block in northern Europe which would outweigh the cracking power of the Hapsburg and shift the balance of the whole continent.

But Axel Oxenstierna discouraged a too rapid conclusion of terms, not trusting his enemies. 'The Bavarian duke', he said, 'is like the Wallensteiner . . . both smooth and false.'[2] Wallenstein too was against the treaty, confident now in his military superiority and knowing that the King's alliances were beginning to fail. The regent of Württemberg was disaffected, the Elector of Brandenburg displeased at the conditions offered for his son's marriage,[3] and the King could never feel sure of John George. While he remained trapped at Nuremberg, Wallenstein's lieutenant, Holk, had invaded Saxony and was systematically devastating the country.[4]

At Nuremberg the army, both man and beast, suffered horribly. A damp summer made the conditions worse,[5] and the shortage of food and fresh water increased the epidemic diseases always prevalent in the camp. Men and horses were dying with terrifying rapidity; the cavalry alone had diminished by nearly three-quarters.

On September 18th the King decided to abandon the position at whatever risk. There were stories of a new peasants' revolt in Austria and a rising of Stephen Ragoczy, Bethlen Gabor's successor, in Transylvania.[6] Gustavus determined to march thither, for he knew that Wallenstein planned to join Holk in Saxony, and hoped that by moving south he would induce him to divide his forces.

As his army marched away, Maximilian once again urged Wallenstein to attack, and once again the general disregarded

---

[1] *Brefvexling*, I, i, pp. 540-3 ff. [2] Ibid., I, vii, p. 574.
[3] Ibid., II, viii, p. 73; SCHULZE, p. 5 f.
[4] SONDEN, *Lars Tungels Efterlämnade Papper. Historiska Handlinger. Nyföljd*, XXII, p. 45.
[5] *Brefvexling*, II, viii, p. 57. [6] SPANHEIM, p. 411.

him.[1] He had a more subtle plan. With the joint armies he intended to race for Saxony; thus either he would come upon John George and Arnim alone and force them to make terms, or he would draw Gustavus off from Austria. But Maximilian had had enough of Wallenstein's plans, and he retired with the rags of his army sulkily to defend Bavaria.

Annoyed, but still set on his original plan, Wallenstein turned north-eastwards, sending word to Holk and Pappenheim, who was on the Weser, to join him. Three armies thus converged upon John George at once. If Gustavus could have trusted the Elector and his general to fight to the last ditch, he might have continued his march on Vienna. But two months ago he had been informed that Arnim had an understanding with the enemy, and John George had spluttered in his cups that he was tired of the King of Sweden's dangerous alliance.[2] In any case the Elector had not the martyr's temperament; from Dresden he could see his people's villages blazing to heaven — torches to light his drinking bouts, mocked the imperial soldiery[3] — and on October 9th he wrote imploring the King's help.[4] Gustavus had not waited for the entreaty; he was already on his way.

On October 22nd he was again in Nuremberg, and could not resist the temptation of turning aside to visit Wallenstein's deserted encampment; all activity was long since silent, but he was sickened there to find the wounded, famished and untended, crawling among the bodies of dead men and beasts.[5] Later he saw the Chancellor Oxenstierna and gave him full instructions for the administration and taxation of the occupied country against the winter. On November 2nd at Arnstadt, he found Bernard of Saxe-Weimar and his troops. There, also, before marching on Leipzig, which had already surrendered to Holk, he wrote to his Chancellor. The winter was coming on, the third winter in Germany, and Gustavus intended to use it to establish his position by law as well as arms. Oxenstierna

---

[1] ARETIN, *Bayerns auswärtige Verhältnisse.* Passau, 1839, I; *Urkunden*, p. 343
[2] IRMER, *Die Verhandlungen Schwedens*, I, pp. 249-50; *Konung Gustaf II. Adolfs Skrifter*, ed. C. G. Styffe. Stockholm, 1861, p. 553.
[3] SONDEN, *Lars Tungel*, p. 611.
[4] HALLWICH, *Briefe und Akten*, III, p. 231 f.
[5] SPANHEIM, pp. 427-8.

was to call a meeting of the four Circles occupied by Swedish troops, those of the Upper and Lower Rhine, of Swabia and Franconia, in order to give the Corpus Evangelicorum legal existence and establish the King as its first president.[1]

On November 6th, Wallenstein and Pappenheim joined forces. Gustavus hesitated; he had little more than sixteen thousand men, his cavalry were very weak, and John George showed no sign of joining him. Four thousand horses had been left dead on the march alone.[2] The imperialists, on the other hand, had twenty-six thousand men. But on the 15th some Croatian prisoners told the King that Wallenstein, apparently thinking the Swedes dared not risk a battle, had sent Pappenheim on to Halle.[3] The occasion could not be lost; hastening forward, Gustavus surprised the imperialists, late in the evening, entrenched in the little town of Lützen, fifteen miles west of Leipzig. It was too dark to try the issue, and Wallenstein, forewarned in the late afternoon of the King's advance, sent a scout pelting after Pappenheim to bring him back.[4] All that night his men worked, setting up batteries in the orchards which flanked the walls of the town, and throwing up hasty earthworks, moving out to their lines by torchlight in the small hours,[5] while Gustavus and his men slept about a mile southeast of Lützen, under the sky in the cold November fields.[6]

The morning of November 16th broke fair, but a thick mist gathered over the flat, sodden country at about ten o'clock and continued for the rest of the day.[7] The ground was perfectly flat, the fields stretching away, almost without cover save for an occasional straggling hedge, on either side of the main road as far as eye could see. The road ran roughly east and west; north of it there was a ditch, and a little farther back three windmills. Between the ditch and the windmills, having Lützen on his right, Wallenstein drew up his forces, placing a line of musketeers in the ditch, whence they could shoot upwards at the bellies of the Swedish horses when they charged. He did not

---

[1] *Brefvexling*, II, i, pp. 855-69.

[2] *Fleetwood. Camden Miscellany*, I, pp. 5-6; *Fyra relationer om slaget vid Lützen. Historisk Tidskrift*, 1932, p. 302.

[3] *Fleetwood*, p. 6.   [4] FOERSTER, *Wallenstein*, II, p. 273.

[5] HALLWICH, *Briefe und Akten*, III, p. 500.

[6] *Fleetwood*, p. 6.   [7] Ibid., I, p. 7.

depart from the time-honoured formation, placing his cavalry
on the wings, his infantry in the centre, his artillery in front of
the infantry. Owing to Pappenheim's absence he had only
between twelve and fifteen thousand men, very ill-armed he
subsequently asserted,[1] and to improve the appearance of his
reduced forces he herded the camp followers out of the
town, grouped them together loosely in squares, the men in
front, provided them with a few standards and hoped that in the

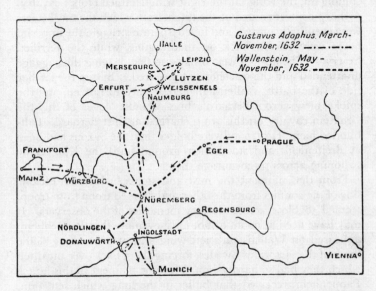

Gustavus Adophus, March-
November, 1632 —.—.—.—
Wallenstein, May-
November, 1632. ———————

grey distance the Swedes would take them for a powerful
reserve.

The King drew up his troops on the south side of the road,
having the town of Lützen a little in front of him and to the
left. His right wing was against a small plantation of trees. He
formed his troops once again in the manner which had been so
successful at Breitenfeld, he himself commanding on the right
wing and Bernard of Saxe-Weimar on the left; but the disposition of the battle, unlike Breitenfeld, was entirely in his hands,
and both left and right wings were drawn up in the Swedish

[1] FOERSTER, *Wallenstein*, II, p. 308.

fashion. On the farther side of the road Holk faced the King, Wallenstein himself was opposite Saxe-Weimar.[1]

As was his custom, the King prayed before the whole army, asking the blessing of God on the Protestant Cause. This was at about eight o'clock and the firing had already begun, but not for two hours did either army move. The Swedes once or twice attempted a feint attack to draw Wallenstein out of his position, but in vain, and at last at ten o'clock, just as the mist was coming up, the King on the right wing charged Holk's cavalry. A sharp contest ensued at the ditch, from which the musketeers were eventually ousted, and in a desperate struggle the imperial horse were driven back on to the guns, while the terrified 'reserves' of camp-followers broke and fled, leaving the baggage unattended and the tracehorses unsecured.[2] But on the farther side of the battle Wallenstein had set fire to Lützen, and the smoke blew across Bernard's lines. Under cover of this the Croatian cavalry on this wing charged against Bernard's half-blinded men. His troops were bolder than the Saxons had been at Breitenfeld, and stood their ground until the King came galloping across to encourage them.

From that moment the mist and smoke, which cut off one side of the conflict from the other and divided troop from troop, seemed to blow across the very memories of the observers. It may have been at noon, or not until evening, that Pappenheim appeared on Wallenstein's left wing and at once charged the flank of the victorious Swedes, forcing them back over the ditch which they had so hardly won. At some moment in this attack Pappenheim received that bullet in the lung which sent him, choking blood, to die in his coach on the Leipzig road. Towards midday the King of Sweden's horse, riderless and wild with pain from a neck-wound, was seen plunging across the field. The imperialists shouted that Gustavus was dead. Octavio Piccolomini swore he had seen him stretched on the ground. Holk spread the news. But on the Swedish side the officers denied it, desperate lest it might be true. It could not be denied for ever, for the King was no longer leading them, and to his army this had but one meaning.

[1] FLEETWOOD, p. 6; FIEDLER, *Diodatis Bericht über die Schlacht bei Lützen. Forschungen zur deutschen Geschichte*, IV. Göttingen, 1865, p. 561.
[2] POYNTZ, p. 126.

Bernard of Saxe-Weimar took command. On the right wing his troops swept forward once again, driving Wallenstein's men back on to flaming Lützen; wheeling, they then charged the centre and seized the batteries at the windmills. On the right, frantic at their King's death, the soldiers cleared the long-contested ditch once again, and put Pappenheim's wild but unreliable cavalry to flight. Three horses were shot under Octavio Piccolomini as he tried to rally them; seven times he was grazed by bullets, but never by word or sign let it be known. At nightfall Wallenstein, crippled with gout, raging with pain and mortification, drew off under cover of darkness to Halle. Exhausted, his men fell and slept by the way, while all night long he sent scouts to find out who was left that could fight. An English captain, roused from the sleep of exhaustion in a ditch, his head propped against his horse's flank, indicated three officers of his company lying close by, but thought there were no other survivors. If there were, he had lost them.[1] Trace-horses were gone, so that the baggage and artillery had to be left, and Holk appears to have been the only man in the imperial army who regarded the engagement as a victory.[2]

In the dank November darkness the Swedes were seeking the body of their King. They found him at last; he had been shot between the ear and the right eye, the wound that killed him, but he had other wounds, a dagger thrust and a shot in the side, two balls in the arm and one — which caused great rumour of treachery — in the back. He lay on what had been the enemy's side of the contested ditch, naked, under a heap of dead. That night, over his whole camp, among Swedes and Germans, Scots, English, Irish, Poles, French and Dutch, among mercenaries as among his subjects, there hung the silence of unutterable sorrow.[3]

VIII

'He thinks the ship cannot sink that carries him', Sir Thomas Roe had said, and in that last year of crowning victories all

---

[1] POYNTZ, p. 126.　　[2] HALLWICH, *Briefe und Akten*, III, p. 503.
[3] There are several accounts of Lützen. I have used chiefly FLEETWOOD'S in the *Camden Miscellany*, vol. I; *Diodatis Bericht üeber Lützen*, HOLK'S account in HALLWICH, *Briefe und Akten*, III, pp. 499-503; *Fyra relationer om slaget vid Lützen. Historisk Tidskrift*, 1932, pp. 299-309; *Swedish Intelligencer*, III, p. 127 f.; MONRO, II, pp. 162-5.

Europe had conspired to think the same. Friends and enemies alike could not conceive that the King should be dead. The first news of Lützen on the Protestant side concealed the shattering fact, and Bernard of Saxe-Weimar deliberately reported only that the King was wounded.[1] Not until November 21st did Oxenstierna know the truth, and for the first time in his life he passed the long night sleepless, grappling with his sorrow.[2] The Queen heard on her way back to Sweden and gave way to a storm of grief. At Vienna, Ferdinand received the news with tears of mingled relief and sorrow,[3] for the quality of the Swedish King was of a kind that he could not but admire; he had done greatly for the Protestants what Ferdinand had tried and failed to do for the Catholics. At Strasbourg men and women who had never set eyes on his face, living, sobbed aloud at the service for his death.[4] They carried the body to Weissenfels, the King going in death, as in life, in the midst of his army between the foot and the horse.[5]

Whatever opinion men might have of the King's motives, his greatness no one could or did deny. But after the first shock his death came as a relief rather than a loss to the majority of his allies. There were even rumours that he had been shot down by one of his own party or by Richelieu's orders. So signal had been his good fortune until this time, that men could not believe he had met the common fate of a soldier in the field. Others saw the direct intervention of God, saying that the Almighty had laid his finger upon him in the critical moment at which he would have ceased to be the liberator and become the conqueror of Germany.

His German allies might wonder if this were true. Had he ever, after all, been anything but a conqueror? He had rolled back the tide of Ferdinand's advance when no one else could, but the price he had asked was a high one. Playing for safety, setting the precarious peace of their land above the freedom of their faith, the Germans had for the most part yielded to imperial tyranny without forcible protest.

---

[1] SONDEN, *Lars Tungel*, p. 72; DITFURTH, p. 261.
[2] ARCHENHOLTZ, II, p. 46.   [3] *Annales*, XII, p. 199.
[4] WALTHER, p. 28.   [5] *Fleetwood*, p. 10.

It was weak, it was cowardly, it was unconstructive, but of the two evils it was their choice, and whatever contempt the hardy Swede might feel for those who dared not defend their religion, he might at least have admitted that they had a better right to choose than he. He had made unwilling heroes and unwilling victims — the Electors of Brandenburg and Saxony, the thirty thousand people of Magdeburg. He had given the Protestant Cause once again a tradition to fight for; he had made bells ring from end to end of Germany, hearts overflow with gratitude, and eyes with tears. But when the bells had clanged into silence and the Golden King had passed on his way, was there much cause left for rejoicing?

The Saxons had paid for the Breitenfeld campaign by a heavy loss of civilian life from plague and starvation.[1] At Magdeburg, Pappenheim had burnt what was left of the town when he evacuated it in the spring of 1632, and the Swedish troops who came in shared the want of the few survivors living in cellars and dug-outs among the ruins.[2] The Alsatian town of Hagenau, three times occupied in eighteen months, lamented: 'We have had blue-coats and red-coats and now come the yellow-coats. God have pity on us.'[3] At Frankfort-on-the-Oder pestilence bred of the rotting bodies of the dead had overwhelmed the survivors.[4] At Stettin and Spandau the Swedes had left the plague, in the towns of Durlach and Lorch, at Würzburg and in the whole province of Württemberg; at Bamberg the bodies lay unburied in the streets, and on both banks of the Rhine there was famine, so that the peasants from miles round came in to Mainz to work on the fortifications for a little bread.[5] The harvest of 1632 promised well, but in Bavaria and Swabia the passing troops trampled it down; in Bavaria there was neither corn left to grind nor seed to sow for the year to come; plague and famine wiped out whole villages, mad dogs attacked their masters, and the authorities posted men with guns to shoot down the raving victims before they could contaminate their fellows; hungry wolves abandoned the woods and mountains to roam through the deserted hamlets,

---

[1] LAMMERT, p. 114; *Theatrum Europaeum*, II, pp. 658, 645.
[2] *Brefvexling*, II, vi, p. 89.   [3] HANAUER, p. 175.
[4] LAMMERT, p. 114.   [5] Ibid., p. 113 f.; DUHR, II, i, p. 406.

devouring the dying and the dead.[1] At Nuremberg, shut in between Wallenstein and the Swedes and crowded with fugitives, they had buried close upon a hundred daily.[2]

The King's discipline had broken down as his army grew[3] and the nucleus of picked soldiers lessened in proportion; but apart from bad discipline, he plundered as no man had plundered before in that conflict, because he plundered systematically to destroy the resources of his enemies. 'Your Grace would not recognize our poor Bavaria', wrote Maximilian to his brother. Villages and convents had gone up in flames, priests, monks and burghers had been tortured and killed at Fuerstenfeld, at Diessen, at Benediktbeuern, in the Ettal.[4]

Moreover, the distress of the defeated imperial soldiery found an outlet in increased brutality; Maximilian's merciless command of no quarter for the stragglers or wounded of the Swedish army[5] was interpreted to cover all who resisted. When the imperialists took Kempten they shot down the burgomaster, set fire to seventy houses, drove some of the inhabitants into the river and slaughtered man, woman and child who came in their way, so that the city became the Magdeburg of the south.[6] At Hagenau plague and want made the soldiers prey even upon each other, and the healthy would plunder their stricken comrades and throw them out, naked, to die in the streets.[7]

However pusillanimous they may have seemed to Gustavus, the German princes did not lament without cause. 'It is hard', wrote the wife of George of Hesse-Darmstadt, 'to hand over the best and most valuable places in our land to a foreign King on so new a friendship, to sacrifice thereby all our undefended country, to make enemies of the neighbours with whom we have lived at peace for countless years, to bring down the Emperor's heavy hand and displeasure upon us, to give help to others but utterly to destroy ourselves.'[8] It was indeed hard, but it was what the King of Sweden demanded.

'Should the war last longer', wrote Arnim, 'the Empire will

[1] LAMMERT, p. 120; Chronik des Jakob Wagner, p. 28.
[2] C. G. VON MURR, Beyträge zur Geschichte des dreissigjährigen Krieges. Nürnberg, 1790, p. 62.
[3] WESTIN, pp. 208-9.   [4] RIEZLER, Geschichte, v, p. 420 f.
[5] Annales, XII, p. 144.   [6] FURTENBACH, Jammerchronik, p. 67 f.
[7] HANAUER, La Guerre de Trente Ans à Hagenau, Colmar, 1909, p. 172.
[8] DROYSEN, Die Verhandlungen über den Universalfrieden, p. 179.

be utterly destroyed. He who has an upright, honest mind must be touched to the heart; when he sees the Empire so afflicted he must yearn after peace. So it is with me. Therefore I have let no opportunity escape ... but have urged peace both on friend and foe ... our beloved Germany will fall a prey to foreign people and be a pitiable example to all the world.'[1] This was not the King of Sweden's view, but it was a more reasonable one than he would ever admit.

The apologists of Gustavus, if such a word may be used for the admirers of an accepted hero of European history, argue that he would have made a strong and lasting peace had he lived. The case must stand on private conviction and not on evidence; he had offered terms to Wallenstein, but they were terms not likely to be accepted while the imperialists had an army in the field. He had failed to make peace at Ferdinand's most defenceless moment in the winter of 1631-32. Gustavus was one of those born conquerors to whom peace is an ideal state, always for excellent reasons unattainable. He had never in his life made any conclusion to a war that was more than an armistice and it was hardly likely that he had changed his character in the course of his last year on earth. Age might have mellowed him but he was thirty-seven when he was killed, and Europe would have had long to wait. Nor is age so infallible a cure for the lust which stirs the blood of a fighter. Wallenstein tired at the end, but Wallenstein was ill as well as ageing, and his temperament, had always been more that of the organizer than of the conqueror. History has too many records of aged warriors, for the mellowing of Gustavus to seem an altogether probable theory.

At some time during his march across Germany, the King had drawn up the so-called Norma Futurarum Actionum, a scheme for the complete reorganization of the Empire, excellent in theory but unobtainable in practice even after victory. All along, his settlement depended on the one element on which he could never count, the agreement of the German rulers. Because he had no true support among these, he never considered modifying his policy. Compromise was not of his nature, and he did not realize that peace in Germany would be impossible without it.

[1] IRMER, *Die Verhandlungen Schwedens*, I, pp. 176, 177.

Had the King entered the war at some genuine personal loss as the ally of the King of Denmark in 1626, that joint intervention would have cut short Ferdinand's advance at the outset, saving Protestant self-respect and German Liberties. Politically the King was justified in not engaging in an undertaking which would have been unremunerative and difficult although far from impossible. In 1630 he was too late to revive the dead cause. Instead he broke the one power which might have united Germany, and set up nothing in its place.

A few days after the battle of Lützen, Frederick of Wittelsbach, who was no longer either Elector Palatine or King of Bohemia, rode into Bacharach on the Rhine. At thirty-six he was a broken man, old before his time and so worn with care that his own brother did not recognize him.[1] Down the Rhine there was famine, and in Bacharach plague; on all sides he saw the ghastly results of the war he himself had caused. He should not have stayed in Bacharach, but the plague caught him before he could fly. It was a slight attack and might have passed, but the news of Lützen and the King of Sweden's death coming at the turning point of the fever, he sank into a heavy gloom and on November 29th died. Dead, as living, he remained a wanderer and an outcast; the last known refuge of the despised exile was a wine-merchant's cellar at Metz.[2]

Thus within a fortnight the successful and the unsuccessful champions of the Protestant Cause had gone. The man had been worse but the Cause had been better in 1619, and the Germans had made their choice. Gustavus might defeat the Emperor, force John George to fight, exploit the policy of Richelieu, but he could not put back the clock. The opportunity that had been lost in 1619 had been lost for ever. He could not alter that numbed willingness of the German Protestants to be crushed; he could break the Hapsburg Empire, but he could build nothing, and he left German politics, as he left her fields, a heap of shards.

[1] ARETIN, *Beyträge*, VII, p. 270.
[2] MOSER, *Neues Patriotisches Archiv*, II, pp. 113-32.

FROM LÜTZEN TO NÖRDLINGEN – AND BEYOND
1632 – 1635

The House of Austria hath a root will up again.

THOMAS WENTWORTH

FROM LÜTZEN TO NÖRDLINGEN—
AND BEYOND
1632—1635

I

THE death of Gustavus kindled once again a spark of hope for peace in Germany, which flickered up only to be ruthlessly extinguished. The war had now lasted for between fourteen and fifteen years, and almost any peace would have been welcome to almost everyone within the Empire. But those who had power to make a conclusion were divided in opinion. Had the choice depended on Ferdinand alone, he was ready to take the hopeful opportunity; so also were John George of Saxony and Arnim; so also was George William of Brandenburg, but his desire was qualified by the fear that Sweden might demand his heritage of Pomerania as the price of withdrawal.

More influential than any of these, Wallenstein for a short while stood guard over imperial policy. He had now unquestionably the greatest military power in Germany, so that his desire for peace had the best prospect of becoming effective. Whether he had in fact any such desire is the crux of the Wallenstein problem, and also the starting-point of those historians who have seen in the last two years of his life the struggle of a nobly constructive statesman to impose a native peace on a Court suborned by Spanish bribes. The theory is equally incapable of proof or disproof. This alone is certain: that if Wallenstein wished for peace he showed phenomenal stupidity in his approach to it, and that his contemporaries credited him neither with honesty nor with public spirit. Wallenstein wanted to retire, more probably because he was growing old and ill than because he longed for general peace. One element alone is constant in all his negotiations at this time — his demand for personal reward. True to the colours of the mercenary, he expected a return for his investment in the war, and it was for that, rather than for the peace of Germany, that he staked his reputation and his life.

Outside the Empire three rulers wanted a settlement: the Archduchess Isabella, the Prince of Orange and the Pope. Urban VIII had already sacrificed his reputation among devout Catholics to the fruitless task of preventing a clash between Hapsburg and Bourbon. He was prejudiced in his methods, but he genuinely sought to lessen the danger of European war.[1] A scandalous outburst in the conclave had been the only result of his well-intentioned but clumsy policy. The Spanish Cardinal Borgia openly accused him of betraying the Church, and in the furious tumult which ensued one prelate, black in the face with wrath, was perceived to tear his biretta in pieces between his teeth. The forcible silencing of Borgia by the Pope's Swiss Guard did no good, for he printed and published his speech throughout Rome.[2] To save his face Urban had to give some grudging help to the Hapsburg cause in Germany.[3]

While there was enmity between France and Spain, Cardinal Carafa had once pronounced, there could never be peace in Germany. Those who wanted the war to continue were Richelieu, Oxenstierna and Olivarez. Richelieu needed it to maintain his power on the Rhine, Oxenstierna needed it because the venture had hitherto been so expensive that he could not return to Sweden without ample indemnification; Pomerania, the price of his withdrawal, could not be had without further fighting, since the Elector of Brandenburg must be satisfied for the robbery by the gift of equivalent land elsewhere. Olivarez wanted war because the Swedish King's death renewed his hope of a Hapsburg advance in Germany and a successful attack on the United Provinces.

Oxenstierna and Richelieu between them could undermine the peace party in Protestant Germany and Europe; Olivarez could assert the financial control of Madrid over Isabella at Brussels and Ferdinand at Vienna. German hopes of peace were in pawn to the political necessities of these three men — and irredeemably.

---

[1] See LEMAN, *Urbain VIII*, *passim*.
[2] Ibid., pp. 134 f., 563-4.
[3] ABREU Y BERTODANO, IV, p. 262 f.

Since the marriage of the Infanta Maria to the King of Hungary in February 1631, things had moved towards a renewed co-operation between Vienna and Madrid. Richelieu must therefore prevent peace both in the Empire and in the Low Countries, and in the opening weeks of 1633 he dispatched two agents, Hercule de Charnacé to The Hague, Manassés de Pas, Marquis de Feuquières, to Germany.[1] Heartless as this behaviour appears, considering the condition of the Empire, it was politically justified and followed naturally from that terror of Spanish power which was the motive force of Richelieu's foreign policy.

Oxenstierna's interests marched with Richelieu's in so far as neither wished for peace. In other respects they were bitterly, although tacitly, in opposition. In his last letter, written on November 9th, 1632, Gustavus had stressed the importance of excluding the King of France from the control of any land in Germany.[2] But after Lützen Richelieu grasped the opportunity to establish the dominance of his master over the Protestant allies. With this in view, he instructed Feuquières to play off the members of the coalition against each other. Saxony was to be prevented from making an independent peace, Brandenburg to be told that the King of France would guarantee Pomerania against the Swedes, Oxenstierna to be dazzled by the suggestion that his son with the help of the French King could secure the hand of Queen Christina. As the same proposition was to be made to the Elector of Saxony, it was touched on with the utmost discretion in both cases. A Protestant confederation was to be formed under John George, through which the King of France could be deftly insinuated into the place left empty by the King of Sweden.[3]

Axel Oxenstierna was in a precarious position. The government of Stockholm had given him unlimited powers in Germany,[4]

[1] AVENEL, IV, pp. 416, 419, 431-4; VIII, pp. 248, 252; FEUQUIÈRES, Lettres et négociations, Amsterdam, 1753, I, pp. 5-6.
[2] Brefvexling, II, i, p. 870.
[3] FEUQUIÈRES, II, i, pp. 10-26.
[4] N. A. KULLBERG, Svenska Riksrådets Protokoll. Händlingar rörande Sveriges Historia, 1878, III, p. 12.

but it was weak, for the accession of the child Queen encouraged the intrigues of a nobility whom the King had controlled but not undermined. The indiscreet, extravagant and vain Queen-mother, a woman still possessing and still conscious of her beauty, was likely to give trouble to Oxenstierna, not because she was essentially hostile to him but because she was easy to prejudice and flatter. With this background, his prosecution of Gustavus's plans in Germany was bound to be slow and uncertain. The foolish bribery of the French ambassadors could not, but necessity might, force him in time to make a partial sacrifice of independence to Richelieu, in order to maintain his position at all.

Axel Oxenstierna received the news of the King's death on the road to Frankfort-on-the-Main.[1] He was on his way to assemble the representatives of the four Circles which were to form the nucleus of the projected Corpus Evangelicorum. Postponing this assembly until the following spring, he turned back from Hanau and travelled rapidly to Saxony. At Christmas he was in Dresden.

The reason for his move was simple. Immediately after the battle of Lützen, Wallenstein had retired to Bohemia. Heavy as his losses had been, they did not account for this hasty action, the springs of which were political. He wished, by proving his goodwill to John George, to tempt him to peace. Even if the Elector refused this bait, he would undoubtedly use the occasion of the King's death to reassert his own interests against those of Sweden. Immediately after Lützen, for instance, he had tried to secure the services of Bernard of Saxe-Weimar for himself.[2]

Oxenstierna had to face yet another peril. No sooner was the death of Gustavus known than the King of Denmark offered to mediate a general peace in the Empire.[3] If there was one thing above all others that must be prevented, it was the dictation of terms by a jealous Denmark.

Hastily pacifying the Elector of Brandenburg by the renewed promise of Queen Christina's hand for his son,[4] Oxenstierna

---

[1] *Brefvexling*, op. cit., I, vii, p. 637.
[2] STRUCK, *Johann Georg und Oxenstierna*. Stralsund, 1899, pp. 19-20.
[3] HALLWICH, *Wallensteins Ende*, Leipzig, 1879, I, pp. 47, 102; IRMER, *Die Verhandlungen Schwedens*, II, pp. 11-12.
[4] A. KÜSEL, *Der Heilbronner Konvent*. Halle, 1878, p. 18.

concentrated on the problem of Saxony. Seldom can he have passed a more unprofitable Christmas than that which he celebrated at Dresden in 1632. The intentions of John George and Arnim were clear from the outset, nor did the eloquence of the Chancellor move them an inch. John George wanted either a separate or a general settlement, Arnim a general peace.[1] Disregarding all protests, they agreed to discuss terms with Wallenstein.

The alliance being all but broken, there ensued a struggle between John George and Oxenstierna for the leadership of the Protestant party in the Empire. On March 18th, 1633, the Chancellor opened the long-planned meeting of the four Circles at Heilbronn, ingeniously evading quarrels over the privileges connected with chairs, stools, and benches by arranging for the deputies to stand throughout.[2] Five weeks later the four Circles agreed to a Treaty with Sweden, creating what was to be known as the League of Heilbronn for the defence of the Protestant Cause in the Empire under Oxenstierna's direction. On two succeeding days he concluded further treaties, one with the free knights of the Empire and one with Philip Lewis of Pfalz-Zimmern, brother of Frederick of Bohemia and regent for the sixteen-year-old Elector Palatine, Charles Lewis, who had succeeded to his father's debts.[3]

These treaties established Oxenstierna in the eyes of the world as the virtual successor of Gustavus. John George, who had thought to wreck the meeting by not attending, had once again miscalculated. By his refusal to come he had tacitly renounced his claim; far from wrecking the assembly, his absence merely ensured the election of Oxenstierna himself as supreme director of the war. If the Chancellor had failed to hold John George to his original obligations, he had effectively saved the situation for Sweden by destroying at a blow all the prestige and half the influence of the lost ally.

Oxenstierna's handling of the French intervention was less effective. Here he was not fighting the drink-sodden John

[1] HELBIG, *Wallenstein und Arnim.* Dresden, 1850, p. 15; HALLWICH, *Wallensteins Ende,* II, p. 254.
[2] *Brefväxling mellan Oxenstierna och Svenska Riksrådet, Händlingar rörande Skandinaviens Historia,* XXV, p. 196.
[3] *Sverges Traktater,* v, ii, pp. 18 ff.; LUNDORP, VI, p. 317 f.

George but the unscrupulous and intelligent Marquis de Feuquières. The French ambassador shone particularly in those qualities on which the reputation of French diplomacy has been built: flexible of method and tenacious of purpose he choked the more rugged growth of Oxenstierna's diplomacy as the ivy chokes the tree. Both of them wanted the support of the German States, and either of them would have used any means to get it. Feuquières had one unfair advantage: his government was more able than that of Sweden to pour out money in bribery.[1] Otherwise his advantage over Oxenstierna was merely that he was apter at diplomacy, saw the opportunity better and struck more swiftly than the northerner, who appears, by contrast, a ponderous bungler. The intentions of both were equally honourable, since each was actuated by the desire to do the best for his country and his religion, Oxenstierna to secure indemnification for Sweden's blood and money, and safety for the Protestants of Germany, Feuquières to protect France from Spain, and the German Catholics from the aggression of their Protestant compatriots. Both acted with equal inhumanity to Germany, but then neither was a German.

Feuquières's first problem was that his instructions were incorrect. In Paris, Richelieu had imagined John George to be master of the situation on the death of Gustavus; he had estimated Oxenstierna too low. No sooner had Feuquières seen the Swedish Chancellor than he recognized this error. Sweden, not Saxony, was the power without whose alliance nothing could be achieved in Germany, and he had the courage to act in the light of his own convictions against the instructions of the Cardinal.[2]

At Heilbronn, to Oxenstierna's unconcealed annoyance,[3] Feuquières persuaded the delegates to accept the King of France as their protector in conjunction with the Swedish government.[4] It might seem that this was a minor achievement, for it gave the King no dominant control in the war, but inevitably the ally with the greater resources would prove the more influential in the end, and Oxenstierna fought the decision to the last. Feuquières inserted another wedge into the

[1] FEUQUIÈRES, passim.
[2] Ibid., I, pp. 75-6, 94, 112, 113, 135-6.
[3] Ibid., pp. 140, 147.
[4] Ibid., pp. 85-8, 217.

Chancellor's arrangements when, by the renewal of the Treaty of Bärwalde, he refused to pay the semi-annual subsidy of half a million livres to the Swedes alone, but insisted that it should go to them on behalf of the Heilbronn League. Oxenstierna, who could not afford to forgo the subsidy, thus had to agree to receive it on terms which bound his German allies still more closely to France and degraded him to the position of a middle-man.[1] The only advantage he gained over Feuquières was on the question of Maximilian, for the preservation of whose neutrality the French government still pleaded in vain.[2]

The foundation of the Heilbronn League marked the virtual end of John George's plan for a general peace. Dismay and distress in Dresden knew no bounds; the threatened dictator-ship of the King of Sweden had been replaced merely by that of Oxenstierna.[3] Above all, Arnim's hopes were destroyed. Judging the moment of disillusionment to be favourable, Wallenstein here intervened, suggesting to the general that he bring the Saxon forces over to join the imperialists and that together they drive the Swedes out of Germany, as six years before they had driven out the Danes. Perhaps it would have been the right thing to do; perhaps it would have succeeded and peace have been the outcome. But here Wallenstein struck against that hard, unimaginative honesty which was the core of Arnim's character. Possibly he saw with his brain that the scheme was feasible, but with Arnim the heart was stronger than the mind, and that rigid, almost tragic sense of honour, the *Aufrichtigkeit* which knows no compromise, the strength and the undoing of the German, stood between him and the betrayal which might have saved his country.[4]

From this moment yet another fissure creeps across the already divided Protestant party, the fissure between the Elector of Saxony and the general of his army. John George was prepared to desert Oxenstierna and make his own peace with Ferdinand. Arnim was not, and in so far as he had power, he still worked

---

[1] FEUQUIÈRES, I, pp. 113, 221; *Sverges Traktater*, v, ii, pp. 12-18.

[2] FEUQUIÈRES, I, pp. 64-5, 141.

[3] *Brefväxling mellan Oxenstierna och Svenska Riksrådet. Händlingar rörende Skandinaviens Historia*, xxv, p. 207; HALLWICH, *Wallensteins Ende*, I, p. 355.

[4] HELBIG, *Wallenstein und Arnim*, p. 18; see also G. DROYSEN, *Holks Einfal in Sachsen. Neues Archiv für Sächsische Geschichte*, I, pp. 53 ff.

for general peace or nothing. He did not, or he would not, see that the League of Heilbronn had so closely riveted the welfare of Protestant Germany to the interests of Oxenstierna and Richelieu that there could now be no general peace within the Empire until either Hapsburg or Bourbon had shattered the rival.

III

Meanwhile, in the Netherlands, Richelieu on the one hand and Olivarez on the other destroyed all hope of peace. In 1632 the Prince of Orange, invading unhindered, had seized Venloo, Roermond, and last of all the great fortress of Maestricht. A more daring and less perceptive leader would have marched on Brussels. Frederick Henry was held back by two considerations: in the first place he was uncertain whether his army would be strong enough to hold the line of communications between the frontier and the Flemish capital,[1] and in the second place neither he nor the government of the United Provinces was altogether certain that the fall of Brussels was desirable. There had been a secret agreement with Richelieu to split the Spanish Nether-lands from end to end, France absorbing the southern and the Dutch the northern half.[2] But Frederick Henry saw that the destruction of Hapsburg power was leading already to the unbalanced aggrandizement of the Bourbon, and was hence-forward determined to preserve at all costs the buffer state between himself and the rising monarchy. Unknown to the Brussels government, the Dutch, their open enemies, were becoming the guarantors of their existence against the aggression of France.[3]

If the ageing Archduchess Isabella hardly grasped this turn in the situation, she understood at least that the retreat of the Dutch meant a tendency towards peaceful settlement, and at this straw she snatched with all that was left of her failing strength. She had good reason. The advance of the Prince of Orange had been assisted by widespread treachery among the

[1] Geyl, pp. 132-3.   [2] Ibid., p. 96.
[3] Waddington, *Les Provinces Unies en* 1630. Paris, 1893, p. 6 f.

Flemish nobility,[1] and although the plot had been discovered in time, its existence revealed to Isabella that the ground, once so firm under her feet, had become a quagmire. The States General, called in September 1632, were loud in their outcry for peace; the occupation of a now ill-paid army, the increase in taxes, the decline of trade as warfare and Dutch competition strangled ports and cities, all drove the deputies to beg for a cessation.[2] With the consent of Madrid, Isabella willingly yielded; a truce was established and deputies chosen to discuss terms with the United Provinces.[3]

The delegates met in the winter of 1632; by the end of November two messages had reached Brussels which changed the face of affairs: the first that the King of Spain's brother was appointed as Governor in succession to the Archduchess, the second that the King of Sweden had been killed at Lützen.[4] The appointment of the Infant Ferdinand, the Cardinal-Infant as he was commonly called, indicated a new effort to revivify Hapsburg influence and popularity in Brussels; the death of the Swedish King meant that the Emperor might again be able to help. In spite of all, the Archduchess, old and wise, would have preferred peace; so would Frederick Henry. But the swelling animosity of Bourbon and Hapsburg struck the power out of their hands. Hercule de Charnacé talked over the Prince of Orange and worked up the war party in the United Provinces,[5] while Olivarez and the King of Spain ceased to treat the peace negotiations with respect. After thirteen months of wasted argument the delegates dispersed.[6]

The King of Sweden's death gave an impetus to the revival which had been for some months preparing in the heart of the Hapsburg dynasty itself. In the younger generation two princes were emerging, on whom the renewed hopes of the family were fixed. By tact, courtesy and discretion, the youthful Cardinal-Infant, brother of Philip IV, and as yet in his early

[1] See WADDINGTON, *La République des Provinces Unies*, Lyons, 1891, pp. 400-5; LUNDORP, IV, pp. 287-9; a full account is in HENNEQUIN DE VILLERMONT, *L'Infante Isabelle*, II, p. 388 f.
[2] GACHARD, *Actes des Etats Généraux en* 1632. Brussels, 1853, pp. 22-60.
[3] Ibid., pp. 76-80, 165-8.
[4] LONCHAY ET CUVELIER, op. cit., II, pp. 659, 664.
[5] PRINSTERER, op. cit., II, iii, pp. 37, 39-40.
[6] GACHARD, pp. 147 f., 162 f.

twenties, had insinuated himself into the graces of Olivarez[1] and thereby smoothed his way to the governorship of the Netherlands. Destined for the Church and raised to the Cardinalate in his childhood, the prince had chafed bitterly at the restraint thus placed alike on his pleasures and his ambition. Nevertheless, he had had the intelligence to exploit the independence of fraternal control to which his ecclesiastical position entitled him.[2] On his appointment to the governorship of the Netherlands he was requested by the Archduchess to lay by his priestly robes as far as possible, since Cardinals as governors had still an unsavoury reputation in Brussels.[3] Nothing could have suited the Cardinal-Infant better, and henceforward the scarlet robe and biretta disappear from his portraits, the slender, oval face is framed in shining flaxen curls, a moustache of startling ferocity garnishes the long upper lip, and the prince, clad in full armour, appears with marshal's baton in hand astride a prancing charger.

There was more in this military gear than mere boyish caprice. The Cardinal-Infant had studied the art of war thoroughly and intended to arrive in the Netherlands at the head of an army. Furthermore, a plan was maturing by which this new army was to be transported overland and used as it passed through Germany to clear the Rhine of enemies.

The second moving spirit of this plan was the cousin of the Cardinal-Infant, the Archduke Ferdinand, King of Hungary and Bohemia, and husband to the Cardinal's sister, the Infanta Maria. It was he who had optimistically approached his father, the Emperor, in the previous year, asking that he, not Wallenstein, be appointed commander-in-chief of the imperial armies. In the ensuing months he had placed himself at the head of a party hostile both to Wallenstein and to Maximilian. This group, if not entirely under the dominance of the Spanish ambassador at Vienna, was at least in very close communication with him. Its chief object was the raising of an army to co-operate with the Cardinal-Infant. The answer which suggested itself in the course of the year 1633 was: Wallenstein's army and Wallenstein's resources but without Wallenstein.

---

[1] *Relazioni dagli Ambasciatori. Spagna*, i, p. 658.   [2] Loc. cit.
[3] LONCHAY ET CUVELIER, ii, p. 659.

The general had forfeited whatever respect or gratitude he had enjoyed at Vienna by his conduct in 1631, his deliberate starvation of Tilly, his betrayal of Mecklenburg to the Swedes, his unscrupulous negotiations with Gustavus and John George, even with the Bohemian exile, Thurn. Bitter necessity alone had caused his recall, and he had shown his animosity towards the Hapsburg dynasty, or so they thought, by quartering his troops in the winter of 1632-33 on imperial lands. In point of fact, military necessity gave him no choice, for he was anxious to caress Saxony into peace by careful treatment and he could have gone nowhere else without grave danger to his and the imperial army.

The situation for the Emperor was intolerable, but there seemed no way out. Any open attack on the general, considering the extent of his power and of his supposed influence with the army, might precipitate some catastrophic treachery. Better to veil mutual suspicion under a pretence of confidence than rush Wallenstein into raising a revolt in Bohemia or going over to the enemy with his troops.

There is no evidence of any definite plot against Wallenstein, for if any such plot existed it was only in the minds of the young Ferdinand and his supporters. For some time even the Spanish party preferred the idea of Wallenstein's continuance in command to that of the inexperienced King of Hungary;[1] the general's own conduct forced them only by degrees to give whole-hearted support to young Ferdinand, and the development of events throughout the year gives proof of no defined scheme on the part of Ferdinand's supporters. But if no connecting thread binds the events of 1633 to the murder of Wallenstein in February 1634, this much at least is clear: the destruction of his personal power was essential to the maturing of the plan for a joint attack on their enemies by the rulers at Vienna and Madrid.

---

[1] GINDELY, *Waldsteins Vertrag*, p. 33; HALLWICH, *Wallensteins Ende*, I, p. 412; see also PEKAŘ, pp. 77-104.

IV

From the beginning of his career Wallenstein had been conscious, perhaps over-conscious, of the hostility of Vienna, and since his dismissal in 1630 the desire for revenge had dominated his policy.[1] Only the means to his end did not always present themselves, and after Lützen he became a prey to uncertainty. Intermittently he seems to have contemplated joining forces with the Saxons, making a private peace with John George in his own interests, leading a revolt in Bohemia. Noble conceptions float hazily in his letters, but not one of them is consistently pursued. In the last year of his life he appears vindictive, changeable, hesitant, a sick, superstitious man surrounded by doctors and astrologers.[2]

At Lützen he had been ill with gout, and his health thereafter broke down completely, carrying the ruin of his mind with it. Grimly significant, the bold signature of 1632 dwindles to a crippled scrawl before the end of 1633.[3] The egomania which had marked his career soared no longer on the wings of genius; even his organizing skill was less, and he parried the attacks of Vienna and Madrid clumsily, arrogantly or not at all. The actions of Wallenstein from Lützen to his murder are the actions of an old and sick man, a man enmeshed in his own illusions, seeking guidance no longer from his own brain but from the revelations of astrologers. In his dual personality the contradiction between the hard-headed man of the world and the superstitious idealist seems to have resolved itself in the victory of the latter. There remained of his once acute worldly perceptions nothing but the mean desire for a personal reward, cutting uncouthly across the grandiose plans with which he fed those with whom he came in contact.[4]

The heaviest loss Wallenstein had suffered at Lützen was that of Pappenheim. Reckless of his men, arrogant and insubordinate, Pappenheim was nevertheless the soldiers' hero:

---

[1] See PEKAŘ, *Wallenstein*, I, p. 51 f.
[2] HALLWICH, *Wallensteins Ende*, II, p. 22.
[3] Parallel facsimiles are given in FOERSTER, *Wallenstein*, III.
[4] VEIT VALENTIN, *Wallenstein after Three Centuries. Slavonic Review*, 1935, p. 160.

tireless, restless, vivid, the first in attack, the last in retreat.[1] Stories of his fantastic courage were told round the camp-fires and he had a legend before he was dead — the hundred scars that he boasted, the birthmark like crossed swords which glowed red when he was angry.[2] He flashes past against that squalid background, the Rupert of the German war. His loyalty to Wallenstein, his affection and admiration,[3] had been of greater effect in inspiring the troops than Wallenstein probably realized. The general owed his power to his control over the army alone, and the loss of Pappenheim was irreparable.

Deceived by his apparent strength, the general did not pause to analyse its cause, and during the year 1633 he forfeited both the loyalty and respect of his men. Immediately after Lützen he signalized his indignation at the defeat by arresting, trying and condemning for cowardice and treachery thirteen officers and five men.[4] In vain his leading subordinates implored him to reconsider the sentences; far from cowing the army, the trials had evoked mutinous murmurs, but Wallenstein would not stay for reason or pity, and on February 14th, 1633, his scapegoats were executed in public at Prague with every circumstance of military ignomithat.[5]

This actual brutality was paralleled in the popular mind by stories about his dangerous humours which doubtless had roots, however slender, in fact. He would have no officers come into his room in jingling spurs, he would have straw laid in the neighbouring streets to mute the rattle of wheels on cobbles, he killed the dogs, cats and cocks wherever he lodged, he had had a servant hanged for waking him in the night, he kept special bravos for the immediate chastisement of visitors who talked too loud.[6]

Wallenstein's conduct justified the rumours; in the opening weeks of 1633 he shut himself away from the world and

[1] *Bandhauers Tagebuch*, p. 268.
[2] KHEVENHÜLLER, *Conterfet Kupfferstich*, Leipzig, 1722, II, p. 261.
[3] FOERSTER, *Wallenstein als Feldherr und Landesfürst*, p. 436.
[4] HALLWICH, *Wallensteins Ende*, I, pp. 41-2.
[5] See SRBIK, *Wallensteins Ende*, Vienna, 1920, pp. 31 ff.; GLIUBICH, p. 368; FOERSTER, *Wallenstein*, II, p. 316; IRMER, *Die Verhandlungen Schwedens*, II, p. 24.
[6] POYNTZ, p. 136; PRIORATO, *Historia delle Guerre*, 1643, p. 98; GINDELY, *Wallenstein während seines ersten Generalats*, I, p. 74.

allowed no one to visit him except his servants, his brother-in-law Trčka[1] and General Holk. Trčka was a cipher; Holk was not a man likely to soothe his temper or replace Pappenheim as a popular figure with the army. A drunken, brutal boor, Holk was competent in a bludgeoning, ruthless manner. 'Hol' Kuh', the peasants called him, clumsily punning on his name and his exploits in plunder. He had once been a Lutheran and remained so in theory, but a popular song put the expressive verse into his mouth:

> Conscience hither, conscience thither,
> I care for nought but worldly honour,
> Fight not for faith, fight but for gold,
> God can look after the other world.[2]

Until a few minutes before his death, it summed up his feelings with tolerable accuracy.

Wallenstein's position with his army was further undermined by reckless recruiting. His personal lands had been invaded in the previous year; for the first time in his military career his funds were unequal to his needs, and he fell back on the old and evil method of selling commissions without inquiring into the credentials of those who bought them.[3]

Meanwhile Maximilian was in a fever of irritation. While Wallenstein marched to Lützen he had fallen back with his few troops under Aldringer to Bavaria and there passed the winter and early spring on tenterhooks of anxiety. A large detachment of the Swedish army under Marshal Horn had pressed up the Rhine during the autumn of 1632 and occupied the greater part of Alsace. Hence it turned eastwards and in the following March joined with an equally large force under Bernard of Saxe-Weimar at Oberndorf in the Black Forest. Their intention was to crush Bavaria.[4] Ever since January

---

[1] The name is Germanized into Terzka, or, in Schiller's *Wallenstein*, into Terzky.

[2] OPEL AND COHN, p. 342:
> Gewissen hin, Gewissen her,
> Ich acht viel mehr die zeitlich Ehr,
> Dien nicht um glauben, dien um Gelt,
> Gott geb, wie es geh in jener Welt.

[3] RITTER, *Deutsche Geschichte*, III, p. 558.

[4] *Brefvexling*, II, viii, pp. 97, 99, 117.

Maximilian had been asking Wallenstein vainly for reinforce-ments.[1] Lacking these, the wretched Aldringer was chivied back into Munich, while many of his over-marched, exhausted troops surrendered to the Swedes.[2] Mercifully for Maximilian, ill-feeling between Bernard and Horn, want and mutiny among the men, held up the attack.[3] In May the Elector, despairing of Wallenstein's help, appealed directly to Holk. A good subordinate, Holk merely passed the letter on.[4] With one of those half-gestures by which Wallenstein intermittently attempted to prove his loyalty, he sent Holk to Eger whence he could watch the progress of events in Bavaria. Whatever confidence he created by this move, he immediately destroyed again by establishing a prolonged truce with Arnim in which terms of peace were discussed with markedly little reference to Vienna.[5] He may have regarded himself as the Emperor's agent in these negotiations, but more probably he was playing for time in order to gauge accurately the best advantage for himself. Since May a confidant of his, the Bohemian exile Kinsky at Dresden, had been working out plans in conjunction with Feuquières and the Swedes, for a national rising in Bohemia.[6] Wallenstein's part in these, if any, must remain doubtful, but it is significant that his chief confidant at this time was his brother-in-law, Trčka, who had burnt his fingers badly in the rising of 1618.

Whatever Wallenstein's motives, his negotiations with Arnim were not supported by any strong desire for peace in Vienna. The party of the young King of Hungary and his friend, Count Trautmansdorff, was growing more effective on the Council than that of the old Emperor and Eggenberg, and in the course of the summer young Ferdinand gained the support of the Spanish ambassador.

The Swedes under Marshal Horn had been for some months threatening Breisach,[7] the fortress which guards the higher

[1] HALLWICH, *Wallensteins Ende*, I, p. 117.
[2] *Brefvexling*, II, viii, p. 119.   [3] Ibid., pp. 97, 110, 124, 126 f.
[4] HALLWICH, *Wallensteins Ende*, I, pp. 98, 149, 224, 230, 239, 260, 273, 300, 312, 327, 379.
[5] Ibid., p. 426.
[6] IRMER, *Die Verhandlungen Schwedens*, II, pp. 136-41; AUBÉRY, *Mémoires pour l'histoire du Cardinal Duc de Richelieu*. Paris, 1860, II, pp. 399-401; FEUQUIÈRES, I, p. 152 f.
[7] *Brefvexling*, II, viii, p. 100.

waters of the Rhine and from whose eminence the traffic up and down the river may be effectively controlled. Should the Emperor, and thereby the King of Spain, lose Breisach, the Cardinal-Infant's plan for transporting an army overland would be scotched at the outset, and he might as well put on his robe and biretta again and devote himself to theology. In May 1633 the Spanish ambassador informed the Emperor that his master would shoulder the expenses of the war, if he might direct it.[1] The Cardinal-Infant had already assembled an army in Italy ready to cross the Alps.[2] But early in July Horn closed in his blockade round Breisach.

Meanwhile on the Saxon border plague devoured Arnim's army and Wallenstein's. The imperialist troops, greedy for plunder, murmured at the enforced idleness.[3] To still their outcry,[4] Wallenstein at length took up arms again and launched Holk, not to the help of Maximilian, but against Saxony, intending by this demonstration of force to induce Arnim, John George and even Bernard of Saxe-Weimar to treat his offers of peace with respect. Plague, the horrible companion of the war, defeated his plan. Holk reached Leipzig, with the pestilence raging among his men, only to find that Bernard would not so much as answer his letters.[5] He had no choice but to fall back once again across country which his own deliberate plundering had stripped bare. Bowed down by useless booty, his men stumbled in the mud and were crushed under wagons and the feet of their comrades. Hungry, mutinous, diseased and weary, they died by the way in ditches and barns, untended, in the stormy August rains.[6] Typhus raged in the army, and other less identifiable diseases. It is not easy to name the epidemic illnesses which consumed the country. Bubonic plague was perhaps what killed Holk.

Coming out to meet them with fresh stores, Colonel Hatzfeld found the old barbarian at Adorf, huddled in his coach, angry and terrified.[7] He had sent out to offer five hundred talers for

[1] HALLWICH, *Briefe und Akten*, IV, pp. 124-6.
[2] LONCHAY ET CUVELIER, III, p. 2.   [3] SRBIK, p. 39.
[4] See GAEDEKE, *Wallensteins Verhandlungen*, p. 173.
[5] HALLWICH, *Wallensteins Ende*, I, pp. 546-7.
[6] GAEDEKE, *Holks Einfall*, p. 153; SONDÉN, *Lars Tungel*, p. 176.
[7] HALLWICH, *Wallensteins Ende*, I, pp. 553-4.

a Lutheran minister to pray with him, but in all that desolate country none could be found; he had forsaken his God, and forsaken of his God he died.[1]

Once again, in September, Wallenstein called a truce, and once again the negotiations came to nothing. No one on the Protestant side believed that the general had the support of Vienna.[2] Rightly so, for by September the breaking-point had come between him and the imperial government. The Duke of Feria, with the advance guard of the Spanish army, was waiting at Innsbruck to march on Breisach; he wanted Aldringer to help him. Throughout August Wallenstein had hesitated to let Aldringer go, and when the Spanish ambassador asked in person for help, had dismissed him with scornful words.[3] On September 29th, 1633, he wrote to the Emperor again asserting his unwillingness to let Aldringer join the Spaniards,[4] but the little self-made soldier from Luxemburg had already fooled him. Seven years before, Wallenstein had called him an 'ink-swiller'; meeting Feria in person at Schongau, the 'ink-swiller' had agreed to put his forces at his disposal whether Wallenstein would or no.[5]

The landslide in the army had begun, and Wallenstein did not realize it. Despising his officers individually, he could not see that his power depended on their goodwill.

On September 29th the armies of Feria and Aldringer met at Ravensburg, on October 3rd they relieved Constance, on the 20th Breisach. Meanwhile, in the east, Wallenstein clumsily attempted to redeem his position. Descending rapidly on Silesia, he surprised the Swedish troops under Thurn and his disorderly lieutenant, the 'brandy-souser' Duval,[6] at Steinau, and within a few days occupied the whole province. But joy gave place to anger at Vienna when they heard that the arch-rebel Thurn had been set free. He had bought his liberty, Wallenstein explained, by surrendering all the fortresses in Silesia;[7] the excuse was sound on military grounds, but taken

[1] GAEDEKE, Holcks Einfall, I, p. 179.
[2] FEUQUIÈRES, II, p. 274; SONDÉN, Lars Tungel, pp. 166, 459-60, 462-4; GAEDEKE, Wallensteins Verhandlungen, II, pp. 305, 339, 341.
[3] IRMER, Die Verhandlungen Schwedens, II, pp. 188-9; HALLWICH, Wallensteins Ende, I, pp. 548 ff.   [4] Ibid., p. 594.   [5] Ibid., p. 583.
[6] GAEDEKE, Wallensteins Verhandlungen, p. 139.
[7] SONDÉN, Lars Tungel, I, p. 190.

in conjunction with the rumours of Wallenstein's understanding with the Bohemian rebels, Thurn's release was highly suggestive.

Meanwhile, Aldringer having gone to Breisach, Bernard of Saxe-Weimar descended on undefended Bavaria. Ferdinand and Maximilian implored Wallenstein to come, receiving only the cynical reply that doubtless Aldringer would help them; he himself could not spare a man from the Bohemian border.[1] On November 14th, 1633, Bernard entered Regensburg.

The city of the Diet, the city which held the line of contact between Bavaria and Bohemia, the city whose name had been the last audible word of the dying Tilly — one man only was responsible for its loss, and that man was Wallenstein. He could partly have saved himself from blame had he stood by his defence, that he could not spare a man from Bohemia. But the danger to Regensburg jolted his sick judgment into further folly, and the news of its capture reached him when he was already marching to its rescue. Miscalculating utterly, he saved neither the city nor his own reputation. He refused to come in time, and by coming at all he proved the frivolity of his first excuse.

Conditions in Bavaria were growing steadily worse: two consecutive years of active fighting across the land, the horrible excesses of Tilly's defeated troops and, later, the deliberate wasting of Gustavus's and Bernard's men, drove the peasantry at last to frenzy. If they had nothing to gain by revolt, they had nothing left to lose. The good harvest of 1632 and the poor, hail-smitten harvest of 1633 had been alike destroyed by the passing armies or ruthlessly collected by the Elector's officials to supply his own troops. When Aldringer attempted to take up winter quarters in the country the rising became general. Maximilian, frightened for once of his own people, attempted to prevent quartering in the worst districts, but the soldiers, driven by necessity, took no notice, and fired on those who resisted them. By the end of December between twenty and thirty thousand peasantry were in arms, holding the roads against Aldringer and his hungry troops.[2] But it was a revolt

[1] HALLWICH, *Wallensteins Ende*, II, pp. 44-66 *passim*.
[2] ARETIN, *Beyträge*, II, iii, pp. 63 ff.

against the quartering, not against the government, for the help offered by Bernard of Saxe-Weimar was not accepted,[1] and Maximilian in the end calmed the rebels by driving Aldringer's troops to find restricted lodging in the calmer districts.[2] Of the two evils he had to choose the less.

Bavaria was not alone in its misery. In spite of the particular request of Ferdinand,[3] in spite of the entreaties of the local authorities,[4] Wallenstein once again quartered his army on the imperial estates in Bohemia. As in the previous year, military exigencies gave him no other choice, but this was no argument against the resentment of Vienna.[5] He lost Regensburg, he allowed Bavaria to be wasted, and he himself ate Bohemia bare. Short of open treachery he had done as much harm as one man could in so short a time to the cause which he was supposed to serve.

Wallenstein himself fixed his headquarters at Pilsen; a lame, bent, nerve-ridden wreck of a man. At Vienna they were openly complaining of him, and Maximilian had written to his agent telling him to join even with the Spanish party to overthrow him.[6] The rank and file of the army were discontented, the higher officers already suspected treason. But Trčka had written to Kinsky, the leading Bohemian exile in Dresden, saying that the general was ready to make terms with Brandenburg, Saxony, Sweden and France, that the time had come 'to throw off the mask'.[7] The time had come, not for Wallenstein to 'throw off the mask' but for others to tear it from him and show him his own reflection, the image of a man drunk with the illusion of a power he no longer possessed.

As early as May 1633 Wallenstein had begun obscure negotiations for the Bohemian Crown through Kinsky in Dresden;[8] in July Feuquières, by the same agency, had promised that France would recognize him as King in return for his treason to the Emperor. In December he seems

---

[1] *Brefvexling*, II, vii, p. 141.
[2] ARETIN, *Beyträge*, II, iii, p. 70 f.
[3] HALLWICH, *Wallensteins Ende*, I, p. 540.
[4] Ibid., II, pp. 153, 157.
[5] ARETIN, *Wallenstein*, I, p. 58.
[6] IRMER, *Die Verhandlungen Schwedens*, III, pp. 68-74.
[7] GAEDEKE, *Wallensteins Verhandlungen*, pp. 214-15.
[8] SONDÉN, *Lars Tungel*, pp. 106-7.

to have made up his wavering mind to accept the offer.[1]

Meanwhile, on the last day of 1633, the Emperor and his council took their decision to be rid of him.[2] Wallenstein's position in his army was the next point to be ascertained, and through his leading subordinates Vienna was already well informed. Aldringer had shown his opinions by obeying the Emperor and not the general, and in the winter of 1633-34 fear of Wallenstein's possible revenge added another motive to his dislike of the commander-in-chief. Holk, whose loyalty was certain, was dead; Octavio Piccolomini, the Italian soldier of fortune who had succeeded to Pappenheim's command, was hand-in-glove with the government at Vienna. Matthias Gallas, the genial, easy-tempered, incompetent general of the artillery, was tempted by the offer of the commandership-in-chief under the King of Hungary. Those who were loyal to Wallenstein numbered only Adam Trčka who controlled eight regiments, Christian Ilow, the quartermaster, the princely soldier of fortune, Franz Albrecht of Saxe-Lauenburg, and a few lesser men. Nevertheless, Wallenstein must be tempted into giving open evidence of treachery before he could be struck down. For this reason it was essential that he should suspect nothing.

His stars fought for the Emperor and the King of Hungary. He trusted rather to the horoscopes of his officers than to their talent, and the horoscopes of Piccolomini and Gallas, of the former in particular, were full of signs which gave him confidence.

In December the Emperor implored him to lighten the contributions imposed on the imperial lands; he refused.[3] In despair, Ferdinand, an old man now and no longer as resilient as in his youth, gave himself up to prayer and fasting, seeking God's guidance to rid him of Wallenstein.[4] The general had indeed gone as far as he safely could, and from now on he felt his way towards open betrayal. He intended to go over to the enemy with his whole army, and on January 12th he called his leading colonels to Pilsen and exacted from them an oath of

[1] FEUQUIÈRES, I, pp. 155-60, 258, 290-1; II, pp. 1-9, 68.
[2] IRMER, *Die Verhandlungen Schwedens*, III, p. 95.
[3] FOERSTER, *Wallenstein*, III, pp. 114-28.
[4] SRBIK, p. 381; GLIUBICH, p. 418.

loyalty to him, telling them that there were plots at Vienna to replace him. Forty-nine colonels signed an obligation to stand by him,[1] and Wallenstein felt safe. It did not cross his mind that the soldier of fortune is an opportunist to whom a signature means little. Unscrupulous himself, he calculated unhesitatingly on the honesty of his subordinates.

News of the Pilsen decision caused more apparent anxiety at Prague than at Vienna. In the Bohemian capital they feared a nationalist revolt — feared, it would seem, rather than hoped for it. At the imperial court the news was, as far as possible, concealed or minimized in its importance.[2] Nevertheless, it hastened the secret decision of the Emperor. On January 24th, 1634, he set his hand to a decree dismissing Wallenstein,[3] and immediately after instructed Count Gallas to consult with Piccolomini how best to take the general, living or dead.[4]

Meanwhile, with Franz Albrecht of Saxe-Lauenburg acting as go-between, Wallenstein worked for an understanding with Arnim and Bernard of Saxe-Weimar. He was anxious to exploit the loyalty shown him at the Pilsen decision before it should cool, but he dared not join Arnim and Bernard until he could be certain they would come half-way to meet him. His cautious hesitation gave Piccolomini and Gallas time to mature their plans.

Wallenstein had his truest henchmen and the soldiers under their command about him at Pilsen, so that any attempt to seize him there would be fatally dangerous. Besides, for the purposes of the Emperor and the young King of Hungary it was essential to avoid any division in the army; a crisis in which a considerable portion of the troops stood by their general would mean only dangerous civil war in Bohemia. The army must be cut away entire from under Wallenstein or the coup would fail.

Early in February wild rumours began to circulate among the officers; Wallenstein was plotting to be King of Bohemia, to make Louis XIII King of the Romans, to give away the Electorates of Saxony, Bavaria, Mainz and Treves to Franz

[1] HALLWICH, *Wallensteins Ende*, II, pp. 136-7.
[2] IRMER, *Die Verhandlungen Schwedens*, III, p. 168; PEKAŘ, p. 600.
[3] FOERSTER, *Wallenstein*, III, p. 177.
[4] SRBIK, pp. 84-6.

Albrecht, Bernard of Saxe-Weimar, Arnim and Marshal Horn, to make Gallas Duke of Mecklenburg, Piccolomini Duke of Milan, Trčka Duke of Moravia, and to cut off Aldringer's head.[1] The skilfully disseminated lies filled the officers of the army with doubts of Wallenstein's sanity; their probable source was the plausible, popular, diplomatic Octavio Piccolomini.[2]

By the first week of February Wallenstein was anxious to move. 'There is not a moment to lose, all is ready', wrote Franz Albrecht to Arnim. He might well think so, for Wallenstein and his party still suspected nothing and Gallas blandly added his wishes for Arnim's coming to the letter.[3] Doubting, the Protestants still hesitated, while at Pilsen from day to day rumours swelled and exploded. A servant of Trčka's had refused admittance to some Franciscan friars, sneering that his master was a good Lutheran; on February 15th at night Piccolomini left the town secretly and none knew why; Wallenstein himself grew doubtful of his strength. Once again he sent for all his leading officers. Aldringer pleaded illness, and Gallas was dispatched to fetch him;[4] neither of them came back. Nor, for that matter, did Piccolomini. On the 18th Franz Albrecht had to admit the possibility of a split in the army. 'They must bend or break', he wrote to Arnim, 'for I see well, they will have to pay for it who stand by Aldringer . . . Most of the officers are here and they have all been fixed.'[5] The last sentence was a lie; a few more than thirty officers only had come to Pilsen for Wallenstein's second meeting and nearly all were nervous and questioning. Franz Albrecht's letter was written on February 18th, and on the same day he set out to implore Bernard of Saxe-Weimar in person to march on Pilsen. He was already too late; on February 18th an imperial decree was published in the further outposts of Wallenstein's army, commanding all officers to take orders in future from Gallas.

On February 20th the second Pilsen meeting took place; Wallenstein saw the colonels first in his bedroom, then asked them to withdraw with Trčka and Ilow; but the best that the

---

[1] See SRBIK, op. cit., p. 82.
[2] Ibid., p. 82.
[3] GAEDEKE, *Wallensteins Verhandlungen*, pp. 259-60.
[4] IRMER, *Die Verhandlungen Schwedens*, III, p. 287.
[5] GAEDEKE, *Wallensteins Verhandlungen*, pp. 281-2.

eloquence and diplomacy of his trusted deputies could extract
from them was a promise that they were willing to stand by him
so long as nothing was intended against the Emperor — and
several of those present refused to sign any undertaking even
with this saving clause.[1]

Then at last Wallenstein and his two remaining conspirators,
Adam Trčka and Christian Ilow, realized their mistake. They
had depended on the army, and the army had deserted them.
With the courage of desperation they made a last throw.
Trčka set out for Prague to raise the capital for Wallenstein;
the general himself was to follow. Two hours later Trčka came
back; he had learnt on the way that Wallenstein's dismissal had
been published at Prague by the officer in command of the
garrison.[2] Still hoping, Wallenstein sent for Colonel Beck, the
supreme commander at Prague who was in Pilsen, and asked
him to go to the capital and denounce the action of his subordinate. He smote against that obstinate imperial loyalty on which
he had not reckoned in an army of mercenaries. They could do
what they liked to him, said Beck, but he would not serve
against the Emperor. There would have been little point in
using the authority which still remained to him to shoot Beck,
and Wallenstein with the last enigmatical and dramatic gesture
of his life, gave his hand to his subordinate as he dismissed him,
saying, 'I had peace in my hands, God is just.'

Meanwhile Trčka was beating the drums for the evacuation
of Pilsen and piling all the treasure he could find into his
baggage wagons. The deserted lodging of Gallas was plundered,
and on February 22nd, 1634, with about a thousand men and a
hundred thousand gulden, Wallenstein, Trčka and Ilow fled
from Pilsen.[3]

Their flight took Piccolomini by surprise. Planning to surround the town with troops loyal to the Emperor and force the
conspirators to surrender, he had stationed men to cover the
road to Vienna lest Wallenstein should attempt anything in that
direction, and the evasion of his quarry northwards, to make a
direct junction with the Saxons, found him at a loss.[4] He

[1] HALLWICH, *Wallensteins Ende*, II, pp. 229-35.
[2] IRMER, *Verhandlungen*, III, p. 289; HALLWICH, *Briefe und Akten*, IV, p. 616.
[3] FOERSTER, *Wallenstein*, III, pp. 230, 254.
[4] IRMER, *Die Verhandlungen Schwedens*, III, pp. 210, 211, 276.

moved to Pilsen to make certain at least of the loyalty of any troops remaining there, and there on February 24th an agitated Irish priest, Father Taaffe, insisted on seeing him. It seemed that he was the confessor of a Colonel Butler who had been marching to Prague with a regiment of dragoons to join the loyal imperialists, when he had run face to face with Wallenstein and his convoy. Commanded to go with the general, he had not dared to disobey, but had contrived to dispatch Taaffe unobserved, carrying a guarantee of loyalty written in English and a verbal message asking what he was to do. Wallenstein was marching for the key fortress of Eger, to join with Arnim and Saxe-Weimar. Piccolomini did not hesitate, and Taaffe rode off at once with the command to Butler to bring in Wallenstein alive or dead.[1]

Before Taaffe could reach him, almost before he had reached Piccolomini, Colonel Butler had taken the law into his own hands. Wallenstein and his companions reached Eger on the evening of the 24th at about five o'clock, where John Gordon, one of Trčka's colonels, received them with apparent willingness. But he opened the gates for fear of Butler's troops as much as Wallenstein's, and when that night he learnt that Butler was loyal to the Emperor, it needed only the firmness of his second-in-command, Leslie, and of Butler himself, to persuade him to betray Wallenstein.[2] The elements in their joint decision are hard to disentangle; Butler at least seems to have felt that he had a duty to rid the Empire of a traitor,[3] but in the behaviour of all three there was much of the mercenary; dangerous as was the deed, the reward would be great. None of them was likely ever again to have so golden an opportunity.

On the following day Ilow attempted in vain to secure further guarantees of loyalty from the officers in the town.[4] Optimistically, he did not regard the failure as grave, for directly afterwards he accepted Gordon's suggestion that he, with Trčka and the Bohemian rebel Kinsky who had joined them, should dine that night with the officers at the castle.[5]

After that it was simple. Butler's dragoons rushed the doors

---

[1] MAILATH, *Geschichte des oesterreichischen Kaiserstaates.* Hamburg, 1842, III, pp. 368-71.
[2] Ibid., pp. 373-5.   [3] Ibid., p. 370.
[4] SRBIK, pp. 385, 390.   [5] Ibid., p. 185.

while the traitors sat at dinner and overpowered them almost at once. Trčka alone, immensely strong, fought his way out into the courtyard. There he was met by a group of musketeers who challenged him for the password. 'Sankt Jakob', he called. It was the word Wallenstein had given. 'House of Austria', they out-shouted him, and battered him down with the butt ends of their muskets, until one of them gave him the *coup de grâce* with a dagger. An Englishman, Captain Devereux, dispatched Wallenstein. Breaking into his lodgings with a few companions, he kicked open the bedroom door to find him undefended. Wallenstein was at the window; turning he faced his murderers, stumbled forward, moaned something which might have been a cry for quarter, and fell transfixed. A huge Irishman picked up the crumpled body and tried to throw it out of the window, but Devereux, with some remnant of decency, stopped him and hastily rolled the corpse in the bloodstained carpet on which it had fallen.[1]

All this time Franz Albrecht of Saxe-Lauenburg had been urging Bernard to march for Eger. But Bernard suspected that Wallenstein was fooling him, and not until February 26th would he agree to set out. Arnim was even more reluctant and did not break camp until the 27th.[2] On the way they learnt that Wallenstein was dead and Eger in the hands of his murderers. Their luckless go-between Franz Albrecht, galloping back with the news that they were on the march, fell all unsuspecting into the hands of Butler's men and was sent prisoner to Vienna. Meanwhile, a sporadic outburst of mutiny was instantly quelled, the suspect officers were placed under arrest, and the army, entire but for a negligible minority, declared its loyalty to the Emperor.[3] The murderers were sent for to Vienna, thanked, fêted and generously rewarded with promotion, money and land.

There was no need to penalize the traitor's family; his wife and young daughter were as harmless as they were innocent, his principal heir was his cousin Max, whose friendship the King of Hungary made haste to win and keep. The organizing genius

---

[1] SRBIK, p. 386; IRMER, *Die Verhandlungen Schwedens*, III, pp. 291-3.
[2] Ibid., pp. 284, 301, 306.
[3] IRMER, *Die Verhandlungen Schwedens*, III, p. 383.
[4] HALLWICH, *Wallensteins Ende*, II, p. 485.

which had kept the army fed had gone, but there was no chance now that supplies would be deliberately cut off, for with Wallenstein perished the privileges which had guarded his estates. Moreover, the Cardinal-Infant was about to cross the Alps with men and money for the Hapsburg cause.

The nightmare of Wallenstein's betrayal had proved itself to be a nightmare only. The greatness which had dazzled Europe and terrified Vienna evaporated at the touch of an assassin. The web of intrigue which had stretched from Paris to Vienna was brushed aside by the conspiracy of three expatriated ruffians in an evening over their cups.[1] Until so near the end he had seemed so terrible; fear gives an edge to the letters of Aldringer, Gallas, Piccolomini, in those last weeks; fear quavers in the obstinate, bewildered words of the officers assembled for that last Pilsen meeting;[2] fear drove the Emperor Ferdinand, day after day, to solitude and prayer.[3] Taaffe had implored Butler to fly alone rather than risk companionship with Wallenstein, Gordon had wished to abandon Eger, his troops and his reputation rather than come into collision with the general's will.[4]

And in the end there was nothing to fear but a crippled man asking for quarter, and nothing left when all was done but carrion for the disposal of Walter Devereux. 'Presently [they] drew him out by the heels, his head knocking upon every stair, all bloody, and threw him into a coach and carried him to the castle where the rest lay naked close together . . . and there he had the superior place of them, being the right hand file, which they could not do less, being so great a general.'[5]

v

The death of Wallenstein had a more profound effect on the Hapsburg than on the Bourbon cause. Although at Frankfort French and Swedish hopes had risen high in the last days of February and the false news that he had seized Bohemia for

---

[1] See Taaffe's relation in MAILATH, III, pp. 373-5.
[2] See HALLWICH, *Wallensteins Ende*.   [3] GLIUBICH, p. 418.
[4] MAILATH, III, pp. 369, 374.   [5] POYNTZ, p. 99.

France preceded by a bare three days the knowledge of his murder,[1] his death left them, but for the disappointment, neither better nor worse off than they had been.

But the revivifying effect on the Hapsburg dynasty was remarkable. The appointment of the already popular King of Hungary to the chief command, and the judicious distribution of rewards to the loyal, soothed and revitalized the imperial army. Matthias Gallas, the new general, was incompetent and self-indulgent, but he had the qualities necessary for the crisis: genial, friendly and unaffected, he liked popularity and aimed to acquire it. Piccolomini, the younger man and his subordinate, was in fact more important, for he had the grasp of actualities, the organizing ability and the tact necessary to tide over the difficult period. A happier combination than these two at this moment could hardly have been found, so favourably did their methods contrast with those of Wallenstein and his hectoring supporters.

In April the King of Hungary was officially proclaimed commander-in-chief. Although it was generally assumed that this young man of twenty-six, with no experience of war, would be merely a figure-head, he was a significant figure-head, since his appointment marked the completion of the Hapsburg plan for a joint and purely dynastic attack on their enemies. It also marked a step forward in the imperial policy of centralization. Since the check at Regensburg in 1630 and the overwhelming advance of the Swedes, the old policy of Ferdinand had been submerged. But his luck had held; in 1630 he had tried in vain to replace Wallenstein by his own son, in 1634 he had achieved it. The fall of Regensburg and the abandonment of Bavaria had driven Maximilian to accept any command rather than that of Wallenstein, and he had welcomed the very appointment which he had prevented four years before.

Underneath the immediate dangers raised by Wallenstein, the situation between the Emperor and the constitutional princes had not altered, and the appointment of the King of Hungary was no less opposed to their interests in 1634 than in 1630. Maximilian, when he wrote in despair to his agent at Vienna, telling him to ally himself even with the Spanish party

[1] FEUQUIÈRES, II, pp. 214, 225-7.

to get rid of Wallenstein, may have done the only thing possible to save Bavaria from destruction, but he was undoing his own policy. Circumstances, not Ferdinand, had been too much for him, and this time indeed the Emperor's luck and not his sense had brought out of Wallenstein's treachery the dynastic achievement on which his heart was set.

Much depended on the use made of his position by the King of Hungary. This was his first open step in the European field, although he had been active on the imperial council since his nineteenth year. Young Ferdinand was the elder of his father's surviving sons by Maria, sister to Maximilian of Bavaria. The surroundings in which the prince had grown up were conventionally perfect. His father and mother, and later his step-mother, lived in unruffled devotion to each other and the children, who were brought up simply and happily in the hills of Styria. Whatever the educational theories of the Styrian household, they were successful in some unusual respects. Cleverer than his father, young Ferdinand never evoked jealousy nor felt resentment; he urged different opinions from the Emperor at the council table, had his own party at Court, criticized his father's policy, particularly his finances, but avoided altogether that ugly antagonism between the ruler and the heir which so often embitters dynastic politics. Father and son admired each other's qualities and compromised on their disagreements.

That young Ferdinand had some exceptional gift for affection is apparent in his relationship with his younger brother, Leopold. This prince, regarding himself as the ablest of the family, deplored his distance from the throne. His brothers were both delicate, and when the eldest, Charles, died in 1619, no one had thought that the second, Ferdinand, would long outlive him. But Ferdinand continued to stand between Leopold and the throne, grew to manhood, married and removed his younger brother by yet another and another life from the inheritance. Leopold, as he grew up, made his annoyance an open secret at Court, yet Ferdinand not only showed no equivalent resentment but set himself to put his brother forward on every possible occasion, to satisfy his lust for power, to consult and pacify him. Leopold's political discontent could not be assuaged, yet in spite of all, the brothers remained the firmest of personal friends.[1]

The King of Hungary had inherited his father's good nature but without his lightness of heart. He had inherited also much of his father's charm. Less garrulous, he was more dignified and not less gracious, and his ability to converse easily in seven languages gave him power to undertake much of his own diplomacy. In appearance he favoured his mother's family and had the melancholy dark eyes, brown hair and strong features of the Wittelsbach. Though he had been educated to enjoy hunting, he preferred to spend his leisure reading philosophy, writing music, carving in ivory, or experimenting in his laboratory. He had on occasion lectured to the Court, the old Emperor beaming on him with proprietary pride. He was quiet, thoughtful, rather melancholy. Unlike his father he was economical to the point of meanness. As a boy, his reserve had made him appear dull-witted, but as he became surer of himself he gave the impression instead of being a profound thinker.[2] Profounder indeed than he was, for when all is said, he was only a decent, imaginative, worried intellectual. He had neither the intense faith in his mission nor the trust in his God which bore up his father; he had not the singleness of purpose which gave the old Emperor a touch of greatness. He was too clever to be happy, not clever enough to be successful. Ferdinand II was either very shrewd or very lucky; Ferdinand III was neither.

The chief influence in Ferdinand's life, from his marriage in 1631 to her death in 1646, was his wife, the Infanta Maria of Spain, sister to the Cardinal-Infant. In a real, if a private sense, this attractive, sympathetic, intelligent woman acted as the connecting link between the Courts of Madrid, Brussels and Vienna.[3] Several years older than her husband, she held his devotion and gave him hers unwaveringly throughout their lives.

As King of Hungary and, later, as Emperor, Ferdinand III played a large part in the history of Europe; it seems therefore

[1] FIEDLER, p. 122.
[2] CARAFA, pp. 268-9; FIEDLER, pp. 189-90, 277-8.
[3] Ibid., p. 279.

only proper that the blank which is usually left for his character should be filled in. There is evidence enough that he impressed his contemporaries more than posterity.

While the situation was thus prepared for the Hapsburg advance within the Empire, the plans of the dynasty elsewhere had matured. The aged Archduchess Isabella died in the winter. Almost with her last words she exhorted Gaston, Duke of Orleans, who had come to visit her, not to desert his mother, now exiled from France.[1] Earlier she had received Princess Margaret of Lorraine, Gaston's wife, with every honour due to a King's daughter.[2] Thus in her last acts she had tried to knit together these vapid malcontents, so that none of them should make peace with the King of France,[3] but remain united, an instrument to be used against the French monarchy. After her death the interim government at Brussels carried out her intentions by completing a treaty of alliance with Gaston of Orleans and inciting the Duke of Lorraine to rebel. Thus once again they set in motion the disturbers of France. In the summer they stifled the cry for peace of their Flemish subjects by dissolving the States General, while the ambassador who had been sent to Philip IV to further the settlement was arrested in Madrid.

The movements of Richelieu completed the other half of the design. He renewed his treaty with the United Provinces,[4] refused to recognize the marriage of Gaston to Margaret of Lorraine and dispatched an army to quell her irrepressible brother, Duke Charles. At Paris, Mademoiselle, the strapping tomboy who was Gaston's only child, bounced about the Louvre singing all the vulgarest songs she could learn against the Cardinal. At seven years old, she was a licensed rebel.[5]

But the centre towards which the policies of Bourbon and Hapsburg pointed was still in Germany, where Feuquières continued, carefully and tactfully, to build up Richelieu's position. In the spring of 1634 the League of Heilbronn met at Frankfort-on-the-Main. In the intervening months since its

---

[1] A. LANGEL, Le Duel de Marie de Médicis et de Richelieu. Revue des Deux Mondes, Nov. 1877, p. 362.
[2] AVENEL, IV, p. 480.   [3] LONCHAY ET CUVELIER, II, p. 718.
[4] AITZEMA, op. cit., II, pp. 94-5.
[5] Mémoires de la Grande Mademoiselle, ed. Petitot, II, xl, p. 373.

last gathering certain mild alterations had taken place; superficially the French and Swedish position seemed much as before, but under the surface Oxenstierna had grown weaker, Feuquières stronger.

Feuquières had the easier task. He had but one object in Germany: to make French protection indispensable. After the formation of the Heilbronn League he set himself to detach the princes and estates one by one from Sweden, exploiting Oxenstierna's organization but driving the wedge of his insinuations and of his generous bribes[1] neatly between him and his allies. Trust in him grew as trust in Oxenstierna waned.

The Swedish Chancellor was not to blame for the lessening of confidence among his allies. He had more to do than one man could easily manage, and the task was proving too much even for him. The army was the trouble. So long as Gustavus had lived, that conglomerate of native Swedish and recruited German troops had some sense of unity. But a storm was blowing up before the King died which broke over Oxenstierna.

There had been four chief armies in the field after Lützen, under Gustavus Horn, Johan Baner, William of Hesse-Cassel and Bernard of Saxe-Weimar. Of these commanders the first two were Swedish marshals, incontrovertibly under the authority of the Swedish government; the third was, except for John George, the only truly independent ally that the King had made, a prince whose small but well-managed forces were treated consistently as an independent, self-reliant unit. The fourth commander, Bernard of Saxe-Weimar, was the difficulty.

This prince was in the same position as Horn or Baner, that of a general under the Swedish Crown.[2] But he had had the impertinence to state that the King was jealous of him, and had clamoured for an independent command even before Lützen;[3] after the battle, which his own dexterity had done much to win, his presence on the scene of action and his admitted ability made him the only man fit to follow the King.

Bernard's character has never been altogether elucidated,

---

[1] FEUQUIÈRES, pp. 96-8, 103, 195, 253, 285.
[2] STRUCK, p. 20, n. 3.
[3] ROESE, *Herzog Bernhard der Grosse.* Weimar, 1828-29, I, p. 174-5.

and neither his writings nor his actions reveal a sympathetic personality. His harsh virtues one would not deny; 'imperare sibi maximum imperium est', he wrote platitudinously in the autograph book of a Saxon worthy,[1] and he was, it is true, self-commanding, temperate, chaste, brave, devout in the practice of his religion. But the face which looks out from contemporary engravings is not prepossessing, with its low forehead, hard, unimaginative eyes and mean, egoistic mouth. His elder brother was that William of Weimar who had attempted to form a Union of Patriots in 1622 and had been taken prisoner at Stadtlohn.[2] This pessimistic, gentle, courteous prince[3] also held a command in the Swedish army, but Bernard brutally pushed him out of his way. An ambitious man, conscious of his nation and of his princely rank, Bernard found Swedish, or indeed any, control galling. On this account a case has been made out for him as a single-minded patriot. The single-mindedness was there, certainly; of the patriotism there is less evidence. 'An excellent commander,' wrote Richelieu, 'but so much for himself that no one could make sure of him.'[4]

The other claimant to command over the two armies was Gustavus Horn. During the King's life, Horn and Oxenstierna had been called his two arms,[5] and the simile was not undeserved, for the marshal was, in his own profession, as reliable and capable as the Chancellor. Horn's commandership-in-chief would certainly have pleased Oxenstierna best, for he was the marshal's father-in-law and they had worked together amicably for many years. Bernard, however, was determined that this should not be; he was reported to have said that a German prince was worth ten Swedish noblemen, and if he might not be above Horn, he would at least be equal and independent. When the two commanders had met on the frontiers of Bavaria in the previous summer, Bernard had arrogantly demanded the title generalissimus, while Horn,

[1] *Melchior Jauch und sein Stammbuch. Archiv für Sächsische Geschichte*, IV, p. 208.

[2] See *supra*, chapters IV, VI.

[3] AUBERY, *Mémoires de Richelieu*, p. 395.

[4] HANOTAUX ET LE DUC DE LA FORCE: *Revue des Deux Mondes*, March 1935, p. 380.

[5] J. V. ANDREAE, *Gustavi Adolphi Suecorum Regis Memoria*. Berlin, 1844, p. 13.

with less arrogance but as much obstinacy, had offered him that of lieutenant-general only.[1] There was, in point of fact, a serious difference both in their political and strategic outlook. Horn, the more constructive if technically the less brilliant soldier, was for concentrating on the head of the Rhine valley and there building up a bulwark against the joint Spanish and Austrian powers. Bernard had more directly personal interests in the war;[2] suddenly in the summer of 1633 he demanded the duchy of Franconia. This move may be interpreted variously; Bernard may have been anxious for a reward as Mansfeld had been; or he may have believed that by seizing land, even under Swedish control, he would be able to assert the interests of the native Germans against the invaders and rescue some at least of the Fatherland. To pacify him, Axel Oxenstierna drew him a patent creating him Duke of Franconia under the Swedish Crown,[3] and partly solved the military problem by agreeing to a free alliance with the new Duke, on the model of that recently renewed with William of Hesse-Cassel.[4]

This kind of ill-feeling did not reassure Oxenstierna's allies, and moreover it provided the opportunity for which Feuquières was watching; as early as April 1633 he had attempted to detach the ambitious Bernard from the Swedes and bind him to France.[5] Further cause for anxiety was given by the actual behaviour of the troops. French subsidies were not paid fast enough, and Oxenstierna's system of distribution broke down badly even before the King's death; afterwards the situation grew steadily worse, culminating in active unrest among both officers and men, and at last in mutiny. The rising was stilled by the partial satisfaction of the demand for pay and by the reckless gift of German estates to the more querulous officers.[6] The danger was past for the moment, but it was not obviated; Oxenstierna realized that he had now both to preserve the peace between his two leading generals, and to keep the

---

[1] *Brefvexling*, II, viii, pp. 126 ff.; PUFENDORF, VIII, p. 40.
[2] K. JACOB, *Von Lützen nach Nördlingen*. Strassburg, 1904, pp. 65-6, 166-7.
[3] *Sverges Traktater*, V, ii, pp. 92-100.
[4] Ibid., pp. 71-4, 105-9.
[5] FEUQUIÈRES, II, p. 96.
[6] *Brefvexling*, II, viii, pp. 97, 110, 124, 248 f.; VI, pp. 51-2.

soldiers contented if the war was to be fought at all; in so far as he calmed the officers with morsels of Germany, he would provoke the annoyance of his German allies in the Heilbronn League. 'J'ai peur', wrote a Dutch politician in April 1634, 'qu'enfin tout ne s'éclate contre les Suédois.'[1]

When the representatives met at Frankfort in the spring of 1634, they treated Oxenstierna's propositions, especially when he spoke of indemnification for Sweden, with open suspicion.[2] This was distressing, particularly as the Chancellor had approached two more divisions of the Empire, the Lower and the Upper Saxon Circles, to join the League,[3] and naturally did not wish to reveal to their ambassadors any discontent among those who were already his allies. An attempt to persuade John George to join the allies ended only in a letter from the Elector warning all honest Germans against specious foreign allies,[4] a statement which cut too dangerously near the bone for Oxenstierna's liking.

Into this uncomfortable situation Feuquières slyly interjected a new proposal of French help. His King was prepared to support the Protestant Cause with money and diplomacy, far more money than the Swedish Crown could give, in return for a very small guarantee. He demanded only the control of the fortress of Philippsburg on the Rhine for the duration of the war.[5] On the right bank of the river, in the lands of the Bishop of Speier and near the junction of the Rhine and Saal, Philippsburg had surrendered to the Swedes early in the year; it was thus technically under the Heilbronn League, and should they decide to hand it over to the French government, Oxenstierna could hardly disagree without precipitating a breach. Such a concession would indicate the definite turning of the balance in favour of Richelieu as protector of German rights.

The proposition was made in July 1634. Meanwhile, in south Germany along the line of the Danube, the armies were once more active. The ravages of the plague and long-drawn hunger[6] hindered the troops of Bernard from carrying out any

[1] PRINSTERER, II, iii, p. 55.   [2] LUNDORP, IV, pp. 425-7.
[3] Brefväxling mellan Oxenstierna och Svenska Regeringen. Handlungen rörande Skandinaviens Historia, XXIX, pp. 251-2.
[4] LUNDORP, IV, pp. 384-9.   [5] Ibid., pp. 416-18; FEUQUIÈRES, II, p. 357.
[6] Brefvexling, II, vii, p. 201.

project until the summer was already advanced. The Cardinal-Infant with twenty thousand men was on his way from Italy; to intercept him Horn besieged the fortress of Überlingen, which guards the southern shore of Constance, along which the Spaniards would march; the town held him up for four weeks before he at length, very much against his will, agreed to join with Bernard[1] in an attempt to shatter the King of Hungary and his army before the Spanish reinforcements could come.

Arnim, acting theoretically in conjunction with a Swedish detachment under Baner, with whom his relations grew daily more embittered and suspicious,[2] had once more invaded Bohemia. This was the occasion, therefore, for Horn and Bernard to fall on the inexperienced King of Hungary and the incompetent Gallas while they were uncertain whether to defend Prague or to march towards the Cardinal-Infant.

On July 12th, 1634, Bernard and Horn met at Augsburg, having about twenty thousand men between them,[3] and marched thence for the Bavarian-Bohemian border. They had information that the King of Hungary was advancing on Regensburg, and they thought that by appearing to join Arnim in Bohemia they would induce him to turn back. On July 22nd they stormed and took Landshut which was occupied by almost all the Bavarian and some of the imperialist cavalry. Aldringer, hastening to the rescue, came too late to organize the resistance and was himself shot, some said by his own men, in the ill-managed retreat.[4] This victory was spectacular enough and, almost at the same moment, Arnim appeared outside the walls of Prague.

The King of Hungary, with unshaken nerve, held on his original course. Horn and Bernard had hardly taken Landshut before they lost Regensburg.[5] Far from hastening back to defend Bohemia, young Ferdinand had profited by the absence of the larger part of the Protestant army to attack their line of communication on the Danube. It was a risk to expose Bohemia so utterly, but he calculated rightly, for no sooner did Regensburg fall than Bernard and Horn swung round and marched

[1] *Brefvexling*, II, viii, p. 275.   [2] Ibid., II, vi, pp. 122 ff., *passim*.
[3] Ibid., I, i, p. 205.
[4] Ibid., II, viii, p. 162; BROHM, *Johann von Aldringen*. Halle, 1882, p. 109.
[5] *Brefvexling*, II, viii, p. 164.

after him, while Arnim at once thought it better to withdraw from Prague and await developments.

The fall of Regensburg was unwelcome to Oxenstierna at Frankfort; still more unwelcome were the messages that came through from Horn and Bernard during the next three weeks. Ferdinand was out-marching them in the race to meet the Cardinal-Infant, and neither Horn nor Saxe-Weimar could force their pestilence-ridden and ill-furnished troops to make the gigantic effort necessary to circumvent the imperial army before the Cardinal should come. On August 16th Ferdinand crossed the Danube at Donauwörth; the Cardinal-Infant was approaching from the Black Forest. It would be only a matter of days until they met. But at Nördlingen, not far from Donauwörth, a strong Swedish garrison lay encamped, and Ferdinand dared not risk a flank attack on his march. He was still some days ahead of Horn and Saxe-Weimar, and turning aside he set himself to reduce the city.

Meanwhile at Frankfort the Heilbronn League was a prey to growing anxiety, which Feuquières was ready enough to fan.[1] Oxenstierna's efforts to reassure his allies were useless, and on hearing that Ferdinand of Hungary had taken Donauwörth, the German representatives agreed to buy Richelieu's support by the preliminary cession of Philippsburg.[2] The articles, which marked the first diplomatic triumph of Feuquières, were signed on August 26th, 1634, about the time when the armies of Horn and Saxe-Weimar, hastening on, came in sight of the King of Hungary's encampment among the wooded hills round Nördlingen.

Horn and Bernard had about twenty thousand men,[3] the King of Hungary about fifteen thousand, and the surrounding country could ill-furnish even one army with supplies. Bernard hoped at first that hunger would force the enemy to retreat without fighting.[4] Both he and Horn, in agreement for once, knew that the town could not be relieved without risking an engagement on singularly difficult and broken ground, and with barely equal numbers.[5] When it became apparent that

---

[1] Feuquières, II, p. 387.
[2] *Sverges Traktater*, v, ii, pp. 200-5.
[3] *Brefvexling*, I, i, p. 205.
[4] Ibid., II, vii, p. 233.
[5] Ibid., p. 231.

Ferdinand intended to wait for the coming of the Cardinal-Infant, they sent for all the scattered troops which they could summon, in the hope that they would force the King of Hungary to retreat before the Spaniards came. Their hope was not realized, for the new troops were so weak, few and dispirited that the King of Hungary did not budge.

Meanwhile the colonel of the garrison at Nördlingen with difficulty prevented the burghers from forcing a surrender. They had, not unnaturally, no desire to share the fate of Magdeburg. Horn contrived to send them messages exhorting them to hold out for six days, and yet another six days, but night after night he could see rockets of distress against the darkened sky, and hear through the day the intermittent thunder of the King of Hungary's cannon bombarding the walls. Once, when a long silence intervened, he was convinced that the town had surrendered.[1]

Among the imperialists there was joyful news of the Cardinal's approach, and on September 2nd the King of Hungary himself went out to meet him. The cousins came together a few miles from Donauwörth and, each dismounting as he saw the other, almost ran into each other's arms.[2] After the long-distance planning of their scheme, it was almost too good to be true that the cousins should be as firm friends in practice as they had long been in theory, but so it was, and the generals who had been set to control them gave way before their combined obstinacy.

On both sides things now moved towards an issue. Horn was anxious to avoid a battle until further reinforcements came, so that the inequality of numbers should be lessened, but both he and Bernard knew that the fall of Nördlingen, coming so soon after the rapid surrender of Regensburg and Donauwörth, would shake the confidence of their German allies, and go far to shatter the Heilbronn League. The political risk of retirement at this eleventh hour was greater than the military risk of staying.[3]

The country south of Nördlingen, with its smooth, rounded

[1] *Brefvexling.*
[2] D. DE AEDO Y GALLART, *Viaje del Infante Cardenal Don Fernando de Austria.* Antwerp, 1635, p. 114.
[3] CHEMNITZ, II, Stockholm, 1653, p. 529.

hills and thickly scattered woods, was unsuited to the type of pitched battle beloved of the seventeenth-century tactician. The imperial and Spanish troops occupied the flatter ground in front of the town itself, and had placed an advance guard on the ridge of a hill which dominated the road to the town. The Swedish army lay on a farther low range of hills, about a mile to the south-west. Should they attempt to relieve the town, they would have to march down into the valley and pass under the menacing outposts of the enemy.

Rashly impulsive, the Cardinal-Infant sent forward some of his musketeers to occupy a small wood on the very fringe of the hill, in the direct path of the enemy's possible advance. The force was too small, and on the evening of September 5th Bernard's troops drove it out and occupied the outpost, thus gaining an important point on the road into the town. The major in command had surrendered and was at once taken before Bernard, whom he found at supper in his coach, apparently in very bad humour. When asked the number of the Spanish reinforcement, the prisoner gave an answer approximating to the truth — about twenty thousand. Bernard swore at him; he had information, he said, that there were not more than seven thousand, and unless the prisoner told the truth he would hang him out of hand. The major stuck to his story and Bernard angrily ordered him away. Horn, who was with him in the coach, said little, but it is clear from Bernard's annoyance, and from the hasty removal of the prisoner, that Horn's decision to fight was still uncertain and liable to be shaken if Bernard's optimistic under-estimate of the Spanish forces proved false.[1]

Meanwhile, not far off, at the imperialist headquarters they were holding a council of war. Gallas openly blamed the Cardinal-Infant for having put too few soldiers in the wood, but the prince quelled him with the unoriginal but comforting statement that what was done could not be undone; for the rest, the two cousins planned the action for the following day with little reference to their elders.[2] They arranged that the

[1] AEDO Y GALLART, p. 127; see also CANOVAS DEL CASTILLO, *Estudios del Reinado de Felipe*. Madrid, 1888, IV, p. 436.
[2] AEDO Y GALLART, p. 128.

forces on the hill should be strengthened so as to be ready for the probable attack of the enemy. The main body of the army was to be massed in the open country before the town, the Germans in front, the Spanish troops behind to reinforce the line where necessary and to beat off any sally from the town itself. The weary garrison of Nördlingen was so small that there was little danger of an effective rear attack. The two princes had thirty-three thousand men — about twenty thousand foot, including the highly trained and disciplined Spanish infantry, and thirteen thousand horse.[1]

In spite of his continued disbelief, Bernard was outnumbered. The united Protestant troops amounted to little more than sixteen thousand foot and nine thousand horse, all suffering from lack of supplies. Yet it was essential to relieve Nördlingen. Consulting together, Horn and Bernard concluded that if they could once dislodge the enemy from the outpost on the hill and occupy it themselves, Ferdinand's position before the town would be untenable and he would have to withdraw. They planned therefore to manœuvre for this position, if possible without provoking a general engagement. Horn on the right wing was to advance by night to the very slopes of the hill and attack it at daybreak. Bernard, on the left, was to follow the valley road into the open plain, draw up his troops before the enemy lines and prevent them by his threatening aspect from reinforcing their fellows on the ridge. The two generals were to work in conjunction, although their spheres of action would be far apart; but they did not allow for the intervening belts of woodland, still in full leaf, which on the morrow prevented each from seeing clearly what the other did. The jealousy between them augured very ill for the conduct of a joint attack, and though in fact neither betrayed the other on the following day, yet each blamed the other afterwards.

From the outset everything went wrong. Horn, or his officers, botched the night advance. The infantry and the light artillery should have gone first, but instead some of the wagons and heavy cannon were sent with the advance guard, and these, sticking and overturning in the narrow muddy lane up the hill-side, caused a clatter which warned the enemy,

[1] AEDO Y GALLART, p. 130.

and a delay which gave them time to entrench themselves ready for the attack.

By the bright sunrise of September 6th Horn had at last got his troops to a sheltered place under the incline of the hill. He intended now to attack with his infantry and, when these had engaged the foremost ranks of the imperialists, to finish the matter with a cavalry charge, taking them unawares in the flank. Having, as he thought, made his intentions plain, the general rode off towards the summit of the hill to reconnoitre the position by daylight. At once one of his colonels, mistaking the situation, ordered the cavalry to charge. Horn's commands were thus reversed and, although his horse chased some of the imperialist defenders off the field, the Swedish infantry now had to attack unsupported by their cavalry and under relentless fire. Nevertheless, the attack was so vigorous and well-ordered that the imperialists, in whom a wholesome terror of the Swedes had reigned ever since Lützen, fled, deserting the batteries. Two accidents cheated the Swedes of their reward. Advancing rapidly upon the position the two brigades of Swedish infantry, each took the other for the enemy, and they could not for some time be separated. Meanwhile a store of gunpowder abandoned by the imperialists exploded in the midst of the victorious troops.

On the opposing side the two princes had found a happier solution of their double responsibility than had Horn and Bernard. As soon as the attack began, they had taken up their position on a small, exposed hillock whence they could follow the fate of both wings at once. Hence they saw the loss of the hill and hence, also, the sudden disorder among the conquering Swedes. At once the Cardinal-Infant detached a Spanish contingent, horse and foot, to prevent the flight of the Germans and renew the assault on the hill. Now would have been the time when Horn would have given anything for his cavalry, which was skirmishing among the fugitives far on the right flank. His disordered infantry collapsed before the Spanish advance, and within an hour he had again lost the summit of the hill.

As the infantry retreated to their first position, they saw through the clearings of the trees some of Bernard's cavalry in flight, and panic which Horn had difficulty to check began to spread among them. Bernard himself was fully engaged in the plain; by judicious and intermittent use of his batteries he sought to prevent his opponents from detaching troops against Horn, but, seeing himself now outnumbered, he dared not provoke a general attack.

Until midday, Horn continued on his hill-side, his lines raked by the enemy's fire. Collecting his cavalry once again, he flung them, horse and foot in succession, against the Spanish position, but in vain. The Spanish infantry in the centre had a trick

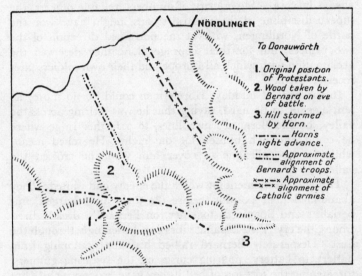

NÖRDLINGEN

To Donauwörth

1. Original position of Protestants.
2. Wood taken by Bernard on eve of battle.
3. Hill stormed by Horn.
—·—·— Horn's night advance.
═══ Approximate alignment of Bernard's troops.
x—x—x Approximate alignment of Catholic armies

equal to any Swedish artifice. As the enemy advanced they knelt down so that the bullets passed over them and then, before the Swedes could reload, were up and had emptied a volley into the advancing ranks. It was their boast that they never wasted a shot.

Time and again the Swedes fell back, leaving their dead; time and again, under Horn's unfaltering hand, they closed up the gashes in their lines and came forward. The Spaniards counted fifteen charges. Each failure increased Horn's determination to succeed. A point had come at which so much had been done that it seemed folly not to do that little more which might turn the scale; always it seemed that the next time must bring the breaking-point. So it went on for seven hours, in the blinding smoke of the guns.

All the time Bernard was battering on the lines before the city, while from their escarpment the King of Hungary and the Cardinal sent couriers this way and that, strengthening here and there a weak point, rushing ammunition to the unceasing guns. Once a captain standing between them was shot down, and often they were implored to leave their exposed position, always in vain.[1] Superiority of numbers, reliable officers, the superb discipline of the Spanish troops, might have won the battle of Nördlingen, without the untrained direction of the two princes, but for their courage alone they deserved the acclamation with which all Europe and their own soldiers later received them.

In the heat of midday, Horn's men could do no more; he sent a scout to Bernard, saying that he was retiring across the valley, behind Bernard's own lines, to a farther ridge where he could entrench himself for the night. He relied meanwhile on his colleague to cover him while he crossed the valley.

This was the moment for which the enemy had waited. They abandoned their position before the town and charged, imperialists and Spaniards together, on Bernard's already tired troops, the cry 'Viva España' vibrating deafeningly through the dust. Desperately Bernard rallied his men, galloping from battery to battery, pouring curses on the sweating gunners, threatening the tortures of hell if they gave way an inch.[2] But he had no chance. Breaking in panic, his men fled, and Horn's exhausted troops, at that moment crossing the valley, received broadside the full impact of the flight. Spent horses dropped under their riders; Bernard's charger fell, but one of his dragoons gave him his own shabby little nag, still brisk and fresh, and on this the prince fled. The rest of the story was tersely dictated by the King of Hungary in his quarters that night. 'The enemy scattered in such a way that ten horses are

---

[1] Gualdo Priorato, *Historia di Ferdinando III Imperatore*. Vienna, 1672, p. 492; Chemnitz, ii, p. 534.
[2] Poyntz, p. 111.

not found together. Horn is taken, Weimar — no one knows whether he be dead or living.'[1]

The victors reckoned the dead of the enemy at seventeen thousand, the prisoners at four thousand,[2] nearly all of whom, officers and men, went into imperial service. The Cardinal-Infant that night took up his quarters in a small farm, handing over the large house which had been found for him to the wounded.[3] Later, he sent fifty of the captured standards to Spain and an image of the Virgin, which he had found with the eyes put out, among the Swedish booty.[4]

A few days later the Emperor, at Ebersdorf near Vienna, on a hunting expedition, came in from his day's sport to find the Empress waiting for him with a messenger newly come from Nördlingen. At the news of the victory, Ferdinand could find no words, the pride of the father, the devotion of the Catholic and the relief of the dynast finding spontaneous issue only in tears of speechless joy.[5] All that had been lost at Lützen had been won again at Nördlingen, and the enemy who had shattered Tilly and the troops of the Catholic League had fallen before the God-directed swords of Ferdinand of Hungary and Ferdinand of Spain.

V I

It looked like the end for the Protestant Cause and the German Liberties; it was the end for Sweden. Never again would Oxenstierna overawe Germany. Forty miles west of Nördlingen, at Göppingen in Württemberg, two days after the disaster, Bernard wrote to Oxenstierna. As late as September

---

[1] *Bandhauers Tagebuch*, p. 313; the account of the battle is composed, except where other references are given, from Horn's account in *Brefvexling*, II, viii; from the Spanish account in AEDO Y GALLART, p. 130 f.; from the contemporary documents in CANOVAS DEL CASTILLO, *Estudios del Reinado de Felipe* IV, pp. 427-42; more recent authorities include LEO, *Schlacht bei Nördlingen*. Halle, 1900, and the brief but masterly comments of DELBRUECK, pp. 243-8.

[2] Oxenstierna, on the other hand, reckoned the total loss at twelve thousand, killed and prisoners. His view is probably as generous on the one side as that of the imperialists on the other. *Brefvexling*, I, i, p. 208.

[3] AEDO Y GALLART, pp. 146-7.

[4] Ibid., p. 151.

[5] PRIORATO, *Historia*, III, 1672, p. 495; *Annales*, XII, p. 1230.

9th, he still had no news of Horn, did not know whether he was alive or dead, captive or free, nor what had become of the Swedish army.[1] He had sent messages to all the scattered garrisons in Franconia and Württemberg, ordering immediate evacuation, so that with such as he could collect of the fliers and with the fresh troops from the garrisons he could make a stand farther west — much farther west. He spoke of holding the Rhine, he who not ten months before had taken Regensburg, he whose troops had held the Wornitz and the Lech. It meant retreat to a defensive position a hundred and fifty miles behind his original line; it meant the total severance of all contact with the Saxons under Arnim and the Swedes under Baner in Silesia. It meant the abandonment of the Duchy of Franconia whose title Bernard carried. And even then, he was uncertain whether he could hold the Rhine.[2]

The news reached Frankfort-on-the-Main, barely outdistancing the fugitive peasants who fled before the Catholic advance like birds before a storm. Once again Oxenstierna passed a sleepless night wrestling with his anxiety.[3] Feuquières was less distressed; for him the defeat of the Swedes, although too drastic to be altogether pleasing, had its fortunate side. The deputies of the Heilbronn League flocked to implore his protection, the two Saxon Circles, terrified at another possible advance of the Roman Church into the north, joined the alliance and all threw themselves on the mercy of Richelieu.[4]

From the religious point of view the Battle of Nördlingen was as shattering a victory for the Catholics as Breitenfeld had been a defeat; dynastically it raised the prestige of the Hapsburg to the heights; in the military field it was the death-blow to the reputation of the Swedish army and the crowning glory of the Spanish;[5] but politically it gave Richelieu the direction of the Protestant Cause and rang up the curtain for the last act of the German tragedy, in which Bourbon, and Hapsburg fought out their struggle openly at last to the inevitable end.

Nördlingen, in so many ways a more dramatic and a more immediate catastrophic battle than Breitenfeld, marks no

---

[1] *Brefvexling*, II, vii, p. 235.
[2] Ibid., I, i, pp. 208-9; FEUQUIÈRES, II, pp. 422, 426, 427-9.
[3] ARCHENHOLTZ, II, p. 46.   [4] FEUQUIÈRES, II, p. 426.
[5] CANOVAS, *Bosquejo Historico*, p. 253.

period in European history. The applause of the one side, the lamentations of the other, which echoed at the time no less loudly than after Breitenfeld, faded into silence. In the struggle between the two dynasties the Bourbon, with sounder politics and more resilient power, must defeat the Hapsburg, cankered with the dry-rot of Spain. The Battle of Nördlingen, the advance which followed, the rejuvenation of the dynasty under the two princes, was nothing but the sudden flaring of a guttering candle. The princes who, on the day after the battle rode along their lines to the re-echoing shouts of 'Viva España'[1] went on their way — the one to long years of anxiety and defeat, the other, happier perhaps, to die in Brussels before the final extinction of the hopes which he had raised.

Immediately after the victory, the King of Hungary urged his cousin to stay in Germany for the autumn and complete the work, but the Cardinal-Infant, not without reason, wished to reach Brussels as soon as he could.[2] The Netherlands were, after all, his true destination. Ferdinand's entreaty did not prevail, and almost immediately after the battle the Spanish and imperialist armies again divided, the Cardinal-Infant making for the Rhine with some German auxiliaries under Piccolomini, the King of Hungary striking westwards across Franconia and Württemberg.

Victory had re-established the morale of the imperial troops, and in the advance across Württemberg they carried everything in front of them. Johann von Werth, the leader of the Bavarian cavalry, a soldier risen from the ranks, and Isolani, the commander of the Croatian contingent, bore down the feeble resistance of the last Protestant outposts. Göppingen fell on September 15th, Heilbronn on the 16th, Weiblingen on the 18th; on the 20th the King of Hungary entered Stuttgart and established the control of the Emperor over all Württemberg. Meanwhile, Piccolomini and the Spaniards made towards the Rhine; on September 18th they took Rothenburg, on the 19th crossed the Main, on the 30th seized Aschaffenburg, on October 15th Schweinfurt, while the Heilbronn League removed hastily from Frankfort to the supposed safety of Mainz. Oxenstierna remained to receive the flying troops, a bare twelve thousand

[1] AEDO Y GALLART, p. 146.   [2] LONCHAY ET CUVELIER, III, p. 21.

379

men, demoralized, mutinous and unpaid.[1] He saw that to save the situation he had no choice but to make Bernard sole commander-in-chief and implore money from Richelieu.[2]

The tide of disaster mounted still, the limbs of the Heilbronn League were lopped off before Oxenstierna's despairing eyes. Nuremberg had been taken on September 23rd, on October 5th Kenzingen, on October 21st Würzburg. In south Germany only Augsburg and the fortress of Hohentwiel held out; on the Main, Hanau; in the southern Rhineland, Strasbourg and Heidelberg. Two of the four Circles in the original Heilbronn League were altogether lost, and of the towns all the chief members in central and south Germany save Augsburg alone. No money could be raised on the taxes of an already exhausted Sweden, where they were talking wildly of immediate peace,[3] and the resources of the German allies were cut off one by one. From Baner in Silesia came depressing news that the Electors of Saxony and Brandenburg were both ready to abandon the Swedes, that the hungry and ill-clad troops in north Germany could get no money from the people, that quarters had been refused to them in Silesia,[4] and that they must withdraw as far as Magdeburg and Halberstadt for the winter.[5]

In these circumstances Bernard and the remnant of the Heilbronn League negotiated desperately with Richelieu. On November 1st, 1634, they signed the so-called Treaty of Paris, by which Louis XIII offered twelve thousand men and half a million livres to be paid at once,[6] in return for a guarantee for the Catholic faith in Germany, the cession of Schlettstadt and Benfeld in Alsace, and the control of the bridge-head at Strasbourg. No truce or peace was to be made without France, nor was her government bound to enter the war openly, nor to promise more than the twelve thousand men.[7] Axel Oxenstierna, who had had to agree to the negotiations, here made his last stand, refusing to ratify the completed treaty in the name of the little Queen of Sweden.[8] His judgment was accurate, for he saw

[1] *Brefvexling*, II, vii, p. 241.   [2] Ibid., I, i, pp. 209-11.
[3] Ibid., II, iii, p. 347 f.
[4] See Baner's letters throughout 1634 in *Brefvexling*, II, vi, pp. 122-50.
[5] *Brefvexling*, I, i, p. 216.   [6] Ibid., p. 224.
[7] *Sverges Traktater*, v, ii, pp. 241-54; LUNIG, v, i, pp. 297-301.
[8] *Brefvexling mellan Oxenstierna och Svenska Regeringen. Händlingar rörande Skandinaviens Historia*, XXXII, pp. 198, 201, 206; XXXIII, p. 3.

that Richelieu, jubilating in the downfall of his too powerful ally, had not yet realized how great was his own peril. When he grasped that, as he must, he would modify his terms. Cool in the midst of overwhelming danger, Oxenstierna played for time.

Early in November the Cardinal-Infant crossed the Flemish frontier and entered Brussels in state, not as a priest but as a soldier, dressed in scarlet and cloth of gold, and girt with the sword of his Burgundian ancestor, Charles V.[1] On the Rhine, Bernard of Saxe-Weimar withdrew to the left bank to join the French troops hastily raised to help him,[2] and the comparative peace of winter settled on Germany.

VII

The winter of 1634-35 was the last respite before the open conflict between Bourbon and Hapsburg, the last moment, in theory at least, when peace for the Empire was possible. It was the period at which John George, dragging the Elector of Brandenburg after him, made a stand for and obtained a settlement; but the terms intended to secure peace were twisted into a new alliance for war.

The negotiations which led to the Peace of Prague on the one hand, to the declaration of war by France on Spain on the other, are significant of a new epoch. The imperial situation had developed a further problem, and the background of the conflict, insensibly changing for the past seventeen years, had completed its metamorphosis. The ageing Emperor, the Electors of Saxony, Brandenburg and Bavaria, the Swedish Chancellor and Richelieu, these still held on their course, but all around them had arisen a new generation of soldiers and statesmen. War-bred, they carried the mark of their training in a caution, cynicism and contempt for spiritual ideals foreign to their fathers.

When lust and private interest gain the upper hand of

[1] AEDO Y GALLART, p. 194.
[2] *Brefvexling*, I, i, p. 224; AVENEL, IV, pp. 603, 618-19.

disorganized society, the most religious of crusades must lose
its sacred character, but the Thirty Years War lost what little
spiritual meaning it had had for other causes. 'The great
spiritual contest', says Ranke, 'had completed its operation on
the minds of men.'[1] The reason was not far to seek. While
increasing pre-occupation with natural science had opened up
a new philosophy to the educated world, the tragic results of
applied religion had discredited the Churches as the directors
of the State. It was not that faith had grown less among the
masses; even among the educated and the speculative it still
maintained a rigid hold, but it had grown more personal, had
become essentially a matter between the individual and his
Creator.

Frederick of Bohemia had lost his crown because he had
offended his subjects in order to obey his Calvinist chaplain;
his son, Prince Rupert, Calvinist in religion and morality,
fought in England for Anglicans and Catholics against Presby-
terians and Independents, because his religion was for him,
as for most of his generation, nobody's business but his own.

Inevitably the spiritual force went out of public life, while
religion ran to seed amid private conjecture, and priests and
pastors, gradually abandoned by the State, fought a losing battle
against philosophy and science. While Germany suffered in
sterility, the new dawn rose over Europe, irradiating from Italy
over France, England and the North. Descartes and Hobbes
were already writing, the discoveries of Galileo, Kepler,
Harvey, had taken their places as part of the accepted stock of
common knowledge. Everywhere lip-service to reason replaced
the blind impulses of the spirit.

Essentially it was only lip-service. The small group of
educated men who appreciated the value of the new learning
disseminated little save the shadow of their knowledge. A new
emotional urge had to be found to fill the place of spiritual
conviction; national feeling welled up to fill the gap.

The absolutist and the representative principle were
losing the support of religion; they gained that of nationalism.
That is the key to the development of the war in its latter period.
The terms Protestant and Catholic gradually lose their vigour,

[1] RANKE, *Sämmtliche Werke*, XXXVIII; *Die römischen Päpste*, p. 376.

the terms German, Frenchman, Swede, assume a gathering menace. The struggle between the Hapsburg dynasty and its opponents ceased to be the conflict of two religions and became the struggle of nations for a balance of power. A new standard of right and wrong came into the political world. The old morality cracked when the Pope set himself up in opposition to the Hapsburg Crusade, and when Catholic France, under the guidance of her great Cardinal, gave subsidies to Protestant Sweden. Insensibly and rapidly after that, the Cross gave place to the flag, and the 'Sancta Maria' cry of the White Hill to the 'Viva España' of Nördlingen.

If Ferdinand of Hungary, who was rapidly filling his father's place at the head of the state, was to control the new situation he must make one essential choice. He must choose whether he would be a German or an Austrian sovereign. He chose Austria. It had long been inevitable that he should. The dynasty belonged in temperament and character to the south; Ferdinand's northward thrust had been buffeted back by the King of Sweden, and he had himself sacrificed Wallenstein's Empire of the Elbe to Spain. Religion, his weapon for the unification of Germany, so powerful long ago in Styria when his world was young, had broken in his hand; all that emerged from his life's work were the confederate states of Austria, Bohemia, Hungary, Silesia, Styria, Carinthia, Carniola and Tyrol, the rough outline of the Austro-Hungarian Empire.

The King of Hungary was neither narrow-minded nor unforeseeing, but his faculties were conditioned by his background, and his actions by his immediate experience. His father had been born and brought up while the shadow of the medieval Empire was still on the dynasty. His birthplace was the provincial court of a Styrian archduke, but the capital of his world was Frankfort-on-the-Main where the imperial elections were held, the spiritual centre of the Holy Roman Empire. To young Ferdinand, Frankfort-on-the-Main had for long been a hostile city, remote beyond the lines of foreign armies, the headquarters of the Swedish invaders. Born in 1608, he could hardly remember a time when the German states had lived in outward peace and open confederation. The Empire was to him no more than a geographical term for a collection of warring fragments. Inevitably he turned to the more obvious solidarity of Vienna, Prague, Pressburg, and built his world on that.

This was the change in the background. There had grown up, too, another problem in the war. From the beginning the question of the mercenary army had been potentially difficult; nearly a generation of warfare had immensely increased its gravity until it became not a subsidiary but a dominant problem. The army as an entity had to be carefully considered and tactfully handled, as tactfully as any political ally. This had been apparent on the imperial side during the counter-plotting of the Viennese government against Wallenstein, on the Protestant side in the negotiations which stilled the mutiny of 1633.

The armies themselves were the last to be affected by the growth of nationalism. The Swedish army had had a strong sense of patriotism when it landed with the King, but since then it had been diluted with so many German and foreign recruits that the original feeling was gone. Certain native regiments in the Spanish army felt strongly for their national honour, and later, in the French army, this emotion was to be developed, but the greater number of the soldiers fighting in 1634 regarded themselves merely as soldiers. All peoples were represented among both parties. Among those who signed the Pilsen manifesto there had been Scots, Czechs, Germans, Italians, Flemish and French, a Pole, a Croatian and a Roumanian. Among the Swedish commanders there were, or had been, the Hessian Falkenberg, the Bohemian Thurn, the Pole Schafflitsky, the Scots Ruthven and Ramsey, the Netherlander Mortaigne, the Frenchman Duval. Among the lesser ranks there were Irishmen, Englishmen, Germans, Bohemians, Poles, French, even occasional Italians. In Bavarian regiments there were Turks and Greeks as well as Poles, Italians and Lorrainers.[1] There were Catholics in Protestant armies, Protestants among the Catholics; an imperialist regiment had once mutinied as a protest against the celebration of Mass.[2]

Among these men, each out for his own livelihood, it was vain to think even of military loyalty when pay or food were short. Of two thousand Württembergers who joined Horn in

[1] RIEZLER, *Geschichte*, VI, p. 164.   [2] Ibid., V, p. 536.

1632 at least half deserted in less than a month;[1] the mixed garrison under Spanish command at Philippsburg gave the place up to the Swedes by the simple means of changing sides;[2] in Silesia, when Wallenstein took Steinau, the discontented 'Swedish' army under Thurn and Duval in the surrounding outposts joined the invaders without hesitation.[3] The case of Arnim, who had held high command on both sides, was paralleled, with less credit, by several others. Werth spontaneously offered to leave the Bavarians for the French,[4] Kratz changed from a responsible position under Wallenstein to a responsible position with the Swedes,[5] Goetz began under Mansfeld and ended under Maximilian of Bavaria, Franz Albrecht of Saxe-Lauenburg fought for the imperialists, for the Swedes, and then for the imperialists again. Even Aldringer was suspected of arranging to change sides just before his death.[6] There were other curious cases. Conrad Wiederhold, governor of Hohentwiel, the fortress overlooking Constance, indignant when his Employer, the regent of Württemberg, bade him evacuate the place to the imperialists, put his own staunch Protestantism above the Duke's feebleness and went on holding the castle — for Bernard of Weimar.

By this time, too, the proportion of the troops to the civilian population had altered radically. Recruiting never ceased in the lands through which the armies passed, and as the life of the peasant and artisan grew harder, the attraction of a soldier's life increased. Ambitious young men were drawn by the tale of those few, those very few, who had risen from the ranks to the highest places of all; their names were a talisman to the new recruit — Werth, Stalhans, St. André.[7] Others thought merely of pay and plunder, of the comparative security of being the robber and not the robbed. With the growth of the armies grew the huge conglomerate mass of the camp followers;

---

[1] *Brefvexling*, II, viii, p. 101. [2] *Annales*, XII, p. 1299.
[3] HALLWICH, *Wallensteins Ende*, I, p. 633.
[4] AVENEL, V, pp. 380-1.
[5] Taken at Nördlingen, he was beheaded as a traitor; he had made the error of deserting from one side to the other without going through the formality of resigning his commission!
[6] H. HALLWICH, *Aldringens letzter Ritt. Mitteilungen der Verein für die Geschichte der Deutschen in Böhmen*, XLV, p. 27.
[7] GRIMMELSHAUSEN, *Simplicissimus*.

it grew faster than the army, so that the old reckoning of a man and a boy for each soldier was no longer adequate, and the women, children, servants and riff-raff who trailed along in the rear outnumbered the soldiers by three or four to one, later even by five to one. It was inevitable that this huge mass, with its particular interests, its future, its women and its children to consider, should exhibit the peculiarities of a self-conscious class and fight for its own advantage. Arnim had, for instance, been afraid that his troops would mutiny if they learnt of his peace negotiations.[1] 'This widespread state', Marshal Baner called his army and, after stilling the mutiny of 1633, Oxenstierna observed that he had elevated the army to the rank of a political Estate;[2] he was not wrong to do so, for they were as large as any Estate in Sweden.

These developments, the shifting of the background and the independent significance of the armies, give its peculiar character to the latter end of the war and more particularly to the negotiations surrounding the Peace of Prague.

VIII

John George and his general had been negotiating for peace throughout 1634, to the profound annoyance of Baner, who was co-operating with Arnim, and of Oxenstierna. The Elector had exerted all his influence to prevent the two Saxon Circles from joining the Heilbronn League, and indeed to break up the League itself.[3] He honestly wanted peace and the expulsion of the invaders, so did also the Emperor, so much so that he was prepared now to do what he had refused to do four years before at Regensburg, namely to abandon the Edict of Restitution. This was the sacrifice of his spiritual to his temporal policy which Eggenberg had advocated all along and which, had he made it at Regensburg in 1630, would have united Germany against Gustavus Adolphus. Since the sacrifice had to be made in the end, it was regrettable that it should not have been made

---

[1] GAEDEKE, *Wallensteins Verhandlungen*, p. 163.
[2] *Brefvexling*, II, vi, p. 529.
[3] *Brefvexling mellan Oxenstierna och Svenska Regeringen. Händlingar rörande Skandinaviens Historia*, xxx, pp. 84-5.

earlier, but Ferdinand was not in the habit of abandoning his policy without a struggle.

Before the Battle of Nördlingen confirmed the Hapsburg position, he had gone so far as to ask only the *status quo* of 1620, but no sooner was the victory won than he increased his claim, and demanded all the land which the Church had regained up to November 1627.[1] There was nothing intolerable in that. Indeed the apparent moral victory of John George's moderate party was complete, for the Edict of Restitution was gone and the Emperor had agreed at last to a compromise. Ferdinand's moral retreat served for cover to his political advance. The winning of John George was likely to go far to reunite the leading princes of Germany under imperial dominance.

This intelligent opportunism may have been in part the work of the King of Hungary who was largely responsible for the negotiations. The terms were temptingly generous. There was complete amnesty for everyone except only the Bohemian exiles and the family of Frederick. John George was to have control of the bishopric of Magdeburg. Above all, private leagues among German princes were henceforward declared illegal, although John George was to continue in semi-independent command of his own army as the Emperor's ally.

In its unheated and reasonable treatment of the problem, its broad basis of compromise, this was the finest work for peace yet achieved on either side — in appearance at least. The soundness of its theory was proved by the acceptance of much of its matter at the ultimate Peace of Westphalia. But its weakness in practice was shown by the events immediately surrounding its ratification. For the negotiators on the imperial side worked with only a partial hope of peace and a shrewd consideration of the possibility of continued war. If the settlement failed as a settlement, it must at least serve to bind John George, and any who cared to follow him, to the imperial cause. The treaty was open to all, and if all the combatants signed it, then it would bring peace indeed; but in the meantime it must be generous enough to tempt as many as possible of the moderates. The refusal to sign must appear wholly unreasonable, so that those who continued in arms — the French, the

[1] HURTER, *Friedensbestrebungen Ferdinands des II*, p. 71.

Swedes and their dwindling allies — should appear as enemies of the commonweal. Such was the theory. If it worked in practice, it would identify the imperial alliance with the general good and assemble the signatories under the Hapsburg banner. But while Swedish troops remained in Germany the war would go on and the Peace of Prague would be only a new and all-embracing alliance in Ferdinand's interests.

At the last minute a dozen obstacles threatened the negotiations. The Emperor had a last qualm over the Edict of Restitution and, for a dizzy moment, contemplated buying the King of France out of the war by the gift of Alsace and thus destroying the financial support of his enemies. The King of Hungary put a stop to this; an Austrian and a Hapsburg before he was a Catholic, he preferred to cede Church land in Germany rather than to give away the dominions of his house and invite France to control the Rhine.

On the Protestant side, the Elector Palatine and the King of England clamoured of betrayal,[1] and nearer home prophets appeared among the people in Saxony itself foretelling a heavenly vengeance on John George if he forsook the Cause. His wife was against the peace[2] and so also was Arnim. The unhappy general had worked hard for a settlement ever since 1632 — when the Peace of Prague was all but concluded he was so filled with joy that he even composed a poem on it[3] — but he could not in honour accept a treaty which excluded the Swedes.[4] He would not buy a useless settlement by the cynical desertion of his allies. The treaty was not a peace, but a new alliance for war — and with the opposite side.

The King of Hungary signed a truce, which later became a final truce, with Saxony at Laun on February 28th, 1635.[5] The emotions of Oxenstierna at this news may well be imagined. The desertion of John George was now inevitable, and he would probably carry with him George William of Brandenburg, who had failed to secure from Sweden a guarantee that he could keep

---

[1] DÄSSLER, Diplomatischer Zusammenstoss zwischen England und Sachsen. Neues Archiv für Sächsische Geschichte, LVI, p. 113 f.

[2] OPEL, Eine politische Denkschrift. Neues Archiv für Sächsische Geschichte, VIII, p. 189; see also HITZIGRATH, Die Publicistik des Prager Friedens. Halle, 1880.

[3] IRMER, Hans Georg von Arnim, Leipzig, 1874, pp. 307. 316 f.

[4] Ibid., p. 316 f.   [5] LÜNIG, VI, i, pp. 391-3.

Pomerania. Richelieu was Oxenstierna's only hope, his only friend even, for Bernard of Saxe-Weimar, with the shameless opportunism of the mercenary, was blackmailing him. Oxenstierna had admitted to Feuquières after Nördlingen that he feared, without the restraining influence of Horn, that Bernard would be dangerous; Feuquières immediately hastened off privately to see Bernard and secure what remained of his army for France.[1] Too wily to be hurried, Bernard temporized, and in the winter of 1634-35 received and apparently considered requests from both Saxony and the Emperor to join them with what was left of his troops.[2] He was thus able to force Oxenstierna, the Heilbronn League and Feuquières to offer him anything that he requested if he would but agree to act in their interests. He played his cards with ruthless skill and secured what he wanted; in the spring of 1635 he was appointed commander-in-chief in Germany both for the Heilbronn League and the King of France. He demanded the power, independent of political control, to wage war and exact contributions as he pleased, and claimed a satisfactory indemnity in case of peace;[3] helpless, the politicians once again bowed before the indispensable soldier.

Oxenstierna's genius was to draw a qualified advantage out of every disadvantage. Although he was dependent on Richelieu to pay Bernard, yet Richelieu was partly dependent on him, since Bernard would not willingly abandon the advantages he could gain from a double mandate of command. So with the Saxon desertion; horrified as Oxenstierna was at the prospect of a hostile eastern and north-eastern Germany, he hastened to point out that Richelieu could not possibly dispense with the Swedish alliance now that the Emperor had strengthened himself by winning John George, and the only support left in the region of the Elbe was a contingent of the Swedish army under Baner.[4]

He had been right not to ratify that treaty of despair signed between the King of France and the Heilbronn League in November, for out of his own disaster, dangers to Richelieu

[1] ROESE, II, pp. 437-9.
[2] Ibid., pp. 444, 447.
[3] Ibid., pp. 457-61, 463-6.
[4] *Händlingar rörande Skandinaviens Historia*, XXXIII, p. 27 f.

were fast growing, and not on his own strength but on Richelieu's fears, he made better terms in the spring. The retreat of Bernard to the left bank of the Rhine, the advance of the Spaniards, within a perilous distance of the French frontier, the appearance of an active governor, the Cardinal-Infant, in the Netherlands, and the sudden revival and reunion of the Spanish and Austrian Hapsburg, awakened Richelieu to the fact that the defeat of the Swedes at Nördlingen had a singularly dangerous side.[1] Before the end of September news came that the Spaniards were raising still more armies in Sicily and Sardinia, and by October he feared sea attack on Provence.[2] Working rapidly, he made a new Dutch alliance in February 1635, the terms of which reflected his fears. Under pressure, he agreed to put an army of thirty thousand in the field against Spain and to leave the direction of the joint war to the Prince of Orange.[3]

Axel Oxenstierna, counting on the usual dilatory opening of the spring campaign, put off the conclusion of terms for another two months. Thinking it best to deal with the slippery Cardinal himself rather than with his still more slippery agents, he came in April to Paris where he was graciously received. The negotiations, in spite of the suspicion of both parties, went well: 'the French manner of negotiating is very strange and depends much on finesse',[4] Oxenstierna once complained, but it seemed that his own nordic method, 'un peu gothique et beaucoup finoise',[5] as Richelieu described it, was a match for it. On April 30th, 1635, they signed the Treaty of Compiègne. By this the French government, in return for the left bank of the Rhine from Breisach to Strasbourg, was to recognize Sweden as an equal ally, to give her the control of Worms, Mainz and Benfeld, to agree to make no peace without her, and to declare open war on Spain.[6] It was the best Oxenstierna could do, and it was infinitely better than the treaty of the

[1] See FEUQUIÈRES, pp. 429-30, 458.   [2] AVENEL, IV, pp. 612, 630.

[3] AITZEMA, II, pp. 117 ff., 198-201; *Mémoires de Frederic Henri*, p. 174; see also WADDINGTON, *La Republique des Provinces Unies*, pp. 421, 432-3; AVENEL, IV, p. 424.

[4] *Brefvexling mellan Oxenstierna och Svenska Regeringen. Händlingar rörande Skandinaviens Historia*, XXXIV, p. 12.

[5] AVENEL, IV, p. 735.

[6] *Sverges Traktater*, V, ii, pp. 18-19; see also *Brefvexling*, I, i, pp. 558-9.

previous November. Richelieu, with the greater resources, was bound to be the dominant partner, but at least the Chancellor had secured partnership and not mere vassalage for himself. Seeing that he had nothing to offer save a virtually bankrupt country under a quarrelsome regency, and Baner's mutinous troops in Halberstadt and Magdeburg, Oxenstierna had squeezed every drop of advantage from the situation.

On May 21st, 1635, in accordance with the obligations of the French government, a herald in the Grande Place at Brussels formally proclaimed that the most Christian King, Louis XIII of France, declared war on his Catholic Majesty, Philip IV of Spain. The technical excuse for the action was that Spanish troops had raided Treves and carried off the Elector prisoner; for the last three years he had been by treaty under the special protection of France.

At Vienna nine days later the terms of the Peace of Prague were published. They were open to any ruler who wished to sign them. The terms had been drawn up wholeheartedly on Saxony's side, and partially at least on the imperial side, with the intention of bringing peace to Germany. But the appearance of France as the ally of Sweden on the left bank of the Rhine, followed by the declaration of war by France on Spain, altered the situation. Those who subscribed to the Peace found that they had not merely to drive Swedish armies out of Germany but French also. And if they closed in conflict with France, they must make common cause with the King of Spain. The Peace of Prague was metamorphosed into an alliance for war, and those who signed it bound themselves to fight the battles of the House of Austria.

'Saxony has made his peace', wrote Richelieu, 'but that will have no effect on us save to make us renew our efforts to keep all in train.'[1] The last act of the German tragedy had begun.

[1] AVENEL, v, pp. 82-3.

THE STRUGGLE FOR THE RHINE
1635 — 1639

Le sentiment de Sa Majesté est, que vous teniez toutes sortes de propositions de paix pour non seulement suspectes, mais même très dangereuses, comme moyens desquels vos ennemis se voudraient servir pour vous surprendre.

FEUQUIÈRES

THE STRUGGLE FOR THE RHINE

I

THE Emperor's position in Germany was stronger than it had ever been. His armies and those of his allies occupied almost the whole right bank of the Rhine, Württemberg, Swabia and Franconia. The Austrian lands could enjoy a respite while these new conquests were bled to support the troops. John George had made himself the subordinate ally of Ferdinand, and Maximilian of Bavaria, protesting but helpless, shortly after did likewise.

He had no choice. If he refused to sign the Peace of Prague the only alternative was to join with Richelieu; but Richelieu and his ally Oxenstierna had alike embraced the cause of his dispossessed and now fatherless Palatine cousins. Neither for the first nor for the last time was Maximilian's retreat cut off by that ambitious folly of 1622. He must subscribe therefore to the Peace of Prague, agree to the dissolution of the Catholic League and the enrolment of all his remaining troops under the imperial command, on the same terms as John George of Saxony. For the first time in his career he was constrained to espouse the cause of the House of Austria without any guarantee of his own control.

Ferdinand sweetened the pill with some cheap concessions. Maximilian was confirmed in his Electorate, his brother in the bishopric of Hildesheim. A further bribe was offered: Maximilian's childless wife had died, and Ferdinand suggested his own daughter, the Archduchess Maria Anna, a princess nearly forty years his junior, as her successor. Maximilian accepted. The marriage was quickly solemnized in Vienna, and within a few weeks the bridegroom paid for his bride by ratifying the Peace of Prague.

The Elector of Brandenburg, the Dukes of Saxe-Coburg,

Holstein, Mecklenburg, Pomerania, the regent of Württemberg, the princes of Anhalt, Hesse-Darmstadt, and Baden, the towns of Lübeck, Frankfort-on-the-Main, Ulm, Worms, Speier and Heilbronn had already set their hands to the deceptive settlement. The constructive diplomacy of the King of Hungary had placed his father at the head of a coalition which isolated the small Calvinist minority and forced them into the unpopular position of disturbers of the peace and allies of the foreigner. The exiled Elector Palatine, the Landgrave of Hesse-Cassel and the Duke of Brunswick-Luneburg were left alone against a united Empire.

Outside Germany the Emperor's position appeared almost equally strong. The enmity of the Swedish government brought him the friendship of Christian of Denmark. He cherished it for an emergency: it might be very convenient to explode a sudden mine behind Oxenstierna's back. Ladislas IV, who had succeeded the wily Sigismund as King of Poland, was at first a less certain ally. He had agreed to a twenty-six years' truce with Sweden and contemplated marrying a no less suspect person than Elizabeth, eldest daughter of Frederick of Bohemia.[1] The King of Hungary intervened with the counter-offer of his sister, the Archduchess Cecilia Renata, incontrovertibly, from all but the personal point of view, the better match. Ladislas let himself be tempted and became once more the ally of Austria.

For the Spanish branch of the family the European situation was equally favourable. England, whose petty onslaughts on. Spanish shipping could be a source of great annoyance, slept while her navy rotted. The attempts of the Dutch and the Swedes to arouse her failed signally. In the Netherlands, the Cardinal-Infant by his tact and charm repeated the feat of Don John sixty years earlier, in pacifying the Flemish;[2] now that France and the United Provinces were both actively in arms against them, they feared that they would be not liberated but torn in pieces between the invaders, and they clung to the House of Austria as to the protectors of their national integrity.

In the United Provinces, although apprehension of the results

---

[1] FEUQUIÈRES, III, p. 41.
[2] GUALDO PRIORATO, *Historia delle Guerre* Part I, p. 240.

of Nördlingen had temporarily silenced it, a very large peace party did exist. The popularity of the Prince of Orange was ebbing; there were many in the state who feared the domination of the House of Orange more than they feared Spain. Inevitably the existence of this group would tell in time on the conduct of the war.

Yet the House of Austria failed to make full use of these advantages, and the revival was foredoomed. Had Philip IV and Olivarez allowed some licence to the strength and intelligence of their allies in Austria and the Netherlands, all might have been well. Instead, they insisted on personally directing affairs, and forced the Emperor to obey them in return for their subsidies. Secretly they annulled the powers of the Cardinal-Infant by giving his nominal subordinate, and their own creature, Aytona, a mandate to place the orders of Madrid above those of the Cardinal.[1] Totally incompetent to solve the simplest problems of their own government, Olivarez and his King were determined on absolute dominance over the men of greater intelligence and better information who were actually on the scene of action in Germany and the Netherlands.

There was no remedy for the Cardinal-Infant's predicament. He was governor under the King of Spain's control and could not protest. The Emperor and the King of Hungary might perhaps have demanded greater liberty, had they not needed the bullion from the Peruvian mines. And in the end they sold themselves for nothing. When, inevitably, disaster overwhelmed the government of Philip IV at home, he himself needed all his money, the supply failed and Spain dragged down Austria in her fall.

I I

The danger inherent in the Hapsburg position was concealed under immediate successes and the years 1635 and 1636 were the most disastrous for the Bourbon and the Swedish cause in all the war. No sooner was the Peace of Prague signed than

[1] LONCHAY ET CUVELIER, III, pp. 18-19.

Baner's troops mutinied. Of the twenty-three thousand men under his command hardly a tenth were Swedes, the rest of all nations, but predominantly German.[1] Saxon agents worked among these men, pointing out that both their duty and their interests should make them desert the Swedes. Their desertion would force Oxenstierna to make peace. By not making peace after Nördlingen he had sacrificed their lives in a hopeless cause, for he could not pay them and there was no hope of victory.[2]

The rising discontent was inadequately stilled in August 1635, Oxenstierna handling the rebellious officers as allies and equals, and signing a formal treaty with them for their allegiance. But the continued agitation of Saxon agents soon had the cauldron boiling again, and Oxenstierna, after a desperate effort to raise money from his allies,[3] left it to Baner to soothe his army by any means he could. The marshal, a coarse, outspoken ruffian, had neither the diplomacy necessary for such a situation nor enough of the brute force which he could doubtless have used effectively had the mutineers been in a minority. By October he was in despair; whole regiments disregarded his orders, and he frankly admitted to Oxenstierna that he intended either to surrender in person to John George or at best to bluff it out and make a private settlement for himself and his few loyal Swedes, letting the mutineers go their own way.[4] This imminent catastrophe, which would have meant the loss of the Elbe valley and the final cutting of communications between Stockholm and the Chancellor on the Rhine, was averted at the last minute of the eleventh hour. The truce signed with Poland released a great number of newly recruited Swedish troops who had been held in readiness against a possible Polish war, and these joined Baner just in time to swing the balance narrowly in his favour.[5] The mutineers, hopeful of a successful campaign and more booty, saw that they could probably get better terms from Baner's fears than from John George. They agreed to remain loyal to Sweden. Actual mutiny was stilled; of the re-establishment of

[1] LORENTZEN, p. 53.
[2] *Händlingar rörande Skandinaviens Histora*, XXXVI, pp. 368 ff.
[3] Ibid., p. 375.
[4] *Brefvexling*, II, vi, p. 225.   [5] LORENTZEN, p. 63.

reasonable discipline there was still no question. 'I must deplore the fact', wrote Baner, 'that every officer gives orders as he pleases.'[1] He could only deplore it, for any injudicious assertion of his authority might precipitate a new crisis. Nevertheless, he used the renewed loyalty of his army to effect a rapid advance before the winter, surprised the outpost of Dömitz on the Elbe and defeated the Saxons at Goldberg, thus encouraging his troops once again to believe in his leadership. There was one advantage to Sweden in the loss of her German allies; the troops could now consider all the country as hostile and replenish their stores by seizure even more drastic than that which they had permitted themselves while the farce of protective alliance continued.

Yet even this advance of the Swedish marshal and his mixed army concealed the controlling hand of France, for the intervention of a French diplomat, had alone completed the Polish truce in time to prevent Baner's disaster.[2]

In the south and south-west matters had taken an even graver turn. After a siege of nearly six months Augsburg surrendered, the imperialists entering a city almost of the dead, in which the people looked like ghosts, and the very soldiers fainted at their posts. They had been eating cats, rats and dogs for three months past, and eight weeks before the surrender the citizens were cutting up the hides of cattle, soaking and chewing them. A woman confessed to having cooked and eaten the body of a soldier who had died in her house. In spite of all, the conquerors celebrated their victory by a banquet, carousing far into the night while the hungry burghers listened and wondered dumbly when and whence provisions would come for them.[3]

Hanau-on-the-Main, in conditions no less horrible,[4] held out with vain heroism for more than eighteen months. Once it was relieved, but was again re-invested and reduced; the commander, a Scot, Sir James Ramsay, by a curious concession obtained liberty to stay in the town as a private person.[5]

---

[1] *Brefvexling*, II, vi, p. 254.
[2] LORENTZEN, p. 63.
[3] *Chronik des Jakob Wagner*, pp. 55-69; *Annales*, XII, p. 1765.
[4] WILLE, *Hanau im Dreissigjaehrigen Krieg*, Hanau, 1888, p. 669.
[5] LUNDORP, IV, pp. 687-8.

The concession was misguided, for Ramsay at a later date used his influence to engineer a rising; the imperialists were too quick for him and he ended his bold if unscrupulous career as a prisoner in their hands.

On the Rhine, Philippsburg and Treves fell to the Spaniards in rapid succession, and Richelieu failing to send troops in time, Bernard could not relieve Heidelberg. In November Gallas invaded Lorraine and here came up with the newly recruited French army under the King in person. 'They were clad all in horsemen's coats of scarlet colour and silver lace;' wrote one of Gallas's astonished men, 'the next day they were all in bright armour and great feathers, wonderful beautiful to behold.'[1] The filthy, vermin-ridden veterans of the imperial army had not for many years seen anything so fine, but cold, hunger and disease made shorter work of the plumed Frenchmen than of Gallas's less decorative troops. Little by little, before the watchful eyes of the imperialists, the gay cavaliers 'sneaked and stole away', leaving Gallas master of the field.[2] But it was winter and bitterly cold; in all the hungry land there was no fodder for man or beast. Plague, bred that year by a drenching spring and a tropical summer, disorganized armies and states alike. Gallas withdrew towards Zabern, took up his winter quarters, commanding the gap in the Vosges and threatened France; but plague and hunger among his men nullified the threat.[3]

That year in the Low Countries the French, invading unexpectedly almost at the same moment as their declaration of war, defeated the Spanish forces near Namur[4] and marched to join the Prince of Orange at Maestricht; he however was dilatory in joining them[5], and the States ungratefully suggested that the French should leave Flanders alone and attack Spain iself.[6] The behaviour of the cautious Dutch arose more from political discretion than military negligence, but it proved more disastrous than could have been wished. It was doubtless difficult to strike a mean between fighting the Spaniards to the death and merely holding them off, but Frederick Henry had

[1] POYNTZ, p. 120.
[2] Ibid., loc. cit.
[3] *Chronik des Jakob Wagner*, p. 32.
[4] AVENEL, V, p. 30.
[5] Ibid., IV, p. 757.
[6] PRINSTERER, II, iii, pp. 78-9.

altogether miscalculated the zeal and popularity[1] of the Cardinal-Infant. Before the end of the year the French had retired in indignation, and Frederick Henry found that he had lost Diest, Goch, Gennep, Limburg, and Schenk. His borders were thus threatened in three places, and Maestricht, his most valuable conquest, was all but cut off.

French arms were more successful in the south, where Richelieu again contemplated forming a North Italian League against the Spaniards,[2] and launched two successful invasions, one against Franche-Comté[3] and another on the Val Telline. This latter was carried out by Rohan, the quondam leader of the Huguenot party, whose religion, it was felt, would endear him to the Protestant anti-Spanish party in the Grisons. This expectation was justified, for the Swiss rose under one of their pastors, the intransigent Jürg Jenatsch, and marched to the conquest and conversion of the Val Telline. Troops were sent from Tyrol and Milan to hold the key position; defeated in four successive engagements, they left Rohan master of the valley for the Swiss pastor, and the French King. But this was the only outstanding achievement of the year 1635, and Richelieu owed it far more to the personality, enthusiasm and religion of Rohan than to his troops.

The diplomacy of the Cardinal and his political ambitions were out of proportion to the military strength of the country. The knowledge of this had driven him to avoid open war for as long as he could. When it became inevitable he urged Feuquières to recruit for him in Germany,[4] complaining anxiously that the troops raised in France were unreliable, ill-trained, inclined to desert and in the main Protestant.[5] The nobility presented another difficulty; since the feudal theory of the army persisted still, it was hard to wage a war without increasing the power of any young nobleman who chose to recruit a troop or even a regiment on his lands, and the nobility as a class, and young noblemen in particular, were Richelieu's bane. He was afraid of any recrudescence of their pretensions against the monarchy. Besides they made

---

[1] *Relazione dagli Ambasciatori. Spagna*, ii, p. 108.
[2] AVENEL, V, pp. 103-8.   [3] Ibid., pp. 209-10.
[4] Ibid., IV, p. 606.   [5] Ibid., pp. 603, 606, 690.

insubordinate soldiers. One young gentleman, who was told that the bad condition of his company would be reported to the King, struck his senior officer a blow on the head, saying: 'Report that to the King.'[1] With troops of this kind Richelieu was unfitted to oppose the Hapsburg and their Spanish army.

Since 1633 he had been trying to win over Bernard of Saxe-Weimar. As always, his actions had a political as well as a military significance; Feuquières had warned him that the German princes were suspicious of French aggression on the Rhine, and he imagined that if he had a German general in his employ he would be more welcome as an ally than if he merely sent French marshals to fight for him.

Bernard had refused the offers made in 1633 because they were not good enough. In 1635 he proved more amenable; he had lost his duchy of Franconia at the battle of Nördlingen, and he knew now that Richelieu, and not Oxenstierna, might secure him something in its place. Already he had settled what that something was to be — the landgravate of Alsace. His ambition sorted well enough with Richelieu's designs, for Alsace conquered by a German in the pay of France would be as useful to him as Alsace conquered by French troops, while the distinction without difference would serve to calm the suspicions of his German allies. By June 1635, he was already spreading the rumour that Alsace was to be ear-marked by the French government as a reward for Bernard.[2]

The prince was not altogether easy to treat with, even though an understanding was ardently desired by both sides. He suspected the French methods of secrecy and took the same pleasure as the King of Sweden in exposing the discreet offers of their government to the judgment of the world. Feuquières approached him quietly one evening as he was riding round his camp with some of his staff and, choosing a moment when Bernard was a little separated from the others, made in low tones an offer of subsidies for the war and a reward afterwards. To his astonishment Bernard, raising his voice to a stentorian shout, announced that he was glad the French government

---

[1] LE COMTE DE CAIX DE SAINT-AYMOUR, *L'enlèvement d'une princesse de Hohenzollern au XVIIᵉ siècle. Revue des Deux Mondes*, July 1915, p. 146.
[2] AVENEL, V, p. 47.

was about to help him and he would hold them to their word, for certainly his men deserved some recompense.[1] Blunt as this method was, it was astonishingly cunning and effective; Richelieu's offer was soon known throughout the army, so that withdrawal was impossible, while Bernard's skilful mention of the interests and deserts of his men naturally enhanced his reputation among the ranks. For the mercenary leader the good opinion of his men was worth more than gold.

The summer's campaign was over before the treaty was signed. Bernard and a force of French auxiliaries under Cardinal de la Valette, after crossing the Rhine at Mainz, were forced to retire again to the left bank for the winter, since Bernard asserted without exaggeration that his officers were threatening to desert and his men were mutinous for lack of money.[2] The situation was grave, but Bernard was clever enough as a diplomatist to make the best use of it for the purpose of forcing up the terms which the French government offered. Richelieu could afford to haggle no more, but in October 1635 signed a contract with Bernard which was subsequently enlarged and ratified after a personal meeting in Paris: Bernard was to support an army of eighteen thousand men, six thousand horse and twelve thousand foot, for which the French government promised him four million livres in the year, together with a personal allowance of two hundred thousand, and the supreme command over any auxiliary troops they cared to send. Peace was not to be concluded unless he received full satisfaction for his losses, and he was to receive as his reward a yearly pension of a hundred and fifty thousand livres and, by a secret clause, the county of Hagenau and the landgravate of Alsace. It was not entirely clear whether Bernard's possession was to be wholly independent, but since the French government had no right save that of conquest by which to dispose of imperial land, the obvious interpretation was that Bernard should conquer Alsace for France and hold it under her. This at any rate was Richelieu's view: Bernard was later to give proof of a somewhat different interpretation. Another secret clause bound the prince to submit to orders from

[1] FEUQUIÈRES, III, pp. 211-13.
[2] Ibid., pp. 260-77.

Paris for the duration of the war.[1] Fertile in expedients, Richelieu took the additional precaution of trying to arrange for the marriage of his new ally to Rohan's daughter and for their double conversion to the Catholic faith.[2] By this scheme he would detach Bernard from his intractable Germanism and make him one with the French nobility; but beyond escorting the young lady two or three times to the theatre, Bernard does not appear to have lent himself to this plan.

Bernard's attitude to the treaty is one of the problems with which the nationalist has been busy for the last hundred years. With Alsace as with Franconia, Bernard may have had some plan for the detachment of these lands from foreign influence and the setting up of a German party based on his own territorial power. With Bernard as with Wallenstein, the sudden ending of his career before the completion of the plan leaves the historian groping. Bernard was highly conscious of his nation and theoretically at least of his duties towards it. He was devout, self-disciplined, masterful — qualities which easily produce in the mind of their possessor that belief in a mission common among fanatical leaders. That he should regard the freeing and uniting of Germany as such a mission is very possible. But such evidence as has survived is inconclusive and much of it at least is capable of another explanation. By profession a leader of one of those dangerous polyglot formations, an army of mercenaries, Bernard had at least some of the characteristics of a mercenary leader. More like Mansfeld than like Wallenstein in the smallness of his own personal resources, a younger son and landless, he was acquisitive of personal possessions. Franconia and Alsace may have meant more to him than Hagenau did to Mansfeld, but there is no proof that they did. The two aspects of Bernard's policy are not irreconcilable; throughout the course of history the patriot has often merged into the adventurer, the adventurer into the patriot, and Bernard himself was probably neither wholly the one nor wholly the other.

Richelieu had now an army, such as Ferdinand had had when he employed Wallenstein. He could not altogether rely on it, he could certainly not command it to do as he chose, but

---

[1] Lünig, viii, pp. 430-2.   [2] Brefvexling, ii, ii, p. 169.

he could rest assured that the soldier of fortune would do nothing to endanger his own future, and something to ensure the success of the government on which he relied for his reward. The only serious danger lay in Richelieu's inability to raise the money for his part of the contract. The Cardinal's administration, so brilliant in other respects, was financially unsound. He had no genius for the organization of revenue and had found the privileges and customs which obscured French finance too thick to cut down. Consequently, now that he had to bear the whole brunt of the war and keep armies on the Flemish, Italian and Spanish frontiers as well as pay Bernard and patrol the coasts, he had no resource but to raise the taxes.

The French taxes were paid in great measure by the poorest and stubbornest class in the country, the peasantry, and these people, the great majority of the population, were the foundation on which the country rested. Thrifty, hardworking and obstinate, they were quick to resent oppression. As early as 1630 the taxation had provoked riots at Dijon, in 1631 in Provence, in 1632 at Lyons. From 1635 onwards the disturbances increased in gravity and frequency, in the Bordeaux district, throughout Gascony and Perigord, in Anjou, in Normandy.[1] Inevitably this tried the resources of the government and drew off troops which should have been used on the frontiers. The complaints of Bernard, whose subsidies remained unpaid and whose troops were poorly reinforced, were met only with useless promises of help.[2]

The weakness of France caused Maximilian of Bavaria once again to initiate a policy. An immediate attack on Paris, he pointed out to the Emperor, would very probably bring the Cardinal to terms and end the war. The plan, received doubtfully at first, at length won the enthusiastic support of the Cardinal-Infant. At midsummer 1636 he asked Maximilian to send him Johann von Werth and the best of the Bavarian cavalry to co-operate with his own troops in Picardy, while Ferdinand arranged with Gallas to invade simultaneously by way of Franche-Comté.[3]

[1] AVENEL, V, p. 485; FAGNIEZ, Le Père Joseph a Ratisbonne. Revue Historique, XXVIII, pp. 306-7.
[2] ROESE, II, pp. 483, 509, 515-17; AVENEL, VI, p. 114; VIII, pp. 306-7.
[3] SCHULZE, pp. 31-40

The Cardinal-Infant's sloth in accepting the plan unhappily robbed it of part of its effect. Werth, imagining that the project was shelved, had allowed the equipment of his troops to get into a bad condition. Nevertheless, he joined the Cardinal-Infant at La Capelle, and the two with an army thirty-two thousand strong[1] swept into Picardy. Together they overran the country between Somme and Oise and sent the French defenders straggling back to Paris. On August 14th they occupied the commanding fortress of Corbie, close to Amiens on the Paris road.

In the south Gallas, assisted by Charles of Lorraine, advanced through the Belfort gap and occupied all Franche-Comté. Meanwhile Werth, outriding the main body of the army, took Roye and Montdidier and reached Compiègne. In Paris all was in tumult. The people cried out against Richelieu, and those nearest to the Court predicted his immediate fall, but both he and his master redeemed their popularity in the crisis. The Cardinal, constant in the face of overwhelming danger, won back the favour of the mob by his rapid measures for the safety of the city, and the King rode out in person to join his troops at Senlis and die in defence of his people.[2]

But the advance suddenly stopped, for Gallas was held up between Champlitte and Langres by Bernard of Saxe-Weimar until his troops melted with desertion and plague, and news of a Swedish advance in Brandenburg forced him to withdraw. The Cardinal-Infant could not risk the attack without him, and in November Maximilian, perturbed by the movements of the Hessian army on his rear, recalled Werth. The invaders both north and south sulkily withdrew.

The failure of the invasion was partly balanced for the Hapsburg by unexpected disaster to Richelieu's policy in the Val Telline. So long as Rohan, the Huguenot leader, was fighting the Catholic Spaniards to win back the valley for the Swiss Protestants, all went well; but when he set about making a peace which would be satisfactory both from the military and

[1] SCHULZE, p. 44 f.

[2] *Brefvexling*, II, ii, pp. 215-16, 222, 230, 231-2; AVENEL, V, pp. 514-674 *passim*; PUYSEGUR, *Mémoires sur les règnes de Louis XIII et XIV*. Paris, 1881, p. 197 f.; VINCART. *Relacion de la Campaña de Flandres en 1636*. Madrid, 1873.

the religious point of view to the government of Catholic France, the Swiss leaders grew indignant. Objecting bitterly to the terms he wished to impose, they went without his knowledge to consult with the Spaniards and, finding them now prepared to buy the right to use the valley at the cost of religious concessions, abandoned their French alliance and virtually expelled Rohan and his troops.[1] In that wild and mountainous country success depended wholly on the goodwill of the people; when Rohan lost that, he lost everything.

While the Hapsburg dynasty maintained its renewed strength in Europe, the Emperor Ferdinand was planning a decisive demonstration of imperial unity in Germany. But for the dispossessed Palatine princes, for Bernard of Saxe-Weimar, for William of Hesse-Cassel and the Duke of Brunswick-Lüneburg, he had all the rulers of Germany on his side. Three electors, Bavaria, Brandenburg and Saxony, were actually in arms for his cause; never before had he had so good a chance of achieving that final confirmation of his power, the election of his son as King of the Romans. To this end, and also for the propagation and confirmation of the Peace of Prague, he called an Electoral meeting, at Regensburg for the autumn of 1636.

He opened this assembly on September 15th[2] and, this time without French intervention, carried it through to a happy conclusion. The birth of a son to the Archduchess Maria Anna, the young wife of the aged Maximilian of Bavaria, seemed like the blessing of Heaven on his return to the Hapsburg alliance. The two other secular Electors, driven to choose between servitude to the Emperor or to Oxenstierna, had chosen the former at the Peace of Prague, and confirmed their choice by declaring war on their one-time ally in the spring of 1636. Lastly, the military prowess and the personal popularity of the young King of Hungary added one puff of wind to the sudden breeze of political confidence which was carrying the tired ship of the old Emperor to port.

On December 22nd, 1636, at Regensburg the King of Hungary was unanimously elected King of the Romans.[3]

[1] AVENEL, V, pp. 762-3; DUMONT, VI, pp. 146-7.
[2] LUNDORP, IV, pp. 576-80.   [3] Ibid., p. 606.

The princes demanded only that he should guarantee the appointment of German officers in the army as far as possible, should desist from unlimited quartering in the Empire, should prohibit his private Austrian chancery from meddling in imperial affairs, and should respect the constitution. This coronation oath was hardly more exacting, and was less likely to be effective, than that which the old Emperor had signed seventeen years before. Thus, at every point, the constitutional policy of Ferdinand II had succeeded: he had reconquered, strengthened and purified the Hapsburg lands of heresy, he had acquired his own army, forced the majority of the German princes to fight his war with and for him, and secured the succession of his son. Constitutionally the assembly of 1636 marks the highest point of Austrian imperial power in Germany.

The rule of the Cardinal-Infant was popular in the Netherlands, and the King of Hungary was ready to ascend the imperial throne over the dead body of the constitutional party. The Val Telline was secure, the right bank of the Rhine occupied, France had been invaded and Paris had all but fallen. A nervous and deserted Oxenstierna, a divided government in the United Provinces, alone clung to Richelieu; of the German opposition there were William of Hesse-Cassel with a small army in East Friesland, and George of Brunswick-Lüneburg with a smaller army on the Weser, both doing nothing, Bernard of Saxe-Weimar demanding French subsidies on the left bank of the Rhine, and the Elector Palatine enlisting the sympathy of the English nobility in London. In the conflict between Hapsburg and Bourbon, victory seemed assured to the House of Austria.

III

Ferdinand II had been as active as ever throughout the Regensburg meeting, attending to the minutest details of every kind. He had busied himself about a stretch of the Danube embankment which had collapsed in Vienna, about a girl who had given herself out for a prophetess in Austria, about some game he had sent to the Queen of Hungary that he feared might have been tough.[1] But his infirmities, asthma in particular, were gaining on him, and he spoke, since the election of his son, cheerfully and hopefully of the next world. 'The Roman Empire needs me no more', he said contentedly, 'for it is already provided with a successor and indeed an excellent one.'[2]

He was only fifty-nine, but ceaseless exertion, heavy meals and religious austerities had made him already an old man. Even the bitter cold of the winter did not deter him from his devotions, and the Empress, waking sometimes in the night, would find him kneeling at the bedside deep in prayer and, stretching out her hand to take his, would implore him in vain to rest.[3] At Sträubing, on the way to Vienna after the meeting, he found his infirmities gathering upon him and wrote to Father Lamormaini for permission to curtail his lengthy morning devotions.[4] The father recognized at once that he must be seriously, if not fatally, ill, and hastened to join him, but Ferdinand struggled forward on the long, cold journey back to Vienna, to reach his capital on February 8th, 1637, a dying man.

He had a tranquil death-bed, propped up among his pillows, fortified by the comforts of the Church, smiling from time to time peacefully at his wife and younger daughter watching by him.[5] In eighteen years of struggle he had never lost confidence in his mission, or in God and at the end he could say 'nunc dimittis' with full contentment, for he had indeed achieved a large measure of his ambition. He had not altogether won back Germany from the heretic, but at the Peace of Prague he had asserted the right of the Church to all she had held in 1624, and this, with the purification of Austria and Bohemia, was a gain of which he might justifiably be proud. At Linz that very year, the sight of the converted people flocking into the churches had moved him to tears of thankfulness.[6] For the

[1] *Briefe Ferdinands II und III und S. von Breuner. Archiv für Oesterreichische Geschichte.* Vienna, 1852; *Notizenblatt,* ii, ii, pp. 152-5.
[2] *Annales,* xii, p. 2415.　　　[3] Ibid., p. 2398.
[4] Dudik, *Correspondenz Kaiser Ferdinands II,* p. 278.
[5] *Annales,* xii, p. 2362.　　　[6] Hurter, *Ferdinand II,* x, p. 118.

rest, he had reunited the Austrian dynasty within itself, grafted it by the marriage of his son to the Spanish tree, successfully reformed the administration of his own lands, destroyed the League and the Union and united most of the ruling princes, whether they would or no, beneath his controlling sceptre. It was an achievement which, seen in the light of his political morality, he might present at the judgment seat of God with a certain modest satisfaction. No qualm of doubt seems to have troubled the calm with which he prepared for his last account. On February 15th at nine in the morning his body and soul parted one from the other, the one to moulder in the vaults of Graz, the other to receive the reward for which he had laboured so long.

His political achievement had cost dear for what it was, too dear had he ever stopped to reckon the cost. On paper, imperial authority might be paramount in Germany; in fact the soldiers alone ruled. The soldiers, not the generals; Baner frankly admitted that he had not the slightest control over his men, and tales were told of the sack of Kempten by the imperialists, of Landsberg by the Swedes, of Calw by the Bavarians, which froze the blood. The imperialists had slaughtered children in the cellars, thrown the women out of the upper windows of the houses and boiled a housewife in her own cauldron. The Swedes had sprinkled gunpowder on their prisoners and set fire to their clothes, the Bavarians under Werth had shut the citizens into Calw, fired the walls, trained guns on the gates and shot at the people as they tried to escape the flames. The stories were exaggerations but based on the increasing and now general barbarity of the war. In sober fact, civilian prisoners were led off in halters to die of exposure by the wayside, children kidnapped and held to ransom, priests tied under the wagons to crawl on all fours like dogs until they dropped, burghers and peasants imprisoned, starved and tortured for their concealed wealth to the uttermost of human endurance with the uttermost of human ingenuity.[1]

The more rapid and widespread movements of the troops

[1] MORGENBESSER, *Geschichte von Schlesien*, Breslau, 1908, pp. 235, 239; NEBELSIECK, *Geschichte des Kreises Liebenwerda*, Halle, 1912, p. 36; RIEZLER, *Geschichte*, V, p. 421; SIERK, pp. 182, 186; EINERT, p. 43.

in the last six years had increased the ravages of plague and hunger beyond all bounds and uprooted the population of central Germany from the soil, turning them into a fluctuating mass of fugitives. This is the only explanation of the total desertion of villages, the dwindling of towns to a tenth and less than a tenth of their original size. The desertion was temporary, and of those who fled many drifted back again, but in the meantime economic life came to a standstill, and some who went as wealthy burghers returned to the charred ruins of their homes with nothing but the rags they wore. Both Saxe-Weimar and Werth made it their business to burn everything they passed in hostile country; Fürth, Eichstätt, Creussen, Bayreuth, Calw, had been laid in ruins, not to speak of innumerable villages, while rats, breeding in huge quantities in deserted cellars and feeding fat in the wake of the armies, devoured the grain which the soldiers left, and ruined the harvests.[1] The gentry, in the effort to maintain their comforts, renounced their established duties and left their homes for the towns, or fell back on the old profession of robbery and raided the passing traveller as in days of old. In Moravia, government officials and local landowners allied themselves with wandering marauders and shared the booty.[2]

The fugitives who fled from the south after Nördlingen died of plague, hunger and exhaustion in the refugee camp at Frankfort or the overcrowded hospitals of Saxony; seven thousand were expelled from the cantons of Zürich because there was neither food nor room for them, at Hanau the gates were closed against them, at Strasbourg they lay thick in the streets through the frosts of winter, so that by day the citizens stepped over their bodies, and by night lay awake listening to the groans of the sick and starving until the magistrates forcibly drove them out, thirty thousand of them. The Jesuits here and there fought manfully against the overwhelming distress; after the burning and desertion of Eichstätt they sought out the children who were hiding in the cellars, killing and eating the rats, and carried them off to care for and educate them; at Hagenau they managed to feed the poor out of

---

[1] *Annales*, XII, pp. 1955-7; CZERNY, *Tourist*, pp. 53-4; LAMMERT, p. 133.
[2] RIEZLER, *Geschichte*, V, p. 538; D'ELVERT, I, p. 451.

their stores until the French troops raided their granary and took charge of the grain for the army.[1]

By the irony of fate the wine harvest of 1634, which should have been excellent, was trampled down by fugitives and invaders after Nördlingen; that of 1635 suffered a like fate, and in the winter, from Württemberg to Lorraine, there raged the worst famine for many years. At Calw the pastor saw a woman gnawing the raw flesh of a dead horse on which a hungry dog and some ravens were also feeding. In Alsace the bodies of criminals were torn from the gallows and devoured; in the whole Rhineland they watched the graveyards against marauders who sold the flesh of the newly buried for food; at Zweibrücken a woman confessed to having eaten her child. Acorns, goats' skins, grass, were all cooked in Alsace; cats, dogs, and rats were sold in the market at Worms. In Fulda and Coburg and near Frankfort and the great refugee camp, men went in terror of being killed and eaten by those maddened by hunger. Near Worms hands and feet were found half cooked in a gipsies' cauldron. Not far from Wertheim human bones were discovered in a pit, fresh, fleshless, sucked to the marrow.[2]

The English ambassador and his suite, travelling to the Electoral meeting at Regensburg, had looked in amazed horror upon a country where the villagers, instead of welcoming them, fled at their approach, thinking them to be more invading soldiers, where the roads were so unsafe that several of the ambassadorial train were set on and murdered within a stone's throw of the highway and not four miles from Nuremberg. The journey was a nightmare to the peaceful Englishmen, and the man who recorded it writes with the air of one not trusting his own eyes, as though he were recording a dream, not a reality. 'From Coln hither [to Frankfort] all the towns, villages and castles be battered, pillaged and burnt'; at Neunkirchen they 'found one house burning when we came and not any body in the village', and later stumbled on two bodies in

[1] BOTHE, *Geschichte der Stadt Frankfurt.* Frankfort, 1929, p. 450; LAMMERT, p. 185; WALTER, pp. 31-2; REUSS, *Alsace*, p. 113; DUHR, II, i, p. 131; WILLE, p. 167.

[2] KAYSER, *Heidelberg*, p. 412; PUFENDORF, VIII, p. 44; REUSS, *Alsace*, p. 129; *Annales*, XII, pp. 2357, 2359; LAMMERT, p. 228.

the streets, one of which had been newly 'scraped out of the grave'. At Eilfkirchen they 'dined with some reserved meat of our own for there was not anything to be found'; at Neustadt 'which hath been a fair city, though now pillaged and burnt miserably . . . we saw poor children sitting at their doors almost starved to death'; at Bacharach 'the poor people are found dead with grass in their mouths'; at Rüdesheim 'His Excellency gave some relief to the poor which were almost starved as it appeared by the violence they used to get it from one another'; at Mainz there were 'divers poor people lying on the dunghills, . . . being scarce able to crawl for to receive His Excellency's alms'; here too the town was 'miserably battered', so that the travellers slept and ate in their boat on the river, throwing the remains to the beggars on the quay, 'at the sight of which they strove so violently that some of them fell into the Rhine and were like to have been drowned'.[1]

Things were worst along the Rhine, but they were bad elsewhere. At Munich Spanish troops passing through left a plague which, within four months, carried off ten thousand.[2] Baner averred there was not a grain of corn left for his men in Anhalt or Halle.[3]

Even in Ferdinand's Styria there had been a rising of the peasants which sent thirty-six of them to the galleys and five to the scaffold.[4] Madness and idealism flickered up among the oppressed in occasional tongues of flame. A dispossessed Protestant farmer in Austria, Martin Leimbauer, collected a band of followers by preaching and prophesying against the government. Arrested, he was released as lunatic, but came back twice again to trouble the government. The third time his own people betrayed him, his headquarters was surrounded and he himself dragged ignominiously from his hiding-place under the outspread skirts of two old women and carried with his young wife prisoner to Linz. Here, after declaring that God had made him his deputy on earth, he broke down under sentence of death and went to the block penitent and a Catholic. His wife, sentenced to perpetual imprisonment, escaped with the hang-

---

[1] CROWNE, pp. 3-4, 8-12, 46, 60-1.
[2] LAMMERT, p. 168.   [3] *Brefvexling*, II, vi, p. 298.
[4] A. MELL, *Windische Bauernaufstand. Mitteilungen des Historischen Vereins für Steiermark*, XLIV, pp. 212-57.

man's assistant on the eve of her husband's execution.[1] With its gross humour, its cynical morality and its touch of spiritual grandeur, the story is typical of its time.

I V

Ferdinand's death fell on the rising trend of a Swedish revival, just before it reached its highest point. He was taken before his eyes could see the real decline of all his hopes. Imperialist troops had been sent to Brandenburg to join with the Saxons against Baner, but the marshal, supported by his able compatriot Torstensson and two Scottish officers, Lesley and King, turned the tables on his assailants. By ingenious manœuvring he cut off their joint forces at Wittstock on the Dosse, a tributary of the Havel. Here on October 4th, 1636, the imperialists took up their position on a hill protected from Baner's troops by a long, narrow belt of wood, dug themselves in, set up their batteries and formed their wagons into a stockade about them. Baner's plan was to draw them out of this strong position and surround them in the plain. Accordingly he arranged that he and Torstensson should march through the wood with half the cavalry and draw the enemy out by appearing, apparently at their mercy, on the lower slopes of the hill. Meanwhile Lesley with the infantry and King with the remaining cavalry should come up through the shelter of the wood and take the enemy unawares on flank and rear.

The ingenious plan all but failed. Baner's advance drew the enemy but their attack was murderous, the Swedish troops were heavily outnumbered, and for an intolerable time neither Lesley nor King appeared. And when Lesley came with the infantry, his onslaught on the imperialist flank only gave Baner and Torstensson a much-needed breathing space, and did not dislodge the imperial batteries from the hill-top. King, who had found the ground impassable and had taken his troops round by a long detour, appeared just as Lesley and Baner thought all was lost. He was just in time, and his coming ended the battle in a matter of minutes; attacked on three sides, the

[1] *Annales*, XII, pp. 1955-8; CZERNY, *Tourist*, pp. 53-4.

enemy commanders preferred flight to surrender. Nineteen standards and over a hundred and thirty-three cannon, with all the baggage and fresh stores of weapons, were left on the hill-top. The powder was only saved from capture by blowing up the wagons.[1]

As a feat of military tactics, Baner's plan had been risky and expensive but successful, and although the victory did not stand in the same rank of importance with Nördlingen, Lützen or Breitenfeld, it went far in popular report to re-establish the shaken reputation of the Swedes. More immediately important, it crippled the military power of the Saxons and left the incompetent George William of Brandenburg defenceless. His lands were rapidly reoccupied, and by May 1637 the armies had made themselves fast on the border near Torgau and were intimidating even John George by savage terrorization. Leipzig had been all but taken, and in the west the vanguard had driven forward almost into Thuringia and occupied Erfurt.

An alteration in the Stockholm government was partly responsible for the revival of Swedish arms. Abandoning the control of German affairs to Richelieu, since he had no other choice, Oxenstierna had returned to his own country to lay a firm hand on the government. He arrived in the capital to find the Queen-mother with her clique of supporters already planning to marry her daughter to a Danish prince;[2] in the meantime she had taken up her residence in a room of which even the windows were covered in black hangings, and was proposing to immure Christina here for the whole length of her childhood, with no better amusement than a collection of fools and dwarfs whose elvish gestures aroused nothing but repulsion in the little Queen. Axel Oxenstierna rescued Christina both from the marriage and the imprisonment. He earned the undying and occasionally effective resentment of the Queen-mother for his pains, but the gratitude of the little Queen, which in the years to come when she became an intelligent woman with a policy of her own, stood often between him and her displeasure.[3]

[1] CHEMNITZ, III, pp. 39-40; *Brefvexling*, II, vi, pp. 856-63. There is an excellent plan of the battle in TINGSTEN, *Baner och Torstensson.*
[2] SCHULZE, *Die Vermählung Friedrich Wilhelms von Brandenburg*, p. 14.
[3] See Christina's Autobiography in ARCHENHOLTZ, II, pp. 46, 63, 66.

With Oxenstierna once again in power at Stockholm, the Swedish marshals could be certain of supplies both of men and money in any serious emergency, of support at all times, and of the firm defence of their north German and Baltic communications against any onslaught from Denmark.

The pendulum which had swung so madly out of equilibrium righted itself slowly. The Swedish advance was paralleled by a signal success in the Low Countries. After a siege which was the talk of Europe for the better part of a year,

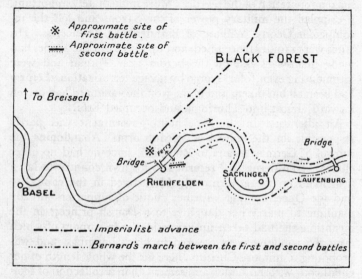

Breda fell to Frederick Henry on October 10th, 1637. It had been twelve years in the hands of the Spaniards, and its loss, besides exposing the border of Brabant, was the first serious check to the Cardinal-Infant. His failure to relieve it discredited him as much as failure in the like case had discredited the Prince of Orange twelve years before.

These two advances at once relieved the pressure on the Rhine, so that Bernard, obeying at last the insistent demands of the French government, after more than two years of penurious defensive, made ready to cross the river. He moved early in February 1638, making for the important bridge at the little town of Rheinfelden, a few miles to the east of Basel. At this point the river runs almost due east and west, Rheinfelden lying on the south, or left bank. Bernard invested it on the south side, and using the ferry at Beuggen a little farther east, transported some of his men to outposts on the north side, whence he intended to attack the bridge-head. The assault was fixed for March 1st, but before it could be made the imperialists under Savelli, an Italian mercenary, and Werth, had hastened up from the Black Forest.

Approaching down the right bank from Säckingen, Savelli's advance guard was sharply beaten off by Bernard's troops. They fell back to their main body and, making a detour through the hilly and wooded country, prepared to attack Bernard's flank. In the brief respite which this manœuvre gave him, Bernard hastily transported some of his artillery and cavalry over the ferry from the left bank. Time was short, and when Savelli reappeared about half Bernard's army was still on the far side of the river.

He had drawn up those troops which he had collected to defend the bridge-head and prevent Savelli from relieving the town. The ground was uneven and the formation scattered, so that united action along the whole front was difficult, and the engagement resolved itself into a series of skirmishes. Savelli, coming in on Bernard's left flank, drove him back in disorder. But on the other side of the field, Bernard's right threw back the imperialist left. The result of these two movements was that both armies turned almost completely on their axes; Savelli, seizing the opportunity, slipped in between Bernard and the bridge, and the day ended with the troops facing each other in positions almost exactly the reverse of those in which they started.

The outlook for Bernard was gloomy. His losses, except in artillery, were not serious, but he was cut off from the rest of his army on the left bank of the river, and he had allowed Savelli to master the bridge and thus control Rheinfelden. There was only one thing to be done — to withdraw to the nearest crossing-place and attempt to reunite his army. With this in view Bernard fell back towards Laufenburg, evading, by a piece of undeserved good luck, the detachments which

Savelli had left in the Black Forest. Here he crossed the Rhine, reassembled his forces and marched down the left bank for Rheinfelden.

Thus at a little after seven in the morning of March 3rd Savelli's outposts were startled by the approach of an army which they believed to be utterly scattered. Leaving the guns, they tumbled back towards Rheinfelden to give the alarm. Bernard stopped only to retrieve several light field-pieces of his own and, trundling these along with him, approached the town. Three times he fired on Savelli's forces as they hastily assembled to defend the city, and before his final charge their lines were already wavering. They broke at once. Bernard's cavalry pursued them, and further troops sallying from the town too late to the help of their comrades were caught between two fires. Half the imperialists fled, half surrendered. Savelli was ignominiously dragged out of a thicket, and Werth, on foot and alone, was recognized and taken in a neighbouring village.[1]

In Paris they sang a Te Deum for Werth's capture,[2] and they had cause, for Bernard, his forces swelled by the prisoners, struck suddenly north again to reduce Breisach, now cut off on all sides.

Fighting a war through untrustworthy allies was a dangerous and skilful task, and Richelieu's success depended on his ability to control both Bernard and the Swedes, and to imbue their separate actions with unity. No sooner was one recalcitrant ally brought into line than the other would be tugging at the halter: while Bernard after months of quiescence had at last justified himself, Richelieu was wrestling with a new Swedish problem. The treaty was running out and Oxenstierna, thinking the moment favourable to free himself of an alliance which had once been necessary but which was always dangerous, decided to make peace on his own account.[3]

He gauged rightly the new Emperor's wish for peace. Should Ferdinand detach him from Richelieu, he would free his own flank of a ceaseless danger and be at liberty to give that help in

---

[1] MUNCH, *Geschichte des Hauses und Landes Fuerstenberg.* Leipzig, 1832, Appendix, Vol. III, *passim*; LEUPOLD, *Journal der Armee des Herzogs Bernhard von Sachsen-Weimar. Basler Zeitschrift*, XI, pp. 303-8, 347-8, 354-61; NOAILLES, *Episodes de la Guerre de Trente Ans*, Paris, 1908, II, pp. 269-80.
[2] AVENEL, VI, p. 140.
[3] PUFENDORF, *De rebus Suecicis*, Utrecht, 1686, VIII, p. 59.

the low Countries, of which his cousin the Cardinal-Infant stood in need. Realizing the new danger, Richelieu dispatched an ambassador to Hamburg to argue with Oxenstierna's plenipotentiary, Adler Salvius. Renewed promises of help, coupled with the Emperor's unwillingness to yield Pomerania, and the hope that Baner might be yet more successful in arms, at length outweighed the Swedish need for peace, and she renewed her old alliance with France by the Treaty of Hamburg.[1]

Ferdinand had failed to detach the allies one from another, and on June 5th, 1638, Bernard of Saxe-Weimar appeared at Breisach. Richelieu speedily made ready to send him French reinforcements, so that the opportunity of mastering this key place in the Hapsburg strategy might not be lost. Hurrying to the rescue, the Bavarian general Goetz was decisively defeated at Wittenweier on July 30th, and six days later Bernard joined with the French under Marshal Turenne. The siege was formed by the middle of August, and in October Charles of Lorraine, rushing troops to the help of the town at the imperial instigation, was cut off and annihilated by a rapid thrust of Bernard at Sennheim.

After this there was no further hope of relief; yet the garrison of Breisach held out from week to week, hoping always that supplies might fail the besiegers as much as the besieged. Hunger alone could reduce Breisach, situated on a steep eminence and protected on one side by the swift-flowing Rhine. Bernard's assaults failed, but time was on his side, for short as supplies might be in his camp, they were shorter still in the town. By November rich burghers' wives were seen in the market bartering their jewellery for a little flour. Horses, cats, dogs, mice were all sold for human food, and the skins of cattle and sheep soaked and cooked. On November 24th one of Bernard's soldiers, a prisoner, died in the castle; before the body could be taken away for burial his comrades had torn it in pieces and devoured the flesh. In the ensuing weeks six other prisoners died and were eaten. On a single morning ten bodies were found in the central square of the town, citizens who had dropped dead of hunger, and by December it was being

[1] FAGNIEZ, II, p. 355; *Sverges Traktater*, v, ii, pp. 424-9.

whispered that poor and orphan children had disappeared.[1]

It seemed impossible that Breisach should hold out so long and so hopelessly. And at this moment, when fortune at last crowned Richelieu's long planning, when the key to the Rhine was all but his, Father Joseph fell ill; day after day they waited in Paris for news of Breisach's surrender, and still the fortress held; day after day the old Capuchin slackened his hold on life. A kindly legend lends to Richelieu one sudden flash of human tenderness. Hastening into the room of the dying man with well-simulated joy, he is supposed to have leaned over the narrow bed and called to him, saying: 'Father Joseph, Breisach is ours.'[2] Twenty-four hours before he died, on December 17th, 1638, Breisach surrendered. They did not know in Paris until the 19th.

Alsace was now occupied from end to end by troops in French pay; Breisach, the key to the Rhine and the gateway to Germany, had fallen. In the east Baner defeated John George near Chemnitz, occupied Pirna and, throwing back the defending army at Brandeis, invaded Bohemia. In Flanders the Cardinal-Infant, unable to check new French inroads, could send no help to Germany, where his fellow-victor of Nördlingen, now Emperor, struggled vainly with inadequate subsidies and bad generals to hold back the rising tide. Piccolomini had gone to the Low Countries, Arnim had resigned, Werth was a prisoner in French hands. In their place Ferdinand relied on Gallas, who grew every year more casual, drunken and incompetent;[3] on Hatzfeld, once a colonel of Wallenstein's, who had indeed made short work of a ridiculously small army under the Elector-Palatine at Vlotho on the Weser, but was otherwise an ungifted hack; on Goetz, a renegade from the other side, of very mild ability, who had replaced Werth as the leader of the Bavarian contingent. Recruiting from the horribly decreased population, raising taxes on the hereditary lands already drained of all blood, paying and feeding the army, weighed ever more heavily on Ferdinand. But in the spring of 1639 a sudden crisis on the Rhine checked Richelieu and gave the Emperor time to consider his line of action.

[1] *Alemannia*, XLII, pp. 55-8; ROESE, II, p. 521.
[2] FAGNIEZ, II, p. 409. [3] FIEDLER, p. 225.

Bernard of Saxe-Weimar asserted his rights against the Crown of France. By the treaty to which he had agreed in 1635 he was to be rewarded by permission to keep Alsace; now that his troops held it he demanded categorically that it should be ceded to him outright, without further consideration of French needs or claims; in the meantime he asserted that Breisach had surrendered not to the King of France but to him, and he intended to hold it. He demanded the integrity of German soil under a German prince, and the right to be treated as an ally on equal terms with Sweden.[1]

v

The soldier of fortune and his reward had been a problem since the beginning of the war. Mansfeld had wanted Hagenau, Wallenstein had wanted Mecklenburg, the Rhenish Palatinate, Brandenburg and Bohemia, the Swedish marshals had asked for estates, Bernard had claimed Franconia and now Alsace. There may have been no more in this than personal ambition, but the peculiar significance of Alsace in later history has invested Bernard's transactions with an aureole which is wholly lacking from those of Mansfeld and the Swedish marshals, if not altogether from those of Wallenstein.

Bernard's reputation as a patriot rests above all on his behaviour in the months succeeding the fall of Breisach. During that time he showed almost open hostility to Richelieu over the question of Alsace, demanding unqualified cession and refusing all compromise. But he was ineffective, if not insincere, as a patriot, because he made no effort either to form a party within the Empire or to win the sympathy of the more influential rulers. On the contrary, he deliberately rejected a plan for the formation of a German party which had been laid before him by the Landgravine of Hesse.

The evidence is once again inconclusive; he may very well have doubted the Landgravine's sincerity. But his failure to make any constructive suggestion himself proves that, whatever the plan behind his opposition to France, it was either

[1] ROESE, II, pp. 528 ff.

chiefly personal or still so rudimentary as to be valueless in German politics.

Bernard made his initial demands in February 1639, asking for the full cession of Breisach and the four so-called 'forest cities', Laufenburg, Säckingen, Waldshut and Rheinfelden.[1] Throughout the spring repeated letters from Paris failed to move him, and when, in June, Marshal Guébriant joined him with fresh troops and further entreaties from Paris, he found him as obstinate as always.[2] No solution could be found, short of confirming that dominating military and territorial power which Bernard claimed — elevating him to the uncontrolled position of a Wallenstein.

Fate stepped in between him and his ambitions. 'Untimely and premature death, for such was the decision of God, commanded the hastening foot to stay in the very midst of its victorious race and marked out the limit to his further ambition.'[3] So runs the grandiose latin of the contemporary account. Less than a week in time divided Bernard the menacing rival from Bernard the lamented hero, for whom the whole Court was commanded to wear black.[4]

He had been intermittently troubled by fever for some months past,[5] and about the middle of July a rapid consuming illness seized him and ended his life in a few days. The end was so timely for Richelieu that many believed that he had poisoned him.[6] The legend is false; an over-tired young man who has for years lived to the uttermost of his strength is as likely to die of a fever as a rash soldier to be killed in battle. Richelieu was as lucky in the death of Bernard as he had been six years before in that of Gustavus.

Bernard himself soon realized that his death was near and, insisting that his doctors keep him alive from hour to hour with stimulants, he composed and dictated his will.[7] On the will, above all, his reputation as a patriot stands. He left Alsace to his elder brother if he would take it — and surely he must have

---

[1] ROESE, II, pp. 528, 536.   [2] Ibid., pp. 539 seq.; AVENEL, VI, pp. 408-10.
[3] Alemannia, 1915, p. 190. 'Mors praecox et immatura, statuente sic aliud Jehova, festinantem et in media victoriarum via currentem pedem, sistere jussit et conatibus ejus ulterioribus finem imposuit.'
[4] AVENEL, VI, p. 462.   [5] Ibid., p. 304.
[6] Brefvexling, II, ii, p. 655.
[7] DROYSEN, Bernhard von Weimar. Leipzig, 1885, II, p. 572.

known that William of Weimar had neither strength nor inclination to do so — failing his brother, to the King of France. Certainly he stipulated that such cession was for the length of the war only but he took no precaution to guarantee this. He left his army entire to his second-in-command, Erlach, a gentleman of Switzerland in whom he had always trusted. He left his best horse to Guébriant, a consolation for his wasted diplomacy.[1] With death so close and so untimely upon him, Bernard might have lifted the veil from his true ambitions by making some last-minute effort to achieve them. But the will, in spite of the undiscouraged efforts of his apologists, remains as obstinately inconclusive as the rest of his policy. It proves nothing save that he realized that Richelieu alone was strong enough to defend the Protestant Cause, and that he had no party in Germany on which to bestow either Alsace or his army.

He made a good end: coldly virtuous, he had few personal sins to trouble him, and as for his public responsibilities, he probably cared as little for the desolation of the Rhineland, for the foul destruction of Landshut or the burning of Bavaria, as had the late Emperor Ferdinand for the total ruin of the Empire. The cause justified all and, whatever his ambitions, there is no doubt that Bernard was as devout a Protestant as Ferdinand had been a Catholic. 'Into thy hands, Lord Jesus, I commend my spirit', he whispered with his last, unwilling breath. He was thirty-five when he died.

On such evidence as there is he can neither be altogether condemned nor altogether acquitted. Death cut short the hearing, opposing to all judgments for good or evil the inconclusive verdict — 'not proven'.

VI

How little Bernard had prepared the German princes for any assertion of national interests was shown by the events which immediately succeeded his death. The masters of Alsace and Breisach were Bernard's soldiers, and their master was Erlach.

[1] ROESE, II, pp. 554-6.

Whoever could come to terms with Erlach gained the Upper Rhine. Of all the rulers in Germany, precisely one made the effort.

Charles Lewis, Elector Palatine, was twenty-three years old, a hard-headed, egocentric, conscientious young man who had learnt early to fend for himself. His misanthropic disbelief in human kind — at home he was nicknamed Timon — was tempered at this period by the reckless optimism of youth. In October 1638 the army he had raised with the help of English money had been destroyed at Vlotho, his younger brother taken prisoner, and he himself barely escaped with his life. Undeterred by this sorry escapade, he set out less than a year later to make himself master of Bernard's army and thereby of the Upper Rhine.

Playing on the Protestant Cause, on his father's wrongs, on his own undoubted German origin and consequent fitness to succeed a fellow German prince, hinting at subsidies from his supposedly wealthy uncle the King of England, Charles Lewis made himself a party in Bernard's army large enough to cause anxiety to Richelieu. He made one childish mistake. Setting out to join the troops, he journeyed straight across France. Richelieu pounced upon him at Moulins and sent him prisoner to Vincennes,[1] where he remained in impotent disgust until Erlach had bartered the army to Louis XIII.

If Bernard is to be a hero, Erlach who contracted his army into the service of Richelieu on his death, and put Alsace and Breisach at their disposal, is the lowest of traitors. But if Bernard was merely an ambitious mercenary leader, then Erlach was neither better nor worse than he, since all he did was to find a new employer for the men whose feeding and pay lay at his charge. The blame, if any, for the loss of Bernard's army to France, lies not with Erlach but with the princes of Germany who made no offer to him. He had to take the best he could get, and the best was Richelieu.[2]

On October 9th, 1639, a treaty was signed between the King of France and the troops henceforward known sometimes as the Weimarians, sometimes as the Bernardines. They

[1] *Brefvexling*, II, ii, pp. 649, 660; AVENEL, VI, p. 601.
[2] See GONZENBACH, *General von Erlach*. Bern, 1880 I, I, p. 203 f.

were to continue in the pay of the French government, to follow the French commander-in-chief on the Rhine, but to keep their own separate entity and their own general who could alone appoint the lesser officers, and were to hold certain fortresses, Breisach in particular, under the French Crown. As Erlach wrote almost apologetically to the Elector Palatine, 'it was impossible to preserve any longer an army which had already suffered much and which the approach of winter threatened with inevitable ruin'.[1]

The treaty, following on the death of Bernard, marks the final abdication of the German extremists from any even partial control in their allies' war. The rulers of Hesse-Cassel continued to assert their independence and stood in relation to Richelieu and Oxenstierna as equal allies, but they steered a narrow course of their own, having neither the military nor the territorial power to affect the progress of the war. Whatever Bernard's intentions, while he had lived there had been a native commander exerting an influence which neither Richelieu nor Oxenstierna could afford to disregard. With his death and the passing of his troops under foreign control, the war degenerated altogether into a contest between the Kings of France and Spain, fought on German soil.

---

[1] See GONZENBACH, I, p. 236 f.

THE COLLAPSE OF SPAIN
1639 – 1643

L'Espagne est comme le chancre qui ronge et mange tout le corps où il s'attache.

RICHELIEU

CHAPTER X

THE COLLAPSE OF SPAIN

I

In Madrid they blamed the Cardinal-Infant for the fall of Breisach; he should, said Olivarez unreasonably, have sent reinforcements to save it.[1] How he was to do this with dwindling financial support and in face of the perpetually contradictory orders he received from Spain, did not appear. But on the Spanish side of the contest troubles gathered so fast that the King and his favourite were only human in transferring the overwhelming blame to others. The disasters of which they were the chief cause were too much for them to bear alone.

Public discontent, which had been an intermittent whisper under Philip II, swelled to a continuous murmur under Philip III, and became by the reign of Philip IV the deafening accompaniment to all he did. More inept tinkering with the currency had produced so startling an inflation that in some districts the people resorted to barter.[2] By the early forties it was estimated that about three-quarters of the goods which came to Spanish ports were carried in Dutch vessels; so ridiculously had the merchant and defence fleets dwindled that this illicit traffic — for the embargo on enemy ships continued — was not only impossible to stop but was actually necessary for the existence of Spain. In 1639 a gigantic Spanish fleet, seventy-seven ships in all, was driven by the brilliant and daring Dutch admiral Tromp to take shelter in neutral English waters, and there, regardless alike of the laws of the sea and the impotent protests of the English, attacked at a disadvantage. Seventy ships were sunk or taken. This colossal victory was the

---

[1] Lonchay et Cuvelier, iii, p. 298.
[2] Canovas del Castillo, *Bosquejo Historico*, pp. 225 ff; *Decadencia de España*, Madrid, 1910, pp. 232-3; E. J. Hamilton, pp. 84, 86.

quietus of Spanish sea-power; staggering since the defeat of 1631, the hollow giant collapsed, never to rise again.

Richelieu meanwhile stretched out his hand to control the border dukedom of Savoy, that small state astride of the Alps which the Hapsburg had long tried to use for a gateway to France. It was ruled now, in the name of her young son, by the widowed Duchess Christina, herself a sister of Louis XIII. By a sudden and almost brutal intervention in the internal affairs of the Duchy, Richelieu established his own control.

As for Germany, Olivarez declared that the Electors of Bavaria and Cologne were in the pay of France, while the Emperor whose reign had opened so hopefully was now a liability. His ministers were faithless, his subjects disloyal.[1] Thus peevishly did Olivarez resent the efforts of Ferdinand to seek his own salvation rather than that of the Spanish monarchy.

In Spain itself the bankrupt Court maintained its façade of dazzling splendour. The King was growing old, his health was failing and he was much given to melancholy and religion; he continued nevertheless to pour out money on masques and theatres, bull-fights, mistresses and bastards.[2] Meanwhile the French defence crystallized into attack both in Flanders and on the Pyrenees. On both fronts the Spaniards still kept the invaders back, but it was a question merely of postponement unless some miracle happened in Madrid.

No miracle happened. In 1640 Catalonia and Portugal burst into revolt. Within a year the mild Duke John of Braganza, borne unwillingly on the current of local discontent, was established under the title of John IV at Lisbon; he obtained a political treaty with France,[3] a truce with the Dutch,[4] commercial agreements with England and Sweden.[5] In Catalonia the revolt was even more dangerous; innocent of intervention until the rebellion broke out, Richelieu had communicated with

[1] CANOVAS DEL CASTILLO, *Estudios del Reinado de Felipe IV*, I, pp. 414-15.
[2] *Relazioni dagli Ambasciatori. Spagna*, II, pp. 11, 107; CANOVAS DEL CASTILLO, *Decadencia de España*, pp. 234 ff.
[3] ABREU Y BERTODANO, V, p. 570.
[4] AVENEL, Additional volume, p. 653.
[5] *Sverges Traktater*, V, ii, pp. 486-500.

the leaders as soon as he realized their importance: By December 1640, he had signed a treaty with the Catalans, and in the new year he was arranging to send the French navy to their help, while they in return elected Louis XIII, Duke of Barcelona, independent of the Spanish Crown.[1]

Thus the Spanish Netherlands were left, a rudderless ship drifting before the gale. The Madrid government, powerless to help them, yet would not renounce its control. Even had Philip been able to spare men or money, he could no longer send them safely by sea or land, for the Dutch held the Narrow Seas and the French Breisach. The great artery of the Hapsburg Empire, from Italy to Flanders, was blocked so that the Val Telline no longer mattered. By the significantly named 'Perpetual Peace' of Milan, the valley was given to the Grisons, and the now useless passes cynically guaranteed to the Spaniards.[2]

In vain now the victory of Nördlingen, in vain the strategy of the Cardinal-Infant on the frontiers of Flanders and Brabant. In 1640 all help was withdrawn, and instead the prince received an entreaty, phrased as a command, to send arms and ammunition to Spain for use against Portugal.[3] Battling with order and contradictory order from Madrid, appeal and counter-appeal, rumour and contradiction from Portugal and Catalonia,[4] the Cardinal-Infant worked unceasingly on. Throughout 1640 he held the Dutch back, and in 1641 all their efforts by land recovered them only Gennep, which they had lost six years before. It could not last; perpetual work, the strain of his uncertain relations with the Spanish Court, and physical exertion in the field wore out the prince's unstable constitution. He sickened in the late autumn of 1641; on November 8th he checked and signed six dispatches to the King of Spain,[5] on November 9th he died. So strong the spirit to the end, so weak the flesh.

---

[1] VASSAL-REIG, *Richelieu et la Catalogne*, pp. 220-30.
[2] ABREU Y BERTODANO, V, p. 313.
[3] LONCHAY ET CUVELIER, III, p. 392.
[4] Ibid., pp. 392 ff.   [5] Ibid., pp. 451-3.

11

Less happy was the fate of his cousin, the Emperor Ferdinand III. While the Spanish monarchy collapsed, he exerted all his strength to keep the Austrian dynasty standing. So near did he come to success, in spite of the complaints and recriminations which assailed him from Madrid,[1] that the tragedy of his failure stood out the more darkly. As King of Hungary he had laid the foundation for a settlement in the imperial interests at the Peace of Prague. As Emperor it remained only for him to follow out the principles he had laid down. Little by little he won to his side, and arrayed in arms against Richelieu and Oxenstierna, all the princes of Germany save only three. One of these, the Elector Palatine, troubled him not at all, for he had no possessions. The second was the selfish dynast George of Brunswick-Lüneburg, who had entered into alliance with Gustavus at the outset and staked the increase of his fortunes on following the Swede; and the last was the Landgrave William V of Hesse-Cassel.

The death of the Landgrave had filled Ferdinand with hopes that his widow, the regent for her young son, would seek peace. He reckoned without the indomitable personality of the Landgravine. A grand-daughter of William the Silent and in her own right Countess of Hanau, Amalia Elisabeth was a woman of immense determination and powerful intellect. She had principles, too, of a kind. She was intensely Calvinist, upright and true to her faith; she was also a dynast and felt it her duty to pass on her husband's estates to her son lessened by not so much as a rood of land, increased if possible.

From the beginning of the war, the ruling families in Hesse-Darmstadt and Hesse-Cassel had regarded each other with cold jealousy. At Darmstadt they had supported the Emperor, at Cassel they had drifted towards his opponents, their progress hastened by the brutal transference of much of their land to their cousins at the Regensburg Electoral meeting of 1623. Their importance to the Protestant party, to the Dutch and French in particular, was not in respect of their lands round Cassel, but

[1] *Relazioni dagli Ambasciatori. Spagna,* II, p. 114.

because they owned also a great part of East Friesland. Added to this, William V was an able general and a respectable statesman, managing to hold his own as an ally of the King of Sweden. His widow was equally determined to make no ignominious peace and to maintain her position as an independent ally of France. Richelieu, she guessed, was likely to exploit her widowhood to force her into a dependent position, so that he could use the small but solid and competent Hessian army as his own.

Amalia Elisabeth was not a far-sighted stateswoman. She has no claim, however nebulous, to have thought or acted on behalf of German integrity. Her principles were sound, but she was not unduly troubled by scruples. In so far as Hesse-Cassel and her son were concerned, she acted with shrewdness, consistency and discretion. The Emperor wooed her to make peace and she signed a truce, but with her eyes fixed on Richelieu, not on Ferdinand. The simple ruse worked. Terrified of her desertion, the Cardinal, who could ill afford to lose her subsidies, her army or her possessions, hastened to offer her terms even more advantageous than those her husband had enjoyed. She signed in rapid succession treaties of independent alliance with the King of France and the Duke of Brunswick-Lüneburg, and this done, callously broke with Ferdinand. In the small circle of her Hessian politics the Emperor had served her turn and been thrown away.

His failure with Amalia Elisabeth did not deter Ferdinand from his policy of separating the allies. An appeal to George of Brunswick-Lüneburg had been treated with contempt,[1] but he was still hopeful of separating Oxenstierna from Richelieu. Throughout 1639 and 1640 his envoys discussed the possibility of settlement at Hamburg. With the offer of Stralsund and Rügen to the Swedish government, Ferdinand came very near to achieving his end, for their treaty with the French was again running out, and there was strong feeling in Stockholm that Richelieu had not justified the hopes placed in him. Swedish diplomats began to demand the direct intervention of the French army in central Germany, complaining that allies who cared for nothing but the Rhine, and left them alone to defend the Elbe and attack

[1] LUNDORP, IV, pp. 905-11.

the Austrian hereditary lands, were not worth having. Richelieu brought them to reason by cutting off supplies altogether, and having thus proved that they were too weak even to make peace without him, renewed the old alliance.[1]

If he could not separate the allies, Ferdinand's best chance was to free himself from his Spanish obligations, since these alone were the cause of French hostility. Trautmansdorff, his most trusted adviser, urged him in this direction, but he had at first to fight against personal prejudices and natural affections too strong to be overcome. The Spanish party was supported by the Empress, a wife as much beloved as loving, and by Ferdinand's ambitious and too much cherished brother, Leopold.

Ceding to the insistence of this party, Ferdinand agreed to make Leopold commander-in-chief.[2] The appointment was a bad one, for the Archduke was no soldier. He was a poor judge of men and none of opportunity. No sooner had he arrived at headquarters than he allowed himself to fall under the influence of the maudlin Gallas. The general had been much blamed for the condition of the troops and for his own intemperance. The Archduke, however, informed Vienna that the lesser officers were to blame and that the general himself had been driven to drink by unsympathetic criticism.[3] Such simplicity does Leopold little credit, and it comes as no surprise that the Archduke was defeated on every occasion when he appeared in battle. Possessed of some real intelligence and great good nature, he was nevertheless incurably conceited; when disappointment finally shook his self-confidence he became unexpectedly embittered and revengeful. The unhappy Leopold, who had imagined himself a more competent Emperor than his brother, proved himself a far less competent general.

The circumstances were certainly not easy, for on both sides theoretical strategy had become useless. The provision of food in a starving country was the guiding consideration of warfare. The movements of the troops could no longer be directed by purely strategic considerations. Great bodies of troops, on either side, would take possession of a district and remain

[1] G. H. BOUGEANT, *Histoire des guerres et des négociations qui précédèrent le Traité de Westphalie.* Paris, 1767, pp. 31 f., 94-104, 116.
[2] DUDIK, *Die Schweden in Böhmen und Mähren.* Vienna, 1879, p. 13 f.
[3] KOCH, *Geschichte Ferdinands III*, Vienna, 1865, I, pp. 179-80.

static from seed time until harvest, sowing and reaping their own grain in country where the peasants were too few to cultivate the soil for them, and selling any surplus.

In the imperial army the decline of Spanish subsidies prevented the regular payment, and the commissariat was abominably mismanaged, neither Gallas nor the Archduke having any gift for organization. 'We might be our own carvers for we had no other pay',[1] wrote one of their men. Central control was relaxed on both sides, and captains took off their companies to forage far afield. An officer with a flair for successful raiding could establish himself as a petty Wallenstein and defy authority indefinitely. The desertion of soldiers from one regiment to another had always been difficult to check, and now the men drifted from one company to another wherever they saw that booty and food were best, without inquiring to what party the captain belonged. 'I wandered . . . I knew not whither and followed I knew not whom',[2] confessed the English mercenary Poyntz without compunction. Ragged bands were scattered across Germany, caring nothing for the cause, knowing nothing of any planned strategy, their chief care to scratch nourishment out of the soil and to avoid serious fighting. They fought only their competitors for food, of whatever party.

This phenomenon created the confused campaigns of the last decade of the war. Fighting was unco-ordinated and spasmodic, the headquarters staff being unable to move the mass of the troops easily or with purpose. The main line of Swedish-imperialist-Saxon warfare was down the Elbe into the Hapsburg lands, the main line of French-imperialist-Bavarian fighting was on the Upper Rhine and across the Black Forest. But intermittent fires, sputtering everywhere, robbed the central offensive of its force and interminably delayed the conclusion. Hard as was a soldier's life, it was the only livelihood open to a great section of the population, and as the proportion of soldiers to civilians increased, the problem of disbanding these great masses of humanity when peace came grew more terrifying.

While the armies, like creeping parasites, devoured the Empire, Ferdinand was planning for peace. At an Electoral

[1] POYNTZ, p. 127.   [2] Ibid., p. 128.

meeting at Nuremberg early in 1640, he had gone so far as to indicate that he would modify the settlement of the Peace of Prague if he could thereby induce the rulers of Hesse-Cassel and Brunswick-Lüneburg and the Elector Palatine to lay down their arms. He found the Electors much of his opinion; even Maximilian grudgingly admitted that he would consider disgorging some of the land he had seized in the Palatinate.[1] With the consent of all the Electors, the Emperor decided to call a Diet before the end of the year.

Ferdinand III opened the Diet at Regensburg on September 13th, 1640, and closed it on October 10th, 1641. During that time the turning-point of the reign was reached, and the slight but definite upward slant of his fortune reached its apex and turned sharply down.

Until January 1641 everything went well. The Emperor's initial appeal for peace and good understanding was well received.[2] On October 9th the Diet agreed to issue safe-conducts to ambassadors from Hesse-Cassel and Brunswick-Lüneburg;[3] on November 4th they agreed to Ferdinand's request that, owing to a Swedish advance, he might quarter troops in and about the city — a demand which at any time in the previous fifty years would have been furiously rejected as an attempt to overawe the meeting;[4] on December 21st they confirmed the present size and subsidization of the imperial army;[5] on the 30th they agreed to an amnesty throughout the Empire, to discuss the question of Swedish satisfaction, and to consider terms for a general settlement on the basis of the Peace of Prague.[6] By January they had even got as far as offering a safe-conduct to Elizabeth of Bohemia and her daughters, should they wish to claim the pension and dowries suitable to a German prince's widow and children.[7] No safe-conduct was offered to her son the Elector Palatine[8] and his brothers, which was hardly remarkable, since one of them was active in the Dutch army, one in the Swedish, one was in Paris, and one had been the Emperor's prisoner for over two years and lost no opportunity

[1] BROCKHAUS, *Der Kurfürstentag zu Nürnberg.* Leipzig, 1883, pp. 99, 126-7.
[2] LUNDORP, op. cit., IV, pp. 863-6.   [3] Ibid., p. 935.
[4] Ibid., p. 954.   [5] Ibid., pp. 1099-112.
[6] Ibid., pp. 1116-18.   [7] Ibid., v, pp. 35-6.
[8] FIEDLER, p. 273.

of asserting the rightness of his father's cause to his exasperated jailers.[1]

In the second week of January 1641, a Swedish army under Baner appeared outside the town, demanding its surrender. The Danube was frozen hard, and the general was prepared to cross the river and surround the town.[2] Ferdinand, with commendable courage and cool judgment, recognized this as a mere demonstration to disperse the meeting and prevent his triumph, and realizing that the enemy had not the resources to maintain their position, refused to let the Diet break up. Instead he fortified the town and strengthened the outlying garrisons. His calculation was right, the river thawed and the enemy withdrew, leaving among other damage the carcasses of twenty of the imperial falcons which had fallen into their hands and which the men, taking them for pheasants, had cooked and eaten.[3] Ferdinand's coolness and judgment won him the final approval of his subject princes. It was the height and the turning-point.

The old constitutional party had collapsed at the Peace of Prague: John George of Saxony altogether, Maximilian of Bavaria for several years. The invasion of Germany by the French and the desertion of the Swedes by almost all their German allies had converted a civil into an external war, and any opposition to the Emperor after the Peace of Prague was bound, of necessity, to place its sponsor in an invidious position. Ferdinand had so arranged matters that imperial policy stood for the integrity of German soil against the French and Swedes. So long as he was not compromised by his Spanish cousins it was morally impossible for any German prince not actually in rebellion to oppose him. But suddenly, at the eightieth session of the Diet, an attack was launched against the Emperor from the Electoral College itself; the representative of Brandenburg emphatically declared that his master did not consider the Peace of Prague in any way suitable as a basis for negotiations. Immediately, in spite of the obstinate resistance of the Electors of Bavaria, Cologne and Saxony,[4] the lesser Protestant princes

---

[1] SCOTT, *Rupert, Prince Palatine*, p. 45.
[2] *Dispacci Ridolfi*, Regensburg, 1871, p. 279.
[3] KOCH, I, p. 256; *Dispacci Ridolfi*, p. 279.
[4] *Urkunden und Aktenstücke zur Geschichte Friedrich Wilhelms*, Berlin, 1864, I, pp. 728-32.

began to accept the leadership of Brandenburg and to identify constitutional opposition to the Emperor with the extreme Protestant party.[1] Fear of external invasion alone had veiled a suspicion which had never ceased to exist, and an unlucky chance had transformed Ferdinand's Diet from a demonstration of imperial unity to a revelation of imperial weakness.

It was only a chance. Ferdinand had called and opened the Diet when old George William was still ruling in Brandenburg under the control of his chief minister Schwarzenberg, a Catholic and a devotee of the imperial house. But George William at little more than forty was already an invalid and his oppressed existence ended on December 1st, 1640. The heir, Frederick William, was twenty years old and unlike his predecessor in all but the height and dignity of his person. Whereas within the manly frame of the father there lurked a timid, dull, unadventuring soul, the no less stalwart frame of the son was alive with a bold, decided, enterprising spirit. Born of the war generation, Frederick William had its opportunism, its unscrupulousness, its disregard of anything but practical considerations.[2] He would have risked and suffered anything for what he took to be the material welfare of his dynasty—to do him justice, perhaps even of his subjects. But he would not have risked a taler for a principle. Later in life he issued a notable manifesto urging the necessity of securing German waterways for the Germans; his object was to secure one particular waterway for himself. Later still he received French subsidies with cynical indifference and baffling secrecy. He bartered Pomerania for Magdeburg and redeemed it by a trick. His internal policy was harsh, salutary, effective and unpopular; his external policy created the Prussian state from the scattered nuclei his father had left him and he must be judged by that creation.

The new Elector's character was still unknown when he succeeded. He had been partly educated in The Hague and had spent much of his time among his cousins, the children of Frederick of Bohemia. He had refused to come home when commanded by his father, and when he ultimately and un-

[1] *Urkunden und Aktenstücke*, I, p. 744.
[2] See his own outline of his methods to the Prince of Orange in 1646. GROEN VAN PRINSTERER, II, iv, p. 172.

willingly obeyed he had lived on the worst terms with Schwarzenberg, whom he suspected of an attempt to poison him.[1]

Since the old Elector's agreement to the Peace of Prague, his troops had been fighting for the Emperor against the Swedes, and ineffective as his military efforts had been, Ferdinand could not afford to lose him, least of all during the Diet where so much depended on an appearance of unity. But under Frederick William affairs in Brandenburg moved fast. The new Elector wanted, above all, peace for his country. He succeeded to lands altogether wasted, occupied by foreign troops or by his own undisciplined army which lived by robbery,[2] to a heritage stripped of all its finest estates by sale and pawn, to an income less than an eighth of that which his father had once enjoyed.[3] He was forced at first to live at Königsberg in Prussia because the roof of his castle at Berlin was falling in, and the province was too short of food to supply the Electoral household.[4] 'Pomerania is lost, Jülich is lost, we hold Prussia like an eel by the tail, and we must mortgage the Mark', lamented one of his advisers.[5]

Frederick William intended neither to mortgage the Mark, nor to lose any more land or money for the Emperor. He at once gave orders that his troops should confine themselves to defensive action; when the Swedes invaded his land he asked them on what terms they would grant him neutrality. In desperation Schwarzenberg tried to work up a mutiny. In January he was dismissed, and died shortly after, probably of the shock.[6]

By the beginning of March 1641, Ferdinand at Regensburg had heard enough to fear a private peace between Brandenburg and Sweden. By May the Elector had dispatched ambassadors to Stockholm; early in July the Swedish government agreed to a military truce, while a longer armistice was contemplated;[7] by the 24th the terms of an indefinite abstention

---

[1] PUFENDORF, *De Rebus Gestis Friderici Wilhelmi*. Leipzig, 1733, XIX, p. 102.
[2] *Urkunden und Aktenstücke*, XV, pp. 259, 322-3; X, p. 61.
[3] PHILIPPSON, *Der Grosse Kurfuerst Friedrich Wilhelm von Brandenburg*. Berlin, 1897, I, p. 29.
[4] Ibid., p. 28; STRECKFUESS, p. 223.
[5] MEINARDUS, *Protokolle und Relationen des Geheimenrates*, Leipzig, 1889, I, p. 45.
[6] *Urkunden und Aktenstücke*, XXIII, pp. 1-8; I, pp. 382-3; XV, pp. 388-9, 398-434.
[7] Ibid., XV, pp. 713-24, 522 ff.; XXIII, I, p. 9.

were privately signed;[1] and early in September the news that Brandenburg and Sweden had suspended hostilities altogether was published by the Electoral representative at Regensburg.[2]

Frederick William had forced Ferdinand's hand. The Emperor genuinely wanted peace, but it must be on terms that did not sacrifice too large a part of what his house had gained after so many years of fighting. He stood by the Peace of Prague, probably not himself realizing that a settlement which had seemed generous before Richelieu's direct intervention in 1635, was not a settlement but a cry of 'no compromise' in 1640. The new Elector of Brandenburg broke down the pretence. An imperial ally, he disregarded the negotiations at Regensburg and made his own truce. It was as if he had stood up openly before Ferdinand's face and accused him of refusing to make peace.

The significance of Frederick William's action was emphasized by a book published some months previously under the title *Dissertatio de ratione status in Imperio nostro Romano-Germanico.* This work was written with such impetus, dramatic skill and logical force that it achieved almost immediately an immense popularity. The identity of its writer was concealed under a punning pseudonym, Hippolithus à Lapide, but he was in fact Bogislav von Chemnitz, later historiographer to the Crown of Sweden. In this well-timed work he analysed the manner in which the Hapsburg dynasty had exploited the imperial constitution for the widening of their personal influence, and revealed with merciless logic the actual weakness of their position, resting as it did on cunning and force and on the exploitation of emergency against the still existent rights of the princes.

Ferdinand had opened the Diet in September 1640 with what he himself thought was an olive branch in his hand. By May 1641 it was the common talk of Europe that he wanted nothing but war,[2] and the negotiations at Regensburg were but a repetition of the brilliant trick he had played at the Peace of Prague: a new and more coercive attempt to hold his allies together and keep the opposing party in the wrong.

Ferdinand was no fool. He saw what had happened and he

---

[1] *Sverges Traktater*, v, ii, pp. 475-83.
[2] *Urkunden und Aktenstücke*, XXIII, i, p. 11. [3] Ibid., pp. 535, 550.

did the only thing possible to meet it. He had held out an olive branch and been told that it was a naked sword. His only hope of saving the reputation of his government lay in proving that his contention was the right one. When he had news that the truce between Sweden and Brandenburg was signed past all revocation, he took it with an excellent grace, the spontaneous pleasure of the genuine peacemaker. This deft movement turned the blow, for Ferdinand's suave agreement disarmed the pugnacious supporters of Brandenburg. Taking the occasion, he asked them to reconsider their views on the Peace of Prague as a basis for general peace. Only the opposition of Brandenburg and the extremists, he asserted, now prevented the opening of a general peace conference. Thus skilfully he threw the accusation of obstruction on to Brandenburg.[1] To evade it the Elector's representatives agreed to the propositions.[2] On November 10th, 1641, Ferdinand dissolved the Diet in person, with this decision: that plenipotentiaries should be chosen for the discussion of peace terms with the rebels and the invaders, on the basis of the Peace of Prague and a general amnesty.[3]

The crisis was postponed, not avoided. Sooner or later Ferdinand would have to open peace negotiations in earnest, and with Frederick William drifting towards friendship with Sweden and France, such peace negotiations might be very disadvantageous to imperial prestige. Sooner or later the sword of war, so indignantly repudiated by both Ferdinand and Frederick William, would have to be lifted again by one or the other.

III

On November 30th, 1641, the imperial decree of amnesty was nailed up at Kölln on the Spree, in the Elector of Brandenburg's lands, but wind and rain reduced it to shreds in the night and buffeted the fragments contemptuously about the street.[4] The incident was too nearly akin to the general opinion of the

[1] *Urkunden und Aktenstücke*, I, p. 775.
[2] Ibid., pp. 775-6. [3] LUNDORP, V, pp. 734-5.
[4] *Urkunden und Aktenstücke*, I, p. 488. The text in LÜNIG, III, ii, pp. 129-33.

Emperor's peaceful intentions not to cause cynical comment among contemporaries.

At Hamburg meanwhile imperial, Swedish and French agents were settling the preliminaries of a peace conference. In succession Ferdinand sent three different ambassadors, not one of whom convinced the Swedes or the French that the imperial government was in earnest. 'They substituted Lützow for Kurtz, Aversberg for Lützow. The men changed but the same tale was told',[1] complained the French ambassador. In fact the situation suited him admirably, since the government in Paris was convinced that delay would bring fresh disasters to the Hapsburg; the government at Vienna was of the opposite opinion. Between them they held up negotiations for weeks and months on one pretext after another. The French demanded a title for the Duchess of Savoy which the Austrians refused to give, and great was the annoyance of both parties when the Danish envoy evolved a solution of the difficulty which neither of them could decently repudiate.[2] The Austrians, however, brought about another deadlock by ratifying the preliminaries in a document of such startling vagueness and irregularity that the French refused to accept it, and the game of postponement went happily on, each party hotly accusing the other of delaying the settlement.[3]

The imperial government showed that easy optimism for which Austria later became famous, and allowed its hopes to be perpetually and unduly raised by small things. Shortly after the Diet the intransigent Duke of Brunswick-Lüneburg died and his heirs deserted the Swedes to make their private peace with the Emperor,[4] thus leaving only Hesse-Cassel and the exiled Elector Palatine in open revolt. Ferdinand counted also on the enmity between Sweden and Denmark, but although he had managed to have Christian IV appointed as a mediator at the peace negotiations, an appointment of which the Swedes loudly and justly complained,[5] there was as yet no open breach.

There was trouble also between Sweden and Brandenburg. The young Queen was unwilling to marry the Elector and the

[1] Leclerc, *Négotiations Secrètes*, The Hague, 1725, I, p. 128 f.
[2] Bougeant, II, pp. 209-12; Lundorp, v, pp. 761, 768-9.
[3] Lerclerc, I, pp. 113-52.   [4] Lundorp, v, pp. 762-8.
[5] Ibid., p. 1067; Bougeant, II, pp. 304-5.

possession of Pomerania was a cause of animated disagreement. Ferdinand had reason to hope for a complete estrangement.[1]

The hostility between Sweden and Denmark, the tension between Brandenburg and Sweden, raised hopes at Vienna which were partly confirmed by events in the field. The situation in the Swedish section of the conflict was singularly dangerous in the two years succeeding Bernard of Saxe-Weimar's death. Johan Baner was a marshal under the Swedish Queen, but he was a nobleman of ancient family and son of a man who had suffered death for rebellion under Charles IX. Like most of the military commanders, Swedish or no, he was ambitious for lands in Germany, and his behaviour during the last years had clearly indicated that he was no less ambitious for private power. The careers of men like Mansfeld, Wallenstein and Bernard opened up possibilities to which no man of ambition could be indifferent. Baner was ambitious, domineering, unscrupulous. Furthermore, the destruction of the greater part of Horn's army at Nördlingen had placed him in a very strong position. For years he remained the one asset of his government. He was the only bastion against the imperialists, Saxons and Brandenburgers in north Germany. He safeguarded the communication line between Sweden and the Rhine or central Germany; withdrawal would render Oxenstierna's alliance valueless to Richelieu and force Sweden into an ignominious peace.

The army under him, ill-paid as it was and often driven into ill-provided quarters by the attacking forces, was singularly unreliable. His reports to Oxenstierna frankly admitted as much. 'Quartermaster Ramm ... has stayed behind in Mecklenburg without my consent, and I do not know what has become of him',[2] he wrote; and again, 'I could do no more than promise [to pay] them again and again in Her Majesty's name ... with the most plausible excuses I could think of';[3] and later, 'There would be no serious gaps in their numbers if only the stragglers, plunderers, and robbers, whose irresponsibility there is ... no means of checking would come back to their colours'.[4]

[1] *Urkunden und Aktenstücke*, XXIII, i, pp. 17 ff.
[2] *Brefvexling*, II, vi, p. 349.   [3] Ibid., p. 529.
[4] Ibid., p. 840.

He admitted that there was no longer any discipline,[1] that the foot soldiers repeatedly exchanged their equipment for food,[2] and over and over again that matters had now reached the last extremity, beyond which there could be no future.[3]

Baner painted the conditions in his army with a full brush, for in fact he managed to carry on. He intended, doubtless, to create the impression that his own resource and intelligence staved off disaster, a story based on the truth if sometimes exaggerated in the telling. It was certainly true, and Oxenstierna knew it, that the government in Stockholm would have been powerless alone to deal with the mutinous bands, and must therefore treat the marshal with the utmost consideration. Rapidly and surely Baner became to Oxenstierna what Bernard had been to Richelieu. At the time of Bernard's death, only lack of money prevented Baner from buying Erlach and the masterless troops over Richelieu's head.[4] Failing in this, he set himself to establish his position by a spectacular offensive. In 1639 he invaded Bohemia, and, but for the skilful defence of Prague by Piccolomini, the unwillingness of the peasants to rise in his favour,[5] and above all the lack of food, would have made himself master of the whole province. 'I had not thought to find the Kingdom of Bohemia so lean, wasted and spoiled,' he wrote to Oxenstierna, 'for between Prague and Vienna all is razed to the ground and hardly a living soul to be seen in the the land.'[6]

He made good use of his opportunities, nevertheless, and the Swedish government were soon electrified by the news that he had opened peace negotiations independently and had toyed with the offer of estates in Silesia and the title of Prince of the Empire.[7] The discovery of his schemes temporarily wrecked them, but he opened a new campaign in 1640 by a spectacular march southward to Erfurt, where he joined with the Bernardine army under the French marshal Guébriant and a contingent from Hesse and Brunswick. Although he now had over forty thousand men, a certain hesitancy appeared in his actions. The imperialists manœuvred, evading a battle, and

[1] *Brefvexling*, II, p. 538. [2] Ibid., p. 530.
[3] Ibid., pp. 400 ff. [4] AITZEMA, II, p. 830.
[5] *Brefvexling*, VI, p. 634. [6] Ibid., p. 625.
[7] BOUGEANT, op. cit., pp. 66-7.

he made no effort to reach the Danube; instead he followed the ancient example of Wallenstein and opened negotiations with the Archduke Leopold. Behind the imperial lines, the Emperor himself regarded these overtures with the utmost suspicion,[1] while in the Franco-Swedish camp an equal uncertainty of Baner's intentions culminated in the resignation of Peter Melander, the Hessian general, who subsequently and somewhat inconsequently took a command in the Bavarian army. The French commander, Guébriant, had more reason to complain, for Baner had again coolly attempted to suborn the Bernardines into leaving the French service for his own.[2]

Failing in this, Baner fell back on the Weser with nothing achieved. His active but unsubtle brain was softening at last under the effect of the heavy drinking in which he had indulged for many years; he was deeply affected by the death in June 1640 of his wife Elisabeth. She had been with him for the greater part of his campaigning, a gracious, gentle, determined woman, who alone knew how to manage her ill-tempered, ambitious, impatient husband. The soldiers, it was said, looked upon her with reverence and affection as a mother, and the wretched civilians had often asked her to stand between them and her husband's exactions; in one town the municipality had even thought it wise to be on good terms with her maid.[3]

At the funeral of his wife the marshal set eyes on the young daughter of the Margrave of Baden, to whom with the disequilibrium of extreme grief he at once addressed his vigorous but now unoccupied affections. The marriage took place within a scandalously short time, and the marshal, with his young bride, proceeded, to the annoyance of the army officers, to spend three-quarters of every night carousing with their friends, and three-quarters of every day in bed.[4]

If this marriage owed its inception largely to Baner's maudlin grief and ill-restrained desires, it owed perhaps a little to the lady's standing in Germany. Baner, as son-in-law to the Margrave of Baden, had got for himself a stake within the Empire

[1] LUNDORP, op. cit., IV, pp. 237-9 f.
[2] NOAILLES, Episodes de la Guerre de Trente Ans, III, p. 147.
[3] M. SCHILLING, Zur Geschichte der Stadt Zwickau, 1639-40. Neues Archiv für Sächsische Geschichte, IX, pp. 291, 298-9.
[4] BOUGEANT, II, pp. 132-3.

which might be useful when he wished to assert himself against the Swedish Crown. He could use the alliance to make himself a party among the German princes. He had had to receive in his camp, much to his annoyance for he detested the amateur soldier,[1] one of the younger brothers of the Elector Palatine, who was learning the art of war. His manner to this prince, offensively cold at first, mellowed into an arrogant familiarity on his marriage and consequent elevation — in his own estimation — to the same social standing.[2]

This was a very small straw in the wind, but Baner's erratic conduct may well have been guided by private ambition; he was in any case becoming so quarrelsome that he was almost useless as an ally. With a sudden return of military energy, he again advanced to Erfurt, where in December 1640 he once more joined with the Bernardines under Marshal Guébriant and with them made a lightning march to Regensburg, even emptying a volley of cannon-shot into the city from the far side of the river. But the weather and his furious disagreements with Guébriant made campaigning impossible, and he withdrew gradually at the end of January 1641 to Zwickau in Saxony and finally to Halberstadt. His actions, in their periodic activity and indolence, in their perpetual shirking of the final attack, have the true stamp of the careerist soldier. He had continued in his efforts to suborn the Bernardines and had managed to provoke them to disorder.[3] But, like Wallenstein before him, Baner misjudged his army. He had never been personally popular and his first wife's death removed a very real element of unity from the command. He was growing more and more careless of discipline, of pay, of provisions, and the army was alive with mutiny.[4] Before it could break out he died, at Halberstadt on May 20th, 1641, and left the Swedish government to deal with a situation which had become as bad as he had ever painted it.

On the news of Baner's death, Oxenstierna appointed Lennart Torstensson as his successor,[5] a soldier who had been trained under Gustavus Adolphus and in whom he felt he could

---

[1] *Brefvexling*, II, vi, p. 802.
[2] *Calendar of State Papers. Domestic*, 1640-1, p. 469.
[3] NOAILLES, III, pp. 180-2.   [4] *Urkunden und Aktenstücke*, I, pp. 537-41.
[5] *Brefvexling*, II, viii, p. 348.

place his trust. But it would be several weeks, if not months, before Torstensson, who was still in Sweden, could take up his post, and in the meantime the task of controlling the army fell upon Karl Gustav Wrangel, an able but not a popular soldier. Under his leadership in June 1641 the army beat off an imperialist force at Wolfenbüttel,[1] but very soon afterwards the murmurs, partially stilled by victory, rose again. Mortaigne, one of the leading officers and a soldier of considerable reputation, led the mutineers. They demanded immediate pay, in default of which they threatened to march off to the Rhineland with the Bernardines and leave the Swedish government without an army.[2] The coming of Torstensson saved the situation.

He arrived in mid-November, a harsh, commanding man, very ill with gout, but undiscouraged either by the doleful reports of Wrangel or by his own crippling illness. He brought with him seven thousand native Swedish troops and, by a stupendous effort, enough money to satisfy the more troublesome of the mutineers. By the judicious distribution of what he had, by leavening the army with the new Swedish recruits, by his own obstinate refusal to be intimidated or impressed by the mutineers, Torstensson at length induced calm.[3]

He was a more reliable leader than Johan Baner had been. His loyalty to the Crown was more certain and he had far greater organizing ability than his predecessor. He needed it. French subsidies were always insufficient and usually late, and they were the only definite resource, that the Swedish army possessed. Torstensson evolved a new method: he no longer recruited men by offering to pay them for their services. To the distressed peasantry, from whom the ever-dwindling troops were perpetually replenished, he offered food, clothing, arms and whatever plunder they were clever enough to secure. He in fact accepted and legalized the situation which already existed, and was thus bound to find money only for the veterans who had been in arms before he came.[4] Plague, hunger, reckless living was year by year decreasing the proportion of such veterans.

---

[1] *Brefvexling*, II, viii, pp. 570-2.
[2] Ibid., p. 352; PUFENDORF, XIII, pp. 37, 52.
[3] CHEMNITZ, IV, pp. 92-104; PUFENDORF, XIII, pp. 52-5.
[4] LORENTZEN, p. 76; MEIERN, *Acta Pacis Executionis*, Hanover, 1736, I, p. 19.

A gang of licensed robbers could only be kept together and forced to do the office of an army by ferocious discipline, and Torstensson was the man for this. He neither cared for nor sought popularity; his men hated him, and he ruled them by terror from the cumbrous litter to which, for the greater part of the time, his illness kept him confined. Had he been a less able soldier he would hardly have escaped some catastrophic mutiny, but his worst enemy could have found no fault with his campaigning. He gave his men plunder and he gave them victory. They cursed his hangings and shootings and floggings, but they did not rise against him.

The coming of Lennart Torstensson destroyed the Emperor's hope of better fortunes. The Swedish marshal opened his campaign in the spring of 1642 by striking straight at the dynastic lands. A Saxon army was heavily defeated at Schweidnitz, with the loss of much artillery and ammunition,[1] and Torstensson swept on unhindered into Moravia. There was little plunder left, but at a certain monastery the soldiers broke open the tombs and cut off the ringed fingers of dead abbots, smashed the vestment chests and marched on to Olmütz with chasubles and altar-cloths slung cloakwise over their dirty leather coats and waving banners with sacred devices.[2] Olmütz fell in June, and Torstensson, brutal and thorough, at once began to fortify the town. Plantations were ruthlessly cut down to build shacks against the winter; the students, the sick and the destitute were expelled as useless,[3] the imperial governor forced, as a dangerous traitor, to leave the town on foot with his wife and children.[4] The local peasantry were suspected of loyalty to the Emperor; Torstensson kept down their petty attacks by burning their villages, torturing and hanging the prisoners and issuing threats of horrible punishment against any who stole from the army.[5]

His outriders meanwhile were within twenty-five miles of Vienna before the imperial generals, the Archduke himself and Piccolomini, could gather a large enough force to march

<hr />

[1] *Brefvexling*, ii, viii, pp. 369, 376.
[2] *Chronik des Minoriten Guardians in Olmütz. Archiv für Oesterreichische Geschichte*, LXII, p. 481.
[3] Ibid., pp. 472, 482; LXV, pp. 322, 348.   [4] Ibid., p. 334.
[5] Ibid., pp. 328-31, 337-8.

against him. Torstensson was cautious. With the main body of his forces he fell back through Silesia to Saxony, here thinking to bring the ill-armed John George to his knees before the imperialist army came up. He was besieging Leipzig when the Archduke Leopold came in sight on November 2nd, 1642. Torstensson withdrew northwards in the direction of Breitenfeld, Leopold pursuing, impetuous for a second Nördlingen. It was a second Breitenfeld.

The Archduke attacked the Swedes by a terrific cannonade with which he hoped to cover his position while the cavalry on the wings formed for action. He used chain shot, still at that date enough of an innovation momentarily to unnerve the Swedish army. Torstensson, however, saw at once that he must engage the superior forces of the enemy while they were still unready and, braving the cannonade, he charged their left wing. The disordered ranks broke at once, and although the Archduke in person galloped to the spot and tried by oaths, threats and blows to rally the fugitives, neither officers nor men took the least notice.

On the opposite side of the field, the imperialist cavalry had beaten back the Swedes, and the imperialist infantry pressed the Swedish centre. Torstensson's victorious cavalry of the right, however, after dispersing the imperialists, came in to the help of the centre and forced the attacking infantry to withdraw. It remained now only for the whole of Torstensson's forces to encircle the isolated right wing of the imperial horse. Some surrendered as they stood, most fled, and the Swedes pursued them for miles across the flat country. Whole companies and troops, flinging down their arms, surrendered to the conquerors and willingly agreed to enter Swedish service. At a low estimate, the Archduke lost a quarter of his army on the field and another quarter to the enemy. The Swedes estimated his dead at nearly five thousand and their prisoners at four thousand five hundred; they had also gained forty-six cannon, fifty wagons of ammunition and the papers and money of the Archduke.[1] He, himself, barely escaping with life and freedom,

---

[1] CHEMNITZ, IV, ii, pp. 139, 142; *Brefvexling*, II, viii, pp. 376-8. The battle is critically described in TINGSTEN, *Johan Baner och Lennart Torstensson*, pp. 213-20. There is also an excellent plan.

retired to Bohemia. Here he tried by court martial the colonel and officers of one whole regiment, which he declared had broken first and wantonly shattered the resistance of the left wing. Defeat embittered his easy temper; he beheaded all the higher officers, hanged the lesser, shot every tenth man in the ranks and broke up the remainder among the rest of the army. This done, he retired to Pilsen to receive the sacrament in public and pray for help.[1]

A few weeks later, bad news came from the opposite quarter of the Empire. Wiederhold, that independent Protestant who had refused to surrender the castle of Hohentwiel to the Emperor eight years before, swooped down on the town of Ueberlingen on the north shore of Constance and seized it for the French.[2]

With the Hapsburg fortunes at this low ebb, the Elector of Mainz had called a Deputationstag at Frankfort-on-the-Main to discuss the problems which had caused, or had subsequently arisen out of, the war.[3] Ferdinand hoped that his assembly would arrogate to itself the right to settle German problems, and that he would thus deprive France and Sweden of any claim to interfere in the affairs of the Empire at the peace discussions. The plan was ingeniously countered by a Swedish move; the Swedish plenipotentiaries at Hamburg issued a manifesto inviting all the Estates of Germany to bring their complaints to an international peace conference.[4]

In the meantime the places of meeting had been fixed at Osnabrück for Sweden, at Münster for France, and the date of assembly fixed for March 25th, 1642. Ferdinand clumsily evaded the issue: he postponed the ratification of the arrangement until the date was past, and issued no credentials for his plenipotentiaries.

The Austrian subterfuges were, however, denounced by this time even by Ferdinand's Catholic allies. Maximilian of Bavaria, whose ever-wandering loyalty had been fixed momentarily by his marriage to the Archduchess, now leaned again to France and carried the Electors of Mainz and Cologne with

[1] CHEMNITZ, IV, ii, p. 153.
[2] HEILMANN, Die Feldzüge der Bayern, Leipzig, 1851, pp. 4-6.
[3] LUNDORP, V, pp. 821-2.
[4] MEIERN, Acta Pacis Westphalicae, Hanover, 1734, I, pp. 11-12.

him. Situated as they were, all three naturally sought to conciliate the dominant power on the Rhine, Mainz and Cologne to secure immediate protection, Bavaria to obtain the confirmation of his Electorate and Rhenish conquests.

Division within the family broke down Ferdinand's powers of resistance. On the death of his cousin, the Cardinal-Infant, Olivarez had at first decided on the Archduke Leopold as his successor.[1] The prince had not shone in Germany, but he was not unintelligent, had something of the Cardinal-Infant's easy charm and was likely to be well received as a prince of the blood by the snobbish Brussels mob and the Flemish officials. Philip of Spain, at first amenable to the suggestion, suddenly changed his mind and declared instead his intention of satisfying the passion for royalty of the Flemish people by appointing his own son, Don John, as governor.[2] Don John was the King's son, it is true, but his mother was the actress Maria Calderon; he was by all reports virtuous and intelligent[3], but he was only twelve years old. The people, from the officials down, were righteously indignant that a bastard was to be set over them, and the inner circle of the government recognized at once that, by appointing a child, Philip was trying to tighten still further the hold of Madrid on their oppressed state. Deferential but persistent protests, at length induced Philip to postpone the sending of Don John indefinitely, and in the meantime to appoint Don Francisco de Melo as regent in the Netherlands.[4]

The situation was not saved. The Austrian family had been bitterly wounded that, after so many years of alliance, the King should prefer his bastard before the eldest Archduke, the avowed leader of the Spanish party in Vienna. The moral bond thus broken by Philip's inept arrogance, it needed only the incompetence of Melo to plunge the Spanish Netherlands into final disaster and give the Emperor one additional stimulus to save himself from the sinking ship of the Spanish monarchy.

---

[1] LONCHAY ET CUVELIER, III, p. 456.
[2] Ibid., p. 459.
[3] *Relazioni dagli Ambasciatori. Spagna*, II, pp. 112, 113.
[4] LONCHAY ET CUVELIER, III, p. 488.

The war between France and Spain progressed fitfully but with an ever-growing balance in favour of France. Richelieu's difficulty to the end was his army; he needed his best men always for Germany, where the danger was greatest, and he did not always trust the noblemen who commanded for him in the Pyrenees, Flanders or Burgundy. He had nevertheless singled out for particular confidence the Duc d'Enghien, eldest son of the Prince de Condé, a man in his early twenties of whom he expected much.[1] At his instance this gentleman was made commander-in-chief of the forces on the Flemish frontier in the winter of 1642.

The Duc d'Enghien had given proof to others of a character less reliable than that with which Richelieu credited him. His temper was so violent, so moody and at times so desperate, when he was a boy, that it had been doubted whether he would grow into sane manhood. By his twenty-second year he had outgrown these failings, but he retained a singularly impulsive and startlingly unconventional manner with a great dislike of contradiction.

The French army, too, had altered during the last years. Richelieu, attempting to save money and curb the power of the commanders, particularly of the nobility, had concentrated more on technical skill than on numbers.[2] With the support of the King he had tried to enforce a more rigorous discipline, threatening Draconian punishments for such minor offences as swearing;[3] he had attempted to reduce the number of camp-followers, and particularly of women, among the troops, not always with success.[4] Furthermore, by smoothing the way as far as possible for promotion by talent and not by influence he had opened a tempting career to the ambitious, intelligent sons of peasants, artisans and shopkeepers, and of course of the impoverished aristocracy. Thus, in the last decade, a highly

[1] HANOTOUX ET LE DUC DE LA FORCE, Revue des Deux Mondes, April 1935, p. 612.
[2] Ibid., March 1935, p. 73 f.
[3] NOAILLES, I, pp. 567-71.
[4] Ibid., loc. cit.; See HANAUER, pp. 190-1, 193, 263 f.

trained machine, particularly remarkable for skill and endurance in siege warfare, had rapidly developed. Nor was it perpetually adulterated by the inclusion of the deserters and prisoners from the opposing side. It evolved and maintained a sense of nationality as strong as that of the Swedes had once been, while prisoners were either rapidly exchanged or, with constructive brutality, drafted into the French navy as galley-slaves.[1]

Richelieu did not live to see the crowning of his long political work by the victory of his last important nominee. The year 1642 was marked by the explosion of the final and most dangerous mine in his path. The King's beautiful favourite Cinq Mars revolted, carrying with him several of the nobility — too few to save his cause, but enough to shake the Cardinal's confidence.[2] For the last time Richelieu triumphed, and Cinq Mars followed earlier leaders of revolt to the scaffold. His victor outlived him less than three weeks. On November 28th, 1642, he was taken seriously ill, and four days later asked permission to resign his office. His body, so long tormented by intermittent and increasing illness, was exhausted at last. The King would not accept the resignation; instead he came to see his minister, sat at his bedside, and fed him with the yolk of eggs, showing in his restrained, inhibited fashion all the tenderness of which he was capable.[3] Their contacts had always been those of the mind only, unsoftened by one touch of emotion, the Cardinal holding to the King as the 'tree-trunk' of the State, the King to the Cardinal as the foundation of his power. Their union had occasionally suffered by those infatuations of the sick and listless King for some young, vivid, healthy thing which could give him the emotional happiness he had found neither in marriage nor in power, but with Louis, for all his unbalanced longings, the head was stronger than the heart, and the domination of Richelieu remained firm.

The King came on December 2nd; on the following night Richelieu received extreme unction and sank slowly into coma. Towards midday on December 4th he died, and the Parisians,

[1] Avenel, v, p. 277.   [2] Ibid., vii, pp. 866-7.
[3] *Un recit inédit de la mort du Cardinal de Richelieu. Revue Historique*, LV. pp. 304-8; Avenel, vi, pp. 507-8, 696, 704.

453

more in curiosity than in sorrow, crowded in to take their last farewell of the man who had never been popular yet always respected, always feared, always in the crisis of their fortunes called upon and trusted.

In the ensuing spring, Enghien, with l'Hôpital and Gassion, two experienced commanders, began operations on the Flemish border. A shadow of uncertainty hung over the campaign for, in Paris, Louis XIII was ill, and his physicians saw little hope of recovery. Richelieu's policy had been taken over, unaltered, by his own latter-day confidant and right-hand man, Cardinal Mazarin. But if the King were to die, his successor would be a child of barely five, under the regency of his mother and a council. While the King lived the restless powers of France, the nobility and the Paris mob, might stomach the guidance of Mazarin, but when that feeble barrier fell it was not likely that they would tolerate the rule of the Spanish queen and the Italian Cardinal.

Under the shadow of these fears, Enghien moved his troops to defend the line of the Meuse. In the Louvre the King lay on his huge bed day after day, but his unhealthy body, which had for the last years never seemed truly alive, was unable to die. The pulse beat obstinately on in the wasted skeleton. Day after day he lay almost motionless, sometimes sinking into troubled sleep, sometimes half-conscious, sometimes speaking, while his wife cried noisily at his bedside. Courtiers and doctors came and went, and among the pompous grandeur and sordid sights of the sick-room, the Dauphin and a little friend played quietly while the Duke of Anjou, on the lap of a strange countess, cried loudly for his nurse who was not privileged to cross the threshold.[1] A little before his death the King woke from a short sleep to see Condé watching him. 'Monsieur de Condé', he said, 'I dreamt that your son had won a great victory.'[2] Early in the morning of May 14th, 1643, he died.

On the evening of the 17th, Enghien had the news, where he lay with his troops somewhere between Auberton and

---

[1] M. L. Cimber, *Archives Curieuses de l'histoire de France*, Paris, 1834, II, v, pp. 427-39.
[2] Ibid., p. 436.

Rumigny,[1] in the flat country to the west of the Meuse, on his march to the relief of Rocroy, a strong frontier fortress besieged by Melo. He thought it wiser at first to say nothing, lest there should be a panic in the army; on the following morning at Rumigny he called a meeting of the officers and informed them of his plans. Rocroy itself stands on an eminence above the surrounding country, but the ground between it and Rumigny is flattish, sandy, and much broken with scrubby woods and narrow marshy streams. Before the town the country opens out and the woods recede. Melo lay with eight thousand horse and eighteen thousand foot between Enghien and the town, well entrenched. The prince's plan was to advance through the narrow defiles of the woods towards Rocroy, leaving the baggage and cannon behind. Should this movement draw Melo from his position, then they would outflank him and approach Rocroy from the rear; should it fail to draw him, then they would force him to try the issue before the town. This scheme laid down, with Gassion's agreement and l'Hôpital's disapproval, Enghien informed the officers of the King's death and appealed for their loyalty to the new sovereign and the regency.[2]

On the following day, May 18th, the first part of the plan was successfully carried out, Melo allowing the whole of the French army, fifteen thousand foot and seven thousand horse, to emerge unmolested from the narrow defiles on to the open ground. He imagined he would do his cause the better service by surrounding and taking the whole French army than merely by putting it to flight. He had the superiority in numbers — although not so great a superiority as he thought — and in training, for he had under his command the flower of the Spanish infantry, the troops of the Cardinal-Infant, the inheritors of the tradition of Spinola. When, however, he saw Enghien's men emerge, he was completely baffled, for the prince so arranged it that the movements of the infantry were partly concealed by those of the cavalry, advancing in front and on both sides. In vain Melo sent out parties to draw off the cavalry that they might estimate the number of the infantry

[1] DE BESSÉ, *Relation des campagnes de Rocroy et de Fribourg*, Paris, 1673, p. 283.
[2] Ibid., pp. 284-6.

in the centre; his scouts failed or brought in such varying reports that he did not know what to believe.

By six in the evening Enghien had drawn his troops up on the plain within cannon shot of the Spaniards. His right wing, where he himself was in command, rested on slightly rising ground, but was partly divided from the opposing cavalry under the Duke of Albuquerque by a thin strip of wood, in which Melo had stationed musketeers to check Enghien's advance. The left wing under Senneterre and l'Hôpital was in lower

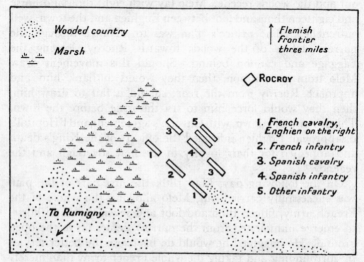

ground, defended from flank attack by a marsh. Melo commanded opposite Senneterre on the Spanish right wing, and the old Flemish general, Fontaine, was in command of the infantry, which occupied the smoothly rising ground in the centre of the Spanish lines. The ground is too little accidented to speak of hills and valleys, but there was a depression between the armies, so that the attackers would start downhill and end by charging uphill.

Six o'clock in the evening was early enough in the fine May weather to open the engagement, and this Enghien would have done, had not Senneterre suddenly, without orders, detached half his cavalry to circumvent the Spaniards and relieve

Rocroy. This movement was ill-considered, as Senneterre had to traverse the marsh on his left flank in full view of the Spanish army, and Melo, seeing his opportunity, was about to charge when Enghien hurried to the spot with reinforcements from the other wing, ordered Senneterre back and covered his retreat. Melo let the opportunity slip, and night fell on the two armies with nothing done.

At daybreak Enghien advanced on the strip of wood between his forces and the opposing Spaniards, and rapidly cleared out the musketeers. This barrier was gone before Albuquerque realized it, and he was still depending on it to protect him when he was engaged simultaneously on the flank by Gassion and in front by Enghien. Albuquerque's troops put up a stout defence but receded and finally broke altogether before the attack. Leaving Gassion to pursue the fugitives, Enghien turned his attention to the centre of the conflict. Far over on his left wing, l'Hôpital's charge had been repulsed by Melo, and his cavalry falling back in disorder might have left the field before he could rally them, had not the reserves come up to support them. Nevertheless, the situation on the left was grave, and in the centre the infantry remained on the defensive, outmatched and outnumbered by the opposing Spanish and Flemish troops.

Taking in the situation at a glance, Enghien rallied his own cavalry and proceeded with the recklessness of genius to cut himself a passage through the Spanish centre. The first line of the enemy infantry, the Spanish veterans, was engaged with the French infantry and pressing them hard; Enghien struck between it and the second and third lines of the Italian, German and Walloon troops. Less well trained than the Spaniards, they soon gave way before the unexpected impact, and Enghien found himself after a sharp struggle on the farther side of the field, in a position to come up on Melo's rear and relieve the attack on the exhausted troops of Senneterre and l'Hôpital. Melo's horsemen, caught between two assailants, broke towards the marsh on their right flank, hotly pursued from both sides, and fled from the field.

The Spanish infantry, about eight thousand strong, were now alone on their slight eminence. If they, by a stupendous feat of endurance, could hold the place until reinforcements were collected, Enghien might yet be defeated. At first it seemed almost that it could be done. The French infantry advanced to within fifty paces, to be met by a sudden hail of musketry fire which sent them back in broken order quicker than they came. Enghien reinforced the line with cavalry, but the mixed attack had as little effect, and three times the French were repulsed with heavy loss of life. Meanwhile, Gassion and Senneterre had pursued the fugitives far enough for safety and returned to the field with their cavalry. Enghien organized a fresh attack, and the Spanish infantry saw that they were now surrounded on all sides. Their leader, Fontaine, killed by a chance shot, and all hope of a successful resistance gone, their officers signalled for a truce.

Enghien was willing enough to grant it on terms. It was already late in the evening and he had no desire to continue the fight à outrance. With a few companions he rode up the hill, but some of the enemy, mistaking this movement for a new attack, opened fire. With cries of indignation the French forces surged forward to protect their leader, the word that he was in danger spreading fast from line to line, until on all sides infantry and cavalry converged on the Spanish position. In vain Enghien shouted to his men to give quarter; furious at the attack on their leader, they cut down all whom they encountered, and the prince himself with difficulty saved some few of the enemy who clung to his stirrups in the mêlée and claimed his personal protection. Night fell on the disaster of the Spanish army; of eighteen thousand infantry, seven thousand were prisoners, eight thousand had been killed, and of those the greater number were Spaniards. Twenty-four cannon, innumerable arms and the military treasury fell into Enghien's hands, and on the following day he entered Rocroy in triumph, a fact recorded to this day on the gates of the little town.[1]

It was the end of the Spanish army. It was true that the cavalry survived, but they were so broken in discipline and

---

[1] The account of the battle is from H. DE BESSE, *Relation des campagnes de Rocroy et de Fribourg*, pp. 287-305; CANOVAS DEL CASTILLO, *Estudios del Reinado de Felipe*, IV, ii, pp. 449-83. See also RODRIGUEZ VILLA, *El Duque de Albuquerque en la Batalla de Rocroy* and M. LE DUC D'AUMALE, *La Première campagne de Condé. Revue des Deux Mondes*, April 1883, pp. 733 ff.

morale as to be useless without that splendid infantry which had been the strength of the army. They had not lost their reputation at Rocroy, as the Swedes had done at Nördlingen, but they had died to keep it. The veterans were gone, the tradition broken, and no one was left to train a new generation. In the centre of their position on the fields before Rocroy there stands to-day a little modern monument, an unassuming grey monolith: the gravestone of the Spanish army; almost, one might say, the gravestone of Spanish greatness.

TOWARDS PEACE

1643-1648

We must die or be slaves for the knife is at our throat.
ISAAC VOLMAR, Imperial plenipotentiary at Münster

TOWARDS PEACE

I

FIVE weeks after Rocroy Ferdinand III gave his imperial sanction for negotiations with France and Sweden on June 23rd, 1643. The congress of Münster did not open until December 4th, 1644; this time the fault was not entirely his. There were three causes for delay: the first a quarrel between the Emperor and the German Estates, the second a weakening in the French position and a breach with the United Provinces, the third a rupture between Sweden and Denmark.

The Emperor had agreed to the meeting of a Deputationstag at Frankfort-on-the-Main, hoping that this assembly would settle the internal difficulties of Germany, above all the religious peace without foreign interference. Whatever allies the contending parties had found, it seemed reasonable to hope that a purely German assembly would be allowed to settle purely German questions. Ferdinand under-estimated the arrogance of the Swedes and French, and over-estimated his own prestige.

Since the implicit accusation made against him by the Elector Frederick William at Regensburg, and more especially since the spreading of that damaging pamphlet, the *Dissertatio de ratione status*, Ferdinand's every action was suspect; at Frankfort-on-the-Main the deputy from Brandenburg indeed accused him of wantonly hindering the peace.[1] Consequently, when first the Swedish[2] and then the French ambassadors,[3] and then again the Swedes,[4] appealed to the German Estates to lay all their grievances before the international congress, the suggestion met with a willing acceptance. Ferdinand issued a counter-appeal in vain;[5] his good faith did not command belief, the more so that he had previously asked the assembly at Frankfort for a subsidy of nearly thirteen million

---

[1] *Urkunden und Aktenstücke*, I, pp. 832-3.
[2] MEIERN, *Acta Pacis*, I, pp. 11-12.   [3] LUNDORP, V, pp. 905 f.
[4] Ibid., pp. 912-13.   [5] MEIERN, *Acta Pacis*, I, pp. 223-8.

gulden, which he could only need if he intended to prosecute the war. Unable to prevent the German representatives from flocking to the peace congress, he denied them the right to vote at Münster or Osnabrück. This was in substance a threat that they should either discuss their grievances at Frankfort or not at all; strong in the support of their foreign allies, and under the leadership of Frederick William of Brandenburg, the Estates protested so vigorously that Ferdinand yielded at last to the inevitable and agreed that the deliberations in Westphalia should have the significance of a Diet; thus any treaty agreed on there and signed by him would become the law of the Empire.[1]

External pressure contributed to his final surrender. The Landgravine of Hesse-Cassel had refused to submit her cause to the Frankfort assembly,[2] an indication that she considered it merely an extension of a prejudiced imperial Court; and Maximilian of Bavaria had threatened to make a separate peace unless Ferdinand would yield.[3] The recalcitrance of the Landgravine was the less important of the two, but it significantly demonstrated that the extremist party would not be satisfied by any settlement at Frankfort. Maximilian's threat was more immediately effective, for his desertion would mean the collapse of imperial arms.

Maximilian's position had altered since the Peace of Prague, in 1635 when he had been deprived of his cherished League and forced to wage war as Ferdinand's ally, almost as his dependant. At that time he had only a rag of an army left, not enough to give him any control over imperial policy, whereas his fellow-ally, John George, had a considerable army with well-distinguished independent rights under a good commander. But while John George had stumbled on in his fuddled way, losing first his commander Arnim and then, little by little, allowing his army to dwindle, Maximilian had so husbanded his resources and improved his army that he had again built up his dominant position. 'He respects the Emperor', said the Venetian ambassador in 1641, 'but he does everything in his own way.'[4] By 1644 he seems to have set his disordered finances

---

[1] STÖCKERT, *Die Reichsstände und der Friedenskongress*, Kiel, 1869, p. 23.
[2] LUNDORP, V, pp. 831-3. [3] KOCH, I, p. 469 f.
[4] FIEDLER, p. 283.

in order again,[1] and his troops had gradually become the backbone of the imperial forces.

Meanwhile the Spanish government drained away Ferdinand's strength: his army, battered and drilled into shape again by the indefatigable Piccolomini, after the second Battle of Breitenfeld,[2] decayed rapidly after Rocroy when Piccolomini's services were demanded in the Netherlands. Robbed of his best commander, Ferdinand had no choice but to appoint Werth, Maximilian's cavalry general, now returned from a French prison, to command the horse. Werth's tactical skill and ingenuity meanwhile made the French professional, known to his employers as Franz von Mercy, the dominant figure on the imperial side, although in fact he was only the commander of the Bavarian troops. In the autumn of 1643 the French, led by Guébriant and relying on the veteran Bernardine army, advanced from Alsace across the Black Forest into Württemberg and took Rottweil. Here Mercy and Werth emphatically turned the tables on them; surprising the troops in their loosely spread quarters near Tuttlingen, they drove them out with heavy loss of baggage and men, and delivered Rottweil. More dismayed than his delegates at Münster would admit, Mazarin hastily collected reinforcements and appointed Turenne to redeem France's reputation, while the imperialists proclaimed their victory to Europe as a sufficient answer to the defeat of Rocroy.[3]

It was not that. But it proved that while Mercy defended Württemberg, Turenne would have serious difficulty in joining forces with the Swedes under Torstensson. It also elevated Maximilian of Bavaria, the master of Mercy and Werth, to the position of an indispensable ally to Ferdinand, and convinced the French government that they must buy Maximilian's friendship once again if they wished to be certain of breaking imperial power. Their conclusions were confirmed by Mercy's siege and reduction of Überlingen in May 1644, and of Freiburg in July.[4] In a three days' battle, in which he was pitted against

[1] DENGEL, *Kardinal Rossettis Wanderung. Forschungen und Mitteilungen zur Geschichte Tyrols und Vorarlbergs*, I. p. 267.
[2] ELSTER, *Piccolomini Studien*, pp. 101 ff.
[3] CHÉRUEL, pp. 475-9; HEILMANN, p. 91; CHEMNITZ, IV, iii, pp. 185-6,
[4] HEILMANN, pp. 97 f., 122-5.

Turenne and Enghien together, Mercy superbly defended his position; he was however outnumbered and Enghien, by a feigned out-flanking movement, which threatened to cut him off from his base in Swabia, forced him to retire.[1]

The Battle of Freiburg was the occasion of so much valour and skill on the French side, that it was later much advertised, but in fact Mercy maintained his original position in Württemberg at the cost of heavy loss to the French army. Bavarian arms remained the chief bulwark of the Empire. So much was this so that when Maximilian threatened to make a separate peace, to withdraw Mercy and leave the gateway of the Empire open to Turenne, Ferdinand could not afford to disregard his threat.

Overreached by his own ally, the Emperor derived some hope from the weakening in the position of France. In the first place the new government was less secure than its predecessor. Richelieu, though never popular, had evoked a certain apprehensive admiration. The people did not feel the same about Cardinal Mazarin. The dapper little Sicilian with his petty personal vanities, his childlike ostentation, his delight in craft and cunning, had no impressive qualities. Equally he had not the comprehensive genius of Richelieu; he never understood or managed to control the internal politics of France. He was essentially a politician, not a statesman.

Yet in some ways this littleness of Mazarin was fortunate. His cunning, his delight in intrigue, his understanding of minute and contradictory side-issues, were exactly suited to the complicated diplomacy of the peace congress at Münster. Richelieu could not have managed the situation better.

Even in internal affairs Mazarin's character gave him one advantage. The late King had appointed the Queen as regent, with a council for her five-year-old son. Anne of Austria, elder sister of the Empress, the King of Spain and the Cardinal-Infant, had been suspected of a leaning towards the Spanish cause while her husband lived, and on his death the Courts of Vienna and Madrid were filled with high hopes. These were rapidly dashed, for Anne of Austria immediately promised

---

[1] HEILMANN, pp. 138-55; BESSE, *Relation de Rocroy et de Fribourg*, pp. 356-7, 365 f.

the Swedish Resident in Paris to stand by her husband's policy[1] and she soon yielded all her powers willingly to Mazarin, who lost no time in reassuring Oxenstierna of his loyalty.[2] The relationship between the Queen and the minister will always remain doubtful; his letters to her are full of a flattering tenderness,[3] but he keeps his distance and one is reminded irresistibly of the reverential flirtation of a Disraeli and a Victoria. Neither Mazarin nor the Queen was yet fifty, and each was attractive to the other sex, the courtly little Cardinal with his bright, appraising eyes and ingratiating smile, the Queen with her indolent grace, smooth, clear complexion and lazy contemplative eyes. The gaiety of her youth had sunk into a tranquil middle age in which it is probable that she agreed to accept rather than to satisfy her minister's adoration.[4]

This friendship of Mazarin and the Queen, the backstairs gossip of the diarist, the ready-to-use material of the romancer, had a definite significance in European history. It kept the regency of France firmly fixed on the road traced out by Richelieu, and destroyed the vain hopes of the House of Austria.

But if the Spanish government could hope nothing from the new regency, it had grounds for hope in another direction. The Battle of Rocroy had destroyed the army which was the sole protection of Flanders; it had made room for France as the dominant power in Europe, not only in the arts but in arms. The doubts which had been growing in the United Provinces for the last thirteen years now became not the accompaniment but the theme of Dutch diplomacy; fear of France overtook and outran fear of Spain. By 1643 the peace and war parties in the Provinces had become respectively the Spanish and the French parties — and the Spanish party was the larger.

The burghers of the United Provinces feared several things. They feared France on their borders and French competition, they feared, superstitiously almost, the secret Roman Catholics in their midst, and they feared the despotism of the House of Orange. Frederick Henry, immensely popular for ten or fifteen

[1] *Hugo Grotii Bref till Svenska Konungahuset. Historiska Handlingar. Ny följd*, XIII, ii, p. 6.
[2] CHÉRUEL, I, pp. 40-1.
[3] MAZARIN, *Lettres à la Reine*, ed. Ravenel. Paris, 1886, pp. 31, 338.
[4] See FEDERN, *Mazarin*, pp. 90-2.

years, had lost favour as he grew older.[1] Subject to recurrent attacks of gout and jaundice, he had become unprepossessing in person and depressed in temper; the caution and moderation which distinguished him in his prime had become, as it were, softened into indecision and languor.[2] More and more he fell under the influence of his wife,[3] and the Princess, once the radiant young beauty Amalia von Solms, was now a stout, vain, exacting woman with ambitions for the dynastic security of her only son. In 1640 she and her husband had married their son, who was only twelve, to the nine-year-old daughter of the English King; this was a suspicious move to the minds of the republican Dutch, and when, very shortly after, civil war broke out in England between King and Parliament, the Dutch Estates sympathized with Parliament while the Prince of Orange unwisely allowed the English Queen and various of the nobility to use The Hague as a base for collecting troops and money for the King. Indeed, so well were the ambitions of Frederick Henry known that the Spaniards had tried to buy him into a private peace with an offer of important lands for his family.[4]

That Frederick Henry spoke French as his native tongue, was the son of a French mother, had married his son to a princess also half French, that Amalia received innumerable gifts from France,[5] all these things made the Dutch burghers suspect that the ambitions of the House of Orange were in some way supported by France. There was no evidence of this except in so far as the French government, a monarchy not quite at ease in dealing with a republic, gave the Prince of Orange the title of 'Altesse'[6] and treated him rather too openly as though he were identical with the Dutch Estates, instead of being merely the Stadholder of six out of seven provinces.

The religious problem also drove the Dutch away from France and towards Spain. The question of toleration for Catholics within the Provinces had always been one of the points on which peace negotiations had foundered; but at least

[1] PRINSTERER, II, iv, p. 272.   [2] HUYGENS, *Mémoires*, p. 90.
[3] PRINSTERER, IV, p. 159.
[4] GEEST, *Amalia van Solms en de Nederlandsche politiek*. Baarn, 1909, p. 21.
[5] DOHNA, *Mémoires*, Königsberg, 1898, p. 31.
[6] AITZEMA, II, p. 417.

the Spaniards handled the question openly. Of recent years the Dutch had nourished a suspicion that the French too had designs on their religious integrity, designs all the more nefarious for being concealed. The French government passed from the hands of one Cardinal into the hands of another, and why were Catholic Cardinals in alliance with Protestant powers except for ulterior motives? Certainly the Catholics of the United Provinces had crystallized the suspicions of the Protestant majority by appealing to the French Queen to intervene in their behalf.[1]

With relations at this tension, one of the French ambassadors, on his way to Münster, passed through The Hague. Claude d'Avaux was a fairly intelligent man; he had done well at Hamburg in dealing with the Germans and the Swedes, but he did not know the Dutch. Very proud of his previous diplomatic successes, very contemptuous of the bovine Hollanders, and far too sure of himself to ask advice from Abel Servien, his colleague, who knew the situation better, he must needs stand up before the Dutch Estates on March 3rd, 1644, and tell them that the King of France thought it would be an excellent thing if they would tolerate the Catholics.[2]

The tempest raised by his speech was so immediate and so violent as nearly to overset the boat of the Franco-Dutch alliance. Only by the most elaborate explanations and the French guarantee that nothing subversive had been intended was the storm momentarily calmed, and even then it was suspended rather than dispersed, and it lowered over the whole of the negotiations at Münster ready to burst again at any minute.[3]

One other danger threatened the French position. The aged Pope Urban VIII died in 1644 and was succeeded by Innocent X. Maffeo Barberini had been devoted to the interests of France; his successor, Giambattista Pamfili, was opposed to them. It would be too high an estimate of the new Pope's policy to say that he was devoted to the interests of Spain. In so far as he stands out at all in Papal history, he stands out as a negative quantity. Depressed, nervous, well-intentioned, he

[1] WADDINGTON, *La République des Provinces Unies*, pp. 383-5.
[2] LE CLERC, p. 193.
[3] CHÉRUEL, pp. 656, 690.

was not a bad man and he was not a bad Pope. Perhaps he was
scarcely a Pope at all. His fame with posterity rests on nothing
that he did, but on the fact that Velasquez painted him. He
lived in the Vatican, played bowls in its magnificent garden,
set his hand to Papal bulls and went through the religious duties
of the Holy Father, but his political and private life were alike
swamped by the activities of an ambitious sister-in-law, who
used his position as a mounting stone for her social elevation
and a missile in her personal quarrels. As for his being a 'Holy
Father' somebody unkindly commented, the very children ran
away from him, 'tant il était effroyable à voir'.[1]

His election, which they at once declared was simoniacal,[2]
meant the removal of a very useful prop to the French government. The whole fantastic alliance of Protestant powers under
a Catholic paymaster, of Sweden, the Provinces, Hesse-Cassel
and the old Heilbronn League under France, had been justified in the eyes of the very Catholic French middle-classes by
the sanction of the Pope. Besides, Urban had lived long enough
to send his own nominee, Fabio Chigi, to represent the Vatican
as one of the mediators of peace at Münster. Now Mazarin
feared that Innocent would withdraw Chigi and send some
Spanish, or Spanish-paid, nuncio to take his place.[3] In fact, he
need not have worried, for Innocent was not a man of action
and Chigi remained. His fears were justified only in Italy, where
the policy of the new Pope led to the rupture of diplomatic
relations between Paris and the Vatican, and a brawl in the
Italian peninsula.[4] This was expensive and unnerving but had
surprisingly little effect in the end on the peace congress in
Westphalia.

The French position was not weakened, in the long run,
as much as the Spaniards hoped in 1644. They were encouraged
nevertheless by current events, by the increasing willingness
of the United Provinces for peace, and their increasing dislike
of the French, by the removal of Papal support from Mazarin,
to seize the opportunity of making an advantageous peace.

[1] *Relazioni Veneziane. Roma*, II, pp. 69-70, 88-9; COVILLE, *Mazarin et Innocent X*, p. 30.

[2] BROSCH, *Geschichte des Kirchenstaates*. Gotha, 1880, I, p. 410.

[3] BOUGEANT, III, pp. 107-8.

[4] See COVILLE, *Innocent X et Mazarin*, for a full account of these difficulties.

Their hope in war destroyed at Rocroy, they snatched at the diplomatic opportunity.

To the French way of thinking, the congress called at Münster and Osnabrück was to settle the war in Germany, in fact to force peace from the Emperor and thus detach him from Spain. The last thing Mazarin wished to see was a general peace in which Spain was included. She was not to creep out of the war to nurse her wounds and come back ten years later, refreshed, to the struggle with France. She was to be left isolated, sword in hand, to fight on to the death. Great, therefore, was the indignation of the French ambassadors when, on arriving at Münster in March 1644 after a bitterly cold journey through melting snow,[1] they found not only an imperial but a Spanish delegate waiting for them. With ready resource they announced that they could not possibly treat with him, since his credentials referred to the King of Spain as King of Navarre and Portugal and Duke of Barcelona;[2] their master, they pointed out, was the only King of Navarre and Duke of Barcelona, and they recognized John of Braganza as the only King of Portugal. Having thus neatly held up the Spanish question, they proceeded to postpone meetings for a still longer period, by a furious dispute with the Spanish delegate as to the precedence of their respective masters.[3]

The dispute between the Emperor and the German Estates, the weakening of the French position and the intervention of Spain, delayed the congress but threatened it with total annihilation less than did the break between Sweden and Denmark which took place at the same time. Ever since his withdrawal in 1629, Christian of Denmark had offered at intervals to 'mediate' between the combatants, and in 1640 he had established himself more or less effectively by means of his delegates as the 'unprejudiced party' in the deliberations at Hamburg. The Swedes, however, had been very far from accepting his impartiality at its face value; he had assisted in the abduction, with her own consent, of the Queen-mother of Sweden, an event which might easily have led to serious internal trouble

[1] OGIER, *Journal du Congrés de Munster*. Paris, 1893, p. 51.

[2] PRESTAGE, *Diplomatic Relations of Portugal to France, England and Holland.* Watford, 1925, p. 17.

[3] FIEDLER, pp. 301-2; MEIERN, *Acta Pacis*, pp. 195-7.

in Sweden. He had signed a commercial treaty with Spain. He had married his son to a daughter of the Elector of Saxony, an open imperial ally. In the spring of 1643 he blockaded Hamburg, and his raising of the Sound tolls in order to meet the perpetual deficit of his budget injured Swedish trade and made him the most hated man on the Baltic.

At this juncture, when Christian had not a friend in the North, Oxenstierna acted, sending instructions to Torstensson in September 1643 to attack the Danish dominions. Waiting only to make certain of his defences on the borders of Bohemia and Moravia, the marshal to the amazement of the Danes turned north-east with the greater part of his army, invaded Holstein in December and overran Jutland before the end of January 1644. Not until this had been accomplished did the Stockholm government deign to issue a manifesto justifying their action. Declaration of war there was none.

Whatever excuse the Swedes had for this conduct, they were much and justly criticized for their manner of action. Popular feeling in The Hague was emphatically for the unoffending Danes. Mazarin was equally indignant, the source of his annoyance being the fear of an untimely revival in Swedish strength which would make them less docile as allies. Indeed he shortly after took the drastic decision to cut off all subsidies unless Torstensson immediately withdrew from Jutland.[1]

Two Danish delegates, all this while, had taken up their residence at Münster and Osnabrück. They now beset the Swedish ambassadors for an explanation of the attack, and getting no satisfaction angrily withdrew from the conference. The gesture proved totally ineffective; the remaining delegates agreed to continue the congress in spite of the rupture.[2]

Nevertheless, the outlook for peace was sadly clouded in the spring of 1644. The Emperor supported the Danes and risked what was left of his resources on equipping an army to support them. This was to attack Torstensson in the rear and force him to surrender. The plan was sound, but the execution would have been laughable had it not been tragic. Gallas, by now rarely more than half-sober, pushed forward unhindered almost

---

[1] MEIERN, Acta Pacis, I, pp. 88-116, 175; BOUGEANT, III, pp. 119-26.
[2] GÄRTNER, Westphalische Friedenscanzlei, Leipzig, 1731, II, pp. 337-9

as far as Kiel; here Torstensson, leaving Wrangel to prosecute the war in Jutland, slipped past the ineffective outposts and marched for the now undefended Hapsburg lands. Gallas, lumbering after him, was met and crushingly defeated at Aschersleben. With what was left of his troops he somehow drifted back to Bohemia.[1] This time no Archduke Leopold stepped forward to say that he was an excellent but much misunderstood commander; of all his army he had brought back a little less than a third — one rumour said only a tenth — and he was commonly known throughout the Empire by the unflattering name of 'der Heerverderber', the spoiler of armies. In the face of bitter and justified abuse he resigned and retired to indulge in private that vice which had been his undoing.

The Danish war petered out. The King himself, commanding his own fleet in a prolonged engagement off Kolberg, prevented an assault on Copenhagen from the sea, but it was clear when Gallas failed him that he would no longer be able to support the war on land.

Meanwhile in Sweden, on September 18th, 1644, Queen Christina, at eighteen years old, became the active ruler. The effect of this change of government was to be felt very soon both at the congress and in the Danish war, for the Queen was no cipher, easily flattered and deceived, but a young person of obstinacy and intelligence. Very much the daughter of her father, she had the courage necessary for the situation and was able the more boldly and easily to abandon a sentimental adherence to his policy. She wanted peace above all things, above even the territorial aggrandizement of Sweden.

With her accession the government at Stockholm ceased obstruction and began to move actively towards a settlement.[2] From that moment the Danish war was virtually discontinued, and the signing of a peace, which was later concluded at Brömsebro, was a foregone conclusion when in November 1644 the Stockholm government agreed to submit the dispute to the mediation of Brandenburg.[3]

The chief obstacles being thus partly smoothed away and

---

[1] CHEMNITZ, III, iv, pp. 167-8.
[2] CHANUT, *Mémoires*, Paris, 1675, I, p. 28.
[3] *Urkunden und Aktenstücke*, XXIII, I, p. 67.

all further excuse for delay overridden, the congress was opened on December 4th, 1644, eighteen months after the Emperor had given it his sanction, and thirty-two months after the date originally fixed for its meeting by the delegates at Hamburg. For all that period, as for three years and ten months after its meeting, the war continued in Germany.

II

There never had been within the Empire any corporate expression of feeling, any channel through which the desire for peace could be expressed. The ruling powers — not merely the princes but any organized body with a means of making itself heard — asked for peace always in a general sense: when it came to practical action they were always prepared to fight for a little longer in order to gain their own particular end — and make a more lasting peace. Even in the last years, at the congress in Westphalia, it was the same. Not only the Elector of Brandenburg, the Landgravine of Hesse-Cassel, the Elector Palatine and a dozen others were prepared to go on and on, always a little longer, to avoid or to obtain something, but even so forlorn a group as the Bohemian Protestant exiles were left at the conclusion of peace still demanding that it be not ratified until their cause was vindicated.

There was, and had been from the beginning, a deep desire for peace in Germany; but it was the mute desire of those unable to express their wrongs, that class from whom the war drew its sustenance, both men and food and money, and who had no means to control or prevent it. The peasant had only one means of making his sufferings known — by revolt; that such revolt invariably ended in defeat for all, and death for the leaders, was no deterrent. Often enough, those who led it had no hopeful illusion that they would be luckier than others, but fought merely for the relief of expressing in action sufferings too deep for words.

In the last eight years of the war there were fewer such risings. The cause was twofold. There must come a point beyond which the human mind, singly and collectively, is

unable to register further suffering or to sink to further degrad-
ation. The accumulated mass of social evidence on the Thirty
Years War proves that that point is far to reach. By the time
the congress met at Münster it had been reached.

In the country at large the soldier ruled, without mercy and
without regard. Torstensson himself compared the sack of
Kremsier in June 1643 to that of Magdeburg;[1] Baner spoke
lightly of shooting down civilians and sacking a town for the
mere offence of refusing food and drink, which it could probably
not have supplied to his men in any case. In Olmütz the
daughters of the richest burghers were forcibly married to
careerist army officers at the request of their colonel.[2] In
Thuringia a father who appealed for justice against a soldier
who had raped and killed his daughter was coarsely informed
by the commanding officer that if the girl had not been so
niggard of her virginity she would still be alive. Here, too, the
Swedes enforced a system by which not only food, shelter and
clothing but arrears of pay were exacted from the townsfolk.[3]
The ports of the Baltic suffered under a continual and increasing strain, as both the Swedes and the Danes levied higher tolls
on their ships and enforced more galling exactions.[4]

But at Münster and Osnabrück, although there was famine
in the surrounding country,[5] supplies did not run short and
nobody was in a hurry. They took six months from the opening
of the congress to decide how the delegates were to sit and who
were to go into the rooms first. The French ambassadors
argued with those of Sweden[6] and Brandenburg[7] as well as
with the Spaniards, and quarrelled with the delegates of the
Hanseatic League,[8] and the Venetian mediator,[9] and even
more fiercely among themselves;[10] the deputies of Brandenburg
and Mainz challenged each other's superiority,[11] as did also the
Venetian mediator and the Bishop of Osnabrück;[12] the chief
French ambassador, Longueville, would not enter until he was

[1] *Brefvexling*, II, viii, p. 408.
[2] *Chronik des Minoriten Guardians*, pp. 466, 469.
[3] EINERT, p. 35. [4] *Brefvexling*, p. 630.
[5] LE CLERC, II, p. 22. [6] Ibid., pp. 22, 25.
[7] MEIERN, *Acta Pacis*, I, p. 393. [8] Ibid., pp. 363-8.
[9] BOUGEANT, II, p. 411.
[10] MEIERN, *Acta Pacis*, I, p. 382; LE CLERC, II, p. 123.
[11] GÄRTNER, V, p. 5. [12] BOUGEANT, III, p. 256.

given the title of 'Altesse',[1] and for the entire duration of the congress could never meet the leading Spanish ambassador because the formalities could not be arranged;[2] the Papal nuncio set up a dais for himself in the chief Church, and the French insisted on his taking it down;[3] the Spaniards raided the house of the Portuguese delegate,[4] the Dutch demanded the precedence of a monarchy,[5] and the servants at the French delegation had a brawl with the street scavengers of Münster, who trundled their loads out of the town every night under their windows, making an intolerable noise and stink.[6] As someone remarked, the child that the French ambassador's wife now carried would be grown-up, dead and buried before the end of the congress.[7]

Another mistake was the continuation of hostilities during the congress; a general cessation of arms would have brought the negotiations more quickly to an end, but while the war continued the diplomats at Münster and Osnabrück allowed their decisions to be influenced by its movements and were always prepared to postpone matters yet a little longer in the hope of some new advantage in the field. The French, above all, with greater resources and less economic and social compulsion than their adversaries, were prepared to postpone a conclusion indefinitely; it was no small part of their tactics to make a parade of their readiness to hold on for ever rather than lose what they wanted. Their chief ambassador, Longueville, planted a garden round his lodgings and sent for his wife to bear him company, merely as a demonstration that he could, and would, stay at Münster for ever. At the same time Mazarin urged his commanders to hasten on affairs by a great show of arms in the field.[8]

Their ambassadors, however, were not very gifted. Claude de Mêsmes, Marquis d'Avaux, had a certain ability but was far too sure of himself to be cautious, and the error he had made in commending Catholic toleration to the Dutch was typical of him. Intolerably haughty and easily offended, he did not get on with the other delegates and least of all with his colleague,

<hr />

[1] MEIERN, *Acta Pacis*, I, pp. 424, 495-6.   [2] FIEDLER, p. 315.
[3] BOUGEANT, II, p. 416.   [4] PRESTAGE, *Diplomatic Relations*, p. 18.
[5] BOUGEANT, III, p. 247.   [6] LE CLERC, II, p. 4.
[7] OGIER, p. 88.   [8] CHÉRUEL, II, pp. 306-7; LE CLERC, III, pp. 136-7.

Servien. 'One would have to be an angel to find a remedy for all your weaknesses',[1] wrote this latter in a fit of passion. Abel Servien, Marquis de Sablé, was less superficially conceited than Avaux, but his letters, and more particularly his quarrels with his colleague, prove that he was no less self-confident. He was Mazarin's right-hand man, and Avaux was both jealous and afraid of him,[2] a feeling which Servien did nothing to alleviate. Cleverer in his dealings with the other delegates, Servien was undoubtedly the better diplomat, but as, at moments of crisis, the two French ambassadors were frequently not on speaking terms, their single or joint ability was often at a discount. The third French ambassador, the Duc de Longueville, had been sent merely to add lustre to the embassy and to keep him out of mischief in France.[3]

Somewhat the same ill-feeling reigned between the Swedish ambassadors. The chief of them, Johan Oxenstierna, had no claim to his position at all save that of being the son of Axel Oxenstierna; he was a large, red-faced, rather stupid man, easily rattled, very haughty, too fond of wine and women.[4] He signalized the hours of his rising, dining and retiring by a fanfare which could be heard all over Osnabrück.[5] His subordinate, Johan Adler Salvius, was one of the few comparatively able men at the congress, determined, clear-headed, resourceful and with a pleasant humour. Oxenstierna was said to be against peace because it would diminish his own and his father's importance. But Salvius had instructions from the Queen to prevent him from needlessly holding up the negotiations; he had her word for it that any peace would be pleasing to her, regardless of the private or public wishes of the Oxenstiernas, father and son.[6] Salvius thus stood in much the same relationship to Oxenstierna as Servien to Avaux: each was the lesser of the ambassadors, yet each was in closer personal touch with the home powers than his superior.

The Spanish ambassador, the Count Guzman de Peñaranda, was not remarkable for intelligence. A handsome man with

[1] Le Clerc, i, p. 102.
[2] Fiedler, p. 300; *Correspondencia diplomatica de los plenipotenciarios Españoles en el congreso de Munster*, 1643-1648, Madrid, 1884, ii, p. 344.
[3] Bougeant, iv, pp. 61-2.   [4] Fiedler, pp. 310-11.
[5] Bougeant, iii, p. 67.   [6] Fiedler, p. 394; Chanut, i, pp. 26, 28, 83.

elegant manners, he was extremely proud and gained the
reputation for being both impulsive and deceitful.[1] He had,
strongly marked, the Spanish tendency to strain over details
and miss the main issue. In so far as Spanish diplomacy
achieved any success at Münster, it was through his singularly
able second, Antoine Brun,[2] a man of letters, a humanist, but
bred of the official class and with all the traditions of bureaucracy at its best, the flair for practical needs and the gift of
compromise.

The chief ambassadors of the United Provinces were Adrian
Pauw for Holland and Jan van Knuyt for Zeeland, between
whom again there was that same element of tension though it
never came to the surface. Pauw represented the peace, or
pro-Spanish party who suspected France; Knuyt the Orange
party with their French leanings. Both were able men, Pauw
perhaps exceptionally so. He was said to be the only man who
had ever outwitted Richelieu.[3] Neither of the Dutchmen
inspired confidence, but they never betrayed themselves and,
although the French and Swedes had the gravest suspicions
of their actions, they could never gain confirmation of them
until it was too late.

The two mediators, or chairmen in the modern sense, were
the Papal nuncio, Fabio Chigi, and the Venetian ambassador,
Alvise Contarini. They exerted just enough influence for
almost everyone to accuse them of prejudice, and just too little
to have any marked effect. Chigi was on the whole easy-
tempered and prepared to smooth matters out as best he could;
Contarini, on the other hand, was more difficult and inclined to
lose his temper completely if contradicted.[4]

For the rest, the hundred and thirty-five deputies[5] assembled
at Münster and Osnabrück included several men distinguished
in other walks of life, theologians, writers, philosophers. But
when the negotiations are considered, one is forced to admit
that, with the exception of Pauw, Brun and Salvius, there is
little evidence of anything save a good-natured or an egotistical

[1] FIEDLER, p. 334; WICQUEFORT, L'Ambassadeur, The Hague, 1681, p. 208.
[2] Ibid., pp. 296-7; see also TRUCHIS DE VARENNES, Un diplomate Franc-
Comtois. Dôle, 1932.
[3] F. DE DOHNA, Mémoires, p. 35.   [4] LE CLERC, III, p. 96.
[5] MEIERN, Acta Pacis, I, p. 9.

muddle-headedness. Even the success of French diplomacy at the end was in great part due to the simplicity of Peñaranda and the victories of Turenne in the field.

One other man who showed, if not outstanding ability, at least great perseverance and great tact, was the imperial ambassador Trautmansdorff. He did not, however, arrive in Münster until the end of November 1645. Until then the imperial case was defended by Isaac Volmar, an acute lawyer and government official, whom the French, however, persistently regarded as unequal to his office by reason of his rank. The Emperor, foreseeing this objection, had appointed the affable Count John of Nassau as a purely decorative addition to the embassy. The French, nevertheless, declared that they would not believe in the Emperor's good faith unless he sent a man whose rank and qualifications were alike equal to the task.[1] It was not, therefore, until Trautmansdorff's arrival, eleven months after the opening ceremony, that anything but the barest preliminaries could be discussed.

III

The congress had been sitting for nearly a year when the delegates found that they were still in doubt as to the *subjecta belligerantia*. A debate was therefore held with the purpose of forming a clear idea of what had been fought for, what was being fought for, and what subjects the peace conference should handle.[2] It is not surprising that they felt the need of greater clarity on these questions. Reduced as far as possible to simplicity, there were four main subjects for discussion: the complaints of the imperial Estates, the conditions of amnesty towards rebels, the satisfaction of foreign allies, and the compensation of the dispossessed. The first group covered nearly all the internal causes of the war; it covered the case of Donauwörth, undecided since 1608; the Cleves-Jülich succession, still only temporarily settled; the vexed problem of the judicial rights of the Reichshofrat; the constitutional rights

---

[1] BOUGEANT, III, pp. 25-6.
[2] MEIERN, *Acta Pacis*, II, p. 75.

of the Emperor; the position of the Calvinists; above all, the distribution of land between Catholic and Protestant rulers.

The second group of problems were those connected with the amnesty; this covered the question of restitution for the Elector Palatine and his uncle the Count of Pfalz-Zimmern, for the Margrave of Baden-Durlach to lands forfeited during the war to Baden-Baden, for the Landgravine of Hesse-Cassel, in the name of her son, to the lands bestowed on Hesse-Darmstadt, and of the return of Protestant exiles to their homes.

The third group, the satisfaction of the allies, overtopped all others in importance at the congress. There could not be peace until the allies were satisfied, whereas in point of fact there could be, and was, peace before all the internal problems were settled. Sweden demanded Pomerania, Silesia less seriously, Wismar, the bishoprics of Bremen and Verden, and money to disband her army. France required Alsace, which her armies had long occupied, with Breisach, the confirmation of her rights to Metz, Toul and Verdun, and in imperial Italy the fortress of Pinerolo. She also required a guarantee that the Emperor would give no further assistance to Spain.

The fourth group was closely allied to both the second and third. It covered the question of compensation for those who had suffered during the war or as a result of the peace. It would include, for instance, the question of recompensing the Elector of Brandenburg should the peace give Pomerania to Sweden, the satisfaction of Maximilian of Bavaria should he have to yield either land or titles to the Elector Palatine.

The congress was divided roughly into two groups: Sweden and the German Protestants at Osnabrück; France, the Emperor and the German Catholics at Münster. At Münster, also, two separate peaces were under discussion: peace between Spain and the United Provinces, and peace between France and Spain. France and Spain had a stake in all these peace conferences, France as the ally of the Dutch in that between Spain and the Provinces, Spain as the ally of the Emperor in that between the Empire, France and Sweden.

The conduct of the peace conference was thus as complicated and as subject to the violent disagreements of the allies as the war itself. The French and Swedes regarded each other with the gravest mistrust, the French being particularly anxious to dispense as far as possible with Swedish interference in Germany. They wanted to create a predominantly Catholic constitutionalist party as a check on the Emperor, whereas the Swedes, hotly supporting the Protestant deputies at Osnabrück, wanted a predominantly Protestant Empire. The Swedes clamoured for the total restitution of the Elector Palatine, the abolition of the Ecclesiastical Reservation, the religious *status quo* of 1618. The French, who never tired of trying to win over Maximilian from the imperial alliance, wanted him to retain his Electorate and the lands he had won, and for the rest supported the German Catholic delegates at Münster in asking for the religious *status quo* of 1627, that fixed by the Peace of Prague.

The nervous exasperation between the French and their Dutch allies continued throughout with varying intensity, while on the opposite side Maximilian of Bavaria kept the Viennese Court in constant apprehension, and the friendship between Austria and Spain was brought more than once almost to breaking point.

The ambassadors of each country had a double task, to negotiate peace for their own government and to divide their enemies one from another. Spanish diplomacy with the Dutch was intended to split up the Franco-Dutch alliance, and in the end did so. Imperial diplomacy with the French was intended to break the Franco-Swedish coalition and set their German allies against them.[1] French diplomacy with the Catholic Germans was directed at detaching Bavaria from Austria.[2] This elaborate game at cross-purposes was further complicated by the presence of various minor powers on the edge of the European conflict, delegates from the King of Portugal, the Swiss Confederation, the Dukes of Savoy and Lorraine.

The war was still in part, if only in a small part, a German civil war, and little as native interests might dominate the congress in Westphalia, they could not be altogether forgotten. Unable to assert control in the war, the two princes who had intermittently attempted to form a German party tried once again to assert themselves at the peace. John George of Saxony and Maximilian of Bavaria did not act in alliance; the centre

[1] CHÉRUEL, II, pp. 122-3. [2] Ibid., p. 754; FIEDLER, p. 327.

481

party had failed too often and too dismally for there to be any question of reviving it. Yet in the intricacies of the negotiations at Münster and Osnabrück the separate threads of Saxon and Bavarian policy tended each to the same end, — the settlement of imperial affairs as far as possible without giving dominant control to any foreign power.

In this swan-song of the two princes, each revealed the singularities which had all along characterized his policy, John George being as always too direct, and Maximilian too indirect, in his plans. John George aimed all along at reconciling the chief quarrels between Catholic and Protestant Germans, in the hope that thus neither party would be tempted to enlist foreign help in the settlement of this central dispute. His policy would have been more effective if it could have achieved an earlier success. Germany settled her religion problem for herself, but not before the French and Swedes had derived what advantage they wished from it.

Maximilian's policy was more complicated. He feared Spain rather than Sweden or France. He therefore required that any demands of France and Sweden should be met outright, Alsace be given to France, Pomerania to Sweden, so that both should be deprived of further excuse to meddle in Germany. This done, he imagined that the deserted Protestants would be easily quelled and a strong Catholic constitutionalist party would be able to assert itself against the Emperor and his Spanish allies without further foreign intervention. He was prepared to sacrifice the territorial integrity of Germany to strengthen her inner solidarity against the Emperor and Spain.[1]

His policy had more influence on the congress than that of Saxony, and this influence was altogether disastrous. He secured Pomerania for Sweden, Alsace for France, without gaining any guarantee that they would refrain from meddling in constitutional problems, and without uniting the Catholic party against the Emperor. The Empire preserved neither her constitutional nor her territorial integrity, the French exploited Maximilian, and the Swedes took no notice of him. The lesser rulers of Germany continued at Osnabrück and Münster to

[1] See H. EGLOFFSTEIN, *Bayerns Friedenspolitik*. Leipzig, 1878, p. 43 and *passim*.

enlist the help of whatever foreign power was likely to be most helpful at the moment. John George and Maximilian managed this last crisis as badly as those which had gone before.

I V

During the first year of the congress, from its opening in December 1644 to the arrival of Trautmansdorff in November 1645, the military situation had darkened for the Emperor. In the New Year of 1645 Torstensson, commanding the Swedes on the Elbe, crossed the Erzgebirge[1] and by the fourth week in February was advancing rapidly on Prague. At Jankau, about nine miles from Tabor, a mixed force of imperialists and Bavarians cut him off and forced him to fight. He had the best of it from the first. The ground was very uneven and thickly wooded, so that the engagement was rather a series of skirmishes than the pitched battle in which the superior numbers of the enemy would have told.[2] Torstensson first outmanœuvred Goetz, the opposing cavalry general, then charging him at a disadvantage scattered his troops. Goetz himself was killed in the flight, and the news of his death spread to the infantry, who fled in panic leaving the guns behind. When the Bavarian cavalry under Mercy and Werth, and the imperialist reserves under Hatzfeld, attempted to hold the Swedes back, their valiant efforts on the difficult ground with inferior numbers led only to a heavy loss of life. General Hatzfeld was taken, and the remnant of the Bavarian and imperialist cavalry fled towards Prague.[3]

Jankau was in some sort the Rocroy of Germany, for it destroyed the Bavarian cavalry, the backbone of the army, just as Rocroy had destroyed the Spanish infantry.[4] More immediately important, it laid Prague open to Torstensson's victorious army. There was panic in the Hapsburg lands.

[1] PAUL GANTZER, *Torstensons Einfall und Feldzug in Böhmen*, 1645. *Mitteilungen des Vereins für die Geschichte der Deutschen in Böhmen*, XLIII, p. 3.
[2] TINGSTEN, *Johan Baner och Lennart Torstensson*, pp. 267-279; see also the excellent plan.
[3] CHEMNITZ, II, v, pp. 40-3; *Brefvexling*, II, viii, pp. 446-8.
[4] Ibid., p. 44.

Ferdinand, himself at Prague, dragged the incompetent Gallas out of his brief retirement to collect and reorganize what was left of the imperial army. He abandoned all hope of saving his capital and left at once, with only a few servants, for Regensburg; thence down the Danube through Linz, where he joined his wife, to Vienna. His own people spoke of this journey as his 'Friedrichsflucht', and indeed he had gone almost as quickly and almost as much alone as the Winter King a quarter of a century before.[1] Ferdinand himself stayed in Vienna, but the extent of his fears may be gauged from the fact that he sent his stepmother and his children to Graz.[2]

The situation was partly saved by the extreme poverty of Bohemia, which could provide wine but no bread for the Swedish soldiery,[3] by the failure of Sigismund of Transylvania on whose help Torstensson counted as, long before, Frederick had counted on Bethlen Gabor,[4] and by the obstinate valour of Brünn which, under a French soldier of fortune, held up the Swedish advance for nearly five months before the invaders at length raised the siege and withdrew again to the borders.[5]

The battle of Jankau proved thus less immediately effective than had been hoped or feared, and its only definite result on the congress at Münster was the Emperor's decision to release the Elector of Treves. This he did at the instance of the Pope, the other spiritual Electors and the French.[6]

Meanwhile the simultaneous invasion of Turenne was checked by Werth who, hastening back from Bohemia, took the French by surprise near Mergentheim and defeated them with considerable loss.[7] Falling back towards the Rhine, Turenne first felt it his duty to resign, but he took courage from Mazarin's unshaken confidence and joined forces with a fresh army under Enghien. In the summer of 1645 they advanced rapidly on the Danube, and effected a junction with a detachment of Swedes under Königsmarck.[8] Cautiously, Mercy withdrew southwards. He was outnumbered and could not hope to do more than hold the line of the Danube. But at this moment Königs-

[1] CHEMNITZ, II, v, p. 45.
[2] Ibid., p. 50.
[3] Ibid., p. 101.
[4] *Brefvexling*, II, viii, p. 637.
[5] D'ELVERT, *Die Schweden vor Brünn*, pp. 51-75.
[6] MEIERN, *Acta Pacis*, I, p. 389 f.
[7] HEILMANN, pp. 200-2, 203-8.
[8] CHEMNITZ, II, v, pp. 118-21.

mark was suddenly recalled to Bohemia, and the position changed. Mercy decided to contest the French advance, and on July 24th, 1645, he entrenched himself on a group of hills to the south-east of Nördlingen, near Allerheim.

When Enghien, in the face of the entrenched Bavarian artillery, gave the order to scale the hill, tradition relates that Mercy flung his arms round his wife's neck in a transport of joy and exclaimed, 'Now they have delivered themselves into our hands'. The story is apocryphal, for Mercy had no wife nor was he given to emotions.[1]

Against all prognostications the *furia Francese* won the position from the Bavarian defence. Yet it was a Pyrrhic victory, for Enghien and Turenne were too tired to pursue, and their losses, in men and officers, were crippling. The Bavarians retreated safely to Donauwörth, their original objective, and entrenched themselves firmly against further attack.[2] One irreparable loss befell the Bavarians and the imperial cause. Franz von Mercy, incomparably the best of their commanders, the man who had held the Black Forest for two years against Turenne and the veteran army of the Bernardines, had been killed.

The invasion of Bohemia and the advance of the French along the Danube had both been partially checked, but neither imperial arms nor imperial diplomacy could check the desertion of the German allies. As early as June 1644 Frederick William of Brandenburg had made his peace with Sweden; this truce left John George alone against Torstensson in the north-east, and Ferdinand was too weak to send troops to help him. His family, who had always disapproved of their father's leaning to the imperial side, urged him to follow Brandenburg's example, and Torstensson, rising to this admirable occasion for freeing his rear and flank of enemies, gave good terms. A preliminary truce was settled at Kötschenbroda in August 1645.[3]

This removal of the last barrier against the Swedish advance

[1] HEILMANN, p. 270; CHEMNITZ, II, v, pp. 186-9.
[2] RIEZLER, *Schlacht dei Allerheim, Sitzungsberichte der Konigliche Bayerische Akademie der Wissenschaften*, 1901; HEILMANN, pp. 270-90.
[3] LUNDORP, v, p. 1031; see also K. G. HELBIG, *Die sächsisch-schwedischen Verhandlungen zu Kötschenbroda und Eilenburg 1645 und 1646. Archiv für Sächsische Geschichte*, v, pp. 269-79.

upon the Hapsburg lands was a crushing blow to Ferdinand. Worse still, it loosened the already weak allegiance of Maximilian, who was far too practical to be left for long alone on a sinking ship. He had already managed through his delegate at Münster to indicate that he was amenable to any private peace in which his interests received proper consideration, and the French government, which had never altogether deserted its old policy of alliance with him against the Hapsburg, welcomed this new chance. The imperial alliance, weakening for the past two years, was held together by a thread in the spring of 1646, a consideration which had noticeable effect on the congress at Münster.

v

At the low tide of the imperial fortunes, on November 29th, 1645, Count von Trautmansdorff entered Münster incognito and late in the evening, bearing with him the personal instructions of the Emperor. Not until the following morning did he give any official intimation of his coming,[1] and then the ingenuity of his arrival was favourably commented on by both sides. The chief French ambassador, Longueville, had entered with ostentatious grandeur, to the exasperation of his opponents.[2] The Spaniard, Peñaranda, had made a laughing-stock of himself by timing a solemn entry in the pouring rain with an inadequate suite, so that the burgomaster and councillors who came to meet him received him very hurriedly, their best clothes smothered under rainproof cloaks, and his train, such as it was, did no justice to itself. Only one carriage was open, and from this a sparkish diplomat bowed gracefully to the sparse spectators, until one of his polite gestures brought him into contact with a stack of earthenware exposed for sale in the narrow street and sent it clattering to the ground, after which he disappeared rapidly inside his carriage.[3] Trautmansdorff, by entering in perfect secrecy, avoided both jealousy and

[1] OGIER, p. 140.
[2] FIEDLER, pp. 314-15; OGIER, op. cit., pp. 125-9.
[3] LE CLERC, op. cit., pp. 376-7.

ridicule, and prepared his adversaries to meet a man of practical good sense and no pretensions.

He paid a visit first to the Spanish, then to the French ambassadors; the latter, who had been ready to be offended at not being visited first, were disarmed almost at once by his good humour.[1] They saw a thick-set, immensely tall, singularly ugly man, with nothing of the aristocrat in his appearance; he was flat-nosed, with high cheekbones and dark, very deepset eyes under thick, frowning brows, his face surmounted by a shabby wig combed forward in a fringe that overhung his eyebrows.[2] It spite of this extraordinary appearance, Trautmansdorff seems to have impressed both them and, later, the Swedes as a straightforward, capable man who knew what his master wanted.

His coming was in itself a final proof that imperial hesitation was over, for Trautmansdorff was the closest friend Ferdinand had; he had been the chief minister in the State ever since Eggenberg died, and the first adviser of Ferdinand himself since he grew to manhood. If any man could interpret accurately the imperial reaction to each new development at Münster and act accordingly, Trautmansdorff was that man. Moreover, he had never belonged to the Spanish party in Vienna; he was indeed very much opposed to it and not beloved of the Empress. His arrival, therefore, was a proof not only of Ferdinand's will to peace but of his abandonment of Spanish interests.

Trautmansdorff found that there had already been an exchange of demands between the French and the imperial ambassadors, ending in a deadlock. Alsace was the cause. Ferdinand had declared that he would not yield Alsace to the French Crown in any circumstances, and there the matter rested. In his opening interview with d'Avaux and Servien Trautmansdorff offered instead Pinerolo, Moyenvic in Lorraine, Metz, Toul and Verdun. This was clearly not enough, considering the exhausted state of Ferdinand, but before he allowed the French to see that he would yield more, Trautmansdorff travelled to Osnabrück and made a last effort to urge the Swedes to a separate peace.[3]

[1] *Correspondencia diplomatica*, I, p. 211; FIEDLER, p. 318.
[2] LE CLERC, I, p. 468.   [3] Ibid., II, b. p. 242.

His machinations were suspected by the French, who learnt shortly after that their agent at Osnabrück, a Monsieur de la Barde, had been refused admittance to the discussions, a fact which they regarded as disturbing.[1] They need not have worried: the only bribe which would make Sweden leave the war separately was Pomerania, and that the Emperor could not yield without the permission of Brandenburg; imploring the Elector to agree to its cession and rely on imperial generosity to give him some adequate recompense, Ferdinand wrote also to Trautmansdorff, secretly, telling him to yield Alsace to France if Sweden and Brandenburg alike proved intractable.[2]

Maximilian's delegate hastened the conclusion. In an interview with Trautmansdorff on March 24th, 1646, he again threatened to make a separate peace with France unless the Emperor offered reasonable terms.[3] Maximilian's calculations were as simple and selfish as ever: in Paris his ambassador was pleading that he was 'old and broken and his children young' and he wanted peace before he died, but what he wanted most of all was French protection against the Swedes and their protégé the Elector Palatine,[4] and he was prepared to do France good service to buy it. He showed throughout a supine indifference to the integrity of the Empire. This was the third time in the last two years that Maximilian had threatened to desert the Emperor, and Trautmansdorff took it seriously.[5] A fortnight later he offered Alsace to the French.[6] Still it was not enough; Servien and d'Avaux promptly asked for Breisach as well. It was on the other bank of the Rhine, but they had conquered it and intended to keep it. Trautmansdorff was indignant, but he was helpless; twice in the course of a month the Bavarian delegate again threatened to make a separate peace,[7] the Swedes had overrun the whole of north Germany, taken the Catholic bishopric of Paderborn and were rumoured to be advancing on Münster to intimidate the im-

[1] Le Clerc, III, p. 18.
[2] *Urkunden und Aktenstücke*, XXIII, i, p. 86; K. Jacob, *Die Erwerbung der Elsass durch Frankreich.* Strassburg, 1897, pp. 316-18.
[3] Cortreius, *Corpus Juris publici.* [4] Chéruel, II, pp. 104, 147-9.
[5] Cortreius, IV, pp. 167-8, 174.
[6] Meiern, *Acta Pacis*, III, pp. 5-7.
[7] Ibid., pp. 3, 22-3; Gärtner, IX, pp. 126-7.

perialist party,[1] and at Osnabrück the Elector of Brandenburg's deputy, Wittgenstein, continued the unending acrimonious argument about Pomerania.

Trautmansdorff gave way, little by little. The Spanish ambassadors implored him to stand firm, but the combination of the French and Bavarian delegates was too strong. On May 11th the French accused him of obstructing negotiations; to meet this he first offered them Alsace in full sovereignty, and then the cession of Benfeld, Zabern and Philippsburg.[2] They still demanded Breisach and, four days later, on the 16th, he yielded.[3]

At the same time the Elector of Brandenburg was weakening. He had himself passed through Westphalia on his way to The Hague. Realizing that Swedish policy clashed too violently with his own, he had abandoned the project of marrying Christina, and was now anxious to link his fortunes to those of the House of Orange, through which he hoped to gain support for his claim in the Cleves-Jülich case. By June 1646, his attitude on the Pomeranian question weakened; by the middle of October he agreed to a compromise dividing Pomerania between himself and the Swedes so that they secured Stettin.[4] Early in November he suddenly attempted to seize Berg, as his rightful part in the Cleves-Jülich succession, and the imperialists, grasping at the clear indication he had now given of a desire to spread westwards towards the dominions of those with whom he was even now seeking a marriage alliance, offered him the bishoprics of Halberstadt and Minden and the reversion of Magdeburg in place of Pomerania. He agreed.[5] On December 7th, 1646, he was contracted to Louise, eldest daughter of the Prince and Princess of Orange, and a week later, under persuasion, agreed to evacuate Berg, in the confident hope that with the support of the Prince of Orange he would gain more in the Cleves-Jülich case by influence than by force.[6]

---

[1] LE CLERC, III, p. 171.
[2] MEIERN, *Acta Pacis*, III, pp. 24-6; *Correspondencia Diplomatica*, I, pp. 302, 305, 318, 319.
[3] Ibid., p. 29.
[4] See *Urkunden und Aktenstücke*, XXIII, i, pp. 81-9; IV, p. 443, 463.
[5] *Urkunden und Aktenstücke*, IV, p. 220 f.; MEIERN, *Acta Pacis* III, p. 752 f.; *Urkunden und Aktenstücke*, XXIII, i, p. 101.
[6] Ibid., IV, p. 245.

In these negotiations over Alsace and Pomerania the rulers had, in both cases, acted as if they were disposing of their personal goods and chattels rather than integral parts of the Empire and several thousands of their subjects. The Pomeranians had themselves sent a deputation to Münster; piteous and persistent, they were left, when all was settled, impotently wailing that they did not wish to be given to Sweden.[1]

The Alsatians fared scarcely better. Here, indeed, there was a curious contradiction, for the Emperor wished to cut off the ceded territory wholly from the Empire, a suggestion which the King of France strenuously opposed.[2] The apparent callousness of Ferdinand and generosity of the French had an obvious cause. Should Alsace be divorced altogether from the Empire, it would betoken nothing save a change of boundary, but should France hold Alsace under the imperial crown, her King could send a representative to the Diet and meddle unceasingly in German affairs. In the end a compromise of such complexity was reached that one writer called it 'une semence éternelle de guerres'.[3] The Emperor ceded his rights in Alsace to the King of France. The extent of those rights remained undefined, and the towns retained their privileges as imperial cities. But in return for the total disarmament of the right bank of the Rhine from Basel to Philippsburg the French agreed not to exact permission to sit in the Diet. Neither party was satisfied and the clauses were so worded that each could retain its pretensions to its own solution.[4]

During all the negotiations the representatives of Strasbourg and the Decapolis, or ten free cities of Alsace, trotted from the French to the Austrian embassy at Münster, patiently presenting their own views. They did not exert the least effect on those who, with reference solely to the King of France, the Emperor and the European situation, were deciding their fate.

---

[1] *Baltische Studien*, IV, v, *passim*; MEIERN, *Acta Pacis*, II, pp. 231-2; Bks. XXIV, XXVI; see also G. BREUCKER, *Die Abtretung Vorpommerns an Schweden*. Halle, 1879.
[2] LE CLERC, III, pp. 102, 161.
[3] VAST, *Les Grands Traités du règne de Louis XIV*. Paris, 1886, p. 7.
[4] See B. AUERBACH, *La France et la Sainte Empire Germanique*. Paris, 1912 pp. 7-36.

VI

The winter of 1646 thus found the allies satisfied in their territorial demands. There remained the problems of the Empire, the quarrels of individual princes, and the question of the constitutional and religious rights for which the war had been fought.

After endless bickering a decision was at last reached for the Palatine Electorate. Maximilian, who appealed for support to the Pope,[1] indignantly repudiated the suggestion that the Electorate should be held alternately.[2] Charles Lewis, the son of Frederick of Bohemia, was equally disgusted by the proposed creation of a new Electorate for him, an Electorate which should bring him back Heidelberg and the Rhenish Palatinate alone, and be the last in precedence in the college. This arrangement, however, suited Maximilian and the French admirably, and they contrived easily enough to talk over the Swedes, who were at first obstinate in defence of Charles Lewis's rights.[3] Deserted by his only powerful allies, weakened by the collapse of his uncle's power in England, the Elector Palatine at length gave in. He had the spirit to strike a medal showing himself in armour with the Palatine lion, wounded and exhausted, at his feet, bearing the inscription 'Cedendo non cedo'.[4]

The Landgravine of Hesse-Cassel, who had succeeded in making herself a valuable asset to both the French and the Swedes in the field, did better than the Elector, who had never been anything but a liability. She was given the greater part of the land she claimed, and more than half a million talers for the satisfaction of her army.[5]

Still more fortunate were the Swiss, who, thanks to the intelligence and political flair of their government, having contrived to keep out of the war hastened to be included in the peace. They had been an independent and growing confederation for upwards of three hundred years, and now included, — beside the

[1] *Quellen und Forschungen aus Italienischen Archiven*, IV, p. 245.
[2] MEIERN, *Acta Pacis*, III, pp. 587-9.
[3] LE CLERC, III, pp. 249, 255.
[4] *Die Schicksale Heidelbergs*, p. 236.
[5] *Sverges Traktater*, VI, i, pp. 209-14.

original cantons of Uri, Schwyz and Unterwalden, Luzern, Zürich, Basel, the Grisons, Solothurn, Sankt Gall, Appenzell and Fribourg; but their existence had never received recognition. This they now demanded and were given.

The question of payment for the Swedish army was more serious. Alexander Erskine, who was dispatched to the congress to defend its interests, declared, truthfully enough, that the troops could not be evacuated unless there were means to pay them. He demanded for this purpose six million talers; the imperialists in answer offered three and in the end compromised on five. [1]

The problem of imperial justice, of the rights of the Reichshofrat and the reversal of the judgment given against Donauwörth in 1608 were, by common consent, shelved until the next Diet; so also, inevitably, was the still unsettled business of the Cleves-Jülich succession. But the question which compelled the interested participation of all parties was that of religion. At first there was a deadlock, for the Catholic delegates at Münster flatly refused to indulge in discussions with the Protestant delegates at Osnabrück, while the mediator, the Papal nuncio, said he would not sit in the same room as a heretic. [2] When these preliminary obstacles had been overcome, each party took an uncompromising stand; the Catholics claimed all the land which the Church had held in 1627, the Protestants demanded a return to the position of 1618. John George performed his greatest service to peace when he induced them to compromise on the situation of 1624. [3]

For the rest, the Edict of Restitution was shelved for ever, and the right of the prince to alter his religion and that of his subjects at will was confirmed. Provision was made for parity between Catholics and Protestants in certain irrevocably divided cities, chief of which were Augsburg and Regensburg.

As a gesture of conciliation, Ferdinand III had, early in the discussions, agreed to recognize Calvinism as a third religion within the Empire, [4] but when all seemed amicably settled he startled the Protestants, profoundly irritated the Catholics and

---

[1] MEIERN, *Acta Pacis*, v, pp. 849-50, 854, 877-83.
[2] Ibid., II, Bk. xv.
[3] Ibid., v, pp. 718-23.
[4] Ibid., II, pp. 8-11. Oct., 45 doc.

jeopardized the still uncertain agreement by an unexpected display of his father's passion. He refused absolutely to concede toleration for the Protestants in the Hapsburg lands, and appealed to the Pope to support him.[1] He refused equally to allow 1624 as the year for the religious land settlement, standing doggedly to that year 1627 which his own diplomacy had won at the Peace of Prague.

Trautmansdorff, who had shown himself diplomatic and good-humoured throughout, now unexpectedly supported his master and said, when he saw the proposed religious settlement, that if the Emperor were a prisoner in Stockholm he would not advise him to sign it. On July 16th, 1647, he had some further speech with Salvius on the subject and, being unable to gain satisfaction, left that night for Vienna. But he left, it was said, looking uncommonly pleased with himself, and indeed he had reason.

VII

All this while the ground had been shifting under the feet of the negotiators, and Ferdinand, despairing when he sent Trautmansdorff in the winter of 1645, was in high hope when he returned eighteen months later.

Eighteen months had witnessed a continuous weakening of the imperial position, but in the summer of 1647 there occurred one of those deceptive turns of fortune which seemed once again to make postponement possible and victory conceivable for the Hapsburg dynasty.

Early in 1646 the Swedish government had yielded at last to the plea of Torstensson for recall on the score of ill-health[2] — he lay often for weeks in his bed, his hands knotted with gout, unable even to sign an order[3] — and appointed Karl Gustav Wrangel as his successor. Proud, truculent, unpopular,[4] Wrangel was nevertheless a skilful general — too skilful to suit

[1] W. FRIEDENSBURG, *Regesten zur deutschen Geschichte aus der Zeit des Pontifikats Innocenz X. Quellen und Forschungen aus Italienischen Archiven*, IV, pp. 251, 254.
[2] CHEMNITZ, II, iii, pp. 29, 79; IV, p. 166.
[3] Ibid., II, vi, p. 200.
[4] CHÉRUEL, III, p. 2; *Detlev von Ahlefeldts Memoiren*, ed. L. Bobé. Copenhagen, 1896, pp. 54-5.

the French. In the summer of 1646 he led a victorious advance against Bavaria. Mazarin, more apprehensive of Swedish conquests than desirious of fresh laurels for the joint armies, did his best to hold back Turenne, or at least to spare Bavaria.[1] But the joint armies of Sweden and France, whether Turenne would or no, could not stay for the niceties of diplomacy. Wrangel wanted a decisive invasion of Bavaria, the men wanted easy plunder.

Johann von Werth, racing to the rescue, turned the tide of advance from Augsburg but could not prevent the invasion which in the autumn of 1646 poured across Bavaria. Maximilian himself, terrified of a peasants' revolt, refused arms to his defenceless subjects and, by destroying mills and storehouses to starve out the invaders, decreed famine for his own people.[2] In the spring he was imploring a truce; in March he signed it, and only in April did Wrangel suspend hostilities.[3]

But Mazarin had a hydra to deal with in the House of Austria, and weak as the monster was becoming, each lopped-off head was replaced by another. The desertion of Bavaria was balanced by a revival. The coming of Trautmansdorff to Münster had seemed to indicate an abandonment of his Spanish policy by the Emperor. The death of his wife, the Infanta Maria, a few months later increased the hope that Ferdinand would break with Spain. Mazarin, snatching at the auspicious moment, had even thought to break the Austro-Spanish alliance and tempt Ferdinand to a rapid peace by offering him as a bride the strapping hoyden, 'Mademoiselle', Gaston of Orleans' daughter. The offer was refused, on the grounds that the Emperor was yet too deep in his sorrow to think of a second union; but genuine though Ferdinand's grief undoubtedly was, it did not prevent him seeking a wife within his own family, and he rejected the French alliance in favour of one of those marriages by which, from time to time, the dynasty reinforced itself. His chosen bride was his cousin, Maria Leopoldina of Tyrol.

---

[1] LE CLERC, III, pp. 189-90, 345, 348.
[2] CZERNY, pp. 91, 95.
[3] LUNDORP, VI, pp. 186-91; *Brefvexling*, II, viii, p. 728.

This betrothal made less stir in Europe than the simultaneous marriage treaty of the King of Spain. Philip IV, having lost both his wife and only son within a few weeks of each other, began, with indecent haste, to seek out a young bride; he was not a very prepossessing husband, old and glum for his forty-odd years, dumbly stupid; as a ruler, a useless idol. He was devoted only to his one remaining child, the scatter-brained little Infanta who despite the formalities of Madrid and the splendours of Versailles remained through life a foolish, impulsive, perpetually sweet-tempered schoolgirl.[1] The Spanish Empire was dead, but the King of Spain sought an Austrian princess in marriage. He sought his own niece, Ferdinand's daughter Maria Anna, and Ferdinand consented.[2]

Nor was this all. To bind his Austrian cousins more firmly to him, Philip yielded to Peñaranda's suggestion, shelved the appointment of his bastard son and made the Archduke Leopold governor of the Netherlands.[3] At the very moment in which Mazarin broke the Bavarian alliance, Spain renewed her hold on Austria. And at that same moment the Spaniards cut away Dutch support from under the Cardinal's feet.

The French in the winter and early spring of 1646 had approached the Spaniards with the suggestion that they should exchange Catalonia, now occupied by French troops, for the Netherlands.[4] The Spaniards took up the plan, whether seriously or because they knew that it would make enmity between the Dutch and French, it is hard to say. In any case, as soon as the projected transaction became known the Dutch, furious at these machinations of an already suspect ally, began to prepare peace-terms acceptable to Spain and in total disregard of French interests.[5]

Not warned by this misfortune, the French let themselves be further deceived by Spanish diplomacy. Philip's son being dead, they encouraged a plan for the marriage of the Infanta, now sole heiress of Spain, to the boy-King of France. This

[1] *Relazioni dagli Ambasciatori. Spagna*, II, pp. 128, 131, 141.
[2] ABREU Y BERTODANO, VII, p. 97 f.
[3] LONCHAY ET CUVELIER, III, p. 615; *Correspondencia Diplomatica*, I, pp. 65-6.
[4] LE CLERC, III, pp. 14, 21; *Correspondencia diplomatica*, I, pp. 281, 285-6.
[5] LE CLERC, III, pp. 49, 83.

time the French concealed all from the Dutch, and their childish duplicity met its due reward when the Spaniards, who had not regarded the scheme seriously, suddenly revealed it all and left the French alone to face the music.[1] This time no denials, no protests, no special deputations availed anything.[2] Even the Swedes were indignant[3] and, finally disgusted with their ally, the United Provinces signed a truce with Spain,[4] leaving their untrustworthy friends to extricate themselves alone.

The abandonment and evaporation of that project for the cession of the Netherlands, drove the French to prosecute the war ardently in the Low Countries. The more so since the Archduke Leopold, travelling rapidly and incognito, had crossed the frontier of Brabant early in the New Year of 1647 and was now preparing for fresh campaigns against France with a zeal reminiscent of the Cardinal-Infant.[5] Bavaria being forced to neutrality, Mazarin designed that Turenne should turn all his forces now in Germany against the Low Countries.[6]

The plan both for Bavarian neutrality and for Turenne's attack on Flanders had one serious weakness. On the Bavarian side Johann von Werth, the general of Maximilian's troops, had no intention of accepting the imposed neutrality and, on the French side, the old Bernardine army had no intention of obeying Turenne. A double mutiny in the summer of 1647 played into the hands of the Hapsburg and for the last time wrecked the matured schemes of France. At the end of June the Bernardines mutinied on the Rhine against their French commanders, at the beginning of July Werth declared his loyalty to the Emperor and not the Elector of Bavaria. No wonder that Trautmansdorff had smiled as he left Münster on the evening of July 16th, 1647.

Maximilian had been on bad terms with Werth for long enough; his discipline was non-existent, his birth was low, his manners revolting, he could barely write, and the Elector, although he admitted him to be an admirable cavalry leader,

[1] Le Clerc, iii, p. 373.
[2] Ibid., p. 387; iv, p. 86 f.   [3] Chanut, i, p. 25.
[4] Abreu y Bertodano, vii, p. 111.
[5] Lonchay et Cuvelier, iii, pp. 625-6, 629.
[6] Chéruel, op. cit., ii, pp. 419, 431, 439.

regarded him openly as a drunken boor and refused to gratify his desire to be named field-marshal. Consequently it had been easy for Ferdinand by a few judicious hints to bribe the unscrupulous and discontented careerist. Late in June Maximilian, hearing something of the plot, sent for his general, but he had no definite evidence, and Werth, confronted with an unsupported accusation, swore his innocence with a cheerful disregard for the pains of hell, and rode back to his men to make all ready for immediate action. In the first week of July 1647 he was marching at the head of his army to join the Emperor.

Meanwhile at Strasbourg the discontent of the Bernardines had come to a head. Turenne had long expected it. Three years earlier a serious mutiny at Breisach had been stilled only by the courage and popularity of Erlach.[1] Since then Erlach had withdrawn and Turenne, who had got on badly with him, got on even worse with his successor, Reinhold von Rosen. The troops were convinced, justly enough, that the French intended to merge them slowly in the main body of the army; they claimed that French officers were appointed over them, that their interests were not considered, and finally that, by the terms of their service, Turenne had no right to order them to Flanders. The mutiny, once started, spread with uncontrolable speed; Rosen, with some mistaken idea of influencing the troops, set himself at the head of them, and when Turenne, somewhat ineptly, arrested him, the Bernardines elected a leader from their ranks and set off four thousand strong, plundering savagely as they went, to join the Swedes.[2]

After that Turenne, seriously weakened, could no longer march on Flanders. Besides, the collapse of Bavarian neutrality made his presence necessary in Germany. But here, too, the mutiny checked his free action, for Wrangel, after a momentary embarrassment,[3] had coolly enlisted the Bernardines, and Turenne refused at first to act in conjunction with an army stuffed with rebels from his own.[4] It would be dangerous to act

---

[1] CHEMNITZ, IV, iv, p. 34; CHÉRUEL, I, p. 710; GONZENBACH, II, p. 45.
[2] HEINRICH ALMANN, Turenne und Reinhold von Rosen. Historische Zeitschrift, XXXVI, pp. 368-409; WALTHER, Strassburger Chronik, p. 40; GONZENBACH, II, pp. 66-71.
[3] Brefvexling, II, viii, pp. 736-7.
[4] CHÉRUEL, III, pp. 63-5.

without the help of the Swedes and, in the circumstances, impossible to act with it.

The Bernardine mutiny was successful from the point of view of the mutineers, but Werth's mutiny benefited only the Emperor. Werth, in fact, had not the character to carry his troops with him; most of his followers went back to Maximilian and he crossed the Austrian frontier almost alone, with a price on his head.[1] Nevertheless, Maximilian had already been frightened out of his peace policy. On September 27th, 1647, the exasperated French ambassadors at Münster learnt that he had rejoined Ferdinand with all his forces.[2] They would have been more distressed still had they known that a little later the one-time Hessian general, Melander, now generalissimus of the imperial and Bavarian troops, had joined with Frederick William of Brandenburg in an attempt to form an eleventh-hour 'German' party and break this foreign-controlled peace.[3]

On January 30th, 1648, Spain and the United Provinces concluded the Peace of Münster.[4] For the wretched Spanish Netherlands it was the end of prosperity; Spain had been prepared to sacrifice the loyal provinces who had fought for her, in order to get better terms for herself. The Scheldt was closed and Antwerp ruined to make way for Amsterdam. But although France was gravely concerned about the peace, it was for no love of Flanders; her ambassadors, after several ineffectual protests,[5] took the decision to call off their own negotiations with the Spanish, citing as their excuse the fact that Peñaranda had left Münster and they could not treat with anyone of less importance. They calculated that they would be able to write off their breaking of their own Dutch alliance against the breaking of the Austro-Spanish pact. The Emperor would not be able to oppose the terms established at Münster and Osnabrück by the assembled German Estates and their foreign allies. When he signed them he would have to renounce all that Spain held in Germany and undertake to help her no more.

[1] RIEZLER, *Die Meuterei Johann's von Werth. Historische Zeitschrift*, LXXXII, pp. 40 ff; PUFENDORF, XIX, p. 34.
[2] OGIER, p. 192.
[3] W. HOFMANN, *Peter Melander Reichsgraf zu Holzappel.* Munich, 1882.
[4] AITZEMA, III, pp. 259 ff.
[5] See CHÉRUEL, II, pp. 359-64.

The success of French diplomacy was sealed by her armies. The desertion of Bavaria forced Turenne to act in unison with Wrangel and abandon his Flemish plan; their differences over the Bernardines shelved, not settled, the two generals at length converged together upon south Germany.[1] On the surface the outlook was not very hopeful. Wrangel, who feared that the end of the war would be the end of his power, had only been forced to act by the appointment of the Queen's cousin as commander-in-chief, and the news that he was on his way to Germany stung the jealous marshal to further effort. If the war had to be ended, better end it himself than leave it to another.[2] He did not, however, hesitate to let it be known that Turenne was trying to evade battle in order to prolong the war.[3] Indeed the weakness of the enemy made further post-ponement impossible to justify. Melander, imperial field-marshal since the previous year, was entrenching himself on the line of the Danube. But the joint Bavarian and imperial armies were outnumbered by the Swedes and French, and Groensfeld, the Bavarian commander, was hampering their joint action by demanding precedence over Melander.[4] In this plight they were surprised in broken, rolling country not far from Augsburg and close to the village of Zusmarshausen. Impeded by an intoler-able train of camp followers — they outnumbered the men, it was reckoned, at the rate of four to one — Melander tried to get the artillery and baggage away, leaving the Italian general Montecuculi to defend the rear; with dogged courage Monte-cuculi retreated from ridge to ridge, using his cavalry to beat off the attacking forces while the infantry withdrew. Melander coming up to his help was mortally wounded. The Italian decided to save the army rather than its impedimenta, now in hopeless confusion, and fell back to Landsberg with the loss of everything except his troops.

In the last, darkest hour Piccolomini came back to Austria to save the situation, but it needed more than his immense energy and tenacity to make an army out of the scattered, demoralized fragments left after Zusmarshausen, and Maximilian did not

---

[1] See CHÉRUEL, II, pp. 536-45, 568-71; III, pp. 63-5, 103.
[2] Ibid., p. 119.   [3] Ibid., p. 142.
[4] STECKZÉN, *Arriärgardesstriden vid Zusmarshausen. Historisk Tidskrift*, 1921, p. 136.

ease matters by arresting Groensfeld for treason directly after the battle.[1]

Turenne and Wrangel, meanwhile, overran Bavaria, wreaking horrible vengeance on the people for the fickle policy of their master. In fact, as Wrangel tersely wrote to the Elector, he had but one way to save his country and that was to make another truce.

A second Swedish army under Königsmarck invaded Bohemia and summoned Prague to surrender. On July 26th, 1648, they took the Kleinseite, and it seemed that all was lost, but the restored Catholic and Hapsburg city fought for its religion and its King as it had never fought before. Taken in 1620 and in 1635 almost without a shot fired, it would have held out in 1648 to the last man. The students, the monks, the burghers defended the Charles Bridge, shoulder to shoulder with the soldiers, never slacking in their efforts. How long they could or would have resisted it is impossible to say. Hope of relief they had almost none, yet for more than three months they held on, and peace, not surrender, ended their long defence.

While the people of Prague stood at bay, Ferdinand, clinging to his religious conviction, his father's heritage, his dynastic obligation, refused to sign the peace. The religious settlement was the ostensible barrier to his signing, yet he had political reasons. Could Ferdinand fail his Spanish cousins when they had made peace with the Dutch and were at last in hopes of meeting the French as equals?[2] His own much beloved brother was supporting that desperate conflict in the Low Countries, confident that he would not be abandoned.

The Archduke had shown himself from the beginning of his governorship an active commander and a firm disciplinarian; he had broken through on the French frontier, reconquering Armentières, Comines, Lens, Landrecies. In those first months of his rule he was strangely unlike the Archduke of later years, that lank, disappointed man who stands in the photographic pictures of David Teniers, waggling an ineffective cane at some favourite masterpiece in a lofty Brussels studio.[3] In that first

[1] Dudik, *Die Schweden in Böhmen*, Vienna, 1879, p. 397.
[2] Chéruel, III, p. 191.
[3] There are several such pictures; a particularly good one is in the Kunsthistorisches Museum at Vienna.

year he seemed the equal of the Cardinal-Infant. And then, at Lens in August 1648, by carelessness, incompetence or bad luck, or by all three, he was trapped by Enghien and his whole army blotted out.[1]

That was the end for Ferdinand. Bavaria lost at Zusmarshausen, Prague beseiged, Leopold broken at Lens. He bowed to the inevitable, accepted the religious settlement and agreed to sign the peace. But the delegates at Münster had not taken three years to make a peace to sign it in three minutes. When Ferdinand's final resolution reached Münster, the key had been lost and it could not be decoded. This delay overcome, there began an interminable discussion of the order in which the treaties should be signed, and not until Saturday, October 24th, nearly three weeks after the solution of all political difficulties, were the actual signatures written. Even on the day the deputies, having waited from nine till one at Münster, were told to come back again at two. Only then did the leading ambassadors appear, and both the treaties of peace were signed. The action was greeted by three successive salvos from seventy cannon ranged on the walls.

That was not the last shot of the Thirty Years War. All those weeks, all those days, all those last futile hours, they had been fighting at Prague, and went on fighting for nine days longer before they, too, had news of the peace.[2] Then they, too, fired their salvo to the skies, sang their Te Deum and rang their church bells because the war was over.

[1] CHÉRUEL, III, pp. 181, 198-9; CANOVAS, *Estudios*, pp. 488-98.
[2] They called an armistice on November 2nd, and news of the peace was confirmed on November 9th; DUDIK, *Die Schweden in Böhmen*, p. 342; PUFENDORF, XX, p. 65.

THE PEACE—AND AFTER

Je crois qu'il se faudra contenter que chacun demeure avec ses prétensions et explique le traité comme il l'entend.

SERVIEN, January 1649

THE PEACE—AND AFTER

I

AFTER thirty years, peace had come to Germany. At Prague the clanging of church bells drowned the last thunders of the cannon. Beacons of joy flamed to the night sky on the hills along the Main.[1] But at Olmütz in Moravia where the Swedish army had lived for eight years the dazed soldiers were sunk in gloom, and in the fields about the town the camp women collected in desolate groups. 'I was born in war,' said one, 'I have no home, no country and no friends, war is all my wealth and now whither shall I go?'[2] Leaving Olmütz, the trail of baggage wagons and stragglers stretched for three miles along the road, while the burghers, as many as were left, gathered together in their long dismantled church to sing their thanksgiving.

'At Thy rebuke they fled; at the voice of Thy thunder they hasted away.

'They go up by the mountains; they go down by the valleys unto the place which Thou hast founded for them.

'Thou hast set a bound that they may not pass over; that they turn not again to cover the earth.'[3]

But for two years after the peace it was still doubtful whether the soldiers might not turn again to cover the earth, and the articles settled at Münster and Osnabrück establish no better peace in Germany than those signed at Prague thirteen years before.

Erskine had made it clear during the negotiations that the interests of the Swedish army, as distinct from the Swedish State, must be considered, and the last delays at Münster arose

[1] BOTHE, *Geschichte Frankfurts*, p. 451.
[2] *Chronik des Minoriten Guardians*, p. 600.
[3] Ibid., p. 610.

from the joint demand by the allies for military quarters for one year more.[1] This was a mere postponement of the critical hour. The French government, still at war with Spain, and in control of its own predominantly native army, had no problem to face. Very different was the position of the Swedish authorities, who had to demobilize nearly a hundred thousand men, of whom the most part were Germans without other hope for the future save that which the career of a soldier had offered them. A small minority in the Swedish ranks were Protestant exiles from the Hapsburg lands, Bohemians and Austrians, who were indignant that the government for which they had fought had sacrificed their interests to make the peace. And there were also the bedraggled remnants of the Bernardine army, who had joined the Swedes in the hope of finding better treatment than with Turenne and were dismayed at the prospect of final disbandment.

On the imperial side the situation was only relatively less menacing. Piccolomini was faced with the task of dispersing about two hundred thousand men and women, robbed of their sole means of existence. The re-absorption of so large a mass in the civilian population would have been complicated even had the soldiers and their families been of more suitable material than they were.

Two dangers were imminent: the first that with the armies still in occupation of the country, the discontent of one or more of the signatories of the peace might lead to renewed war while the means were to be had; the second, that the soldiers should take the law into their own hands, mutiny against their generals and continue to live as heretofore on the spoil of the country, no longer as armies but as robber bands. Both dangers were real enough. At Vienna they feared that Swedish and Bavarian troops would join forces against the peacemakers.[2] The appointment of Christina's cousin, Charles Gustavus, to the chief command did not increase political confidence: the prince was young, ambitious and warlike, and it was galling to him that he should have no more glorious task assigned to him than the demobilizing of an army.

Meanwhile the signal failure of the negotiations in West-

phalia to settle certain problems, subjected the whole instrument to dangerous criticism. Neither Catholics nor Protestants
were contented with the compromise decision in regard to their
relative possessions. Moreover, no arrangement had been made
for the execution of this part of the settlement, and any attempt
to force it into effect might easily re-awaken the war.

The Papal nuncio introduced another jarring note by
denouncing the whole settlement as contrary to the interests
of the Church; the Spanish government protested angrily to
the Emperor because he had basely deserted them; the freebooter Charles of Lorraine was totally excluded from the
treaty and continued to hold the fortress of Hammerstein on
German soil, regardless of protests; the Spaniards announced
their intention of remaining in Frankenthal; the Duke of
Mantua protested because the French government had handed
over part of his lands without so much as asking his permission.[1]

Five and a half years after the signing of the peace, in May
1654, the last hostile garrison withdrew from Germany.
For the first two years of that period the continuance of war
was still highly probable, for the last three years only local
dangers threatened the general security.

Peace had been proclaimed at Prague in mid-November
1648. Until the end of December the Swedish and imperial
commanders repeatedly conferred together, which led the
populace fondly to expect prompt demobilization. By the end
of the year the generals had made only one step forward —
that of deciding on the exact amount of the interim contribution to be levied on the Emperor's subjects for the support of
the troops until their disbandment.[2] The disbanding itself
had not even been discussed, and all arrangements were
postponed until a new congress should meet at Nuremberg to
consider the execution of the terms and the manner of
demobilization.

Great was the dismay throughout Germany when the
amount of the interim assessment was made known. At
Strasbourg the news damped the rejoicings[3], and Charles

[1] B. Erdmannsdörffer, *Deutsche Geschichte*. Berlin, 1892, pp. 5-6; Lorentzen,
pp. 179-81, 189.
[2] Ibid., p. 155.   [3] Walther, p. 41.

Gustavus nearly shattered the peace itself by sending troops into the bishopric of Liège to extract the money at the sword's point.[1] But so intense was the longing for an end that the majority of the people spared no effort to raise the gigantic sums demanded, and with the help of Swiss and native bankers covered the whole assessment.[2]

The onus now rested on the generals, Charles Gustavus, Wrangel and Piccolomini, who acquitted themselves of the task with unexpected success. By September 1649 Charles Gustavus was able to celebrate the happy conclusion of the chief points at issue by entertaining his colleagues to a Peace Banquet in Nuremberg, and here it was that Wrangel, gaily firing off his pistol at the ceiling, remarked that he had no further use for ammunition.[3] Charles Gustavus, meanwhile, had reconciled himself to his task and was showing the same genius, courage and discretion in demobilizing as he was later to show in leading armies. By dismissing supernumerary officers and drafting incomplete companies together, he first brought the nominal strength of the army into proportionate relationship with its actual strength. Regiments which he suspected of mutinous intention he broke up and scattered in different districts, so that revolt would not easily spread, and when mutiny in fact occurred he crushed it with merciless thoroughness.

On both sides the rulers attempted to alleviate the situation by drafting some of the men on to the land, a plan which achieved only a very mediocre success in Bavaria, in Hesse, in the Palatinate.[4] On the whole the discontented soldier preferred to fend for himself. Captains and whole companies deserted, marching off to hire themselves to the French, the Spaniards, the Duke of Savoy, the Venetians, the English, the Prince of Transylvania, even the Tsar of Russia. But there was a glut of soldiers on the market, and late-comers found no welcome. Others merely took to the hills and woods and became robber bands. In one or two districts it was necessary — although apparently not for long — to keep a small armed force against

---

[1] MEIERN, *Acta Executionis*, II, p. 686 f.
[2] LORENTZEN, pp. 179-81, 189.
[3] MEIERN, *Acta Executionis*, II.
[4] RIEZLER, *Geschichte*, v, p. 660; LORENTZEN, p. 207.

these marauders,[1] and for many years after the war merchants preferred to travel in great companies and well guarded.

More than once the situation was dangerous. Among the Swedish forces there were mutinies at Überlingen, Neumarkt, Langenarch, Meinau and Eger. A serious outbreak at Schweinfurt had to be quelled by Wrangel in person. Several regiments managed to seize the money sent to their commander to pay them off and make away with it whither they listed. In Anhalt in July 1650, a band of mutineers, more dangerous and more successful than any hitherto, had to be outmanœuvred, surrounded and shot down.[2] A mutiny among the Bavarian troops was stamped out with the same ruthlessness, the Elector bringing up the heavy artillery to mow down the mutineers, and fifteen of the ringleaders being hanged for the assertion of what appeared to them to be their rights.[3]

As late as the summer of 1650 the discovery that imperial troops were being drafted into the Spanish armies brought forth indignant protests from the Swedes and French, and for a few days it seemed at Nuremberg that war was imminent. Demobilization was said to have stopped, nay there were reports that the Swedes were recruiting. But the crisis passed, and on July 14th, 1650, the negotiators met for the last time at a huge banquet given in their honour, this time by Piccolomini. He had set up a gigantic tent outside the town, decorated with mirrors, candelabra, flowers and symbolic insignia. Outside there was a cardboard fortress crammed with fireworks. After the usual unpleasantness, caused this time by Wrangel and a certain imperial general quarrelling for the superior place, the guests sat down at five in the evening to an enormous meal at which, to the accompaniment of deafening salvos, they drank the health of the peace and of everyone present. When they had finished, Piccolomini himself touched off the fuse which sent the cardboard fortress shooting to heaven in a whirl of rockets. For the populace there was a mild, hollow lion with an olive branch fixed in its harmless paw, from whose jaws issued a continuous stream of wine.[4]

The principal negotiators having left, the conference sat

[1] Lorentzen, p. 204. [2] Ibid., pp. 188-9.
[3] Riezler, *Geschichte*, v, p. 658. [4] Meiern, *Acta Executionis*, ii, pp. 444-6.

for a year longer to settle various minor points. Even then several problems remained unsolved. The Spaniards did not withdraw from Frankenthal until the Emperor ceded them Besançon in 1653; Charles of Lorraine did not leave Hammerstein until early in 1654, and in May of the same year the Swedish garrison at Vechta had the doubtful honour of being the last to quit Germany. But the evacuation had been continuous ever since the conference met at Nuremberg in 1649, and by the harvest of 1650 most districts in Germany felt that they could now safely celebrate the return of peace. Remarkable in those pitiful little demonstrations of thanksgiving was the part played by the children, school-children in white with green crowns at Dollstedt singing in procession,[1] school-children speaking a welcome to the long-exiled Elector Charles Lewis on the frontiers of the Palatinate.[2] These were the future, the hope — perhaps in some places the only hope.

II

This was not the first time that Germany had been subjected to continuous war for over a generation, but a legend surrounds this war which makes it unique in German, if not in European history. Until at least the middle of the nineteenth century no estimate of the loss in life and wealth was too extravagant for belief. The population was supposed to have sunk by three quarters, the loss in live stock and wealth to have been far greater, agriculture to have been restored to its pristine flourishing condition in some districts only after two centuries, commerce to have perished altogether in innumerable centres; every ill which affected the body politic was readily ascribed to the Thirty Years War, from the vagaries of the imperial constitution to the late development of a German overseas Empire.

The more critical research of the last three generations has revealed two hitherto unnoticed aspects of the problem: the first that Germany in 1618 was already far gone on the road

[1] FREYTAG, *Bilder aus der deutschen Vergangenheit*. Leipzig, 1859, II, p. 202.
[2] L. HÄUSSER, *Geschichte der rheinischen Pfalz*. Heidelberg, 1856, II, p. 583.

to destruction; the second that contemporary figures are unreliable. Princes seeking to evade financial responsibilities, states claiming damages, citizens asking exemption from taxes — all these naturally painted the condition of their country in the dreariest colours. In the list of damages drawn up for the Swedish government, the number of villages destroyed was represented in some districts as more than the total number of those known to have existed.[1] Journalists and pamphleteers on both sides wrote in a perpetual superlative which defeats its object.

Yet this exaggeration is in itself significant for, at least in official documents, it would not have been possible without some element of truth to bear it out; and if contemporary writers wail in too long-sustained and high a monotone, that is significant, if not of a fact, at least of a mood which must have had root somewhere in actuality. Whether Germany lost three-quarters of her population, or a small percentage, it is certain that never before, and possibly never since, in her history had there been so universal a sense of irretrievable disaster, so widespread a consciousness of the horror of the period which lay behind.

In collecting the comparatively few reliable facts, in sifting the mass of exaggerated legends and statements, an acute contrast between the general and the particular makes itself bewilderingly apparent. The individual peasant suffered atrociously during the war; defenceless, he was exposed to heavy taxation, plunder, violence and exile. Yet the peasantry in general emerged from the war in a stronger position with regard to the rest of society than any they had yet held. The gentry depended on their labour to restore the land to prosperity, a task for which their numbers were relatively small. This gave them for once a chance to assert themselves effectively.[2] In the sphere of ordinary household economics there is the same contradiction. From about the year 1622, and for the next fifty years, prices were steadily falling.[3] This movement was accompanied by a general rise in the level of wages, so that the

[1] DUDIK, *Die Schweden in Böhmen*, p. 377.
[2] WUTTKE, *Gesindeordnung und Gesindezwangsdienst*, Leipzig, 1893, pp. 62, 69-70.
[3] ELSAS, pp. 22-5.

cost of living fell and the standard rose throughout the Thirty Years War. All this did not in the slightest degree palliate the suffering caused by intermittent and local famine, by plunder, persecution and emigration. Reduced to the impersonality of a graph, the price of wheat in Augsburg certainly ran downhill, but each sudden upward thrust of the line, however temporary, meant hunger and death.[1]

The accounts and figures of contemporaries, exaggerated as they are, give at least a general impression of conditions as they appeared to those who in 1648 were faced with the task of rebuilding Germany. True or false, they have a human value, which, meaningless though it may be to the economist, is important to the historian. The Swedes alone were accused of destroying nearly two thousand castles, eighteen thousand villages and over fifteen hundred towns.[2] Bavaria claimed to have lost eighty thousand families and nine hundred villages, Bohemia five-sixths of its villages and three-quarters of its population. In Württemberg the number of the inhabitants was said to have fallen to a sixth, in Nassau to a fifth, in Henneberg to a third, in the wasted Palatinate to a fiftieth of its original size.[3] The population of Colmar was halved, that of Wolfenbüttel had sunk to an eighth, of Magdeburg to a tenth, of Hagenau to a fifth, of Olmütz to less than a fifteenth.[4] Minden, Hameln, Göttingen, Magdeburg, by their own account, stood in ruins.[5]

So far the legend. Where more solid proof is to be found the figures, if they do not bear out, at least provide some justification for the tradition. The population of Munich numbered twenty-two thousand in 1620, seventeen thousand in 1650; Augsburg forty-eight thousand in 1620, twenty-one

[1] ELSAS, pp. 34-5, 41-2, 48-9, 54.
[2] DUDIK, Die Schweden in Böhmen, p. 37.
[3] MEIERN, Acta Pacis, v, p. 774; INAMA-STERNEGG, Die Volkswirtschaftliche Folgen des dreissigjährigen Krieges. Historische Taschenbuch. Vierte Folge, v, p. 16; SPIELMANN, Geschichte von Nassau. Wiesbaden, 1910, I, p. 86; BRÜCKNER, Beitrag zur Statistik und Geschichte des dreissigjährigen Krieges. Zeitschrift für Deutsche Kulturgeschichte, 1857, pp. 212-13; HÄUSSER, Geschichte der Rheinischen Pfalz, II, p. 583.
[4] REUSS, Alsace au XVIIe siècle, pp. 110-12; HEINEMANN, Geschichte von Braunschweig. Gotha, 1892, III, p. 100 f.; HAENDKE, Deutsche Kulturgeschichte im Zeitalter des dreissigjährigen Krieges. Leipzig, 1906, p. 186; HANAUER, p. 397; D'ELVERT, IV, pp. xxix, cclxxvi.
[5] HEINEMANN, p. 100 f.

thousand in 1650.[1] Chemnitz sank from nearly a thousand to under two hundred, Pirna from eight hundred and seventy-six to fifty-four.[2] The population of Marburg, eleven times occupied, dwindled by half and the municipal debt rose to seven times its original size; two hundred years later the burghers were still paying interest on loans raised during the war.[3] The population of Berlin-Kölln decreased by a quarter, that of Neu Brandenburg by nearly a half. In the Altmark Salzwedel, Tangermunde and Gardelegen had lost a third of their people, Seehausen and Stendal more than half, Werben and Osterburg two-thirds.[4] As many as two hundred ships had sailed yearly across the Sound from the ports of East Friesland in 1621; by the last decade of the war the average number in a year was ten.[5]

'I would not have believed a land could have been so despoiled had I not seen it with my own eyes,' declared General Mortaigne in Nassau.[6] And there is evidence enough of such wasting in the drastic efforts of the rulers to revive cultivation.

The loss in agricultural land and live stock is difficult to reckon, since reliable figures rarely exist for the period both immediately before and immediately after the war. It is an easy error to attribute to the war a poverty in cattle and agriculture by which a district may always have been distinguished. Bitterly as they complained, the armies contrived to live on the land to the end, managed to keep some at least of their cavalry mounted on four-footed beasts — apparently not always on horses! — and to get their baggage wagons drawn for them. Again, far as the marauding troops would sometimes wander from their base, a village away from a road, or sheltered in the dead end of a remote valley, might escape altogether.

Leipzig went bankrupt in 1625, but the financial position of the municipality had been insecure before.[7] Some towns experienced very little set-back, a few even derived advantage

[1] ELSAS, p. 79.   [2] WUTTKE, Gesindeordnung, p. 65.
[3] KUERSCHNER, Geschichte Marburgs, pp. 135-6, 149, 150, 151, 166.
[4] KAPHAHN, Die wirtschaftliche Folgen des dreissigjährigen Krieges, Gotha, 1911, pp. 37, 45.
[5] HAGEDORN, Ostfrieslands Handel und Schiffahrt, Berlin, 1912, p. 504.
[6] INAMA-STERNEGG, p. 11.
[7] KROKER, Handelsgeschichte der Stadt Leipzig, Leipzig, 1925.

from the war. Erfurt attempted to set up a rival annual fair when Leipzig was occupied by troops in 1632-33.[1] The population of Würzburg rose steadily.[2] Bremen contrived to monopolize the English linen market,[3] Hamburg had engrossed the sugar and spice trade of its rivals and came out of the Thirty Years War one of the finest towns in Europe, able to compete in the Baltic with Sweden and the United Provinces.[4] The county of Oldenburg, thanks to the enlightened dishonesty of its ruler, had executed so intricate a dance among the shifting alliances as always to be not only on the winning side but in a position to prevent occupation by the troops. Frankfort-on-the-Main, after the lean years which followed Nördlingen, emerged again comparatively wealthy, comparatively prosperous. The population of Dresden made up on the harbouring of exiles what it lost by plague, and had neither grown nor diminished in the course of the war.[5]

Above all it must be remembered that the destructive powers of the armies were infinitely less than they are now. The lack of any authority to protect the civilian, the inadequacy of charitable services, the total absence of discipline in the modern sense, made the immediate pressure of the war overwhelming. But there was no organized deportation, no annihilation bombing, no scientifically planned destruction. The buildings destroyed were wooden houses, quickly rebuilt; stone and brick mocked the rage of the seventeenth-century soldier. Recovery was therefore in many districts so rapid as to have produced, in certain sceptics, a doubt of the actual horror of the war.

In actual money the losses were never so great as the complaints of the authorities suggest. Much of the wealth seized as war-contributions merely changed hands, flowing back into the pockets of the people in payment for the needs of the soldiery. Comparatively little was saved and sent back to foreign banks and foreign lands by thrifty generals.[6] That little would be abundantly balanced by the money which flowed

[1] KROKER, p. 128. [2] ELSAS, p. 79.
[3] B. HAGEDORN, Ostfrieslands Handel und Schiffahrt, p. 510.
[4] AUBÉRY DU MAURIER, Mémoires de Hambourg, p. 28 f.
[5] MÜLLER, Dresden im dreissigjährigen Kriege. Neues Archiv für Sächsische Geschichte, XXXVI, p. 248. [6] KAPHAHN, pp. 56-7.

into the country through the armies from Spain, Sweden, the United Provinces, and above all from France.

Nevertheless, the shortage of capital during the war itself was, at least locally, very strongly marked. Between 1630 and 1650 only two and a half million talers were minted by the Saxon government, as opposed to more than twice that number in the last twenty years of the previous century.[1] The steadily decreasing yield of taxes is proof of the devaluation of property and the decline in prosperity of the taxpayer. It is a grievous thought that the takings of the Leipzig beer-cellar sank to less than a quarter.[2]

On occasion the peasantry did well out of the financial chaos. Soldiers did not stop to bargain, and the village boy who exchanged a mug of beer for a silver chalice[3] did well out of the deal. In Augsburg during the Swedish occupation several ingenious peasants managed to buy plundered cattle at ridiculous prices, the soldiers having no idea of the value of the animals they had stolen.[4] The breakdown of authority also gave great opportunities to the unscrupulous. When their timorous neighbours had fled, certain bold farmers could sometimes make easy money by selling the produce of their neighbours' lands, the wood in particular, as if it was their own.[5] Towards the end of the war, indeed, a generation had grown up who knew how to make the best of the unusual freedom which had arisen from the weakness of civil authority.

The incredible decrease in population claimed for so many districts was to some extent the outcome of temporary emigration, and a careful consideration of conditions in Germany both before and after the war reveals the fact that society was dislocated rather than destroyed. But the marks of that dislocation remained long after the limbs had been re-integrated.

The actual loss of population is hard to gauge with accuracy. A detailed inquiry into the conditions of the Altmark reveals a decrease of two-fifths in the towns, of one half in the open country.[6] This loss affected the male and female population

---

[1] WUTTKE, *Gesindeordnung*, p. 66.   [2] Ibid., pp. 63, 64; KROKER, pp. 129, 130.
[3] EINERT, p. 52.   [4] WAGNER.
[5] EHRENBERG, *Aus dem dreissigjährigen Kriege.* (*Altona unter Schauenburgischen Herrschaft*, v. Altona, 1892), p. 33.
[6] KAPHAHN, p. 98.

almost equally, for it must be remembered, in calculating the damages done by the war, that the mortality among the civilian population was certainly as great in proportion, if not greater, than among the armies. There was no difficult social problem such as arises from a war in which the casualties are confined largely to the males.

The old legend that the population dropped from sixteen to four million people, rests on imagination: both figures are incorrect. The German Empire, including Alsace but excluding the Netherlands and Bohemia, probably numbered about twenty-one millions in 1618, and rather less than thirteen and a half millions in 1648.[1] Certain authorities believe that the loss was less,[2] but these are for the most part writers of a militaristic epoch, anxious to destroy the ugly scarecrow which throws so long a shadow over the glorious past.

III

The breakdown of social order, the perpetual changing of authority and religion in so many districts, contributed to that disintegration of society which was more fundamentally serious than the immediate damages of war.

The slight improvement in the position of the peasant which had resulted in some districts from the slackening of the central authority was not firmly enough established to outlast the conditions which had produced it. In Saxony in particular the coming of peace was marked by the peevish outcry of the nobility for government help against the peasants. Of old the serf had not been able to leave the land, but in the chaos of war many had drifted into the towns and learnt trades; these came back to improve the standard of living at home, and the sons and daughters of labourers were now growing up to increase the family income by plying domestic industries.[3]

---

[1] ELSAS, p. 78.
[2] HOENIGER, *Der dreissigjährige Krieg und der deutsche Kultur. Preussische Jahrbücher*, CXXXVIII, pp. 421, 425-6. He makes very light of the war. To his mind, it had the excellent effect of breeding a race of soldiers.
[3] WUTTKE, p. 68.

So long as the war lasted, the landed aristocracy viewed these proceedings with impotent dismay, but when peace came all was changed. In Saxony they compelled the Elector — who owed them money — to issue a series of laws forbidding the peasant either to leave his village or to ply any industry in his home.[1] In this way the one improvement brought about by the war was effectively destroyed.

The advance and the decline of the landless peasant was most strongly marked in Saxony, but the same process in a less exaggerated form took place in nearly all districts. The economic results of this shameless class-legislation were less disastrous than the social. The landed gentry wished to make their lands prosperous, and if they were narrow-minded, they were not essentially bad, masters. In the years following the war there was everywhere scientific and intelligent development of the land. But morally and socially the evil results of this oppression were undeniable. Feudal barriers were re-created where feudal obligations had long ceased to exist, and the seeds of a caste-consciousness, which still persists, took root and flourished.

The same distinctions existed between town and country, between merchant and peasant and noble, and these were strengthened by the efforts of the dominating classes to maintain their social position in spite of economic distress. Meanwhile the devastation of war had brought into existence a class of landless nobility, pretentious parasites who lived on their kinsfolk and on their wits and preyed on society for generations to come. In spite of that levelling of classes which some claim to be the effect of acute and prolonged emergency, the social hierarchy emerged from the war as rigid as before. Rarely a successful general managed to buy an estate, or marry into the nobility and found a new noble family. Johann von Werth retired with immense wealth and took a Fräulein von Kuefstein to wife; the peasant-born Melander became a Count and died worth a quarter of a million talers. But these appear to be unusual cases. In spite of the booty accumulated by privates, it was extremely difficult to rise from the ranks. Even the foreign adventurers who distinguished themselves were

[1] WUTTKE, pp. 72, 77.

almost always of noble if impoverished families. Piccolomini came of the distinguished Sienese dynasty, Isolani claimed noble ancestors in Cyprus, the Swedish officers were almost all of the landed class.[1] Even men like the murderers of Wallenstein styled themselves gentlemen. Social castes defied the pressure of military necessity, and although there were many uneducated boors among the officers of both sides, the great majority claimed nevertheless to come of families bearing coat armour. The distinction, absurd in every practical sense, was highly significant in the eyes of contemporaries. It is notable that among the foreign mercenaries names of an aristocratic flavour predominate — Devereux, Ruthven, Montecuculi. Among the Germans, scions of ancient families are no less frequent among the officers in 1648 than in 1618. They are Falkenberg and Kuefstein still, not Müller and Schmidt.

If the war had no effect in mixing classes, it had a slight effect in mixing races. The influx of Spanish, Swedish, Italian, Croatian, Flemish, and French soldiery must have had some influence on the racial composition of the masses. It cannot have had very much on that of the middle and upper classes. Of a fundamental alteration in the physical characteristics of the people there is of course no question. The Germans had not absorbed recurrent waves of Goth, Vandal, Frank, with strains of Hun, Slav and Viking, to be altered out of recognition by the birth of a few thousand hybrid babies. The racial influence of the Swedish occupation on the Czechs rests on popular belief alone, and certainly the numerous 'Schwedenschantz' in Germany almost all owe their name to the corruption of some older form.[2]

Some have said that German militarism may be traced to the war. But in fact the Germans had always produced a large number of military adventurers from the Crusades to the sixteenth century. If the war taught the people anything it taught them a slavish endurance: if it is to this that its apologists refer, there may be some truth in their contention, since that quality appears to be an essential element in the militarism of the twentieth century.

[1] DELBRUCK, p. 20.
[2] HEBBE, *Svenskarna i Böhmen*. Stockholm, 1932, pp. 135-50.

The commercial middle-classes, long declining in influence, had been altogether undermined by the war; the bourgeoisie of the future was composed not of independent merchants but of dependent officials, not a free and experimental, but a parasitic and conservative, class.[1] By becoming satellites of the governing class and identifying their interests with those of the rulers, the townsfolk virtually destroyed the buffer state between nobility and peasantry.

The importance and the culture of the small town survived, but it was dependent now on the goodwill of the prince who extended his protection over reviving urban life, and exploited the walled cities as strategic points for the defence of his lands. The spontaneous and lively art of the municipality gave way before the restrained and genteel culture of the provincial Court. It was an imitative rarified culture, remote from the life of the people, remote often from the natural expression of the Germans, but at its best international, civilized and significant, as the culture of the small town could never be. Losing its national rigidity, German art was merged in the main stream of European development, which meant at that time in the culture of France.

The nationalist regrets the change; an ill-founded belief in the merits of purity blinds him to the virtues of the foreign and the hybrid. Are the arts to be so bounded by the meaningless frontiers of geography that we are to deplore the soaring light of Tiepolo's ceiling at Würzburg, the Parisian elegance of the Zwinger at Dresden? Are we to stop our ears to the music of the eighteenth century because it derived so much from lands beyond the German border?

German racial consciousness survived the war in a form as aggressive as before. The people resented the French culture from the moment of its coming, and not only because it came with invasion and imperial defeat. The Austrians, the defeated, received it best and made the best use of it. In the north and west they accepted it resentfully, gracelessly, but accepted it none the less. The princes gave them no alternative and left middle-class writers to protest in vain — Philander von Sittewald crying in the wilderness against a younger generation for

[1] Gebauer, *Deutsche Kulturgeschichte*, p. 111.

whom everything must be *à la mode* and who characterized their dislikes as 'altfränkisch', as we some years ago called ours 'Victorian'.[1]

For this submergence of German culture the war was not in itself responsible. French fashions triumphed the world over, in Italy, in England, in the United Provinces, even in Sweden and Denmark.

IV

The political effects of the war were more distinct than its social and economic results. The actual boundaries of the Empire had changed. The acceptance of the independence of Switzerland and the United Provinces merely confirmed an already existent situation. Alsace and Hither-Pomerania, on the other hand, although still technically part of the Empire, were virtually under the control of foreign powers, a cession which in the case of Alsace at least was to become permanent. The mouths of the four great rivers were thus in foreign hands: the delta of the Rhine under Spanish and Dutch control, the Elbe under Danish, the Oder under Swedish, the Vistula under Polish. The situation with regard to the Elbe and the Vistula was what it had been in 1618, but the establishment of the aggressive power of Holland in virtual possession of the outlet from the Rhine,[2] and the seizure of the Oder by the Swedes, were bound to react unfavourably on what remained of German commerce and self-respect.

Within the Empire it is difficult to analyse the political changes in their exact relationship to the war. The elements out of which the conflict had arisen had resolved themselves into a new formation, and some at least had disappeared in the process. The shifting of the balance between Church and State was in process in 1618 and might well have completed

[1] See SITTEWALD, *Visiones de Don Quevedo*, Part II, *passim*; K. BIDERMANN, *Der dreissigjährige Krieg und seine Wirkungen auf die gesellschaftlichen und die sittliche Zuetande Deutschlands. Zeitschrift für Deutsche Kulturgeschichte*, 1856, p. 165.

[2] It will be remembered that by the Peace of Münster the Scheldt had been closed to traffic, so that all Rhine commerce now had to pass through the Dutch ports.

itself without unnecessary bloodshed. Calvinism, although not officially recognized, was practised by more of the population before than after the war. The struggle against absolutism in Germany had been hampered from the outset by the jealousies of the privileged classes. If the triumph of the princes and their separatist tyrannies, over the Emperor on the one hand and the Estates on the other, was not certain in 1618, it was at least highly probable.

The war hastened the development by leaving the princes as the only power to whom the disorganized people could turn. Authority seemed necessary for the survival of the State; despotism was more practically effective than self-government, bureaucracy more stable than elective choice.

The Empire sank to the level of a geographical term. Ferdinand III had entrenched himself in his father's creation of 'Austria'; it was as King-Emperor of Austria and her surrounding provinces that he had acted at Münster and was to act afterwards. By confirming the princes in their right to make their own foreign alliances, the peace completed the disintegration of the Empire as an effective State. Out of its decay arose, living and self-conscious, Austria, Bavaria, Saxony and Brandenburg — the Prussia that was to be.

By shattering Austria, France had opened the way for a new power in Germany. Frederick William of Brandenburg and his descendants saw to it that the new power should not be Bavaria or Saxony or a revived Austria. It is true that Frederick William was not altogether the product of the war: if the background of his youth had toughened certain qualities in him, his abilities were his own. The war gave him his chance: he made his own use of it.

Yet the war contributed in north Germany to that suspicion of the Hapsburg which crystallized ultimately into hatred and made them the scapegoats for all disaster. They had sacrificed the Empire to Austria, they had bought peace at the expense of the Holy German Land. Their policy, it was averred, gave the Swedes control of the Oder and threw Alsace into the greedy maw of France. In vain to argue that they had in fact fought manfully to unite an unwilling Germany, and that the Swedes had taken advantage of the separatism of the princes to set foot on the Baltic coast. In vain to show conclusive proof that Maximilian of Bavaria had forced an unwilling Emperor to sacrifice Alsace. The psychological fact remains that hatred and blame became, after the Thirty Years War, the natural reaction of the north towards the dynasty which ruled in the south. If the war had done nothing else, it had made inevitable the estrangement of Germany and Austria.

A claim has often been made that but for the war Germany would have become the greatest, or at least one of the greatest, colonial powers in Europe. The assumption rests on an unsteady foundation. The Empire in 1618 showed no signs of developing as a colonial power; she had not in the mildest degree entered into competition with the Dutch, the Spanish, or the English. Commerce, and more particularly marketing and exchange, had been her gifts, gifts not necessarily the same as those needed for pioneer colonization. The decline of urban enterprise was one of the most distressing elements in the Germany of 1618. Only a sudden and improbable revival, together with the emergence of some strong guiding power, could have converted the Empire of 1618 once more into a leading commercial state.

The undertakings of Spain, Portugal, England, the United Provinces, were based either on the deliberate policy of a State strong enough to subsidize colonial ventures, on private enterprise backed by immense private resources, or on the desperate need to find a land free of religious tyranny. In the Empire there was no central authority, private wealth was declining, and the principle of *cujus regio ejus religio* meant that a man could have some degree of freedom of conscience without crossing the Atlantic. No one would deny that the late coming of Germany into the field of colonial development has been unfortunate, but it had nothing to do with the Thirty Years War.

v

Germany's tragedy was essentially her own. Without extenuating the actions of Richelieu, Olivarez, the two Ferdinands and the King of Sweden, it is yet possible to see that the opportunity was made *for* and not *by* them. Always it proved so easy to separate political allies, to exploit the private interests of rulers and set them at loggerheads one with another. Brandenburg and Saxony were separated and singly subdued, when in 1631 the Leipzig manifesto gave some faint hope of a German party between the clash of foreign interests. Saxony and Bavaria were brought separately into the Peace of Prague and tricked into allying themselves with the Emperor, when in 1635 there had seemed to be a united movement towards a settlement. It is not surprising that the clear-headed egoism of a ruler like the Landgravine of Hesse-Cassel, or even of an adventurer like Bernard of Saxe-Weimar, has been acclaimed and twisted into evidence of German patriotism, for it is so great a relief in that limbo of muddled intentions to find any ruler with a clear conception of policy.

The responsibility for the catastrophe is so diffused as to defy any effort to localize it. In a sense every man and woman of influence in every German state must stand accused of the dreadful lethargy which allowed the war to spread. Yet the greater the power the greater the responsibility, and the accusation must be heaviest against those who could in fact have stopped the war and did not.

Frederick and Ferdinand, the protagonists of 1618, can at least claim the justification that each thought himself to be fulfilling the mandate of a Higher Power. Their actions must be judged accordingly. It was not so with John George and Maximilian, and it is fair to apply other standards to them. Each of them was sane enough to draw advantage from the conflict. They should have been sane enough to prevent its continuance. They held the balance at the beginning, and might so easily have held it at the end.

With a certain poetic completeness, they were among the few who saw the beginning and the end, John George dying full of years in his palace at Dresden in 1654, his children and grandchildren about him, and Maximilian, three years earlier, in a bare room at Ingolstadt with the Jesuit fathers at his side.

These two, had they been able to sink their parochial ambition, could have formed a central party strong enough to curb Ferdinand's ambition, to stifle Frederick's war, without

Spanish intervention on one side or French on the other. They had attempted the task in 1620 when they allied themselves with Ferdinand in order to prevent his appeal to Spain. But Maximilian had sacrificed his position to scramble vulgarly for Frederick's lands and title, and John George was powerless alone. His demand for Lusatia was an error, but at least Lusatia was Ferdinand's to give. It was not so with the Palatinate, and Maximilian's claim was a dangerous and criminal blunder. Afterwards he could never redeem his position. The Electorate stood always between him and his duty as a German. He could never trust his fortunes to a centre party, because no centre party could give its full approval to the bare-faced robbery he had committed under the imperial sanction. It drove him into the Spanish camp against his will when the Swedes came in and French protection failed him; it drove him at the end to do yeoman service for France at the Peace of Westphalia, to wrench Alsace from the body of the Empire and give it to Mazarin. The cession of Alsace was the price which Germany paid that Maximilian might keep the Palatinate.

He had it in him to be a constitutionalist; he was a clever man and he resented the interference of the foreigner in German affairs, but his own misdeed drove him from the German to the Spanish camp, from the Spanish to the French. Had he at the essential moment thought of Germany and not of Bavaria, he could have ended the war; he had all the cards in his hand in 1620 and he threw them all away. Judged by the provincial standard of the single state he ruled, he might pass for a great man; he extended its frontiers and became the first secular prince of Germany. Judged by the wider standard of the nation to which he belonged and the Empire to which he himself boasted his unfaltering loyalty, he must be either a dupe or a traitor — perhaps a little of both.

John George of Saxony struggled longer and with less opportunity to prevent the forces of Europe from closing in across his country. In 1624 and in 1631 he emerged as the potential leader of a central German party, to be swamped first by the obstinate fears of Maximilian and later by the King of Sweden. Yet again in the years between Gustavus's death and the Peace

of Prague he rose to the surface and attempted valiantly to stem
the flood, battling with the cross-currents of Swedish, French
and Spanish intervention. Unsupported, he was dragged out of
his course by the perversion of the Peace of Prague into an
imperial coalition for war. That perversion, the result of French
and Swedish conflict as much as of Hapsburg design, forced the
patriot Arnim to resign. John George, who could not leave
his post, remained to drift miserably with the tide.

It was not a brilliant career, but it was at least a career of honest
intentions, and posterity, while it may regret that John George
was unequal to his trust, cannot accuse him of betraying it.

VI

In Germany the war was an unmitigated catastrophe. In
Europe it was equally, although in a different way, catastrophic. The peace, which had settled the disputes of Germany
with comparative success because passions had cooled, was
totally ineffectual in settling the problems of Europe. The
inconclusive and highly unpopular cession of Alsace led direct
to war; the seizure of half Pomerania by the Swedish Crown was
only less disastrous because the Swedish Crown was palpably
too weak to hold it. The insidious growth of Bourbon influence
on the Rhine, and Mazarin's deliberate policy of seizing good
strategic points on the frontier, vitiated the settlement. The
Peace of Westphalia was like most peace treaties, a rearrange-
ment of the European map ready for the next war.

The Peace has been described as marking an epoch in
European history, and it is commonly taken to do so. It is
supposed to divide the period of religious wars from that of
national wars, the idealogical wars from the wars of mere
aggression. But the demarcation is as artificial as such arbitrary
divisions commonly are. Aggression, dynastic ambition and
fanaticism are all alike present in the hazy background behind
the actual reality of the war, and the last of the wars of religion
merged insensibly into the pseudo-national wars of the future.

At Lissa in Poland the Bohemian Protestant exile Comenius
wrote: 'They have sacrificed us at the treaties of Osnabrück . . .

I conjure you by the wounds of Christ, that you do not forsake us who are persecuted for the sake of Christ.' From the Vatican, Innocent X solemnly condemned the peace as 'null, void, invalid, iniquitous, unjust, damnable, reprobate, inane, empty of meaning and effect for all time'. After thirty years of fighting the extreme Catholics and the extreme Protestants were left still unsatisfied. Both Ferdinand and Christina had to prohibit their clergy from publicly condemning the peace,[1] and the Bull issued with all the prestige of the Vatican was as ineffective in practical politics as the appeal of the exiled Bohemian.

After the expenditure of so much human life to so little purpose, men might have grasped the essential futility of putting the beliefs of the mind to the judgment of the sword. Instead, they rejected religion as an object to fight for and found others.

As there was no compulsion towards a conflict which, in despite of the apparent bitterness of parties, took so long to engage and needed so much assiduous blowing to fan the flame, so no right was vindicated by its ragged end. The war solved no problem. Its effects, both immediate and indirect, were either negative or disastrous. Morally subversive, economically destructive, socially degrading, confused in its causes, devious in its course, futile in its result, it is the outstanding example in European history of meaningless conflict. The overwhelming majority in Europe, the overwhelming majority in Germany, wanted no war; powerless and voiceless, there was no need even to persuade them that they did. The decision was made without thought of them. Yet of those who, one by one, let themselves be drawn into the conflict, few were irresponsible and nearly all were genuinely anxious for an ultimate and better peace. Almost all — one excepts the King of Sweden — were actuated rather by fear than by lust of conquest or passion of faith. They wanted peace and they fought for thirty years to be sure of it. They did not learn then, and have not since, that war breeds only war.

[1] CHANUT, p. 367.

BIBLIOGRAPHICAL NOTE

The sources from which this book is taken are given at the foot of each page. I have followed the usual practice of giving the full title and date of each authority the first time it is cited; thereafter titles are given in an abbreviated form.

A full bibliography of the Thirty Years War will be found in the latest edition of Dahlmann-Waitz, *Quellenkunde zur deutschen Geschichte* and the continuations which bring it up to date, listed in Gebhardt, *Handbuch der deutschen Geschichte*, I, p. xvii (Stuttgard, 1954).

A number of biographies, monographs and works on special aspects of the Thirty Years War have appeared since this book was first published in 1938. General works include W. F. Reddaway, *History of Europe*, 1610–1715 (London, 1948); G. Pagés, *La Guerre de Trente Ans* (Paris, 1939). The relevant volume of the new *Cambridge Modern History* is shortly to be published.

By far the most important biography is Michael Roberts, *Gustavus Adolphus: A History of Sweden*, 1611–32 (London, 1953, 1958), which contains a comprehensive bibliography. Other biographies include Francis Watson, *Wallenstein, Soldier under Saturn* (London, 1938); Aldous Huxley, *Grey Eminence* (London, 1940) a study of Father Joseph. Carl Burckhardt, *Richelieu: Der Aufstieg zur Macht* (Munich, 1935) is available in an English translation (London, 1940) but does not take the story beyond 1630. The monumental life of Richelieu by Gabriel Hanotaux, of which the first volume appeared in 1893, reached completion in six volumes with the assistance of the Duc de la Force in 1947.

Franco-Spanish relations are treated by Auguste Leman, *Richelieu et Olivares, leurs negociations sècretes de* 1636 *à* 1642 (Lille, 1938). The relations of Spain and Austria are treated in Bohdan Chudoba, *Spain and the Empire*, 1519–1643 (Chicago, 1952) a work which makes interesting use of Spanish and Czech sources; also by G. Mecenseffy, *Habsburger im* 17*ten Jahrhundert* (Vienna, 1955). A valuable study of the declining power of Spain will be found in J. H. Elliott, *The Revolt of the Catalans* (Cambridge, 1963).

Past and Present for November 1954 contains an article by J. V. Polisensky which is helpful on the Czech element in the war and the economic background.

Of outstanding importance for the economic and especially the agricultural and population changes caused by the war is Günther

Franz, *Der Dreissigjährige Krieg und das deutsche Volk*, third revised edition (Stuttgart, 1961).

On the question of propaganda in the war, especially pictorial propaganda, there is an attractive and valuable book by Elmer A. Beller, *Propaganda in Germany during the Thirty Years War* (Princeton, 1940) with numerous illustrations.

There is a recent study of the peace treaty by Fritz Dickmann, *Der Westfälische Frieden* (Münster, 1959).

TABLE SHOWING THE MARRIAGES OF THE HAPSBURG DYNASTY

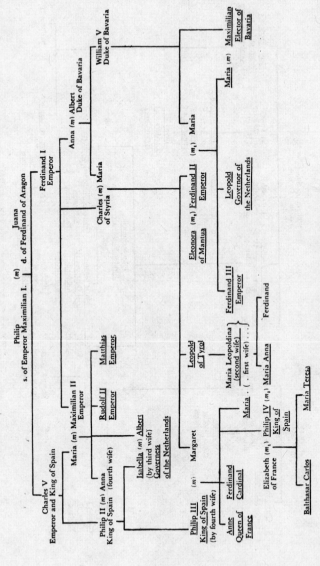

Persons mentioned in connection with the war are underlined.

TABLE SHOWING THE CONNECTIONS OF THE LEADING PROTESTANT DYNASTIES

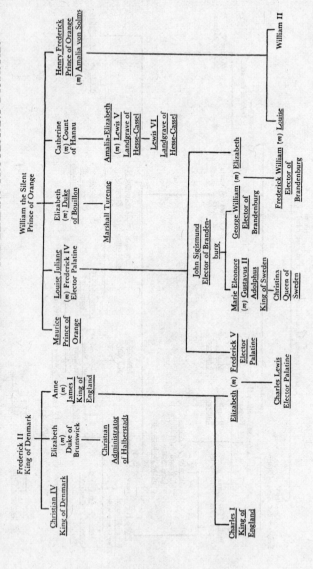

Persons mentioned in connection with the war are underlined.

530

INDEX

531

INDEX

532

INDEX

INDEX

INDEX

537

INDEX

Marie de Medici, Queen-mother of France, 113, 187-8, 308
Mark, 48-9, 439
Martinitz, Jaroslav, 76-9
Matthias, Emperor, 51, 55, 65, 71, 73-4, 77-8, 82, 84, 90
Maurice, Landgrave of Hesse-Cassel, 42, 46, 180, 209
Maurice, Prince of Orange, 28, 85, 98, 110, 113, 121-2, 131, 137, 156, 183, 192, 201, 272
Maurice, Prince Palatine, 131
Maximilian, Duke, later Elector of Bavaria, 18, 59, 62-4, 84, 89-90, 96, 107, 115, 117, 163-5, 167, 180-3, 213-14, 215, 314-15, 330, 344, 352-3, 437, 509
  and the Bohemian revolt, 93, 98-9, 121-30
  and the Electorate, 133-4, chapter IV, ii, iv; 222, 226, 395, 436, 480
  his policy, 192-4, 233, 254, 482, 522-4
  and Wallenstein, 199-200, 220-1, 227-8, 238, 263, 265, 320-3, 348-50, 361-2
  and the Edict of Restitution, 239-44
  and the French, 258, 261-2, 278, 291-3, 308-10, 317-18, 430, 450-1, 481, 499-500
  and the French invasion, 405-7
  and Mercy, 464-6
  at the Peace of Westphalia, 480-3, 486, 488, 491, 494
  and Werth, 496-8
Mazarin, Cardinal, 454, 465-7, 470-2, 476-7, 484, 494-6, 524-5
Mecklenburg, 41, 206, 220, 225, 226, 228, 232-3, 237, 239, 282, 285, 288, 293, 306, 321, 345, 421
Mecklenburg, Dukes of, 212, 219, 223, 227, 277, 283, 306, 396
Meinau, 509
Melander, Peter, Hessian, later imperialist, general, 445, 498, 499, 517
Melo, Francisco de, Spanish general, 451, 455-7
Memmingen, 263
Mercy, Franz von, Bavarian general, 465-6, 483-5
Mergentheim, 484
Merseburg, 294
Metz, 156, 332, 480, 487
Meuse, 454, 455
Mexico, 24
Milan, 24, 50, 401
Milan, Perpetual Peace of, 431
Milanese, the, 50, 114, 235
Minden, 244, 489, 512
Mingolsheim, 151

Mittelwalde, 217
Mitzlaff, Joachim, Protestant general, 224
Moldau, 119, 120, 126, 141
Montdidier, 406
Montecuculi, Raymond, Count, imperialist general, 499
Montferrat, 235
Montpelier, 18
Monzon, Peace of, 208
Moravia, 24, 69, 89, 90, 91, 94, 118, 128, 141, 142, 167, 172, 177-8, 192, 216, 217-18, 411, 448, 472
Morgan, Charles, Colonel, 208
Mortaigne, Gaspard Corneille de, Swedish general, 447, 513
Mosel, 40
Moulins, 424
Moyenvic, 487
Mühlhausen, 107, 116, 131-2, 134, 227, 233, 282
Mulde, 40
Munich, 41, 128, 130, 254, 318-19, 349, 413, 512
Münster, 34, 152, 183-4, 239, 450, 459
Münster, Congress of, chapter XI
Münster, Peace of, 498

Namur, 400
Nancy, 308
Naples, 24
Nassau, 256, 512, 513
Nassau, Count John of, 479
Neckar, 40, 151-2, 154
Netherlands (see Spanish Netherlands, United Provinces, etc.)
Neubrandenburg, 223, 286, 513
Neuburg, 34
Neuburg, Prince of, 162, 260
Neumarkt, 509
Neustadt, 413
Nordhausen, 34, 282
Nördlingen, 241, 303, 370
Nördlingen, Battle of, 371-7, 378-9, 383, 387, 390, 397, 402, 411, 431, 514
Nördlingen, second Battle of, 485
Norma futurarum actionum, 331
Normandy, 405
Norway, 28
Nuremberg, 32, 34, 107, 119, 168, 282, 306, 314, 319, 320-3, 330, 380, 412, 436, 507, 508, 509, 510

Oberndorf, 348
Oder, 32, 41, 103, 210, 234, 284, 285-6, 520, 521
Oise, 406
Oldenburg, 514

538

INDEX

INDEX

INDEX

JONATHAN CAPE PAPERBACKS